IUSTITIA DEI

SECOND EDITION

A HISTORY OF THE CHRISTIAN DOCTRINE OF JUSTIFICATION

The doctrine of justification was of major importance at the time of the Reformation, and continues to be of immense significance in modern ecumenical dialogues. This book, which appeared in its first edition in 1986, represents the first major study of the doctrine since 1870. Its many acclaimed features include a detailed assessment of the semantic background of the concept in the thought world of the ancient Near East, a thorough examination of the development of the doctrine during the medieval period, and a careful analysis of the sixteenth-century debates over the doctrine. This revised and updated edition brings together into a single volume the enormous amount of material from the two-volume first edition, while adding new sections dealing with recent developments in Pauline scholarship and ecumenical debates over the doctrine. It will be an essential resource for anyone wanting to understand historical theology, sixteenth-century church history or the modern ecumenical debates between Protestants and Roman Catholics.

Alister McGrath is the Principal of Wycliffe Hall, Oxford and a Research Lecturer in Theology at the University of Oxford. His major academic works include *The Genesis of Doctrine* (1990), *The Intellectual Origins of the Reformation* (1987) and *Luther's Theology of the Cross* (1987). He is also the editor of the *Blackwell Encyclopaedia of Modern Christian Thought* and the author of a number of acclaimed student textbooks on Christianity and Christian theology.

IUSTITIA DEI

SECOND EDITION

A HISTORY OF THE CHRISTIAN DOCTRINE OF JUSTIFICATION

ALISTER E. McGRATH

CAMBRIDGE
UNIVERSITY PRESS

PUBLISHED BY THE PRESS SYNDICATE OF THE UNIVERSITY OF CAMBRIDGE
The Pitt Building, Trumpington Street, Cambridge CB2 1RP, United Kingdom

CAMBRIDGE UNIVERSITY PRESS
The Edinburgh Building, Cambridge CB2 2RU, United Kingdom
40 West 20th Street, New York, NY 10011–4211, USA
10 Stamford Road, Oakleigh, Melbourne 3166, Australia

First published in two volumes in 1986

Volume I
First paperback edition 1989
Reprinted 1993, 1997

Volume II
Reprinted 1991
First paperback edition 1993
Reprinted 1994, 1996

Second edition in one volume 1998

Printed in the United Kingdom at the University Press, Cambridge

Typeset in Plantin 10/12 pt[CE]

A catalogue record for this book is available from the British Library

Library of Congress cataloguing in publication data
McGrath, Alister E., 1953–
Iustitia Dei: a history of the Christian doctrine of
justification / Alister E. McGrath. – 2nd edn.
p. cm.
Includes bibliographical references and indexes.
ISBN 0 521 62426 6 (hardcover). – ISBN 0 521 62481 9 (pbk.)
1. Justification – History of doctrines.   I. Title.
BT764.2.M43   1998   97–45969   CIP
234′.7′09–dc21
ISBN 0 521 62426 6 hardback
ISBN 0 521 62481 9 paperback

Contents

Contents

Contents

Preface

> But pardon, gentles all,
> The flat unraised spirits that hath dar'd
> On this unworthy scaffold to bring forth
> So great an object: can this cockpit hold
> The vasty fields of France? or may we cram
> Within this wooden O the very casques
> That did affright the air at Agincourt?
>
> Henry V, *Chorus* 8–14

The history of the development of the Christian doctrine of justification has never been written. It is this deficiency which the present volume seeks to remedy. It will be evident, however, that the vast scope of the subject under consideration has resulted in certain inevitable restrictions being placed upon the material here presented. A full treatment of the subject would not be confined to the historical and theological aspects of the matter, but would also deal with the related juristic, semantic, political, moral and metaphysical issues which have shaped the Christian discussion of justification down the ages. It is hoped, however, that the significance of this shortcoming will greatly be diminished by judicious use of the vast body of scholarly material available in the learned literature. Inevitably, pressure upon space means that the established results of scholarship must frequently be referred to, rather than reproduced. In effect, the present study is a bibliographical essay which records, correlates, and where possible extends, the present state of scholarly work on the development of the Christian doctrine of justification. It is not merely a catalogue of the doctrines of justification associated with theologians of alleged importance to the development of that doctrine, but is an attempt to record its continuous development within the western theological tradition.

Preface

It is customary to present an *apologia* for a work which may appear to cover much familiar ground. The following considerations suggest that a new study of the development of the Christian doctrine of justification is necessary. First, there has been no major study of the development of the doctrine since the classic study of Albrecht Ritschl, *Die christliche Lehre von der Rechtfertigung und Versöhnung*, published in 1870. The value of that work, now over a century old, is greatly reduced by Ritschl's moralist pre-suppositions, which seriously prejudice his analysis at points, particularly in the case of the young Luther. Secondly, Ritschl's work deals with the development of the doctrine from the eleventh century to the nineteenth, restricting its discussion of the post-Reformation period to its development within German Protestantism. It will therefore be clear that his work requires extension to include the first ten centuries of Christian history, post-Reformation Roman Catholic theology, and later nineteenth- and twentieth-century developments. Thirdly, the vast scholarly undertakings which have given the modern period the magnificent critical editions denied to Ritschl (such as the Weimar Luther edition) have also cast new light on the theology of the medieval period, calling into question most of Ritschl's conclusions. There is an urgent need to correlate these findings and to reappraise the development of the doctrine of justification in the medieval period accordingly. Fourthly, the new interest in ecumenism makes an informed discussion of the development of the doctrine of justification essential. It is thus hoped that the present volume will at least serve to introduce the subject to a wider circle than would otherwise be the case.

The importance of the present study is threefold. First, the historical study of the development of any Christian doctrine from its origins to the present day is inherently significant, in that it illustrates the factors which have influenced the development of doctrine in general. The doctrine of justification, like other doctrines, was discussed in terms of certain semantic, ontological and juristic assumptions, which were questioned, criticised and replaced as the development of Christian theology proceeded. The development of the doctrine of justification is thus a paradigm for the study of ideological interaction in the development of doctrine, illustrating how theological and secular concepts were related as theologians responded to the cultural situation of their period.

The study is also of theological importance. The theological situation today demands both a *restatement* and a *reinstatement* of the Christian doctrine of reconciliation. The essential prerequisite of any attempt to interpret, reinterpret or restate that doctrine is a due appreciation of the historical origins and subsequent development of the concept. It is clearly of little value to attempt to develop or defend theories of justification, reconciliation or atonement which can be shown to rest upon some misunderstanding of a Hebrew root, which represent a recent distortion of an older and more considered doctrine, or which represent a conditioned response to a specific cultural situation that no longer pertains today (a theme which I explored in my 1990 Bampton Lectures at Oxford University). Of the several concepts that have been used within the Christian tradition to articulate the reconciliation effected by God with the world through Christ, perhaps the most important is that of justification. The present study is thus offered as a resource to stimulate and inform this theological need.

In the third place, the study is of importance as a resource for the dialogue between Christians of different traditions, most notably those whose present identities are shaped by the European Reformation of the sixteenth century. The doctrine of justification came to assume a major, possibly pivotal, rôle at that time, with debates over the issue contributing significantly to the emergence of divisions within western Christianity. As pressure grows for Christians to attempt to settle their differences (or at least to understand one another better), an informed understanding of the sixteenth-century debates over the doctrine of justification clearly has a major rôle to play. It is no accident that discussions over this doctrine have played a major role in ecumenical dialogues since 1980.

The first edition of this work appeared in two volumes in 1986, and quickly established itself as the definitive work on the subject. The need for a new edition has been clear for some time. The inconvenience of the original format has resulted in the new edition appearing in a single volume, merging the two volumes of the original. In addition to general updating, substantial additional material has been provided in two areas which have emerged as important in recent years: the 'new perspective' on Paul, which has called into question the general Lutheran understanding of the pivotal role of justification in Paul's writings (§39); and the discussion of the doctrine of justification in recent official ecumenical consultations (§40). With these two new sections, the work may be regarded as a continuous analysis of the reflection within the church on Paul's views on justification during the first two millennia of the Christian era.

Some readers of the first edition expressed puzzlement that there was to be found no specific treatment of Paul's view on justification. It may be helpful to such readers to recall that every generation believed that it had understood Paul correctly, and was duly puzzled when its own settled convictions were called into question by a later generation. What one generation takes to be an accurate analysis of Paul is seen by later scholarship as that generation's analysis of Paul, reflecting its own values, presuppositions, goals and prejudices. The present volume can thus be seen, at one level, as a continuous analysis of the church's interpretation of Paul on justification, which takes no fixed view on what the correct interpretation of Paul should be.

It will be clear that this work has built significantly on the achievements of previous generations of scholarship. If the present work represents an improvement on that which has gone before, it is partly due to the immense researches of others, on which I have been able to draw. Like someone who contemplates a vast landscape, I have been able to see further by standing on the shoulders of others.

We are like dwarves sitting upon the shoulders of giants. We see more, and things that are more distant, than they did, not because our sight is superior to theirs or because we are taller than they were; but because they raise us up, and by their great stature add to ours. (John of Salisbury, *Metalogicon* III, 4)

Oxford   Pentecost, 1997

Acknowledgements

One of the greatest pleasures of scholarship is to be able to acknowledge the assistance which others so generously rendered. I owe sincere thanks to Fr Fergus Kerr O.P., Professor Oliver O'Donovan and Fr Edward Yarnold S.J., who read an earlier draft of this work and made invaluable comments upon it. I also owe thanks to many others, who assisted me in various ways: Fr M. D. Chenu, O.P., Fr Cassian Reel O.F.M.Cap., Beryl Smalley, Peter Southwell and Fr Adolar Zumkeller O.E.S.A. Of the many libraries which were used during the course of this work, I particularly wish to acknowledge the invaluable assistance of the staff of the Bodleian Library, Oxford and Cambridge University Library. I also owe a considerable debt to Merton College, Oxford and St John's College, Cambridge for academic research awards which permitted me to undertake the present work, and Wycliffe Hall, Oxford, for providing me with the facilities to complete it. Finally, I wish to thank the officers of Cambridge University Press, particularly Dr Robert Williams, for their encouragement and support during the closing stages of this work.

1 · Prolegomena

§1 The subject defined

The nature and significance of the Christian doctrine of justification are best appreciated when the nature of Christianity is considered. The central teaching of the Christian faith is that reconciliation has been effected between God and sinful man through Jesus Christ, and that this new relation between God and man is a present possibility for those outside the church, and a present actuality for those within its bounds. Although the manner in which this relationship is conceived and proclaimed generally reflects the contemporary cultural context, the assertion that a *new relationship* – however this is articulated – is thus possible is essentially independent of cultural considerations. It will therefore be clear that the question of how the saving action of God towards mankind in Christ may be appropriated by the individual is of central significance. The Christian doctrine of justification is not, however, merely concerned with the question of what man must do if he is to enter into a relationship with God through Christ, but also with establishing its presuppositions and consequences.

The Christian doctrine of justification, which forms the subject of the present study, thus constitutes the real centre of the theological system of the Christian church, encapsulating the direct and normative consequences of the historical revelation of God to mankind in Jesus Christ. There never was, and there never can be, any true Christian church without the doctrine of justification, for the community of faith cannot exist without proclaiming, in word and sacrament, the truth of what God has done for man in Christ. It is this truth which called the church into being, and it is this truth which must be expressed in her life and doctrine. In the Christian doctrine of justification, we are concerned with the turning of the godless man against his godlessness; with his transformation from man *without*

I

God to man *with* God, *for* God and *before* God; with his transition from *homo peccator* to *homo iustus*. The doctrine defines the conditions under which man's broken relationship with God may be restored, and the nature of that transition itself. Without the recognition of the *necessity*, the *possibility* and the *actuality* of such a transition, there can be no community of faith – and it is in this sense that the *articulus iustificationis* is the *articulus stantis et cadentis ecclesiae*.[1]

The Christian faith is centred upon the person of Jesus Christ. The centrality of the mystery of the person of Christ to her faith is ultimately an expression of his church's conviction that God was in Christ reconciling the world to himself. The creeds of Christendom may not explicitly state a doctrine of reconciliation, but its thread runs throughout their fabric. *Qui propter nos homines et propter nostram salutem descendit de coelis!* Wherever the church commemorates, celebrates and proclaims the passion of her redeemer and the benefits which she thereby receives, she rehearses her faith in the reconciliation he accomplished on her behalf, and which called her into being. Who Christ is becomes known in his saving action; who man is becomes known through his being the object of that saving action. The doctrine of justification thus encapsulates the essence of the Christian faith and proclamation, locating the essence of Christianity in the saving action of God towards mankind in Jesus Christ. The fundamentally soteriological orientation of the patristic Trinitarian and Christological debates demonstrates the centrality of the concept of reconciliation, however expressed, to the positive articulation of the Christian message. Indeed, the dissociation of these dogmas from their soteriological contexts results in their becoming abstract to the point of irrelevance.

The *concept of justification* and the *doctrine of justification* must be carefully distinguished. The *concept* of justification is one of many employed within the Old and New Testaments, particularly the Pauline corpus, to describe God's saving action towards his people. It cannot lay claim to exhaust, nor adequately characterise in itself, the richness of the biblical understanding of salvation in Christ. The *doctrine* of justification has come to develop a meaning quite independent of its biblical origins, and concerns the *means by which man's relationship to God is established*. The church has chosen to subsume its discussion of the reconciliation of man to God under the aegis of justification, thereby giving the concept an emphasis quite absent from the New Testament. The 'doctrine of justification' has come to bear a meaning within dogmatic theology which is quite independent of its Pauline origins, so that even if it could be shown that it plays a minimal role in Pauline soteriology, or that its origins lie in an anti-Judaising polemic quite inappropriate to the theological circumstances of today, its significance would not be diminished as a result. That it was justification, rather than some other soteriological metaphor, which was singled out in this manner may be regarded as an accident of history, linked to several developments.

1. The rise in Pauline scholarship during the theological renaissance of the twelfth century, and particularly the use of Pauline commentaries as vehicles of theological speculation.

2. The generally high regard for classical jurisprudence within the western church.

3. The semantic relationship between *iustitia* and *iustificatio*, which allowed the theologians of High Scholasticism to find in the cognate concept of justification a means of rationalising the divine dispensation towards mankind in terms of justice.

4. The emphasis placed upon an already important concept by Luther's theological difficulties concerning how the statement 'God is just' could be gospel, so that the Reformation came to be perceived to be inextricably linked with the doctrine of justification.

5. The discussion of the reconciliation of man to God under the aegis of the doctrine of justification by the Council of Trent in its sixth session.

The history of the doctrine of justification has its sphere within the western church alone. The Orthodox emphasis upon the economic condescension of the Son leading to man's participation in the divine being is generally expressed in the concept of deification (θεοποίησις or θέωσις) rather than justification.[2] Three factors may be identified which account for this development.

1. The different understandings of the operation of the Holy Spirit associated with the western and eastern churches. The west has tended to subordinate the work of the Holy Spirit to the concept of grace, which is interposed between God and man. The Orthodox stress upon the immediacy of the divine, and the direct encounter of man with the Holy Spirit naturally leads to this encounter being expressed in terms of deification.[3]

2. The concept of deification is particularly suited to a marriage with neo-Platonism, a marriage particularly associated with the mystical works of pseudo-Dionysius, whose use of neo-Platonist concepts to articulate his theology of redemption resulted in a philosophical Christianity of a profundity quite unparalleled in the

west. It was only when his works became available in Latin translation that the theologians of the west began to respond to his
influence[4] – by which time, a western theological tradition of a very
different cast had already become firmly established. The great
theologians of the medieval period, such as Thomas Aquinas, may
have modified their doctrines of justification to accommodate his
insights, but they were already constrained by tradition to the
category of justification, rather than deification.

3. The eastern church never developed the interest in Roman law
which is so characteristic of the early theologians of the Latin west
which, coupled with the character of the Latin language itself (see §2)
led to the western commitment to justification as *the* fundamental
soteriological metaphor. It may therefore be noted that the
astonishing use of the concept of justification in the works of Cyril
Lucaris (1572–1638) merely illustrates his unusual relationship with
the Reformed church of his day,[5] rather than any inherent trends
within Orthodox theology itself. The great schism between east and
west finds expression at a far deeper level than the mere politics of the
matter might suggest.

The present study is therefore concerned with the attempts of the
western church to analyse the presuppositions and consequences of
her proclamation of salvation in Christ from the earliest of times to
the present day.

§2 The conceptual foundations of the Christian doctrine of justification

'I am not ashamed of the gospel, for it is the power of God for
salvation to everyone who has faith . . . for in it the righteousness of
God is revealed' (Romans 1.16–17). For Paul, the revelation of the
righteousness of God *is* the gospel.[1] But what is this tantalising
'righteousness of God'? As the present study will make clear, the
interpretation of the 'righteousness of God' within the western
theological tradition has been accompanied by the most intractable
difficulties. The concept of *justification* is inextricably linked with that
of *righteousness*, both semantically and theologically.[2] Central to the
Christian understanding of the economy of salvation is the conviction
that God is righteous, and acts in accordance with that righteousness
in the salvation of mankind. It is clear, however, that this conviction
raises certain fundamental questions, not least that of which concept
of 'righteousness' can be considered appropriate to a discussion of the

divine dispensation towards mankind. The relationship between God and man, according to the Christian understanding, may be characterised in three propositions:

1.   God is righteous.
2.   Man is a sinner.
3.   God justifies man.

The quintessence of the Christian doctrine of justification is that these three propositions do not constitute an inconsistent triad. God, in his righteousness, justifies the sinner. The proclamation of this justification to those outside the church has always been accompanied by speculation within the church as to how it is possible for God, being righteous, to justify sinners in the first place. It is therefore of considerable importance to consider the various understandings of the concept of 'righteousness' or 'justice' which have been employed in the articulation of the doctrine of justification.

Modern theological vocabularies contain a host of Hebrew, Greek and Latin words, most of which possess, in their original contexts, a richness and depth of meaning which cannot possibly be conveyed by the mere translation of the word into English. Such an enterprise involves not merely the substitution of a modern word for the original, but the transference of the latter from its own proper conceptual framework to one in which its meaning is distorted. This problem has long been recognised. Jesus ben Sira, presumably in an attempt to divert attention from the absence of a Hebrew original, complained that 'things originally spoken in Hebrew do not have the same force when they are translated into another language ... with the law, the prophets and the rest of the writings, it makes no small difference when they are read in their original language' (Ecclesiasticus, prologue). The conceptual foundations of the Christian doctrine of justification may be sought in the Old Testament, in a milieu quite different from that of western Europe, where it received its systematic articulation. The transference of the concept from this Hebraic matrix to that of western Europe has significant consequences, which we shall explore in the present section.

The primary source for Christian theological speculation is Holy Scripture: indeed, Christian theology may be regarded as an extended commentary upon the biblical material. It is therefore evident that Christian theology will contain a number of important concepts originating from a Hebraic context, and that the transference of these concepts from their original context may result in a shift in meaning with unacceptable theological consequences. In particular, it must be pointed out that the equation of Hebraic and western concepts of 'righteousness' is frequently implicit in theological works, so that western concepts of justice are employed in the articulation of the Christian doctrine of justification. A study of the classic western understandings of justice suggests that these are essentially *secular* and *practical*, and therefore quite unsuited to a discussion of the 'righteousness of God'. The present section, dealing with the Hebrew, Greek and Latin understandings of 'righteousness', is therefore intended as a prolegomenon to the study of the doctrine of justification. Although not strictly a part of the history of the doctrine itself, the question exercised such an influence over the subsequent discussion of justification that its omission at this stage is impossible.

The etymology of the terms ṣedeq and ṣᵉdāqâ is generally accepted to be obscure, and it is quite possible that the original meaning of the grapheme ṣdq is lost beyond recovery. Recent theories of the historical background of the Hebrew language have tended to divide the Hamito-Semitic languages into two groups: the archaic southern Cushitic and Chadic languages, and the more progressive northern group of languages, including the Semitic languages, the Berber languages of north Africa, and ancient Egyptian and Coptic.[3] The triliteral root is a conspicuous feature common to all the languages of the northern group, and it is possible to argue that at every level – whether semantic, grammatical or phonological – features of these languages are theoretically derivable from a common source. When the etymology of the grapheme ṣdq is examined, using other ancient near eastern languages as models, a spectrum of possible meanings emerges, of which the most fundamental appears to be that of *conformity to a norm*.[4] This observation is confirmed by the fact that the dominant sense of the terms ṣedeq and ṣᵉdāqâ appears to be that of 'right behaviour' or 'right disposition'.[5] That similar understandings of 'righteousness' were common in the ancient world is demonstrated by the close semantic association between the ideas of 'righteousness' and 'truth' in the Aryan ṛtá- and Iranian aša.[6]

The validity of such an appeal to etymological considerations has been criticised by Barr,[7] who illustrates the alleged inadequacy of the tool with reference to the English word 'nice'. The etymology of the word indicates that it derives from the Latin *nescius*, presumably *via* the Old French *nice*, thereby suggesting that its meaning should be 'silly' or 'ignorant' – which is clearly of little use in determining its late twentieth century usage. Barr neglects, however, to point out that etymological considerations *can* give an indication of the *early* meaning of a term, despite the connotations it may develop later as a consequence of constant use. Whilst the derivation of 'nice' from 'nescius' does not allow its modern meaning to be established, it is perfectly adequate to allow its *sixteenth*-century meaning to be established, it then bearing the sense of 'silly' or 'ignorant'. As the enterprise in question is to establish the meaning of the term in texts of widely varying age, etymological arguments are perfectly acceptable in an attempt to establish its *early* meaning: the later meaning of the term, of course, cannot be determined by such considerations, as nuances not originally present make their appearance. Thus in later Hebrew, ṣᵉdāqâ came to mean 'almsgiving', a meaning which cannot be derived from etymological considerations alone. Here, as elsewhere, the semantic connection between a grapheme and the meaning of a word appears to have eventually become so strained as to have almost snapped completely. However, as we shall indicate below, this later meaning of the word ṣᵉdāqâ can be understood on the basis of its etymology.

The *oldest* meaning of ṣᵉdāqâ, as judged by its use in the Song of Deborah (Judges 5.1–31), appears to be 'victory'.[8] This meaning appears to be retained in some later texts,[9] although it is clear that the nuances associated with the term have altered. In this early passage, which contains many unusual grammatical forms and rare words, God is understood to have demonstrated his 'righteousness' by defending Israel when her existence was threatened by an outside agency. Underlying this understanding of *iustitia Dei* is the conceptual framework of the covenant: when God and Israel mutually fulfil their covenant obligations to each other, a state of righteousness can be said to exist – i.e., things are ṣaddîq, 'as they should be'. Thus Israel's triumphant victories over her enemies were seen as proofs of the ṣidqôt 'ᵃdoñay,[10] the *iustitiae Dei* of the Vulgate. Even where the term 'righteousness' is not found, it seems that a clear connection is understood to exist between God's activity as a judge and Israel's victory over her neighbours.[11]

At this stage in the history of Israel, the 'righteousness' of the covenant does not appear to have been considered to have been under threat from within Israel itself, but merely from external agencies. However, with the establishment of Israel came the rise of prophecy, and the threat posed to the covenant relationship from within Israel herself became increasingly apparent. This insight was expressed by the prophets in terms of the *conditional election* of Israel as the people of God. For the prophets, ṣᵉdāqâ was effectively that condition or state which was required of Israel if her relationship with God was to continue.[12] Although there are many instances where ṣᵉdāqâ can be regarded as corresponding to the concept of *iustitia distributiva*, which has come to dominate western thinking on the nature of justice (despite the rival claims of *iustitia commutativa*), there remains a significant number which cannot. An illustration of this may be found in the Old Testament attitude to the poor, needy and destitute. As we have noted, ṣᵉdāqâ refers to the 'right order of affairs' which is violated, at least in part, by the very existence of such unfortunates. In his ṣᵉdāqâ, God must deliver them from their plight – and it is *this* aspect of the Hebrew concept of ṣᵉdāqâ which has proved so intractable to those who attempted to interpret it solely as *iustitia distributiva*. It is clear that this aspect of the Hebraic understanding of 'righteousness' cannot be understood in terms of an impartial judge who administers justice according to which party has broken a universally accepted law.

It is to the genius of Cremer that we owe the fundamental insight that ṣᵉdāqâ, in its basic sense, refers to an actual relationship between two persons, and implies behaviour which corresponds to, or is consistent with, whatever claims may arise from or concerning either party to the relationship. The relationship in question is that presupposed by the covenant between God and Israel, which must be considered as the ultimate norm to which ṣᵉdāqâ must be referred. The Hebrew concept of ṣᵉdāqâ stands in a class of its own – a class which Cremer brilliantly characterised as *iustitia salutifera*.[13]

The strongly soteriological overtones of the term ṣᵉdāqâ can be illustrated from a number of passages in which 'righteousness' and 'salvation' are practically equated, particularly from Deutero-Isaiah:

> I will bring my ṣᵉdāqâ near, it is not far away,
> And my salvation will not be delayed.[14]

This is not, it must be emphasised, to say that 'righteousness' and 'salvation' are treated as being synonymous: rather, they are regarded as being inextricably linked on account of the covenant relationship between God and Israel. Semantic and theological considerations combine to give the Old Testament concept of the 'righteousness of God' such strongly soteriological overtones, which the western concept of *iustitia distributiva* cannot convey. The later meaning of ṣᵉdāqâ in post-biblical Hebrew ('almsgiving') can thus be seen as the development of a trend already evident in passages such as Psalm

112.9 and Daniel 4.27 (Aramaic 4.24: although this section of the book of Daniel is written in Aramaic, rather than Hebrew, the same word is used in each language). The 'right order of affairs' is violated by the existence of the poor and needy; it is therefore a requirement of ṣᵉḏāqâ that this be remedied by the appropriate means. Thus the sense which ṣᵉḏāqâ assumes in the Targums and Talmud ('benevolence' in general, or 'almsgiving' in particular) can be seen to represent a natural development of the soteriological nuances which had been associated with the term from the earliest of times, rather than the final rupture of the semantic connection between a word and its root.[15]

The difficulties attending the translation of the Old Testament into any second language, whether modern English or Hellenistic Greek, are well illustrated by the application of semantic field theory. The *semantic field*[16] of a word includes not merely its synonyms, but also its antonyms, homonyms and homophones. As such, it is much broader than the *lexical field*, which may be defined very precisely in terms of words which are closely associated with one another. The enormous size of such semantic fields may be illustrated from the associative field of the French word *chat*, which is estimated to consist of some two thousand words.[17] The translation of a word into a different language inevitably involves a distortion of the semantic field, so that certain nuances and associations present in the original cannot be conveyed in a translation, and new nuances and associations not already present make their appearance. The word chosen to translate the original will itself have a well-established semantic field, so that an alien set of associations will be imposed upon the word in question. This difficulty is well illustrated in the two non-contiguous semantic transitions of importance to our study, ṣᵉḏāqâ → *iustitia*, and haṣdîq → *iustificare*, whether these proceed directly, or indirectly through the Greek of the Septuagint (LXX). We shall consider these semantic transitions individually.

1 ṣᵉḏāqâ → δικαιοσύνη → *iustitia*

The considerable influence of Greek philosophy and culture upon Christian thought in its formative period has been well documented.[18] This influence is also mediated through the LXX, whose origins date from the beginning of the third century BC.[19] The term δικαιοσύνη had by then acquired a generally Aristotelian sense, so that by δικαιοσύνη we may understand something very similar to *iustitia distributiva.*[20] Aristotle's ethical thinking is to be set in the context of the political community, the πόλις, so that 'righteousness' is defined teleologically, in terms of the well-being which it brings to the political community as a whole. Lower beings, such as the animals, and higher beings, such as the gods, were excluded from any discussion of δικαιοσύνη precisely because they were not members of the contracting political community. The sphere of δικαιοσύνη is defined as that of the πόλις, so that the concept of the 'righteousness of God' has no immediate practical significance.

It is evident that this understanding of 'righteousness' is quite different from that signified by the Hebrew word ṣᵉḏāqâ. In particular, δικαιοσύνη is a secular concept incapable of assuming the soteriological overtones associated with the Hebrew term. Whilst the translators of the LXX appear to have attempted consistency in this translation of Hebrew terms,[21] they were unable to accommodate the meaning of ṣᵉḏāqâ by the simple substitution of δικαιοσύνη in every case. Of particular interest is the translation of ṣdq in the construct form (e.g., at Leviticus 19.36, Deuteronomy 25.15 and Ezekiel 45.10). The Hebrew has the sense of 'accurate' – i.e., in the case of Leviticus 19.36, the weights are 'as they are intended to be' – accurate. Thus the στάθμια δίκαια of the LXX are clearly nothing more than accurate weights. Similarly, the 'sacrifices of righteousness' (Deuteronomy 33.19; Psalm 4.6; 51.21) appear to be nothing more than 'correct sacrifices' – i.e., those which are 'in order' under the cultic circumstances, rather than ethically or forensically 'righteous'. The basic meaning of the ṣdq-group as 'conformity to a requirement' is well illustrated by the use of ṣdq in the construct form – a meaning for which there was no satisfactory Greek equivalent. While the δικ-lexical group appears to have been considered capable of translating the ṣdq-group in the majority of cases, the soteriological connotations of ṣᵉḏāqâ were occasionally so strong that it could not be translated by δικαιοσύνη, the translators being forced to use ἐλεημοσύνη.[22] This would be expected to have at least one very significant consequence for the Greek reader of the Old Testament, unfamiliar with its Hebrew original: here he might encounter a reference to God's δικαιοσύνη, there to his ἐλεημοσύνη – and yet the same Hebrew word, ṣᵉḏāqâ, might lie behind both. The reader, unaware that the same Hebrew word was being 'translated' in each case, might conceivably set God's 'righteousness' and 'mercy' in opposition, where no such tension is warranted on the basis of the text itself.

For the first fifteen hundred years of her existence, the western church's theologians depended mainly upon Latin translations of the bible, chiefly the Vulgate, for their theological deliberations. As most theologians of the period did not have access to the original Hebrew version of the Old Testament – assuming, of course, that they knew Hebrew[23] – their interpretation of *theologoumena* such as *iustitia Dei* and *iustificare* would ultimately be based upon the Latin version of the bible available to them. It is therefore of importance to consider the difficulties attending the translation of essentially Hebraic concepts, such as 'justification', into a Latin linguistic and conceptual framework. By the second century A.D., the Latin term *iustitia* had acquired well-established juristic connotations which were to exert considerable influence over future theological interpretation of such *theologoumena*. The Ciceronian definition of *iustitia* as *reddens unicuique quod suum est* had become normative. Iustitia virtus est, communi utilitate servata, suam cuique tribuens dignitatem.[24] In effect, the Ciceronian definition encapsulates the western concept of *iustitia distributiva*, the 'due' of each man being established through the *iuris consensus*, and embodied in *ius*. The tension between this concept of 'righteousness' and that of the Old Testament will be evident.

The most important book of the Old Testament, as judged by its influence upon the development of the Christian doctrine of justification, is the Psalter, the subject of major commentaries by Augustine, Peter Lombard and Luther, to name but three. The Vulgate, as we know it, contains Jerome's translation of the Hebrew books of the Old Testament, with the *exception* of the Psalter. The Psalter found in the Vulgate is the *Psalterium Gallicum*, Jerome's second revision of the Old Latin Psalter, itself based upon Origen's recension of the LXX version.[25] His later *Psalterium iuxta hebraicam veritatem* never gained general acceptance. The difference between the two Psalters may be illustrated from their translations of Psalm 24.5 (Vulgate 23.5):

Psalterium Gallicum:
accipiet benedictionem a Domino et *misericordiam* a Deo salvatore suo.
Psalterium iuxta hebraicam veritatem:
accipiet benedictionem a Domino et *iustitiam* a Deo salutari suo.
Here the Gallic Psalter follows the LXX, and the *Psalterium iuxta hebraicam veritatem* the original Hebrew.

Although it is clear that considerable confusion could potentially have arisen through such translations, two important factors served to greatly reduce this possibility.

1. The Vulgate itself is not consistent in its translation of the LXX.

Thus the LXX ἐλεημοσύνη, translating ṣᵉḏāqâ, is translated as *iustitia* at Psalm 35.24 and elsewhere. The reasons for this inconsistency are not clear.

2. The two passages in the Psalter which appear to have exercised the greatest influence over western conceptions of *iustitia Dei* are Psalm 31.1 (Hebrew and Vulgate: 30.2) and 71.2 (Vulgate: 70.2).[26] In both these passages, the Psalmist appeals to God, in his righteousness, to deliver him:

> In you, O Lord, do I take refuge,
> Let me never be put to shame.
> *In your righteousness* deliver me and rescue me.

In both cases, the LXX translated ṣᵉḏāqâ as δικαιοσύνη, and the Vulgate thence as *iustitia*. The strongly soteriological sense of *iustitia* could thus be appreciated, as is borne out by the study of the exegesis of such passages in the early medieval period.

2 haṣdîq → δικαιοῦν → *iustificare*

The Hebrew term haṣdîq, usually translated 'to justify', cannot bear the negative sense 'to condemn' or 'to punish', its primary sense apparently being 'to vindicate', 'to acquit', or 'to declare to be in the right'.[27] The difficulty faced by the LXX translators was that the corresponding Greek verb δικαιοῦν differed from haṣdîq in two important respects.

1. In its classical usage, δικαιοῦν with a *personal* object almost invariably seems to be applied to someone whose cause is *unjust*, and thus bears the meaning of 'to do justice to' – i.e., 'to punish'. Although it is possible to adduce occasional classical references in which δικαιοῦν may conceivably be interpreted as assuming a *positive* sense – i.e., to 'right an injustice suffered'[28] – it may be emphasised that this is extremely unusual. In general, the classical usage of δικαιοῦν is such that it is highly unusual to find it applied, with a personal object, in the sense of 'to justify' – and yet it is this positive sense which constitutes the *norm* for the Septuagintal use of the verb. Indeed, there are no known occurrences of δικαιοῦν in a negative sense in any part of the Septuagint for which there exists a Hebrew original.[29] It is therefore clear that the Septuagintal usage of the term represents a significant shift away from the classical meaning of the term towards that of the corresponding Hebrew term – a shift which might prove stultifying to a Greek reader of the Old Tes-

tament, not familiar with the Hebrew original. No example of the classical use of δικαιοῦν can be adduced from the LXX, and the normal meaning it assumes in the LXX can only be adduced in a few isolated and controversial passages in classical Greek literature.

2. In classical Greek, δικαιοῦν with a personal object *applied to a person whose cause is unjust* invariably assumes the negative meaning 'to punish'. The Septuagintal use of the verb in an identical context demands that it assumes a *positive* meaning – i.e., 'to justify', 'to declare to be in the right', or 'to acquit'. For example, Isaiah 5.22–3 (LXX) follows both the wording of the Massoretic text very closely, giving the following translation: οὐαὶ ... οἱ δικαιοῦντες τὸν ἀσηβῆ ἕνεκεν δώρων καὶ τὸ δίκαιον τοῦ δικαίου αἴροντες. The substance of the complaint is that certain men are, for the sake of financial considerations, δικαιοῦντες τον ἀσηβῆ. This complaint does not make sense if the classical sense of δικαιοῦν (e.g., as it is encountered at Ecclesiasticus 42.2) is presumed to apply: if the unjust are punished – i.e., have 'justice done to them' – there can be no cause for complaint. The complaint does, however, make sense if the term is presumed to have a Hebraic background, in that the substance of the complaint is then that certain men have been bribed to declare the guilty to be innocent. It is clear that the term δικαιοῦν, although of classical Greek provenance, has assumed a Hebraic meaning as a consequence of its being used to translate the ṣdq-words. The Greek reader of the Old Testament, unfamiliar with the Hebraic background to such material, would find passages such as the above highly perplexing. The *locus classicus* for the secular Greek use of the verb is Book V of Aristotle's *Nicomachean Ethics*, in which the passive form of δικαιοῦν, (δικαιοῦσθαι) is clearly and unequivocally understood to be the antithesis of ἀδικεῖσθαι and the passive equivalent of the active δικαιοπραγεῖν, as may be seen from the statement ἀδύνατον γὰρ ἀδικεῖσθαι μὴ ἀδικοῦντος, ἢ δικαιοῦσθαι μὴ δικαιοπραγοῦντος.[30] It is clear that the passive meaning of the verb is 'to have justice done to one'. If this classical Aristotelian understanding of δικαιοῦσθαι is applied to the Septuagintal translation of Isaiah 43.26, an apparent absurdity results. Israel is there invited to confess her sins, ἵνα δικαιωθῆς. It is not clear why this should move Israel to confess her sins, as in the classical sense of the verb, her punishment will follow as a matter of course. Of course, if it is assumed that the verb has taken on the meaning of haṣdîq, the meaning becomes clear and comprehensible: Israel is invited to confess her sins, in order that she may be acquitted of them. A similar

conclusion must be drawn in the case of Micah 6.11 (LXX), εἰ δικαιωθήσεται ἐν ζυγῷ ἄνομος καὶ ἐν μαρσίππῳ στάθμια δόλου; in which it is clear that the rhetorical question expects an answer *in the negative*.

It is therefore clear that, under the influence of the Hebrew original, the Septuagintal verb δικαιοῦν came to assume a meaning quite distinct from its classical origin. Furthermore, such a meaning must have become widespread and accepted within Greek-speaking Judaism – otherwise, the Septuagint would have been incomprehensible at points. It is clear that this inherent difficulty reflects the quite different semantic fields of the ṣdq- and δικ-words.

A difficulty of a quite different nature arose in the translation of terms such as haṣdîq or δικαιοῦν into Latin. The verb *iustificare*, employed for this purpose, was post-classical, and thus required interpretation. The general tendency among Latin-speaking theologians was to follow Augustine of Hippo (see §4) in interpreting *iustificare* as *iustum facere*. Augustine's etymological speculations have been the object of derision for some considerable time – for example, his impossible derivation of the name *Mercurius* from *medius currens*.[31] His explanation of the origins of the term *iustificare* is, however, quite plausible, for it involves the acceptable assumption that *-ficare* is the unstressed form of *facere*. While this may be an acceptable interpretation of *iustificare* considered in isolation, it is not an acceptable interpretation of the verb *considered as the Latin equivalent of* δικαιοῦν. This point may be developed with reference to the related case of the Greek and Latin understandings of the concept of 'merit'.[32]

Whilst Tertullian has frequently been singled out as the thinker who shackled the theology of the western church to a theology of 'works' and 'merit', there are reasons for supposing that whatever blame is due may be more fairly attributed to the Latin language itself. In Greek, 'merit' tends to be treated as a quality, so that it is essentially adjectival. Thus 'merit' is essentially a matter of estimation. The Latin term *meritum*, however, is a participial form of *mereri*, itself a deponent form of *mereo*, derived from the Greek verb μερόμαι – 'to receive one's share'. The transferred meaning of this thus becomes 'to deserve' or 'to be worthy of something'. There is, however, no Greek verb which bears quite this sense, for desert is treated essentially as a matter of estimation, rather than a quality in itself. The 'estimation' in question cannot be transferred to its object. The Latin approach to the question, however, involves the identification of the quality of the object which occasioned such an estimation. In other words, the Greek verb refers to something outside the person in question (i.e., the estimation in which he is held by others, and which cannot be treated as a quality), whereas the Latin refers to the qualities of the person in question (i.e., what it is about him that has caused the estimation in which he is held by others). Thus the nearest Greek equivalents to *mereri* are probably the passive form ἀξιοῦσθαι or the periphrastic ἄξιος εἶναι – but in each case, the reference is still to the estimation in which the individual is held, rather than to his 'merit'. It is of considerable interest to note that the Latin *meritum* and its cognates derive from the Greek μερόμαι rather than ἀξιοῦσθαι. The Latin notion of 'merit' clearly refers to the *right* of the individual to the particular estimation in which he is held by others, or the reward which results from this. This is clearly stated by Hilary of Poitiers: '*Mereri* is predicable of the person whose own act is the origin of the acquisition of merit for himself.'[33] This observation goes some considerable way towards explaining why the Greek-speaking church never developed a theology of 'merit' in a manner comparable to that of the Latin west.

If this illustration of the relationship between ἀξιοῦσθαι and *mereri* is applied to the related case of δικαιοῦσθαι and *iustificari*, it would appear that the Greek verb has the primary sense of being *considered* or *estimated* as righteous, whereas the Latin verb denotes *being* righteous, the reason why one is *considered* righteous by others. Although the two are clearly related, they have quite distinct points of reference.

'Messieurs, l'Angleterre est une île.' Jules Michelet prefaced his lectures on British history by pointing to a single geographical factor which had such a decisive influence upon his subject, and which was all too easily overlooked. As we begin our study of the development of the Christian doctrine of justification, it is necessary to observe that the early theologians of the western church were dependent upon Latin versions of the bible, and approached their texts and their subject with a set of presuppositions which owed more to the Latin language and culture than to Christianity itself. The initial transference of a Hebrew concept to a Greek, and subsequently to a Latin, context point to a fundamental alteration in the concepts of 'justification' and 'righteousness' as the gospel spread from its Palestinian source to the western world. Viewed theologically, this transition resulted in a shift of emphasis from *iustitia coram Deo* to *iustitia in hominibus*. This shift in emphasis and reference from God to man is

Prolegomena

inevitably accompanied by an anthropocentricity in the discussion of
justification which is quite absent from the biblical material. The
subsequent development of the theology of justification within the
western church would be concerned with the elucidation of this
iustitia in hominibus – i.e., with questions such as: what was the nature
of this righteousness within man, how did it get there, and where did
it come from? These questions are largely the result of a changed
linguistic and conceptual framework resulting from the transference
of originally Hebraic concepts to the western Latin-speaking world.
The shifts in meaning we have noted for the non-contiguous semantic
transitions ṣᵉḏāqâ → δικαιοσύνη → *iustitia* and haṣdîq →
δικαιοῦν → *iustificare* must be regarded as being of decisive
importance in the shaping of the western discussion of justification.
As we begin the study of the development of the doctrine of
justification within the western church, it must be appreciated that
the Latin language itself has had a far greater influence upon that
development than has been generally appreciated.

2. The fountainhead: Augustine of Hippo

Introduction

The theology of the medieval period may be regarded as thoroughly Augustinian, a series of footnotes to Augustine, in that theological speculation was essentially regarded as an attempt to defend, expand, and where necessary modify, the Augustinian legacy. The doctrine of justification is of particular significance in this respect, in that the medieval period witnessed a decisive shift in emphasis away from speculation concerning the *person* of Christ to speculation concerning the *work* of Christ. While the patristic period witnessed considerable interest in the question of who Christ *was*, the medieval period recognised the need to amplify the somewhat unsatisfactory patristic replies to the question of what Christ *did*. An awareness of the leading features of Augustine's doctrine of justification is therefore an essential prerequisite to a correct understanding of the medieval discussion of the doctrine of justification. In the present chapter, we propose to indicate the main features of Augustine's soteriology, after considering the early confusion on the matter within the pre-Augustinian tradition.

§3 The pre-Augustinian tradition

The patristic era is that of the exploration, and where possible the reduction, of the tension existing between the need to retain a traditional *corpus* of belief as the *regula fidei*,[1] and the need to expand and develop that *corpus* in the face of opposition from both within and without the Christian community. The earlier patristic period represents the age of the exploration of concepts, when the proclamation of the gospel within a pagan culture was accompanied by an exploitation of both Hellenistic culture and pagan philosophy as vehicles for theological advancement. This tentative exploration of the conceptual world is particularly well illustrated by the rise and subsequent decline of the Logos-Christology. The use of such concepts in Christian theology was not, however, without its risks: it was not sufficient merely to baptise Plato and Plotinus, for the tension which existed between the essentially Hebraic concepts which underlie the gospel and the Hellenism of the medium employed in its early formulation and propagation remains unresolved. Whilst it is evident that some form of adaptation may be necessary in order to give the gospel more immediate impact on its introduction to an alien culture, it is equally evident that such an adaptation may result in both compromise and distortion of the characteristic and distinctive elements of the gospel. An excellent example of the influence of a Hellenistic milieu upon Christian theology is provided by the doctrine of the ἀπάθεια of God,[2] which clearly demonstrates the subordination of a biblical to a philosophical view of God.

Part of the fascination of the patristic era to the scholar lies in the efforts of its theologians to express an essentially Hebraic gospel in a Hellenistic milieu: the delights of patristic scholarship must not, however, be permitted to divert our attention from the suspicion voiced by the Liberal school in the last century – that Christ's teaching was seriously compromised by the Hellenism of its earliest adherents.[3] The early history of the development of the Christian doctrine of justification lends support to such a suspicion. In particular, it can be shown that two major distortions were introduced into the *corpus* of traditional belief within the eastern church at a very early stage, and were subsequently transferred to the emerging western theological tradition. These are:

1. The introduction of the non-biblical, secular Stoic concept of αὐτεξουσία or *liberum arbitrium* in the articulation of the human response to the divine initiative in justification.

2. The implicit equation of ṣᵉdāqâ, δικαιοσύνη and *iustitia*, linked with the particular associations of the Latin term *meritum* noted earlier (p. 15), inevitably suggested a correlation between human moral effort and justification within the western church.

The subsequent development of the western theological tradition, particularly since the time of Augustine, has shown a reaction against both these earlier distortions, and may be regarded as an attempt to recover a more biblically orientated approach to the question of justification. The *pre*-Augustinian theological tradition, however, may be regarded as having taken a highly questionable path in its articulation of the doctrine of justification in the face of pagan opposition. The Pelagian controversy may be regarded as having highlighted the two points noted above, although not in the precise form in which they are there stated, so that considerable attention was subsequently paid to their more precise formulation. It is therefore advisable to follow late medieval theological scholarship in drawing a distinction between the *modus loquendi theologicus* prior and subsequent to the Pelagian controversy.[4]

The history of early Christian doctrine is basically the history of the emergence of the Christological and Trinitarian dogmas. Whilst the importance of soteriological considerations, both in the motivation of the development of early Christian doctrine and as a normative principle during the course of that development, is generally conceded,[5] it is equally evident that the early Christian writers did not choose to express their soteriological convictions in terms of the concept of justification. This is not to say that the fathers avoid the term 'justification': their interest in the concept is, however, minimal, and the term generally occurs in their writings as a direct citation from, or a recognisable allusion to, the epistles of Paul, generally employed for some purpose other than a discussion of the concept of justification itself. Furthermore, the few occasions upon which a specific discussion of justification can be found generally involve no interpretation of the matter other than a mere paraphrase of a Pauline statement. Justification was simply not a theological issue in the pre-Augustinian tradition. The emerging patristic understanding of matters such as predestination,[6] grace and free will[7] is somewhat confused, and would remain so until controversy forced a full discussion of the issue upon the church. Indeed, by the end of the fourth century, the Greek fathers had formulated a teaching on human free will based upon philosophical rather than biblical foundations. Standing in the great Platonic tradition, heavily influenced by Philo, and reacting against the fatalisms of their day, they taught that man was utterly free in his choice of good or evil. It is with the Latin fathers that we observe the beginnings of speculation on the nature of original sin and corruption, and the implications which this may have for man's moral faculties.[8]

'It has always been a puzzling fact that Paul meant so relatively little for the thinking of the church during the first 350 years of its history. To be sure, he is honored and quoted, but – in the theological perspective of the west – it seems that Paul's great insight into justification by faith was forgotten.'[9] In part, the early patristic neglect of the Pauline writings may reflect uncertainty concerning the extent of the New Testament canon.[10] As the Pauline epistles came to be accorded increasing authority within the church, so their influence upon theological debate increased correspondingly. Thus the end of the period of oral tradition (c. 150) may be considered to mark a return to Paulinism in certain respects, so that writers such as Irenaeus of Lyons may be regarded as representing the gospel more accurately than Ignatius of Antioch.[11] It must also be appreciated, however, that the early fathers do not appear to have been faced with a threat from Jewish Christian activists teaching justification by works of the law, such as is presupposed by those Pauline epistles dealing with the doctrine of justification by faith in most detail (e.g., Galatians). The only patristic work which appears to presuppose this specific threat is the tract *de his qui putant se ex operibus iustificari*[12] of Mark the Hermit (fl. c. 431), probably dating from the early fifth century. The main external threat to the early church, particularly during the second century, appears to have been pagan or semi-pagan fatalisms, such as Gnosticism, which propagated the thesis that man is neither responsible for his own sins, nor for the evil of the world. It is quite possible that the curious and disturbing tendency of the early fathers to minimise original sin and emphasise the freedom of fallen man[13] is a consequence of their anti-Gnostic polemic. Whilst it is true that the beginnings of a doctrine of grace may be discerned during this early period,[14] its generally optimistic estimation of the capacities of fallen humanity has led many scholars to question whether it can be regarded as truly Christian in this respect.

The pre-Augustinian theological tradition is practically of one voice in asserting the freedom of the human will. Thus Justin Martyr rejects the idea that all human actions are foreordained on the grounds that this eliminates human accountability.[15] This argument is supplemented by an appeal to scriptural texts apparently teaching man's freedom of action, such as Deuteronomy 30.19: 'I have set before you life and death, the blessing and the curse; therefore choose life, that you may live.' It must be pointed out, of course, that Justin's defence of the free will is not in any way specifically *Christian*, in any way linked to the Incarnation, for example. With the obvious exception of the use of biblical quotations, Justin's anti-fatalist arguments can be adduced from practically any of the traditional pagan refutations of astral fatalisms, going back to the second century B.C.[16] Furthermore, the biblical quotations which Justin does employ can be shown to be predominantly from the Old Testament, and traditionally used in *Jewish* refutations of such fatalisms. Thus

Philo of Alexandria had earlier used an anti-fatalist argument practically identical to Justin's, down to the citation from Deuteronomy 30.19.[17]

Whilst Justin's defence of the freedom of the will does not appear to have been occasioned by Gnosticism, its rise appears to have had a profound effect upon his successors. While there is still uncertainty concerning the precise nature of Gnosticism, it may be noted that a strongly fatalist or necessitarian outlook appears to be characteristic of the chief Gnostic systems.[18] Far from recognising the limitations of man's free will, many early fathers enthusiastically proclaimed its freedom (ἐλευθερία) and self-determination (αὐτεξουσία): ἐλεύθερον γὰρ καὶ αὐτεξούσιον ἐποίησεν ὁ θεος ἄνθρωπον.[19] The introduction of the *secular* concept of self-determination (αὐτε-ξουσία) into the theological vocabulary of Christendom is of particular significance, particularly in view of its later application in the Macarian homilies.[20] There man's self-determination is proclaimed to be such that he can apply himself either to good or evil.[21] God cannot be said to force the free will, but merely to influence it.[22] While God does not wish man to do evil, he cannot compel him to do good.[23] John Chrysostom's defence of the power of the human free will was so convincing that it was taken up by many Pelagian writers: 'good and evil do not originate from man's nature itself, but from the will and choice alone'.[24] This localisation of the origin of sin in the misuse of the human free will was a theological commonplace by the fourth century.[25] The patristic discussion of human freedom received significant development by the Cappadocians. Gregory of Nyssa distinguished two types of freedom: structural freedom, by which Adam was able to communicate with God and all of his creation; and functional freedom, by which man has freedom of choice. The former was lost at the Fall, but by proper use of the latter, man is able to regain it.[26] Nemesius of Emesa may be regarded as having developed this idea along Aristotelian lines, thus providing an important link between the latter patristic and early scholastic understandings of human freedom.[27] Nemesius' distinction between the *voluntarium* and *involuntarium*, and his emphasis upon the role of *consilium* in decision-making, leads to his insistence that the human reason itself is the basis of man's freedom.

The western theological tradition was somewhat slower to develop than the eastern, and in the course of that development, the theological vocabulary of the east became current in the west. This necessitated the translation of Greek theological terms into Latin, with inevitable shifts in their meanings as a result. It is almost certain too that the western theological tradition owes much of its vocabulary to Tertullian. Thus it is due to his influence that the term *persona* came to translate ὑπόστασις, despite the rival claims of *substantia*.[28] And it is the same writer who introduced to the west the Latin term which would now become the equivalent of αὐτεξουσία – *liberum arbitrium*.[29] It may be noted that αὐτεξουσία concerns ἐξουσία, 'authority-to-act', and has at best remote associations with the concepts of 'will' or 'choice'. The idea of 'will' (*voluntas*) may, indeed, be argued only to have become fully articulated when the Latin language became the normal vehicle of Christian philosophical expression. The weakness of Pauline influence in the early church may be illustrated from the fact that two non-Pauline, non-biblical terms (αὐτεξουσία and *liberum arbitrium*) came to be introduced into the early Christian discussion of man's justification before God. While the introduction of the equally non-biblical term ὁμοούσιος in the fourth century occasioned considerable protest,[30] no objections appear to have been raised to the introduction of the term αὐτεξουσία to refer to man's autonomy in justification. Yet, like the ἀπάθεια of God, the 'self-determination' of the human free will is not so much a Christian idea, as a philosophical idea of its early Hellenistic milieu. Whereas Christian theology has had to wait until the twentieth century for a convincing critique of the former, Augustine's penetrating theological critique of the latter was not long delayed.

The earliest known Latin commentary upon the Pauline epistles is that of Ambrosiaster.[31] Most modern commentators on this important work recognise that its exposition of the doctrine of justification by faith is grounded in the contrast between Christianity and Judaism: there is no trace of a more universal interpretation of justification by faith meaning freedom from a law of works – merely freedom from the Jewish ceremonial law. The Pauline doctrine of freedom from the works of the law is given a specific historical context by Ambrosiaster, in the Jewish background to Christianity. In other respects, Ambrosiaster is more akin to Pelagius than to Augustine. The Pelagian controversy had yet to break, and much of Ambrosiaster's teaching seems strange in the light of that controversy. Like many of his contemporaries, for example, he appears to be obsessed with the idea that man can acquire merit before God, and the associated idea that certain labours are necessary to attain this.[32] Similar ideas have often been detected in the writings of Tertullian, leading some commentators to suggest that his theology is merely a republication of that of Judaism,[33] others charging him with uniting Old Testament legalism with Roman moralism and jurisprudence.[34] His most debatable contribution to the developing western tradition on justification, his introduction of the term *liberum arbitrium* aside, is his theology of merit. For Tertullian, the man who performs good works can be said to make God his debtor: bonum factum deum habet debitorem, sicuti et malum: quia iudex omnis remunerator est causae.[35] The understanding of the 'righteousness of God' as *reddens unicuique quod suum est* underlies this teaching. A similar tendency can be detected in his teaching that man can 'satisfy' his obligation to God on account of his sin through penance.[36] Indeed, Tertullian has exercised a certain fascination over legal historians, who have noted his introduction of legal terms such as *meritum* and *satisfactio* into theology with some interest.[37] The concept of a divine obligation to man thus makes its appearance in the western theological tradition in a somewhat naïve form, and once more it is due to the religious genius of Augustine that the concept was subjected to penetrating criticism.

For the first three hundred and fifty years of the history of the church, her teaching on justification was inchoate and ill-defined. There had never been a serious controversy over the matter, such as those which had so stimulated the development of Christology over the period. The patristic inexactitude and naïveté on the question merely reflects the absence of a controversy which would force more precise definition of the terms used. If the first centuries of the western theological tradition appear be characterised by a 'works-righteousness' approach to justification, it must be emphasised that this was quite innocent of the overtones which would later be associated with it. This 'works-righteousness' ceased to be innocent and ingenuous in the system of Pelagius and his followers, and came to threaten and obscure the gospel as the message of the free grace of God. It is therefore to Augustine of Hippo that we turn for the first definitive statements of the western doctrine of justification.

§4 Augustine of Hippo

According to Isidore of Seville (c. 560 – 636), the following cautionary lines were written above the cupboard which housed the works of Augustine in the Seville library:

> Mentitur, qui te totum legisse fatetur,
> An quis cuncta tua lector habere potest?[1]

It is certain that no writer, other than those of scripture, has exercised so great an influence over the development of western Christian thought as Augustine of Hippo. This influence is particularly associated with, although by no means restricted to, the theological renaissance of the twelfth century, and the Reformation of the sixteenth. Anselm of Canterbury spoke for the theological tradition of the west when he equated orthodoxy with conformity to the writings *catholicorum patrum et maxime beati Augustini*.[2] *All* medieval theology is 'Augustinian', to a greater or lesser extent. It is, however, remarkable that although much attention has been paid in the literature to Augustine's doctrine of *grace*, there is a virtual absence of studies dealing with his doctrine of *justification*. This *lacuna* is all the more astonishing when the significance of Augustine's understanding of justification to his social and political thought is considered. The significance of Augustine's doctrine of justification to the present study relates to its subsequent influence upon the medieval period and beyond. Augustine's doctrine of justification is the first discussion of the matter of major significance to emerge from the twilight of the western theological tradition, establishing the framework within which the future discussion of the justification of man before God would be conducted.

It is important to appreciate that Augustine's doctrine of justification underwent significant development. For example, prior to his elevation to the see of Hippo Regis in 395, Augustine appears to have held precisely the same opinion which he would later condemn – the Massilian attribution of the *initium fidei* to the human free will. Some thirty years after his consecration, Augustine conceded that his earlier works, particularly his *Expositio quarundam propositionum ex epistula ad Romanos* (394), should be corrected in the light of his later insights concerning the doctrine of grace.[3] When did Augustine change his mind on this crucial matter? Fortunately, we have his own answer to this question: it was 'in the first of two books written to Simplicianus',[4] written in late 396 or early 397. This work is generally regarded as containing the key to Augustine's changed views on justification.[5] In view of the fact that the Pelagian controversy would not break out until early the following century, it is important to appreciate that Augustine appears to have developed his new understanding of justification – which would henceforth bear the epithet 'Augustinian' – in a non-polemical context. It is not correct to suppose that Augustine's doctrine of justification is merely a reaction against Pelagianism.

Prior to 396, Augustine appears to have seen the spiritual life as an ascent to perfection.[6] This understanding of the Christian life is particularly well expressed in his early conviction that man can take the initiative in this spiritual ascent to God by believing in him, and calling upon God to save him.[7] Augustine was forced to reappraise this youthful opinion in 395, when his Milanese acquaintance Simplicianus posed a series of questions relating to predestination. Why did God hate Esau? Augustine appears to have avoided issues such as this up to this point, but was now obliged to consider the question – and as a result, he appears to have abandoned his earlier attempts to uphold the unrestricted freedom of the will. Among the important changes in his thinking on justification as a result of his reflections on Romans 9.10–29, the following may be noted.

1. Man's election is now understood to be based upon God's eternal decree of predestination.[8] Augustine had earlier taught that man's temporal election of God is prior to God's eternal election of man.

2. Man's response of faith to God's offer of grace is now understood to be in itself a gift of God.[9] Augustine abandons his earlier teaching that man's response to God depends solely upon his unaided free will.

3. While conceding that man's free will is capable of many things, Augustine now insists that it is compromised by sin, and incapable of leading to man's justification unless it is first liberated by grace.[10] In view of the fact that Augustine's teaching on justification altered so radically at this point, and that he is generally regarded as having worked within the same basic conceptual framework for the next thirty years,[11] it is clearly important to exclude any writings prior to his elevation to the episcopacy[12] from our analysis of his mature doctrine of justification, which henceforth would be known as the 'classic Augustinian theology of grace'.[13] We begin our analysis of this theology by considering one of its most difficult aspects – Augustine's teaching on the *liberum arbitrium*.

Luther's 1525 treatise *de servo arbitrio* derives its title from a phrase used in passing by Augustine in the course of his controversy with the Pelagian bishop Julian of Eclanum.[14] In selecting this phrase, Luther appears to claim the support of Augustine for his radical doctrine of the *servum arbitrium*. A consideration of Augustine's background, however, suggests that it is improbable that he held such a doctrine. He had been engaged in anti-Manichaean polemic for some time, defending the catholic teaching against its fatalist opponents. *De*

libero arbitrio (388–95) was written against precisely such necessitarian teachings (e.g., that evil is natural, and not the work of the
human free will). Although Augustine would later modify his earlier
views on the nature of man's *liberum arbitrium*,[15] it is important to
appreciate that the central thesis of the existence of such a *liberum
arbitrium* was neither rejected nor radically altered.

In many respects, Pelagianism may be regarded as the antithesis of
Manichaeism: whereas the latter rejected the existence of free will,
the former exaggerated its role in justification. Augustine's first
anti-Pelagian work, *de peccatorum meritis et remissione* (411), opened
the attack against Pelagianism with the assertion that it attributed too
much to man's *liberum arbitrium*, and thereby effectively denied the
need for special grace. It must be stressed that Augustine does not
refute the error by *denying* man's free will. Augustine insists that the
need for grace can be defended without denying man's *liberum
arbitrium*. His discussion of human freedom in justification proceeds
upon the assumption that both grace and free will are to be affirmed,
the problem requiring resolution being their precise relationship.
God has given man free will, without which he cannot be said to live
well or badly,[16] and it is on the basis of his use of this *liberum arbitrium*
that he will be judged.[17] Grace, far from *abolishing* man's free will,
actually *establishes* it.[18] How can this be so?

Augustine, reacting against the Pelagian exaggeration of fallen
man's abilities, maintained that man possesses *liberum arbitrium* and
denied that he possesses *libertas*.[19] The sinner has free will, but it is
unable to function properly, and thus to allow him freedom. 'The free
will taken captive (*liberum arbitrium captivatum*) does not avail, except
for sin; for righteousness it does not avail, unless it is set free and
aided by divine action.'[20] By *libertas*, Augustine means the power to
choose and accomplish good – a power which fallen human nature
does not possess. However, this loss of *libertas* does not imply the loss
of *liberum arbitrium*. The human will cannot be likened to a scale, in
whose balance-pans the arguments for and against a possible course of
action are carefully weighed before any action is taken (i.e., *libertas
indifferentiae*), as Julian of Eclanum insisted to be the case. While
Augustine allows that the scales in question really do exist, and are
capable of operating, he argues that the balance-pans are loaded on
the side of evil, yielding a judgement invariably biased towards evil.
Although Adam possessed *liberum arbitrium* before the Fall, man's
free will is now compromised by sin, so that it is now *liberum arbitrium
captivatum*. The free will is not lost, nor is it non-existent: it is merely

incapacitated, and may be healed by grace.[21] In justification, the *liberum arbitrium captivatum* becomes the *liberum arbitrium liberatum* by the action of healing grace. Hence the possibility of not sinning cannot exist in fallen man, although Augustine is at pains to point out that this does not exclude man's natural freedom. God would not command us to do something unless there was free will by which we could do it.[22] Augustine's ethics presuppose that man's destiny is determined by merit or demerit, which in turn presuppose – at least for Augustine – free will. Thus Augustine's doctrine of *liberum arbitrium* is to be sharply distinguished from Luther's doctrine of *servum arbitrium*: 'If there is no such thing as God's grace, how can he be the saviour of the world? And if there is no such thing as free will, how can he be its judge?'[23] Augustine's concept of *liberum arbitrium captivatum* resolves the dialectic between grace and free will without denying the reality of either.

For Augustine, man's *liberum arbitrium captivatum* is incapable of either desiring or attaining justification. How, then, does faith, the fulcrum about which justification takes place, arise in the individual? According to Augustine, the act of faith is itself a divine gift, in which God acts upon the rational soul in such a way that it comes to believe. Whether this action on the will leads to its subsequent assent to justification is a matter for man, rather than God. Qui fecit te sine te, non te iustificat sine te.[24] Although God is the origin of the gift which man is able to receive and possess, the acts of receiving and possessing themselves can be said to be man's.

To meet Pelagian evasions, Augustine drew a distinction between *operative* and *cooperative* grace (or, more accurately, between operative and cooperative modes of gratuitous divine action: Augustine does not treat them as distinct species). God *operates* to initiate man's justification, in that he is given a will capable of desiring good, and subsequently *cooperates* with that good will to perform good works, to bring that justification to perfection. God operates upon the bad desires of the *liberum arbitrium captivatum* to allow it to will good, and subsequently cooperates with the *liberum arbitrium liberatum* to actualise that good will in a good action. Man's justification is therefore an act of divine mercy, in that he does not desire it (because the *liberum arbitrium captivatum* is incapable of desiring good) nor does he deserve it (because of his sin and lack of merit). On account of the Fall, man's free will is weakened and incapacitated, though not destroyed. Thus man does not wish to be justified, because his *liberum arbitrium captivatum* is incapable of desiring justification;

however, once restored to its former capacities by healing grace, it recognises the goodness of what it has been given. God thus cures man's illness, of which the chief symptom is the absence of any desire to be cured. This apparent contradiction has, of course, been criticised for failing to respect man's free will.[25] In response to this, it must be pointed out that the divine justification of the sinner in the manner outlined above does not in any way compromise man's free will, understood as *liberum arbitrium liberatum*, nor his *libertas*: the only 'free will' which is compromised is the *liberum arbitrium captivatum*, itself a crippled parody of the real thing. The compromise of the *liberum arbitrium captivatum* is necessary in order that the *liberum arbitrium liberatum* may be restored.

Once justified by divine action, the sinner does not at once become a perfect example of holiness. Man needs to pray to God continually for his growth in holiness and the spiritual life, thereby acknowledging that God is the author of both. God *operates* upon man in the *act* of justification, and *cooperates* with him in the *process* of justification.[26] Once justified, the sinner may begin to acquire merit – but only on account of God's grace. Merit is seen to be a divine, rather than a human work. Thus it is clearly wrong to suggest that Augustine excludes or denies merit;[27] while merit *before* justification is indeed denied, its reality and necessity *after* justification is equally strongly affirmed.[28] It must be noted, however, that Augustine understands merit as a gift from God to the justified sinner,[29] and does not adopt Tertullian's somewhat legalist approach to the matter.[30] *Hominis bona merita, Dei munera*. Eternal life is indeed the reward for merit – but merit is itself a gift from God, so that the whole process must be seen as having its origin in the divine liberality, rather than in man's works.[31] If God is under any obligation to man on account of his merit, it is an obligation which God has imposed upon himself, rather than one which is imposed from outside, or is inherent in the nature of things. Fidelis Deus, qui se nostrum debitorem fecit, non aliquid a nobis accipiendo, sed tanta nobis promittendo.[32] The classic Augustinian statement on the relation between eternal life, merit and grace is the celebrated *dictum* of Epistle 194: 'When God crowns our merits, he crowns nothing but his own gifts.'[33] The possibility of a preparation of grace, whether meritorious or not, such as that associated with the Franciscan school in the medieval period, cannot be adduced from the mature writings of Augustine, although traces of such a doctrine may be found in his writings prior to 396.[34]

Central to Augustine's doctrine of justification is his understanding of the 'righteousness of God', *iustitia Dei*.[35] The righteousness of God is not that righteousness by which he is himself righteous, but that by which he justifies sinners.[36] The righteousness of God, veiled in the Old Testament and revealed in the New, and supremely in Jesus Christ, is so called because, by bestowing it upon man, God makes him righteous.[37] How is it possible for God, being just, to justify the ungodly? Augustine shows relatively little interest in this question, giving no systematic account of the work of Christ.[38] Instead, he employs a series of images and metaphors to illustrate the purpose of Christ's mission. Of these, the most important is generally agreed to be his demonstration of the divine love for man, *ad demonstrandum erga nos dilectionem Dei*.[39] Other metaphors and images which he uses to express his understanding of Christ's work include mediation,[40] sacrifice,[41] deliverance from the power of Satan,[42] or an example to be imitated.[43] It must be emphasised that it is manifestly an imposition upon Augustine's theology to develop a systematic account of the work of Christ, for the bishop is primarily concerned with the question of *how* God justifies man, rather than how God *is able* to justify him. Like Luther, he employs a wide range of images and metaphors to illustrate the nature of Christ's mission, and declines to commit himself exclusively to any one of these.

As noted above, God's prevenient grace prepares man's will for justification. Augustine understands this grace to be intimately involved with the sacrament of baptism: however, while he insists that there can be no salvation without baptism (or, more accurately, without what baptism represents) it does not follow that every baptised sinner will be justified, or finally saved. The grace of final perseverance is required if a Christian is to persevere in faith until the end of his life. It is clear that this raises the question of predestination: God may give the regenerate faith, hope and love, and yet decline to give them perseverance.[44]

While Augustine occasionally appears to understand grace as an impersonal abstract force, there are many points at which he makes a clear connection between the concept of grace and the operation of the Holy Spirit. Thus regeneration is itself the work of the Holy Spirit.[45] The love of God is shed abroad in our hearts by the Holy Spirit, which is given to us in justification. The appropriation of the divine love to the person of the Holy Spirit may be regarded as one of the most profound aspects of Augustine's doctrine of the Trinity.[46] *Amare Deum, Dei donum est*.[47] The Holy Spirit enables man to be inflamed with the love of God and the love of his neighbour – indeed,

the Holy Spirit himself *is* love.[48] A man who has faith and not love –
and this is perfectly possible, given Augustine's strongly intellectualist concept of faith – is nothing. Faith can exist without love, but is of
no value in the sight of God.[49] God's other gifts, such as faith and
hope, cannot bring us to God unless they are accompanied or
preceded by love.[50] The motif of *amor Dei* dominates Augustine's
theology of justification, just as that of *sola fide* would dominate that
of one of his later interpreters. Faith without love is of no value. So
how does Augustine understand those passages in the Pauline corpus
which speak of justification *by faith* (e.g., Romans 5.1)? This question
brings us to the classic Augustinian concept of 'faith working through
love', *fides quae per dilectionem operatur*, which would dominate
western Christian thinking on the nature of justifying faith for the
next thousand years. The process by which Augustine arrives at this
understanding of the nature of justifying faith illustrates his desire to
do justice to the total biblical view on the matter, rather than a few
isolated Pauline gobbets. In *de Trinitate*, Augustine considers the
difficulties arising from I Corinthians 13.1–3,[51] which stipulate that
faith without love is useless. He therefore draws a distinction between
a purely intellectual faith (such as that 'by which even the devils
believe and tremble' (James 2.19)) and true justifying faith, by
arguing that the latter is faith *accompanied by love*. Augustine finds
this concept conveniently expressed within the Pauline corpus at
Galatians 5.6: 'In Christ Jesus neither circumcision nor uncircum-
cision avails anything, but *faith that works through love*.'[52] Although
this is open to a Pelagian interpretation, this is excluded by Augustine's insistence that both the faith and love in question are gifts of God
to man rather than man's natural faculties. Augustine tends to
understand faith primarily as an adherence to the Word of God,
which inevitably introduces a strongly intellectualist element into his
concept of faith,[53] thus necessitating its supplementation with *caritas*
or *dilectio* if it is to justify man.[54] Faith alone is merely assent to
revealed truth, itself adequate to justify.[55] It is for this reason that it is
unacceptable to summarise Augustine's doctrine of justification as
sola fide iustificamur – if any such summary is acceptable, it is *sola
caritate iustificamur*.[56] For Augustine, it is love, rather than faith,
which is the power which brings about the conversion of man. Just as
cupiditas is the root of all evil, so *caritas* is the root of all good. Man's
personal union with the Godhead, which forms the basis of his
justification, is brought about by love, and not by faith.[57]

Augustine understands the verb *iustificare* to mean 'to make righteous', an understanding of the term which he appears to have held throughout his working life.[58] In arriving at this understanding, he appears to have interpreted -*ficare* as the unstressed form of *facere*, by analogy with *vivificare* and *mortificare*. Although this is a permissible interpretation of the *Latin word*, it is unacceptable as an interpretation of the *Hebrew concept* which underlies it (see §2). The term *iustificare* is, of course, post-classical, having been introduced through the Latin translation of the bible, and thus restricted to Christian writers of the Latin west. Augustine was thus unable to turn to classical authors in an effort to clarify its meaning, and was thus obliged to interpret the term himself. His establishment of a relationship between *iustificare* and *iustitia* is of enormous significance, as will become clear.

Augustine has an all-embracing understanding of justification, which includes both the *event* of justification (brought about by operative grace) and the *process* of justification (brought about by cooperative grace). Augustine himself does not, in fact, distinguish between these two aspects of justification: the distinction dates from the sixteenth century. However, the importance of Augustine to the controversies of that later period make it necessary to interpret him in terms of its categories at this point. The renewal of the divine image in man, brought about by justification, may be regarded as amounting to a new creation, in which sin is rooted out and the love of God planted in the hearts of men in its place, in the form of the Holy Spirit. God's new creation is not finished once and for all in the event of justification, and requires perfecting,[59] which is brought about by cooperative grace collaborating with the *liberum arbitrium liberatum*. Whilst *concupiscentia* may be relegated to the background as *caritas* begins its work of renewal within man, it continues to make its presence felt, so that renewed gifts of grace are required throughout man's existence, as sin is never totally overcome in this life.[60]

Man's righteousness, effected in justification, is regarded by Augustine as *inherent* rather than *imputed*, to use the vocabulary of the sixteenth century.[61] A concept of 'imputed righteousness', in the later Protestant sense of the term, would be quite redundant within Augustine's doctrine of justification, in that man is *made righteous* in justification. The righteousness which man thus receives, although originating from God, is nevertheless located within man, and can be said to be *his*, part of his being and intrinsic to his person. An element which underlies this understanding of the nature of justifying righteousness is the Greek concept of deification, which makes its appearance in the later Augustinian soteriology.[62] By charity, the Trinity itself comes to inhabit the soul of the justified sinner,[63] although it is not clear whether Augustine can be said to envisage a 'state of grace' in the strict sense of the term – i.e., a habit of grace, created within the human soul.[64] It is certainly true that Augustine speaks of the real interior renewal of the sinner by the action of the Holy Spirit, which he later expressed in terms of participation in the divine substance itself. However, it seems most prudent to state that Augustine's theological vocabulary was not sufficiently developed to allow us to speak of his teaching 'created grace' in the later sense of the term. The later Augustine frequently uses phrases which are strongly reminiscent of the Cappadocians – e.g., *Deus facturus qui homines erant, homo factus est qui Deus erat*[65] – and frequently places the concepts of adoptive filiation and deification side by side in his discussion of justification. There is thus a pronounced element of participation in Augustine's later understanding of the nature of justifying righteousness, even if it is not possible to speak of a 'state of grace' in the strict sense of the term. God has given man the power both to receive and participate in the divine being.[66] By this participation in the life of the Trinity, the justified sinner may be said to be deified.[67] Augustine's understanding of adoptive filiation is such that the believer does not merely receive the *status* of sonhood, but *becomes* a son of God. A real change in man's *being*, and not merely his *status*, is envisaged in his justification, so that he *becomes* righteous and a son of God, and is not merely *treated as if he were* righteous and a son of God.

For Augustine, justification includes both the beginnings of man's righteousness before God and its subsequent perfection, the event and the process, so that what later became the Reformation concept of 'sanctification' is effectively subsumed under the aegis of justification. Although Augustine is occasionally represented, on the basis of isolated passages, as understanding justification to comprise merely the remission of sins, it is clear that he also understands it to include the ethical and spiritual renewal of the sinner through the internal operation of the Holy Spirit. Justification, according to Augustine, is fundamentally concerned with 'being made righteous'. But what does he understand by *iustus* and *iustitia*? With this question, we come to the relation between Augustine's doctrine of justification and his ethical and political thought.

According to Augustine, the *iustitia* of an act is to be defined both in terms of the substance of the act itself (*officium*) and its inner motivation (*finis*). The correct motivation for a righteous action can only come about through operative grace and the interior action of the Holy Spirit within the believer. Righteousness, itself regarded as a gift of the Holy Spirit, consists both in the possession of a good will (effected by operative grace) and in having that potentiality actualised through cooperative grace. It will therefore be clear that Augustine understands *iustitia* participationally, rather than relationally.[68] Everyone who is incorporated into Christ can perform an action which is *iustus*.[69] In other words, Augustine defines *iustitia* in such a manner that, by definition, only Christians may perform good actions. This is well illustrated by his famous example of the two men,[70] one of whom does not hold a 'true and catholic faith in God', yet leads a morally blameless life, and another, who holds such a faith and yet leads a morally inferior existence. Which is the superior in the sight of God? For Augustine, it is the latter, on account of his faith, even though the former may be superior morally. Had the former faith, he would be the superior in the sight of God. This example illustrates the difference between the inherent moral value of an act itself (*officium*), and the inner motivation which establishes the theological foundation for the righteousness of an act (*finis*). A correct inner motivation is only possible through *fides quae per dilectionem operatur*. It may be noted that Augustine does *not* deny pagans the ability to perform morally good acts, as some have represented him as doing. These works are good, considered as *officium* – i.e., they are good *coram hominibus*, but not *coram Deo*. The moral and meritorious realms are scrupulously distinguished by Augustine. Pagans may practise continency, temperance, even *caritas humana*[71] – yet these are not virtues *coram Deo*.[72] The *virtutes impiorum* are *iustae* in terms of their *officium*, but have no value in obtaining felicity.[73] In itself, such an act may be good – but if performed outside the specific context of faith, it is sterile or even sinful.[74] The crucial distinction between the *virtutes impiorum* and *virtutes piorum* lies in justification, by which God makes godly those who were once ungodly (*ex impio pius fit*). Thus Augustine's moral theology (i.e., his theology of *iustitia*, applied to the individual) can be seen to be closely related to his doctrine of justification. The bridge between the moral and the meritorious, between the human and the divine estimation of an act, lies in the justification of the ungodly.

Augustine's political theology (i.e., his theology of *iustitia*, applied to the community) is of considerable inherent interest, and is also closely associated with his doctrine of justification. *De civitate Dei* (413–26) contains a critique of the Ciceronian understanding of the basis of social justice of decisive importance to our study. It is only within the city of God that the true divine justice, effected through justification, may be found.[75] Augustine's concept of *iustitia* within the *civitas Dei* is based on his concept of God as *iustissimus ordinator*, who orders the universe according to his will.[76] The idea of *iustitia* involved can approach that of a physical ordering of all things, and is also reflected in the right ordering of human affairs, and man's relationship to his environment.[77] For Augustine, *iustitia* is practically synonymous with the right ordering of human affairs in accordance with the will of God.[78] It may be noted that Augustine's quasi-physical understanding of justice reflects his hierarchical structuring of the order of being: *iustitia* is essentially the ordering of the world according to the order of being, itself an expression of the divine will. God created the natural order of things, and therefore this natural order of things must itself reflect *iustitia*. Thus God created man as he ought to be – i.e., he created man *in iustitia*, the correct order of nature. By choosing to ignore this ordering, man stepped outside this state of *iustitia*, so that his present state may be characterised as *iniustitia*. Justification is therefore essentially a 'making right', a restoration of every facet of the relationship between God and man, the rectitude of which constitutes *iustitia*. *Iustitia* is not conceived primarily in legal or forensic categories, but transcends them, encompassing the 'right-wising' of the God–man relationship in its many aspects: the relationship of God to man, of man to his fellows, and of men to their environment. Justification is about 'making just' – establishing the rectitude of the created order according to the divine intention. Although it is clear that justification has legal and moral ramifications, given the wide scope of Augustine's concept of *iustitia*, it is not primarily a legal or moral concept.

It is therefore clear that the interpretation of *iustitia* is dependent upon its particular context. What is *iustum* in the case of the relationship between God and man may not be *iustum* in the case of man's relationship to his fellows, so that the analogical predication of human concepts of *iustitia* to God cannot be regarded as inherently justifiable. This point is particularly well illustrated by Augustine's critique of the Ciceronian definition of *iustitia* as *reddens unicuique quod suum est*, 'giving to each his due'.[79] While Augustine is prepared to use this secular definition at points,[80] it is clear that his own concept of *iustitia* is grounded firmly in the divine will. In the course of his controversy with Julian of Eclanum, Augustine found it necessary to counter the application of a secular concept of justice to rationalise the divine dispensation towards mankind.[81] Julian defined justice in terms of God rendering to each man his due, without fraud or grace, so that God would be expected to justify those who merited his grace on the basis of their moral achievements. This approach yielded a doctrine of the justification of the *godly*, whereas Augustine held the essence of the gospel to be the justification of the *ungodly*. In countering Julian's concept of *iustitia Dei*, Augustine appealed to the parable of the labourers in the vineyard (Matthew 20.1–16) to demonstrate that *iustitia Dei* primarily refers to God's fidelity to his promises of grace, irrespective of the merits of those to whom the promise was made (see further §6).

Augustine's fundamental concept of *iustitia* is that of the submission of the individual's whole being to God. While this theme of submission to God may reflect the neo-Platonist notion of the acceptance of the established order of the universe, it is possible that Augustine's understanding of *iustitia* within the *civitas Dei* is based upon ideas similar to those to be found in the *Divinae Institutiones* of Lactantius (c. 250–317). The political theology developed by Lactantius was particularly suited to the new Christian empire, then developing under Constantine. Here *iustitia* is practically equated with *religio*: 'justice is nothing other than the pious and religious worship of the one God'.[82] This definition could be interpreted as an extension of the Ciceronian understanding of *iustitia* as 'rendering to each his due' to include man's proper obligation to God, whose chief part is worship. In *de civitate Dei*, Augustine subjected Cicero's classic definition of the *res publica*[83] by making *iustitia* an essential element of the *iuris consensus*: where there is no true *iustitia*, there is no true *ius*. Whereas Cicero taught that *iustitia* was based on *ius*, arising from the *iuris consensus*, Augustine argued that *ius* itself must be regarded as based on *iustitia*. Thus for Augustine there can be no *res publica* without there being true *iustitia* within the community – i.e., a right ordering of all its relationships in accordance with the divine purpose.[84] Where this justice does not exist, there is certainly no 'association of men united by a common sense of right and a community of interest' (as Cicero had defined the *res publica*). It is only in the *civitas Dei* that true justice exists: in the city of men, only vestiges of this true justice may be found. It is clear that Augustine understands all human *ius*, in so far as it is just, to derive ultimately from an eternal divine law: 'there is nothing just or legitimate in temporal law save what men have derived from the eternal law'.[85] Whilst God's law is eternal and unchanging, the positive laws which govern men's relationships may vary from place to place, and yet still reflect that divine law.[86] Although it is only in the regenerate that *vera iustitia* is possible, through their justification, there remain some *vestigia supernae iustitiae* even in the unjustified, and it is such vestiges which form the basis of human ideas of justice as they find their expression in human legal and political institutions. Without such vestiges, Augustine insists, there could be no justice of any sort among men.[87]

The student of Augustine's doctrine of justification can only admire the astonishing comprehensiveness of its scope. Quid est enim aliud, iustificati, quam iusti facti, ad illo scilicet qui iustificat impium, ut ex impio fiat iustus?[88] Augustine's discussion of *iustitia*, effected only through man's justification, demonstrates how the doctrine of justification encompasses the whole of Christian existence from the first moment of faith, through the increase in righteousness before God and man, to the final perfection of that righteousness in the eschatological city. Justification is about 'being made just' – and Augustine's understanding of *iustitia* is so broad that this could be defined as 'being made to live as God intends man to live, in every aspect of his existence', including his relationship with God, with his fellow men, and the relationship of his higher and lower self (on the neo-Platonic anthropological model favoured by Augustine). That *iustitia* possesses legal and moral overtones will thus be evident – but this must not be permitted to obscure its fundamentally *theological* orientation. By justification, Augustine comes very close to understanding the restoration of the entire universe to its original order, established at creation, an understanding not very different from the Greek doctrine of cosmic redemption. The ultimate object of man's justification is his 'cleaving to God', a 'cleaving' which awaits its consummation and perfection in the new Jerusalem, which is even now being established. Aeterno creatori adhaerentes, et nos aeternitate afficiamur necesse est.

3. The development of the doctrine in the medieval period

Introduction

The terms 'medieval' and 'Middle Ages' are modern, signifying the period of transition between the intellectual glories of antiquity and those of the modern period. Although phrases similar to 'medieval' are encountered in the medieval period itself, their meaning is quite distinct from the modern sense of the term. Thus Julian of Toledo uses the phrase 'middle age' (*tempus medium*) in an Augustinian sense to refer to the period between the incarnation and the second coming of Christ.[1] The question as to when the 'Middle Ages' can be said to have begun has vexed historians for some time, and the answers given to this question depend upon the criterion used in its definition. The practically simultaneous suppression of the Athenian Platonic academy and the establishment of Montecassino in 529 are regarded by many as marking, although not in themselves causing, the transition from late antiquity to the medieval period. For the purposes of the present study, the medieval period is regarded as having been initiated through Alaric's conquest of Rome in 410, with the resulting gradual shift in the centres of intellectual life from the Mediterranean world to the northern European world of Theodoric and Charlemagne, and later to the abbey and cathedral schools of France, and the universities of Paris and Oxford. While Augustine's world was that of the *imperium Romanum*, that of his later interpreters would be the courts and monasteries of northern Europe.[2]

Associated with this shift in the intellectual centres of Europe was a related shift in the method employed by the theologians of the medieval period. The accumulated body of tradition associated with the world of antiquity – which included both pagan philosophy and patristic theology – was assimilated and incorporated into the emerging theological literature. Prosper of Aquitaine's *Liber sententiarum ex operibus Augustini* may be regarded as an early example of this

37

phenomenon.[3] The medieval period was characterised by its attempts to accumulate biblical and patristic material considered to be relevant to particular issues of theological interpretation, and by its attempt to develop hermeneutical methods to resolve the apparent contradictions encountered in this process.[4] These collections of patristic 'sentences' appear to have been modelled upon the codifications of the canonists, who initially grouped their collected decretals chronologically, and later according to subject.[5] An examination of such collections of patristic 'sentences' suggests that they were largely drawn from the works of Augustine. The most famous such collection, the *Sententiarum libri quattuor* of Peter Lombard, has been styled an 'Augustinian breviary', in that its thousand citations from Augustine comprise four-fifths of the work.[6] The high regard in which Augustine was held during the theological renaissance of the late eleventh and twelfth centuries ensured that the framework of the medieval discussion of justification was essentially Augustinian. The theology of the period may be regarded as a systematic attempt to restate and reformulate Augustine's theology to meet the needs of the new era then developing.[7] The development of the doctrine of justification during the medieval period may be considered primarily as the systematisation, clarification and conceptual elaboration of Augustine's framework of justification, where possible restating the dogmatic content of his works in the accepted categories of the day.

The period saw the concept of justification developed as the metaphor most appropriate for the articulation of the soteriological convictions of the western church. Associated with this development were two factors of particular importance, which we shall consider before turning to the development of the doctrine of justification during the period.

1. The transference of the discussion of the salvation of mankind from the *mythological* to the *moral* or *legal* plane.

2. The earlier medieval use of Pauline commentaries as vehicles for theological development, which inevitably led to Pauline concepts, such as justification, being incorporated into the *modus loquendi theologicus* of the later medieval period.

The early patristic discussion of the redemption of mankind in Christ frequently took the form of the portrayal of a cosmic battle between God and the devil, with its *locus* in the cross of Christ. This theme would later pass into the medieval tradition in the notion of the 'Harrowing of Hell'.[8] Associated with the image of a cosmic battle fought between God and the devil over man are several concepts which indicate the crude realism of its mythology – for example, the ideas of the devil possessing rights over man (the *ius diaboli*), of God entering into a transaction with the devil, or of God deceiving the devil.[9] The theological renaissance of the late eleventh century saw this structure being subjected to a devastating theological criticism, particularly by Anselm of Canterbury, largely on account of the conviction that *iustitia Dei*, the 'righteousness of God', necessarily entailed that God acted righteously in all his actions, including the redemption of mankind (see §6). This fundamental conviction led to the medieval construction of theories of redemption in which emphasis was laid upon the moral or legal propriety of both the redemption of mankind in the first place, and the means subsequently employed by God in this redemption. It is possible to argue that it is with Anselm's insights that the characteristic thinking of the western church on the means of the redemption of mankind may be said to begin.[10] The emphasis which is then laid upon the moral or legal character of God inevitably leads to increased interest in the precise nature of *iustitia Dei*, and the question of how *iustitia Dei* and *iustitia hominis* are correlated. The recognition of the cognate relationship between *iustitia*, *ius* and *iustificatio* served to further enhance the importance of the concept of justification as a soteriological metaphor.

The importance of the influence of Pauline commentaries to the development of theology during the earlier medieval period has been well documented,[11] and it is possible to demonstrate that the development of the various theological schools of the period may be illustrated with reference to this literary genre. These commentaries are known to have been of particular importance in the early systematisation of theology during the medieval period:[12] a survey of the commentaries on Romans alone – the most important of the Pauline epistles, judged from the standpoint of the development of the doctrine of justification – suggests that practically every theologian of note during the early medieval period used such a commentary for both the positive statement and development of his own characteristic theological positions.[13] It was therefore inevitable that these theological positions would be influenced, to a greater or lesser extent, by the Pauline material with reference to which they were developed and expounded. The discussion of questions such as the salvation of the Old Testament patriarchs, and the relation between faith and works, are but two examples of pertinent theological questions which such theologians were thus obliged to discuss with reference to the concept of justification. Thus the distinction between *iustificatio per legem* and *per fidem* was frequently used by these theologians in connection with *heilsgeschichtlich* questions such as the salvation of Abraham,[14] usually discussed with reference to Romans 4.4, whilst the discussion of the relation between faith and works would often involve discussion of the apparent differences on the matter between Paul and James[15] – again, with explicit reference to the concept of justification. Thus the early use of such Pauline commentaries as vehicles for positive theological articulation and development assisted the establishment of justification as *the* most important soteriological concept, precisely because it was used by Paul in connection with those soteriological issues which attracted the attention of the theologians of the period. By the time the later *Commentaries on the Sentences* and *Summae* had replaced these commentaries, the influence of the Pauline material upon which the earlier commentaries were based was so great that it had made an indelible impression upon the emerging medieval theological vocabulary. Furthermore, the tendency of early medieval systematic works other than Pauline commentaries to use a *heilsgeschichtlich* format in presenting their material,[16] which necessitated a careful distinction between the times of the law and gospel, naturally led to an appeal to the Pauline concepts of *iustificatio per legem* and *per fidem* in an attempt to clarify the difference between the two periods. In other words, the actual systematic presentation of theology itself during the early medieval period may be regarded as having further enhanced the importance attached to the metaphor of justification by medieval theologians.

The present chapter documents the development of particular aspects of the doctrine of justification during the medieval period, and illustrates how Augustine's basic insights into the framework of the doctrine of justification were preserved, while being developed to meet the needs of the new era in theology which was dawning.

§5 The nature of justification

What is signified by the word 'justification'?[1] As noted previously (§§2, 4), the Latin term *iustificatio* is post-classical, and almost entirely restricted to theological contexts. The Vulgate uses the term to translate the Greek δικαίωσις, although the plural *iustificationes* is occasionally encountered,[2] when the term is used to translate δικαιώματα. Augustine's interpretation of *iustificare* as *iustum facere* (see

§4), based on the assumption that *-ficare* was the unstressed form of *facere*, was universally accepted during the medieval period, almost certainly reflecting the considerable esteem in which the opinions of the bishop were held. Although *iustificare* is occasionally interpreted as *iustum habere*,[3] it is clear that this is intended to refer to *iustificatio coram hominibus* rather than *coram Deo*.[4] The characteristic medieval understanding of the nature of justification may be summarised thus: justification refers not merely to the beginning of the Christian life, but also to its continuation and ultimate perfection, in which the Christian is made righteous in the sight of God and the sight of men through a fundamental change in his nature, and not merely his status. In effect, the distinction between justification (understood as an external pronouncement of God) and sanctification (understood as the subsequent process of inner renewal), characteristic of the Reformation period, is excluded from the outset. This fundamental difference concerning the *nature* of justification remains one of the best *differentiae* between the doctrines of justification associated with the medieval and Reformation periods.[5]

An examination of the early vernacular works appears to confirm this conclusion concerning the ubiquity of the Augustinian interpretation of the significance of 'justification'. The most convenient vernacular works to study in this respect are the Old English homilies of Wulfstan (d. 1023) and Ælfric (c. 955–1020),[6] and the Gothic Bible, the *Vulfila*. Wulfstan does not, in fact, mention the term 'justification' in his homilies, and it is with the latter works that we are chiefly concerned. The Old English church was generally able to express Christian ideas by giving new meanings to existing words in the vernacular, or by forming new compounds of words already in use.[7] Occasionally, this seems to have been impossible, with the result that 'loan words' were introduced – for example, *dēofol* (for the Latin *diabolus*) and *biscop* (for the Gallo-Roman *ebescobu* – cf. Latin *episcopus*). The theological vocabulary of Old English frequently had recourse to literal translations of Latin words – for example, *gecyrrednyss* for the Latin *conversio*. The subsequent disappearance of most of these words may be attributed to the Norman Conquest of 1066. Thus *hǣl* (salvation), *ǣrist* (resurrection) and others disappeared, whilst *God*, *heofon* and *hel* remained. The Old English terms for 'justification' and its cognates appears to have suffered the former fate, *gerihtwīsung* being replaced with the Middle English *iustification* and *gerihtwisian* with *iustifien*, both presumably derived from the Old French *justification* and *justifier*. This disappearance may be illustrated from the translation of Psalm 143.2 from a fourteenth century vernacular source, where the Romance theological term seems out of place among its Anglo-Saxon neighbours:

> Lorde, they seruaunt dragh neuer to dome,
> For non lyuyande to the is justyfyet.[8]

Ælfric regularly translates *iustificatio* by *gerihtwīsung*,[9] and in this he follows what appears to be a traditional interpretation of the Latin text.[10] It is clear that the Old English term is an interpretation, rather than a mere translation, of the original Latin term. A factitive, rather than declarative, interpretation of the term is indicated by the fact that Ælfric uses the phrase *rihtwise getealde* to mean 'reckoned righteous',[11] so that the most appropriate contemporary translation of *gerihtwīsung* would appear to be 'putting right', or 'rightwising'. A similar interpretation can be adduced from the Gothic version,[12] traditionally held to have been translated directly from the Greek by the Arian bishop Ulphilas (d. 383). Although the value of this source is seriously diminished by its fragmentary character,[13] it is clear that the factitive interpretation of δικαιοῦσθαι can be demonstrated in the Gothic version of the Pauline epistles. Thus δικαιοῦν, as it occurs in Galatians 2.16, is translated as *raihts wairthan*,[14] which clearly bears the sense of 'becoming righteous'.[15] It may be noted, however, that δικαιοῦν is not translated regularly as *raihts wairthan* in the Gothic version of the gospels – for example, it is translated as the comparative *garaithoza* at Luke 18.14. This interesting interpretation arises through misreading δεδικαιωμένος as the comparative form of δικαίος, and ἤ as 'than', as is indicated by the following *thau*.

The systematic discussion of the *inner structure* of justification dates from the beginning of the twelfth century, with the formulation of the *processus iustificationis*. This discussion is an important development in the history of the doctrine of justification, as it marks an attempt to correlate the process of justification with the developing sacramental system of the church. Its beginnings may, however, be discerned at a much earlier period in the history of doctrine. Thus Augustine distinguished three aspects of the justification of the ungodly:

Iustificatio porro in hac vita nobis secundum tria ista confertur: prius, lavacro regenerationis, quo remittuntur cuncta peccata; deinde, congressione cum vitiis, a quorum reatu absoluti sumus; tertio, dum nostra exauditur oratio, qua dicimus, *Dimitte nobis debita nostra.*[16]

Bruno the Carthusian also distinguished three aspects of the process of justification.[17] A more detailed discussion of the inner structure of justification may be found in Hervaeus of Bourg-Dieu's comments on Romans 3.20: the recognition of sin is followed by the operation of healing grace, which leads to a love for righteousness:

Per legem enim cognitio peccati; per fidem impetratio gratiae contra peccatum; per gratiam sanatio animae a vitio peccati; per animae sanitatem libertas arbitrii; per liberum arbitrium, iustitiae dilectio; per iustitiae dilectionem legis operatio.[18]

The sequential ordering of the process, with one element leading to another in a causal sequence, foreshadowed the twelfth-century discussion of the *processus iustificationis*.

Initially, the theologians of the twelfth century envisaged the *processus iustificationis* as consisting of three elements. Peter Manducator defined the sequence as follows: tria enim sunt, in quibis iustificatio consistit, scilicet primarie gratie infusio, cordis contritio, peccati remissio.[19] As a study of twelfth-century works indicates, the terminology of the *processus iustificationis* is still fluid, and although the threefold structure appears fixed, its elements were still not clearly defined. For example, the *processus* is elsewhere defined as consisting of *gratiae infusio, liberi arbitrii cooperatio, et consummatio*.[20] Occasionally, a threefold scheme is encountered which omits any reference to the infusion of grace, such as *peccati desertio, propositum non peccandi de cetero, dolor de peccato preterito*.[21] Nevertheless, it is clear that a threefold process, which is initiated through the infusion of grace and terminates in the remission of sin, was widely accepted as normative. Although it must be conceded that the *processus* does not in itself represent an important advance, in that the three elements involved had long been recognised as closely inter-related, it does represent an important advance in the *systematic discussion of justification*, in that the three elements are now linked as the 'process of justification'.

Although the threefold scheme appears to have gained considerable acceptance in the twelfth century, it was a fourfold scheme of the inner structure of justification which would finally become accepted as normative. The threefold *processus* recognised a single notion of the *liberum arbitrium*, which subsequently came to be divided into two components: a movement of the free will towards God, and a movement of the free will away from sin. As stated by Peter of Poitiers, the scheme has the following form:

Sciendum est autem quod ad iustificationem impii quatuor occurunt: infusio gratiae, motus surgens ex gratia et libero arbitrio, contritio, peccatorum remissio. Nullum istorum prius est aliquo eorumdem tempore, sed tamen naturaliter praecedit gratiae infusio et per ordinem sequuntur alia tria, non tempore, sed natura. Sciendum est autem quod quodlibet istorum quatuor dicitur iustificatio, nec unum potest esse in homine sine aliis tribus.[22]

The infusion of grace thus initiates a chain of events which eventually leads to justification: if any of these events may be shown to have taken place, the remaining three may also be concluded to have taken place. The fourfold *processus iustificationis* differs from the threefold scheme in including a dual, rather than a single, motion of the human free will, otherwise retaining the same overall structure. It was taken up by the first Summist, William of Auxerre, in the form *infusio gratiae, motus liberi arbitrii, contritio, peccatorum remissio*,[23] and was accepted in this form by the doctors of the early Dominican and Franciscan schools.[24] The inclusion of *contritio* in the *processus* is of no small significance, as it greatly assisted the correlation of the *processus* with the sacrament of penance in the thirteenth century (see §8).

The justification of the fourfold *processus iustificationis* within the early Dominican school is of particular interest, as it demonstrates the considerable influence of Aristotelian physics upon theological speculation within that school.[25] Albertus Magnus defined justification as a *motus* from sin to grace and rectitude.[26] Having already applied the Aristotelian theory of motion, as stated in the celebrated maxim of Aristotelian physics, *omne quod movetur ab alio movetur*, to a physical *motus* such as free fall, or a theological problem of *motus* such as the existence of God,[27] the same principle is applied to the analysis of the inner structure of the *motus* of justification. The explicit application of the Aristotelian theory of generation to the transition from nature to grace leads to a fourfold *processus iustificationis*, with a dual motion of the free will. This application of Aristotelian physics to the *motus* of justification is particularly associated with Thomas Aquinas. Having stated the *processus iustificationis* to be:

1.   the infusion of grace;
2.   the movement of the free will directed towards God through faith;
3.   the movement of the free will directed against sin;
4.   the remission of sin;

Thomas now justifies this on the basis of Aristotelian physics. By nature, the movement of the mover must come first, followed by the disposition of the matter, or the movement of that which is to be moved, followed by the final termination of the motion when the objective of the movement has been achieved.[28] Thus the infusion of grace must precede the remission of sin, as the infusion of grace is the efficient cause of that remission. Thus the *motus* which is justification ends in the remission of sin, which may be considered as the *terminus* of the infusion of grace.[29] As every movement may be said to be defined by its *terminus*, justification may thus be said to consist of the remission of sin.[30]

Some commentators have misunderstood Thomas' occasional definition of justification solely in terms of the remission of sin, representing him as approaching a forensic concept of justification. It will be clear that this is a serious misunderstanding. Where Thomas defines justification as *remissio peccatorum*, therefore, he does not exclude other elements – such as the infusion of grace – from his definition, for the following reasons. First, justification is thus defined without reference to its content, solely in terms of its *terminus*. Such a definition is adequate, but not exhaustive, and should not be treated as if it were. Second, Thomas' understanding of the *processus iustificationis* means that the occurrence of any one of the four elements necessarily entails the occurrence of the remaining three. The definition of *iustificatio* as *remissio peccatorum* therefore expressly *includes* the remaining three elements.

Having established that the remission of sin is the final element in the *processus iustificationis*, Thomas argues that the element intervening between the initial (i.e., *infusio gratiae*) and the final (i.e., *remissio peccatorum*) elements must be the disposition of the object of justification – i.e., the *motus mobilis*, the movement of that which is to be moved. As justification is *motus mentis*, this disposition must refer to the human free will, which precedes justification itself by nature.[31] This consideration leads to a definition of justification as *quidam motus quo humana mens movetur a Deo a statu peccati in statum iustitiae*,[32] and allows a threefold *processus iustificationis* to be established: *infusio gratiae, motus liberi arbitrii, remissio peccatorum*. Tradition had by now, however, established a dual motion of the free will in justification, in faith and contrition,[33] so that it was necessary to resolve the *motus mobilis* into two elements. Thomas achieves this by applying a further axiom of Aristotelian physics – that 'in movements of the soul, the movement to the principle of understanding or to the end of the action comes first'[34] – to the *motus animi* of justification. Thus a movement of the *liberum arbitrium* towards God must precede its motion against sin, as the former is the cause of the latter.[35] This teaching, found in the *Summa Theologiae*, is of particular interest, as it represents an abandonment of his earlier teaching, that there should be no intermediates between the influence of grace and the remission of sin.[36]

In justification, according to Thomas, man is translated from a state of corrupt nature to one of habitual grace; from a state of sin to a state of justice, with the remission of sin.[37] But how is this state of justice to be conceived? As noted earlier (§4), Augustine's understanding of *iustitia* embraces practically the entire ordering of the universe, so that justification can be understood as the restoration of man to his correct place in the hierarchy of being, including the establishment of the correct relationship between the various existential strata within man, on the basis of the neo-Platonist anthropological model favoured by Augustine. Thomas' discussion of the question involves a crucial distinction between the *virtue* of justice, and the *supernatural habit* of justice, infused by God. *Iustitia acquisita*, the virtue of acquired justice,[38] may be considered either as particular justice, which orders man's actions relating to his fellow men, or as legal justice, as defined by Aristotle.[39] *Iustitia infusa*, however, on the basis of which man is justified, comes from God himself, through grace.[40] Failure to appreciate this distinction will lead to the quite untenable conclusion that Thomas teaches justification purely through self-endeavour or moral attainment. Justification is concerned with justice in the sight of God, *iustitia quae est apud Deum*.[41] *Iustitia infusa* is that justice which is infused into man by God, by which man's higher faculties are submitted to God. In essence, it may be noted that Thomas' concept of infused justice is very similar to Aristotle's notion of metaphorical justice,[42] which refers primarily to a rectitude of order within man's interior disposition. It is this infused justice, and this justice alone, which is the basis of man's justification.

The characteristically Augustinian understanding of justification as the restoration of man to his proper place in the created hierarchy of being is reflected in Thomas' discussion of why justification is properly named after justice, rather than faith or love. Although both faith and love are involved in justification,[43] and although their supernatural habits are infused in its course, Thomas insists that the transformation which is called 'justification' is properly named after justice alone on account of the all-embracing character of the latter, which refers to the entire rectitude of order of the human soul, with all its faculties. Faith and love refer only to specific aspects of this order, whereas justice embraces man's higher nature in its totality.[44]

It may be noted at this point that Thomas' understanding of justification as a *motus mentis* reflects his intellectualist understanding of human nature; if the higher nature is subordinate to God, it will be enabled to restrain the lower nature. Man's intellect is restored through justifying faith, so that he is able to avoid *mortal* sin; although the higher nature subsequently restrains the lower, it is unable to overcome it entirely, so that man is still unable to avoid *venial* sin after justification.[45] Thus even the man who is in a state of grace cannot be said to be free from sin. Thomas' exposition of Romans 7 is of particular interest in this respect, as he clearly understands the chapter to refer to the Christian constituted in grace.[46] Justification is about 'being made just': the precise nature of this 'making just' is, however, carefully defined in terms of the rectitude of the human mind so that it, acting as a secondary cause, may bring all that is subordinate to it into conformity with the exemplar established for it by God. The *event* of the infusion of the habit of justice must therefore be followed by the *process* of the submission of the lower to the higher nature; in this understanding of the dual nature of justification, Thomas remains faithful to the teaching of Augustine.

Thomas' understanding of justification as a *motus mentis* allows him to apply the Aristotelian theory of motion to its presuppositions, as well as its interior structure, and is of particular interest in relation to his discussion of the need for a disposition towards justification on the part of the sinner.[47] The early Franciscan school, however, developed a more psychological approach to justification, reflecting an Augustinian illuminationist epistemology which is not characteristic of the Dominican school. The general features of the early Franciscan teaching on the nature of justification may be found in Bonaventure's *Itinerarium mentis in Deum*, which develops a hierarchical concept of justification which clearly reflects the influence of Dionysius. The three fundamental operations of grace in justification are the *purification*, *illumination* and *perfection* of the soul.[48] Christ performed three acts which re-established and reordered man's supernatural life towards God: he purged our guilt, enlightened us by his example, and perfected us by enabling us to follow in his footsteps. The Christian is required to respond to these in three hierarchical acts by which he can appropriate their benefits. These three aspects of the justification of the sinner correspond to the 'Three Ways' which are so characteristic of Bonaventure's spirituality, distinguished by their goals rather than their relation in time. The *stimulus conscientiae* motivates the way of purification, the *radius intelligentiae* the way of illumination, and the *igniculus sapientiae* the way of unity with God. From the moment of its first infusion, sanctifying grace takes over the substance and faculties of the soul, setting each in its respective place, and ordering the soul that it may be conformed to God.[49] The process of justification involves the destruction of the passions which threaten the development of man's new life, so that man can rediscover the image of God within himself. Thus the soul, reconstituted by grace, can begin its ascent towards the goal of supernatural perfection. It will be clear that Bonaventure's understanding of the nature of justification differs from that of Thomas only in emphasis: both understand justification as the establishment of rectitude within man's higher nature, whether this be considered as *mens* or *anima*. Bonaventure's teaching was developed by his Italian disciple Matthew of Aquasparta, who discussed justification in terms of six stages: the hatred of sin and the love of good; regeneration; the reforming and reordering of man's nature; the generation of virtues; conversion to, and union with, God; and remission of sin.[50] His emphasis upon the regeneration of the sinner and his ultimate union with God point to a psychological approach to justification more characteristic of Bonaventure than Thomas.

The medieval statements concerning the nature of justification demonstrate that justification is universally understood to involve a real change in its object, so that regeneration is subsumed under justification. As John of La Rochelle pointed out, unless justification did produce a real change in man, it would appear to serve no useful purpose:

Homo est iustificatus. Si nihil ponitur in eo, nulla mutatio fit a parte ipsius, nec est proximus bono aeterno quam prius; si ponitur aliquid, id dico esse gratiam.[51]

This statement is of particular interest, as it involves the appeal to the reality of a change in man arising through his justification in the refutation of the earlier opinion, gratia ponit nihil in anima.[52] Whilst justification was universally understood to involve the regeneration of man, the opinion that an *ontological* change is thereby effected within man is particularly associated with the period of High Scholasticism and the development of the concept of created grace. The earlier medieval theologians expressed the change effected in justification in terms of a particular presence of God in his creature, which did not necessarily effect an ontological change. Thus the *Summa Fratris Alexandri*, written after 1240, developed the Augustinian concept of the indwelling of God in his creatures by declaring that God is present in all his creatures, but that only some (i.e., those who are justified) may be said to possess him. All creatures can participate in God – only the justified can be said to actually possess that divine presence. The *Summa* conceives a special presence of God in the justified, such that an ontological change occurs in the soul. The presence of God in the justified sinner necessarily results in *created* grace – a created grace which can be conceived as a conformity of the soul to God.[53] This special presence of God in the souls of the justified must be distinguished from the general presence of God in the world, and from the unique union between God and man achieved in the hypostatic union. In this, the *Summa* makes an important advance on Peter Lombard's discussion of the divine presence in all creatures; in angels and the souls of the justified through indwelling grace, and in Christ *non per adoptionis sed per gratiam unionis*.[54]

The later medieval period saw the rise of the opinion particularly associated with the *via moderna* according to which the relationship between God and man was to be understood *covenantally* rather than *ontologically*.[55] Although this opinion involves the linking of justification with the extrinsic denomination of the divine acceptation, the *de facto* necessity of a habit of grace in justification continued to be maintained. Although the ultimate reason for man's acceptation lies in the divine decision to accept, the fact remains that *de potentia Dei ordinata* the infusion of grace, the indwelling of the Holy Spirit, and the divine acceptation coincide. The rejection of the metaphysical necessity of such a habit of grace must be carefully distinguished from the assertion of its *de facto* necessity within the context of the covenant which governs the divine dispensation towards mankind. The necessity of a habit of created grace in justification is radically contingent, a *necessitas consequentiae* rather than a *necessitas consequentis*; however, as theology is concerned with the articulation of the divine dispensation towards mankind as it now pertains, man's justification before God must be considered to involve an ontological change within him. *De potentia Dei ordinata* the habit of created grace is the middle term between sinful man and his acceptation by God in justification: it need not have been so, but the fact remains that it is so. The essential contribution of the *via moderna* to the medieval understanding of the nature of justification is its emphasis upon the *contingent* nature of the ontological change which occurs within man in justification. It is only by confusing the actual divine dispensation *de potentia ordinata* with a hypothetical dispensation *de potentia absoluta* that any continuity with the Reformation understandings of the nature of justification may be maintained.

Associated with the *via moderna* in particular is the weakening of the link between the elements of the *processus iustificationis*. As noted above, the four elements of the process were regarded as essentially aspects of the one and the same transformation, causally linked by their very nature (*ex natura rei*). From the time of Duns Scotus onwards, this view was subjected to increasing criticism. The infusion of grace and the remission of sin came increasingly to be seen as fundamentally distinct, coexisting and causally related only through the divine ordination (*ex pacto divino*). One may take place without the other. Scotus states four reasons why the remission of sin and the infusion of grace cannot be regarded as aspects of one and the same change (i.e., justification):[56]

1.   The remission of sin is multiple, as God forgives each committed sin individually, whilst the infusion of grace is single.
2.   Infusion of grace can occur without remission of sin, and *vice versa*. Thus God infused grace into Adam in his state of innocence without remitting his sin, as he did also with the good angels.
3.   There is no necessary correlation between sin and grace as opposites.
4.   Sin cannot be regarded simply as the privation of grace, which would be necessary if justification were regarded as the transition from a privation to its corresponding quality.

Furthermore, Scotus points out that infusion of grace is a *real* change in man, whilst the remission of sin is a *mutatio rationis*, an ideal change within the divine mind and not within man himself. As the concepts of the infusion of grace and the remission of sin have totally different points of reference, they cannot be allowed to be causally related as in the traditional *processus iustificationis*. Since their relationship does not derive from the nature of the elements themselves, it must derive from the divine will – i.e., it is arbitrary. Without in any way challenging the *de facto* relationship of the elements of the *processus iustificationis*, Scotus demonstrated that this relationship was itself radically contingent, the consequence of divine ordination rather than the nature of the entities themselves. This point, which relates to the nature of the causal processes involved in justification, will be developed further in our discussion of the rôle of supernatural habits in justification (see §13).

The medieval concept of justification includes the renovation as well as the forgiveness of the sinner: in iustificatione animarum duo concurrunt, scilicet remissio culpae et novitas vitae per gratiam.[57] Although some theologians appear to define justification solely as the remission of sins,[58] it must be pointed out that this is a consequence of their use of Aristotelian categories in their discussion of justification: as a *motus* may be defined by its *terminus*, justification may be defined as the remission of sins. The entire medieval discussion of justification proceeds upon the assumption that a *real* change in the sinner is effected thereby. This observation is as true for the *via moderna* as it is for the earlier period.[59] It is quite untenable to suppose that the Reformation distinction between justification and regeneration can be adduced from the medieval period, when it is clear that the universal opinion is that such a distinction is excluded from the outset. Indeed, the *modernus* Gabriel Biel explicitly contrasts a forensic justification before a secular judge with justification as transformation in relation to God, the spiritual judge.[60] In the later medieval period, the *de facto* necessity of a habit of created grace in justification is maintained, even by those theologians who otherwise stood closest to the Reformers.[61] As we have insisted, the notional distinction between *iustificatio* and *regeneratio* provides one of the best *differentiae* between Catholic and Protestant understandings of justification, marking the Reformers' complete discontinuity with the earlier western theological tradition. From its beginning to its end, the medieval period saw justification as involving a real change in the sinner – an understanding which precludes the Reformation distinction between *iustificatio* and *regeneratio* from the outset.

§6 The righteousness of God

What is signified by the 'righteousness of God', and how is it manifested? What does it mean to affirm that God is 'righteous'? The importance of these questions was emphasised by the patristic exegesis of Romans 1.17,[1] in which Paul practically equates *iustitia Dei* with the gospel. An examination of the medieval exegesis of Romans 1.17 indicates that there was an early consensus among Pauline exegetes that *iustitia Dei* was to be understood as referring primarily to God's righteousness as demonstrated in the justification of the ungodly, *iustificatio impii*, in accordance with his promises of mercy. In general, two main lines of interpretation may be distinguished in the early medieval period.

1. A subjective understanding of the construction *iustitia Dei* – i.e., *iustitia Dei* is the righteousness by which God is himself righteous.

This interpretation, which appears to stem from Ambrosiaster, emphasises the maintenance of the divine integrity in justification. God, having promised to give salvation, subsequently gives it, and as a result is deemed to be 'righteous' – i.e., faithful to his promises. The 'righteousness of God' is therefore demonstrated in his faithfulness to his promises of salvation: iustitia est Dei, quia quod promisit dedit, ideo credens hoc esse se consecutum quod promiserat Deus per prophetas suos, iustum Deum probat et testis est iustitiae eius.[2] The gospel is therefore understood to manifest the divine righteousness in that God is shown to have fulfilled the Old Testament promises, made in the prophets and elsewhere, of salvation for his people.

2. An objective interpretation of the construction iustitia Dei – i.e., iustitia Dei is the righteousness whose origin is God, given to the sinner in his justification, rather than the righteousness by which God is himself just. This interpretation, which appears to stem from Augustine (see §4), treats the construction iustitia Dei as an example of genitivus auctoris: iustitiam Dei vocat gratiam, non qua ipse iustificatur, sed qua hominem induit.[3]

In both cases, the 'righteousness of God' is understood to refer to his gracious act of justification, rather than to a divine property which stands over and against man. In the case of the subjective interpretation of the construction, iustitia Dei is understood to refer to the general framework within which the justification of man takes place (i.e., the promises of the Old Testament), whereas the objective interpretation of the construction refers to the immediate means by which that justification takes place (i.e., the 'righteousness' which God bestows upon the sinner, in order that he may be 'made just'). It will be clear that the two interpretations of the construction iustitia Dei are complementary rather than mutually exclusive, and it is not uncommon to find both interpretations within the same work. Iustitia Dei is thus understood to be set in a soteriological context, referring to the salvation of mankind, whether as a consequence of God's faithfulness to his promises of mercy, or of the bestowal of divine righteousness upon the sinner.

It can, however, be shown that a third interpretation of the concept existed in the earlier medieval period, apparently corresponding to a form of popular Pelagianism. Iustitia Dei is here understood to refer to the divine attribute by which God rewards man according to his just deserts. God, in his righteousness, will reward those who act justly and punish those who act unjustly – thereby justifying the godly, and punishing the ungodly. Iustitia enim tua est, ut qui fecerit voluntatem tuam, transeat a morte in vitam, per quam et ego nunc eripi deprecor.[4] This corresponds to what might be called a 'popular catholic' understanding of justification, according to which justification is understood to be dependent upon man's efforts to emulate the example which is set him in Christ. While the early exponents of this theology of justification insisted that man cannot justify himself,[5] it may be pointed out that the orthodoxy of this position is superficial. As justification is defined as the *divine* judgement that man is righteous, it follows as a matter of course that man is not competent to pronounce this judgement himself, and thereby usurp the place of God. Justification is God's judgement upon man, made upon the basis of whether he has emulated the *iustitia Dei* revealed to man in Christ – i.e., the divine standard of righteousness, which man must imitate. Pelagius' interpretation of the concept of the 'righteousness of God' is of particular interest in this respect, as it is taken to refer to the righteousness which God gives to man in Christ *as his example*, so that his justification may be attributed to his own moral efforts to imitate *iustitia Dei, per exemplum Christi*, through the free and autonomous exercise of *liberum arbitrium*. A similar, although more developed, understanding of *iustitia Dei* can be found in the writings of Julian of Eclanum.[6] God deals with man in equity, totally impartially, considering only his merits and demerits in justification, reddentem sua unicuique sine fraude sine gratia, id est sine personarum acceptione.[7] In effect, Julian applies a *quid pro quo* understanding of justice to the divine dealings with men – an understanding of *iustitia* which found its classic expression in the Ciceronian definition of *iustitia* as habitus animi, communi utilitate conservata, suam cuique tribuens dignitatem (see §§2, 4). For Julian, God rewards man according to his merits – otherwise, God is made guilty of a gross injustice. Julian singles out several aspects of Augustine's theology of grace for particular criticism on the basis of this understanding of *iustitia Dei* – for example, his understanding of the nature of original sin, and the doctrine of the justification of the *un*godly. If God is to reward man *sine personarum acceptione*, he must reward them on the basis of what they *have done*, rather than on the basis of who *they are* – i.e., they must be rewarded on the basis of merit. This Ciceronian understanding of *iustitia Dei* had earlier been criticised by Augustine (see §4), who pointed out that the Parable of the Labourers in the Vineyard (Matthew 20.1–10) gave a more reliable insight into the divine justice than Julian's Ciceronian analogy. Every man was rewarded with his denarius, irrespective of the period he actually spent working: although the workers had no claim to the denarius in terms of the work they had performed, they *did* have a claim on account of the promise made to them by the owner of the vineyard. By analogy, man has no claim to grace on the basis of his works (i.e., on a *quid pro quo* basis), but such a claim on the basis of the obligation of God to fulfil his promise.

JULIAN: Est igitur procul dubio iustitia, sine qua deitas non est; quae si non esset, deus non esset; est autem Deus, est itaque sine ambiguitate iustitia. Non est autem aliud quam virtus omnia continens et restituens suum unicuique sine fraude sine gratia; consistit autem maxime in divinitatis profundo.
AUGUSTINE: Definisti esse iustitiam virtutem omnia continentem et restituentem suum unicuique sine fraude sine gratia. Proinde videmus eam sine fraude restituisse denarium eis, qui per totum diem in opere vineae laboraverant; hoc enim placuerat, hoc convenerat, ad hanc mercedem se fuisse conductos negare non poterant. Sed dic mihi, quaeso te: quomodo eis sine gratia tantundem dedit, quit una hora in illo opere fuerunt? An amiserat fortasse iustitiam? Cohibe itaque te potius; neminem quippe fraudat divina iustitia, sed multa donat non merentibus gratia.[8]

This criticism of the predication of the Ciceronian concept of *iustitia* to God would be continued by the theologians of the early medieval period. Thus Remigius of Auxerre pointed out that human concepts of justice involved the rendering of good for good, and evil for evil – yet God rendered good for evil when he justified sinful man.[9] If God's dealings with men are to be rationalised on the basis of justice, human ideas of justice must give way to those of God. A somewhat different approach to the question may be found in Atto of Vercelli's gloss on Romans 1.17. Here the legal category of justice is retained, along with a Ciceronian interpretation of *iustitia* – but it is interpreted in terms of Christ's obedience to the law:

Iustitia enim Dei in eo revelatur ex fide in fidem. Iustitia dicitur, quasi iuris status. Iustitia ergo est, cum unicuique proprium eius tribuitur: unde et iustus dicitur, eo quod ius custodiat. Iustitia autem Dei Christus est, quae revelatur in eo.[10]

In effect, this marks a development of Ambrosiaster's approach to *iustitia Dei*, in that God's faithfulness to his promise of mercy is now expressed in legal terms – i.e., 'faithfulness' is interpreted in terms of 'keeping the law'. It may, however, be emphasised that while the earlier medieval period is characterised by its conviction that God's righteousness is somehow grounded in his promise of mercy, there is no real attempt to establish the precise relationship between *iustitia*

Dei and *misericordia Dei*: most theologians were content merely to affirm that God, in his righteousness, was faithful to his promises.[11]

The theological renaissance of the late eleventh and twelfth centuries[12] saw the 'righteousness of God' being discussed in terms of two separate, although clearly related, questions:

1. What concept of *iustitia* is appropriate to characterise God's dealings with men?
2. How is it possible, given the limitations of human language, to speak of God being 'righteous' in the first place?

We shall consider these questions separately.

The first major discussion of the first point is due to Anselm of Canterbury. It must be pointed out that Anselm's soteriology has frequently been criticised as 'legalist', typical of the Latin 'impulse to carry religion into the legal sphere'.[13] This misguided and discredited criticism of Anselm, however, brings us to the very point which confronted Anselm as he began his attempt to defend the rationality of the incarnation of the son of God: what was the relationship between the 'righteousness of God' and the ideas of 'righteousness' taken from 'ordinary human life'?

God is wholly and supremely just.[14] How can he then give eternal life to one who deserves eternal death? How can he justify the sinner? This is the central question with which Anselm is concerned in *Cur Deus homo* (1098). Earlier, Anselm had wrestled with substantially the same problem in the *Proslogion* (1079):

Verum malis quomodo parcis, si es totus iustus et summe iustus? Quomodo enim totus et summe iustus facit aliquid non iustum? Aut quae iustitia est merenti mortem aeternam dare vitam sempiternam? Unde ergo, bone Deus, bone bonis et malis, unde tibi salvare malos, si hoc non est iustum, et tu non facis aliquid non iustum?[15]

Initially, Anselm locates the source of God's mercy in his *bonitas*, which may be contrasted with his *iustitia*. He then proceeds to argue, however, that despite the apparent contradiction between the divine *misericordia* and *iustitia*, God's mercy must somehow be grounded in his justice. Anselm resolves this dilemma by arguing that God is just, not because he rewards according to merit, but because he does what is appropriate to him as the highest good, *summum bonum*: ita iustus es non quia nobis reddas debitum, sed quia facis quod decet te summe bonum.[16] The explicit criticism of the Ciceronian definition of *iustitia* as *reddens unicuique quod suum est* will be evident. A similar pattern may be seen in *Cur Deus homo*, where Anselm notes various interpretations of the concept of *iustitia*, before selecting that which is most appropriate for his purposes: *iustitia hominis*, which pertains under law;[17] *iustitia districta*, beyond which 'nothing more strict can be imagined' – Anselm presumably therefore understands *iustitia hominis* as *iustitia aequitatis*[18] – and supreme justice, *summa iustitia*.[19] The concept of justice which Anselm selects as most appropriate to characterise God's dealings with men is, as in the *Proslogion*, justice understood as action directed towards the highest good. As that highest good includes the redemption of fallen mankind, the salvation of man may be regarded as an act of divine justice. In the course of the discussion, however, it becomes clear that Anselm understands the concept of *rectitudo* to underlie that of *iustitia*, and to determine its basic meaning.

According to Anselm, justice is a 'rectitude of will served for its own sake (*rectitudo voluntatis propter se servata*)'.[20] Similarly, truth must be defined in terms of rectitude: non aliud ibi potest intelligi veritas quam rectitudo, quoniam sive veritas sive rectitudo non aliud in eius voluntate fuit quam velle quod debuit.[21] The relationship between rectitude, truth and justice could be expressed as follows:

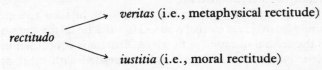

rectitudo

veritas (i.e., metaphysical rectitude)

iustitia (i.e., moral rectitude)

Anselm clearly assumes that the three concepts are closely linked: habes igitur definitionem iustitiae, si iustitia non est aliud quam rectitudo. Et quoniam de rectitudine mente sola perceptibili loquimur, invicem sese definiunt veritas et rectitudo et iustitia.[22] The concepts of 'truth' and 'righteousness' had, of course, been long recognised to have close conceptual connections,[23] and Anselm may be regarded as establishing the conceptual foundation of both to be 'rectitude'. *Iustitia* has as its fundamental sense the moral rectitude of the created order, established by God at creation, and in itself reflecting the divine will and nature. This moral ordering of the universe extends to the relationship between man and God, and man and his fellow men. Anselm appears to use the term *rectitudo* to describe the basic God-given ordering of the universe, and employs the term *iustitia* in a number of derivative senses, each of which may be traced back to the fundamental concept of rectitude. God's moral governing of the universe clearly involves both the divine regulation of the affairs of men, and also the self-imposed regulation by which

God governs his dealings with men – and it is not possible to argue that the laws governing each are the same. In its fundamental sense, *iustitia* merely refers to rectitude; it remains to be seen what form this ordering may take with respect to the various aspects of creation. The justice which regulates the affairs of men (e.g., the Ciceronian and Justinian principle of *reddens unicuique quod suum est*) cannot be considered to be identical with the justice which regulates God's dealings with man.

Man was created in a state of *iustitia originalis*, which was forfeited at the Fall. It may be noted that the concept of 'original justice' is understood by Anselm to refer to the initial moral rectitude of man within the created order. For Anselm, the basic requirement of *iustitia* is that rational creatures be subject to God,[24] which merely amounts to a statement of the place of man in the hierarchical moral ordering of creation. This moral ordering of creation, itself an expression of the divine will, allots a specific place to man, with a concomitant obligation that he submit his rational nature to God. This moral ordering of the universe was violated by man at the Fall, so that man's present state is that of *iniustitia*, understood as the privation of *iustitia* rather than as a positive entity in itself. The essence of original sin is the inherited lack of moral rectitude in the will of fallen man.[25] Man's violation of the moral order of creation means that he is no longer capable of submitting his rational nature to God – and therefore that he is incapable of redeeming himself. If man is to be redeemed, a divine act of redemption is required *which must itself be consonant with the established moral order of the universe*. God, having created the moral order of the universe as an expression of his nature and will, is unable to violate it himself in the redemption of mankind.

This important point is made with particular clarity at that point in *Cur Deus homo* at which Anselm considers the question of why God cannot simply forgive sins as an act of mercy.[26] For Anselm, God's freedom in will and action is limited by his own nature. God is not free to do anything which violates his own nature, since this involves a contradiction. Thus what is *iustum* cannot become *iniustum* simply because God wills it, as such an alteration involves a radical change in the divine nature itself. God's character as *summa iustitia* is expressed in the moral order of creation, and the free forgiveness of sins through mercy alone would violate this ordering. God's attributes are essential to his being, and not mere accidents which he may change at will. Anselm's theological insight is that the divine attributes must coexist within the limiting conditions which they impose upon each other. Thus the rectitude of the established moral order requires that God redeem man in such a way that his own nature as *summa iustitia* is not contradicted.

In a very brief, but highly significant, review of the accounts traditionally given of the redemption of mankind in Christ, Anselm makes it clear that he is not satisfied with their failure to explain *why* God chose to redeem man – at best, they were merely descriptions of *how* God redeemed man, offering no explanation for why God should choose to redeem man in the first place, nor the particular mode of redemption selected. Anselm therefore presents an account of the redemption of mankind, based on *iustitia*, which demonstrates:

1.   that the redemption of mankind is necessary *as a matter of justice*;
2.   that this redemption is effected in a manner that is consonant with the divinely established moral ordering of the universe.

We shall consider these points individually.

If *iustitia Dei* is understood as a *lex talionis*, or in the Ciceronian sense of *reddens unicuique quod suum est*, it is clearly impossible, in Anselm's view, to consider God's act of redemption as an act of justice. It is for this reason that Anselm does not employ these concepts of justice in his soteriology. For Anselm, the moral ordering of the universe was violated by the sin of man, so that the present state of affairs is that of a privation of justice – i.e., *iniustitia*. As whatever is unjust is a contradiction of the divine nature, it is therefore imperative that the moral rectitude of the created order be restored. God, as *summa iustitia* is therefore obliged, by his very nature (since to permit a state of injustice to continue indefinitely is tantamount to a contradiction of his nature) to restore the rectitude of the created order by redeeming fallen man – *as an act of justice*.

Anselm prefaces his discussion of the method by which God redeemed mankind by considering the rival theory of the *ius diaboli*, the 'devil's rights'. This theory may be illustrated from the tract *de redemptione humana*, attributed to Bede,[27] in which it is argued that, while the death of Christ is a free act of divine love, the choice of the means employed to effect man's deliverance from the devil is necessarily dictated by the fact that the devil is *justly* entitled to punish sinners. The origins of this teaching may be traced back to Gregory the Great, who taught that the devil had acquired a legal right over sinners as a consequence of the Fall, but had no such right over anyone who was sinless. Christ therefore assumed the form of man in order to deceive his opponent, who naturally assumed that he, like the rest of humanity, was a sinner. As the devil thus brought about the crucifixion of the sinless Christ contrary to justice his own legitimate power over sinners was justly abolished.[28] This theory makes its appeal to justice – but it is a very different concept of justice to that employed by Anselm. For Anselm, justice relates to the moral ordering of creation, which the devil himself, as a rational creature, is subject to. The devil clearly violated this order in his seduction of man, and cannot be regarded as having any *just* claim over man. Himself a rational creature, the devil is obliged to submit his rational nature to God – only if he were not part of God's creation, and could therefore stand aloof from its moral ordering, could the devil claim any 'right' over man. By his own violation of *iustitia*, the devil had lost any claim to *ius* over man. Anselm therefore dismisses the theory of the work of Christ which had been current for so long, and with it, an unacceptable concept of *iustitia Dei*: non video quam vim habeat.

Anselm's own theory may be stated as a series of propositions, if the numerous digressions are ignored. When this is one, the centrality of the concept of *iustitia* to his argument becomes apparent:

1. Man was created in a state of original justice for eternal felicity.
2. This felicity requires the perfect and voluntary submission of man's will to God – i.e., *iustitia*.
3. Man's present state is that of *iniustitia*.
4. Either this must result in man's being deprived of eternal felicity, or else the situation must be rectified by an appropriate satisfaction.
5. This satisfaction must exceed the act of disobedience.
6. Man cannot offer to God anything other than the demands of *iustitia*, and on account of his present *iniustitia*, he cannot even do that.
7. Therefore God's purpose in creating man has been frustrated.
8. But this is unjust, and poses a contradiction to the divine nature.
9. Therefore a means of redemption must exist if justice is to be reestablished.
10. Man cannot redeem himself, being unable to make the necessary satisfaction for sin.
11. God could make the necessary satisfaction.
12. Since only God can, and only man ought to, make the necessary satisfaction, it must be made by a God-man.
13. Therefore the incarnation is required as an act of justice.

The importance of justice at this stage in the argument is often overlooked. The 'syllogism' – Aristotle, it must be recalled, had yet to be rediscovered! – which demonstrates the 'necessity' of the incarnation may be stated thus:

A.   Only man ought to make satisfaction for sin – but he cannot.

B.   Only God can make the necessary satisfaction – but he is under no obligation to do so – indeed, he ought not to do so.

It is clear that this primitive 'syllogism' could lead to two conclusions.

1.   A God-man both cannot and ought not to make such a satisfaction.

2.   Only a God-man both can and ought to make such a satisfaction.

From a purely dialectical standpoint, the work in question could equally well be entitled *Cur Deus non homo*. However, as justice demands that man's predicament be resolved, Anselm feels himself justified in drawing the second conclusion, and overlooking the first.

The weak point in Anselm's soteriology is generally considered to be his theory of satisfaction,[29] which we do not propose to discuss further. The essential point, however, is that Anselm considers, presumably on the basis of the established satisfaction-merit model of the penitential system of the contemporary church, that the payment of a satisfaction by the God-man would be regarded by his readers as an acceptable means of satisfying the demands of moral rectitude without violating the moral order of creation. For our purposes, this aspect of Anselm's soteriology is subsidiary, the main element being his development of *iustitia Dei* as action directed towards the highest good, and thus embracing the redemption of mankind. Anselm's soteriology is dominated by the understanding of justice as moral rectitude, and it marks a decisive turning point in the medieval discussion of the 'righteousness of God'.

The theory that the devil has rights over man, which God was obliged to respect, continued to influence theologians for some time after Anselm's death. Thus the school of Laon, marked by its extreme theological conservatism, taught that the devil had gained just possession of man because man had freely enslaved himself to the devil as a consequence of his sin. God is therefore obliged to respect the *ius diaboli*.[30] The theological justification provided for the incarnation by the school of Laon is that it is only God who has the *ability* and only man who has the *obligation* to overcome the devil: by logic similar to that employed by Anselm of Canterbury, the necessity of the incarnation is then deduced. The devil has no *ius* over the God-man, and by his abuse of his legitimate power, the devil forfeits his *ius* over man.[31]

This position was subjected to a penetrating theological critique by Peter Abailard. While in no way denying that the devil exercised *potestas* over man *de facto*, Abailard insisted that this power was not acquired or administered *de iure*. By seducing man, the devil acquired no rights over man: diabolus in hominem quem seduxit nullum ius seducendo acquisierit.[32] If the devil has any power over sinful man, he possesses it solely by divine permission, in that God has allotted him the function of captor of sinful man in the economy of salvation. Outside the realm of this divine permission, the devil has no rights over man. As the devil does not possess even this limited *potestas* by an absolute right, God is at liberty to withdraw it. A similar position is adopted by Hugh of St Victor, who argues that although man is justly punished by the devil, his dominion over man is held unjustly: iniuste ergo diabolus tenet hominem, sed homo iuste tenetur.[33] The school of Abailard, as might be expected, upheld their master's teaching that the devil had *potestas* over man *de facto* but not *de iure*.[34] Bernard of Clairvaux, an opponent of Abailard on so many matters, concedes that the devil's power over man may be said to be just in that it derives from God, but unjust in that it was usurped by the devil.[35] The classic position characteristic of the later twelfth century is summarised in the teaching of Peter of Poitiers: the devil has no right to punish man, but on account of his sin, man deserves to be placed under his power.[36]

The significance of the critique of the *ius diaboli* lies in the concept of *iustitia* employed to characterise God's dealings with the devil. If *iustitia* is understood to entail the respect of established *ius* – i.e., the situation as it exists *de facto* – then God is obliged to respect the dominion of the devil over man. If *iustitia* is conformity to the divine will, the devil has no *de iure* rights over man, having abused the limited and conditional rights which some theologians were prepared to allow him in the context of the economy of salvation. The general rejection of the *ius diaboli* by the theologians of the twelfth century is therefore of considerable significance in the development of the articulation of the 'righteousness of God'.

A further theological development of significance is associated with Peter Abailard. Throughout his writings, there is an analogical predication to God of the definition of *iustitia* taken directly from Cicero: iustitia virtus est, communi utilitate servata, suam tribuens dignitatem.[37] In effect, it is this concept of *iustitia* which underlies Abailard's rejection of the *ius diaboli*: the devil, by insisting upon more than his due, stepped outside the boundaries of *iustitia*. Although Augustine had earlier subjected the theological application of the Ciceronian concept of *iustitia* to a penetrating critique (see §4), most theologians of the late twelfth century returned to the Ciceronian concept of *iustitia* to clarify the apparently related concept of *iustitia Dei*. The widespread use of the concept within the Abailardian school[38] suggests the influence of Abailard in this respect. While Godfrey of Poitiers followed Stephen Langton in distinguishing three aspects of the term *iustitia*, he appears to have introduced a significant innovation – the opinion that *iustitia reddit unicuique quod suum est* is attributed to *Augustine*.[39] William of Auxerre, the first Summist, distinguished the specifically theological use of the term from its ordinary sense,[40] noting that justice and mercy were not opposed in the former case. Simon of Hinton also reproduces the Ciceronian definition, again attributing it to Augustine.[41] The application of this concept of *iustitia* to the specific matter of justification may be illustrated from the *de virtutibus* of John of La Rochelle:

iustitia est sua cuique tribuens, Deo, sibi, et proximo. De hac etiam dicitur Matth. VI: primum querite regnum Dei et iustitiam eius. Hec est iustitia generalis que iustificatur impius, cuius sunt due partes: declinare a malo et facere bonum. Huius etiam iustitie generalis partes sunt latria, dulia et obedientia.[42]

It will be clear that the justification of man is seen as an act of divine justice, rendering to man his due for his efforts to avoid evil and do good. This understanding of *iustitia Dei* is clearly closely linked to a doctrine of merit, by which the divine justification of man may be rationalised on the basis of justice, understood as *reddens unicuique quod suum est*. It will also be evident that this approach requires reference to the divine equity as much as to the divine justice – i.e., God justifies those who merit it *sine gratia sine fraude sine personarum acceptione*.

A somewhat different approach to the matter is found in the works of Hugh of St Victor. His discussion of justification involves the distinction between *iustitia potestatis* and *iustitia aequitatis*. The former, also referred to as *iustitia secundum debitum facientis*, is such that the agent (i.e., God) is permitted to do anything within his power, provided that it is not unjust. The latter, or *iustitia secundum meritum patientis*, is that which relates to man as the object of the divine justification, and is such that he is permitted to have whatever he is entitled to, irrespective of whether he wants it.[43] Applying these concepts of justice to man's justification, Hugh argues that God is able to justify man justly, although it may reasonably be pointed out that Hugh's definitions of justice lead to the conclusion that whatever God wills for man is just, whether justification or condemnation, by virtue of the power of the divine will.[44]

The middle of the thirteenth century saw the introduction of the Aristotelian concept of justice into the theology of the western church. Thus Albertus Magnus' commentary on Book III of the *Sentences* appears to demonstrate familiarity with Book V of the *Nicomachean Ethics*,[45] while his commentary on Book IV (1249) makes use of a translation of this work for the first time.[46] While this introduction allowed a classification of the various senses which the term *iustitia* could bear, it does not appear to have had a significant effect on the medieval discussion of the 'righteousness of God'. The basic concepts employed remain the same, despite differences in terminology. Of far greater importance is the emergence of a clear distinction between the *intellectualist* and *voluntarist* approaches to the question of *iustitia Dei*, which may be illustrated from the works of Thomas Aquinas and Duns Scotus respectively.

Thomas rejected the opinion that *iustitia Dei* is merely an arbitrary aspect of the divine will. To assert that *iustitia* ultimately depends upon the will of God amounts to the blasphemous assertion that God does not operate according to the order of wisdom.[47] Underlying *iustitia* is *sapientia*, discernable to the intellect, so that the ultimate standard of justice must be taken to be right reason.[48] This intellectualism is particularly evident in Thomas' discussion of the rationale of the salvation of mankind in Christ. For Thomas, the deliverance of mankind through the death of Christ is the most appropriate mode of redemption, and can be established as such on rational grounds. After listing the five reasons which lead to this assertion, Thomas concludes: et ideo convenientius fuit quod per passionem Christi liberaremur, quam per solam Dei voluntatem.[49] Underlying this point is Thomas' critique of a voluntarist interpretation of *iustitia Dei*, according to which God's justice demanded Christ's passion as a *necessary* satisfaction for human sin: iustitia Dei exigebat ut homo a peccato liberaretur, Christo per passionem suam satisfaciente. Thomas argues that human sin counts as *culpa*, and as such must be treated as coming under private, rather than public, law. If God is considered as judge (*iudex*), then he is not at liberty to remit an offence (*culpa*) without satisfaction, as the offence in question has been committed against a higher authority (e.g., the king), on whose behalf the judge is obliged to act. However, as God is the supreme and common good of the universe (*supremum et commune bonum totius universae*), it follows that the *culpa* in question has not been committed against some higher authority than God, but against God himself. And just as it is perfectly acceptable for an individual to forgive an offence against himself without satisfaction, so God may forgive the sinner without the *necessity* of satisfaction.[50] An interpretation of *iustitia Dei* which insists upon the absolute necessity of satisfaction – and Thomas appears to have Anselm of Canterbury in mind – is to be rejected in favour of one by which satisfaction is recognised to be most appropriate to right reason, and *universally* recognised as such by rational beings.

This point becomes clearer when the voluntarist interpretation of *iustitia Dei* is considered. Although the origins of this approach are especially associated with Duns Scotus,[51] it would find its most thorough development in the soteriology of the *via moderna*. Gabriel Biel insists upon the priority of the divine will over any moral structures by declaring that God's will is essentially independent of what is right or wrong; if the divine will amounted to a mere endorsement of what is good or right, God's will would thereby be subject to created principles of morality. What is good, therefore, is only good if it is accepted as such by God:

Nihil fieri dignum est nisi de tua benignitate et misericordia voluntate dignum iudicare volueris, neque enim quia bonum aut iustum est aliquid, ipsum Deus vult, sed quia Deus vult, ideo bonum est et iustum. Voluntas nanque divina non ex nostra bonitate, sed ex divina voluntate bonitas nostra pendet, nec aliquid bonum nisi quia a Deo sic acceptum.[52]

The divine will is thus the chief arbiter and principle of justice, establishing justice by its decisions, rather than acting on the basis of established justice. Morality and merit alike derive from the divine will, in that the goodness of an act must be defined, not in terms of the act itself, but in terms of the *divine estimation of that act*. Duns Scotus had established the general voluntarist principle, that every created offering to God is worth precisely whatever God accepts it for: dico, quod sicut omne aliud a Deo, ideo est bonum, quia a Deo volitum, et non est converso; sic meritum illud tantum bonum erat, pro quanto acceptabatur.[53] The consequences of this principle for the doctrine of merit will be explored in §10. Applying this principle to the passion of Christ and the redemption of mankind, Scotus points out that a good angel could have made satisfaction in Christ's place, had God chosen to accept his offering as having sufficient value: the merit of Christ's passion lies solely in the *acceptatio divina*.

A further development of the medieval discussion of the 'righteousness of God' is also accepted with Duns Scotus. This development is essentially grammatical, and concerns the distinction between *univocity* and *equivocity*: a term is strictly univocal when it signifies the things it represents by means of one concept and one grammatical mode of signification.[54] The earlier medieval theologians had distinguished two main senses of the term *iustitia* – *iustitia distributiva* and *condecentia bonitatis*[55] – permitting *iustitia* and *misericordia* to be correlated within the context of the economy of salvation. The *locus classicus* for this interpretation of the 'righteousness of God' was due to Thomas Aquinas: misericordia non tollit iustitiam, sed est quaedam iustitiae plenitudo.[56] This approach to the matter was precluded by Scotus' insistence upon the univocity of *iustitia*: in Deo non est nisi unica iustitia . . . Nullam iustitiam habet nisi ad reddendum suae bonitati vel voluntati, quod eam condecet.[57] Scotus' Aristotelian interpretation of *iustitia Dei*, linked with his insistence upon the univocity of the term, led to a hiatus being imposed between *iustitia* and *misericordia*:[58] the 'righteousness of God' cannot find its expression in man's justification, which must now be seen as an aspect of the divine mercy.[59]

One of the most significant developments in relation to the medieval understanding of the 'righteousness of God' took place within the *via moderna*, and is of particular importance in relation to the developing theology of the young Luther.[60] Gabriel Biel's doctrine of justification is based upon the concept of a *pactum* between God and man (see §11) which defines the conditions which man must meet if he is to be justified, as well as emphasising the divine reliability. The present order of salvation, although radically contingent, is nevertheless totally reliable and strictly immutable.[61] Thus God, having freely and of his *liberalitas* determined to enter into such a binding contract with man, is now obliged to respect the terms of that covenant; deus dat gratiam facienti quod in se est necessitate immutabilitatis et ex suppositione quia disposuit dare immutabiliter gratiam facienti quod in se est.[62]

The establishment of such a reliable moral framework within which justification takes place allows Biel to resolve a difficulty which had previously impeded theologians from applying the Ciceronian definition of *iustitia* directly to God. The Ciceronian, Justinian and Aristotelian concepts of *iustitia* are based upon the notion of a contracting community, the *res publica* or πόλις, which establishes the *iuris consensus*. The direct application of such concepts of *iustitia* to God was rendered problematical by the absence of a theological equivalent to this contractual framework. The postulation of a *pactum* between God and man eliminates this difficulty, the *pactum* effectively functioning as the *iuris consensus* which is required if *iustitia Dei* is to be defined in terms of *reddens unicuique quod suum est*. Furthermore, studies of the medieval discussion of the concept of the divine self-limitation (as expressed in the *pactum*) have demonstrated how the theologians of the period found the terminology of Canon Law – particularly *iustitia* – to be an ideal vehicle for its articulation.[63] Under the terms of the covenant (*pactum*), God is obliged to reward the man who does *quod in se est* with grace *as a matter of justice*, in that he is rendering to him that to which he is entitled. The *pactum* determines *quod suum est*, and specifies the conditions upon which the *viator* may receive it. Biel is able to correlate the divine justice and divine mercy by pointing out that the present order of salvation, to which God is now irrevocably committed as a matter of justice, is ultimately an expression of the divine mercy. *Stante lege*, God is necessarily obliged to reward the *viator* who does *quod in se est* with *quod suum est* – i.e., justifying grace. In his mercy, God established an order of justice to which he is presently and irrevocably bound. Failure on the part of God to honour the pactum would result in his being unjust, which is inconceivable: ita etiam quod stante sua promissione qua pollicitus est dare vitam eternam servantibus sua mandata, non posset sine iniusticia subtrahere eis premia repromissa.[64] It is therefore up to the individual, knowing the divine will, to conform himself to it if he wishes to be justified.[65] It is therefore clear that Biel understands *iustitia Dei* to refer to equity within the context of the *pactum*, by which God has established his dealings with men upon a reliable basis.

It is this understanding of the 'righteousness of God' which is reproduced by Martin Luther in the earlier part of his *Dictata super Psalterium* (1513–15), as may be judged from his scholion on Psalm 9.9 (Vulgate: 10.9):

Iustitia autem dicitur redditio unicuique quod suum est. Unde prior est equitas quam iustitia et quasi prerequisita. Et equitas meriti distinguit, iustitia premiae reddit. Sic Dominus iudicat orbem terrae in equitate (quia omnibus idem est, vult omnes salvos fieri) et iudicat in iustitia, quia reddit unicuique suum premium.[66]

Luther here reproduces the key aspects of Biel's understanding of *iustitia Dei*: *iustitia* is understood to be based upon divine equity, which looks solely to man's merits in determining his reward within the framework established by the covenant: hinc recte dicunt doctores, quod homini facienti quod in se est, Deus infallibiliter dat gratiam.[67] Luther's theological breakthrough is intimately connected with his discovery of a new meaning of the 'righteousness of God',[68] and it is important to appreciate that his earlier works are characterised by the teaching of the *via moderna* upon this matter.

The second question concerning the 'righteousness of God' raises the whole issue of the analogical nature of theological language. How is it possible to speak of God being 'righteous' (*iustus*)? As we noted earlier (§2), the biblical material upon which the medieval commentators based their exegesis contained a Hebraic concept of the 'righteousness of God', *iustitia salutifera*, which bore little resemblance to the concept of *iustitia distributiva* characteristic of western European thought. As such, it was difficult to argue from human to divine justice, a point which was frequently emphasised by early biblical commentators with reference to the problem of the 'transference of meaning'.[69] Peter Abailard thus urged extreme caution when employing terms borrowed from their everyday context (*translata a consuetis significationis*) in statements concerning God,[70] although he appears to have overlooked his own principle when analogically predicating human concepts of justice to God, as we noted above.

This use of human concepts of justice, applied analogically to God, was criticised by several theologians of the twelfth century, most notably by Alan of Lille. According to Alan, every term which is predicated of God is necessarily transferred from its proper meaning (*transfertur a sua propria significatione*). Recognising that God can only be described as *iustus* by an indirect transference of the term from its proper signification, Alan insists that this transference be understood to refer solely to the word (*nomen*) thus transferred, and not to its signification (*res*):

Deus est iustus, hoc nomen *iustus* transfertur a sua propria significatione ad hoc ut conveniat Deo, sed res nominis non attribuitur Deo.[71]

In other words, the statement 'Deus est iustus' contains the term *iustus* transferred from a particular human context – but the term cannot be allowed to bear precisely the same meaning in this statement as it assumes in that specific human context. Even though the same term *iustus* is predicated by God in the statement 'Deus est iustus' as in the analogical statement 'Socrates est iustus', it cannot be allowed to bear the same signification in each case. On account of its transference from its proper context, the word acquires a 'borrowed meaning'[72] which, although analogous to its original meaning, is not identical with it. Thus divine justice is not the same as human justice, so that the statement 'Deus est iustus' cannot be allowed to have the same point of reference as 'Socrates est iustus'. This leads to the inevitable conclusion that, since the 'borrowed meaning' of *iustus* is unknown, and almost certainly unknowable, the statement 'Deus est iustus' has no meaning. If we do not know precisely what meaning the term *iustus* assumes in the statement 'Deus est iustus', we cannot know what the statement means.[73] Most theologians of the twelfth century thus preferred, like the Benedictine Hugh, Archbishop of Rouen, to seek refuge in the divine incomprehensibility: Deus enim semper est id quod est, qui determinari seu describi vel diffiniri non potest, quia incomprehensibilis est.[74]

The question of how God may be described as *iustus* raises the related question of how his attributes may be discussed. What does it mean to speak of God's wisdom, righteousness, etc.? The rise of the Ockhamist epistemology in the late fourteenth century led to the existence of such attributes being called into question.[75] Henry of Ghent maintained the reality of such divine attributes. If the mental distinction between essence and attributes in God rested upon a comparison with reference to the same qualities in creatures, the existence of the divine attributes would come to be dependent upon creatures – which Henry considered impossible. Therefore the divine attributes must be considered to differ by an internal relation of reason, independent of any intellectual comparison with the same qualities among creatures. Godfrey of Fontaines, however, argued that the basis of the distinction between the divine attributes must be considered to lie in creatures, rather than in God himself. Godfrey, like most of his contemporaries, accepted that the distinction between the divine attributes was purely mental, but insisted that the distinction must originate outside the mind. Whilst Henry located the origin of this distinction in God himself, Godfrey located it within creatures. The distinction between the attributes must rest upon a comparison within the intellect between God himself and the diversity which exists in his creatures, as otherwise God, being supremely simple, would only be conceived as one. The divine attributes, therefore, are contained virtually within the divine essence as the source of all perfection, and are known only by comparison with what approximates to them – i.e., by the recognition on the part of the human intellect of a similarity between God and creature in respect of the quality involved. As such forms and qualities in creatures owe their existence and origin to the divine ideas and their perfection in God, the existence of such a similarity, albeit only to a limited and determinate extent, is to be expected.

By contrast, William of Ockham rejected both opinions. The

distinction between the divine attributes on the part of the human intellect owes nothing either to any such distinction in God himself, nor to any comparison with himself or anything else. According to Ockham, God's attributes, such as his *iustitia*, *misericordia*, etc., cannot be said to correspond to anything real within God himself, but arise purely and simply from the multiplicity of acts of human cognition involved.[76] Thus *iustitia Dei* cannot be allowed to have any real existence within God, as it is a consequence purely of the act of cognition on the part of the human intellect. The only distinction that may be allowed among the divine attributes is that they are different concepts within the human mind: they do not denote a formal distinction within God, nor do they correspond to any distinction *in* him, or *in relation to* him. The concepts involved are neither *really* nor *formally* identical with the divine essence. The fact that such conceptual distinctions are known by the human intellect cannot be allowed to impose such a distinction upon the object of the intellect, so that any diversity which may be posited among the divine attributes cannot be allowed to correspond to a diversity within God himself, but merely to concepts which are distinguished by the intellect. God, as supremely simple, is either apprehended totally, or not at all, and as a consequence his attributes are merely the product of the human intellect. Whereas God is real, his attributes are not (unless, of course, concepts are allowed to be real). The essence of Ockham's important criticism of the real existence of the divine attributes is that they are not founded in being. A twofold distinction must therefore be made:[77]

1. The divine attributes, taken absolutely for the perfection which is God himself.
2. The divine attributes, taken as concepts which can be predicated of God.

If the attributes of God are understood as in (1), there is no real distinction between them; if they are understood as in (2), the attributal distinction is purely mental, and has no foundation in reality. Either way, it makes little sense to speak of *iustitia Dei*, and still less to speak of a tension between *iustitia* and *misericordia* in God.

Ockham's critique of the divine attributes does not appear to have had any real significance upon the later medieval discussion of *iustitia Dei*, which tended to proceed on the assumption that a real distinction could be drawn between *iustitia* and *misericordia Dei*. The problem of defining that 'righteousness', however, proved to be intractable. The medieval period can be characterised by its insistence that God's mercy, righteousness and truth were simultaneously manifested in his salvation of mankind, a point often made in connection with the Christological exegesis of Psalm 85.10 (Vulgate: 84.11):

> Misericordia et veritas obviaverunt sibi,
> Iustitia et pax osculatae sunt.

The theologians of the medieval period were convinced that God's righteousness was expressed in the manner in which he chose to redeem mankind in Christ. The difficulties associated with this understanding of the 'righteousness of God', particularly in connection with the correlation of *iustitia Dei* and *iustitia hominis* were never, however, fully resolved.

§7 The subjective appropriation of justification

The medieval theological tradition followed Augustine of Hippo in insisting that man has a positive role to play in his own justification. Augustine's celebrated *dictum* 'Qui fecit te sine te, non te iustificat sine te'[1] virtually achieved the status of an axiom[2] in the medieval discussion of justification. The definition of the precise nature of this human rôle in justification was, however, the subject of considerable disagreement within the medieval theological schools. The development of the various traditional positions on the question, which forms the subject of the present section, is conveniently discussed under three headings:

1. the nature of the human free will;
2. the necessity and nature of the proper disposition for justification;
3. the origin, application and interpretation of the axiom *facienti quod in se est Deus non denegat gratiam*.

Before considering these three aspects of the appropriation of justification, it is necessary to make two observations. First, it is impossible to discuss the medieval understandings of the subjective appropriation of justification without reference to the rôle of the sacraments in justification, to be discussed in the following section (§8). Second, the medieval discussion of the appropriation of justification is not conducted in terms of the concept of justification *by faith*. Justifying faith is universally understood to be a gift of God bestowed upon man as a consequence of his disposition towards justification. In effect, the possibility of justifying faith being a human work is excluded from the outset. The medieval discussion of the appropriation of justification is primarily concerned with establishing the conditions upon which justifying grace and faith are bestowed upon the individual by God. In the present section, the three aspects of the question of the subjective appropriation of justification identified above will be considered individually.

1 The nature of the human free will

The influence of Augustine upon the medieval discussion of justification is probably at its greatest in connection with the relation between grace and free will. Although the term *liberum arbitrium* is pre-Augustinian and un-biblical (§3), Augustine succeeded in imposing an interpretation upon the term which allowed a profoundly biblical understanding of human bondage to sin and need for grace to be maintained, while simultaneously upholding the reality of human free will. This understanding of the nature of the human free will would be clarified in the course of a series of controversies immediately succeeding Augustine's death, in addition to two during his lifetime – the Pelagian and Massilian controversies.

In essence, Pelagianism must be seen as a reforming movement in the increasingly corrupt world of the later Roman empire, especially critical of the growing tendency to see in Christianity an almost magical way of obtaining salvation in the next world without undue inconvenience in the present. It was primarily against this moral laxity that Pelagius and his supporters protested,[3] apparently unaware that their chief theological opponent shared precisely the same concern. Augustine's account of the origin of the Pelagian controversy relates how Pelagius was outraged by the much-cited prayer from his *Confessions*, 'Give what you command, and command what you will.'[4] To Pelagius, these words suggested that man was merely a puppet wholly determined by divine grace, thereby encouraging moral quietism of the worst order. For Pelagius, moral responsibility presupposed freedom of the will: I ought, therefore I can. The fundamental doctrine of Pelagius' theological system is the unequivocal assertion of the autonomous and sovereign character of the human *liberum arbitrium*: in creating man, God gave him the unique privilege of being able to accomplish the divine will by his own choice, setting before him life and death, and bidding him choose the former – but permitting the final decision to rest with man himself. Pelagius found particularly offensive the suggestion that man's *liberum arbitrium* was diseased, compromised or handicapped in any way, so that it has an inherent bias towards evil-doing. While Pelagius conceded that Adam's sin had disastrous consequences for his posterity, he insisted that these arose by *imitation*, rather than by *propagation*. There is no congenital fault in man, and no special or general influence upon him to perform evil or good. God, having created man, is unable to exert any influence upon him, except through external non-coercive means (i.e., *gratia ab extra*). In part, the confusion surrounding Augustine's controversy with Pelagius arises from the fact that Pelagius appears to understand by *grace* what Augustine understands by *nature*. Thus when Augustine and Pelagius agree that man stands in need of grace, the latter merely means *general* grace, given in the endowment of nature, enabling man to perform God's will with his natural faculties.

The real *locus* of the Pelagian controversy lies in Augustine's doctrine of prevenient grace. Pelagius understands grace as *gratia ab extra*, an external, non-coercive grace of knowledge such as the Decalogue or the example of Christ. A man can, if he so chooses, fulfil the Law of Moses without sinning. It is this concept of grace which ultimately leads to the harsh doctrine of *impeccantia*: as the Law *can* be fulfilled, so it *must* be fulfilled. This 'theology of example' may be seen in both Pelagius' emphasis upon the need for *imitatio Christi* and in the assertion that it is by the *example* of Adam's sin that his posterity is injured. The Pelagian analysis of volition in terms of *posse, velle, esse* is particularly well suited to an exemplarist soteriology: the external example demonstrates the *posse*, thereby stimulating the *velle*.

The Massilian controversy appears to have arisen over Augustine's doctrine of predestination. The term 'semi-Pelagian' is a seriously misleading anachronism which has no place in this discussion.[5] The term 'Massilian' is used by Augustine himself, and eliminates the unjustified comparison with Pelagianism implicit in the term 'semi-Pelagianism'. Augustine described the Massilians as holding doctrines which 'abundantly distinguished them from the Pelagians', which appears to amount to a rejection of Prosper of Aquitaine's description of them as the *reliquiae Pelagianorum*. He notes their chief error to lie in their teaching on predestination.[6] The same cannot be said of Faustus of Riez, who asserted that man's free will was capable of taking the initiative in his salvation. If the term 'semi-Pelagian' is merited by any Massilian, it is by Faustus. Vincent of Lérins appears to have formulated his canon within the specific context of his refutation of Augustine's predestinarianism. The nature of truly catholic doctrine is that it is *quod ubique, quod semper, quod ab omnibus creditum est*.[7] As Augustine's doctrine of predestination failed to conform to this triple test of ecumenicity, antiquity and consent, it cannot be regarded as catholic. A more positive approach to Augustine's teachings is found in the writings of John Cassian. Like Vincent, he rejected the Pelagian doctrine of the free will, apparently accepting Augustine's theology of grace in its entirety, with the specific exception of his doctrines of predestination and irresistible grace.[8] In particular, it may be noted that he appears to have grasped and upheld the Augustinian concept of the dialectic between the *liberum arbitrium captivatum* and *liberatum*: 'He is truly free who has begun to be your prisoner, O Lord.'[9] Cassian's emphasis upon the reality of the human free will has its context in monastic asceticism, with its characteristic emphasis upon the need for exertion in the spiritual life. Cassian wrote primarily for monks, who may be regarded as having been initiated into the Christian life. It may therefore be assumed that when Cassian speaks of grace, he intends *cooperative*, rather than *operative* grace to be understood (to use Augustine's terms). If Cassian appears to be a 'synergist', it is because, like Augustine, he asserts the synergy of grace and free will *after* justification. Furthermore, it may be pointed out that Cassian's emphasis upon *prayer* as a means for improving the spiritual condition is a sign of the *importance* he attaches to grace, rather than of his *rejection* of its necessity, as some have supposed.

The Synod of Jerusalem (July 415) and the Synod of Diospolis (December 415) led to mild censure of Pelagianism, with the influence of Augustine much in evidence. Neither of these Synods can be considered to be significant in comparison with the Council of Carthage (418),[10] whose canons would receive wide acceptance in the catholic church, and feature prominently in medieval discussions of the nature of the Pelagian error. Of these canons, the most important is the fifth, which teaches the impotence of the human free will unless aided by grace, and the further necessity of grace to enable man to fulfil the commandments of the law.[11] The Council of Ephesus (431) condemned both Nestorianism and Pelagianism (this latter in the form associated with Caelestius), although the council does not appear to have recognised the close theological connection between the heresies so ably summarised in Bishop Gore's *dictum*, 'The Nestorian Christ is the fitting saviour of the Pelagian man.'[12]

The most specific attack upon Pelagianism to be found in a fifth century authoritative source is that of the *Indiculus de gratia Dei* (431), usually regarded as the work of Prosper of Aquitaine. Its chapters explicitly reject the Pelagian understandings of the nature of grace and the capabilities of man's free will. A man cannot rise from the depths of Adam's sin unless the grace of God should lift him up.[13] Even after justification, man requires God's grace if he is to persevere.[14] The most important statement of the document relates to the effects of grace upon free will: the *Indiculus* makes it clear that grace *liberates* rather than *abolishes* man's *liberum arbitrium*.[15]

The definitive pronouncement of the early western church on the Pelagian and Massilian controversies may be found in the Second Council of Orange (529). The Council declared that to teach that the 'freedom of the soul' remained unaffected by the Fall was Pelagian.[16] The Faustian doctrine of the *initium fidei* – i.e., that man can take the initiative in his own salvation – was explicitly rejected: not only the *beginning*, but also the *increase* of faith, are alike gifts of grace.[17] While the Council declared that man's *liberum arbitrium* is injured, weakened and diminished, its existence was not questioned.[18] Although the Council declined to teach the doctrines of double predestination and irresistible grace, it must be pointed out that it is questionable whether these may be considered as authentically *Augustinian*, in that they are not *explicitly taught by Augustine*, even though they may appear to *follow logically* from his teaching. If the epithet 'Augustinian' is understood to mean 'conforming to doctrines explicitly taught by Augustine after 396', it may be asserted that Orange II endorses an Augustinian doctrine of justification.

Although it might therefore appear that the medieval period was thus bequeathed an accurate and definitive account of Augustine's teaching on justification, three factors conspired to generate considerable confusion over this matter. It is a curious and unexplained feature of the history of doctrine that the canons of Orange II appear to have been unknown from the tenth to the middle of the sixteenth centuries.[19] The theologians of the medieval period thus did not have access to this definitive statement of an Augustinian doctrine of justification, and appear to have been unaware of its existence. Second, much of Pelagius' work was mistakenly ascribed to Jerome during the medieval period, with the inevitable result that Jerome and Augustine were thought to have radically different theologies of justification. For example, Peter Lombard found himself in some difficulty as he tried to reconcile Augustine's opinion concerning man, *posse peccare et non posse non peccare etiam damnabiliter*, with the affirmation *hominem semper et peccare et non peccare posse*, which he attributes to Jerome's *Explanatio fidei catholicae ad Damasum*.[20] In fact, the Lombard is unwittingly citing from Pelagius' *Libellus fidei ad Innocentium*! Third, many pseudo-Augustinian works were in circulation in the medieval period, frequently teaching a doctrine of justification which owed more to Pelagius or Faustus of Riez than to Augustine.[21] An excellent example is provided by Pelagius' *Libellus fidei*, which we have already noted to have been attributed by some (e.g., Peter Lombard) to Jerome: elsewhere, this same Pelagian work is attributed to Augustine as *Sermo* 191! A further example is provided by the famous maxim *si non es praedestinatus, fac ut praedestineris* ('If you are not predestined, endeavour to be predestined'), to be discussed in §12. Although fourteenth century source-critical studies achieved a certain degree of resolution of these difficulties, the fact remains that the great theological renaissance of the twelfth century would take place without access to the authentically Augustinian teaching of the sixth century church on the relation between grace and free will. This point is of particular importance in connection with the development of the teaching of Thomas Aquinas on the *initium fidei*, which will be discussed further below.

Despite these circumstances, the twelfth century witnessed considerable agreement on the issues of grace and free will. The profession of faith, composed by Leo IX in 1053, contained a clear statement of the relationship between the two: grace precedes and follows man, yet in such a manner that it does not compromise his free will.[22] Anselm of Canterbury defined free will as the power (*potestas*) of preserving the *rectitudo voluntatis*: man, though fallen, still possesses this *potestas*, and can therefore be said to possess *libertas arbitrii*. However, no power is capable of actualising its potential unaided,[23] and if the *potestas* of the human free will is to be reduced to *actus* it must be actualised by God's general or special *concursus*. In effect, Anselm's definition of free will is such that a positive answer to the question of whether man can justify himself is excluded from the outset: as only God can convert *potestas* to *actus*, so only God can justify.

This concept of the divine actualisation of *potestas* found its expression in the thirteenth-century doctrine of the *concursus simultaneus*. There was, however, considerable confusion concerning the precise means by which potency was reduced to act: according to some, the agent involved was the Holy Spirit, whilst others considered it to be actual or habitual grace.[24] Later, the axiom *omnis actus perfectus a forma perfecta* would be employed in the discussion of the question.[25] Underlying these developments, however, is the basic conviction, expressed by Peter Lombard in his *Sentences*, that man's *liberum arbitrium* cannot do good unless it is first liberated (*liberatum*) and subsequently assisted by grace.[26] The subsequent confusion concerning the precise nature of the *concursus* unquestionably reflects a corresponding prior confusion concerning the nature of grace itself, so characteristic a feature of early scholasticism (see §9).

The medieval ignorance of the canons of Orange II is of particular importance in relation to the evaluation of the 'Pelagianism' of the teaching on man's *liberum arbitrium* associated with the *via moderna*. We shall illustrate this with reference to Gabriel Biel. The relevance of Gabriel Biel's doctrine of *liberum arbitrium* to the development of Luther's doctrine of *servum arbitrium* has been emphasised,[27] as it is now generally accepted that Luther's *Disputatio contra scholasticam theologiam* (1517) is specifically directed against Biel, rather than against 'scholastic theology' in general.[28] Following the common teaching of the *via moderna*, Biel declines to distinguish man's intellect and will, so that *liberum arbitrium*, *libertas* and *voluntas* are regarded as being essentially identical. This approach to the question leads to a strong assertion of the freedom of the will, as *libertas* is regarded as a corollary of rationality. That the will is free is evident from experience, and requires no further demonstration.[29] For Biel, free will is the power of the soul which allows the *viator* to distinguish and choose between good and evil, by which he is distinguished from other animals.[30] The theological consequences of Biel's doctrine of *liberum arbitrium* may be stated as follows:[31]

1. The human free will may choose a morally good act *ex puris naturalibus*, without the need for grace.[32]
2. Man is able, by the use of his free will and other natural faculties, to implement the law *quoad substantiam actus*, but not *quoad intentionem praecipientis*.[33] In other words, man is able to fulfil the external requirements of the law by his own power, but is unable to fulfil the law in the precise manner which God intended.
3. *Ex puris naturalibus* the free will is able to avoid mortal sin.[34]
4. *Ex puris naturalibus* the free will is able to love God above everything else.[35]
5. *Ex suis naturalibus* the free will is able to dispose itself towards the reception of the gift of grace.[36]

It is this final aspect of Biel's teaching on the capacities of fallen man's free will which has claimed most attention, and has frequently given rise to charges of Pelagianism or 'semi-Pelagianism'.[37] These charges are quite without foundation. As Biel himself makes clear, his discussion of man's rôle in his own justification must be set within the context of the divine *pactum*. The requirement of a minimum response on man's part of the divine offer of grace is totally in keeping with the earlier Franciscan school's teaching, such as that of Alexander of Hales or Bonaventure. Biel has simply placed his theology of a minimum human response to the divine initiative in justification on a firmer foundation in the theology of the *pactum* thereby safeguarding God from the charge of capriciousness. Biel's modern critics' surprise at the absence of contemporary criticism of his teaching as Pelagian[38] simply reflects the fact that, by the standards of the time, Biel's doctrine of justification would not have been considered Pelagian. The sole legitimate criteria by which the 'Pelagianism' of Biel's doctrine of justification may be judged are the canons of the Council of Carthage – the only criteria which medieval doctors then possessed, for reasons we have already noted. Biel's high regard for the tradition of the church is such that he accepts whatever the church defined as being *de fide*. Biel's attitude to tradition is such that, had he known of the decrees of Orange II, he would have incorporated their substance into his doctrine of justification as *determinationes ecclesiae*.[39] If Biel's theology is to be stigmatised as 'Pelagian' or 'semi-Pelagian', it must be appreciated that he suffered from an historical accident which affected the entire period up to the Council of Trent itself. If orthodoxy is to be determined with reference to *known authoritative pronouncements of the church*, orthodoxy would undergo a radical change with the rediscovery of these canons. Those who were orthodox by the standards of 1500 – among whom we may number Gabriel Biel! – may no longer have been so by 1550. Biel himself is aware of the decrees of the Council of Carthage, and makes frequent reference to Canon 5 in particular, which he states thus: 'Qui dixerit, quod sine gratia possumus mandata Dei implere per liberum arbitrium, anathema sit.'[40] Biel's careful distinction between the implementation of the law *quoad substantiam actus* and *quoad intentionem praecipientis* ensures his conformity to the teaching of this canon.

It is clear that the charge of 'Pelagianism' or 'semi-Pelagianism' brought against Biel stands or falls with the definition employed. If it is taken to mean that the *viator* can take the initiative in his own justification, the very existence of the *pactum* deflects the charge: God has taken the initiative away from man, who is merely required to *respond* to that initiative by the proper exercise of his *liberum arbitrium*. However, neither the Pelagian nor Massilian controversies operated with so sophisticated a concept of causality as that employed by the theologians of the *via moderna*, expressed in the *pactum*-theology, so that the application of epithets such as 'Pelagian' to Biel's theology of justification must be regarded as historically unsound. In terms of the historical controversies themselves, Biel must be regarded as totally innocent of both errors.

In general, although the assertion that man possesses the freedom to respond to the divine initiative in justification is characteristic of the medieval period, this consensus was accompanied by widespread disagreement as to the precise nature of the freedom in question, and whether it could be regarded as given in nature or acquired through grace. This point becomes particularly clear in the medieval discussion of the axiom *facienti quod in se est Deus non denegat gratiam*, to which we shall shortly return. Our attention now turns to the medieval opinions concerning a disposition for justification.

2 *The necessity and nature of the proper disposition for justification*

What happens before the sinner is justified? Is justification preceded by a preparation on the part of the sinner to receive the gift which God subsequently gives him? And if this is the case, is God *obliged* to bestow the gift in question upon the sinner on account of his having prepared himself to receive it? The twelfth century saw a growing conviction that a preparation was required of man for justification. Peter of Poitiers used a domestic analogy to illustrate the rôle of such a preparation for justification. A man may clean out his house and decorate it in order to receive an important guest, so that all will be ready when he arrives. This preparation, however, does not necessitate the arrival of the guest, which depends only upon the guest's love for his host.[41]

The necessity of a preparation or disposition for justification was insisted upon by both the early Franciscan and Dominican schools, although, as we shall demonstrate, for very different reasons. The pre-Bonaventuran Franciscan school demonstrates a certain degree of uncertainty on the question, partly due to a related uncertainty in relation to the concept of created grace. Alexander of Hales may have seemed to limit man's rôle in justification to not resisting grace,[42] but his teaching was developed by John of La Rochelle in a significant direction. John insists upon the need for a disposition for justification in man, in that the recipient of uncreated grace – i.e., the Holy Spirit – is unable to receive it unless his soul has first been prepared for it. The need for such a disposition does not result from any deficiency on the part of God. John draws a distinction between sufficiency on the part of the agent (i.e., God) and on the part of the recipient in justification. God is all-sufficient in justification, but the recipient of uncreated grace must first be disposed for its reception by created grace.[43] Odo Rigaldi likewise distinguished between the gift of the uncreated grace of the Holy Spirit and the disposition of the human soul towards the reception of this gift by created grace.[44] It may be noted that Odo appears unclear as to what created grace actually *is* – he seems to regard it as a hybrid species.[45] This unclarity was resolved by the *Summa Fratris Alexandri*[46] in what appears to have been the first systematic discussion of the nature of created grace. The *Summa* begins by considering the concept of uncreated grace,[47] which transforms the human soul in justification: gratia ponit aliquid in anima. If uncreated grace did not alter the soul in justification, there would be no difference between the justified and the unjustified sinner. Uncreated grace may therefore be considered as the *forma transformans* and created grace as the *forma transformata*.[48] This important interpretation of the nature of created grace points to its being a quality of the soul – i.e., a *disposition*, rather than a *substance*. The Holy Spirit can be said to dwell in the souls of the justified as in a temple: this is impossible unless there is something within the soul which, although not itself the temple, is capable of transforming the soul into such a temple capable of receiving the Holy Spirit.[49] This interpretation of the nature and function of created grace is closely linked with the anthropology of the early Franciscan school, according to which the human soul is not naturally capable of receiving grace. In order for the human soul to receive grace, it must first be disposed to receive it. By contrast, the early Dominican school maintained that *anima naturaliter est gratiae capax*, reflecting a quite different understanding of man's pristine state. The disposition of the human soul for the reception of uncreated grace is understood by the *Summa* to be a quality of the soul brought about by the action of grace, and which may be termed *created grace*. It will, however, be clear that there was still uncertainty as to whether *gratia creata* was to be considered as the *disposition towards the reception of uncreated grace* or the *result of the reception of uncreated grace*.

This basic teaching of the early Franciscan school was developed along psychological lines by Bonaventure.[50] Human nature is sufficiently frail that it is simply incapable of receiving the gift of sanctifying grace unless it is prepared beforehand.[51] This disposition towards justification is effected with the assistance of prevenient grace, *gratia gratis data*, and cannot be effected by the unaided free will.[52] The transition from nature to grace is effected by prevenient grace disposing the human soul to receive the supernatural gift of habitual grace.[53] Matthew of Aquasparta reports the opinion that a preparation for justification is useless and unnecessary, since grace is given to man according to his natural aptitudes and capacities.[54] This opinion is to be rejected, he argues, as being improbable and contrary to experience: man cannot prepare himself for justification without *gratia gratis data*, which moves and excites the will to detest sin and desire justification.[55] Following Bonaventure, Matthew emphasises the frailty of human nature: just as a man cannot look at the sun until he has become accustomed to its brilliance by appropriate preparation, so the free will cannot prepare itself for the light of grace unless itself moved by grace.[56] In effect, actual grace is conceived as a medium between the states of nature and supernature: it is impossible to proceed directly from one to the other, and *gratia gratis data* provides the intermediate position by which the transition may be effected.[57] Richard of Middleton distinguished between a *proximate* and a *remote* disposition towards justification.[58] Man may dispose himself towards his own justification by virtue of his own powers: this disposition, however, is remote, and not an immediate disposition towards justification, which may only be effected through actual grace exciting and illuminating man's mind.[59] It is clear that Richard understands actual grace to refer primarily to a special supernatural motion directly attributable to the Holy Spirit.[60] Unlike habitual grace, no disposition is required for actual grace. Thus Roger of Marston emphasised that the gift of actual grace is the first gift by which God prepares the human will for grace, and does not itself require any preparation for justification.[61]

In general, the strongly Augustinian illuminationism of the early Franciscan school led to a theology of justification in which the necessity of a disposition or preparation towards justification was maintained on the grounds of the frailty of the unaided human intellect. Just as man's intellect was incapable of attaining and comprehending divine truth unless illuminated directly by God,[62] so man's will was incapable of desiring or attaining justification unless similarly illuminated (see §15).

The early Dominican school also taught the need for a disposition for justification, but for quite different reasons. The axiom *naturaliter est anima gratiae capax* is particularly associated with the early Dominican school,[63] and on the basis of this anthropology there would appear to be no *prima facie* case for the necessity of a disposition towards the reception of grace. If man's soul is naturally capable of receiving grace, there would seem to be no compelling reason to posit such a necessity. The early Franciscan school, it will be recalled, posited the necessity of such a disposition on the grounds that a transformation of the natural state of the human soul was required in order for it to be *capax gratiae*. It is therefore important to observe that the theologians of the school, particularly Thomas Aquinas, deduced the necessity of such a disposition *on the basis of the Aristotelian analysis of motion*.[64] Grace, being a form, exists as a disposition in the subject who receives it. Application of the Aristotelian theory of generation to this results in the deduction of a stage of preparation. Albertus Magnus did not develop this question at any length,[65] and it is with Thomas Aquinas that its full statement may be found.

In his *Commentary on the Sentences* (1254–7), Thomas considers the question *utrum homo possit se praeparare ad gratiam sine aliqua gratia*.[66] His answer involves distinguishing two understandings of grace, either as the arousal of man's will through divine providence, or as a habitual gift in the soul.[67] In both cases, a preparation for grace is necessary, in that justification, being a *motus*, requires premotion on the basis of the Aristotelian theory of generation. Omne quod movetur ab alio movetur. Grace, being a form, exists as a disposition in the subject who receives it. How can the human free will be prepared to receive the gift of habitual grace? Thomas points out that the preparation cannot take the form of a second habitual gift, as this would merely result in an infinite regression of habitual gifts: some gratuitous gift of God is required, moving the soul from within.[68] Whilst man is converted to his ultimate end by the prime mover (God) he is converted to his proximate end (i.e., the state of justification itself) by the motion of some inferior mover.[69]

In the *Commentary on the Sentences*, Thomas had treated the premotion required for justification as being external and natural – the examples which he provides of such premotions include admonition by another person, or physical illness.[70] In the later *Quaestiones disputatae de veritate* (1256–9), however, Thomas acknowledges an internal means of premotion, *divinus instinctus secundum quod Deus in mentibus hominum operatur*,[71] although it appears that his most characteristic position remains that man can naturally dispose himself towards the reception of grace. The *Summa contra Gentiles* (1258–64) is generally regarded as marking a turning point in Thomas' teaching on the nature of the preparation for justification. It appears that the pseudo-Aristotelian *Liber de bona fortuna* first came to Thomas' attention during this period,[72] as it is cited for the first time at III, 89 and frequently thereafter.[73] In this work, Thomas described the 'errors of the Pelagians' as lying in the assertion that the beginning of man's justification is the work of man, whilst its consummation is the work of God.[74] The crucial statement which marks Thomas' changed views on the question is the following: 'Matter does not move itself to its own perfection; therefore it must be moved by something else.'[75] Therefore, man cannot move himself to receive grace, but is moved by God to receive it.[76] The *Quodlibetum primum*, dating from the second Paris period, attributes the beginnings of man's justification to an internal operation of God, by which God acts on the will internally to cause it to do good.[77] The essential difference between Thomas' early and mature opinions on the question, as determined from the *Commentary on the Sentences* and the *Summa Theologiae* respectively, is that whilst in both he asserted the need for premotion for the *motus mentis* of justification, the early opinion that the 'inferior mover' causing the premotion was man himself was rejected in favour of the later opinion that the 'inferior mover' was God himself. Man's preparation for justification is thus understood to be a divine work, so that no preparation is required for man's justification which God himself does not provide.[78] The preparation for grace in man is the work of God as the prime mover and of the free will as the passive entity which is itself moved.[79] Thomas' discussion of the justification of man therefore proceeds along thoroughly Aristotelian lines, pre-supposing that there are two unequal stages in the process: the *praemotio* (i.e., the preparation for justification as the proximate end), and the *motus* itself (i.e., the movement from the natural to the supernatural planes, with the infusion of supernatural justice). We have already emphasised the rôle of Aristotelian physics in Thomas' deduction of the *processus iustificationis* (see §5). It may be noted that Thomas understands the priority of the premotion over the motion to be *by nature* and not *in time*: the two may coincide temporally, as in the case of the conversion of Paul.[80]

The later medieval period saw the need for a human disposition towards justification accepted as axiomatic. The disputed aspects of the matter related primarily to the question of whether this disposition was itself a work of grace, or a purely human act performed without the aid of grace. Thus Luther's mentor Johannes von Staupitz affirmed the necessity of a proper disposition for justification, even though he stressed the moral impotence of fallen man and taught gratuitous election *ante praevisa merita*.[81] This brings us to the question of the *nature* of the disposition towards justification, which was practically invariably discussed in terms of the axiom *facienti quod in se est Deus denegat gratiam*. It is to this axiom that we now turn.

3 The axiom 'facienti quod in se est Deus non denegat gratiam'

This axiom is probably best translated as: 'God will not deny grace to the man who does his best.'[82] The essential principle encapsulated in the axiom is that man and God have their respective rôles to play in justification; when man has fulfilled his in penitence, God will subsequently fulfil his part. The theological principle underlying the axiom may be shown to have been current in the early patristic period – for example, it is clearly stated by Irenaeus: 'If you offer to him (i.e., God) what is yours, that is faith in him and subjection, you shall receive his, and become a perfect work of God.'[83] The medieval period saw this axiom become a dogma, part of the received tradition concerning justification. The final verbal form of the axiom can be shown to have been fixed in the twelfth century,[84] an excellent example being provided by the *Homilies* of Radulphus Ardens:

Est ergo, acsi dicat Dominus: Facite, quod pertinet ad vos, quia facio, quod pertinet ad me. Ego facio, quod amicus, animam meam pro vobis ponendo; facite et vos, quod amici, me diligendo et mandata mea faciendo.[85]

It may, of course, be pointed out that the logic underlying Radulphus' version of the axiom is that man should do *quod in se est* because Christ has already done *quod in se est*. In other words, Christ has placed man under an obligation to respond to him. This logic was, however, generally inverted, to yield the suggestion that God's action was posterior, rather than prior, to man's. The idea that man could, by doing 'what lies within him' (*quod in se est*) place *God* under an obligation to reward him with grace is particularly well illustrated from the works of Stephen Langton[86] and others influenced by him. The use of *debere* by an anonymous twelfth century writer in this connection is of significance: si homo facit, quod suum est, Deus debet facere, quod suum est.[87] A slightly different approach to the matter is based on James 4.8: 'Draw near to God, and he will draw near to you.' This was interpreted by some twelfth century theologians, such as Robert Pullen, to mean that man, by drawing near to God, placed God under an obligation to draw near to man.[88]

The relationship between the human penitential preparation for justification and the divine justification of man which followed it was the subject of considerable discussion among twelfth century theologians. In general, the possibility of the preparation for grace being the efficient cause of justification was rejected: most theologians appear to have adopted a solution similar to that of Alan of Lille. According to Alan, man's preparation for justification could be likened to opening a shutter to let sunlight into a room. The act of penitence was the *causa sine qua non* and the *occasio*, but not the *causa efficiens*, of justification:

(Poenitentia) est tamen causa sine qua non, quia nisi homo poeniteat, non dimittitur a Deo peccatum. Sic sol domum illuminat quia fenestra aperitur, non tamen apertio fenestrae est causa efficiens illuminationis, sed occasionalis tantum, sed ipse sol est causa efficiens illuminationis.[89]

In effect, man's preparation for justification may be regarded as the removal of an obstacle to grace (*removens prohibens*). This analysis was placed upon a firmer basis by Hugh of St Cher, who distinguished three aspects of the remission of sin: actus peccandi desertio, maculae sive culpae deletio, reatus solutio. The act of sinning is an obstacle to grace, and man, by ceasing to perform acts of sin, removes this obstacle and thus prepares the way for grace to be infused into his soul:

Desertio actus peccandi habilitat hominem, quo facto ingreditur gratia. Actus enim peccandi obstaculum est gratie. Et loquitur Ambrosius sicut communiter dicitur, quod ille qui aperit fenestram, intromittit solem, id est facit aliquid, quo facto sol ingreditur.[90]

Although only God is able to forgive sin, man is able to set in motion a series of events which culminate in forgiveness of sins by the act of ceasing to perform acts of sin, which lies within his own powers. Man does what is asked of him, and God subsequently does the rest.

The origins of the interpretation of the axiom characteristic of the early Franciscan school can be found with John of La Rochelle. Man cannot dispose himself adequately for grace, so that the required disposition must be effected by God. God will, however, effect this disposition, if man does *quod in se est*. John uses Alan of Lille's analogy of the opening of a shutter to illustrate this point: the opening of the shutter permits the light of the sun to dispel darkness, just as the act of doing *quod in se est* permits the grace of God to dispel sin. Although man does not have the power to dispel darkness, he does have the power to initiate a course of action which has this effect, by opening a shutter and thus remove the obstacle to the sun's rays; similarly, although man does not have the ability to destroy sin, he can remove the obstacles to divine grace, which then effects the required destruction of sin.[91] God continually bestows grace through his generosity, and by doing *quod in se est*, man removes any obstacles in the path of that grace.[92] Odo Rigaldi similarly teaches that grace is given to the man who disposes himself to receive it by doing *quod in se est* – for example, by attrition. The subsequent gift of grace transforms this to contrition, which leads to the remission of sins.[93] Whilst this disposition towards grace cannot be considered to be meritorious in the strict sense of the term (i.e., *de condigno*), it can be considered meritorious *de congruo* (see §10).[94] The *Summa Fratris Alexandri* considers the case of the good pagan, who is ignorant of the Christian faith, and argues that if he does *quod in se est* – which is clearly understood as a purely natural act – God will somehow enlighten him, in order that he may be justified.[95] Man prepares himself for justification by receiving the *dignitas congruitatis* which arises from the proper use of his natural faculties of reason or free will.[96] Similarly, Bonaventure argues that, although *gratia gratis data* stirs the will, it remains within the power of the human free will to respond to or reject this excitation. Bonaventure frequently stresses that God does not justify man without his consent,[97] giving grace in such a way that the free will is not coerced into accepting it.[98]

The interpretation of the axiom within the early Dominican school is somewhat confused, as Thomas Aquinas presents radically different interpretations of the axiom in the *Commentary on the Sentences* and the *Summa Theologiae*. In the *Commentary*, Thomas concludes his discussion of the question *utrum homo possit se praeparare ad gratiam sine aliqua gratia* with a *prima facie* Pelagian interpretation of the axiom: man can prepare himself for justification by virtue of his own natural abilities, unaided by grace.[99] This disposition is meritorious *de congruo*.[100] Thomas emphasised that God is continuously offering his grace to man, and anyone who does *quod in se est* necessarily receives it.[101] In effect, this represents a further development of Alan of Lille's analogy of the opening of a shutter. Philip the Chancellor had earlier applied the Aristotelian categories of material and formal causality to the sun and the opening of the shutter respectively, so that the formal (i.e., the immediate) cause of justification is the human preparation for justification, understood as the removal of obstacles to grace. Thomas is thus able to formalise his causal scheme in Aristotelian terms, further enhancing the Aristotelian cast of his discussion of the doctrine of justification.

Critics of Thomas' early teaching on justification, particularly within the early Franciscan school, pointed out that he allowed a purely natural disposition towards justification, which was clearly contrary to the teaching of Augustine.[102] It is therefore important to appreciate that his mature teaching, as expressed in the *Summa Theologiae* (1266–73), is significantly different. Later commentators frequently emphasised these differences: for example, several fifteenth-century manuscripts refer to *conclusiones in quibus sanctus Thomas videtur contradicere sibi ipso*, or *articuli in quibus Thomas aliter dixit in Summa quam in scriptis sententiarum*, or – more diplomatically! – *articuli in quibus frater Thomas melius in Summa quam in scriptis sententiarum dixit*.[103] Whilst Thomas continues to insist upon the necessity of a preparation for justification, and continues to discuss this in terms of man's doing *quod in se est*, he now considers that this preparation lies outside man's purely natural powers. As he now understands the matter, man is not even capable of his full *natural* good, let alone the *supernatural* good required of him for justification. The preparation for justification is itself a work of grace,[104] in which God is active and man passive. For Thomas, the axiom *facienti quod in se est* now assumes the meaning that God will not deny grace to the man who does his best, in so far as he is moved by God to do this: Cum dicitur homo facere quod in se est, dicitur hoc esse in potestate hominis secundum quod est motus a Deo.[105] It is highly significant that Thomas does not follow the early Franciscan school in applying the axiom to the good pagan in the *Summa*, even where it would be expected at IIa–IIae q. 10 a. 1.[106] Thomas now understands *quod in se est* to mean 'doing what one is able to do when aroused and moved by grace', thus marking a significant departure from his earlier interpretation of the concept. A similar interpretation of *quod in se est* is encountered in the writings of Peter of Tarantaise.[107]

A further development may be noted in relation to Thomas' teaching on the meritorious character of the disposition towards justification. In the *Commentary*, Thomas allows that such a disposition is meritorious *de congruo*.[108] In the later *de veritate*, however, we find an unequivocal assertion that there are no merits save demerits prior to justification,[109] a view which finds fuller expression in the *Summa Theologiae*. Although Thomas is prepared to allow that a justified sinner can merit *de congruo* the first grace for another person,[110] he is not prepared to allow the individual's preparation for his own justification to be deemed meritorious, even in this weak sense of the term.[111] Significantly, Peter of Tarantaise – who reproduces Thomas' interpretation of *quod in se est* – declines to follow him in this matter, teaching that the preparation for justification is meritorious *de congruo*.[112] It is thus clear that there was some confusion within the early Dominican school upon this matter.

An examination of the writings of later medieval theologians of the Augustinian Order reveals a lack of agreement concerning the interpretation of the axiom. Thomas of Strasbourg states that the man who does *quod in se est* cannot be regarded as preparing himself for justification: man's rôle in his own justification lies in his consenting to the divine action which is taking place within him.[113] In this he is followed, as in so many other matters, by Johannes von Retz.[114] Thomas is, however, prepared to allow that this disposition towards justification is meritorious *de congruo*.[115] Retz' rejection of the possibility of a purely *natural* disposition for grace is of interest, as it proceeds upon Aristotelian presuppositions. Justification involves a transition from form to matter. Just as a natural form is converted to natural matter by a natural agent, so the conversion of a supernatural form to supernatural matter requires the action of a supernatural agent moving the soul – i.e., divine grace.[116] While the theologians of the Augustinian Order continued the common teaching of the necessity of a disposition towards justification, the older Augustinian theologians were prepared to allow this disposition was meritorious *de congruo*, whereas the theologians of the *schola Augustiniana moderna* tended to exclude this possibility. Thus Thomas Bradwardine, Gregory of Rimini, Johannes Klenkok, Angelus Dobelin, Hugolino of Orvieto and Johannes Hiltalingen of Basel rejected the opinion that the disposition for justification was meritorious *de congruo*.[117] A similar position is associated with Luther's mentor at Wittenberg, Johannes von Staupitz,[118] although his regent of studies at Erfurt, Johannes de Paltz, allowed that such a disposition was meritorious *de congruo*.[119]

The theologians of the *via moderna* adopted a much more positive attitude to the axiom *facienti quod in se est*. Underlying this attitude is the theology of the *pactum*, by which a distinction is to be made between the inherent value of a moral act and its ascribed value under the terms of the covenant between God and man. Just as in today's economic system, paper money has a much greater ascribed value than its inherent value on account of the covenant on the part of the issuing agency or bank to pay the bearer the equivalent sum in gold upon request, so in the Middle Ages the king appears to have been regarded as entitled to issue 'token' coinage, often made of lead, which had a negligible inherent value, but which would be redeemed at its full ascribed value at a later date.[120] In the meantime, the ascribed value of the coins was vastly greater than their inherent value, on account of the promise of the king expressed in the covenant regulating the relationship between the *valor impositus* and *valor intrinsecus*. Such analogies from the economic system of the period lent themselves particularly well to illustrate the important distinction, characteristic of the *via moderna*, between the moral and the meritorious value of an act. Just as a major discrepancy could arise within an economic system between *bonitas intrinseca* and *valor impositus*, given a firm and binding contract on the part of the king, so a similar discrepancy could arise between the moral value of an act (i.e., its *bonitas intrinseca*) and its meritorious value (i.e., *valor impositus*), given a comparable covenant on the part of God. Although human acts have negligible inherent value in themselves by God's absolute standards, he has entered into a *pactum* with man by virtue of which such acts have a much greater contracted value – sufficient to merit the first grace *de congruo*. Just as a king might issue a small leaden coin with negligible inherent value, and a considerably greater ascribed value which permitted it to purchase goods, so man's moral acts, although in themselves incapable of meriting grace, have a much greater contracted value adequate for this purpose.

The essential point emerging from this analysis of the context in which the characteristic interpretation of the axiom *facienti quod in se est* associated with the *via moderna* is set is this: man's disposition cannot be said to cause his justification on account of its own nature (*ex natura rei*), but only on account of the value ascribed to it by God (*ex pacto divino*). This point is made by Ockham, again using the illustration of the king and the small lead coin.[121] A similar analogy is used by Robert Holcot, who pointed out that a small copper coin may buy a loaf of bread, despite the much greater inherent value of the latter.[122] Failure on the part of God to honour his contractual obligation by rewarding the man who did *quod in se est* with grace would amount to a contradiction of the divine nature.[123] While God is not bound by absolute necessity (i.e., *necessitas consequentis*) to act in this way, he has imposed upon himself a conditional necessity (i.e., *necessitas consequentiae*) which he is bound to respect.[124] Gabriel Biel interprets the axiom *facienti quod in se est* to mean that God is under obligation to give the first grace to the man who desists from sin. However, this does not mean that man is capable of remitting his own sin. As Biel emphasises, the link between doing *quod in se est* and the remission of sin is provided by the covenant, rather than the nature of the entities in themselves. Alan of Lille and the early Franciscan school illustrated the axiom with reference to a shutter and the rays of the sun, as noted above: implicit in this analogy is an *ontological* concept of causality (see §§7, 9). The nature of the entities (i.e., the shutter and the sun's rays) is such that the removal of the obstacle permits the sunlight to enter the room. Biel and the *via moderna* operated with a concept of *covenantal* causality, by which the relationship between man's action and the divine response is a consequence of the divine ordination, rather than the nature of the entities in themselves. By the *pactum*, God has graciously ordained that such an act may be accepted as worthy of grace. Biel reproduces the earlier Franciscan teaching, by which man's disposition towards justification may be regarded as removing an obstacle in the path of divine grace:

Anima obicis remotione ac bono motu in deum ex arbitrii libertate elicito primam gratiam mereri potest de congruo. Probatur: quia actum facientis quod in se est Deus acceptat ad tribuendum gratiam primam, non ex debito iustitiae, sed ex sua liberalitate; sed anima removendo obicem, cessando ab actu et consensu peccati et eliciendo bonum motum in Deum tamquam in suum principium et finem, facit quod in se est; ergo actum remotionis obicis et bonum motum in Deum acceptat Deus de sua liberalitate ad infundendum gratiam.[125]

Following the general teaching of the Franciscan schools, Biel holds this disposition towards justification as meritorious *de congruo*. Although man is able to remove an obstacle to grace, Biel insists that it is God, and God alone, who remits sin – but by virtue of the *pactum*, man is able to act in such a manner as to oblige God to respond thus.[126]

The pastoral significance of the axiom may be illustrated with reference to the sermons of Johannes Geiler of Keisersberg, cathedral preacher at Strasbourg from 1478 to 1510.[127] In his exposition of the Lord's Prayer, Geiler stresses that if a man's prayer is to be heard, he must do *quod in se est*. Each of the seven petitions of the Lord's Prayer presupposes that man is already doing what lies within his powers. Thus man prays to God that he might be given his daily bread

– but this presupposes that man does *quod in se est* by cultivating the fields.[128] The same principle is elaborated with reference to Matthew 6.26, which refers to the birds of the air being fed by their heavenly father. Geiler observes that this does not mean that the birds sit on their branches all day, doing nothing: they too must do *quod in se est*, going out early in the morning looking for food.[129] It is therefore only to be expected that Geiler should apply the same principle to man's justification, for which he considers preparation to be essential: 'Fools expect to have this gold without paying for it – that is, without a disposition for grace.'[130] Just as the wind does not enter into a sail until the sailsman first turns the sail directly into the wind, so the wind of the Holy Spirit only enters a soul which has been prepared to receive it. Man must therefore dispose himself towards the reception of grace by doing *quod in se est*.[131] The pastoral orientation of Geiler's sermons is evident from the fact that the axiom is usually expressed in the imperative form: fac quod in te est!

The use of the axiom remained a commonplace in the early sixteenth century, and is encountered in the earlier writings of Martin Luther.[132] Luther's continuity with the *via moderna* is particularly evident in the *Dictata super Psalterium* (1513–15), and may be illustrated from his comments on Psalm 114.1 (Vulgate: 113.1):

Hinc recte dicunt doctores, quod homini facienti quod in se est deus infallibiliter dat gratiam et licet non de condigno sese possit ad gratiam praeparare, quia est incomparabilis, tamen bene de congruo propter promissionem istam dei et pactum misericordiae.[133]

In this, as in so many other respects, the young Luther demonstrated his close affinity with the theology of justification associated with the *via moderna*.

The discussion of the subjective appropriation of justification presented in the above section may have conveyed the impression that the theologians of the medieval period understood justification in purely individualist terms, teaching that justification is solely concerned with the individual *viator* and his status *coram Deo*. This is, in fact, not the case. The medieval discussion of justification proceeds upon the basis of certain explicit presuppositions concerning the community within which this justification takes place. Justification takes place within the sphere of the church, being particularly associated with the sacraments of baptism and penance, so that it is impossible to discuss the medieval understanding of the subjective appropriation of justification without reference to the relationship between justification and the sacraments. The present section, therefore, may be regarded as having dealt with the individualist aspects of the appropriation of justification; the following section, which considers the relation between justification and the sacraments, may be considered to deal with the communal aspects of the appropriation of justification.

§8 Justification and the sacraments

The systematic development of sacramental theology is a major feature of the medieval period, particularly between the years 1050–1240.[1] Associated with this development is the specific linking of justification with the *sacramenta mortuorum*, baptism and penance, and hence with the sacramental system of the church. The earlier medieval writers, such as Cassiodorus and Sedulius Scotus, had identified baptism as the justifying sacrament.[2] The ninth century, however, saw the Anglo-Irish system of private penance become widespread in Europe, with important modifications to the theology of penance following in its wake. Although earlier writers considered that penance could only be undertaken once in a lifetime, as a 'second plank after a shipwreck' (*tabula secunda post naufragiam*),[3] this opinion was gradually abandoned, rather than refuted, as much for social as for pastoral reasons. Thus the eighth-century bishop Chrodegang of Metz recommended regular confession to a superior at least once a year,[4] whilst Paulinus of Aquileia advocated confession and penance before each mass. Gregory the Great's classification of mortal sins became incorporated into the penitential system of the church during the ninth century,[5] so that private penance in the presence of a priest became generally accepted.[6] Penitential books began to make their appearance throughout Europe, similar in many respects to those which can be traced back to sixth-century Wales.[7] The spread of the practice in the Carolingian church appears to have been due to the formidable influence of Alcuin, who has greater claim than any to be considered the founder of the Carolingian renaissance.[8] It is therefore of considerable significance that Alcuin specifically links penance with justification: non dubitamus circa fidem iustificari hominem per poenitentiam et conpunctionem.[9] Associated with this correlation between justification and penance is a maxim which represents a conflation of Ezekiel 18.21 and 33.12: in quacumque hora conversus fuerit peccator, vita vivet et non morietur.[10] The essential feature of this development is that justification is understood to *begin* in baptism, and *to be continued* in penance. A further development of this idea may be found in the works of Rabanus Maurus, who became the leading proponent of private confession in the Frankish church after Alcuin: justification is here linked, not merely with penance, but with sacerdotal confession.[11] The relationship between justification, baptism and penance was defined with particular clarity in the ninth century by Haimo of Auxerre:

Redemptio nostra qua sumus redempti, et per quam iustificamur, passio Christi est quae, iuncta baptismo, iustificat hominem per fidem: et postmodum per poenitentiam. Ita enim illa duo mutuo sunt coniuncta, ut unum sine altero hominem non possit iustificare.[12]

The possibility of constructing a totally sacramental economy of salvation was demonstrated by Bruno of Cologne in the late eleventh century. Like most of his contemporaries, Bruno defined grace in non-ontological terms, understanding it as the remission of sin:

determinat quidem Paulus gratiam Dei, quotquot peccata sint, in baptismo omnia dimittere, sed postquam iustificati sunt, si iterum peccant, non sicut prius ex gratia, sed merito poenitentiae dimittentur peccata.[13]

The emerging understanding of the *processus iustificationis* (see §5) further assisted the integration of justification within the sacramental system of the church. Of particular significance in this respect is the occasional inclusion of a fifth element in the traditional fourfold *processus iustificationis* to allow the direct correlation of justification with the temporal remission of sin.[14]

The relationship between justification and the sacraments of baptism and the sacraments of baptism and penance was to preoccupy most, if not all, of the theologians of the twelfth century. How can infants or imbeciles, who are incapable of any rational act, be justified by baptism?[15] No general solution to the problem may be said to have emerged during the period, at least in part due to the fact that there was a general failure to distinguish between habit, act and virtue. Anselm of Canterbury taught that infants are treated *quasi iusti* on account of the faith of the church.[16] In this, he was followed by Bernard of Clairvaux, who noted that, as it was impossible to please God without faith, so God has permitted children to be justified on account of the faith of others.[17] This was given some theological justification by Peter Manducator, who argued that as children are contaminated by the sins of another (i.e., Adam) in the first place, it is not unreasonable that they should be justified by the faith of others.[18] Peter Abailard was sceptical as to whether an infant was capable of an act of faith: given that this possibility appeared to be excluded, he derived some consolation from the idea that infants who die before maturity are given a perception of the glory of God at their death, so that charity may be born within them.[19] Gilbert de la Porrée is typical of the many who declined to speculate on the mysterious operation of the Holy Spirit, which none could fathom.[20]

The origins of the generally accepted solution to this difficulty date from the closing years of the twelfth century, with the introduction of the Aristotelian concept of the *habitus*. Thus Alan of Lille, one of the more speculative theologians of the twelfth century, distinguished between *virtus in actu* and *virtus in habitu*.[21] An infant may be given the habit of faith in baptism as the *virtus fidei in habitu*, which will only be manifested as the *virtus fidei in actu* when the child reaches maturity and becomes capable of rational acts. The lack of agreement which characterised the twelfth century is well illustrated from the letter of Innocent III, dated 1201, in which he declined to give any definite positive statements on the effects of baptism, merely noting two possible opinions: (1) that baptism effects the remission of sins; (2) that baptism effects the infusion of virtues as habits, to be actualised when maturity is reached.[22]

Although baptism had been recognised as a sacrament from the earliest of times,[23] the same recognition had not always been extended to penance. Hugh of St Victor had defined a sacrament as a 'physical or material object admitted to the perception of the external senses, representing a reality beyond itself by virtue of having been instituted as a sign of it, and containing within it some invisible and spiritual grace, in virtue of having been consecrated'.[24] It is clear that this definition of a sacrament, which insists upon the presence of a physical element, leads to the exclusion of penance from the list of sacraments. Peter Lombard's definition of a sacrament[25] is therefore as interesting for what it does *not* say as for what it does, as no reference is made to the need for a 'physical or material element from without'. It is this decisive omission which allowed the Lombard to include penance among the seven sacraments – an inclusion which is of major significance to the development of the doctrine of justification within the sphere of the western church.

The necessity of sacerdotal confession for the remission of sins in penance was insisted upon by many of the earlier medieval theologians. Honorius of Autun,[26] Hervaeus of Bourg-Dieu[27] and Bruno of Asti[28] all use the Pentateuchal leper-cleansing ritual to illustrate the need for sacerdotal confession: the sinner's faults are only cleansed when they are confessed before a priest. Just as baptism effects the remission of *original* sin, so confession effects the remission of *actual* sin.[29] This distinction leads to the obvious conclusion that regular confession is to be encouraged, in order to receive absolution. Such exhortations to confession were generally accompanied with an appeal to texts such as Isaiah 45.22, Joel 2.12 or Zechariah 1.3: *convertimini ad me, ait Dominus exercituum, et convertar ad vos.*[30] It must be emphasised, however, that these exhortations to confession are set within the context of the reconciliation of a lapsed believer, a justified sinner who wishes to be restored to fellowship within the church, and are not capable of a Pelagian interpretation. They refer to the restoration of justification, rather than its inception – i.e., the second rather than the first justification, to use the terms of a later period. The use of such texts, and the maxim *in quacumque hora*, noted above, indicates a growing awareness of the association of the recovery of justification with the sacrament of penance, which involves the confession of sin, penance and absolution. It may be noted, however, that there was no general agreement upon the necessity of *sacerdotal* confession: in the twelfth century, for example, the Abailardian school rejected its necessity, whilst the Victorine school insisted upon it.[31]

The integration of justification within the context of the sacrament of penance was greatly assisted by two developments. First, the general acceptance of Peter Lombard's *Sentences* as the basis of theological discussion during the thirteenth century led to justification being discussed with reference to the *locus* of distinction seventeen of the fourth book of the *Sentences* – i.e., within the specific context of the sacrament of penance. Second, the development of the *processus iustificationis* (see §5) had led to contrition and remission of sins being identified as its third and fourth elements respectively – both of which could be correlated with the sacrament of penance. The justification of the sinner was therefore explicitly linked with the sacramental system of the church. This connection may be regarded as having been unequivocally established through the decrees of the Fourth Lateran Council (1215), which laid an obligation upon believers to confess their sins to their priest annually:

Omnis utriusque sexus fidelis, postquam ad annos discretionis pervenerit, omnia sua solus peccata saltem semel in anno fideliter confiteatur proprio sacerdoti, et iniunctam sibi poenitentiam pro viribus studeat adimplere.[32]

The early discussion of penance involved the distinction of three elements: contritio cordis, confessio oris, satisfactio operis.[33] It seems that the earlier medieval discussion of the matter led to the greatest emphasis being placed upon the third element, satisfaction – an observation which is of considerable importance in connection with Anselm of Canterbury's understanding of the incarnation of the Son of God. For Anselm, the satisfaction-merit model provided by the penitential system of the church of his time provided a suitable paradigm for the divine remission of sin through the death of Christ, which his readers would have accepted as just.[34] By the early twelfth century, however, the emphasis appears to have shifted from satisfaction to contrition, with increasing emphasis being placed upon the inner motivation of the penitent, rather than on his external achievements made as satisfaction for sin. Thus Peter Abailard defined *poenitentia* in purely psychological terms: dolor animi super ea, in quo deliquit, cum aliquem scilicet piget in aliquo excessisse.[35] His respect for tradition is such, however, that he does not deny the *de facto* necessity of both confession and satisfaction, subject to qualification on account of possible mitigating circumstances.[36] This contritionism was developed by Peter Lombard, who stressed that contrition was the sole precondition for forgiveness: the function of the priest in the sacrament of penance was purely declarative, in that he merely certifies that the penitent has been justified and reconciled to the church.[37]

The precise relationship between justification and penance was the subject of considerable debate during the twelfth century. Peter of Poitiers drew attention to a possible misinterpretation of the relationship between the two: as man can lose the first grace through sin, and subsequently have it restored through penance, it might appear that the first grace can be merited by penance. Peter rejected this interpretation on the basis of its failure to recognise that man can only *regain* the first grace in this manner: it is only the man who has already received *gratia prima* who can be justified again by penance.[38] Simon of Tournai argued that whilst prayers and alms qualify man for becoming good, they cannot be said to make man good in themselves – man only becomes good through the grace of God.[39] Penance, apart from grace, does not justify. Alan of Lille similarly emphasised the unmerited character of grace in his discussion of the relation between justification and penance: the true efficient cause of justification is not penance,[40] as might be thought, but the gracious will of God.[41] Penance is merely the *occasio* and *conditio sine qua non* of justification (see §7). However, it will be clear that the location of any type of cause of justification within the penitent is of significance, in that it naturally leads to the discussion of the nature of the act or disposition required of the penitent if justification is to occur. It is for this reason that the establishment of the triple order of *contritio cordis, confessio oris* and *satisfactio operis* within the sacramental system of the church[42] is of such importance, as it allows the necessary steps for the justification of the penitent to be definitely established, in order that the penitent may be assured that he *has* been justified. The psychological aspects of the sacrament of penance must not be overlooked.

The classic medieval representation of the three steps leading to penitential justification may be found in Dante Aligheri's *Purgatorio*. As the poet awakes from his dream, he finds that he has been carried up to the gate of purgatory, before which lie three steps which he must first climb:

> Là ne venimmo; e lo scaglion primaio
> bianco marmo era sì pulito e terso,
> ch'io mi specchiai in esso qual io paio.
> Era il secondo tinto più che perso,
> d'una petrina ruvida ed arsiccia
> crepata per lo lungo e per traverso.
> Lo terzo, che di sopra s'ammassiccia,
> porfido mi parea sì fiammeggiante
> come sangue che fuor di vena spiccia.[43]

The three steps represent the three penitential elements, which Dante presents in the different order of confession, contrition and satisfaction. As the poet faces the first step of polished white marble, he sees himself reflected as he really is, and so is moved to recognise, admit and confess his sin. The second step is black, cracked in the shape of a cross, symbolising the contrite heart, whilst the third, redder than blood spurting from a vein, symbolises Christ's atoning death, to which must be added the satisfaction of the penitent if it is to be made complete.

The most important criticism of the 'contritionist' understanding of penance, associated with Peter Lombard, is due to Duns Scotus. If contrition is required as a necessary disposition for the reception of sacramental grace, the role of the *sacrament* of penance is called into question. If justification through the sacrament of penance is contingent upon an antecedent disposition of contrition, the sacrament can no longer be said to be effective *ex opere operato*, but only *ex opere operantis*.[44] The alternative, according to Scotus, is 'attritionism'. Attrition is essentially repentance for sin based on fear of punishment, whilst contrition is a repentance for sin grounded in a love for

God.[45] According to Scotus, the sinner may be justified in two possible ways:

1. He may be attrite to a sufficient degree to merit grace *de congruo*.
2. He may be attrite to a minimal extent (*parum attritus*) which, although inadequate to merit justifying grace *de congruo*, is sufficient to effect justification *ex pacto divino*, as mediated through the sacrament of penance.

It will be clear that the first alternative is of major importance, as it allows the possibility of *extrasacramental justification*. If the attrition is of sufficient intensity, God informs it by grace, converting it to contrition *directly* by the extrinsic denomination of the *acceptatio divina* (see §§10, 13) and thereby effectively bypassing the sacrament of penance. In the second alternative, Scotus defines the concept of *parum attritus* as not placing an obstacle in the path of sacramental grace (*non ponere obicem*) through the avoidance of mortal sin – a teaching which has frequently been criticised for its moral laxism.[46] This device allows the *ex opere operato* efficacy of the sacrament of penance to be maintained. Whereas Thomas Aquinas integrated contrition within the sacrament of penance, thus effectively excluding the possibility of extrasacramental justification, Scotus allows for this possibility by means of an attrition of sufficient intensity to merit *de congruo* its conversion to contrition, and thus to merit the first grace. It may be noted that the two modes of penitential justification are essentially the same, the difference lying in the fact that they are mediated through different secondary causes. Both presuppose, and are based upon, the divine acceptation.

Scotus' doctrine of the *parum attritus* appears to challenge the medieval consensus concerning the inability of the *viator* to know with absolute certainty whether he is in a state of grace: if he can assure himself that he is *parum attritus*, he may rely upon the *ex opere operato* efficacy of the sacrament to assure himself that he is in a state of grace.[47] Although Scotus does indeed state that a greater degree of certitude may be achieved by this mode of justification than by the extrasacramental mode,[48] he does not retract or qualify his specific magisterial rejection of the possibility of certitude of grace made elsewhere.[49] It must therefore be assumed that Scotus did not intend to teach the absolute certitude of grace in this matter.

Scotus' position was criticised by many of his contemporaries and successors, particularly by Gabriel Biel.[50] Biel insisted that justification by perfection attrition (i.e., Scotus' extrasacramental mode of justification) must always be taken as implying the intention of confession, and is therefore implicitly linked with the sacrament of penance.[51] In this, Biel appears to be reverting to a principle established by the early Franciscan school, that the intention to confess (*propositum confitendi*) is an integral element in the definition of true penance: a man cannot be truly penitent if he does not wish to confess his sins to a priest. Biel does not exclude the possibility of *pre*-sacramental justification, but declines to allow that this may be considered to be 'extra-sacramental', a second path to justification apart from the sacrament of penance.[52] It will be evident, however, that Biel's emphasis upon the need for contrition in penance lays him open to the same charge which Scotus earlier directed against Peter Lombard – that sacramental efficacy is thence defined *ex opere operantis* rather than *ex opere operato*. Biel himself avoids this difficulty by stating that the *viator* is able, through the use of his own natural faculties, to elicit an act of love of God for his own sake, on the basis of which the infusion of *gratia prima* takes place. It must be emphasised that this act of love of God for his own sake is to be set within the context of the sacrament of penance, even though Biel observes that it is not necessary, in principle, for justification and sacramental absolution to coincide in time: man's reconciliation to the church *must* be effected through the sacrament of penance, which is therefore necessarily implicated in justification. In effect, Biel appears to be saying that man's presacramental justification must be declared *in foro ecclesiae* by sacramental absolution before it can be deemed to be justification.[53] Like the earlier Franciscan school, Biel anchors justification to the sacrament of penance by means of the *propositum confitendi*.[54] A further criticism which Biel directs against Scotus' doctrine of the *modus meriti de congruo* (as he terms Scotus' extrasacramental mode of justification) is that it is based upon an act of attrition, whose intensity, degree and duration are unknown to anyone, and are not specified by Holy Scripture: as such, it is therefore impossible to be sure that the correct act has been performed for the correct duration.[55] Biel rejects the idea of a fixed duration and intensity on the part of the penitent, insisting upon the need for *amor amicitie super omnia propter Deum* in its place. It will be clear that this doctrine is essentially an extension of Biel's interpretation of *facienti quod in se est* from the *first* justification to the *second* justification. *De potentia ordinata* God is obliged to reward the man who does *quod in se est* with grace, an obligation which exists as much in regard to the sacrament of penance as to the bestowal of the first grace. As Biel pointed out, we do penance, not so that God 'would change his judgement in response to our prayer, but so that by our prayer we might acquire the proper disposition and be made capable of obtaining what we request'.[56]

An attack of a somewhat different type was, however, developed during the fifteenth century, with potentially significant consequences for the sacramental economy of salvation. The Vulgate translated the inauguration of Christ's preaching, 'Repent (μετανοεῖτε), for the kingdom of God is at hand' (Mark 1.14), as follows: 'Do penance (*poenitentiam agite*), for the kingdom of God is at hand.' The double reference of the Latin *poenitentia* (i.e., it can mean 'repentance' or 'penance') served to establish a link between the sinner's inward attitude of attrition and the sacrament of penance. The rise of the new critical philology in the Quattrocento called this link into question. Thus Lorenzo Valla challenged the Vulgate translation of New Testament texts such as the above.[57] In this, he was followed by Desiderius Erasmus, whose *Novum instrumentum omne* (1516) reproduced Valla's challenge to the Vulgate translation of μετανοεῖτε. Thus in the 1516 edition, Erasmus translated the Greek imperative as *poeniteat vos* ('be penitent'), and in the 1527 edition as *resipiscite* ('change your mind'), further weakening the link between the inward attitude of repentance and the sacrament of penance. The full significance of this philological development would, however, only be appreciated in the first phase of the Reformation of the sixteenth century, and did not pose a serious challenge to the correlation of justification and the sacraments in the late medieval period.

In conclusion, it may be stated that the medieval period saw the justification of the sinner firmly linked to the sacramental life of the church, a sound theological link having been established between justification and the sacraments.[58] This linking of justification to the sacramental system of the church has profound theological and pastoral consequences, of which the most important is the tendency to assert *iustificatio extra ecclesiam non est*.[59] Although the theologians of the medieval period were aware that God was not bound by the sacraments, the tendency to emphasise the reliability of the established order of salvation, of which the sacramental system is part, can only have served to convey the impression that the sinner who wishes to be reconciled to God must, *de facto*, seek the assistance of a priest. The explicit statement of the sacramental economy of salvation may be regarded as complete by the thirteenth century, and to have survived the only serious theological attack to be made upon it during the medieval period. The Psalmist exhorted his people to 'enter his gates by confession': the theology of the medieval period ensured that the only manner in which God's gates could be entered was through the sacraments of baptism and penance.[60]

§9 The concept of grace

The earlier medieval writers tended to conceive grace primarily in Augustinian terms, including elements such as the restoration of the divine image, the forgiveness of sins, regeneration and the indwelling of the Godhead.[1] In the present section, we are particularly concerned with three aspects of the development of the concept of grace which are of importance to the overall scheme of the development of the doctrine of justification. These are:

1. The development of the concept of the supernatural in the articulation of the nature and the effects of grace.
2. The distinction between *gratia gratis data* and *gratia gratum faciens*.
3. The distinction between operative and cooperative grace.

We shall consider these points individually. Before this is possible, however, a serious difficulty in terminology must be noted. The terms *gratia gratis data* and *gratis gratum faciens*, used extensively in this section, and elsewhere in this study, are conventionally translated as *actual grace* and *sanctifying grace*. These translations are, in fact, anachronisms, dating from the post-Tridentine period. *Gratia gratis data* is probably better translated as *prevenient grace*, although even this is not totally satisfactory. In view of the widespread tendency to translate *gratia gratis data* as 'actual grace', and the absence of any generally accepted alternative, however, we feel we have no alternative but to continue this practice, having drawn attention to its deficiencies.

The emergence of the concept of the supernatural[2] is associated with the late twelfth century. The theologians of the earlier medieval period had generally been content to assert that grace is a gift of God, which cannot be merited, and appealed to the cognate relationship of the terms *gratia*, *gratis* and *gratuita* in support of this contention. It will be clear that his discussion of the nature of grace merely postponed the inevitable question which could not be ignored: what is the relation of God's grace to his other gifts? Grace is indeed the free gift of God – but are *all* of God's gifts to be identified as his grace? In other words, is the characteristic feature of grace to be located purely in the fact that it is freely bestowed by God? The eleventh and twelfth century discussions of this question made it clear that a careful and systematic distinction between *naturalia* and *gratuita* was required if confusion was to be avoided.[3] The distinction which required elucidation was between *datum* (i.e., that which is already given in nature) and *donum* (i.e., the subsequent and additional gift of grace). As we have noted, confusion over precisely this point prevailed during the Pelagian controversy (see §7).

The first instance of a systematic distinction between *datum* (i.e., nature) and *donum* (i.e., grace) may be found in the ninth century, with Scotus Erigena.[4] Scotus makes a clear distinction between the natural and supernatural orders: donum gratiae neque intra terminos conditae naturae continetur neque secundum naturalem virtutem operatur, sed superessentialiter et ultra omnes creatas naturales rationes effectus suos peragit.[5] Of particular importance in this respect is Scotus' explicit reference to *gratia supernaturalis* in this context.[6] Phrases indicating that the realm of grace was increasingly conceived in supernatural terms – e.g., *supra naturam* or *ultra naturam* – are encountered with increasing frequency in the following centuries.[7] The first major step towards the definition of the concept of the supernatural may be regarded as having been taken by Simon of Tournai, who argued that the *datum* is the purely natural, whilst the *donum* is the purely spiritual:

Datis autem subsistit homo, quod est et qualis est naturaliter; donis vero qualis est spiritualiter. Ex datis ergo contrahit naturalem; ex donis, spiritualem.[8]

This attempt to define the nature of grace in terms of the dialectic between the natural and the spiritual did not, however, really meet the problem. Similar remarks may be made concerning Peter of Poitiers' attempt to define the distinction between *naturalia* and *gratuita* in terms of their origins:

Naturalia dicunt illa quae habet homo a nativitate sua, unde dicuntur naturalia, ut ratio, ingenium, memoria, etc. Gratuita sunt illa quae naturalibus superaddita sunt, ut virtutes et scientiae; unde etiam dicuntur gratuita, quia a Deo homini per gratiam conferuntur.[9]

Whilst it is impossible to point to any single theologian who may be credited with making the crucial distinction between nature and supernature in defining the essence of grace, it would seem that if anyone is entitled to this claim, it is Praepositinus of Cremona.

Standing at the dawn of the thirteenth century, Praepositinus argued that there must be a higher order than nature itself, and deduced its existence from considerations such as the following. Reason is the highest thing in nature, yet faith must be considered to transcend reason. Therefore faith must be regarded as transcending the natural, being itself something which is beyond nature (*supra naturam*).[10] This distinction can also be applied to the virtues. For example, in his polemic against the teaching of Hugh of St Victor, William of Auxerre distinguished a purely natural *amor amicitiae erga Deum* from a meritorious love for God.[11] On the basis of such considerations, William argued for two distinct orders of being. Even though there is a tendency here to define grace purely in terms of the meritorious, it is clear that significant progress towards the classic definition of supernature has been made. The turning point in achieving this definition appears to have been due to Philip the Chancellor, who distinguished the natural order from the 'more noble' supernatural order: to the former belong reason and natural love, to the latter faith and charity.[12] This important distinction allowed justification to be resolved into a twofold operation.

1. The natural: grace operates on the will, effecting its moral goodness.

2. The supernatural: grace effects the meritoriousness of human acts, raising them from the purely natural plane to that of the supernatural.

In one sense, it could be argued that this is not a new development at all, for these effects of justification had been generally accepted since the time of Augustine. Philip's achievement, however, is to distinguish the two aspects of justification in terms of two levels of being, thereby removing much of the confusion surrounding the matter. Whilst the theologians of the earlier twelfth century tended to define grace in terms of merit, the theologians of the closing years of the century generally regarded merit as the consequence of the transference of an act from the natural (i.e., morally good) to the supernatural (i.e., meritorious) plane, in a transition effected by grace. This distinction, once made, became generally accepted: thus Thomas Aquinas stated that 'when someone is said to have the grace of God, what is meant is something supernatural (*quiddam supernaturale*) in man which originates from God'.[13]

The earlier medieval period was characterised by confusion concerning the various manners in which grace could be understood. Peter Lombard drew a distinction between *gratia gratis dans* (i.e., the uncreated grace which is God himself) and *gratia gratis data* (i.e., the grace of justification).[14] This latter concept, however, was clearly ill-defined, and it became a task of priority to clarify what was meant by the term. Bonaventure noted the general tendency to conceive grace in the broadest of terms, and demonstrated the advantages of restricting the term to *gratis gratis data* and *gratum faciens*.[15] The distinction between *gratia gratis data* and *gratia gratum faciens* appears to have been established by the dawn of the thirteenth century, although confusion in relation to the terms employed is frequently encountered. In broad terms, *gratia gratum faciens* came to be understood as a supernatural habit within man, while *gratia gratis data* was understood as external divine assistance, whether direct or indirect. Initially, this clarification took place by cataloguing the senses in which *gratia gratis data* could be understood. For example, Albertus Magnus distinguishes the following eight senses of the term:[16]

1. rational nature and its powers;
2. natural moral goodness;
3. Adam's supernatural gifts prior to the Fall;
4. imperfect movements towards salvation;
5. inspiration, thaumaturgy and similar gifts;
6. the assistance of the angels;
7. the indelible character received in the sacraments of baptism and confirmation;
8. the divine *concursus*.

Although Bonaventure concludes that the divine *concursus* should be excluded from this list,[17] the concept of *gratia gratis data* is still conceived in the broadest of terms:

Vocatur hic gratia gratis data, quidquid illud sit, quod superadditum est naturalibus, adiuvans aliquo modo et praeparans voluntatem ad habitum vel usum gratiae, sive illud gratis datum sit habitus, sicut timor servilis, vel pietas aliquorum visceribus inserta ab infantia, sive sit etiam aliquis actus, sicut aliqua vocatio vel locutio, qua Deus excitat animam hominis, ut se requirat.[18]

It would seem that the general concept which underlies Bonaventure's catalogue of instances of *gratis gratis data* is that of anything which prepares or disposes man towards the gift of *gratia gratum faciens*. A similar degree of ambiguity is evident from the earlier writings of Thomas Aquinas. Thus Thomas uses the term *gratia gratis data* in a flexible manner, apparently regarding the concept as being beyond meaningful definition.[19] In contrast, the concept of *gratia gratum faciens* appears to have been relatively well characterised by this point.[20] Further confusion, however, existed concerning the distinction between operative and cooperative grace,[21] an important feature of Augustine's theology of justification (see §4). We shall illustrate this point with reference to the developing insights of Thomas Aquinas on this matter.

It is important to appreciate that Thomas Aquinas' understanding of both the nature and the operation of grace underwent considerable development during his lifetime. In his early discussion of grace in the *Commentary on the Sentences*, Thomas poses the following question, to answer it in the negative: utrum gratia sit multiplex in anima?[22] The reply given to this question illustrates his early confusion concerning the concept of actual grace. A distinction may be made between grace and the virtues: if grace is to be identified with these, it must follow that there are many graces, which is impossible. Although it might appear that the distinctions between prevenient and subsequent, operative and cooperative grace seem to point to the multiplicity of grace, these distinctions in fact merely reflect the various effects of the one grace. In other words, the distinction between *gratia praeveniens* and *subsequens*, *operans* and *cooperans*, are purely notional and not real. Grace produces in us a number of effects, and the multiplicity of the effects of grace does not necessitate the deduction of a multiplicity of graces. The effect of operative grace is to produce a good will within man, and that of cooperative grace to actualise this good will in a good performance – which amounts to an exact restatement of the teaching of Augustine on this matter. Thus internal acts are to be attributed to operative grace, and external acts to cooperative grace. This understanding of grace may be summarised as follows:

$$
Gratia
\begin{cases}
formaliter
\begin{cases}
operans \text{ (making man acceptable to God)} \\
cooperans \text{ (making man's deeds acceptable to God)}
\end{cases} \\
effective
\begin{cases}
operans \text{ (making man's will desire good)} \\
cooperans \text{ (actualising man's good will in good deeds)}
\end{cases}
\end{cases}
$$

This simple division of grace, based simply upon the distinction between the formal and effective aspects of operative and cooperative grace, is of particular significance in that the entire analysis of the nature of grace proceeds without reference to *gratia gratis data*!

In his discussion of the matter in the later *de veritate*, a slightly different question is posed: utrum in uno homine sit una tantum gratia gratum faciens?[23] In his answer to this question, Thomas makes an important and explicit distinction between *gratia gratis data* and *gratia gratum faciens*, the former being more a loose catalogue of various possibilities rather than a precise catalogue, and is hence evidently multiple. *Gratia gratum faciens*, however, is something quite different. If this type of grace is understood as referring to every aspect of the divine will, such as good thoughts or holy desires, it is clearly multiple. This simple admission of the multiplicity of *gratia gratum faciens* represents a clear and significant development in Thomas' theology of grace. In his earlier *Commentary on the Sentences*, Thomas had insisted upon the simplicity of *gratia gratum faciens*, whilst conceding the multiplicity of its effects. The multiplicity of the division of graces is purely notional, reflecting the effects of the one *gratia gratum faciens*. Thomas now appears to introduce a distinction between the habitual gifts of grace, and grace understood as the effects of the gratuitous will of God. This more complex division may be summarised as follows:

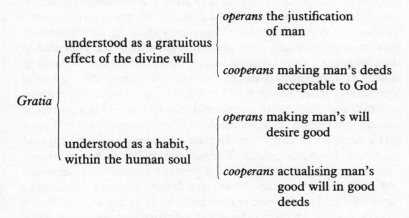

Here the distinction between formal and efficient causality is retained, but is transferred from the distinction between the external and internal operation of grace (see above) to the distinction between *operation* and *cooperation*. Thus, on the basis of Thomas' statements in *de veritate*, the habitual gift of grace may be said to act as follows:

$$\textit{Gratia} \text{ (understood as a habit)} \begin{cases} \textit{formaliter} \rightarrow \textit{operans} \\ \\ \textit{effective} \rightarrow \textit{cooperans} \end{cases}$$

This has the important consequence of excluding the possibility of operative grace acting *efficiently*, which Thomas had upheld in the *Commentary on the Sentences*. It is clear, however, that the distinction between the formal and efficient causality of habitual grace leads to consequences which are merely distinct at the *notional* level, whilst the distinction between formal and efficient causality in the case of grace, understood as an effect of the divine will, leads to consequences which are distinct *in fact*. This clearly marks a significant departure from the Augustinian understanding of the distinction between operative and cooperative grace – indeed, it seems that Thomas is so dissatisfied with Augustine's understanding of the concepts that he practically abandons them. Whereas Augustine taught that operative grace excites the will to desire good, and that cooperative grace subsequently actualises this good will in good deeds, Thomas now explicitly teaches that *cooperative* grace both excites the will to good desires and also externalises this in external action. This opinion would, however, soon be abandoned.

Thomas' mature discussion of the nature and divisions of grace, as presented in the *Summa Theologiae*, is of particular interest. Thomas' attempt to correlate Augustine's teaching on the relation between good will and good performance, which first appeared in the *Commentary on the Sentences*, only to be rejected in *de veritate*, makes its reappearance in the *Summa Theologiae*, although in a significantly modified form. The Augustinian distinction between operative and cooperative grace, originally introduced in a polemical context to meet the Pelagian distinction between good will and good performance, was simply inadequate to convey the metaphysical aspects of the matter which Thomas considered to be important. Thomas introduces the distinction between *actus interior voluntatis* and *actus exterior voluntatis* to express the substance of Augustine's earlier distinction.[24] Grace is now understood either as a habit or a motion, both of which may be either operative or cooperative. Such is man's frailty that, once in a state of habitual grace, he requires a continual and unfailing supply of actual graces (note the deliberate use of the plural) if he is to grow in faith and charity. The new understanding of the divisions of grace may be represented as follows:

$$
Gratia
\begin{cases}
Motus
\begin{cases}
\textit{operans}: \text{moves the will to interior action} \\
\textit{cooperans}: \text{moves the will to exterior action}
\end{cases} \\
Habitus
\begin{cases}
\textit{operans}: \text{justifies man} \\
\textit{cooperans}: \text{functions as the principle of} \\
\qquad\qquad\quad \text{meritorious action}
\end{cases}
\end{cases}
$$

Habitual grace is *operative*, in so far as it heals man's wounded nature and justifies him, rendering him acceptable to God; and *cooperative*, in so far as it is the basis of man's meritorious action. Grace, understood as *motus*, operates on man's will in order that it may will good – in this matter, God is active and the free will passive. Grace, understood as *motus*, then cooperates with the will to achieve the good act itself. In this matter, the will is active, and may be said to cooperate with grace. The most important point which may be noted concerning this new interpretation of the nature and divisions of grace is that actual grace is now assigned a definite role in man's justification.

It is clear that Thomas' changing views on the nature and divisions of grace are complex and difficult to follow. It is therefore important to identify any underlying factors which may explain the leading features of these changes. The decisive alteration which appears to underlie Thomas' changing views on the nature and divisions of grace appears to be his growing pessimism concerning man's natural faculties, which we noted earlier (§7) in relation to Thomas' teaching on the nature and necessity of man's preparation for justification. In his early period, Thomas regarded a preparation for justification as necessary, yet possible without the assistance of grace. As such, the concept of *gratia gratis data* had no significant role to play in man's justification. In his later period, Thomas taught that the beginning of man's conversion must be seen as an internal operation of grace,[25] thus necessitating the implication of *gratia gratis data* prior to man's justification. Further, in his early period, Thomas appears to have regarded man's natural capacities to be such that, once justified, no further assistance in the form of grace was required: *gratia gratum faciens* alone is treated as being *gratia operans et cooperans*.[26] Thomas cited with approval Averroës' statement to the effect that the possession of a habit allows the will to be transformed to action spontaneously.[27] Thomas, while conceding that man is far from perfect, appears to have considered this deficiency to be remedied by the possession of habitual grace. This conclusion is confirmed by two additional considerations. First, the further interference of God in man's life is to be rejected as amounting to a violation of man's dignity. Second, the mere external action of God would not bring about any permanent change in man. Divine action may make a particular action good, but it fails to bring about any fundamental alteration within man himself. Man would remain as deficient after this external intervention as he was before it, and so a means of grace is to be rejected in favour of an internal change within man, which is articulated in terms of the habitual gift of *gratia gratum faciens*. Thomas' discussion of the same point in *de veritate* suggests that he is no longer content with this understanding of the nature of habitual grace. No matter how perfect the habit may be, man is sufficiently frail that he requires the continual assistance of further divine graces functioning as *gratia cooperans*[28] – i.e., acting on man who is already in a state of habitual grace. No habit or set of habits is sufficiently efficacious to make man's operation truly good,[29] as God alone is capable of perfect action. Thomas makes it clear that he now regards man as requiring actual grace before and after his conversion: the internal change wrought within him by the habit of created grace requires further supplementation by external graces.

It is thus fair to suggest that Thomas' developing understanding of the divisions of grace reflects his new insights into man's impotence, which we noted earlier in relation to man's disposition for justification (see §7).

The development of the concepts of *gratia gratis data* and *gratia gratum faciens* in the later medieval period is shrouded in obscurity at present, as it is not clear how the precise relationship between the habit of created grace and the extrinsic denomination of the divine acceptation was understood in the fourteenth and fifteenth centuries.[30] We shall return to this question in connection with the related question of the formal principle of justification, to be discussed in §13. We conclude the present section by summarising the classic Thomist understanding of the nature and divisions of grace, as stated in the *Summa Theologiae*. Grace may be defined according to whether it is *actual* or *habitual*, and according to whether it *operates* upon man, or *cooperates* with him. Actual grace, *gratia gratis data*, may be conceived as a series of transient effluxes of divine power or influence, given over and above the realm of nature, which impinge upon man's will in order to incline it or assist it to particular actions.

The earlier distinction between *prevenient* and *subsequent* grace must therefore be understood to apply only to *actual* grace. Quite distinct from this is habitual or sanctifying grace, *gratia gratum faciens*, which takes the form of a permanent habit of the soul, infused into man by God, and which may be considered to amount to a participation by man in the divine being. Although permanent in the individual who has been justified, the habit may be lost by mortal sin, and must be regained in penance. The combination of these categories leads to four main categories of grace:

Actual operative: this grace inclines man's will to desire good, and operates without the need for a response from man.

Actual cooperative: this grace assists the renewed will to actualise its good intentions in the form of external actions, and requires the cooperation of the will.

Habitual operative: this is the formal principle of justification within the Thomist understanding of the process.

Habitual cooperative: this is the formal principle of merit within the Thomist system, and requires man's cooperation.

It is to the question of merit that we now turn.

§10 The concept of merit

The medieval discussion of merit may be regarded as based upon Augustine's celebrated maxim: si ergo Dei dona sunt bona merita tua, non Deus coronat merita tua tanquam merita tua, sed tanquam dona sua.[1] When God crowns man's merits, he merely crowns his own gifts to man, rather than some attribute of man which it is obliged to acknowledge, respect and reward. The early Latin fathers, prior to the Pelagian controversy, do not appear to have considered merit to involve any real claim on the part of man to divine reward on the basis of his efforts.[2] Merit appears to have been understood simply as a divine gift to the justified sinner, relating to the bestowal of eternal life, rather than of the first grace, and based upon divine grace rather than upon divine justice or an obligation arising from the nature of merit in itself. Non debendo enim sed promittendo debitorem se Deus fecit.[3] Despite the semantic associations of the Latin term *meritum* (see §2), the early use of the term appears to have been quite innocent of the overtones of 'works-righteousness' which would later be associated with it.

The theological renaissance of the eleventh and twelfth centuries saw several developments of decisive importance in connection with the concept of merit. Of these, the most significant is the shift in the context in which merit was discussed. For Augustine, the purpose of man's temporal existence was 'to win the merit by which we may live in eternity'.[4] The context in which Augustine's doctrine of merit is set is clearly that of the final gaining of eternal life, rather than of man's initial justification. When God 'crowns his merits', he does so, not by *justifying* man, but by bestowing upon him *eternal life*. For Augustine, merit both presupposes and expresses grace. The eleventh and twelfth centuries, however, saw the question of merit discussed within a quite different context – the gratuity of *gratia prima*. Is man capable of meriting his initial justification? The fact that this question was universally answered in the negative[5] is at least in part a consequence of the Augustinian background to the early medieval discussion of merit, in that merit is *per definitionem* a consequence of grace.

The Augustinian interpretation of merit as *gratis pro gratia* can be illustrated from many works of the eleventh and twelfth centuries,[6] but is particularly associated with Gilbert de la Porrée (sometimes referred to as 'Gilbert of Poitiers') and his school,[7] among whom we may number Cardinal Laborans, Odo of Ourscamp, Alan of Lille and Radulphus Ardens. The axiom 'Christus solus meruit' is of particular importance in this connection, as it summarises the opinion, characteristic of the *Porretani*, that only Christ may be said to merit anything in the strict sense of the term.[8] The systematisation of theological discourse during the twelfth century, however, led to a growing realisation that the strict sense of merit as *meritum debitum* was quite inadequate to deal with the spectrum of meanings of the term if the utter gratuity of justification and the necessity of a human disposition or preparation for justification were to be simultaneously upheld (see §7). It can be shown that a distinction came to be drawn between the concepts of *merit* and *congruity*: while man cannot be said to merit justification by any of his actions, his preparation for justification could be said to make his subsequent justification 'congruous' or 'appropriate'. Thus a manuscript source of the late twelfth century makes a clear distinction between the two concepts, digno, dico, non dignitate meriti, sed dignitate congrui.[9] The sense which is clearly intended here is that of a congruity which cannot be considered meritorious in the strict sense of the term. This concept of merit appears to have found its most important application in connection with the question of whether Mary can be said to have merited to bear the saviour of the world.[10] The answer given to this question was that Mary could not be thought of as having merited this distinction in the strict sense of the term, although it was appropriate or congruous that she should have been favoured in this manner. The concept of *meritum congruitas* or *meritum interpretativum* thus passed into general circulation, being understood as a form of merit in the weakest sense of the term. This distinction between merit in the strict sense of the term and it its weaker sense of 'propriety' passed into the theological vocabulary of the thirteenth century as the concepts of *meritum de condigno* and *meritum de congruo*. Although these precise terms can be shown to have been used occasionally in the late twelfth century,[11] they do not always bear precisely the same meaning as they would in later periods. Furthermore, the concept of congruous merit, which was initially used chiefly in connection with the question of the propriety of Mary's bearing the saviour of the world came to be used increasingly in a quite distinct context – that of the meritorious character of man's disposition towards justification (see §7). Thus whenever a theologian of the twelfth century concedes merit prior to justification, the 'merit' in question is not merit in the strict sense of the term, but *meritum de congruo*.[12]

The concept of congruous merit has been the subject of considerable criticism on the part of Protestant historians.[13] For Adolf von Harnack, the concept represented the total disintegration of the Augustinian doctrine of grace. It is, of course, possible to sustain this extravagant thesis with reference to certain theologians of the *via moderna*. Thus Durandus of St Pourçain appears to have regarded *meritum de congruo* as *meritum ante gratiam*:[14] the sole difference between *meritum de congruo* and *meritum de condigno* is that the former exists prior to grace, and the latter subsequent to it. However, an analysis of the origins of the concept, and the intentions which underlie it, conspire to invalidate such criticism. In particular, three points may be noted.

1. The pastoral intention of the concept cannot be overlooked.[15] Although man has no claim to justification on the basis of divine justice, he may look towards the divine generosity and kindness for some recognition of his attempts to amend his life in accordance with the demands of the gospel. It may be pointed out that the concept of a disposition towards justification which is meritorious *de congruo* is particularly associated with the Franciscan Order and the school of theology which came to be associated with it. The pastoral emphasis upon God's kindness towards sinful mankind finds its appropriate expression in the concept of congruous merit.

2. The human activity, which counts as the disposition towards justification, must be regarded as being already set within the context of grace.[16] Even in the later *via moderna*, the axiom *facienti quod in se est Deus non denegat gratiam* (see §7) is always understood as an expression of and a consequence of divine grace. Those theologians who taught that man could prepare himself for justification in a manner which was meritorious *de congruo* invariably insisted that this be understood as a consequence of divine grace. Man's justification must be seen as a divine *gift*, rather than as a divine *reward*.

3. The theologians of the period explicitly taught that man required the assistance of actual grace before he is capable of disposing himself *proximately* towards justification, although they might concede that man is capable of disposing himself *remotely* towards justification through the proper exercise of his natural unaided faculties. Those theologians who held that a proximate disposition towards justification was meritorious *de congruo* thus presupposed the implication of *gratia gratis data* (and not merely the *concursus generalis*) in effecting this necessary disposition.

The concept of condign merit was employed to express the notion of a self-imposed obligation upon the part of God to reward man's efforts. The notion of obligation, which is essential to the concept of merit *de condigno*, may be detected in the early twelfth century. Peter the Chanter explicitly implicated the notion of obligation in his definition of merit: mereri est de indebito debitum facere.[17] In this, he was followed by Alan of Lille, who listed four elements essential to true merit, the fourth being of particular importance:

Ad hoc enim, ut aliquis proprie dicatur aliquid mereri, quattuor concurrunt: ut opus quod agit eius proprie sit; ut apud alium mereatur; ut apud talem qui potestatem habet remunerandi; ut de indebito fiat debitum.[18]

The notion of *de indebito debitum facere* is taken up by theologians of the early thirteenth century, such as Stephen Langton[19] and Godfrey of Poitiers,[20] and is stated with particular clarity by William of Auvergne, who defines merit thus:

meritum ergo proprie et rectissima diffinitione obsequium est retributionis obligatorium, hoc est quod recipientem sive illum, cui impenditur, retributionis efficit debitum.[21]

Merit may therefore be defined as an act performed by man which places God under obligation to him. It must be pointed out, however, that this obligation on the part of God is usually understood to arise as a consequence of his gracious decision to allow himsef to be placed under obligation to man in this manner.[22] A similar definition of merit may be shown to have characterised the writers of the early Franciscan school, such as Odo Rigaldi[23] and Bonaventure,[24] as well as the first Summist, William of Auxerre.[25]

The introduction of Aristotelian physics had a pronounced and profound effect upon the early Dominican school. We have already noted the considerable influence of Aristotelian physics upon Thomas Aquinas' teaching upon the nature of justification (see §5) and the necessity of a disposition for justification (see §7). It can be shown that Aristotelian considerations also exercised a considerable influence upon the early Dominican school's teaching on merit. Roland of Cremona defined merit thus: mereri est motum ex virtute gratuita et libero arbitrio elicere in via militiae; et aliquem mereri sibi est motum virtutis pro se elicere.[26] The essence of merit is here understood to lie in its being a *motus* intermediate between man's initial state and the final state of eternal life. In this, we can see the beginnings of the tendency, which would become particularly clear in the writings of Thomas Aquinas, to conceive merit *ontologically*, rather than in terms of a personal obligation of God to the individual Christian. Whereas the earlier medieval theologians had understood merit to refer essentially to the obligation of God towards man, the theologians of the early Dominican school tended to understand merit in terms of ontological participation in the divine nature itself. This may be contrasted with the teaching of the early Franciscan school, which retained the older personal understanding of merit.[27]

A significant feature of the medieval understanding of condign merit is that merit and its reward are understood to be proportionally related. Thus Roland of Cremona states that merit *de condigno* is not called merit *de digno* precisely because the initial 'cum' indicates the association between the merit and its reward: ipsum autem cum adiungitur ibi ad notandum associationem meriti cum praemio.[28] This idea can be found stated with particular clarity in the writings of Odo Rigaldi[29] and Bonaventure.[30] Of considerable significance is the assertion, first clearly encountered in the writings of William of Auxerre, that the relation between merit and reward can be established as a matter *of justice*.[31] This aspect of the matter is taken up by Thomas Aquinas: unde sicut reddere iustum pretium pro re accepta ab aliquo, est actus iustitiae; ita etiam recompensare mercedem operis vel laboris, est actus iustitiae.[32] Thomas, however, emphasises that the term 'justice' is used in this context in a sense significantly different from its normal use.

Although merit *de condigno* is often referred to as 'true' merit, to distinguish it from merit *de congruo*, it must be appreciated that Thomas understands neither type of merit to represent a just claim on man's part before God. Justice, in the strict sense of the term, can only exist among equals. Just as Aristotle excluded animals and gods from his concept of justice on the grounds that there existed too great a dissimilarity between them and men to allow their inclusion in the contracting political community, so Thomas argues that there is too great a dissimilarity between man and God to allow anyone to speak of man having a 'just' claim before God. 'It is obvious that there is the greatest inequality between God and man, for they are infinitely different, and all of man's good comes from God.'[33] Thus one cannot speak of *iustitia secundum absolutam aequalitatem* in this context, but only of *iustitia secundum proportionem quandam*. Although one can speak of justice and merit in terms of the relationship between God and man, it must be appreciated that merit in this context must be understood as merit on the basis of *iustitia secundum praesuppositionem divinae ordinationis*, rather than on the basis of *iustitia secundum absolutam aequalitatem*. The merit in question is thus merit *secundum quid* – a merit before God which is essentially distinct from all human merit. Merit before God is based upon a divine ordination according to which he will reward a particular work with a specified reward. God cannot be thought of as man's debtor – if God is in debt to anyone, he is in debt to himself, as he has ordained that he will reward such acts in this manner.[34] Merit arises from grace, in that God can be said to bestow quality upon his creatures in an act of grace. Merit is therefore not based upon strict justice, but upon *iustitia secundum quid*, 'a sort of justice', which is based upon God's decision to reward his creatures. In effect, Thomas develops Augustine's principle, that merit is based upon the divine promise, to the effect that *all* merit before God is 'improper' merit, in the sense that it is not based upon strict justice between equals.

It is possible to distinguish between an *intellectualist* and a *voluntarist* approach to the relation between the moral and the meritorious. The former, which is particularly associated with the theologians of the twelfth century and the early Dominican and Franciscan schools, recognises a direct correlation between the moral and the meritorious value of an act, the transition between the two being effected by grace or charity. This relationship is frequently indicated by the use of terms such as 'comparabilis', 'associatio', 'aequiparari' or 'proportionalis'. While there was general agreement that the merit of an act *coram Deo* was a consequence of God's graciousness and liberality in accepting it as such, rather than its inherent value, there was division between the early Dominican and Franciscan schools on whether this merit was to be conceived *ontologically* or *personally*. Although the intellectualism of the early Franciscan school stands in contrast to the voluntarism of the later Franciscan school, an essential continuity between the schools is demonstrated in their mutual tendency to conceive merit in *non-ontological categories*.

The voluntarist position is particularly associated with the later Franciscan school and the *via moderna*. Its fundamental and characteristic feature is the recognition of a discontinuity between the moral and the meritorious realms, the latter being understood to rest entirely upon the divine will itself. For Scotus, every created offering is worth exactly what God accepts it for, and nothing more: dico, quod sicut omne aliud a Deo, ideo est bonum, quia a Deo volitum, et non est converso: sic meritum illud tantum bonum erat, pro quanto acceptabatur.[35] The meritorious value of an act need therefore have no relation to its moral value, as it rests upon God's estimation alone. This position is developed with particular clarity in the works of William of Ockham, and we shall illustrate it with reference to these.

For Ockham, the decision as to what may be deemed to be meritorious or demeritorious lies entirely within the scope of the divine will, and no reference whatsoever need be made to the moral act in question. There is a fundamental discontinuity between the moral value of an act – i.e., the act, considered in itself – and the meritorious value of the act – i.e., the value which God chooses to impose upon the act. Moral virtue imposes no obligation upon God, and where such obligation may be conceded, it exists as the purely contingent outcome of a prior uncoerced divine decision. This aspect of Ockham's teaching has been the subject of considerable criticism, as it appears to suggest that the relation between the moral and the meritorious domains is purely arbitrary.[36] Although Ockham insists that an act can only be meritorious if it is performed in a state of grace,[37] it appears that he regards this as merely a *conditio sine qua non*, secondary in importance to the divine acceptation.[38] For Ockham, an act can only be meritorious *de potentia ordinata* (see §11) if it is performed in a state of grace – but the meritorious *value* of that act is determined solely through the divine will. God is not bound by the moral value of an act, but is free to impose whatever meritorious value upon that act which he may deem appropriate. The relationship between the moral and meritorious values of an act is purely contingent, a consequence of the divine will, and not merely a necessary consequence of the nature of the act itself which God is obliged to respect. Ockham's concept of *covenantal causality* (see §13) necessitates his rejection of an *ex natura rei* causal relationship between the moral and meritorious realms. Ockham uses the dialectic between the two powers of God (see §11) to demonstrate that *de potentia absoluta* an act which is now deemed meritorious might have been demeritorious, even though precisely the same act is involved in each case.[39]

Ockham's discussion of the nature of congruous merit is of particular significance, as it appears to underlie the criticisms of Thomas Bradwardine and Gregory of Rimini directed against the 'modern Pelagians'. According to Ockham, God rewards virtuous acts performed outside a state of grace with congruous merit.[40] However, Ockham insists that this 'merit' carries with it no claim to eternal life, which arises only on account of merit *de condigno*.[41] All that Ockham intends to convey by the notion of congruous merit is that man is capable of acting in such a way that God may bestow upon man a habit of grace – which, as we noted earlier, is the general understanding of the concept at the time. The *function* of the concept within the context of Ockham's soteriology is that it forms the necessary (understood as *necessitas consequentiae*, rather than *necessitas consequentis*) bridge between the states of nature and grace, and between the moral and theological virtues. It is often asserted that Ockham's optimism concerning man's abilities leads him into Pelagianism or 'semi-Pelagianism': it may, however, be pointed out that Ockham's optimism concerning man relates solely to his *moral* capacities, and that the radical discontinuity which Ockham recognises between the moral and meritorious values of an act means that man's moral abilities are largely irrelevant, as the ultimate grounds of merit lie outside of man, in the extrinsic denomination of the divine acceptation. As we have pointed out, the meritorious value of an act lies in the divine estimation of that act rather than in its inherent moral value. Ockham's theology of merit allows him to take a favourable view of man's moral capacities, while at the same time totally destroying the theological foundation upon which man's acts might be considered as capable of meriting grace or eternal life. It is one of the most brilliant aspects of Ockham's theology of merit that he permits man's moral acts to have a considerable inherent moral value, while simultaneously establishing that the moral value of an act is irrelevant in determining its meritorious value, by locating the *ratio meriti* in the extrinsic denomination of the *acceptatio divina*. It will be clear that Ockham's teaching on this matter has been subject to a considerable degree of misrepresentation and misunderstanding, both by his contemporaries and by his modern critics.[42]

Of Ockham's contemporary critics, his fellow Englishman Thomas Bradwardine may be singled out for particular comment. Bradwardine totally rejected the concept of congruous merit prior to grace,[43] insisting that merit was the consequence of grace: unless the tree is itself good, it cannot bear good fruit. A similar position is associated with Gregory of Rimini.[44] In response to the opinion which was more associated with Ockham's followers than with Ockham himself, that man can merit justification *de congruo* by an act of contrition,[45] Gregory denies that contrition is a possibility apart from grace. A rather different, and somewhat startling, approach to the question is associated with John Wycliffe, the later English follower of Bradwardine.[46] Wycliffe totally rejected the concept of *condign* merit, even after the bestowal of grace, on the grounds that the concept implied that God rewarded man's acts *de pura iustitia*, as if they were entirely performed by man himself without the assistance of divine grace. Wycliffe defines congruous merit as merit which arises through God rewarding those human acts which result from the influence of divine grace – and hence altogether excludes the concept of condign merit from consideration:

Et est duplex meritum, scilicet de congruo et de condigno: de congruo quando aliquis meretur de pura gracia premiantis, ut puta, quando premians prevenit cooperando omne meritum merentis . . . de condigno autem dicitur quis mereri, quando meretur de pura iusticia ab alico premiante, quod fuit quando premians non graciose coagit cum illo.[47]

Unlike Bradwardine, who conceded both congruous and condign merit after justification, Wycliffe conceded *only* congruous merit, and that *only after* justification. A similar position is associated with Huss,[48] who pointed out that *pura iustitia* implied an equality between God and man which simply did not exist, except in the form of *equalitas proportionis*:

Qui ergo dicunt, quod non potest homo mereri vitam aeternam de condigno, attendunt equalitatem quantitatis; qui autem dicunt, quod homo potest mereri de condigno attendunt equalitatem proporcionis.[49]

It is therefore impossible for man to merit eternal life *de condigno*, even when in a state of grace: non potest pura creatura de condigno *mereri vitam eternam.*[50] It is instructive to recall that Thomas Aquinas made a similar observation concerning the concept of *iustitia* implied by the concept of condign merit, but did not feel that the 'secundum quid' character of the resulting merit was sufficient reason to reject the concept. The criticisms of Wycliffe and Huss appear to be directed against a misunderstanding or misrepresentation of the nature of condign merit which does not correspond to the teaching of any of the theological schools of the period, in that the existence of a proportional relationship between an act and its reward was not held to imply an equality between man and God.[51]

The later *via moderna* may be regarded as continuing the teaching of Ockham on the nature of merit. Gabriel Biel emphasised that the concept of congruous merit is based upon the divine liberality rather than the divine justice. Man's disposition towards justification is regarded as meritorious *non ex debito iusticie sed ex sola acceptantis liberalitate.*[52] As we have noted above, it is clear that the teaching of the *via moderna* concerning congruous merit was criticised in certain quarters as exhibiting Pelagian tendencies. It is therefore of particular interest to note the defence of the doctrine provided by the noted early sixteenth-century Tübingen exegete Wendelin Steinbach. Steinbach points out how the early church was confused concerning the concept of merit, but that the concept was now sufficiently well understood to avoid a Pelagian misunderstanding of the concept of congruous merit: et tamen hodie non est absonum dicere, quod peccator mereatur bonis operibus de genere vel impetret de congruo a Deo iustificari et graciam sibi infundi.[53]

The continuity between the late medieval and Reformation periods may also be demonstrated from John Calvin's teaching concerning the merits of Christ. The later Franciscan school, the *via moderna* and the *schola Augustiniana moderna* regarded the *ratio meriti* as lying in the divine good pleasure; nothing was meritorious unless God chose to accept it as such. This teaching was extended to include the work of Christ: the *merita Christi* were regarded as being grounded in the *acceptatio divina*. There are excellent reasons for suggesting that Calvin himself encountered such a teaching during his formative Paris years.[54] It is therefore of some considerable interest that Calvin reproduces the essential features of this late medieval understanding of the *ratio meriti Christi*. This point can only fully be appreciated by considering the *Institutio* of 1559 (II.17.1–5), a section which is based upon an exchange of letters between Calvin and Laelius Socinus. In 1555, Calvin responded to questions raised by Socinus concerning the merit of Christ and the assurance of faith,[55] and appears to have incorporated these replies into the 1559 *Institutio* without significant modification. In the course of this correspondence, Calvin's strongly voluntarist understanding of the *ratio meriti Christi* becomes apparent. Although the evident similarity between Calvin and Scotus on this question has been noted in the past,[56] it has not been fully appreciated that Scotus merely marks a point of transition in the medieval discussion of the question of the *ratio meriti*, so that the main theological schools of the fourteenth and fifteenth centuries adopted a similarly voluntarist understanding of the criterion of merit. In other words, there has been a tendency in the past to assume that this similarity between Scotus and Calvin *reflects the specific influence of Scotus* upon Calvin, whereas it actually reflects a more general influence of later medieval theology. Calvin insists that 'apart from God's good pleasure, Christ could not have merited anything': nam Christus nonnisi ex Dei beneplacito quidquam mereri potuit.[57] Christ's work is meritorious *pro nobis* for the simple reason that God has ordained that it will be so, and accepted it as such. The fact that Calvin's discussion of the *ratio meriti Christi* is continuous with that of the *via moderna* suggests that Calvin encountered such an opinion at Paris, perhaps through the influence of John Major. Whatever the historical explanation of this continuity with later medieval thought may be, however, it serves to indicate that there is a closer relationship between late medieval theology and that of the Reformation than many have realised.

§11 The dialectic between the two powers of God

From the discussion of merit presented above, it will be clear that the concept of God being under an obligation to justify man if he does *quod in se est* is a commonplace in the later medieval discussion of justification.[1] But in what sense may God be said to be under an *obligation* to man? Is not this a compromise of the divine freedom and omnipotence? It is this question which forms the context of the dialectic between the two powers of God, which is one of the most important and most frequently misrepresented aspects of the late medieval discussion of justification, and which we propose to discuss in the present section.

The problem identified above is recognised by Augustine, who presented the outlines of a solution which would be taken up and developed by the theologians of the medieval period, particularly by those of the *via moderna*. For Augustine, the divine *obligation* to man arises purely from the divine *promises* made to man: non debendo enim, sed promittendo debitorem se deus fecit, id est non mutuo accipiendo.[2] If God is under any obligation to man, it is as a consequence of his non-coerced decision to place himself under such an obligation by means of his promises to mankind. We have already noted the significance of the divine promises to man in relation to Augustine's understanding of *iustitia Dei* (see §§4, 6). It is clear that Augustine understands the concept of divine obligation to man as an expression of the divine sovereignty, as it demonstrates God's ability to limit his own course of action.[3] This point was taken up and developed during the theological renaissance of the twelfth century, but assumed a new significance in the thirteenth century as a consequence of Averroist determinism. Thus Thomas Aquinas points out that, while God is omnipotent, there are many things which he could do which he wills not to do. From an initial set of possibilities, limited only by the condition that the outcome must not involve contradiction, God willed to actualise a specific subset. In that God could have willed a different subset of possibilities, and was not coerced in his selection, the subset selected for actualisation cannot be regarded as resulting from absolute necessity. However, in that God has chosen to act in this particular manner, the subset of unwilled possibilities must be considered to be set aside as only hypothetically possible.[4] These two sets of possibilities represent the two spheres of the power of God. God's *absolute* power refers to the initial set of possibilities which are open to divine actualisation, which is limited only by the condition that their actualisation does not involve contradiction. Of these initial possibilities, only a small number are selected for actualisation. Their actualisation results in the present order as we know it, the realm of God's *ordained* power. This realm represents the subset of possibilities which God chose to actualise – and having chosen them, he abides by them. Thus there is no absolute necessity for God to choose any particular course of action within the context of the ordained order; however, having chosen to establish the present order, God is under a self-imposed obligation to himself to respect it. Such considerations underlie the important distinction between *necessitas consequentis* (a necessity which arises through the inherent nature of things) and *necessitas consequentiae* (a necessity which arises through the establishment of a contingent order of existence). This important distinction between an *absolute* necessity and *self-imposed conditional* necessity is of vital

§11 The dialectic between the two powers of God

importance to a correct understanding of the medieval discussion of justification.

The thirteenth century saw the rise of Averroist determinism at Paris, posing a serious threat to the concept of the divine freedom. Among the propositions which were condemned at Paris in 1277 were several which denied or seriously questioned the omnipotence and freedom of God.[5] According to Siger of Brabant, God *necessarily* produces everything which proceeds directly from him.[6] The essential problem which these opinions raise may be stated in terms of two propositions:

1.   God is free, and not bound by any external factors in his action.
2.   God acts *reliably* in his dealings with mankind.

The Averroist controversy made it a matter of urgency to develop a conceptual framework within which both these propositions could be maintained simultaneously. In its original form, the dialectic between the two powers of God was conceived as a solution to this dilemma, and is particularly associated with Henry of Ghent and Duns Scotus. For Scotus, the divine freedom may be upheld in connection with his primordial decision as to which of the possibilities open to initial actualisation would subsequently be actualised. God's freedom in this respect is demonstrated by the non-coerced character of this decision, in that God was free from external constraints (save that contradiction must not result) in his decisions concerning the nature of the present established order. Scotus is thus able to reject the idea that God acts of absolute necessity – i.e., *necessitas consequentis*. Once having determined the nature and character of the established order, however, God has placed himself under a contingent, conditional and self-imposed obligation to respect the order which he has established – and which may therefore be regarded as totally reliable. The present obligation to man on the part of God is a consequence of, as well as an expression of, his freedom. By his absolute power (*de potentia absoluta*) God is totally free in his decisions; by his ordained power (*de potentia ordinata*) God is totally reliable in his actions. The two propositions noted above may therefore be maintained simultaneously without contradiction.

The development of this dialectic between the absolute and ordained power of God is particularly associated with William of Ockham.[7] Like Scotus, Ockham uses the tension between what is *de facto* and what might have been *de possibili* to safeguard the divine freedom in the face of Greco-Arabian determinism. Although

Ockham frequently refers to the first article of the Creed, 'credo in deum patrem *omnipotentem*',[8] it is clear that he understands this omnipotence to have been qualified and circumscribed by his decision to become God the creator. It must be stressed that Ockham does not teach that God is currently able to do one thing *de potentia absoluta*, and the reverse *de potentia ordinata*: as he frequently emphasises, there exists only one power in God at present, and that is his ordained power, itself an expression of his contingent decision to create the established order:

Circa primum dico quod quaedam potest Deus facere de potentia ordinata et aliqua de potentia absoluta. Haec distincto non est sic intelligenda quod in Deo sint realiter duae potentiae quarum una sit ordinata et alia absoluta, quia unica est potentia in Deo ad extra, quae omni modo est ipse Deus. Nec sic est intelligenda quod aliqua potest Deus ordinate facere et aliqua potest absolute et non ordinate, quia Deus nihil potest facere inordinate. Sed est intelligenda quod 'posse aliquid' quandoque accipitur secundum leges ordinatas et institutas a Deo; et illa dicitur Deus posse facere de potentia ordinata.[9]

Where Ockham appears to go further than Scotus is in the *use* he makes of the dialectic between the powers of God. For Ockham, the dialectic between the powers of God was a critical tool for theological analysis: we shall illustrate this point with reference to his critique of the necessity of created habits in justification (see §13). Thus while Peter Aureole insisted upon the absolute necessity of a created habit in justification, Ockham pointed out that God was free to choose an alternative mode of justification, had he chosen to do so. Without rejecting their *de facto* implication in justification, Ockham demonstrated that created habits were not involved as a matter of *absolute* necessity.

Ockham's use of the dialectic between the two powers of God as a critical theological tool was misunderstood at an early stage. In 1326 a commission of six theologians censured 51 articles taken from Ockham's writings, including a number of relevance to the doctrine of justification. Some six centuries later, the report of these *magistri* was rediscovered,[10] allowing us to establish both the precise nature of the condemned propositions, as well as the reasons for their condemnation. The four propositions which concern us are the following:

1.   *de potentia Dei absoluta* a man may make good use of his will by his purely natural powers, which God may accept as meritorious.[11] The *magistri* pronounced this to be Pelagian 'or worse', as it overthrew the habit of charity altogether.[12]

2.   *de potentia absoluta* God may accept a man *ex puris naturalibus* as worthy of eternal life without his possessing habitual grace, or damn him without his having sinned.[13]

3.   *de potentia absoluta* God may accept a man *ex puris naturalibus* as worthy of eternal life without his possessing a habit of charity. Taking these two propositions together, the *magistri* pronounced that they were Pelagian, in that they taught that man could be accepted to eternal life by his natural abilities.

4.   *de potentia absoluta* God may remit sin without the infusion of grace.[14] This proposition follows from the others, and the *magistri* duly repeat their charge of Pelagianism.

The text of the condemned propositions makes it explicit that they are intended to be understood as discarded hypothetical possibilities, pertaining *de potentia absoluta* but not *de potentia ordinata*. The *magistri*, however, insisted that the addition of the phrase *de potentia Dei absoluta* made no difference to the sense of the propositions.[15] It is clear that this amounts to a culpable misunderstanding of Ockham's intentions: Ockham merely exploits the tension between what *might have been* and what *actually pertains* to demonstrate the contingency and reliability of the established order. As we have noted, Ockham insists that there is only one power in God: God only has one course of action open to him at present, irrespective of what his initial options were. If both the absolute and ordained powers of God were understood to pertain now, the charge of Pelagianism against Ockham could be regarded as justified. The fact remains, however, that it is manifestly obvious that this is not what Ockham meant.

That Ockham is not guilty of Pelagianism in these propositions may be confirmed by considering the position of Gregory of Rimini, one of the most ferociously anti-Pelagian theologians of the medieval period, on the same questions. Like Ockham, Gregory emphasises that, while God is not bound by any absolute necessity to accept a man to eternal life if he possesses a habit of charity, he has ordained that *de potentia ordinata* the possession of such a habit will result in the glorification of the *viator*. Gregory thus draws three conclusions:[16]

1.   *De potentia absoluta* God may accept a man as *gratus* without a habit of created grace.

2.   *De potentia absoluta* God is not obliged to accept as *gratus* the *viator* who is in possession of such a habit.

3.   *De potentia absoluta* God may accept an act as meritorious even if it is performed outside a state of grace.

It is clear that these propositions correspond to those of Ockham which were condemned at Avignon, and that they represent hypothetical possibilities *de potentia Dei absoluta* which do not pertain *de facto*. Furthermore, a careful examination of the writings of the *modernus* Pierre d'Ailly suggests that the critique of the necessity of grace is justification, conducted *via* hypothetical speculation *de potentia absoluta*, is specifically aimed at *created habits of grace*, and not the uncreated grace of the Holy Spirit himself.[17] In effect, the necessity of a created infused habit of grace in justification may be regarded as the consequence of the intrusion of Aristotelianism within the sphere of the doctrine of justification, and the application of 'Ockham's Razor' – in this case, supported by a critique based upon the dialectic between the two powers of God – leads to the rejection of the absolute necessity of such a habit. The fact that the Tridentine decree on justification declines to affirm the necessity of a created habit of grace or charity in justification may be regarded as demonstrating that the hypothetical critique of the concept had made its point well.

The soteriological point which theologians of the *via moderna* used the dialectic between the two powers to emphasise is that the present established order of salvation, although radically contingent, is totally reliable. God is not obliged by any external constraints to justify man: however, having determined to do so by a free and uncoerced act of self-limitation, he abides by that decision. By his absolute power, God retains the *ability* to do many things which he does not *will* to do. The established order of salvation, to which scripture and tradition bear witness, is an expression of the divine will, and circumstances under which God would act contrary to his established and revealed will can never arise. To the objection that, because the present order depends upon the divine will, the possibility that God might revoke this order through a further act of will cannot be ignored, the theologians of the *via moderna* responded by appealing to the unity of intellect and will within God: God's actions are always totally consistent and reliable. God always acts justly, not because he acts in accord with generally accepted standards of justice, but because he possesses an inward sense of justice which is manifested in his actions and which is consistent with his nature, even though this lies beyond human knowledge.

The use of the dialectic between the two powers of God within the *via moderna* has often been illustrated with reference to the writings of Gabriel Biel, and it is necessary to challenge a serious and influential misrepresentation of Biel's teaching on the *potentia Dei absoluta*. Carl Feckes argues that Biel used the absolute power of God as a convenient vehicle for conveying his own true theology, while retaining traditional teaching in connection with the ordained power of God. In other words, Biel states *de potentia absoluta* what he would have stated *de potentia ordinata*, were it not for fear of recrimination by the ecclesiastical authorities.[18] This criticism of Biel is impossible to sustain, particularly when it is appreciated that the use to which Biel puts the tool of the dialectic between the two powers of God is that of not merely *defending* the established order of salvation against divine capriciousness, but also of providing a firm theological foundation (in the concept of the *pactum*) upon which the established order of salvation may be more securely grounded. This misrepresentation of Biel's thought has also had considerable influence in connection with the related question of the influence of later medieval theology upon the young Martin Luther: if what Biel *really* meant is to be determined from his statements concerning the *absolute* power of God, then Luther's early opinions should be compared with Biel's opinions *de potentia Dei absoluta*. This inevitably leads to the simplistic and quite unjustifiable conclusion that Luther merely states *de potentia ordinata* what Biel stated *de potentia absoluta* – which is as much a caricature of Luther's thought as it is of Biel's![19] Feckes' interpretation of Biel appeared in 1925; the first significant criticism of his approach appeared in 1934, with the publication of Paul Vignaux' highly influential study on fourteenth-century theology,[20] which included a careful study of Ockham's 'voluntarism'.[21] The established order of salvation is not arbitrary but rational, and its rationality can be demonstrated on the basis of probable, though not necessary, arguments. According to Vignaux, the hypothetical order *de potentia absoluta* represents the order of divine logic, in that the possibilities open to divine actualisation are non-contradictory; the actual order *de potentia ordinata* is the order of divine mercy, in that God has voluntarily made himself a debtor to those who possess divine grace in order that they might be justified. Vignaux developed this point in 1935, in his highly acclaimed study of the young Luther,[22] in which he emphasised that it was a total misrepresentation of Biel's thought to argue that the absolute power pertained to the order of reason and law, while the ordained order pertained solely to the arbitrary *de facto* situation.[23] The established order, Vignaux stressed, demonstrates simultaneously the divine justice and the divine mercy. On the basis of this, subsequent studies have emphasised the innocence of Biel's use of the dialectic between the two powers of God,[24] although criticism has frequently been directed against the amount of theological energy wasted on hypothetical speculation *de potentia Dei absoluta*.[25] Similar criticism was directed against the device in the fifteenth century, as may be seen from Erasmus' comments concerning the theological questions which were perplexing the Paris *théologastres* in the final decade of the century. Two such questions may be noted:

1.   Can God undo the past, such as making a harlot into a virgin?[26]
2.   Could God have become a beetle or a cucumber, instead of man?[27]

In fact, both these questions raised serious theological issues, similar to the question of the necessity of created habits in justification, which could not be resolved without the appeal to the dialectic of the two powers of God.[28]

The understanding of divine self-limitation associated with the *via moderna* is particularly associated with a 'covenant' (*pactum*) between God and man. It must be emphasised that this *pactum* should not be confused with the early form of the social contract theory which is so characteristic a feature of the political thought of Marsilius of Padua. The *pactum* is ordained and instituted unilaterally by God, as an act of kindness and generosity towards man. Strictly speaking, it is necessary to recognise two covenants, one pertaining to the natural order, relating to all mankind, by which God commits himself to upholding the created universe and the laws which govern it; the other pertaining to the theological order, relating to the church, by which God commits himself to the salvation of sinful mankind. It is with this latter covenant that we are chiefly concerned. At the heart of this concept of the covenant lies a major break with the rationalistic limitations of the Aristotelian concept of God, and a return to a more biblical concept of God who, though omnipotent, has entered into a covenant with the descendants of Abraham. The existence of this covenant affirms God's commitment both to the salvation of mankind and the means ordained towards this end, particularly the sacramental system of the church (see §8). It is this *pactum* which forms the fulcrum about which the doctrines of justification associated with the *via moderna* turn.[29]

In his discussion of sacramental causality, Thomas Aquinas notes the following opinion concerning the relationship between the sacraments and grace:

Quidam tamen dicunt quod non sunt causa gratiae aliquid operando: sed quia Deus, sacramentis adhibitis, in anima gratiam operatur. Et ponunt exemplum de illo qui, afferens denarium plumbeum, accipit centum libras ex regis ordinatione: non quod denarius ille aliquid operetur ad habendum praedictae pecuniae quantitatem; sed hoc operatur sola voluntas regis.[30]

Thomas rejected this opinion on the grounds that 'a lead coin is no more than a certain kind of sign of the royal ordination directing that the man who presents it is to receive a sum of money'. However, the opinion rejected by Thomas would become an important feature of later medieval understandings of justification, especially within the *via moderna*. Under the terms of the *pactum* between God and man, God has ordained that he will accept human acts as worthy of eternal life. This act of divine will is completely contingent and uncoerced: nevertheless, it is also totally reliable. The *pactum* encapsulated the general medieval conviction that God had imposed upon himself an obligation to man, and that his decision, though contingent, was totally reliable. We have already noted the characteristic teaching of the *via moderna* concerning the dichotomy between the moral and the meritorious realms (see §10): *de potentia ordinata*, however, the relationship between the moral and the meritorious value of an act was established by the *pactum*. We have already discussed this point in relation to the teaching of the *via moderna* on the meritorious character of the disposition towards justification (see §7). The *pactum* determines the relation between the *bonitas intrinseca* and the *valor impositus* of man's moral actions, and thus provides the foundation for the justification of the sinner. While the divine freedom was safeguarded through the absolute power of God, the divine reliability was safeguarded through the ordained power, as expressed in the *pactum*. The emphasis placed by the theologians of the *via moderna* upon the *contingency* and *reliability* of the established order of salvation is particularly well demonstrated by the young Luther's discussion of the reasons why faith and grace are implicated in justification:

Immo et fides et gratia, quibus hodie iustificamur, non iustificarent nos ex seipsis, nisi pactum Dei faceret. Ex eo enim precise, quia testamentum et pactum nobiscum foecit, ut qui crediderit et baptisatus fuerit, salvus sit, salvi sumus. In hoc autem pacto Deus est verax et fidelis et sicut promisit, servat.[31]

The most important use to which the dialectic between the two powers of God was put in the medieval period was the demonstration of the radical contingency of the rôle of created habits in justification, associated with which is the development of the concept of 'covenantal causality'. This topic will be further explored in §13. Our attention is now claimed by the question of the relationship between predestination and justification.

§12 The relation between predestination and justification

The first systematic discussion of the relation between predestination and justification is encountered in the works of Augustine of Hippo.[1] Although earlier writers appear to have realised that Paul's discussion of the rejection of Israel, contained in Romans 9–11,[2] raised the question of predestination, their chief concern appears to have been the defence of what they understood to be an authentically Christian understanding of free will in the face of astral fatalisms, such as Gnosticism. The confusion between the concepts of predestination and fatalism or determinism unquestionably served to lessen patristic interest in the idea of *divine* predestination, with the inevitable result that the early patristic period is characterised by a theological optimism quite out of character with the Pauline corpus of the New Testament.[3] It is with Augustine that attention is first directed to the idea that God exercises more control over the entire process of salvation than might at first seem to be the case.

As noted earlier (§4), Augustine appears to have first confronted the problem of predestination in the course of his correspondence with Simplicianus of Milan.[4] Around 395, Simplicianus found himself perturbed by several issues arising from his reading of Romans 9–11. Why did God hate Esau? And was the idea that God hardened Pharaoh's heart compatible with the Christian understanding of the nature of God and of human freedom? Simplicianus' attempt to persuade Ambrose of Milan to discuss the problem appears to have resulted in failure: the bishop seems to have considered that the writings of Paul posed no problems which could not be resolved simply by reading him aloud.[5] Simplicianus then turned to Augustine for guidance, and by doing so appears to have occasioned the characteristic theological position generally known as 'Augustinianism', which would have so incalculable an effect upon subsequent western theological speculation concerning the relation between predestination and justification.

The essence of Augustine's position upon this question may be summarised in the statement that man's *temporal* election, or justification, is the consequence of God's *eternal* election, or predestination.[6] Thus Augustine interprets the hardening of Pharaoh's heart as a consequence of divine predestination, understood as a positive action on God's part.[7] However, Augustine totally excludes the possibility of an arbitrary *fiat* on the part of God in this respect by emphasising that predestination is based upon and is ultimately an expression of divine justice. Augustine demonstrates that the hardening of Pharaoh's heart is based upon justice in three ways:

1. The hardening of Pharaoh's heart must be seen as a consequence of his previous sins.[8]
2. The hardening of Pharaoh's heart is not totally a work of God: Pharaoh must be regarded as having contributed to the hardening of his heart by his own free will.[9] Even in his discussion of predestination, Augustine insists upon the reality of the human free will.
3. God's judgement, whether open to public scrutiny or not, is always just.[10] God is just, so that whether he hardens a man's heart is not an arbitrary matter, but a matter of justice.

Even in the famous letter to Sixtus, written at the close of the Pelagian controversy, Augustine insists upon the total justice of divine predestination. God determines the destinies of men on the basis of justice. Augustine frequently emphasises the role of the divine wisdom in predestination, intending by this to draw attention to the distinction between predestination and fatalism.[11] The total sovereignty of God in election is maintained: man's justification is preceded by the stirring of his will by God – and God, in his wisdom, has determined only to prepare the wills of a few.[12] For Julian of Eclanum, any such teaching called into question the divine justice; Julian, however, employed a concept of *iustitia Dei* which Augustine was not prepared to sanction.[13]

Augustine declined to draw from his doctrine of predestination the conclusion that God predestined some to eternal life and others to damnation, or the related conclusion that Christ died only for the elect. These conclusions, however, would be drawn – and opposed! – with considerable frequency thereafter. The first theologian who can legitimately be styled 'predestinarian' is the fifth-century Gallic priest Lucidus, whose views were condemned at the Council of Arles (473). Of particular importance are his assertions that Christ did not die for all men, that the divine grace is irresistible, and that those who are lost, are lost through God's will:

(Lucidus) dicit quod Christus Dominus et Salvator noster mortem non pro omnium salute susceperit; quid dicit quod praescientia Dei hominem violenter impellat ad mortem, vel quod cum Dei pereant voluntate qui pereunt.[14]

This condemnation was endorsed by Orange II (529), which specifically anathematised anyone who believed that some are predestined to evil by God.[15] Although some have argued that the council's condemnation was directed against Augustine, the fact remains that Augustine did not explicitly teach a doctrine of *double* predestination.

The most significant predestination controversy of the medieval period erupted in the ninth century, centring on the Benedictine monk Godescalc of Orbais (often incorrectly referred to as 'Gottschalk').[16] Until recently, our knowledge of this controversy stemmed chiefly from the accounts of Godescalc's supporters and opponents. The original text of Godescalc's chief writings was rediscovered in the first half of the present century,[17] with the result that we are now in a position to assess the significance of the great predestinarian controversy of the ninth century with some accuracy.

Godescalc's doctrine of double predestination, *praedestinatio gemina*, is a logical consequence of a fundamentally Augustinian understanding of the relation between nature and grace. Where Godescalc appears to have differed from Augustine is in the rigour with which he deduced the necessity of double predestination from the prevenience of grace in justification. Every rational creature, whether human or angelic, continually needs divine grace if he is to be acceptable to God.[18] This necessity of grace extends also to the proper functioning of the human free will, which is unable to will or to do good apart from grace.[19] With total fidelity to Augustine, Godescalc asserted that man's free will is only truly free when it has been liberated by grace.[20] So far, Godescalc and Augustine are in agreement – yet Augustine teaches predestination *ad vitam*, whilst Godescalc teaches *praedestinatio gemina*. How does this difference arise, given the evident similarities in premises between the two men?

It seems that the fundamental principle upon which Godescalc based his doctrine of double predestination is that of the divine immutability: credo et confiteor deum omnipotentem et incommutabilem praescisse et praedestinasse angelos sanctos et homines electos ad vitam gratis aeternam.[21] If there is in God no new judgement or decision, then all must be predestined. The possibility of any such new judgements or decisions is excluded on the grounds that 'if God does something which he has not done through predestination, he will have to undergo change'[22] – which is quite unthinkable, given Godescalc's doctrine of the immutability of God. If God damns anyone, he must have determined to do so from all eternity, in that he is otherwise subject to change. Therefore,

Godescalc concluded, both the salvation of the elect and the reprobation of the damned are predestined from all eternity. It is possible
that this radical departure from the teaching of Augustine on this
matter may have been occasioned by the teaching of Isidore of
Seville, who explicitly taught that 'there is a double predestination,
of the elect to rest and of the damned to death. Both are caused by
divine judgement.'[23] Godescalc frequently refers to the great Spanish
bishop with approval in relation to his teaching on predestination.[24]

If some are predestined to evil, it follows that Christ cannot have
died for all men, but only for those predestined to life. This conclusion is unhesitatingly accepted by Godescalc.[25] The text frequently
cited against him in relation to this point was I Timothy 2.4, which
refers to God desiring 'all men to be saved'. Godescalc rejected the
suggestion that this reference implied that God desired all men in
general to be saved, interpreting it instead as an affirmation that
whoever is saved, is saved by divine predestination.[26]

The most sophisticated critique of Godescalc's doctrine of predestination was due to the Irish head of the cathedral school in Paris,
John Scotus Erigena. In his *De divina praedestinatione*, written
c. 850, Scotus criticised Godescalc for his misinterpretation and
improper use of theological language. Terms such as 'predestination'
and 'foreknowledge' are predicated of God metaphorically (*trans-
lative de deo predicari*), so that the precise meaning of the term
'predestine' cannot be assumed to be the same in the following
statements:

1.   God has predestined the elect to salvation.
2.   God has predestined the wicked to damnation.

Although this would not satisfy Prudentius of Troyes,[27] it served to
draw attention to some of the difficulties attending the debate.

The most implacable opponent of the views of Godescalc was
Hincmar of Reims, who accused *isti moderni praedestinatiani* of teaching that 'the necessity of salvation has been imposed upon those who
are saved, and the necessity of damnation upon those who perish'.[28]
This was unacceptable, as it appeared to deny the reality of human
free will, which Hincmar asserted to be real, even if weakened by the
Fall (*per se sufficiens sibi ad malum, languidum autem atque invalidum
ad omne bonum*).[29] Hincmar also asserted that Godescalc's statements
amounted to a contradiction of the teaching of Augustine, and cited
the pseudo-Augustinian treatise *Hypognosticon*[30] in support of his
refutation of the Benedictine:

Praedestinatio quippe a praevidendo et praeveniendo vel praeordinando futurum aliquid dicitur; et ideo Deus cui praescientia non accidens est, sed essentia fuit semper, et est, quidquid antequam sit praescit, praedestinat; et propterea praedestinat, quia quale futurum sit praescit ... Sed non omne quod praescit, praedestinat. Mala enim tantum praescit, bona vero et praescit et praedestinat. Quod ergo bonum est, praescientia praedestinat, id est, priusquam sit in re praeordinat.[31]

Citing this work as 'Augustine's book on predestination', Hincmar insisted that predestination and foreknowledge must be distinguished. As Florus of Lyons – a moderate supporter of Godescalc – pointed out, this restricted predestination to the elect, while allowing the divine foreknowledge to apply to both the elect and damned.[32] Florus himself had no difficulty in rejecting the Augustinian provenance of the treatise in question.[33]

In 849, Hincmar convened a synod at Quiercy, which condemned the opinions of Godescalc, and deprived him of his orders. The synod was reconvened by Hincmar in 853, and issued a renewed censure of predestinarianism in the form of four *capitula*:[34]

1. Predestination is to be distinguished from foreknowledge. God can be said to predestine to eternal life, but he cannot be said to predestine to punishment. A distinction is made between the predestination of punishment, and predestination *to* punishment. In effect, this amounts to a restatement of the teaching of the pseudo-Augustinian *Hypognosticon*, noted above. For Hincmar, 'God had predestined what divine equity was going to render, not what human iniquity was going to commit'[35] – i.e., God has predestined that he will reward evil with punishment, but *not* the evil that will be thus punished.

2. Man's *libertas arbitrii*, which was lost in Adam, has been restored in Christ.[36] This *capitulum* is extremely unsatisfactory, as it manifestly confused *liberum arbitrium* and *libertas arbitrii* – i.e., natural and acquired freedom. A similar weakness may be noted in the first *capitulum*, which asserts that God created man 'righteous, without sin, and endowed with *liberum arbitrium*'.[37] As Florus of Lyons pointed out, this statement of free will was utterly devoid of any reference to divine grace.[38] Florus found a similar weakness in the same *capitulum*, in that it appeared to make grace a mere consequence of divine foreknowledge.[39] The confusion of nature and grace is one of the most striking features of the first two *capitula* of this synod.

3. God wills to save all men, rather than just the elect.[40]

4. Jesus Christ died for *all* men, and not just for a section of

humanity.[41] Again, this amounts to a restatement of Hincmar's position that Christ had suffered and died for all men, even if they refused to accept his gift of redemption.[42] *Sanguis Christi redemptio est totius mundi.*[43] For Hincmar, God was evidently guilty of injustice if Christ was permitted to die for the elect alone.[44] The teaching of this *capitulum* was criticised by Florus of Lyons on the grounds that it implied that the blood of Christ was shed in vain (*esse inane et vacuum*) if it was shed for those who did not believe in it.[45] Florus himself argued that Christ's blood was not shed for all men, but for his church, i.e., 'all believers in Christ who have been or now are or ever will be'.[46]

Florus himself drew upon seven 'rules of faith' in which a careful distinction is made between the concepts of predestination and foreknowledge, and for which he claimed the authority of both scripture and the fathers:[47]

1. The predestination and foreknowledge of God are, like God himself, eternal and unchangeable.

2. There is nothing in all creation which is not foreknown or predestined by God himself.

3. Anything which may be said to have been predestined may also be said to have been foreknown, just as whatever may be said to have been predestined may also be said to have been foreknown. Nothing exists which can be said to have been predestined but not foreknown, and vice versa.

4. The good works of both men and angels may be said to be foreknown and predestined by God, while their evil works may be said to be foreknown, but not predestined, by God. The evident tension between this statement and the previous two is not discussed at any length.

5. God's foreknowledge and predestination cannot be said to impose necessity upon anyone. This point had been made against Hincmar by supporters of Godescalc, such as Ratramnus[48] and Servatus Lupus.[49]

6. These concepts of foreknowledge and predestination are implied by Holy Scripture, even at those points at which they are not explicitly stated.

7. None of those who are elect may ever perish, just as none of those who are damned can ever be saved.

The pronouncements of the Synod of Quiercy were overturned by the Council of Valence (855).[50] Whereas Quiercy had insisted that there is *una Dei praedestinatio tantummodo*, Valence asserted a double predestination, *praedestinatio electorum ad vitam et praedestinatio impiorum ad mortem*.[51] It must be emphasised that the Council understood this latter predestination to be essentially different from the predestination of the elect: in electione tamen salvandorum misericordiam Dei praecedere meritum bonum; in damnatione autem periturorum meritum malum praecedere iustum Dei iudicium.[52] The canons of Valence were reaffirmed four years later at a local synod held in Langues. In that same year, it is reported that Nicholas I issued a declaration endorsing the doctrine of double predestination, and the associated teaching that Christ died only for the elect.[53] It is impossible to confirm this report, as no such papal declaration is known to exist. Hincmar, writing in 866, declared his belief that the alleged declaration was a fraud.[54]

The ninth-century debate on predestination was not continued in subsequent centuries. The tenth century is generally regarded as a period of stagnation or decline,[55] and the theological renaissance of the late eleventh and twelfth centuries saw little attention being paid to the question. In general, two schools of thought concerning the motivation of divine predestination may be discerned:

1. The general opinion, which recognised that there was no basis whatsoever in man for either predestination to glory or reprobation, the difference resting solely in the divine will itself. This opinion was supported by Peter Lombard in his *Sentences*,[56] and in this he was followed by the majority of the theologians of High Scholasticism, and particularly by the theologians of the early Dominican school. Thus Thomas Aquinas taught that the divine decision in man's election was necessarily free and uncoerced, made without reference to man's foreseen merit or demerit.[57]

2. The minority opinion, according to which there is some basis in the man for both predestination and reprobation. This opinion is particularly associated with the early Franciscan school, such as Alexander of Hales and Bonaventure. Predestination is understood as an act of intellect, rather than will: the divine will must be informed by the intellect before the decision to elect or reject, and the information supplied by the intellect relates to the foreseen use of the grace granted to the individual in question.[58]

Duns Scotus departed from the early Franciscan school's teaching on predestination by insisting that predestination was an act of the divine *will* rather than the divine *intellect*. Predestination is understood as an act of will by which God, electing a rational creature, ordains him to grace and glory, or the act of intellection which *accompanies* (and not, as in the case of the earlier Franciscan school, *precedes*) this election.[59] Scotus understands predestination as *praedestinatio ad vitam*, to be distinguished from reprobation. One of the most important aspects of Scotus' doctrine of predestination is the means by which he deduces the gratuity of predestination. Scotus appears to be the first theologian to use the principle *omnis ordinate volens prius vult finem quam ea quae sunt ad finem* to demonstrate the utter gratuity of predestination.[60] Before Scotus, the gratuity of predestination had been deduced from the *datum* of the gratuity of grace. For Scotus, however, the volition of the end itself must precede the volition of the means to that end – i.e., God wills the final glorification of man before he wills the means by which this end may be achieved. As grace is merely the means to the end of predestination, it is improper to deduce the gratuity of predestination from that of grace, in that grace is logically posterior to predestination. Therefore the election of a soul to glory must precede the foreknowledge of merits, and hence be without any foundation outside the divine will. The logical priority of predestination over the means by which it is attained inevitably means that the *ratio praedestinationis* lies in the divine will itself. Predestination is therefore totally gratuitous, in that it represents an act of divine will, uninformed by the intellect's analysis of any *ratio praedestinationis in creatura*. The *processus praedestinationis* is therefore such that eternal life precedes merit in terms of its logical analysis, but is consequent to it in terms of its execution in time.[61]

This analysis runs into difficulty in the case of reprobation. Following the teaching of the early Franciscan school, Scotus refuses to concede that God actively wills reprobation. Citing the axiom *non prius est Deus ultor quam aliquis sit peccator*, Scotus argues that the foreknowledge of sin must precede reprobation.[62] As all good is to be attributed principally to God, and all evil to man, Scotus argues that different processes must be considered to operate in the cases of predestination and reprobation.[63] As predestination is an act of the divine will, rather than the divine intellect, Scotus rejects the opinion that foreknowledge is a cause of predestination: the decision of God to predestine a soul to glory does not depend upon information about the soul in question being made available to the divine will by the divine intellect. It is clear that predestination is thus understood to be an active decision on the part of God, rather than the essentially passive endorsement of a prior human decision. This stands in contrast to Scotus' teaching on reprobation, which is understood to be a passive act of divine permission in regard to human sin. The distinction may be illustrated by considering the cases of Peter and

Judas. The former was predestined by God independent of foreknowledge of his merit: God prepared for Peter the means of grace by which he might be glorified. In the case of Judas, however, God merely recognises his sin and punishes him for it. This points to an important difference between Thomas Aquinas and Scotus: for the former, God predestines first to grace and subsequently to glory; for the latter, God predestines first to glory and then to grace. It also illustrates a significant difference between the intellectualism and the voluntarism of the early and later Franciscan schools respectively. The intellectualist approach to predestination involves the intellect informing the will concerning the foreseen use an individual will make of a gift of grace, thus permitting the will to make an informed decision. The *ratio praedestinationis* and *ratio reprobationis* are both located in the creature. The voluntarist approach, however, necessarily locates the *ratio praedestinationis* in the divine will, and Scotus' fidelity to the teaching of the earlier Franciscan school on the *ratio reprobationis* appears to involve him in a serious contradiction, in that his voluntarist presuppositions dictate that it should also be located in the divine will.

Scotus' doctrine of predestination has important consequences for his soteriology in general. As is well known, Scotus regards the Fall of man and the incarnation of the son of God as being essentially independent of each other. The incarnation did not occur as a consequence of human sin. For Scotus, Christ in his human nature was first in the order of the divine foreknowledge, predestined before all other creatures. The *processus praedestinationis* places the predestination of creatures *after* the predestination of the incarnation, as may be seen from the following *ordo praedestinationis*. First, God, apprehends himself by means of the *summum bonum*; second, he apprehended all other creatures; third, he predestined some to glory and thence to grace; fourth, he performed what might be termed an act of omission, by not predestining the remainder; fifth, he foreknew that they would fall in Adam; sixth, he preordained the remedy for the Fall of man, in that man might be redeemed by the passion and death of the son of God. Thus Christ in the flesh was first predestined to grace and glory, in common with the elect, although prior to them; only after the divine foreknowledge of the Fall of man was his incarnation ordained as a remedy for the sin of man. Scotus supports this teaching by arguing that a physician necessarily wills the health of his patient before he specified the remedy which will cure him.[64] In other words, the elect are predestined to grace and glory *before* (both *logically* and *chronologically*) Christ's passion was ordained as a means to that end. As we have already noted (§10), this has significant consequences for his doctrine of the *meritum Christi*.

This doctrine of predestination was developed in a significant direction by William of Ockham, who also remained faithful to the Franciscan teaching that reprobation is based upon a quality within man, rather than an act of divine will. For Ockham, *praedestinare*, in its active mood, refers to the future bestowal of eternal life upon an individual, just as *reprobare* refers to the infliction of punishment upon him. It is clear that both verbs have a specifically future reference, so that any proposition which contains the verbs must necessarily refer to the future.[65] Thus the proposition *Petrus est praedestinatus* is not necessarily true, as the verb here appears with reference to the past.[66] The statement can only refer to a future instant during which God will bestow eternal life upon Peter – and only at that instant can the proposition be said to be true. Of course, its truth at that instant guarantees its truth in the past, so that the proposition is then recognised always to have been true. However, the fundamentally eschatological orientation of Ockham's concept of predestination prevents any positive statement concerning the truth of the proposition from being made until that point has been reached. For Ockham, predestination signifies three entities: God, man, and eternal life. Ockham rejects any understanding of predestination as a real relation additional to God's own necessary being, or as a *relatio realis* added to man by virtue of his being predestined.[67] Predestination is defined solely in terms of the final gift of eternal life, given by God to man.

Ockham's discussion of the *cause* of predestination is generally regarded as being extremely difficult to follow. First, it may be noted that Ockham's understanding of predestination is such that, strictly speaking, it is impossible to speak of it having a cause in the first place. Ockham is only prepared to discuss predestination in terms of the priority of propositions. Ockham provides the following causal sequence of propositions, apparently in the form of an enthymene, to illustrate this point:[68]

1. This man will finally persevere.
2. Therefore he will be predestined.

The non-syllogistic character of the argument may, of course, be rectified by supplying the assumed major premise: 'a man who finally perseveres will be predestined'. Whilst this constitutes the only permissible statement on the relationship between predestination and human merit which is possible, given Ockham's definitions of the terms, it must be pointed out that there are several passages in which he refers to the relationship between predestination and merit in more traditional terms. On the basis of a careful examination of such passages, it appears that Ockham allows both a general *praedestinatio cum praevisis meritis* and a special and distinct *praedestinatio ex gratia speciali*, both possible *de potentia ordinata*. Some will be saved on account of their merits, as without acting freely they would not merit their salvation. As predestination is equivalent to being given eternal life, these individuals may be said to have merited their pre-destination, *provided that* the explicitly future reference of this statement is acknowledged. Only when eternal life is finally bestowed upon an individual can he be said to be predestined, and only then can the causality of the matter be properly discussed. In the case of other individuals (St Paul being isolated as a specific example), pre-destination is regarded as arising for no other reason that that God desires their salvation without merit.

The obscurity surrounding Ockham's pronouncements upon pre-destination has led to a number of questionable conclusions being drawn in connection with them. Oberman concludes that Ockham taught predestination *post praevisa merita*,[69] which, in addition to being a questionable interpretation of Ockham's teaching in the first place, compounds the confusion still further by introducing the terminology of Protestant Orthodoxy where it is clearly totally out of place and seriously misleading. As we have argued elsewhere,[70] Ockham's doctrine of predestination is best approached through the writings of Gabriel Biel, which may be treated as a commentary upon Ockham. Biel himself pronounced his *Collectorium* to be an attempt *dogmata et scripta venerabilis inceptoris Guilelmi Occam Angli indagatoris acerrimi circa quattuor sententiarum libros abbreviare*. In fact, Biel's discussion of predestination represents a considerable expansion, rather than an abbreviation, of Ockham's statements on the matter.[71] We therefore propose to analyse Biel's doctrine of predestination as an influential late medieval interpretation of Ockham's teaching on the matter.

Oberman's analysis of Biel's doctrine of predestination is confused by his use of the categories of predestination *post praevisa merita* and *ante praevisa merita*. We have already noted this point in relation to his analysis of Ockham's teaching on the matter. Biel, naturally, does not use either phrase,[72] nor the conceptual framework within which

Protestant Orthodoxy discussed the doctrine of justification. Biel, it must be emphasised, is entitled to be interpreted by the standards of, and within the context of his own conceptual framework, rather than an alien framework imposed upon him. Following Ockham, Biel understands the term predestination to have a specifically future reference. If an individual receives eternal life, he may be said to be predestined *at that moment* – but not before. If God chooses to accept the *viator* to eternal life at the end, that man may be said to be predestined from that moment, and from that moment only. Of course, his predestination at that moment demonstrates his predestination at earlier points – but it is impossible to verify the statement until the actual bestowal of eternal life takes place. The statement ' "A" is predestined' cannot be verified until 'A' actually has eternal life bestowed upon him by God.[73] Oberman has argued that Biel cannot have a meaningful doctrine of predestination on the grounds that his Pelagian doctrine of justification makes predestination not merely superfluous, but actually destructive.[74] Oberman's criticism of Biel may be rejected, however, for two reasons. First, it is dependent upon Oberman's prior conviction that Biel teaches a Pelagian doctrine of justification, which is questionable (see §7). Second, Oberman misunderstands Biel to refer predestination to *justification*, whereas it is clear that Biel refers it to the final bestowal of eternal life. This misunderstanding appears to have arisen through Oberman's approaching Biel through the later Protestant understanding of the nature of predestination, evident in his unjustifiable use of terms such as *praedestinatio ante praevisa merita*. The justification of the sinner does not demonstrate his predestination, which is only demonstrated by his final glorification. Man's justification does not necessarily imply his future glorification.

A consideration of Biel's discussion of the grounds of merit (*ratio meriti*) makes Oberman's thesis even more improbable. Eternal life cannot be merited *de congruo*, but only *de condigno* by the *viator* in possession of a habit of grace.[75] The ultimate grounds of merit, however, lie in the divine will (see §10), which leads to a hiatus between the moral and the meritorious realms. The *ratio meriti* lies outside of man, in the extrinsic denomination of the divine acceptation. Applying these observations to Biel's doctrine of predestination, we find that we are forced to draw a conclusion very different from that of Oberman. Like Ockham, Biel recognises two modes of predestination, which may be termed *praedestinatio cum praevisis meritis* and *praedestinatio ex gratia speciali*. The former term is to be preferred to Oberman's anachronistic and misleading *praedestinatio post praevisa merita*. It will be evident that if an individual, such as St Paul, is predestined *ex gratia speciali*, the *ratio praedestinationis* will lie outside man. Some commentators, however, appear to assume that the general mode of predestination *cum praevisis meritis* locates the *ratio praedestinationis* within man, so that man may be said to occasion his own predestination. It will be evident that this is not the case. Even in this mode of predestination, the *ratio praedestinationis* lies outside of man, precisely because the *ratio meriti* lies outside of man in the extrinsic denomination of the *acceptatio divina*. If the grounds of man's predestination by this mode is his merit, it must be conceded immediately that the grounds of this merit lie outside of man, in the extrinsic denomination of the *acceptatio divina*. This observation leads to the following important conclusion: predestination *cum praevisis meritis* is itself predestination *ex gratia speciali* mediated through the secondary cause of merit. The two types of predestination are essentially the same, except that one proceeds directly, and the other indirectly through secondary causes. The situation may be represented as follows:

1.   Predestination *ex gratia speciali:*
    acceptatio divina → *ratio praedestinationis.*
2.   Predestination *cum praevisis meritis:*
    acceptatio divina → *ratio meriti* → *ratio praedestinationis.*

In both cases, the ultimate grounds of predestination lie outside of man, in the extrinsic denomination of the divine acceptation. Viewed from the standpoint of the divine acceptation, the two modes are essentially the same: the essential difference between them is that one proceeds directly, the other indirectly. In both cases, however, the *ratio praedestinationis* is one and the same, the *acceptatio divina*, external to man and outside his control.

A very different understanding of the nature of divine predestination, however, emerged during the fourteenth century, and is particularly associated with the academic Augustinian revival at Oxford, and especially at Paris, usually known as the *schola Augustiniana moderna*.[76] In many respects, the *schola Augustiniana moderna* may be regarded as developing a doctrine of predestination similar to that of Godescalc of Orbais. Although Augustine himself did not explicitly teach a doctrine of double predestination,[77] there were those who argued that it represented the logical outcome of his doctrine of grace, and hence claimed the support of the African bishop for their teaching. The origins of this sterner understanding of predestination are usually considered to lie in the anti-Pelagian polemic of the English secular priest, Thomas Bradwardine.

In his witty caricature of fourteenth century theology, Chaucer derided those who studied

> ... the holy doctor Augustyn
> or Boece, or the bishop Bradwardyn.[78]

This reference to Bradwardine may well reflect a revival of interest in his works, due to the influence of Wycliffe. Bradwardine's chief work, *de causa Dei contra Pelagianum* is a somewhat tedious rambling work aimed at certain unnamed *Pelagiani moderni*, presumably the Oxford circle based upon Merton College in the fourteenth century, noted for their Ockhamism.[79] According to Bradwardine's own account of the history of his religious opinions, he himself was attracted to Pelagianism in his early days as a philosophy student at Oxford.[80] However, this youthful espousal of some form of Pelagianism – and Bradwardine never favours us with an explicit definition of the term – was to evaporate when confronted with Romans 9.16, which was to become the *Leitmotif* of his mature theology. It is quite possible that Bradwardine's conversion to a theocentric doctrine of grace prior to his inception as a theological student exemplifies the Augustinian *cognitio* through *illuminatio*.[81] Whilst Bradwardine's theological sources in *de causa Dei* are primarily scriptural, it is clear that his interpretation of these sources is based upon Augustine, whom he values above all others as their interpreter.[82] Although Bradwardine follows Augustine faithfully in defending the existence of a weakened free will against those, such as *vani astrologi*, who maintained a psychological determinism,[83] he departs significantly from Augustine's teaching in relation to the Fall. For Bradwardine, man's need for grace is a consequence of his creatureliness, rather than of the Fall: even when in Paradise, man was impotent to do good. This departure from Augustine is also evident in connection with his teaching on predestination. Although Bradwardine follows Augustine in discussing predestination within the context of the question of final perseverance, his explicit teaching on *double* predestination at once distinguishes him from the authentic teaching of Augustine. Bradwardine's doctrine of predestination is essentially supralapsarian, although it may be noted that he is careful to locate the origin of evil in secondary causes, so that God may be said to predestine *to* evil, but not to *predestine* evil. It may be noted in this respect that Bradwardine's discussion of contingency appears to contain several novel elements: contingency is understood not merely to include the non-necessary, but also to express the principle that events may occur at random or by chance, apart from God's providential direction. In rejecting this understanding of contingency, Bradwardine appears to teach that all things happen of necessity, in that God may be said to cause and direct them. On the basis of such presuppositions, it may be conceded that Bradwardine's doctrine of double predestination expresses a metaphysical, rather than a theological, principle.

In the nineteenth century, Bradwardine was widely regarded as having prepared the way for the Reformation through the questions which he raised, and through the influence which he mediated through Wycliffe and Huss.[84] This view cannot be maintained in its original form. Thus while Bradwardine emphasised the role of the divine will in predestination, Wycliffe saw predestination as a form of divine truth, known to God by means of the ideas themselves before their actualisation. Thus Wycliffe's doctrine of predestination is not based upon a free decision of the divine will: his understanding of necessity is such that the reprobate are damned by foreknowledge, rather than an unconditional act of divine will.[85] In primis suppono cum doctore secundo, quod omnia quae eveniunt sit necessarium evenire:[86] Wycliffe's determinism, as stated in this celebrated *locus*, may possibly reflect the influence of Bradwardine. It is also quite possible that Wycliffe's determinism is a necessary consequence of his doctrine of real universals and possibilities.[87] The attribution of Wycliffe's form of determinism to the influence of Bradwardine is rendered questionable by two considerations. First, Bradwardine's understanding of *necessitas antecedens* presupposes the real existence of human free will – a freedom which Wycliffe explicitly rejects. Second, Bradwardine explicitly condemns as *heretical* the thesis that everything which occurs, takes place by absolute necessity – yet it is precisely this thesis which some argue Wycliffe derived from Bradwardine. A more realistic estimation of Bradwardine's significance is that he established an academic form of Augustinianism, based primarily upon his anti-Pelagian writings, which eventually became characteristic of the *schola Augustiniana moderna*. Two factors, however, combined to reduce Bradwardine's influence over this school. First, Bradwardine was not a member of a religious order, which would propagate his teaching. By contrast, Gregory of Rimini's teaching was extensively propagated within the Augustinian Order. Second, the Hundred Years War resulted in Oxford becoming isolated as a centre of theological study, with Paris gaining the ascendancy. The *schola Augustiniana moderna* thus came to be based on Paris, even though it is possible to argue that its origins lay at Oxford.

A doctrine of double predestination, similar in respects to that of Bradwardine, is associated with Gregory of Rimini.[88] Predestination is defined as the divine decision to grant eternal life, and reprobation as the decision not to grant it[89] – and *both* are understood to be acts of divine will. Predestination and reprobation are not based upon foreknowledge of the use made of free will, not of whether an obstacle will be placed in the path of grace:

Mihi autem videtur quod ex dictis scripturae et sanctorum sequuntur hae conclusiones cum quarum omnium veritate non state veritas alicuius modi dicendi de praedictis. Harum prima est, quod nullus est praedestinatus propter bonum usum liberi arbitrii quem Deus praescivit eum habiturum qualitercumque considereter bonitas eius.

Secunda, quod nullus est praedestinatus quia praescitus fore finaliter sine obice habituali et actuali gratiae. Tertia, quod quemcumque Deus praedestinavit gratis tantummodo et misericorditer praedestinavit. Quarta, quod nullus est reprobatus propter malum usum liberi arbitrii quem illum Deus praevidet habiturum. Quinta, quod nullus est reprobatus quia praevisus fore finaliter cum obice gratiae.[90]

The exclusive location of both predestination and reprobation in the divine will runs counter to the general opinion of the period, which tended to locate the cause of reprobation at least partly in man himself. Gregory's views were widely propagated within the Augustinian Order, by theologians such as Hugolino of Orvieto,[91] Dionysius of Montina,[92] Johannes Hiltalingen of Basel,[93] Johannes Klenkok[94] and Angelus Dobelinus.[95]

The renewed interest in, and increasing understanding of, Augustine in the fourteenth and fifteenth centuries is reflected in the increasingly critical approach adopted to the *dictum*, widely attributed to Augustine: si non es praedestinatus, fac ut praedestineris. 'If you are not predestined, endeavour to be predestined!' Johannes Eck, later to be Luther's opponent at the Leipzig Disputation of 1519, described this *dictum* as a 'teaching of Augustine which is better known than the history of Troy':

Ex data distinctione clare potest haberi verus sensus propositionis divini Augustini, quae est notior alias historia Troiana: 'Si non es praedestinatus, fac ut praedestineris' . . . Recipit ergo veritatem, quando intelligitur de praedestinatione secundum quid et secundum praesentem iusticiam, et est sensus:

Si non es praedestinatus, scilicet per praesentam gratiam, *fac* poenitendo et displicentiam de peccatis habendo *ut praedestineris* gratiam acquirendo, a qua diceris praedestinatus secundum praesentem iusticiam.[96]

In adopting this approach to the *ratio praedestinationis*, Eck appears to have believed himself to remain faithful to the teaching of the early Franciscan school.[97] For Eck, the *dictum* represented a significant development of the axiom *facienti quod in se est Deus non denegat gratiam* (see §7). The *viator*, by doing *quod in se est*, could ensure that he would receive the grace necessary for him to be 'predestined'. Predestination may therefore be regarded as the divine counterpart to man's doing *quod in se est*,[98] so that the *viator* may reassure himself concerning his predestination by performing good works. It is, of course, significant that Eck refers predestination to justification, rather than to the final future bestowal of eternal life. The non-Augustinian character of this *dictum* was increasingly recognised during the closing years of the medieval period. For example, Johannes Altenstaig's celebrated theological dictionary of 1517 attributes the maxim to an unnamed doctor: unde quidam doctor; si non est praedestinatus, fac ut praedestineris. Unde in potestate tua est damnari vel salvari.[99] In the same year, Johannes von Staupitz published his famous series of lectures on predestination, *Libellus de exsecutione aeternae praedestinationis*, in which he supported his argument to the effect that man's temporal election is posterior to the eternal divine election with a denial of the Augustinian provenance of the maxim.[100]

Finally, it is appropriate to inquire into the *function* of doctrines of predestination within the context of medieval theologies of justification. This function is best demonstrated by considering the profile of Duns Scotus' doctrine of justification. Scotus' doctrine of justification resembles an Iron Age settlement, containing a highly vulnerable central area surrounded by defensive ditches. The two defensive ditches in Scotus' doctrine of justification are his doctrines of absolute predestination and divine acceptation, which emphasise the priority of the divine will in justification. The central area, however, is highly vulnerable to the charge of Pelagianism, in that Scotus insists upon the *activity* of the human will in justification. Any study of Scotus' doctrine of justification which does not take account of the theological context in which it has been placed (i.e., the doctrines of the *acceptatio divina* and absolute predestination) will inevitably conclude that Scotus is guilty of Pelagianism or some kindred heresy. The charges of Pelagianism or 'semi-Pelagianism' brought against Scotus by an earlier generation of scholars are now appreciated to be hopelessly inaccurate,[101] although it is relatively easy to understand how these arose. It will, of course, be evident that a weakening of these outer defences without a concomitant strengthening of the inner structure of the doctrine of justification will make such a doctrine increasingly vulnerable to a Pelagian interpretation. It is the opinion of several scholars of the later medieval period that precisely such a weakening may be detected in the soteriology of the *via moderna*,[102] although we have reservations concerning such conclusions. In effect, the theologians of the *via moderna* appear to have recognised the close interconnection between the doctrines of predestination and divine acceptation, with the result that the two outer ditches have become merged into one, although the basic profile of their doctrines of justification remains similar to that of Scotus.

§13 The critique of the rôle of supernatural habits in justification

We have already noted how justification is invariable understood to involve a real change in the sinner (see §5), and not merely an external pronouncement on the part of God. This change was generally regarded as involving the infusion of a supernatural habit of grace into the soul of man (see §9). It will be clear, however, that there remains an unresolved question concerning the relationship between these aspects of justification. Are these habits infused into man in order that he may be regarded as acceptable by God? Or is man regarded as acceptable by God, as a result of which the supernatural habits are infused? Although these two may be regarded as being essentially simultaneous, there still remains the question of their *logical* relationship. Is the infusion of supernatural habits theologically prior or posterior to the divine acceptation? It is this question which lay at the heart of the fourteenth-century debate on the rôle of supernatural habits in justification, which forms the subject of the present section.

The starting point for this discussion is generally agreed to be Peter Lombard's identification of the *caritas* infused into the soul in justification with the Holy Spirit.[1] For Thomas Aquinas, this opinion is impossible to sustain, as the union of the uncreated Holy Spirit with the created human soul appeared to him to be inconsistent with the ontological distinction which it was necessary to maintain between them.[2] Thomas therefore located the solution to the problem in a created gift which is itself produced within the soul by God, and yet is essentially indistinguishable from him – the supernatural habit.[3] The general teaching of the early Dominican and Franciscan schools is that the immediate or formal cause of justification, and hence of divine acceptation, is the infused habit of grace. This opinion is also characteristic of the *schola Aegidiana*, the early school within the Augustinian Order, as may be illustrated from the position of Thomas of Strasbourg on this matter: nullus potest esse formaliter Deo gratus, nisi sit informatus gratia a Deo creata.[4] The possibility of a purely extrinsic acceptation is rejected on the grounds that a real change must occur in man if he is to be acceptable to God, and that such a change is effected solely by a created habit of grace.[5] Grace is *aliquid creatum in anima*, which alone renders man acceptable to God.[6] The general consensus of the thirteenth century was thus that *gratiae infusio* was prior to *acceptatio divina*.

The fourteenth century saw this consensus shattered through the systematic application of the dialectic between the two powers of God (see §11) and the concept of covenantal causality. The origins of this critique of the role of supernatural habits in justification is generally regarded as owing its origins to Duns Scotus, whose teaching on the matter we shall consider in detail.[7] The terms *acceptatio* or *acceptio*, first extensively employed by Scotus, are of biblical provenance.[8] Scotus notes three general senses of the term: simple contemplation; efficacious volition; and the divine acceptation which not merely wills a thing to be, but also accepts it according to the greater good.[9] It is in this final sense that the term is used in Scotus' analysis of the seventeenth distinction of the first book of the Lombard's *Sentences*. Scotus' interpretation of the Lombard at this point is based upon two explicitly acknowledged presuppositions: the reality of the justification of sinners (*iustificatio impii*), and the real possibility of human merit. It is significant that Scotus regards these as *articuli fidei*, and derives them from the Apostles' Creed.[10] The theological problem which requires resolution is the following: how *can* God justify sinners and permit human merit? The explicit linking of these two questions is of considerable significance, as essentially the same solution emerges to both: the *ratio iustificationis* and *ratio meriti* are identical, in that they must both be located in the extrinsic denomination of the *acceptatio divina*.

Scotus' insistence upon the unity and the simplicity of the divine will leads him to the conclusion that the divine will cannot be altered from within. If God wills to accept something, or if he wills not to

146

accept something else, the reason for the distinction must be regarded as lying outside the divine will itself, if a serious internal contradiction is not to result. That God should choose to save *this* man and to reject *that* man must reflect a fundamental difference between the two men in question, as the divine will is unable, according to Scotus, to move itself to accept one and not the other without external causes. Whether a man is accepted or not must depend upon the man himself. The obvious difficulties which this assertion raises in relation to his teaching on predestination (see §12) are not discussed. Therefore, Scotus argues, there must be a habit within man, by which he can be accepted at a given moment in time, whereas previously he was not regarded as acceptable. This difference, Scotus argues, is the habit of charity.[11] This is the first of four arguments which Scotus brings forward in support of his contention that a habit of charity is required *de potentia ordinata* for justification. His second argument is based upon the immutability of the divine will, and has already been touched upon above. As the divine will is immutable, the diversity apparent in the fact that God accepts some, and not others, must arise on account of a similar diversity within the individuals in question. There must therefore be something inherent within the individual which leads to this diversity of judgement – and Scotus identifies this as the presence, or absence, of the created habit of charity.[12] His third argument is based upon privation. Man is not born in a state of justice, so he is unable to increase in justice unless it is by means of a supernatural habit. If this were not the case, man could be both a friend and enemy of God, both loved and not loved. Therefore there must exist a supernatural habit which can account for this transition from being an enemy of God to being a friend of God – and this is the habit of charity.[13] Finally, Scotus argues that those who deny the necessity of such a habit *de potentia Dei ordinata* must be considered as asserting that an individual is as acceptable to God *before* penitence as *afterwards* – which is heretical.[14] Scotus thus insists that a habit of charity is required for justification *de potentia Dei ordinata*.

Having established this conclusion, Scotus begins to employ the dialectic between the two powers of God to qualify his conclusions. By his absolute power, God was not under any compulsion whatsoever to accept a soul to eternal life on account of its possession of a created habit of charity, nor was he obliged to employ such intermediates in justification in the first place. God need not do anything by second causes which he could do directly himself. God has ordained, however, that such a habit of charity is required for acceptation and justification. This necessity, however, does not arise through the nature of divine acceptation itself (*ex natura rei*), but merely arises on account of the laws which God has established by his ordained will (*ex pacto divino*). By God's absolute power, a quite different set of laws might have existed in connection with divine acceptation. Whilst the laws relating to divine acceptation through created habits may be considered to be utterly reliable,[15] they must also be considered to be equally contingent.

This leads to Scotus' important discussion of whether this created habit of charity can be said to be the formal cause of justification, in which the maxim *nihil creatum formaliter est a Deo acceptandum* plays an important rôle. Scotus begins his discussion by citing Augustine in support of the general consensus of the period to the effect that those who are accepted by God are distinguished from those who are not by their possession of a created habit of charity.[16] This does not, however, mean that the habit of created charity may be regarded as the formal cause of divine acceptation, considered from the standpoint of the one who elicits the act of acceptation (i.e., God), as this must be regarded as lying within the divine will itself.[17] A distinction must be made between the primary cause of divine acceptation (i.e., a *necessary* cause, arising out of the nature of the entities in question) and the secondary cause of divine acceptation (i.e., a *contingent* cause, which has its *esse* solely in the divine apprehension). On the basis of this distinction, Scotus argues that the created habit of charity must be regarded as a secondary cause of divine acceptation. God ordained from all eternity that the created habit of charity should be the *ratio acceptandi*, so that its importance in this connection is contingent, rather than necessary, deriving solely from the divine ordination, and not from any universally valid law. In effect, this amounts to an unequivocal statement of the concept of *covenantal causality*, noted earlier (see §11). The inner connection between acceptation and the habit of charity does not lie in either the nature of acceptation or the habit of charity, but solely in the divine ordination that there should be a causal relationship between them, which has now been actualised *de potentia Dei ordinata*.[18]

A further aspect of Scotus' teaching on acceptation which should be noted is his distinction between divine acceptation of a person and divine acceptation of his acts. The *acceptatio personae* takes priority over the *acceptatio actus*.[19] As it is the acceptation of the person which gives rise to the acceptation of his acts, it will be clear that the *ratio meriti* lies outside man in the divine acceptation itself. Furthermore, a distinction must be drawn between acceptation to eternal life and acceptation to grace. The former relates to the *end* of justification, the latter to its *means*. In keeping with the general Scotist principle (see §12) that the end is willed before the means to this end, it follows that acceptation to grace is posterior to acceptation to eternal life. Acceptation to grace is merely *acceptatio secundum quid*, as it presupposes *acceptatio simpliciter* – i.e., acceptation to eternal life.[20] As we noted earlier (see §12), the general profile of Scotus' doctrine of justification is thus such that the fundamental gratuity of justification and predestination are maintained, despite the apparent threat posed to this gratuity by Scotus' insistence upon the activity of the human will.

Scotus' teaching on the secondary and derivative rôle of the created habit in justification was criticised by Peter Aureole,[21] who is generally regarded as being the most important theologian in the period between Scotus and Ockham. He appears to have been dissatisfied with the Aristotelianism of his period, in that both his psychology and his noetic are fundamentally Augustinian in character.[22] It is interesting to note that Peter is heavily dependent upon Durandus of St Pourçain, mediated through the quodlibetal questions of Thomas of Wilton.[23] While Peter's epistemology is characterised by his rejection of any realist understanding of universal concepts,[24] it must be pointed out that it is inaccurate to characterise his epistemology as 'nominalist' in the usual sense of the term: his understanding of the role of *conceptio* in cognition suggests that his particular form of 'nominalism' should be styled *conceptualism*. Peter's theology of justification is of particular interest on account of his explicit and penetrating criticism of Scotus on two matters: the type of denomination required for divine acceptation, and the rôle of the divine will in predestination.

In marked contrast to Scotus, Peter maintains that for a soul to be *accepta Deo*, a habit of charity is necessary. In his rejection of Scotus' maxim *nihil creatum formaliter est a Deo acceptandum*, Peter argues that the necessity of the intrinsic denomination of the habit of charity for divine acceptation is itself the consequence of a primordial divine ordination. His teaching on the matter may be summarised in the three propositions which he advances in support of this contention:[25]

1. divine acceptation is the natural and necessary result of the presence of a created form in the soul;[26]
2. this form is not itself the consequence of divine acceptation, but itself renders the soul acceptable to God by the application of the divine love;[27]

3.　　　　this form, by which the soul is accepted, is some habitual love of God, directly infused into the soul by God himself, and which does not arise from man's natural powers.[28]

Peter then identifies this *aliqua forma creata* as the habit of charity, directly infused by God himself into the soul of the *viator*. Thus the extrinsic denomination of the divine acceptation is itself based upon the intrinsic denomination of the infused habit of charity.

Peter's criticism of Scotus' doctrine of absolute predestination is based on related considerations. Scotus had taught that God first predestined a soul to glory, and then to grace *quasi posterius*. For Peter, this failed to do justice to the universal saving will of God. The divine will must extend to the salvation of all men, not merely to those who are predestined. Peter eliminates this apparent arbitrariness on the part of God by insisting that the formal cause of divine acceptation must be considered to be the intrinsic denomination of the habit of charity. By doing this, he effectively reduces predestination to an act of divine power, based upon foreknowledge.[29]

It will be clear that the fundamental disagreement between Peter and Scotus relates to the question of the causality of the supernatural habit of charity. For Scotus, the causality of the habit in connection with divine acceptation is *covenantal*, reflecting the divine ordination that such a causality should exist. For Peter, the causality is *ex natura rei*, itself a consequence of the nature of the created habit of charity and the act of divine acceptation. The nature of the entities implicated in the act dictates that such a causal connection is necessary, independent of any divine ordination concerning it. Once the habit of charity has been infused into the soul of the *viator*, God is obliged, by the very nature of things, to accept that *viator*.

Peter's association of the priority of habit over act was rejected by William of Ockham. After stating Peter's three theses, Ockham begins his criticism mildly enough: ista opinio non videtur mihi vera.[30] The first thesis to which he refers is that a created form in the soul is by its very nature (*ex natura rei*) pleasing to God, so that it results in divine acceptation and the bestowal of grace. Ockham immediately demonstrates the *contingency* of this thesis: *de potentia absoluta*, God may bypass created habits, preparing and accepting the soul to eternal life in the absence of any such habit. God's granting eternal life and the beatific vision to an individual is in no way a consequence of or dependent upon the possession of such a created habit.[31] To those who object that it is only by virtue of the possession of such a habit that a *viator* becomes worthy of eternal life, Ockham replies that all that is actually necessary is that God disposes the *viator* towards eternal life.

Ockham's second argument against Peter is that both being loved and being hated by God are effects of the divine will. To be hated by God, however, does not necessarily result in *aliqua forma creata detestabilis* formally inhering within the soul of the *viator* who is hated by God. It is therefore inconsistent to assert that such a created form is required within the soul of a *viator* if he is to be *loved* by God, while not simultaneously asserting that such a form is required if he is to be *hated* by God. The inconsistency involved is further emphasised by Ockham in connection with the action of the sacrament of baptism. If Peter's thesis is valid, according to Ockham, it must follow that a sinner who is newly converted and baptised would be loved and hated *at the same time*, as the habits of mortal sin and charity would coexist.

Ockham's critique of Peter continues with a strong statement of the priority of acts over habits. The meritorious nature of an act is not located in the fact that the *viator* is in possession of a created habit of charity. Merit has its origin in the uncoerced volition of the moral agent. The criterion of merit or demerit is what God chooses to accept or reject, lying outside the moral agent, and not reflecting any quality (such as a created habit) inherent to the *viator*. God can do directly what he would normally do by a supernatural habit. Although God is *now* obliged to justify man by means of created supernatural habits, this does not reflect the nature of things, but simply the divine ordination. After considering the opinion of Thomas Aquinas on the *ratio meriti*, Ockham concludes:

Ideo dico aliter ad quaestionem, quod non includit contradictionem aliquem actum esse meritorium sine omni tali habitu supernaturali formaliter informante. Quia nullus actus ex puris naturalibus, nec ex quacumque causa creata, potest esse meritorius, sed ex gratia Dei voluntari, et libere acceptante. Et ideo sicut Deus libere acceptat bonum motum voluntatis tamquam meritorium quando elicitur ab habente caritatem, ita de potentia sua absoluta posset acceptare eundem motum voluntatis etiam si non infunderet caritatem.[32]

De facto, a created habit is implicated in divine acceptation – but this implication arises *ex pacto divino*, not *ex natura rei*. While not questioning the *de facto* necessity of such habits in justification, Ockham demonstrated their radical contingency, and thus undermined the conceptual foundations upon which the *habitus*-theology had been established in the thirteenth century.

Ockham's basic position was defended by Gabriel Biel,[33] in that the *de facto* necessity of habits in justification was maintained, while their absolute necessity was rejected. That habits are implicated in the divine acceptation is a matter of theological contingency: nihil creatum potest esse ratio actus divini.[34] Biel, however, defends the traditional teaching on the rôle of created habits in justification with considerable skill. Particular attention should be paid to his argument that actual grace is inadequate to cope with the ravages of human sin: as God cannot accept indifferent or sinful acts, the *viator* would be required to avoid these totally at all times – which is clearly an impossibility. Biel stresses the reality of venial sin, and points out that the concept of *habitual* grace allows for a certain degree of indifference of sinfulness to coexist with acceptability.[35] It must be conceded, however, that the precise significance of the concept of created grace within the context of the soteriology of the *via moderna* is open to question, in that the theological foundations of the concept, laid in the earlier medieval period when the concept of ontological (i.e., *ex natura rei*) causality had been regarded as self-evident, appear to have been quite demolished through the application of the dialectic between the two powers of God and the concept of covenantal (i.e., *ex pacto divino*) causality. The arguments for the necessity of created grace originally rested upon the apparent necessity of created habits in effecting the transformation from *homo peccator* to *homo iustus* and his acceptance by God. The new emphasis upon the priority of acts over habits called this presupposition into question.

The theologians of the *schola Aegidiana* (i.e., the early school of theology within the Augustinian Order, based upon the teaching of Giles of Rome) taught that divine acceptation was contingent upon a created habit of grace. We have already noted this point in relation to Thomas of Strasbourg. This teaching is maintained by several later theologians of the Augustinian Order, such as Johannes von Retz: (nullus) potest esse formaliter carus vel gratus nisi informatus gratia a Deo creata.[36] The *schola Augustiniana moderna*, however, followed Scotus and the *via moderna* in teaching the priority of the act of divine acceptation over the possession of created habits. This development is associated with the theologian usually regarded as having established the theological foundations of the *schola Augustiniana moderna*, Gregory of Rimini.

Gregory distinguished two modes by which a soul is accepted by God:[37]

1. An *intrinsic* mode, by a habit of grace informing the soul;
2. An *extrinsic* mode, by which the divine will accepts the soul directly to eternal life.

Grace may therefore be understood either as an intrinsic created gift, or as the extrinsic divine acceptation. The former, however, must be regarded as contingent, in that God must be at liberty to do directly what he would otherwise do indirectly, through created intermediates. Thus God normally accepts the *viator* on the basis of created grace informing the soul: however, as God himself is the prime cause of the secondary cause of acceptation (i.e., the habit of created grace), he must be regarded as at liberty to bypass the intrinsic mode of acceptation altogether. Distinguishing between created and *un*created grace, Gregory argues that the uncreated gift itself (i.e., the Holy Spirit) is itself sufficient for acceptation without the necessity of any created form or habit. Gregory is thus able to maintain the possibility of a purely extrinsic justification by simple acceptation: a habit bestowed upon the *viator* does not bestow any benefits which cannot be attributed to the Holy Spirit himself.[38]

This logico-critical approach to the rôle of created habits in justification was developed by Hugolino of Orvieto, who is distinguished in other respects as being one of the most conservative anti-Pelagian theologians of the Augustinian Order.[39] Like Gregory, Hugolino was concerned to preserve the divine freedom in man's justification, particularly in relation to created habits. The primacy of acts over habits is maintained uncompromisingly: no created grace, whether actual or habitual, can render a man *gratus*, *carus*, or *acceptus ad vitam aeternam* before God as its formal effect. In common with Gregory, Hugolino regards the formal cause of justification to be the extrinsic denomination of the divine acceptation.[40] If the possession of a habit of charity were the formal cause of justification, Hugolino argues that it would follow that a creature (i.e., the created habit) would effect what was appropriate to the uncreated grace of the Holy Spirit, which is unthinkable. Hugolino thus assigns a minimal rôle to created habits in justification, tending to see justification as a direct personal act of God himself. Hugolino's extensive use of the dialectic between the two powers of God has raised the question of the influences of the *via moderna* upon his theology, although it is difficult to demonstrate the positive influence of the *via moderna* upon his theology.[41] Hugolino's views on divine acceptation appear to be derived from Scotus, probably *via* Gregory of Rimini, rather than from Ockham.

A similar critique of the rôle of created habits in justification can be shown to characterise the writings of later theologians of the Augustinian Order. Hugolino's teaching was developed by his junior in the

Order, Dionysius of Montina, who lectured on the *Sentences* at Paris in the academic year 1371–2.[42] A similar critique was developed by Alphonsus of Toledo.[43] Johannes Klenkok insisted that God could undoubtedly remit sin without the necessity for any created qualities within the soul: immo mihi plus valeret solus Deus me in via dirigens quam quaecumque tales qualitates.[44] A similar conclusion is drawn by Johannes Hiltalingen of Basel.[45] The position of Angelus Dobelinus is less certain, although he is clearly unhappy about the underlying rationale for the necessity of created habits in justification.[46] Dobelinus himself clearly attached considerably greater importance to the uncreated gift of the Holy Spirit than to created habits. In this, he may be regarded as having been followed by Johannes von Staupitz, who emphasised the priority of *gratia increata* over *gratia creata*: the movement of the soul towards God in justification is effected by none other than the Holy Spirit himself.[47] Indeed, there are grounds for suspecting that Staupitz may have abandoned the concept of a created habit of grace altogether.[48]

This late medieval critique of the rôle of created habits in justification, with an increased emphasis upon the rôle of uncreated grace in the person of the Holy Spirit, constitutes the background against which Luther's early critique of the rôle of habits in justification should be seen.[49] Luther argues that the habit required in justification is none other than the Holy Spirit: habitus adhuc est spiritus sanctus.[50] There is every reason to suppose that Luther's critique of the rôle of created habits in justification, and his emphasis upon justification as a personal encounter of the individual with God, reflects a general disquiet concerning the theological foundations of created grace, and a decisive shift away from created grace towards the uncreated grace of the Holy Spirit in the late medieval period.

The question of the nature of the formal, or immediate, cause of justification is of particular significance in three respects.

1. It permits the teachings of the early and later Franciscan schools on justification, which are in other respects very similar, to be distinguished.

2. It allows the *schola Aegidiana* to be distinguished from the *schola Augustiniana moderna*.

3. It emerged as an important issue in its own right at the Council of Trent. The Tridentine discussion of the question can only be understood in the light of the medieval discussion of the question.

4. The medieval schools of thought on justification

Introduction

The late eleventh and early twelfth centuries saw a remarkable advance and consolidation within the church and society as a whole, in literature, science, philosophy and theology.[1] In part, this renaissance must be regarded as a direct consequence of increasing political stability in western Europe, a fact which is recognised by several writers of the period, such as Andrew of St Victor: ab otiosis enim et in tempore otii et non a discurrentibus et perturbationis tempore sapientia discitur.[2] The rise of canonical theology had been greatly stimulated by the emergence of the church as a unifying social force during the Dark Ages, and its development was to reach its zenith during the twelfth century, under Gratian of Bologna and Ivo of Chartres. The Berengarian and Investiture controversies[3] further stimulated the need for systematic codification in theology. This need for theological development and codification was met by the monastic and cathedral schools, which quickly became the intellectual centres of a rapidly developing society. It is a simple matter to demonstrate that each of these schools developed its own particular and characteristic stance on theological and spiritual matters, and it is the purpose of the present chapter to document the different interpretations of the doctrine of justification which emerged from such schools in the medieval period.

The ninth century saw the development of St Gall, Reichenau, Tours, Mainz, Corbie, Laon and Reims as theological centres.[4] The rise of the great cathedral schools in the eleventh century appears largely due to the instructions issued in 1079 to his bishops by the reforming pope Gregory VII, to the effect that all bishops should 'cause the discipline of letters to be taught in their churches'.[5] By the year 1197, which witnessed the death of Peter the Chanter,[6] Paris had become established as the theological centre of Europe. During the course of the twelfth century, the Parisian schools of the Ile de la Cité and the abbeys of the Left Bank would far surpass in importance those of Leon, Chartres, Bec, Reims and Orléans, which had dominated the eleventh century. The rise of the Left Bank schools was largely a consequence of the migration of masters from the Ile de la Cité to evade the jurisdiction of the chancellor. The masters' practice of placing themselves under the jurisdiction of the independent congregation of St Geneviève would only receive formal papal authorisation in 1227, but was a widespread practice in the late twelfth century. The second half of the twelfth century was dominated by the schools based upon masters such as Peter Abailard, Gilbert of Poitiers, Peter Lombard and Hugh of St Victor. These schools were, however, of relatively little significance in connection with the development of the doctrine of justification, and as we have already noted their contributions in connection with individual aspects of this development in the previous chapter, we do not propose to discuss them any further.

A development which, though not theological in itself, was to have an incalculable effect upon the development of the medieval understanding of justification was the establishment of the Dominican and Franciscan schools at Paris in the early thirteenth century. The Friars Preachers arrived at Paris in 1218 and the Friars Minor the following year. Until the arrival of the friars at Paris, teaching at the University of Paris had been solely the responsibility of the secular clergy. Neither the Dominicans nor the Franciscans can be regarded as having come to Paris with the object of founding theological schools, which makes subsequent events all the more significant. By the year 1229, both Orders were established at their Parisian houses, at which they carried out teaching, in addition to their other work. Theology was taught at the university by secular masters, who held eight chairs of theology according to the decree of Innocent III of 14 November 1207.[7] By 1229, this number had risen to twelve, of which three were reserved for canons of Notre Dame.[8] In 1229 a dispute arose which led to the 'Great Dispersion' of masters and students between March 1229 and April 1231. Although the masters left Paris for other centres of study, the friars continued their work. As they were not subject to the normal university discipline, they were not obliged to join the general exodus. Among those who left Paris for Cologne was a certain Boniface, who left vacant his chair of theology. His place appears to have been taken by Roland of Cremona, a Dominican student of the secular master John of St Giles. Roland was granted his licence in theology by William of Auvergne, bishop of Paris, over the head of his chancellor. The second Dominican chair was established the following year, when John of St Giles himself entered the Dominican Order on 22 September 1230. This second chair of theology would thereafter be known as the 'external' chair, reserved for Dominican masters from outside Paris. The Franciscan chair was established in 1236 or 1237, when an English secular master, Alexander of Hales, caused a sensation by joining the Friars Minor. By 1237, therefore, three of the twelve chairs in theology at the University of Paris were reserved for members of the Dominican or Franciscan Orders. The establishment of these chairs may be regarded as marking the first phase of the conflict between the friars and the secular masters which was so characteristic a feature of the university during the thirteenth and fourteenth centuries: the secular masters appear to have been convinced that the friars deliberately remained in Paris during the Dispersion to take advantage of their absence.[9]

The significance of the University of Paris to our study may also be illustrated from the later medieval period, in that both the *via moderna* and the *schola Augustiniana moderna* were well represented in its faculties in the fourteenth and fifteenth centuries. The faculty of arts at Paris initially attempted to stem the influence of the *via moderna*: on 29 December 1340, a statute condemning the *errores Ockanicorum* took effect.[10] Henceforth any candidate wishing to supplicate for the degree of Master of Arts at Paris would have to swear that, in addition to being under the age of twenty-one and having studied arts for six years, he would observe the statutes of the faculty of arts *contra scientiam Okamicam*, and abstain from teaching such doctrines to his pupils.[11] The ineffectiveness of these measures may be judged from the career of the noted *modernus* Pierre d'Ailly, who was appointed chancellor of the university in 1389.[12] Paris would remain a stronghold of the *via moderna* until the sixteenth century. During the fourteenth century, the *schola Augustiniana moderna* appears to have become established at the university through the activity of Gregory of Rimini and his followers, such as Hugolino of Orvieto.[13] The historical significance of both these movements, however, is largely due to their influence upon the development of the Reformation in general, and the theology of Martin Luther in particular,[14] with the result that they are usually discussed with relation to the late medieval universities of Germany, rather than Paris itself.[15]

In the following sections, we shall characterise and compare the five main schools of thought on justification during the medieval period. In view of the importance of the *via moderna* and *schola Augustiniana moderna* to the development of the theology of the Reformation, we propose to consider these in more detail than the other three.

§14 The early Dominican school

On 24 June 1316, a decree of the provincial chapter of the Dominican Order in Provence was promulgated, stating that the works of Albertus Magnus, Thomas Aquinas and Peter of Tarantaise were to be regarded as normative in doctrinal matters.[1] Of these three doctors, however, it is clear that Thomas was regarded as pre-eminent: in 1313, the general chapter of the Order ruled that no friar of the Order was to be permitted to undertake theological studies at Paris without three years' study of the works of Thomas, and that no *lector* was to be permitted to mention opinions contrary to his teaching, unless such opinions were refuted immediately.[2] It will be clear, of course, that these rulings were made without apparent reference to the diversity of opinion which may be found within Thomas' writings, which we have noted during ·the course of the present study. Thus his doctrine of justification as stated in the *Commentary on the Sentences* (1252–6) is quite distinct from that stated in the *prima secundae* of the *Summa Theologiae* (1270), as noted above (see §§7, 9). There appears to have been some confusion within the early Dominican school as to which of these works should be used in ascertaining the authentic position of the Angelic Doctor. It may be pointed out that the distinctive contribution of Johannes Capreolus to the development of the later Thomist school was his insistence that the *Summa* represents the final determination and retraction of Thomas' earlier statements.[3]

Along with other Parisian masters of the period, Roland of Cremona is known to have developed an interest in Aristotle,[4] and this interest is reproduced by his successors within the early Dominican school. Of particular importance in this respect is his ontological interpretation of merit (see §10), and the definition of justification as a *motus* from sin to rectitude. The Aristotelian foundations of Thomas Aquinas' teaching on the *processus iustificationis* (see §5) and the necessity of a disposition towards justification (see §7) are particularly significant examples of the theological influence of the Stagirite over the theology of the early Dominican school. The positive estimation of Aristotle is one of the most prominent features of the early Dominican school, and is particularly evident when contrasted with the strong Augustinianism of the early Franciscan school.

One of the most important aspects of the early Dominican school's teaching on justification relates to the question of 'original justice', *iustitia originalis*. The thirteenth century witnessed considerable discussion of the question of whether the first man was created in a state of grace or a purely natural state. The general consensus in the earlier part of the period was that Adam was created in the integrity of nature, but not in a state of grace. If Adam received the gift of sanctifying grace, he did so voluntarily.[5] In his earlier works, Thomas Aquinas appears to register a hesitant disagreement with the opinion of Albertus Magnus on this question. It seems clear that Thomas favoured the opinion that Adam received grace at the instant of his creation, as judged from his discussion of the matter in the *Commentary on the Sentences*.[6] This opinion is unequivocally stated in the later disputed questions *de malo*,[7] where it is stated that *iustitia originalis*, which Adam received at the moment of his creation, included sanctifying grace (*gratia gratum faciens*).[8] This same view is put forward in the *Summa Theologiae*, in an important discussion of the Old Testament *locus* which usually constituted the point of departure for speculation on this matter: Deus fecit hominem rectum (Ecclesiastes 7.30).[9] What can this mean except that God created man, and then bestowed original justice upon him? The basis of this original justice must be considered to be the supernatural submission of the will to God, which can only be effected through sanctifying grace: radix originalis iustitiae, in cuius rectitudine factus est homo, consistat in subiectione supernaturali rationis ad Deum, quae est per gratiam gratum faciens.[10] This original justice pertains to the essence of the soul, and is inherent within man.[11] Thomas is careful to point out this does not amount to an equation of nature and grace.[12] For Thomas, the *status naturae integrae* is merely an abstraction: not even Adam could ever be said to have existed in this state, for at the instant of his creation he was endowed with the *donum supernaturale* of *gratia gratum faciens*. Although nature must be regarded as being good, it is nevertheless incomplete, and requires ordering towards its principal good (i.e., the enjoyment of God) through the aid of supernatural grace. It therefore follows that original sin may be formally defined as the privation of original righteousness. Although Thomas follows Albertus Magnus in adopting Anselm of Canterbury's definition of original sin as *privatio iustitiae originalis*, it is necessary to observe that he uses the term *iustitia* in a significantly different sense from Anselm.

The prime effect of the first sin, according to Thomas, is thus the instantaneous fall of Adam from the *supernatural* plane to which he had been elevated at the moment of his creation through *gratia gratum faciens* to the purely *natural* plane. The human nature which is transmitted to us from Adam is thus nature deprived of the supernatural gifts once bestowed upon Adam, but capable of receiving such gifts subsequently: anima naturaliter capax gratiae.

The general characteristics of the early Dominican school at Paris, as exemplified by Thomas Aquinas, may be summarised as follows.

1. The possibility of man meriting justification *de congruo* is rejected on the basis of the general principle that all merit presupposes grace. It must be pointed out that this opinion is characteristic of the *Summa Theologiae* but *not* of the earlier *Commentary on the Sentences*, in which a congruously meritorious disposition for justification is upheld. There appears to have been some confusion within the early Dominican school upon this matter.

2. The possibility of man knowing with absolute certitude whether he is in a state of grace is rejected.[13] God is totally beyond man's comprehension, and although the *viator* may know in a conjectural manner whether he has grace – e.g., by observing whether he takes delight in God – he cannot know *beyond doubt* whether he is in a state of grace. It may be noted that this represents the general medieval opinion on this question, rather than the peculiar teaching of the early Dominican school.

3. Original righteousness is understood to include the gift of sanctifying grace, so that the formal element of original sin may be defined as *privatio iustitiae originalis*.

4. The formal cause of justification is defined to be the habit of created grace.

5. The principle of merit is understood to be the habit of created grace.

6. The necessity of a human disposition towards justification is maintained, on the basis of the Aristotelian presupposition that motion implies premotion.

7. A strongly maculist position is adopted in relation to the conception of Mary.[14]

§15 The early Franciscan school

The early Franciscan school of theology owed its origins to its first great Parisian master, Alexander of Hales. The work which is generally known as the *Summa Fratris Alexandri*, long thought to be an authentic work of Alexander's, is now regarded as being composite.[1] Alexander's authentic lectures on the *Sentences*, generally considered to date from 1222–9, were discovered in the form of students' notes in 1946.[2] On the basis of these, and a series of disputed questions which antedate his joining the Franciscan Order, it is possible to argue that the main features of the early Franciscan school's teaching on justification are essentially identical with the early teaching of Alexander of Hales. In other words, Alexander does not appear to have modified his theology significantly upon joining the Friars Minor, and subsequent Franciscan masters perpetuated his teachings as the authentic teaching of their Order. This may be illustrated with reference to his teaching on original justice.

Alexander notes that there are two opinions concerning Adam's pristine state: the first is that he was created in a purely natural state; the second that he was created in a state of *gratia gratum faciens*.[3] The opinion adopted is a consequence of the interpretation of Ecclesiastes 7.30, *Deus fecit hominem rectum*. Alexander draws a distinction between natural and gratuitous justice, and argues that the verse in question clearly refers to a state of natural justice.[4] In this, he was followed by Odo Rigaldi, who taught that Adam was created in a state of purely natural justice and innocence, relying upon actual grace (*gratia gratis data*), rather than *gratia gratum faciens*.[5] Bonaventure similarly states that man was not endowed with *gratia gratum faciens* at his creation,[6] while recognising his endowment with *gratia gratis data*.

The characteristic features of the early Franciscan school's teaching on justification are the following.

1. The possibility of man meriting justification *de congruo* is upheld.
2. The possibility of absolute certitude of grace is rejected.
3. Original righteousness is understood to include the gift of actual grace; the opinion that the gift included *gratia gratum faciens* is rejected.
4. The formal cause of justification is understood to be a created habit of grace.
5. The formal principle of merit is understood to be a created habit of grace.
6. The necessity of a human disposition towards justification is maintained upon Augustinian psychological grounds.
7. A maculist position is adopted in relation to the conception of Mary.

The early Franciscan school can be shown to have found itself in difficulty towards the end of the thirteenth century in relation to its understanding of the relationship between nature and grace. The Augustinianism of the early school is not restricted to its soteriology and psychology, but extends also to its epistemology. The early Franciscan school adopted the Augustinian doctrine of divine illumination,[7] which is actually an elaboration of a metaphor which Augustine himself used in an attempt to explain how God makes himself understood to man. God is to the human mind what the sun is to the physical world. Just as a physical object cannot be seen without the light of the sun, so the mind is unable to perceive spiritual truths without divine illumination. Just as the sun is the source of the light by which man is able to see physical objects, so God is the course of the spiritual light by which man is able to apprehend divine truth. It will be evident that this concept betrays considerable affinity with the Platonic notion of the Good as the sun of the intelligible world. The fundamental difficulty which faced the early Franciscan proponents of divine illumination was that it was far from clear as to whether this illuminating influence of God was to be considered as a *natural* or *supernatural* light: was it *naturalia* or *gratuita*? Scotus' radical criticism of Henry of Ghent's illuminationism[8] led to the characteristically abstractionist epistemology of the later Franciscan school, and considerable unease concerning illuminationism may be detected in the final years of the early Franciscan school. Thus Peter Olivi stated that he supported the doctrine of divine illumination merely because it happened to be the traditional teaching of his order, while even Matthew of Aquasparta was unable to decide whether divine illumination counted as a 'somewhat general influence' or a 'special influence' of God. The essential problem underlying this question is that of the relationship between nature and grace, and it is precisely this difficulty which emerged from the early Franciscan discussion of the nature and necessity of a human disposition for justification. The essential difficulty facing the early Franciscan theologians was that the transition from nature to grace was *prima facie* impossible. The transition between opposites was held to be impossible without an intervening stage – but how is this *tertium quid* to be understood? The concept of *gratia gratis data* did not appear to resolve the difficulty, as the ontological chasm between nature and grace remained. It must be emphasised that this difficulty arises through the early Franciscan understanding of *iustitia originalis*: for the early Dominican school, man was *naturally* capable of grace, having been created with this facility; for the Franciscans, however, the possession of *gratia gratum faciens* was not included in the original endowment of nature. The problem of the ontological transition implicit in justification had not been resolved by the time Richard of Middleton's *Commentary on the Sentences* appeared at some point shortly after 1294. The period of the early Franciscan school may be regarded as closing at this point, in that a new approach to the problem was being developed which would avoid this difficulty. The solution of this difficulty, however, involved the abandonment of much of the earlier Franciscan pre-suppositions concerning the nature of grace and its rôle in justification, and the period of the later Franciscan school may thus be regarded as beginning at this point.

§16 The later Franciscan school

The early Franciscan school looked to Bonaventure for its inspiration and guidance; the latter Franciscan school substituted for him the colossal figure of Duns Scotus. Although there are undoubtedly Augustinian elements in Scotus' theology, it is quite clear that there has been a decisive shift away from Augustinianism towards a more Aristotelian metaphysics, particularly in connection with epistemological matters. Furthermore, Scotus' discussion of justification is quite distinct from that of Bonaventure at points of major importance, among which may be noted his teaching on the relationship between the elements of the *processus iustificationis* (see §5), on the possibility of extrasacramental justification (see §8), on the cause of predestination (see §12) and on the formal principle of merit and justification (see §13). This latter is of particular significance in relation to the major difficulty we noted in the previous section in connection with the early Franciscan school's teaching on the relationship between nature and grace. For Scotus, the volition of the end necessarily precedes the volition of the means to that end, so that the precise means by which justification occurs is of secondary importance to the fact that God has ordained that it *will* occur. The increasing emphasis upon the priority of the extrinsic denomination of the divine acceptation (see §13) over the possession of a habit of grace inevitably led to a marked reduction in interest in the question of how such a habit came about in the soul. Furthermore, Scotus' concept of covenantal causality eliminated the ontological difficulty felt by the theologians of the early Franciscan school over the possibility of the transition from nature to grace: for Scotus, God had ordained that this transition could be effected through a congruously meritorious disposition towards justification, so that there was no difficulty in abolishing the hiatus between the states of nature and grace. Scotus' approach to the question which posed such difficulties for his predecessors in the Franciscan Order may therefore be said to have resolved the problem in two ways. First, the question was discussed in a significantly different context: for Scotus, the divine acceptation was prior to the possession of a habit of grace, whereas the theologians of the early Franciscan school regarded divine acceptation as posterior to, and contingent upon, the possession of a habit of grace. Second, the *ex natura rei* concept of causality, which posed such difficulties for the theologians of the early Franciscan school, was replaced with an *ex pacto divino* concept, which eliminated the difficulty at once. These alterations, however, resulted in significant changes in Franciscan teaching on justification, which will be noted below.

Scotus' theology of justification, which may be regarded as characteristic of the later Franciscan school, has already been discussed at some length in terms of its individual aspects. There remains, however, one aspect of his teaching which was the subject of considerable confusion in the medieval period itself, and which requires further discussion. This is the question of the possibility of the certitude of grace. The Council of Trent witnessed a significant debate among the assembled prelates[1] over Scotus' teaching on this matter, reflecting the considerable difficulty in interpreting Scotus' pronouncements concerning it. This difficulty chiefly arises from the fact that Scotus never treats the matter *ex professo*, although he comments upon it briefly in his discussion of the possibility of extrasacramental justification (see §9). In general, however, it is clear that Scotus rejects the possibility of such certitude. A man who is conscious of having elicited an act of love for God is not able to conclude that he is in possession of an infused habit of charity as a result. He cannot deduce this from either the substance or the intensity of the act itself, nor from the pleasure or ease with which he elicits the act. If such a conclusion were possible, the *viator* could know for certain that he was in a state of charity.[2] It is, however, impossible for the *viator* to know whether he is worthy of love or hate. The impossibility of such certitude is particularly emphasised by Scotus in connection with the reception of the sacraments.[3] It may be concluded that Scotus adopts the general position of the twelfth and thirteenth centuries by declining to allow the *viator* anything other than *conjectural* certainty, and rigorously excluding the possibility of *absolute* certitude, of grace.

A development of major importance within the later Franciscan schools concerns the doctrine of the Immaculate Conception.[4] This doctrine is of subsidiary importance in relation to the development of the doctrine of justification, in that it relates to the extent of Christ's redeeming work. Prior to Scotus, there appears to have been a general maculist consensus. Thomas Aquinas states this consensus as follows: sanctificatio beatae virginis non potuit esse decenter ante infusionem animae quia gratiae capax nondum fuit, sed nec etiam in ipso instanti infusionis.[5] The most devastating argument against the concept of the Immaculate Conception, as used by the theologians of the early Dominican school, such as Albertus Magnus and Thomas Aquinas, is that the exemption of Mary from sin would limit the perfection of the work of Christ, who must be considered to have died for *all* mankind without exception. It is a reflection of Scotus' subtlety that he is able to turn this argument *against* the doctrine into an argument *for* it. If Christ is the most perfect redeemer, it must be conceded that he is able to redeem at least one person in the most perfect manner possible. As it is more perfect to preserve someone from sin than to liberate them from it, it follows that the most perfect mode of redemption is preservation from sin. Turning his attention to the pressing question of who that single person might be, Scotus argues that it is appropriate that the person concerned should be the mother of the redeemer himself.[6] Scotus' second argument in defence of the Immaculate Conception is the Anselmian principle that the highest possible honour consistent with scripture and tradition should be ascribed to Mary.[7]

Scotus' influence within the Franciscan Order was such that the doctrine of the Immaculate Conception had become the general teaching of the Order by the middle of the fourteenth century,[8] and rapidly became accepted within the *via moderna* and *schola Augustiniana moderna*. The doctrine is particularly useful in distinguishing the later Franciscan and Dominican schools of theology, although Dominican theologians associated with the *via moderna* – such as Robert Holcot – appear to have experienced some difficulty in accommodating the tension between the teaching of their *Orders* and their *schools*.[9]

The leading features of the later Franciscan school's teaching on justification may be summarised as follows:

1.   The possibility of man meriting justification *de congruo* is upheld.
2.   The possibility of absolute certitude of grace is rejected.

3. Original righteousness is understood to refer to the gift of actual, rather than habitual, grace.

4. The formal cause of justification is understood to be the extrinsic denomination of the divine acceptation. The intrinsic denomination of the created habit of charity is relegated to the status of a *secondary* formal cause of justification.

5. The formal principle of merit is understood to be the extrinsic denomination of the divine acceptation. Every act of man is worth precisely what God chooses to accept it for.

6. The necessity of a preparation for justification is upheld. The psychological justification for this preparation, associated with the earlier Franciscan school, appears to be abandoned.

7. Mary must be regarded as exempt from the common human condition of original sin, and thus as standing outside the scope of Christ's normal mode of redemption. This does not, however, mean that Scotus denies that Christ redeemed Mary, as some have suggested: rather, a different mode of redemption is envisaged in this specific case.

§17 The *via moderna*

In the present study, the term *via moderna* has been employed to refer to the theological school based upon the teachings of William of Ockham, including such theologians as Pierre d'Ailly, Robert Holcot, Gabriel Biel and Wendelin Steinbach. The term 'Nominalism' has frequently been employed in the past to designate this school, and we therefore propose to indicate the reasons for preferring the term *via moderna*.

Until recently, it was generally considered that pre-Reformation catholicism had been captured by a single school of 'Nominalism', which was everywhere in control of the teaching of Christian doctrine.[1] In part, the assertion of the dominance of this 'crippled parody of true scholasticism'[2] has arisen through the questionable presuppositions and methods of an earlier generation of Reformation historians, who tended to base their estimations of the nature of pre-Reformation catholicism solely upon studies of German academic theologians of the late fifteenth century, such as Gabriel Biel, in an attempt to elucidate the background against which the emergence of the theology of the young Luther must be understood. Unfortunately, the results of these early studies were applied uncritically to catholicism throughout Europe, on the unjustified and inherently unjustifiable assumption that the situation in the German universities accurately reflected late medieval theology in general.

This situation, however, is rapidly being remedied. A series of seminal studies have drawn attention to the astonishing diversity of theological opinion within the movement originally known as 'Nominalism', so that it is now recognised that it is quite improper to speak of a homogeneous 'Nominalist' theology in the first place. A series of studies published in the third and fourth decades of the present century drew attention to the existence of two diametrically opposed trends within 'Nominalism' in relation to the powers of human nature and the dynamics of grace.[3] Hence William of Ockham, Robert Holcot and Gabriel Biel came to be seen as promoting an optimistic view of human nature, allowing man a positive rôle in his own justification, while others, such as Marsilius of Inghen, Gregory of Rimini and Heinrich Totting von Oyta were critical of such views, asserting a doctrine of grace which must be considered to be more Augustinian in character. The most important monograph to appear during this early period was Cardinal Ehrle's justly celebrated study *Der Sentenzenkommentar Peters von Candia* (1925), in which the multiplicity of opinions within the allegedly homogeneous 'Nominalist' school of the fourteenth and fifteenth centuries was adequately demonstrated for the first time. On the basis of his studies, Ehrle argued that the term 'Nominalism' was sufficiently ill-defined as to be misleading.[4] This point was further emphasised by Lang, who pointed out that many of those who accepted Ockham's *philosophy* were considerably more sceptical concerning his *theology*,[5] so that the fact that a thinker of the fifteenth century held an Ockhamist epistemology could be not regarded as implying that he held a 'Nominalist' doctrine of justification. In a highly significant study, Hochstetter drew attention to the fact that it was improper to equate 'Nominalism' and 'Ockhamism' in the first place,[6] in that the term 'Nominalist' tended to be applied to the followers of Ockham *by their opponents*.

The term 'Nominalism' was first used in the twelfth century to refer to the anti-realist position on the question of universals, otherwise known as 'Terminism', and is used to designate an epistemological, rather than a theological, aspect of a writer's doctrine. As such, the term should be applied primarily to thinkers of the twelfth century: as Vignaux has pointed out, when a writer of the thirteenth century refers to the *nominales*, he has the logicians of the previous century in mind.[7] The term is not generally used to refer to Ockham by his contemporaries, although Ehrle notes that a condemnation of 1472 includes Ockham among the *nominales*.[8] It is, however, quite absurd to assume that Ockham's position on the question of universals should dictate the remainder of his philosophical and theological system, so that the epithet 'Nominalist' may be considered a convenient means of encapsulating his entire thought in a single term. The fundamental contention of nominalism or terminism, in its strict and proper epistemological sense, is that all things which exist to the mind are merely particulars: there is no genuine or objective identity in things which are not in themselves identical. This may be contrasted with the realist position, which concedes the existence of universals, arguing that the apparent situation is the real situation. It should be noted, of course, that realism and nominalism are not directly opposed, in that realism is effectively the *via media* between nominalism and universalism.[9] Thus Ockham's rejection of a 'common nature' and his emphasis upon the knowledge of the particular indicate a nominalist epistemology. But what, it may reasonably be asked, are the theological consequences of such an epistemology?

Elsewhere, we have shown how Ockham's nominalism is of significance in relation to his Christology.[10] Whereas the theologians of the *via antiqua* – such as the Albertists, Thomists and Scotists – found no difficulty with the concept of *humanitas* denoting a universal human nature, Ockham's nominalism required him to hold that it denotes individual *homines*. The point is well made by Martin Luther, who shares Ockham's terminism in this respect:

Terministen hieß man eine secten in der hohen schulen, unter welchen ich auch gewesen. Die selbigen haltens wider die Thomisten, Scotisten und Albertisten und hießen auch Occamisten von Occam, ihrem ersten anfenger, und sein die aller neuesten secten, und ist die mechtigste auch tzu Paris. Der hader war, ob *humanitas* und dergleichen wordt eine gemeine menscheit heiße, die in allen menschen were, wie Thomas und die andern halten. Ja, sagen die Occamisten oder Terministen, es sey nichtes mit solcher gemeiner menschheit, sondern der Terminus 'homo' oder menschheit heist alle menschen insonderheit, gleichwie ein gemalt menschen bilde alle menschen deutet.[11]

It is not, however, clear that such logical considerations in relation to the signification of terms have any bearing on the doctrine of justification. Thus Martin Luther, Gregory of Rimini,[12] Hugolino of Orvieto,[13] William of Ockham, Robert Holcot and Gabriel Biel may all be regarded as nominalists on the basis of the sole acceptable criterion – their position on the question of universals. It will, however, be evident that the six writers have very different doctrines of justification, the first three adopting radically Augustinian positions, and the remainder positions which approach, although do not strictly constitute, Pelagianism. This point serves to illustrate the general conclusion of modern late medieval scholarship, that there were many doctors who shared common nominalist epistemological presuppositions who otherwise had little, if anything, in common. The publication of an increasing number of theological treatises by *moderni* has made it abundantly clear that a nominalist epistemology (i.e., Terminism) can be associated with such an astonishing variety of theological positions that it conveys no useful information concerning a given 'Nominalist's' theology. Just as the theologians of an earlier period (such as the early Dominican and Franciscan schools) were generally realist, those of the later medieval period were generally nominalist. It is therefore necessary to find an acceptable alternative designation for theologians such as Ockham, Holcot and Biel.

How then, may the distinctive school of thought traditionally known as 'Nominalism' be designated? One possible way of avoiding the difficulties noted above is to define 'Nominalism' as the characteristic theological position of Ockham *cum suis*,[14] and ignore the fundamentally epistemological reference of the term. This pragmatic approach to the difficulty is, however, quite unacceptable, not least because it means that it inevitably perpetuates the myth of the homogeneity of late medieval thought. In addition, it will be clear that the specific meaning of the word 'Nominalism' will alter with each successive study of the thought of Ockham and his circle. Furthermore, it is important to establish whether writers who have traditionally been designated as 'Nominalists' through the questionable presuppositions and research methods of earlier generations of scholars actually merit the description in the first place, which evidently requires that some criterion be accepted for the purpose other than the loose descriptive definition suggested. Recent research, however has discredited this approach for a rather different, and totally unexpected, reason. In an important study, Schepers demonstrated that Oxford radical 'Nominalism' *was a specifically anti-Ockhamist movement*.[15] Robert Holcot and Adam Wodeham have now been identified as the chief proponents of Ockham's system after his departure from England in 1324, and the Dominican William of Crathorn and the Franciscan Walter Chatton as their radical opponents.[16] There is thus every reason to suppose that Ockhamism was a non-radical system, with Ockham being regarded as a reactionary by those who wished to develop his nominalism fully. If the term 'Nominalism' is employed to refer to the teachings of Ockham *cum suis*, it will therefore be clear that there were others with at least as great, and almost certainly a considerably greater, claim to represent a 'Nominalist' theology.

For reasons such as those we have outlined above, we refuse to employ the term 'Nominalist' in the present study, preferring to adopt the increasingly common alternative *via moderna*,[17] which refers primarily to a theological method, based on the application of the dialectic between the two powers of God and the concept of covenantal causality, rather than the *corpus* of doctrines resulting from its application. Although the theologians of the *via moderna* generally adopted a nominalist epistemology, in common with their contemporaries, their characteristic soteriological opinions were quite independent of this nominalism. The characteristic features of the doctrines of justification associated with the theologians of the *via moderna* are similar to those of the later Franciscan school. Despite the nominalism of the former and the realism of the latter, their doctrines of justification are substantially identical. Where differences exist between the two schools, they are primarily concerned with the *conceptual framework* within which the justification of the *viator* was discussed, rather than the *substance* of their teaching on justification. Indeed, the *via moderna* may be regarded as having exploited the dialectic between the two powers of God and the concept of the *pactum* (see §11) to place the teaching of the later Franciscan schools upon a firmer conceptual foundation. Furthermore, the differences which exist between the later Franciscan school and the *via moderna* in relation to the conceptual framework within which justification was discussed do not appear to have any *direct* bearing upon the epistemological differences between the schools.

The context within which the question of the possibility of the justification of the *viator* is set by the theologians of the *via moderna* is that of the *pactum* between God and man. God has ordained to enter into covenantal relationship with man by virtue of which he will accept human acts as being worthy of salvation, even though their intrinsic value is negligible. This distinction between the *intrinsic* and *imposed* value of moral acts is of decisive importance, as it permits the axiom *facienti quod in se est Deus non denegat gratiam* (see §7) to be interpreted in a sense which allows a man to play a positive rôle in his own justification, without elevating that rôle to Pelagian proportions. In this way, the theologians of the *via moderna* were able to maintain the teaching of both the early and later Franciscan schools concerning man's meritorious disposition towards justification, while establishing a conceptual framework within which this teaching could be safeguarded from the charge of Pelagianism. Linked with this was the related concept of *covenantal causality*, by which the theologians of the *via moderna* were able to avoid the ontological difficulties experienced by the early Franciscan school concerning the transition from nature to grace.

One aspect of the soteriology of the *via moderna* which is of particular interest is the Christological lacuna within their understanding of the economy of salvation.[18] It is quite possible to discuss the justification of the *viator* within the terms set by the theologians of the *via moderna* without reference to the incarnation and death of Christ. This point is best seen by considering the following question: what, according to the theologians of the *via moderna*, is the difference between the justification of man in the period of the Old Testament and in the period of the New? Biel's understanding of the covenant between God and man is such that God rewards the man who does *quod in se est* with grace, irrespective of whether this pertains under the old or new covenants. The Old Testament character of the ethics of the *via moderna* has frequently been noted:[19] it does not appear to have been fully appreciated, however, that this arises from the simple fact that the Old Testament scheme of justification is essentially the same as the New. Both the Old and the New Testaments hold out the promise of rewards to those who do good.[20] Whilst the new covenant abrogates the ceremonial aspects of the old, the moral law of the Old Testament remains valid.[21] Christ is therefore more appropriately described as *Legislator* than *Salvator*: Christ has fulfilled and perfected the law of Moses in order that he may be imitated by Christians.[22] Caritatem precipuit Christus legislator noster et tamquam signum suae legis ac discipulatus praestituit.[23] The justice which is required of man in order that he may be justified is the same in the Old and New Testaments: ubera hec due sunt partes iustitiae, declinare scilicet a malo et facere bonum.[24]

The characteristic features of the doctrines of justification associated with the *via moderna* may be summarised as follows. It must be emphasised that the following features pertain *de potentia Dei ordinata*.

1. The necessity of man meriting justification *de congruo* is maintained, this being regarded as effecting the transition between the moral and the meritorious planes within the terms of the *pactum*.

171

2.	The possibility of man knowing with absolute certitude whether he is in possession of grace is rejected, although various degrees of conjectural certainty are conceded. In view of the total reliability of the *pactum*, however, the uncertainty is understood to arise through man's inability to know whether he has done *quod in se est*.[25]

3.	Original righteousness is understood to include the gift of actual, but not sanctifying grace. The state of pure nature is thus understood to include the *influentia Dei generalis* alone.[26]

4.	The formal cause of justification is defined as the extrinsic denomination of the divine acceptation. It is not clear what rôle created habits play within the soteriology of the *via moderna* (see §13).

5.	The formal principle of merit is defined as the extrinsic denomination of the divine acceptation.

6.	The necessity of a human disposition towards justification is maintained, on the grounds that it constitutes the contracted link between the realms of nature and grace within the terms of the *pactum* – i.e., within the context of *ex pacto divino* causality, it functions as the cause of the infusion of grace. The difficulties associated with the early Franciscan school – which arise from an *ex natura rei* understanding of causality – are thus avoided.

7.	A strongly immaculist approach is generally adopted to the question of the conception of Mary.

§18 The medieval Augustinian tradition

In the previous section, we noted how the questionable presuppositions and methods of earlier generations of Reformation historians led to a distorted understanding of the nature and influence of the *via moderna*. A distorted impression of the 'medieval Augustinian tradition' has also arisen for similar reasons. The tendency on the part of an earlier generation of historians to approach the late medieval period with the concerns and presuppositions of the Reformation itself (particularly in relation to Martin Luther) resulted in the identification of 'Nominalism' and 'Augustinianism' as two theological movements within the later medieval period which were totally and irreconcilably opposed. In particular, the conflict between the 'Nominalism' of Gabriel Biel and the 'Augustinianism' of Johannes von Staupitz was assumed to be a general feature of the period between the death of Duns Scotus and Luther's revolt against the theology of Gabriel Biel in 1517. A study of the interaction between 'Nominalists' and 'Augustinians' in the fourteenth and fifteenth centuries, however, indicates that this dichotomy is more easily suggested than demonstrated. The highly questionable methods of earlier Reformation historiographers thus resulted in an estimation of pre-Reformation catholicism being deduced which reflects solely or largely the interests, concerns and presuppositions of modern Luther scholars.

Recently, this trend has been reversed, with increasing attention being paid to the theology of the later medieval period as a subject of importance in its own right, independent of its relation to the Reformation, with a considerable number of important studies being published on medieval Augustinian theologians.[1] As a result, we are now in a position to evaluate the nature and influence of the 'medieval Augustinian tradition'. In the present section, we propose to consider whether any 'medieval Augustinian tradition' can be identified with a coherent teaching on justification.

As noted in the previous section, there is a growing tendency to reject the idea of 'Nominalism' as a homogeneous school of thought during the later medieval period. It is not generally appreciated, however, that this has important consequences for the definition of 'Augustinianism' during the same period, in that the latter was usually *defined in relation to 'Nominalism'*. Once the idea of a homogeneous school of 'Nominalism' is rejected, the point of reference for the definition of 'Augustinianism' is removed. The vast amount of research undertaken on theologians of the Augustinian Order during the present century has made it clear that a dichotomy between 'Augustinianism' and 'Nominalism' is quite untenable. A phenomenally wide spectrum of theological opinions existed at the time, so that the use of the terms 'Nominalist' and 'Augustinian' *as correlatives* is now obviously inappropriate.

The situation has been still further confused by the variety of interpretations placed upon the term 'Augustinian' by historians and theologians alike. At least four senses of the term may be distinguished in writings of contemporary medieval scholarship.[2]

1. The theology of the Latin west in general, in so far as it represents a refraction of that of Augustine.
2. The theology of the Augustinian Order (i.e., the Order of the Hermits of St Augustine), whether this theology may happen to correspond to the teaching of Augustine or not. As used in this sense, the term 'Augustinian' has the same significance as 'Franciscan' or 'Dominican' (see §§14–16): an 'Augustinian' theology need therefore bear no relation to that of Augustine, just as that of

the early Franciscan school bears no relation to that of Francis or that of the early Dominican school to Dominic.

3. The theology of a specific group within the Augustinian Order, which corresponds to a greater extent with the teaching of Augustine.

4. A theology which corresponds to that of Augustine, particularly in relation to his teaching on original sin and predestination, irrespective of whether the theologian in question belonged to the Augustinian Order.

This confusion is particularly well illustrated by the attempt of A. V. Müller to demonstrate that Luther stood within a school of theologians which represented a theology more Augustinian than that of Thomas Aquinas or Bonaventure.[3] In particular, Müller argued that Luther's concept of *iustitia duplex* could be traced back to a theological school which included Simon Fidati of Cascia (d. 1348), Hugolino of Orvieto (d. 1373), Agostino Favaroni (d. 1443) and Jacobus Perez of Valencia (d. 1490).[4] A similar thesis was defended, although for rather different reasons, by Eduard Stakemeier, who argued that the doctrine of double justification associated with Girolamo Seripando during the Tridentine proceedings on justification represented an Augustinian theological tradition which could only be properly understood when set within the context of the theological tradition of the Augustinian Order – to which both Seripando and Luther belonged.[5] It is, however, quite impossible to sustain the thesis that both Luther and Seripando represent possible variations on a basically Augustinian theology of justification, in Stakemeier's sense of the term.[6] Not only does Luther's implacable hostility to the doctrine of double justification exclude such a thesis from the outset:[7] the important study of Henniger demonstrated that Augustine himself knew nothing of such a doctrine of double justification,[8] so that the use of the epithet 'Augustinian' was quite inappropriate to characterise Seripando's doctrine of justification. There are, in fact, serious difficulties attending *any* attempt to characterise the theology of any later medieval thinker as 'Augustinian' (in the sense of 'corresponding to the thought of Augustine himself'), as we shall make clear in what follows.

It is necessary to make a clear distinction between the *dogmatic content* of Augustine's theology, and the *terms and concepts* which he originally employed to express this content. In particular, it may be emphasised that Augustine's theological vocabulary was frequently developed in a polemical context, in conscious opposition to his

Pelagian or Donatist opponents, so that the form of his responses was frequently determined by the prior questions or objections of his opponents. An excellent example of this is provided by his distinction between operative and cooperative grace, which met the needs of the moment, but proved less valuable to his later interpreters. The theological renaissance of the twelfth century was almost entirely based upon the works of Augustine, as we have already noted. It soon became clear, however, that this involved the introduction of terms and concepts unknown to Augustine (such as the distinction between congruous and condign merit) in an attempt to preserve the *dogmatic content* of his theology, while expressing it in a more systematic form.

The essential point which we wish to make is the following: by the close of the thirteenth century, the dogmatic content of Augustine's theology had become expressed in terms and concepts unknown to Augustine himself. Once such developments had taken place, there was no real possibility of abandoning them. Thus the only theologians of the later medieval period who can lay claim to be 'Augustinian' in the strict sense of the term are those who were sufficiently reactionary, not merely to retain the dogmatic context of Augustine's theology, but also the terms in which he himself expressed it. However, as theologians who wished to express opinions closer to those of Augustine than their contemporaries were obliged to use the theological vocabulary of their day if they wished to engage in dialogue with their contemporaries, it will be evident that few, if any, 'Augustinian' theologians can be adduced.

The term 'Augustinian' must therefore be used in a qualified sense, signifying 'retaining the *dogmatic content*, if not the *conceptual forms*, of Augustine's theology'. There are, however, serious objections even to this modified definition of the term. For example, we have already drawn attention to the numerous pseudo-Augustinian works in circulation in the medieval period (see §7), many of which were clearly opposed to the teaching of Augustine on justification. Furthermore, the general tendency of the age to use collections of Augustinian 'sentences', rather than the original works of Augustine, inevitably led to Augustinian citations being used out of context, with an inevitable distortion in their meaning. An excellent example of this phenomenon has been noted in the cases of Duns Scotus and Gabriel Biel, who both manage to achieve a complete inversion of Augustine's teaching on the relation between grace and free will by confusing an image used by Augustine himself with a similar image found in the pseudo-Augustinian *Hypognosticon*.[9] Most significantly of all, the criterion of the 'Augustinianism' of a theologian usually employed in this context is his teaching on predestination and related matters, as noted above. This is open to question, as it appears to rest upon the presupposition that Augustine's doctrine of predestination is more characteristically 'Augustinian' than the remainder of his teaching, such as his doctrine of the church. Thus John Huss, usually identified as a late medieval 'Augustinian', may well justify this epithet in relation to his soteriology – yet his ecclesiology is radically non-Augustinian. It is this fundamental point which underlies the famous epigram: 'The Reformation, inwardly considered, was just the ultimate triumph of Augustine's doctrine of grace over Augustine's doctrine of the church.'[10]

The criterion usually employed in establishing the 'Augustinianism' of a theologian is whether he taught that anything in man himself could be said to cause his subsequent justification. The rejection of any such *ratio iustificationis ex parte creaturae* is usually taken as evidence of a theologian's 'Augustinianism'. This criterion, however, is open to question, as such a rejection may arise for thoroughly non-Augustinian reasons. This may be illustrated with reference to Thomas Bradwardine, who rejects the thesis that anything in man is the cause of his justification for the following reasons:

Prima, quod nihil potest quicquam movere sine Deo idem per se et proprie commovente. Secunda, quod nihil potest quicquam movere sine Deo immediate idem movente. Tertia, quod nihil potest quicquam movere sine Deo idem movente immediatius alio motore quocunque. Quarta, quod nulla propositio tribuens quodcunque creatum cuicunque causae secundae, est immediata simpliciter.[11]

God is the efficient, formal and final cause of everything which occurs concerning his creatures, so that the creature has no rôle to play in the causal sequence whatsoever. The reasons for Bradwardine's rejection of any *ratio iustificationis ex parte creaturae* are thus Aristotelian in nature, rather than Augustinian, and clearly raise questions relating to the rôle of the Fall in this theology. Man's need for grace is a consequence of his creatureliness, rather than his sinfulness as a result of the Fall. There is thus no fundamental difference between man's pristine and fallen states in this respect, as in both he is a creature. It is difficult to see how such a theologian can be deemed to be 'Augustinian', in view of the critical rôle of the Fall and human sin in Augustine's theology. It is almost certain that Gregory of Rimini, the great fourteenth-century theologian of the

Augustinian Order, singles out Bradwardine for special criticism for his un-Augustinian views on the Fall.[12] A more sustained critique of Bradwardine upon this point may be illustrated from the writings of other members of the Augustinian Order at the time, such as Johannes Klenkok, who studied at Bradwardine's university, Oxford, in the decades following the appearance of *de causa Dei*.[13] Klenkok's critique of Bradwardine is very similar to that of his fellow-Augustinian Hugolino of Orvieto:[14] both Augustinian theologians regarded Bradwardine as perpetrating a metaphysical determinism which owed nothing to Augustine. Similar criticisms were made by the later Augustinians Johannes Hiltalingen of Basel[15] and Angelus Dobelinus, the first professor of theology at the university of Erfurt.[16]

A more significant approach to the 'medieval Augustinian tradition' is to study theological currents prevalent within the Augustinian Order during the later medieval period. When this is done, it is possible to distinguish two main schools of thought within the Order during the period: the *schola Aegidiana* and the *schola Augustiniana moderna*. We shall consider these two schools individually.

The school of thought which developed during the fourteenth century, based upon the writings of Giles of Rome, was known as the *schola Aegidiana*,[17] suggesting that Giles was regarded as a theological authority by those who followed in his footsteps within the Order. Although the theory that members of the Augustinian Order were obliged to swear fidelity to the teachings of Giles of Rome at the time of their profession has not stood up to critical examination,[18] it is nevertheless clear that a school of thought developed within the Order which remained faithful to his teaching. This fidelity is particularly clear in relation to his teaching on original righteousness.[19] Thus Dionysius de Burgo regarded Giles of Rome and Thomas Aquinas as being theological authorities of equal importance, although his occasional preference for *doctor noster Aegidius* is noticeable.[20] Thomas of Strasbourg refers to Giles as *doctor noster*, and cites him with sufficient frequency to suggest that he regards him as a theological authority of some considerable weight.[21] Johannes von Retz, the second member of the Augustinian Order to become professor of theology at Vienna, cited both Giles of Rome and especially his follower Thomas of Strasbourg extensively.[22] Johannes Hiltalingen of Basel considered that the theologians of the Augustinian Order could be regarded as constituting a distinct theological school, although he neglected to mention which particular features were characteristic of this putative 'school'.[23] It seems, however, that the characteristic features of the *schola Aegidiana* are due to Giles of Rome himself, the strongly Augustinian character of his theology being slightly modulated with Thomism at points.[24] The strongly Augustinian cast of the *schola Aegidiana* may be particularly well seen in the emphasis placed upon the priority of *caritas* and *gratia* in man's justification.[25]

It seems, however, that the *schola Aegidiana* gave way to the *schola Augustiniana moderna* during the fourteenth century. It is generally accepted that the period of medieval Augustinian theology can be divided into two periods: the first encompassing the period between Giles of Rome and Thomas of Strasbourg, and the second the period between Gregory of Rimini and the early sixteenth century. The theologians of the Augustinian Order appear to have been significantly influenced by theological currents from outside their Order, as may be seen from their changing understandings of the nature of the conception of Mary. The earlier theologians of the *schola Aegidiana*, such as Giles of Rome, Albert of Padua, Augustinus Triumphus of Ancona and Gregory of Rimini were strongly maculist in their Mariological persuasions.[26] However, from the late fourteenth century onwards, the theologians of the Augustinian Order came to adopt the immaculist position. Thus beginning with Johannes Hiltalingen of Basel, Henry of Freimar, and Thomas of Strasbourg, and continuing into the fifteenth and early sixteenth centuries with Jacobus Perez of Valencia,[27] Johannes de Paltz[28] and Johannes von Staupitz,[29] the theologians of the Augustinian Order moved away from the teaching of the *schola Aegidiana* in this respect. Although similar divergences from other characteristic teachings of the *schola Aegidiana*, such as their understanding of *iustitia originalis*,[30] may also be detected, the most fundamental difference relates to the method employed in theological speculation.

In the previous section, we noted the emergence of the logico-critical attitudes of the *via moderna* within the German universities of the late fourteenth and early fifteenth centuries, and the resulting polarisation between *antiqui* and *moderni*. In the late fourteenth century, precisely such a polarisation between the methods and presuppositions of the *via antiqua* and *via moderna* took place within the Augustinian Order itself.[31] While the *antiqui* were primarily concerned with establishing accurately the opinions of writers such as Augustine on the basis of historico-critical studies, the *moderni* employed the logico-critical device of the dialectic between the two powers of God (see §12) to 'correct' such opinions.[32] One such 'correction' was the critique of the role of created habits in justification (see §13). Although the theologians of the *schola Aegidiana* held that the formal cause of justification was the created habit of grace, the theologians of the *schola Augustiniana moderna* adopted the characteristic position of the later Franciscan school and the *via moderna* – that the *ratio iustificationis* was the extrinsic denomination of the divine acceptation.[33] By the late fifteenth century, a theology of justification had developed within certain sections of the Augustinian Order which can only be regarded as a hybrid species, retaining much of the authentic theological emphases of Augustine (e.g., the emphasis upon man's depravity, and the priority of *caritas* in justification), while employing methods (such as the dialectic between the two powers of God) which owed more to the *via moderna*.[34] This point serves to emphasise the total futility of attempting to make a sharp distinction between 'Augustinian' and 'Nominalism' in the later medieval period: not only did many Augustinians adopt a nominalist epistemology (such as Gregory of Rimini and Hugolino of Orvieto) – they also incorporated significant elements of 'Nominalism' into their discussion of justification. Indeed, it may be argued that it is precisely this variation between individual 'Augustinian' theologians in relation to the extent to which they appropriated elements of 'Nominalism' which has caused such confusion in the present century concerning the characteristics of a putative school of 'Augustinian' theology in the medieval period.

It will therefore be clear that it is impossible to speak of a single homogeneous 'medieval Augustinian tradition' during the Middle Ages in relation to the doctrine of justification. Two such traditions may be identified:

1. The school of thought, often referred to as the *schola Aegidiana*, which is based upon the teaching of Giles of Rome, which understood the created habit of grace to be the *ratio iustificationis*.

2. The later school of thought, usually referred to as the *schola Augustiniana moderna*, mediated through Gregory of Rimini and Hugolino of Orvieto, which had serious reservations concerning the rôle of created habits in justification, and which placed increasing emphasis upon the uncreated grace of the Holy Spirit and the extrinsic denomination of the divine acceptation. It is within this latter tradition that Martin Luther's early critique of the rôle of created habits in justification should be understood.[35]

5. The transition from the medieval to the modern period

§19 Forerunners of the Reformation doctrines of justification?

It is clearly of considerable interest to establish the relationship between the doctrines of justification associated with the emerging churches of the Reformation of the sixteenth century and those associated with earlier periods in the history of doctrine. The historical importance of this question will be self-evident, in that the character, distinctiveness and final significance of any movement in intellectual history is invariably better appreciated when its relationship to comparable movements which preceded it are positively identified. It is for this reason that considerable attention is currently being directed towards establishing the precise relationship between the thought of the late medieval period and that of the Reformation. It must be appreciated, however, that scholarly interest in the *historical* aspects of the question concerning the continuity of the late medieval and Reformation periods has tended to obscure the theological aspect of the question, which was considered to be more significant at the time of the Reformation itself. The fundamental theological question which is thus raised is the following: can the teachings of the churches of the Reformation be regarded as truly catholic?[1] In view of the centrality of the doctrine of justification to both the *initium theologiae Lutheri* and the *initium Reformationis*,[2] this question becomes acutely pressing concerning the doctrine of justification itself. If it can be shown that the central teaching of the Lutheran Reformation, the fulcrum about which the early Reformation turned, the *articulus stantis et cadentis ecclesiae*,[3] constituted a theological *novum*, unknown within the previous fifteen centuries of catholic thought, it will be clear that the Reformers' claim to catholicity would be seriously prejudiced, if not totally discredited.

The question of the historical continuity between the teaching of the churches of the Reformation and that of earlier periods in relation to justification thus became acutely pressing. For the Roman Catholic opponents of the Reformation, such teachings represented theological innovations. For Bossuet, the Reformers had significantly altered the common teaching of the catholic church upon this central doctrine and by doing so, had forfeited their claims to orthodoxy and catholicity:

The church's doctrine is always the same ... the Gospel is never different from what it was before. Hence, if at any time someone says that the faith includes something which yesterday was not said to be of the faith, it is always *heterodoxy*, which is any doctrine different from *orthodoxy*. There is no difficulty about recognising false doctrine: there is no argument about it: it is recognised at once, whenever it appears, merely because it is new.[4]

This was such a serious charge that the theologians of the Reformation were obliged to meet it, which they did in two manners.

1. The claim was rejected out of hand, it being asserted that the Reformation represented a long-overdue return to the truly catholic teaching of the church, which had become distorted and disfigured through the questionable theological methods of later medieval theology. Particular emphasis was laid upon the alleged concurrence of the Reformation teachings on justification with those of Augustine.[5]

2. The claim was conceded, to varying extents, but was qualified in an important respect. The doctrines of justification associated with the Reformation only represent innovations if orthodoxy is determined by the decrees of the corrupt late medieval church. A dichotomy was posited between the corrupt official teaching of the church, and the faithful catholic teaching of individual 'proto-Reformers', which would eventually triumph at the time of the Reformation.[6] It is this thesis which is usually stated in terms of the existence of 'Forerunners of the Reformation'.[7] In the present section, we are particularly concerned with the historical task of establishing areas of continuity and discontinuity between the late medieval period and that of the Reformation. In view of the theological importance of the question, however, we shall examine both of the positions identified above.

From the analysis of the late medieval schools of thought on justification presented in the present study, it will be clear that there existed considerable diversity of opinion on the matter during the later medieval period. This diversity represents a particular instance of the general pluralism of late medieval religious thought, which is usually argued to originate from the fourteenth century.[8] The

Tridentine decree on justification may be regarded as an attempt to define the limits of this pluralism, if not to impose a unity upon it.[9] But are the characteristic features of the Reformation doctrines of justification foreshadowed in the doctrinal pluralism of the late medieval period? Before attempting to answer this question, the characteristic features of such teachings must first be identified.

The first era of the Reformation witnessed a broad consensus emerging upon both the *nature* of justification and the *context* in which it was set. The following three features are characteristic of Protestant understandings of the *nature* of justification over the period 1530–1730:[10]

1. Justification is understood to be the forensic declaration that the Christian is righteous, rather than the process by which he is made righteous, involving a change in his *status* before God, rather than his *nature*.

2. A deliberate and systematic distinction is made between the concept of *justification* itself (understood as the extrinsic divine pronouncement of man's new status) and the concept of *sanctification* or *regeneration* (understood as the intrinsic process by which God renews the justified sinner).

3. The formal, or immediate cause, of justification is understood to be the alien righteousness of Christ, imputed to man in justification, so that justification involves a *synthetic* rather than an *analytic* judgement on the part of God.

In defining these features as characteristic of Protestant understandings of justification, it must be emphasised that neither Martin Luther nor Huldrych Zwingli understood justification in precisely this manner. The consolidation of these features as characteristics of Protestantism appears to have been achieved through the considerable influence of Philip Melanchthon. It is nevertheless clear that Luther's doctrine of the *iustitia Christia aliena* laid the conceptual foundation for such a doctrine of forensic justification.[11] In effect, Luther must be regarded as a figure of transition, standing at the junction of two rival understandings of the nature of justification. As we demonstrated earlier (see §5), the medieval theological tradition was unanimous in its understanding of justification as both an act and a process, by which both man's status *coram Deo* and his essential nature underwent alteration. Although Luther regarded justification as an essentially unitary process, he nevertheless introduced a decisive break with the western theological tradition as a whole by insisting that, through his justification, man is *intrinsically* sinful yet *extrinsically* righteous.[12] It is at this point that it is possible to distinguish the otherwise similar teachings of Luther and Johannes von Staupitz on justification.[13]

It must be emphasised that it is totally unacceptable to characterise the doctrines of justification associated with the Reformation solely with reference to their anti-Pelagian character, or their associated doctrines of predestination. Although an earlier generation of scholars argued that the Reformation resulted from the sudden rediscovery of the radical anti-Pelagianism of Augustine's soteriology, it is clear that this judgement cannot be sustained. The emergence of the *schola Augustiniana moderna* (see §18) in the fourteenth century was essentially an academic movement based upon the anti-Pelagian writings of Augustine,[14] and the possibility that both Calvin and Luther, as well as other Reformers such as Peter Martyr Vermigli, demonstrate continuity with this late medieval Augustinian school calls this judgement into question.[15] In its radical anti-Pelagianism, the Reformation, in its first phase, demonstrated a remarkable degree of continuity with well-established currents in late medieval thought. This is not, of course, to say that the Reformation was *typical* of the late medieval period, but merely to observe that the Reformation demonstrates strong affinities with one of the many theological currents which constituted the flux of late medieval theology. Equally, the Reformers unhesitatingly rejected the necessity of created habits of grace in justification, a tendency which is evident from Luther's *Randbemerkungen* of 1509–10 onwards.[16] By doing so, they reflected the general tendency of the period, particularly within the *via moderna* and *schola Augustiniana moderna*, to locate the *ratio iustificationis* primarily in the extrinsic denomination of the divine acceptation (see §13). The covenantal, rather than ontological, and voluntarist, rather than intellectualist, foundations of late medieval theology may also be argued to have passed into the theology of the first phase of the Reformation. It will therefore be clear that many of the fundamental presuppositions of the soteriology of the late medieval period passed into the early theology of the Reformation. Within the flux of late medieval theology, currents may easily be identified which demonstrate various degrees of continuity with the emerging theologies of justification associated with the first phase of the Reformation.

These areas of continuity, nevertheless, relate to the *mode* of justification, rather than to its *nature*. Despite the disagreement within the various theological schools concerning the manner in which justification came about, there was a fundamental consensus on what the term 'justification' itself signified. Throughout the entire medieval period, justification continued to be understood as the process by which a man is made righteous, subsuming the concepts of 'sanctification' and 'regeneration'. *Iustificare* was understood to signify *iustum facere* throughout the period. Albrecht Ritschl is thus correct when he states that:

> We shall ... search in vain to find in any theologian of the Middle Ages the Reformation idea of justification – the deliberate distinction between justification and regeneration ... Their deliberate treatment of the idea of justification proceeds rather on the principle that a real change in the sinner is thought of as involved in it – in other words, the Reformation distinction between the two ideas is at the outset rejected.[17]

The significance of the Protestant distinction between *iustificatio* and *regeneratio* is that a fundamental discontinuity has been introduced into the western theological tradition *where none had existed before*. Despite the astonishing theological diversity of the late medieval period, a consensus relating to the *nature* of justification was maintained throughout. The Protestant understanding of the *nature* of justification represents a theological *novum*, whereas its understanding of its *mode* does not. It is therefore of considerable importance to appreciate that the *criterion employed in the sixteenth century* to determine whether a particular doctrine of justification was Protestant or otherwise was *whether justification was understood forensically*. The fury surrounding the Osiandrist controversy only served to harden the early Protestant conviction that any doctrine of justification by inherent righteousness was inherently anti-Protestant.[18] The history of the Reformation itself, especially as it concerns Osiander and Latomus, demonstrates that the criterion employed *at the time* to determine whether a given doctrine was Protestant or otherwise primarily concerned the manner in which justifying righteousness was understood. It would therefore appear to be historically unsound to use any other criterion in this respect.

Once this point is conceded, we may return to a consideration of the two main lines of defence of the catholicity of Protestant doctrines of justification encountered during the first phase of the Reformation. The first such approach, which is particularly associated with Philip Melanchthon, is to argue that the Reformation understandings of justification represent a legitimate interpretation of the theology of Augustine, so that the Lutheran Reformation may be regarded as recovering the authentic teaching of the African bishop from the distortions of the medieval period.[19] However, it will be clear that the medieval period was astonishingly faithful to the teaching of Augustine on the question of the nature of justification, where the Reformers departed from it. Melanchthon himself appears to have been unaware of this point, as Latomus pointed out with some force.[20] A more forceful statement of the same position is associated with the Scottish Protestant polemicist James Buchanan (1804–70), who declared his intention to:

prove as a matter of FACT . . . that the Protestant doctrine of justification was not a 'novelty' introduced for the first time by Luther and Calvin . . . and that there is no truth in the allegation that it had been unknown for fourteen hundred years before the Reformation.[21]

Thus he indignantly rejects any suggestion that the Reformers were theological innovators, or that 'Augustine knew nothing of a forensic justification by faith', teaching instead 'the opposite doctrine of a "moral" justification by infused or inherent righteousness'.[22]

If the catholicity of Protestant understandings of the nature of justification is to be defended, it is therefore necessary to investigate the possible existence of 'Forerunners of the Reformation doctrines of justification' – i.e., writers from the later medieval period itself who, in conscious opposition to what they deemed to be the corrupt teaching of the contemporary church, foreshadowed the teaching of the Reformers on the point at issue. Although this approach yields valuable results in the area of sacramental theology and ecclesiology, particularly in connection with the opinions of Wycliffe and Huss, it fails in relation to the specific question of the nature of justification and justifying righteousness. It is, of course, possible to argue that later medieval teaching on *predestination* establishes the case for 'Forerunners of the Reformation doctrines of justification'.[23] However, as we shall indicate below, this appears to rest upon a fallacy.

In an important study, Oberman argued that Dettloff was unable to distinguish the 'nominalistic' and 'scotistic' traditions on justification (i.e., the teachings of the *via moderna* and the late Franciscan school)

because he concentrated on the doctrine of justification, which in the late medieval sources is always associated and connected with a discussion of predestination. These differences do not appear in an analysis of the *content* of statements on justification, but rather in the different *context* of justification, namely, in the diverging ways of understanding the doctrine of predestination.[24]

This point is unquestionably valid: precisely because there was a fundamental continuity within the medieval tradition concerning the *content* of justification, differences between theologians had to be sought elsewhere, in their discussion of its *context*. It may, however, be noted that analysis of the doctrine of predestination does not exhaust an analysis of a writer's views on the context of justification, which must also be regarded as including his statements concerning the possibility or otherwise of extrasacramental justification. Nevertheless, this cannot be regarded as an adequate scholarly foundation for dealing with the relationship between the doctrines of justification of the late medieval period and the Reformation – precisely because there exist such significant differences between their understandings of the *nature* of justification that an inquiry into its *mode* is no longer necessary. The appeal to writers' statements concerning *predestination* in an attempt to elucidate their doctrines of *justification* is legitimate *only when their statements are otherwise indistinguishable*. In the case of the later Franciscan school and the *via moderna*, such statements are near-identical (see §§16, 17), so the appeal is proper. Nevertheless, in the case of late medieval theology and the theology of the first phase of the Reformation, statements concerning justification are immediately distinguishable without the necessity of appealing to their statements concerning predestination. In this case, there is a remarkable degree of continuity between the statements of certain strands of late medieval thought (e.g., the *schola Augustiniana moderna*) and that of the Reformation, despite the fact that their statements pertaining to the *content*, as opposed to the *context*, of justification (to use Oberman's terms) are grossly different. It will therefore be clear that the application of this method to study the continuity between the thought of the later medieval period and the first phase of the Reformation is seriously misleading, as well as being unjustifiable.

The essential feature of the Reformation doctrines of justification is that a deliberate and systematic distinction is made between *justification* and *regeneration*. Although it must be emphasised that this distinction is purely notional, in that it is impossible to separate the two within the context of the *ordo salutis*, the essential point is that a notional distinction is made where none had been acknowledged before in the history of Christian doctrine. A fundamental discontinuity was introduced into the western theological tradition where none had ever existed, or ever been contemplated, before. The Reformation understanding of the *nature* of justification – as opposed to its *mode* – must therefore be regarded as a genuine theological *novum*.

Like all periods in the history of doctrine, the Reformation demonstrates both continuity and discontinuity with the period which immediately preceded it. Chief among these discontinuities is the new understanding of the nature of justification, whereas there are clearly extensive areas of continuity with the late medieval theological movement as a whole, or well-defined sections of the movement, in relation to other aspects of the doctrine, as noted above. That there are no 'Forerunners of the Reformation doctrines of justification' has little theological significance today, given current thinking on the nature of the development of doctrine, which renders Bossuet's static model, on which he based his critique of Protestantism, obsolete. Nevertheless, the historical aspects of the question continue to have relevance. For what reasons did the Reformers abandon the catholic consensus on the nature of justification? We shall discuss this matter in our study of the development of the doctrine from the Reformation to the present day.

6. The development of the doctrine in the Reformation period

Introduction

The leading principle of the Reformation is generally considered to be its doctrine of justification.[1] This is not, in fact, correct. It is certainly true that the *articulus iustificationis* is the leading feature of the theology of Martin Luther,[2] and that his enormous influence over the evangelical faction within Germany and elsewhere inevitably led to this high estimation being reflected elsewhere. Thus by the beginning of the seventeenth century the *articulus iustificationis* appears to have been generally regarded as the *articulus stantis et cadentis ecclesiae*, the 'article by which the church stands or falls'.[3] Nevertheless, as will become clear in the present study, the origins of the Reformed church owe little, if anything, to Luther's insights into justification. The relation between Luther's own theological insights and the dawn of the Reformation itself is now appreciated to be an historical question of the utmost complexity,[4] and it must be emphasised that it is no longer possible to assert with any degree of certainty that the Reformation began as a consequence of Luther's new insights into man's justification *coram Deo*, although it is unquestionably true that Luther's own personal theological preoccupations centred upon this matter. The present chapter is concerned with the documentation and critical analysis of the understandings of justification associated with the Reformation in Germany and Switzerland – in other words, with the origins and subsequent development of the Lutheran and Reformed churches. In view of the crucial importance of the development of Martin Luther's theological insights to any account of the origins of the Reformation, we begin by considering his break with the theology of the medieval period associated with his 'discovery of the righteousness of God', and the leading features of his doctrine of justification.

The Reformation is often portrayed as a rediscovery of the Bible, particularly of the Pauline corpus. Although there is undoubtedly truth in this description, it is considerably more accurate to portray it as a rediscovery of Augustine's doctrine of grace, with a subsequent critique of his doctrine of the church.[5] In an age which witnessed a general revival of Augustinian studies,[6] this new interest in Augustine must be regarded as an aspect of the Renaissance in general, rather than a feature peculiar to the Reformers. What was unquestionably new, however, is the use to which the Reformers put Augustine. The most accurate description of the doctrines of justification associated with the Reformed and Lutheran churches from 1530 onwards is that they represent a radically new interpretation of the Pauline concept of 'imputed righteousness' set within an Augustinian soteriological framework. The leading primary characteristics of Protestant doctrines of justification, as established from the literary output of the theologians of the Lutheran and Reformed churches over the period 1530–1700, may be summarised as follows:

1. Justification is defined as the forensic *declaration* that the believer is righteous, rather than the process by which he is *made* righteous, involving a change in his *status* rather than his *nature*.

2. A deliberate and systematic distinction is made between *justification* (the external act by which God declares the sinner to be righteous) and *sanctification* or *regeneration* (the internal process of renewal within man). Although the two are treated as inseparable, a notional distinction is thus drawn where none was conceded before.

3. Justifying righteousness, or the formal cause of justification, is defined as the alien righteousness of Christ, external to man and imputed to him, rather than a righteousness which is inherent to him, located within him, or which in any sense may be said to belong to him. God's judgement in justification is therefore *synthetic* rather than *analytic*, in that there is no righteousness within man which can be considered to be the basis of the divine verdict of justification; the righteousness upon which such a judgement is necessarily based is external to man.

It is clearly of importance to account for this new understanding of the nature of justifying righteousness, with its associated conceptual distinction between justification and sanctification. Attempts on the part of an earlier generation of Protestant apologists to defend this innovation as a recovery of the authentic teaching of Augustine, and of their Catholic opponents to demonstrate that it constituted a vestige of a discredited and ossified Ockhamism, can no longer be taken seriously. It is the task of the historian to account for this new development, which marks a complete break with the tradition up to this point.[7]

It must be made clear that it is quite inadequate to attempt to characterise the doctrines of justification associated with the Reformation by referring merely to their anti-Pelagian structure. Such doctrines of justification can be adduced from practically every period in the history of doctrine, particularly in the later medieval period (such as within the *schola Augustiniana moderna*). The notional distinction, necessitated by a forensic understanding of justification, between the external act of God in pronouncing sentence, and the internal process of regeneration, along with the associated insistence upon the alien and external nature of justifying righteousness, must be considered to be the most reliable *historical* characterisation of Protestant doctrines of justification. As the Osiandrist controversy made clear, an anti-Pelagian doctrine of justification could still be rejected as unrepresentative of the Reformation *if justifying righteousness was conceived intrinsically*. Indeed, precisely this controversy may be considered to have exercised a decisive influence in establishing the concept of forensic justification as characteristic of the Reformation. As the history of the Reformation itself demonstrates, the criterion employed at the time to determine whether a given doctrine of justification was Protestant or not was whether justifying righteousness was conceived extrinsically. This criterion served to distinguish the doctrines of justification associated with the magisterial Reformation from those of Catholicism on the one hand, and the radical Reformation on the other.[8]

In view of the significance of the concept of the imputation of righteousness both as an idea itself, and as a criterion of the Protestant character of a doctrine of justification, much of the present chapter is concerned with documenting its development within the churches of the Reformation. The importance of the concept is also reflected in other parts of the present volume, particularly in the attention paid to the late sixteenth- and early seventeenth-century disputes over the formal cause of justification.

The present chapter begins by documenting Martin Luther's break with the soteriology of the *via moderna*, traditionally regarded as marking a pivotal point in the history of the Reformation.

§20 Luther's discovery of the 'righteousness of God'

In an earlier section (§6), we drew attention to the fact that in the period 1508–14 the young Luther appears to have adopted an understanding of the 'righteousness of God' essentially identical to that of the *via moderna*. The continuities between the young Luther and late medieval theology over the period 1509–14 include several matters of significance to his understanding of justification. Thus the young Luther rejected the implication of supernatural habits in justification,[1] following both the *via moderna* and the *schola Augustiniana moderna* in doing so (see §13). Of particular importance is the observation that in this period he developed an understanding of man's involvement in justification which is clearly based upon the *pactum*-theology of the *via moderna*,[2] and the interpretation of the axiom *facienti quod in se est Deus non denegat gratiam* characteristic of this school of thought.[3] Over the period 1514–19, however, Luther's understanding of justification underwent a radical alteration. The nature and date of this alteration have remained a matter of controversy within contemporary Luther scholarship, justifying extensive discussion of the question in the present section.

One of the most important sources for our understanding of this radical alteration in Luther's doctrine of justification is the 1545 autobiographical fragment,[4] in which Luther records his intense personal difficulties over the concept of the 'righteousness of God'.

Interim eo anno [1519] iam redieram ad Psalterium denuo interpretandum, fretus eo, quod exercitatior essem, postquam S. Pauli Epistolas ad Romanos, ad Galatas, et eam, quae est ad Ebraeos, tractassem in scholis. Miro certe ardore captus fueram cognoscendi Pauli in epistola ad Rom., sed obstiterat hactenus non frigidus circum praecordia sanguis, sed unicum vocabulum, quod est Cap. 1: Iustitia Dei revelatur in illo. Oderam enim vocabulum istud 'Iustitia Dei', quod usu et consuetudine omnium doctorum doctus eram philosophice intelligere de iustitia (ut vocant) formali seu activa, qua Deus est iustus, et peccatores iniustosque punit.[5]

The modern preoccupation of scholars with this autobiographical fragment dates from 1904, when the distinguished Catholic historian Heinrich Denifle argued that Luther's discussion of the term *iustitia Dei* indicated a near-total theological ignorance and incompetence.[6] In a remarkable appendix to his intensely hostile study of the development of Lutheranism, Denifle produced a detailed analysis of the exposition of Romans 1.16–17 by some sixty doctors of the western church, indicating that not one of them, from Ambrosiaster onwards, understood *iustitia Dei* in the sense Luther notes in the above citation.[7] However, the conclusion which Denifle drew from this demonstration – that Luther was either ignorant of the Catholic tradition, or else deliberately perverted it – was clearly unjustified.

Luther made no global reference to the tradition of the western church upon the matter, but referred specifically to the doctors who taught *him* – an unequivocal reference to the *moderni* at Erfurt, under whom he received his initial theological education. There is every indication that Luther is referring to the specific concept of *iustitia Dei* associated with the *via moderna*: God is *iustus*, in the sense that he rewards the man who does *quod in se est* with grace, and punishes the man who does not. In view of Gabriel Biel's unequivocal assertion that man cannot know for certain whether he has, in fact, done *quod in se est*,[8] there is clearly every reason to state that Luther's early concept of *iustitia Dei* was that of the righteousness of an utterly scrupulous and impartial judge, who rewarded or punished man on the basis of an ultimately unknown quality. The autobiographical fragment clearly indicates that Luther's difficulties over the concept of the 'righteousness of God' were resolved *by* (although not necessarily *in*) the year 1519.[9] An analysis of Luther's lectures on the Psalter (1513–15), on Romans (1515–16), and on Galatians (1516–17)[10] indicates that Luther's understanding of this theologoumenon in particular, and his theology of justification in general, appears to have undergone a significant alteration over the period 1514–15, with the crucial step apparently dating from 1515.

Luther's early understanding of justification (1513–14) may be summarised as follows: man must recognise his spiritual weakness and inadequacy, and turn in humility from his attempts at self-justification to ask God for his grace. God treats this humility of faith (*humilitas fidei*)[11] as the precondition necessary for justification under the terms of the *pactum* (that is, as man's *quod in se est*), and thus fulfils his obligations under the *pactum*, by bestowing grace upon him.[12] It is clear that Luther understands man to be capable of making a response towards God without the assistance of special grace, and that this response of *iustitia fidei* is the necessary precondition (*quod in se est*) for the bestowal of justifying grace.[13] Although some Luther scholars have argued that Luther's understanding of the term *iustitia Dei* appears to have undergone a significant alteration during the course of his exposition of Psalms 70 and 71,[14] it is clear that Luther has merely clarified the terminology within his *existing* theological framework, so that the precise relationship of the various *iustitiae* (specifically, the *iustitia* which man must possess if he is to be justified (that is, *iustitia fidei*) and the *iustitia* by which God is obliged to reward this righteousness with grace (that is, *iustitia Dei*)) implicated in the process of justification is clarified.[15]

Luther still expounds with some brilliance the *pactum*-theology of the *via moderna*.

A decisive break with this theology of justification is evident in the Romans lectures of 1515–16. Three major alterations may be noted, leading to this break. First, Luther insists that man is *passive* towards his own justification.[16] Although not denying that man has *any* rôle in his justification, Luther clearly states that man is not capable of initiating the process leading to justification. Whereas in the *Dictata super Psalterium*, man was understood to be *active* in the process of his justification (in that he was able to turn to God in humility and faith, and cry out for grace), Luther now unequivocally states that it is God who turns man towards him.[17] Second, he insists that man's will is held captive by grace, and is incapable of attaining righteousness unaided by divine grace.[18] One should speak of *servum potius quam liberum arbitrium*, as Augustine reminded Julian of Eclanum (§§4, 7). Third, and perhaps most significant of all, Luther states that the idea that man can do *quod in se est* is nothing more and nothing less than Pelagian, even though he once held this position himself.[19] Despite the fact that his theology of justification up to this point was based upon the explicitly stated presupposition that man was capable of doing *quod in se est*, he now concedes the Pelagianism of the opinion that salvation is dependent upon a decision of the human will.[20] Even though he continues to identify *fides* and *humilitas* for some time to come, it is clear that a genuine and radical alteration in his theology of justification has taken place. Although he may not have arrived at any dramatically new understanding of the *nature* of faith, he has certainly arrived at a radically new understanding of *how faith comes about in the first place*.

The recognition that God bestows the precondition of justification upon man inevitably involves the abandonment of the soteriological framework underlying the *pactum*-theology of the *via moderna*. Luther's early interpretation of *iustitia Dei* was based upon the presupposition that God, in his equity (*equitas*) rewarded the man who had done *quod in se est* with justifying grace, *sine acceptione personarum*. The divine judgement is based solely upon the divine recognition of an individual's possessing a quality which God is under an obligation to reward. If God himself bestows this quality upon man, the framework of *equitas* and *iustitia* essential to the *pactum*-theology of the *via moderna* and the young Luther can no longer be sustained, in that God is open to the charge of *inequitas*, *iniustitia*, and *acceptio personarum*. The essential feature of Luther's theological breakthrough is thus the destruction of the framework upon which his early soteriology was based, and *thence* the necessity of reinterpretation of the concept of *iustitia Dei*. It is therefore clear that an important change in Luther's understanding of justification took place at some time in the year 1515.

How, then, does this relate to the experience described in the autobiographical fragment of 1545? The first point which should be noted is that the fragment does not state that Luther's discovery *took place* in 1519, or that it was essentially the recognition that *iustitia Dei* was none other than *iustitia qua nos Deus induit, dum nos iustificat*, as some more superficial discussions appear to suggest; if this were the case, we should be forced to conclude that Luther merely came to a conclusion identical to that already reached by Karlstadt in 1517, in a work known to have been read by Luther (see §22). Rather, the fragment states that his theological insights were *complete* by 1519, and also that these insights involved not merely the rethinking of the specific theologoumenon of *iustitia Dei*, but also *sapientia Dei*, *fortitudo Dei* and *gloria Dei*. Second, it is clear that the concept of *iustitia Dei* as *iustitia activa* which Luther describes in the fragment is that associated with the soteriology of the *via moderna*.[21] As we suggest elsewhere, however, Luther's discovery of the 'wonderful new definition of righteousness'[22] is essentially programmatic, and capable of being applied to other divine attributes, such as those referred to in the autobiographical fragment, leading ultimately to the *theologia crucis*, the 'theology of the cross',[23] in which there is currently such considerable interest in systematic theological circles.

Although Luther indeed recognises that *iustitia Dei* is not to be understood as the righteousness by which God is himself just, but the righteousness by which he justifies the ungodly, this does not exhaust his understanding of the concept, nor is it sufficient to characterise it adequately. Indeed, Luther's unique interpretation of the 'righteousness of God' could not be distinguished from Augustine's interpretation of the same concept if it were. The following characteristics of Luther's concept of *iustitia Dei* may be established on the basis of an analysis of the later portions of the *Dictata super Psalterium* (1513–15), and the Romans lectures (1515–16). *Iustitia Dei* is:

1. A righteousness which is a gift from God, rather than a righteousness which belongs to God.
2. A righteousness which is revealed in the cross of Christ.
3. A righteousness which contradicts human preconceptions.

While the first of these three elements unquestionably corresponds to an important aspect of Augustine's concept of *iustitia Dei*, the remaining two serve to distinguish Luther and Augustine on this point. For Luther, the 'righteousness of God' is revealed exclusively in the cross, contradicting human preconceptions and expectations of the form that revelation should take. This insight is essentially methodological, as the autobiographical fragment indicates, and is capable of being extended to the remaining divine attributes – such as the 'glory of God', the 'wisdom of God', and the 'strength of God'. All are revealed in the cross, and all are revealed *sub contrariis*, contradicting human expectations. It is this understanding of the nature of the revelation of the divine attributes which underlies Luther's *theologia crucis*, and which distinguishes the 'theologian of glory' from the 'theologian of the cross'.

Initially, Luther could not understand how the concept of a 'righteous God' was gospel, in that it appeared to offer nothing other than condemnation for sinful man. On the basis of the Ciceronian concept of *iustitia* as *reddens unicuique quod suum est*, underlying the concept of *iustitia Dei* associated with the *via moderna*, the man who failed to do *quod in se est* was condemned. The fundamental presupposition at the heart of this soteriology is that man is indeed capable of *quod in se est* – in other words, that man is capable of meeting the fundamental precondition of justification through his own unaided faculties. The essential insight encapsulated in Luther's breakthrough of 1515 is that God himself meets a precondition which man cannot fulfil – in other words, that God himself bestows upon man the gift of *fides Christi*. It is this insight which underlies Luther's remarks of 1517, paralleling the statements of the 1545 fragment: 'Mira et nova diffinitio iusticie, cum usitate sic describatur: "Iusticia est virtus reddens unicuique, quod suum est." Hic vero dicit: "Iusticia est fides Ihesu Christi."'[24] We shall return to consider Luther's concept of *fides Christi* in the following section.

In turning to assess the *significance* of Luther's 'discovery', we are confronted with what appears to be a paradox. Luther's most important insight, judged in terms of its perceived significance to him in his autobiographical reflections, actually has relatively little, if anything, to do with the origins of the Reformation. The Reformed wing of the Reformation was not initially concerned with the general question of man's justification, let alone the particular question of the proper interpretation of the 'righteousness of God'. As we shall indicate later (§22), the Reformation within the Wittenberg theological faculty was based upon essentially Augustinian insights similar to the three we noted in the Romans lectures of 1515–16. Although these insights lay behind Luther's changing conception of the 'righteousness of God', the early Lutheran Reformation did not perceive the two matters to be so intimately related, or that their relation was theologically significant. Indeed, it is clear that many of the Reformers (such as Melanchthon and Calvin) actually reverted to concepts of the 'righteousness of God' which were remarkably similar, if not identical, to that rejected by Luther. Furthermore, the historical origins of the Lutheran Reformation do not appear to have been related primarily to the theologoumenon of *iustitia Dei*. In terms of its historical and theological dimensions, therefore, the Reformation cannot be considered to be closely linked with Luther's discovery. This is not to say that the 'discovery' was of no significance, in that it appears to have been the catalyst for the development of Luther's *theologia crucis*, perhaps one of the most powerful and important understandings of the nature of Christianity ever to have been formulated – but not an understanding which was taken up and developed in the sixteenth century, even within the evangelical faction at Wittenberg itself. The origins of the Reformation at Wittenberg are more complex than might be imagined, and there are excellent reasons for suggesting that it was initially based directly upon Augustine, rather than Luther's interpretation of him.

The importance of Luther's 'theological breakthrough' – a term which, incidentally, is greatly to be preferred to the inappropriate 'Turmerlebnis' or 'reformatorische Entdeckung'[25] – thus relates to Luther's personal theological development, over which it may easily be shown to have exerted an influence which was nothing less than decisive. It is all too easy, however, to equate Luther's personal preoccupations and beliefs with those which would initially lead to, and subsequently shape the thought of, the Reformation as a whole. As noted in the introduction to the present chapter, the relationship between *initia theologiae Lutheri* and *initia Reformationis* is now appreciated to be far too complex to permit the conclusion that Luther's discovery of the 'righteousness of God' *initiated* the Reformation. To illustrate this point, we must consider the remarkable doctrines of justification associated with the early Reformed theologians, such as Zwingli, over which Luther's influence appears to have been minimal.[26] In the following section, however, we are concerned with the broad features of Luther's doctrine of justification from 1515 onwards, particularly as it functions as a point of transition from late medieval thought to Protestantism.

§21 Martin Luther on justification

'Alas, gone is the horseman and the chariots of Israel!' With these words, Melanchthon broke the news of Luther's death in 1546 to the assembled students at Wittenberg. In view of the considerable influence which Melanchthon subsequently came to exercise over the Lutheran church, one may wonder whether he consciously saw himself as playing Elisha to Luther's Elijah. For reasons which will become clear, however, Luther's mantle would fit no man – neither Melanchthon nor Amsdorf.

It was Luther above all who saw the *articulus iustificationis* as *the* word of the gospel, to which all else was subordinate. The doctrine of justification which he propounded was to cause him to reject the papacy and the church of his day, not on the basis of any *direct* ecclesiological argument, but upon the basis of his conviction that the church of his day was committed to doctrines of justification which were nothing less than Pelagian.[1] The priority of his soteriology over his ecclesiology is particularly evident in his remarkable statement of 1535, to the effect that he will concede the Pope his authority if the latter concedes the free justification of sinners in Christ.[2] The cornerstone both of Luther's theological breakthrough and his subsequent controversy with the church of his day appears to have been based upon his insight that man cannot initiate the process of justification, and his conviction that the church of his day had, by affirming the direct opposite, fallen into the Pelagian error. It is, of course, obvious that this was not the case: he appears to have been familiar with the academic theology of the *via moderna* at first hand, and does not appear to have known any of the rival soteriologies – such as that of the *schola Augustiniana moderna* (despite his being a member of the Augustinian Order).[3] In view of the fact that the soteriology of certain Reformed theologians (such as Peter Martyr Vermigli and John Calvin) may reflect precisely this soteriology,[4] it is necessary to treat Luther's inadequate and ill-informed generalisations concerning the theology (especially the *pastoral* theology) of the late medieval church with considerable caution.

Following his decisive break with the soteriology of the *via moderna* in 1515, the general lines of the development of Luther's theology are clear. The important concept of *iustitia Christi aliena*, the 'commerce of exchange' between Christ and the sinner, and the *totus homo* theology all make their appearance in the Romans lectures of 1515–16; the *theologia crucis* emerges over the period 1516–19; the place of good works in justification is clarified in the 1520 *Sermo von den guten Werken*; and the crucial distinction between forgiving grace and the gift of the Holy Spirit is made clear in what is perhaps the most impressive of Luther's early works, *Rationis Latomianae confutatio* (1521). We shall consider these points individually.

It is important to appreciate that Luther's theology of justification cannot be characterised solely with reference to the strongly anti-Pelagian cast which that theology increasingly assumed from 1515 onwards. One of its most distinctive features is its explicit criticism of Augustine, evident from the same period. This point was raised by Karl Holl's interpretation of Luther's understanding of justification as a progressive *reale Gerechtmachung*.[5] For Holl, the solution to *das eigentliche Rätsel von Luthers Rechtfertigungslehre* lay not in a doctrine of double justification,[6] nor in a juxtaposition of *Rechtfertigung* and *Gerechtmachung*,[7] but in a proleptic understanding of the basis of the analytic divine judgement implicit in the process of justification. Holl illustrated this concept with reference to the analogy of a sculptor and his vision of the final product which motivates and guides him as he begins work on a block of crude marble;[8] similarly, God's present justification of the sinner is based upon his anticipation of his final sanctification, in that man's present justification takes place on the basis of his foreseen future righteousness. This influential interpretation of Luther was, according to some critics, actually a confusion of Luther's views with those of early Lutheran Orthodoxy,[9] requiring modification on the basis of the 1521 treatise *Rationis Latomianae confutatio*, to which we shall shortly return. Nevertheless, Holl's exposition of the dialectic between the sinner's state *in re* and *in spe* does indeed correspond closely to the sanative concept of justification, frequently employed by Luther in the 1515–16 Romans lectures. This clearly raises the question of precisely what *was* distinctive about Luther's early teaching on justification.

The key to Luther's distinctive early understanding of the process of justification, particularly his difference with Augustine, lies in his anthropology.[10] Departing radically from Augustine's neo-Platonist anthropology, Luther insists that the Pauline antithesis between *caro* and *spiritus* must be understood theologically, rather than anthropologically. On an anthropological approach to the antithesis, *caro* is the 'fleshly', sensual or worldly side of man, whilst *spiritus* represents man's higher nature, orientated towards striving towards God. For Luther, it is the whole man (*totus homo*) who serves the law of God and the law of sin at one and the same time, and who thus exists under a double servitude.[11] The one and the same man is spiritual and carnal, righteous and a sinner, good and evil.[12] It is on the basis of this anthropology that Luther bases his famous assertion that the believer is *iustus et peccator simul*.[13] How, then, may the believer be distinguished from the unbeliever on the basis of this anthropology? The answer lies in the frame of reference from which the *totus homo* is viewed – *coram Deo* or *coram hominibus*. For Luther, the believer is righteous *coram Deo*, whereas the unbeliever is righteous *coram hominibus*:

Sancti Intrinsece sunt peccatores semper, ideo extrinsece Iustificantur semper. Hypocrite autem intrinsece sunt Iusti semper, ideo extrinsece sunt peccatores semper. Intrinsece dico, i.e. quomodo in nobis, in nostris oculis, in nostra estimatione sumus, Extrinsece autem, quomodo apud Deum et in reputatione eius sumus. Igitur extrinsece sumus Iusti, quando non ex nobis nec ex operibus, Sed ex sola Dei reputatione Iusti sumus.[14]

The believer is thus *iustus apud Deum et in reputatione eius*, but not *iustus coram hominibus*. The justified sinner is, and will remain, *semper peccator, semper penitens, semper iustus*.[15] This point is important, on account of the evident divergence from Augustine. For Augustine, the righteousness bestowed upon man by God in his justification was recognisable as such by man – in other words, the justified sinner was *iustus coram Deo et coram hominibus*.[16] It will therefore be clear that Luther was obliged to develop a radically different understanding of the nature of justifying righteousness if he was to avoid contradicting the basic presuppositions implicit in his *totus homo* anthropology. This new understanding is to be found in the concept of *iustitia Christi aliena*, which is perhaps the most characteristic feature of his early understanding of justification.

For Luther, the gospel destroys all human righteousness,[17] in that man is forced to recognise that he is totally devoid of soteriological resources, and thus turns to receive these resources *ab extra*. Man is justified by laying hold of a righteousness which is not, and can never be, his own – the *iustitia Christi aliena*, which God mercifully 'reckons' to man. 'The Christ who is grasped by faith and lives in the heart is the true Christian righteousness, on account of which God counts us righteous and grants us eternal life.'[18] The essence of justifying faith is that it is *fides apprehensiva* – a faith which seizes Christ, and holds him fast, in order that his righteousness may be

ours, and our sin his. This *commercium admirabile* is explained by
Luther on the basis of the analogy of a human marriage: *sponsus et
sponsa fiunt una caro.*[19] For Luther, man may thus only progress in the
spiritual life by continually returning to Christ, *semper a novo
incipere.*[20] Thus Luther interprets *semper iustificandus* as 'ever to be
justified anew', while Augustine treats it as meaning 'ever to be made
more and more righteous'.[21] Luther does not make the distinction
between justification and sanctification associated with later Protestantism, treating justification as a process of becoming: *fieri est
iustificatio.*[22] Justification is thus a 'sort of beginning of God's
creation', *initium aliquod creaturae eius*, by which the Christian waits
in hope for the consummation of his righteousness: 'sicut nondum
sumus iustificati, et tamen sumus iustificati, sed iustitia nostra pendet
adhuc in spe'.[23] Like a sick man under the care of a doctor, who is ill
in re yet healthy *in spe*,[24] the Christian awaits in hope the final
resolution of the dialectic between righteousness and sin. This
sanative aspect of his early teaching on justification corresponds
closely to the teaching of Augustine on the matter. Justification is
regarded as a healing process which permits God to overlook the
remaining sin on account of its pending eradication. There is thus
clearly a proleptic element in this understanding of justification, as
Holl suggests. However, Luther's equation of *iustitia* and *fides Christi*
– foreshadowed in the concept of *iustitia fidei* in the *Dictata super
Psalterium* – is potentially misleading on this point. The distinction
between Luther and Augustine on this aspect of justification is best
seen from Luther's discussion of the relation between grace and faith.

Luther's concept of faith represents a significant departure from
Augustine's rather intellectualist counterpart. The strongly existentialist dimension of faith is brought out with particular clarity in
the 1517 Hebrews lectures. Whereas a purely human faith acknowledges that God exists,[25] or – in a speculative manner – that 'Christ
appears before the face of God for others', a true justifying faith
recognises, in a practical manner, that 'Christ appears before the face
of God for us' (*Christus apparuit vultui Dei pro nobis*).[26] Only this latter
faith can resist the assaults of *Anfechtung*.[27] Whereas *fides informis* is
like a candle, all too easily extinguished by the winds of *Anfechtung*,
true justifying faith is like the sun itself – unaffected by even the most
tempestuous of winds.[28]

The most significant discussion of faith, however, may be found in
the 1521 treatise *Rationis Latomianae confutatio*, in which, on the
basis of an exegesis of John 1.17, *gratia* is identified with *favor Dei*,

and *veritas* with *iustitia seu fides Christi* – both of which are given in Christ. Gratiam accipio hic proprie pro favore Dei, sicut debet, non pro qualitate animi, ut nostri recentiores docuerunt, atque haec gratia tandem vere pacem cordis operatur, ut homo a corruptione sua sanatus.[29] For Luther, the grace of God is always something external to man, and an absolute, rather than a partial, quality. Man is either totally under grace or totally under wrath. In contrast to this, faith (and its antithesis, sin) are seen as internal and partial, in that the man under grace may be partially faithful and partially sinful. Faith is thus seen as the means by which the man under grace may depend and grow in his spiritual life.[30] Luther thus abandons the traditional understanding of the rôle of grace in justification (see §9) by interpreting it as the absolute favour of God towards an individual, rather than a quality, or a series of qualities, at work within man's soul. Grace is no longer understood as a new nature within man. This latter rôle is now allocated to *fides Christi*.

It is important to appeciate that Luther insists that the distinguishing mark of faith is the real and redeeming presence of Christ. Faith is *fides apprehensiva*, a faith which 'grasps' Christ and makes him present. By arguing that grace and faith are given in Christ, Luther is able to assert at one and the same time that the righteousness of the believer is, and will remain, extrinsic to him,[31] whilst Christ is nonetheless really present within the believer, effecting his renovation and regeneration. Furthermore, by insisting that faith is given to man *in* justification, Luther avoids any suggestion that man is justified *on account of* his faith: justification is *propter Christum*, and not *propter fidem*. The reinterpretation of grace as an absolute external, and faith as a partial internal, quality permits Luther to maintain what is otherwise clearly a contradiction within his theology of justification – his simultaneous insistence upon the external nature of the righteousness of Christ, and the real presence of Christ in the believer. The divine *reputatio iustitiae* does not, therefore, imply that man can be said to *possess* righteousness: sola autem reputatione miserentis Dei per fidem verbi eius iusti sumus.[32] Although Luther does not develop a theology of *iustitia imputata* at this point, it is clear that his anthropological presuppositions dictate that justifying righteousness be conceived extrinsically, thus laying the foundations for the Melanchthonian doctrine of the imputation of the righteousness of Christ to the believer (see §22). The origins of the concept of 'imputed righteousness', so characteristic of Protestant theologies of justification after the year 1530, may therefore be considered to lie with Luther.

One of the most significant aspects of Luther's break with the soteriology of the *via moderna* lies in his doctrine of the *servum arbitrium*.[33] The 1517 *Disputatio contra scholasticam theologiam* asserted that the unjustified sinner can only will and perform evil.[34] The Heidelberg disputation of the following year included the assertion: liberum arbitrium post peccatum res est de solo titulo, et dum facit quod in se est, peccat mortaliter.[35] It is difficult, at this stage, to draw any clear distinction between Augustine and Luther on the powers of the *liberum arbitrium post peccatum*, partially because it is not clear precisely what Luther understands by the term *liberum arbitrium* (for example, if it is assumed that he is referring to Augustine's *liberum arbitrium captivatum*, the proposition is clearly Augustinian). It is therefore important to observe that the condemnation of Luther's teaching in the papal bull *Exsurge Domine* of 15 June 1520 is curiously phrased, and should probably be interpreted to mean that the condemned forty-one propositions are *variously* heretical *or* scandalous *or* false *or* offensive to pious ears *or* misleading to simple minds, rather than that each and every proposition is to be condemned on all five grounds.[36] The thirty-sixth proposition, which appears to affirm an essentially Augustinian doctrine, may therefore be regarded as having been condemned for stating an orthodox Catholic dogma in an offensive or potentially misleading manner.

In his subsequent pronouncements upon free will, however, Luther appears to move increasingly away from Augustine. Both in his defence of the thirty-sixth proposition and the anti-Erasmian *de servo arbitrio* of 1525, Luther appears to adopt a form of necessitarianism, either as the main substance of his defence of the *servum arbitrium*, or at least as an important supporting argument. His assertions that Wycliffe was correct to maintain that all things happen by absolute necessity,[37] and that God is the author of all man's evil deeds,[38] have proved serious obstacles to those who wish to suggest that Luther was merely restating an Augustinian or scriptural position. In particular, three significant points of difference between Augustine and Luther should be noted in this respect:

1. For Luther, it is God who is the author of sin: Deus operatur et mala opera in impiis.[39] For Augustine, it is man who is the author of sin.

2. The slavery of man's will is understood by Luther to be a consequence of his creatureliness, rather than his sin (the affinities with Thomas Bradwardine here are evident).[40]

3.   Luther explicitly teaches a doctrine of double predestination, whereas Augustine was reluctant to acknowledge such a doctrine, no matter how logically appropriate it might appear.

Some scholars have argued that Luther's doctrine of justification and of the *servum arbitrium* are related as the two sides of a coin,[41] so that a statement of the one amounts to a statement of the other. It must, however, be pointed out that Luther's doctrine of justification is not exhausted or adequately characterised by a statement of the doctrine of the *servum arbitrium*. Essential to his understanding of justification is the concept of *iustitia Christi aliena*, which is not necessarily implied by the doctrine of the unfree will. If man's free will is enslaved, it is certainly true that he cannot justify himself – but this does not place God under any obligation to justify him by means of an extrinsic righteousness, provided the source of justifying righteousness is conceded to be none other than God himself. That man's will is enslaved is one matter; that God should choose to justify him in one specific manner as a result is quite another. As we shall indicate, the history of Lutheran theology indicates that a wedge was driven between the concepts of an alien justifying righteousness and an enslaved will at a comparatively early stage, the former being consistently maintained as *de fide*, the latter being abandoned or reduced to the mere assertion that man cannot justify himself – a far cry from its original meaning. This implicit criticism of Luther by Lutheranism may be taken as demonstrating that there is no fundamental theological connection between the two concepts. They are two essentially independent statements about justification, related only by the personality of Luther. With his death, that relation ceased to exist within Lutheranism.

A point upon which Luther has been consistently misunderstood concerns the relationship between faith and works in justification. Luther's theological breakthrough was intimately linked with the realisation that man was not justified upon the basis of any human work, but through the work of God within man.[42] Luther's intense hostility towards anyone who wished *per legem iustificari*,[43] thus compromising the *virginitas fidei*,[44] led him to develop an understanding of the relationship between law and gospel which allocated the former a specific, but strictly circumscribed, rôle in the Christian life.[45] Luther does not, as he is frequently represented, reject the necessity of good works in justification: *opera sunt necessaria ad salutem, sed non causant salutem, quia fides sola dat vitam*.[46] He frequently appeals to the biblical image of the good tree which bears good fruit, thus testifying to, rather than causing, its good nature.

Estque necessario effectus fidei et fructus et fit ad salutem, non meretur salutem. Estque necessario effectus in christiano, qui iam salvus est in fide et spe et tamen tendit in ista spe ad salutem revelandam.[47]

In his later period, particularly in those writings dating from 1534–5, Luther distinguished two dimensions to justification: Duplex in scripturis traditur iustificatio, altera fidei coram Deo, altera operum coram mundo.[48] It is clear that he is not developing a doctrine of 'double justification' (see §25) at this point, but merely identifying one element of the *usus legis in loco iustificationis*. The good works of the justified demonstrate the believer's justification *by God*, and cannot be considered to cause it:

Tamen non sequitur, quod opera ideo salvant, nisi valde necesse intelligamus, quod oporteat esse internam et externam salutem sive iustitiam. Opera salvant externe, hoc est, testantur nos esse iustos, et fidem esse in homine, quae interne salvat, ut Paulus inquit: Corde creditur ad iustitiam, ore fit confessio ad salutem. Externa salvatio ut fructus ostendit arborem bonam, ostendit fidem adesse.[49]

Before documenting the manner in which Luther's doctrine of justification was appropriated or modified within the early Reformation, it is important that we should attempt to establish the points of contact with the earlier medieval tradition. Luther represents a figure of theological transition, standing between two eras, and it is clearly of some interest to characterise the modifications which took place. In view of the fact that he knew little at first hand of the early Dominican school, or the early or later Franciscan schools, and of the restricted influence of both German mysticism and the *schola Augustiniana moderna*,[50] we are particularly concerned with his relation to Augustine and the *via moderna*.

It is possible to characterise the relation between Luther and Augustine on justification as follows:

1. Luther and Augustine both interpret *iustitia Dei* as the righteousness by which God justifies sinners, rather than as the abstract divine attribute which stands over and against mankind, judging on the basis of merit. In this respect, Luther is closer to Augustine than the *via moderna*, although the nature of Luther's understanding of *iustitia Dei* is more complex than is usually appreciated.[51]

2. Augustine understands *iustitia Dei* to be contiguous with *iustitia hominum*, in that it underlies human concepts of *iustitia*. For Luther, *iustitia Dei* is revealed only in the cross of Christ, and, if anything, contradicts human conceptions of *iustitia*.

3. Whereas Luther's doctrine of justification is based upon the concept of *servum arbitrium*, Augustine's is based upon that of *liberum arbitrium captivatum*, which becomes *liberum arbitrium liberatum* through the action of *gratia sanans*. Luther does not appear to envisage a liberation of *servum arbitrium* after justification, in that the servitude of man's will is seen as a consequence of his creatureliness, rather than his sinfulness. The differences between Luther and Augustine on predestination, noted above, also reflect this point. Although the phrase *servum arbitrium* derives from Augustine, it is not typical of his thought (see §§4, 7).

4. Luther and Augustine concur in understanding justification as an all-embracing process, subsuming the beginning, development and subsequent perfection of the Christian life. This is one of the clearest *differentiae* between Luther and later Protestantism, and places Luther closer to the position of the Council of Trent than is generally realised.

5. Whereas Augustine understands the believer to become righteous in justification, participating in the divine life and being, Luther is reluctant to admit that man becomes righteous in justification. If anything, man becomes more and more aware of his sinfulness, and of his need for the alien righteousness of Christ. Intrinsically man is, and will remain, a sinner, despite being extrinsically righteous. Luther explicitly criticises Augustine on this point. Although Luther makes frequent reference to the righteousness of believers, his equation of *iustitia* and *fides Christi* makes it clear that he is not referring to the morality of believers, but to the real and redeeming presence of Christ. The strongly Christological orientation of Luther's concept of the righteousness of believers sets him apart from Augustine on this point.

6. Luther and Augustine work with quite different anthropological presuppositions, with important consequences for their understandings of faith and sin.

It will therefore be clear that Luther's relation to Augustine is ambivalent. While one can point to elements in his thought which are clearly Augustinian, there are points – particularly his doctrine of *iustitia Christia aliena* – where he diverges significantly from Augustine.

Luther's relation to the *via moderna* is more complex, and remains the subject of investigation. There can be no doubt that Luther's early theology, up to the year 1514, as well as some elements which persist until 1515, is essentially that of the *via moderna*. This is particularly evident in the case of his understanding of the covenantal foundations of justification, his interpretation of the axiom *facienti quod in se est Deus non denegat gratiam*, his understanding of the theologoumenon *iustitia Dei*, and his critique of the implication of created habits in justification. It is also clear that Luther's 1517 dispute against 'scholastic theology' is actually directed specifically against Gabriel Biel. The question which remains to be answered, however, is whether Luther appropriated any elements of the theology of the *via moderna* in his *later* theology of justification.

At one stage, it was considered that Luther's doctrine of the imputation of righteousness and the non-imputation of sin represented one such element. Thus de Lagarde suggested that the background to Luther's doctrine was to be found in the dialectic between the two powers of God.[52] *De potentia sua absoluta*, God may accept a man without the grace of justification. Thus Luther may be regarded as stating *de potentia ordinata* what Biel stated *de potentia absoluta* concerning divine acceptation. It may, however, be pointed out that where Biel and Ockham understand the *locus* of the doctrine of the *acceptatio divina* to be the divine will, Luther actually locates it Christologically. A similar argument was advanced by Feckes, based upon the presupposition that Biel actually states *de potentia absoluta* what he would like to have stated *de potentia ordinata*, but could not on account of possible criticism from the ecclesiastical authorities.[53] As Feckes' attempt to relate Biel and Luther is based upon this discredited understanding of Biel,[54] it cannot be sustained. Furthermore, as Vignaux has pointed out, this possibility is excluded by Luther himself, particularly by theses 56 and 57 of the *Disputatio contra scholasticam theologiam*.[55] Neither Biel nor Ockham, of course, develops a doctrine of the imputation of righteousness, which enormously weakens the case for any putative positive influence from the *via moderna* in this respect. We must look elsewhere for the origins of Luther's understanding of the *reputatio* of the *iustitia Christi aliena* to believers.

The influence of the *schola Augustiniana moderna* upon Luther is much more difficult to assess. It is clear that there are excellent reasons for believing that Luther did not encounter this school, even in the person of Johannes von Staupitz, during his theological education.[56] Furthermore, Luther does not appear to have encountered Gregory of Rimini's writings until 1519.[57] It is therefore impossible to maintain that his distinctive views on justification derive from this school. Thus Luther and Staupitz, although having a common Augustinian soteriological framework, differ totally on the question of the nature of justifying righteousness: for Staupitz, justifying righteousness is *iustitia in nobis*, whereas for Luther it is *iustitia extra nos*.[58]

The influence of mysticism upon Luther's theology of justification has been difficult to ascertain. Several scholars have identified elements of his thought on justification in the teachings of the later German mystics, such as Tauler, and have suggested that these should be regarded as 'Forerunners of the Reformation'.[59] There can be no doubt that Luther was familiar with such writings, in that he edited *Eyn theologia deutsch* in 1516 and 1518, and appears to have annotated Tauler's sermons extensively in 1519. Tauler's discussion of fallen human nature demonstrates an anthropological pessimism paralleling that of Luther: man is fallen, poisoned and introverted.[60] The possibility of man attaining salvation unaided is, however, upheld by Tauler. Furthermore, salvation is understood in terms of a direct, unbroken and unmediated mystical fellowship with God: the Christological concentration evident in Luther's concept of the *commercium admirabile* is quite absent. Tauler's essentially neo-Platonist anthropological and theological presuppositions lead to his conceiving salvation in terms of a substantive union between God and man. Luther's insistence upon the exclusive location of all soteriological resources outside man stands in diametrical opposition to Tauler's concern to promote the *Seelengrund*, and Gerson's concern to enhance the soteriological possibilities of *synteresis*.[61] While it is quite possible that Luther may have derived his concept of *Anfechtung* from late medieval mysticism,[62] it is impossible to argue that any of the crucial elements in his early theology of justification (such as the concept of *iustitia Christi aliena*) derive from such a source.

Whatever the origins of Luther's distinctive ideas on justification, it is clear that they exercised an immediate influence upon the development of the Lutheran Reformation at Wittenberg. Nevertheless, Luther's ideas were not universally accepted, and were subjected to a gradual process of modification in the years leading up to the Formula of Concord. In the following section, we shall consider the origins and subsequent development of this process of modification of Luther by Lutheranism.

§22 Justification in early Lutheranism 1516–80

The year 1516 witnessed considerable discussion within the theological faculty at the University of Wittenberg concerning the nature of Augustine's teaching on justification. In a disputation of 25 September 1516, Luther had suggested that Karlstadt should check the teachings of the *scholasticos doctores* against the writings of Augustine to discover the extent to which they diverged from him.[1] Setting off for Leipzig on 13 January 1517, Karlstadt managed to equip himself with a copy of the works of Augustine, and hence realised the radical discrepancy between his own position and that of Augustine.[2] As a result, Karlstadt was moved to arrange a public disputation on 26 April 1517, in which, to Luther's delight, he defended 151 Augustinian theses.[3] His particular attraction to Augustine's strongly anti-Pelagian *de spiritu et litera* led to his lecturing, and subsequently publishing a commentary, upon this important work. The result of Karlstadt's conversion to the *vera theologia* in 1517 was that the Wittenberg theological faculty was committed to a programme of theological reform by the year 1518, based extensively upon the anti-Pelagian writings of Augustine.

It is at this point that differences between Luther and Karlstadt are clearly discernible. In his works dating from this early period, Karlstadt appears as a remarkably faithful interpreter of Augustine, where Luther often appears as his critic. Thus Karlstadt follows Augustine in developing an antithesis between law and *grace*,[4] rather than *gospel*, and emphasises the priority of *grace*,[5] rather than *faith*. Most significantly of all, the Augustinian understanding of the *nature* of justification is faithfully reproduced. Of particular importance is his unequivocal assertion that justifying righteousness is inherent to man, and that it *makes* him righteous:

Non est sensus, quod illa iusticia dei sit per legem testificata, qua deus in se iustus est, sed illa, qua iustificat impium, qua induit hominem, qua instaurat imaginem dei in homine; de hac iusticia, qua deus suos electos iustos et pios efficit, tractamus.[6]

It is clear that Karlstadt follows Staupitz in this understanding of the nature of justifying righteousness,[7] and knows nothing of Luther's concept of justifying righteousness as *iustitia Christi aliena*. Indeed, the Christological emphasis evident in Luther's theology of justification by this stage is quite absent from Karlstadt's theology of justification,[8] which continues to be primarily a theology of the *grace of God*. It will also be clear that this passage calls into question the suggestion that Luther discovered an essentially *Augustinian* concept of *iustitia Dei* in late 1518 or early 1519 (see §20): precisely this concept of *iustitia Dei* is faithfully reproduced in Karlstadt's lectures and published commentary on Augustine. Similarly, Karlstadt follows Augustine in defining justification in terms of the non-imputation of sin, rather than the imputation of righteousness. In his writings for the period 1519–21, Karlstadt faithfully reproduces the Augustinian concept of justification as the non-imputation of sin and the impartation of righteousness, and does not develop Luther's extrinsic concept of justifying righteousness.[9] As we indicated earlier, Luther's extrinsic conception of justifying righteousness is partly a consequence of his *totus homo* anthropology, which differs significantly from Augustine's neo-Platonist understanding of man. Karlstadt adopts an essentially Augustinian anthropology, in which justification is conceived as a renewal of man's nature through a gradual eradication of sin. *Iustus ergo simul est bonus et malus, filius dei et seculi*.[10] Although this is clearly similar to Luther's assertion that the justified believer is *simul iustus et peccator*, it is clear that the two theologians interpret the phrase differently. For Luther, what is being stated is that the believer is *extrinsically righteous* and *intrinsically sinful*; for Karlstadt, what is being stated is precisely what Augustine intended when he stated that the justified sinner is *partly* righteous and *partly* sinful (*ex quadam parte iustus, ex quadam parte peccator*).[11]

There are therefore excellent reasons for suggesting that Karlstadt's doctrine of justification over the period 1517–21 is essentially Augustinian, lacking the novel elements which distinguish Luther's teaching of the time from that of the African bishop. A similar conclusion must be drawn concerning the theology of Johann Bugenhagen over the period 1521–5. In his 1525 lectures on Romans, Bugenhagen identifies the three elements of justification as *remissio peccatorum*, *donatio spiritus* and *non-imputatio peccati*.[12] Even when commenting on Romans 4.5–6, where Erasmus had retranslated the Vulgate reference to *reputatio iustitiae* as *imputatio iustitiae*, Bugenhagen still interprets the text as referring to the *non-imputation of sin* rather than the *imputation of an alien righteousness*.[13] Where Bugenhagen speaks of *imputatio* in a specifically *Christological* context, he is referring to the fact that the sin of the believer is not imputed to him on account of Christ: *iusti non imputante deo propter Christum peccatum*.[14] More generally, however, his concept of the non-imputation of sin is discussed in a pneumatological context; the renewing work of the Holy Spirit within man permits God not to impute his sin: *quod non imputetur reliquum … quia spiritu contranitimur peccato*.[15] Although Bugenhagen thus develops a doctrine of justification which is essentially Augustinian, omitting any reference to the imputation of the alien righteousness of Christ, it is clear that he has moved away from Augustine on points of significance. In particular, grace is conceived extrinsically, as *favor Dei*:

Praeterea in hoc loco vides quam insipienter errent, qui gratiam dei, de qua loquuntur scripturae per quam solam salvamur, describunt esse habitum in hominem sive qualitatem, cum sit favor potius in deo bene volente nobis ut filiis.[16]

In this, Bugenhagen is clearly dependent upon Melanchthon's 1521 *Loci*.[17] In view of Melanchthon's importance in establishing a forensic concept of justification as normative within Protestantism, it is appropriate to consider his contribution at this point.

Although an Erasmian on his arrival at Wittenberg in 1518, Melanchthon appears to have adopted Luther's *totus homo* anthropology at an early stage,[18] regarding sin as permeating even man's higher faculties. While his baccalaureate theses of September 1519 appear to develop a theology of justification which parallels that of Luther rather than Karlstadt,[19] it is clear from his writings of the period 1519–20 that he still tends to conceive justification ethically at points, as 'mortification of the flesh and our affections'.[20] Nevertheless, by 1521 Melanchthon appears to have grasped much of Luther's distinctive understanding of justification, and incorporated it into the first edition of the *Loci communes* of that year. This is particularly clear in the *locus de gratia*, in which grace is unequivocally defined extrinsically as *favor Dei*: non aliud enim est gratia, si exactissime describenda sit, nisi dei benevolentia erga nos.[21] Nevertheless, in his early works, Melanchthon still tends to conceive justification in factitive, rather than declarative, terms.[22] Thus a conspicuous feature of these works is his emphasis upon the rôle of the *person* of Christ in justification; for example, the 1523 *Annotationes in Evangelium Iohannis* develops the idea that justification involves a personal union between Christ and the believer.[23] This contrasts significantly with his later emphasis upon the more abstract concept of the *work* of Christ associated with his doctrine of forensic justification, which becomes particularly evident from his writings dating from after 1530.

In his writings subsequent to 1530, Melanchthon increasingly emphasises the notion of *iustitia aliena* – an alien righteousness, which is imputed to the believer. Justification is then interpreted as *Gerecht-*

sprechung, being 'pronounced righteous' or 'accepted as righteous'. A sharp distinction thus comes to be drawn between justification, as the external act in which God pronounces or declares the believer to be righteous, and regeneration, as the internal process of renewal in which the believer is regenerated through the work of the Holy Spirit. Whereas Luther consistently employed images and categories of personal relationship to describe the union of the believer and Christ (such as the *commercium admirabile* of a human marriage paralleling that between the soul and Christ), Melanchthon increasingly employed images and categories drawn from the sphere of Roman law. Thus Melanchthon illustrates the concept of forensic justification with reference to a classical analogy: just as the people of Rome declared Scipio to be a free man *in foro*, so God declares the sinner to be righteous *in foro divino*.

Iustificatio significat remissionem peccatorum et reconciliationem seu acceptationem personae ad vitam aeternam. Nam Hebraeis iustificare est forense verbum; ut si dicam, populus Romanus iustificavit Scipionem accusatum a tribunis, id est, absolvit seu iustum pronuntiavit. Sumpsit igitur Paulis verbum iustificandi ex consuetudine Hebraici sermonis pro acceptatione, id est, pro reconciliatione et remissione peccatorum.[24]

Significantly, Erasmus uses the forensic concept of *acceptilatio* (the purely verbal remission of a debt without payment) in the 1516 *Novum instrumentum omne* of 1516 as an illustration of the meaning of the verb *imputare*. We shall return to this point towards the end of the present section.

The Augsburg Confession (1530) contains a brief statement on justification in its fourth article, which does not refer to the imputation of the alien righteousness of Christ, but merely restates the Pauline idea (Romans 4.5) of 'faith being reckoned as righteousness':

Item docent, quod homines non possint iustificari coram Deo propriis viribus, meritis aut operibus, sed gratis iustificentur propter Christum per fidem, cum credunt se in gratiam recipi et peccata remitti propter Christum, qui sua morte pro nostris peccatis satisfecit. Hanc fidem imputat Deus pro iustitia coram ipso.[25]

The formula *propter Christum per fidem* is significant, in that it defines the correct understanding of the formula 'justification *sola fide*'. The sole grounds for man's justification lie, not in man himself or in anything which he can do, but in Christ and his work alone. Man is not justified on account of his faith (which would be justification *propter fidem*), nor must faith be seen as a human work or achievement: strictly speaking, faith is a reception by man of the gracious deed of God in Christ.

In the *Apologia* (1530) for the Confession, Melanchthon develops the concept of imputation – hinted at in the above article – in a significant direction. Just as a man might pay the debt of a friend, even though it is not his own, so the believer may be reckoned as righteous on account of the alien merit of Christ.[26] Making Luther's critique of Augustine's concept of justifying righteousness explicit, Melanchthon states that justification is to be understood forensically, as the declaration that the believer is righteous on account of the alien righteousness of Christ: iustificare vero hoc loco forensi consuetudine significat reum absolvere et pronuntiare iustum, sed propter alienam iustitiam, videlicit Christi, quae aliena iustitia communicatur nobis per fidem.[27] Thus justification does not signify 'making righteous', but 'pronouncing righteous'.[28] There is no righteousness within man, or inherent to him, which can be regarded as the basis of his justification: man is justified on the basis of an external and alien righteousness, which is 'reputed' or 'imputed' to him. Propter Christum coram Deum [sic] iusti reputemur.[29] It will be clear that these statements of the imputation of righteousness go far beyond the traditional Augustinian statements concerning justification as the non-imputation of sin, and contradict such statements which define justification as 'making righteous'. It might, therefore, appear reasonable to conclude that the teaching of the Lutheran church with respect to justification had been defined and distinguished from that of Augustine at this point. In fact, this is not the case.

Alongside statements which explicitly define the forensic character of justification, and which clearly *exclude* a factitive interpretation of justification, we find statements which explicitly define justification in factitive terms. Significantly, such statements tend to be found near the beginning of the *Apologia* for the fourth article, whereas those denying the factitive character of justification tend to be found towards its end. For example, an early paragraph defends the forensic dimension of justification by appealing to its factitive aspect: et quia iustificari significat ex iniustis iustos effici seu regenerari, significat et iustos pronuntiari seu reputari.[30] This ambiguity on the part of Melanchthon has led to considerable confusion among his modern interpreters.[31]

The subsequent history of the evangelical faction within Germany, particularly in the aftermath of Luther's death (1546), the defeat of the Smalkadic League (1547) and the imposition of the Augsburg

Interim (1548) is that of controversy over the doctrine of justification. These controversies related to three main areas of the doctrine: the objective grounds of justification (the Osiandrist and Stancarist controversies); the necessity of good works after justification (the Antinomian and Majorist controversies); and the subjective appropriation of justification (the Synergist and Monergist controversies). We shall consider these areas individually.

1 The Objective Grounds of Justification: The Osiandrist and Stancarist Controversies

Among Melanchthon's contemporary critics was Andreas Osiander, leader of the evangelical faction in Nuremburg from 1522 to 1547. For Osiander, the Melanchthonian concept of justification as *Gerechtsprechung* was totally unacceptable: saving righteousness was none other than the essential indwelling righteousness of Christ, arising from his divinity, rather than his humanity.[32] Justification must therefore be understood to consist of the infusion of the essential righteousness of Christ. Although some of his critics, such as Martin Chemnitz, argued that this made justification dependent upon sanctification, it is clear that this is not the case. Osiander merely reacted against what he regarded as the unacceptably extrinsic conception of justification in the *Apologia* by emphasising those scriptural passages which speak of Christ indwelling within the believer.[33] Furthermore, Osiander claimed, with some reason, the support of Luther in his views on the significance of the indwelling of Christ: the increasing emphasis within the German evangelical faction upon the work of Christ imputed to man inevitably led to a reduction in interest in the rôle of the person of Christ within man, and thus to a certain indifference to Luther's high estimation of this aspect of man's justification. Osiander's views merely served to harden German Protestant opinion against the concept of justification by inherent righteousness, and it was left to Calvin (§23) to demonstrate how Osiander's legitimate protest against the externalisation of Christ might be appropriated while maintaining a *forensic* doctrine of justification.

Francesco Stancari maintained a totally antithetical position, and cited Melanchthon in his support (to the latter's horror). Whereas Osiander maintained that Christ's *divinity* was the ground of man's justification, Stancari argued that the implication of Christ's divinity in man's justification was quite unthinkable, involving logical contradiction (such as the fact that Christ's divine nature had to function both as mediator and offended party). The objective basis of man's justification was therefore Christ's *human* nature alone. On account of Christ's obedient suffering upon the cross in his human nature, his *acquired* (not *essential!*) righteousness was imputed to man as the basis of his justification.[34]

These controversies thus identified the need for clarification of the Augsburg Confession's unclear statements on the nature of justifying righteousness and the person of the Redeemer.

2 The Role of Works in Justification: The Antinomian and Majorist Controversies

Perhaps through his emphasis on the priority of faith in justification, Luther had often seemed to imply that good works were of no significance in the Christian life (see §21). His position on this matter was clarified in his later writings, and may be stated as follows: works are a condition, but not a cause, of salvation.[35] Luther is prepared to concede that if no works follow faith, it is certain that the faith in question is dead, and not a living faith in Christ.[36] The 1520 sermon on good works states that 'faith in Christ is the first, highest and most sublime good work', adding that 'works are not pleasing on their own account, but on account of faith'.[37] Melanchthon, however, always entertained a much more positive understanding of the rôle of the law in the Christian life. In his *Annotationes in Evangelium Matthaei*, justification is understood as a new capacity to fulfil the law,[38] and the 1521 *Loci* defined Christian freedom as a new freedom to fulfil the law spontaneously.[39] The 1527 *Articuli de quibus egerunt per visitatores* reproduced these views, and placed the preaching of the law as the heart of Christian instruction, insisting that without the law, both repentance and faith were impossible. These views outraged Johann Agricola, who argued that repentance was a consequence of the gospel, not the law. Although Agricola was restrained in his antinomianism, he would unquestionably have agreed with Jakob Schenk's suggestion that Moses ought to be hanged.

The Majorist controversy initially concerned Georg Major's justification of the failure of the Leipzig Interim to stress the exclusive rôle of faith in justification. Although it is clear from his 1552 tract *Auf des ehrwürdigen Herrn Nikolaus von Amsdorfs Schrift Antwort* that Major was totally committed to the principle of justification *sola fide*, he nevertheless stated his conviction that Luther taught that good works were necessary for salvation. Flacius immediately pointed out that this excluded both infants and the dying from being saved. Nikolaus von Amsdorf replied to Major initially with the assertion that the law had no rôle in justification whatsoever, and subsequently with the suggestion that good works were positively detrimental to salvation.[40] The related dispute *de tertio usus legis* arose over similar views expressed by Luther's pupils Andreas Poach and Anton Otho.[41] By 1560, it was clear to all that the sixth article of the Augsburg Confession required clarification if serious internal disunity on this point was to be brought to an end.

3 The Subjective Appropriation of Justification: The Synergist and Monergist Controversies

Luther's insistence upon man's utter passivity in justification, especially evident in his defence of the thirty-sixth proposition and *de servo arbitrio*, remained characteristic of his teaching on justification throughout his life. It is therefore important to note Melanchthon's growing unease concerning this aspect of Luther's theology. The 1535 edition of the *Loci* suggested, and the 1543 edition made explicit, that Melanchthon no longer agreed with Luther on this point: justification was now to be attributed to three contributing factors – the Word of God, the Holy Spirit, and the faculty of the human will. For Melanchthon, man possesses the *facultas applicandi se ad gratiam* prior to justification. As a result, nobody is drawn to God unless he wishes to be drawn.[42] Similarly, Melanchthon's early commitment to the doctrine of predestination *ante praevisa merita* in the 1521 *Loci* is replaced by that of predestination *post praevisa merita* by 1535.[43] It is possibly this change of heart which underlies the omission of an *articulus de praedestinatione* in the Augsburg Confession.[44] Melanchthon's views were defended by Strigel,[45] and subjected to heavy criticism by Amsdorf and Flacius. The occasion of the synergist controversy was the publication of Johann Pfeffinger's *Propositiones de libero arbitio* (1555), which asserted that the reason why some responded to the gospel and others not, was to be found within man himself, rather than in an extrinsic prior divine decision. Thus the ultimate difference between David and Saul, or between Peter and Judas, must lie in their respective free wills. Although Pfeffinger was careful to insist that God retains the initiative (and, indeed, the upper hand) in justification, he nevertheless stated that it is the human free will which decides whether or not the Holy Spirit enters into an individual's life. This concept of *liberum arbitrium in spiritualibus* was violently opposed by the monergists Amsdorf and Flacius,[46] with the result that the matter came to a head at the Weimar Colloquy (1560). In this dispute, Strigel suggested that the human free will was injured and weakened through original sin, although not completely destroyed. He illustrated this Augustinian position (see §§4, 7) by comparing the effect of sin upon the free will with that of garlic juice upon a magnet: once the obstruction has been removed, the power of the magnet is restored. Flacius replied by accusing Strigel of externalising sin and proceeded to develop Luther's analogy of the passivity of man in justification in a manner which seemed Manichaean to those observing the debate. Nevertheless, it was once more clear that clarification of man's rôle in his own justification was required if further internal dissent was to be avoided.

Clarification of these three areas would be provided by the Formula of Concord, drawn up in March 1577. Before considering the manner in which the Formula settled these disputes, it is necessary to return to the question of the nature of justification and justifying righteousness, in order to note that substantial internal agreement had been reached within Lutheranism and the Reformed church on this matter in the intervening period. This is best illustrated from Martin Chemnitz' *Examen Concilii Tridentini* (1563–73), an authoritative work which clearly established the difference between the Lutheran church and Augustine on these points. Chemnitz notes that there are two approaches to the term 'justification': the Latin approach, which interprets justification as *iustum facere*, and the Hebrew approach, which interprets it as *absolutio a peccato seu remissio peccatorum et imputatio iustitiae Christi*.[47] The former corresponds to that of Augustine and subsequently the Roman Catholic approach, and the latter to the Lutheran. The Latin approach involves the interpretation of justification as the infusion of righteousness,[48] whereas Chemnitz argues, on the basis of an analysis of secular Greek sources, that the verb δικαιοῦν must be interpreted as *verbum forense*: Germani *Rechtfertigen* plane Graeco more in significatione forensi usurpant.[49] Augustine is guilty of misrepresenting Paul,[50] particularly in relation to the matter of imputation.[51]

This position was endorsed by the third article of the Formula of Concord.[52] Justification is defined in forensic terms, and it is made clear that it is not faith which is reckoned as justifying righteousness, but the righteousness of Christ imputed to us.[53] Vocabulum igitur *iustificationis* in hoc negotio significat iustum pronuntiare, a peccatis et aeternis peccatorum suppliciis absolvere, propter iustitiam Christi, quae a Deo fidei imputatur.[54] The individual teachings of both Osiander and Stancari are rejected,[55] in favour of justification by the mediatorial righteousness of Christ as both God and man.[56] The Majorist controversy was ended through the fourth article of the Formula, which asserted that good works were obligatory, in that they are commanded, as well as being an appropriate expression of faith and gratitude to God;[57] they are not, however, mandatory or necessary *for salvation*.[58] Works are and remain the effects of justifying faith, and must not be confused with the cause of that faith. The synergist and monergist controversies were ended with the explicit condemnation of the synergist position.[59] Strigel's analogy of the magnet and garlic juice is explicitly rejected.[60] The text (John 6.44) which Melanchthon had interpreted (with the aid of Chrysostom) to mean that God only drew to himself those who wished to be drawn, is now interpreted in an anti-Melanchthonian sense, meaning that the free will is totally impotent and dependent upon grace. Whereas, since 1535, Melanchthon had recognised three concurrent causes of justification (the Word, the Holy Spirit, and man's will), thus permitting man a say in his own justification, the Formula recognised only one such cause – the Holy Spirit.[61]

It might therefore be thought that the Formula endorses the monergist position. In fact, it does not, as may be seen from its statements on predestination. The doctrine of double predestination – so important a feature of Luther's *de servo arbitrio* (see §21) – is explicitly rejected in favour of a doctrine of predestination based upon the *benevolentia Dei universalis*. A careful distinction is made between *praedestinatio* and *praescientia*: the former extends only to the children of God,[62] whereas the latter extends to all creatures as such.[63] The *causa perditionis* is defined to be man, rather than God[64] – a conclusion, incidentally, which stands in contrast to Luther's 1525 assertion that the only centre of freedom which cannot be said to be necessitated by another is God himself. Furthermore, Luther's doctrine of the *servum arbitrium* is radically undermined by the assertion that the free will may, under the influence of grace, assent to faith.[65] Although the Formula specifically rejects any suggestion of cooperation between man's will and the Holy Spirit,[66] it is clear that this is directed against Melanchthon's opinion that man can cooperate with God *apart from grace*. The Formula envisages the human *liberum arbitrium* as being liberated by grace, whereas Luther regarded it as being permanently enslaved through human creatureliness (see §21).

The emphasis upon the concept of forensic justification in both the Formula of Concord and Melanchthon's *Apologia* of 1530 raises the question of the origins of the concept. It is clear that the extrinsic conception of justifying righteousness which is fundamental to the notion of forensic justification is due to Luther (see §21). Although Luther incorporates traces of legal terminology into his discussion of justification,[67] it seems that the origins of the concept lie with Erasmus' 1516 translation of the New Testament. The concept of forensic justification is particularly well illustrated by the analogical concept of *acceptilatio* – indeed, this latter concept was frequently employed by the theologians of later Orthodoxy in their discussion of the nature of forensic justification. 'Acceptilation' is a Roman legal term, referring to the purely verbal remission of a debt, as if the debt has been paid – whereas, in fact, it has not. As we have noted, Melanchthon frequently uses classical legal analogies and categories in his discussion of theological concepts, and it is therefore important to note that Erasmus' *Novum instrumentum omne* of 1516 provided not merely a new Latin translation of the Greek text of the New Testament, but also extensive notes justifying departure from the Vulgate text, which often appeal to similar classical antecedents. Of particular interest are his alterations to Romans 4.5. Where the Vulgate read 'Credidit Abraham deo et reputatum est illi ad iustitiam', Erasmus altered the translation to 'Credidit aut Abraham deo et imputatum est ei ad iustitiam.' The potentially forensic implications of this new translation of the Greek verb λογίζηται were pointed out by Erasmus himself: the basic concept underlying 'imputation' was termed 'acceptilation' by the jurisconsults.[68] In view of the fact that Melanchthon knew and used this New Testament text – the best of its age – he could hardly have failed to notice the forensic implications of the concept of 'imputation' as the purely verbal remission of sin, *without* – as with Augustine, Karlstadt and Bugenhagen – the prior or concomitant renewal of the sinner. It would therefore have been a remarkable coincidence, to say the least, that Erasmus should choose to illustrate the meaning of the term 'imputation' with a classical analogy which would later become normative within Protestant Orthodoxy in the definition of the concept of forensic justification – although the concepts of *acceptatio* and *acceptilatio* were frequently confused! – if his original use of the analogy had not been taken up and developed by Melanchthon. A forensic doctrine of justification, in the proper sense of the term, would result from linking Erasmus' interpretation of the concept of imputation with Luther's concept of an extrinsic justifying righteousness – and it seems that Melanchthon took precisely this step.

It will therefore be clear that the Formula of Concord marked not only the ending of an important series of controversies in the Lutheran church immediately after Luther's death; it also marked the victory and consolidation of the critique of Luther from within Lutheranism itself. Luther's concept of justification, his concept of the presence of Christ within the believer, his doctrine of double predestination, his doctrine of *servum arbitrium* – all were rejected or radically modified by those who followed him. It would be improper to inquire as to whether this critique and modification was justified; it is, however, right and proper to note that it took place, as it is only on the basis of this recognition that the full significance of the contribution of Lutheran Orthodoxy to the development of our doctrine may be appreciated.

§23 Reformed doctrines of justification 1519–60

It is a fact, the significance of which is all too easily overlooked, that most of the major Reformers, with the notable exception of Luther, were humanists. In the case of the Reformed church, the influence of humanism was decisive.[1] Although Erasmus' interest in the doctrine of justification appears to have been minimal, it is clear that it is strongly (though not exclusively) moralist in tone.[2] Although it is possible to describe Erasmus' thought as 'Christocentric', this should be understood to refer to the centrality of the *lex Christi* to his ethics.[3] Erasmus thus emphasises the tropological sense of scripture, by which he is able to demonstrate the continuity of the *lex evangelica* from the Old Testament to the New.[4]

The influence of Erasmus over both Zwingli and Bucer appears to have been considerable,[5] and may go some way towards explaining the strongly moralist doctrines of justification associated with these two key theologians of the early Reformed church. Zwingli's theological development appears to have been decisively influenced by his near-fatal illness during an outbreak of the plague at Zurich in August 1519. During the course of this illness, Zwingli appears to have realised that he was nothing but a plaything in the hands of the Almighty; whether he was saved or not was a matter of the divine good pleasure:

Wilt du dann glych
tod haben mich
in mitz der tagen min,
so sol es willig sin.[6]

The strongly determinist cast to Zwingli's thought – probably owing more to Seneca than to St Paul – which is reflected in his emphasis upon an omnipotent and sovereign God contrasts with Luther's quest for a gracious God. In his understanding of justification, Zwingli departs considerably from Luther. In his early humanist period, Zwingli's understanding of justification appears to have been primarily ethical. His contemporaries within the *Christianismus renascens* movement regarded him as a fine exponent of the *philosophia Christi*,[7] with its emphasis upon moral integrity.[8] Zwingli's statements concerning the 'law of the living spirit' are of particular importance in this connection: he defines this law as the 'leading and instructing which God offers to us out of a true understanding of his word'.[9] For Zwingli, the 'righteousness of faith',[10] based upon obedience to God, must be contrasted with 'self-righteousness', based upon self-confidence. The similarities between Erasmus and Zwingli on the *lex evangelica* are evident, particularly in their subordination of justification to regeneration. In fact, Zwingli rarely uses the term 'justification' or 'justified', tending to use the term *rechtglöbig* ('right-believing') instead. Thus he indicates that *der rechtglöbige mensch* submits himself to the law willingly, in contrast to the unbeliever.[11] Zwingli's emphasis upon the moral character of the 'new man' (*wiedergeborene und neue Menschen*)[12] leads him to understand justification to be based upon an *analytic*, rather than a *synthetic*, divine judgement. It is this aspect of Zwingli's theology which led Melanchthon to hint darkly at Marburg of the works-righteousness of the Swiss Reformers: incommode enim loquuntur et scribunt de hominis iustificatione coram Deo, et doctrinam de fide non satis inculcant, sed ita de iustificatione loquuntur, quasi opera, quae fidem sequuntur, sint iustitia hominis.[13]

A similarly moralist approach to justification may be found in the writings of Johannes Oecolampadius, whose strong emphasis upon the importance of regeneration in the Christian life inevitably led to man's justification being subordinated to his regeneration. As Oecolampadius remarks in the course of his comments on Hebrews 10.24, the Christian must continually examine himself to see if the faith which he professes is manifested in good works. As Strohl has noted, Oecolampadius' chief concern appears to have been the ethical dimension of faith.[14] Similarly, Christ's death upon the cross exemplifies the divine love for man, which is intended to move man to moral excellence.[15] Here, as with Zwingli, we find the moral protests of the early Swiss Reformers passing into their theology: the man who has true faith is the man of moral integrity – whose faith may be proved by precisely that integrity. Similarly, Heinrich Bullinger insisted that justification did not mean the imputation of righteousness, but the actualisation of righteousness.[16] As with later Pietism, man's justification is confirmed by moral action.

The most significant exposition of the doctrine of justification within the early Reformed church is due to Martin Bucer, and it is here that we find the still-inchoate moralism of Zwingli being developed into a strongly Erasmian doctrine of justification. Even from his earliest period, Bucer was strongly inclined towards Erasmianism.[17] Although Bucer was clearly influenced by Luther, following their meeting at Heidelberg in 1518, it is significant that Bucer tended to interpret much of Luther's teaching in Erasmian terms, and to pass over many of his more distinctive ideas altogether.[18] Bucer's preoccupations are clearly moralist, as may be seen from his reduction of 'doctrine' to 'ethics' on the basis of his philological exegesis of the concept of *torah*: for Bucer, the whole of scripture is thus *lex*.[19] This moralist approach to scripture is reflected in his doctrine of justification, which represents a significant modification of that of Luther.

Bucer develops a doctrine of *double* justification: after a 'primary justification', in which man's sins are forgiven and righteousness imputed to him, there follows a 'secondary justification', in which man is *made* righteous: the *iustificatio impii*, expounded by Bucer on the basis of St Paul, is followed by the *iustificatio pii*, expounded on the basis of St James.[20] While Bucer is concerned to maintain a forensic concept of primary justification, he stresses the need for this to be manifested as good works in the secondary justification. Although man's primary justification takes place on the basis of faith alone (*sola fide*), his secondary justification takes place on the basis of his works. While Bucer maintains the forensic nature of the primary justification, he stresses the need for this to be manifested in good works. Although this secondary justification appears to be equivalent, in respects, to the later concept of sanctification, it is still conceived in primarily moralist terms.

The question which necessarily follows from this analysis is this: did Bucer actually teach a doctrine of double justification *stricto sensu*

– in other words, that the formal cause of justification is both imputed and inherent righteousness? Bucer's involvement in the drawing up of the 'Regensburg Book' (*Liber Ratisboniensis*), with its important article on justification, is certainly highly suggestive in this respect.[21] The most adequate answer to this question appears to be that Bucer did not intend his doctrine of justification to be an eirenicon, as did Gropper and Pighius (see §25), but rather intended to forge a secure theological link between the totally gratuitous justification of the sinner and the moral obligations which this subsequently placed upon him. The righteousness and good works which are effected by the Holy Spirit are to be seen as the visible evidence of man's unmerited acceptance in the sight of God. Just as a good tree produces good fruit, so the justified sinner must produce good works.[22] It is on account of his preoccupation with the ethical dimensions of the apparently anti-moral doctrine of justification *sola fide* that Bucer has been styled 'the Pietist among the Reformers'.[23] Bucer clearly considers the rôle of piety in the Christian life to be of sufficient importance to require explicit incorporation into a doctrine of justification. Faith must produce 'die ganze Frommheit und Seligkeit', and Bucer ensures this by establishing the following *ordo salutis*:[24]

$$praedestinatio \rightarrow electio \rightarrow vocatio \rightarrow iustificatio \rightarrow glorificatio$$

in which *iustificatio* is understood to have two elements: an initial justification by faith, and a subsequent justification by works.

The important point we wish to emphasise is that Bucer implicates human moral action under the aegis of justification, whereas others (such as Melanchthon) implicated them under the aegis of regeneration or sanctification, which was understood to be a quite distinct element in the *ordo salutis*. Bucer does not, as one of his recent interpreters suggests, include sanctification in the *ordo salutis*:[25] what was later termed *sanctificatio* by Calvin is termed 'secondary justification' or *iustificatio pii* by Bucer.

An important element of the theology of justification of later Reformed Orthodoxy (see §24) can be detected in the writings of the Zurich Reformers dating from the third decade of the sixteenth century.[26] The notion of a 'covenant' or 'testament', an important element of the soteriology of the *via moderna* (§§11, 17) and the young Luther (§20), is evident in that of Zwingli and Bullinger.[27] The concept of a 'covenant' between God and man served two purposes:

the *hermeneutical* function of establishing a basis upon which the unity of the Old and New Testaments might be defended;[28] and the *soteriological* function of establishing the basis upon which man might be justified.[29]

The most significant contribution to the development of the early Reformed doctrine of justification was due to John Calvin.[30] Although the 1536 edition of the *Christianae religionis institutio* contains a few scant lines on justification, that of 1539 and subsequent editions describe the doctrine of justification as the 'main hinge upon which religion turns', and the 'sum of all piety'. The terse statements of that first edition concerning justification are, however, significant:

> Saepe de fidei iustitia disputatur, pauci assequuntur, quomodo fiamus iusti fide. Addamus hanc esse Christi iustitiam, non nostram, in ipso, non in nobis sitam, sed imputatione nostram fieri, quoniam accepta nobis fertur. Ita non vere nos esse iustos sed imputative, vel non esse iustos, sed pro iustis imputatione haberi, quatenus Christi iustitiam per fidem possidemus, res plana erit et expedita.[31]

This brief statement makes explicit a concept of forensic justification, which is developed in subsequent editions. Man is not made righteous in justification, but is accepted as righteous, not on account of his own righteousness, but on account of the righteousness of Christ located outside of man. Calvin's brief discussion of the nature of imputation parallels that of Erasmus' *Novum instrumentum omne* (1516), noted above. In later editions, this understanding of justification is developed (and never, apparently, modified).

For Calvin, a man may be said to be justified when he is accepted by God as if he were righteous:

> Ita nos iustificationem simpliciter interpretamur acceptionem qua nos Deus in gratiam receptos pro iustis habet. Eamque in peccatorum remissione ac iustitiae Christi imputatione positam esse dicimus.[32]

Calvin himself has no hesitation in acknowledging the strongly forensic character of this concept of justification, particularly in his polemic against Osiander.[33] It will also be clear that the emphasis placed by Calvin upon the *acceptatio divina* parallels that of the *via moderna* and the *schola Augustiniana moderna* (§§13, 17, 18), suggesting an affinity with the voluntarism and extrinsicism of these late medieval movements.[34] As there is no basis in man for his divine acceptation, his righteousness in justification is always *extra seipsum*; our righteousness is always *non in nobis sed in Christo*.[35] Although Calvin may be regarded as following Melanchthon in this respect,[36] he nevertheless preserves an important aspect of Luther's understanding of justification which Melanchthon abandoned – the personal union of Christ and the believer in justification. Calvin speaks of the believer being 'grafted into Christ', so that the concept of *incorporation* becomes central to his understanding of justification. The *iustitia Christi*, on the basis of which man is justified, is treated as if it were man's within the context of the intimate personal relationship of Christ and the believer.

Non ergo [Christum] extra nos procul speculamur, ut nobis imputetur eius iustitia: sed quia ipsum induimus, et insiti sumus in eius corpus, unum denique nos secum efficere dignatus est: ideo iustitiae societatem nobis cum eo esse gloriamur. Ita refellitur Osiandri calumnia, fidem a nobis censeri iustitiam; quasi Christum spoliemus iure suo, quum dicimus fidei nos ad eum vacuous accedere, ut eius gratiae locum demus, quo nos ipse solus impleat. Sed Osiander hac spirituali coniunctione spreta, crassam mixturam Christi cum fidelibus urget.[37]

Calvin's polemic against Osiander concerns the nature, rather than the existence, of the union of Christ and the believer; Osiander understands the union to be physical, where Calvin regards it as purely spiritual.[38] The two consequences of the believer's incorporation into Christ are *iustificatio* and *sanctificatio*, which are distinct and inseparable.[39] Thus where Bucer speaks of *iustificatio pii* or 'secondary justification', Calvin speaks of *sanctificatio*; where Bucer links the first and second justifications on the basis of the regenerating activity of the Holy Spirit, Calvin relates them on the basis of the believer's *insitio in Christum*. Justification and sanctification are aspects of the believer's new life in Christ, and just as one receives the whole Christ, and not part of him, through faith, so any separation of these two soteriological elements – which Calvin refers to as *les deux principales grâces*[40] – is inconceivable. It is instructive to compare Bucer and Calvin on the *ordo salutis*:

Bucer: *electio* → *iustificatio impii* → *iustificatio pii* → *glorificatio*

$$\text{Calvin: } electio \rightarrow unio\ mystica \left\{ \begin{array}{c} iustificatio \\ sanctificatio \end{array} \right. \rightarrow glorificatio$$

The strength of Calvin's understanding of justification thus becomes apparent, in that it is evident that justification is now conceived *Christologically*, thus permitting the essentially moral conception of justification associated with Zwingli and Bucer to be discarded. Where Zwingli and Bucer tended to make justification dependent

upon the believer's regeneration through the renewing work of the
Holy Spirit, which enabled him to keep the law and imitate the
(external) example of Christ, Calvin understands both justification
and sanctification to be the chief *beneficia Christi*, bestowed simultaneously and inseparably upon the believer as a consequence of his
insitio in Christum. Calvin thus implicates Christ *intrinsically*, where
Zwingli and Bucer implicated him *extrinsically*, in the *ordo salutis*.
This new approach to justification may be regarded as a recovery –
whether conscious or unconscious – of Luther's realist conception of
justification as the personal encounter of the believer with God in
Christ, while simultaneously the extrinsicism of the Melanchthonian
concept of justification is retained. Like Luther, Calvin stresses that
faith is only implicated in justification to the extent that it grasps and
appropriates Christ.[41] Indeed, faith may be said to play its part in
justification by insisting that it does *not* justify, attributing all to
Christ.[42] In other words, the possibility that the slogan 'justification
sola fide' will be understood as 'justification *propter fidem*' is excluded
from the outset: justification can only be *propter Christum*. Faith is
but the vessel which receives Christ – and the vessel cannot be compared in value with the treasure which it contains.[43] Faith may thus
be said to be the instrumental cause of justification.[44] It will,
however, be clear that Calvin is actually concerned not so much with
justification, as with incorporation into Christ (which has, as one of
its necessary consequences, justification). It is this point which goes
some considerable way towards explaining the lack of importance
which Calvin appears to attach to justification in the 1559 *Institutio*.

It is a well-known fact that, in the 1559 edition of this work,
Calvin defers his discussion of justification until Book III, and it is
then found only after a detailed exposition of sanctification. This has
proved a serious embarrassment to those who project Luther's
concern with the *articulus iustificationis* on to Calvin, asserting that
justification is the 'focal centre' of the *Institutio*.[45] In fact, Calvin's
concern is with the manner in which the individual is incorporated
into Christ, and the personal and corporate consequences of this
insitio in Christum – of which justification is but one. Calvin thus
expresses systematically what Luther grasped intuitively – the recognition that the question of justification was essentially an aspect of
the greater question of man's relation to God in Christ, which need
not be discussed exclusively in terms of the category of justification.[46] In effect, all the watchwords of the Reformation relating
to this theme – *sola fide*, *sola gratia*, and even *sola scriptura* – may be

reduced to their common denominator: justification is *through Christ alone*.

Calvin may be regarded as establishing the framework within which subsequent discussion of justification within the Reformed school would proceed, as well as exemplifying a trend which becomes increasingly evident in the Protestantism of the following century – the increasing diminution of the perceived significance of the *locus iustificationis*. Calvin did not, however, initiate this trend: as we have argued in the present section, the early Reformed church never attached the same importance to the *articulus iustificationis* as did the early evangelical faction within Germany (apparently on account of the personal influence of Luther). Zwingli's early concern with *Christianismus renascens* and Bucer's Erasmian concept of *lex Christi* had little bearing on the doctrine of justification, and, if anything, appear to have exercised a negative influence upon its evaluation. The supposition that the Reformation was homogeneously concerned with the *articulus iustificationis*, even in its initial phase, cannot be sustained on the basis of the evidence available, in that this evidence indicates that the high estimation of and concern for this article was restricted to the initial phase of the German Reformation.

With the death of Calvin, a new phase in the development of Reformed theology took place, which resulted in the emphasis shifting still further away from justification. The rise of Reformed scholasticism led to the recognition of predestination as the central dogma of the Reformed church,[47] even though this emphasis is absent from Calvin's 1559 *Institutio*. Whereas the Lutheran church was initially faced with a series of controversies relating to justification (§21), those now facing the Reformed church would concern predestination. In the following section, we shall consider the development of the doctrine of justification within Lutheran and Reformed Orthodoxy, and establish their points of convergence and divergence.

§24 Justification in Protestant Orthodoxy

The remarkable ease with which a new scholasticism established itself within the churches of the Reformation is one of the more significant aspects of the intellectual history of that period.[1] The need to systematise both Reformed and Lutheran dogmatics was partly a consequence of the perceived need to defend such theologies, and to distinguish them not merely from that of the Council of Trent, but also from one another. The rise of Confessionalism led to a new emphasis upon doctrinal orthodoxy as conformity to the confessional documents of Protestantism, and the use of increasingly subtle and refined concepts in order to defend their theological coherence. This is particularly evident in the case of the doctrine of justification, in which the differences between the two chief Protestant confessions were well established by the year 1620.

Reformed theology was quicker to develop a new scholasticism than its Lutheran counterpart. The general drift of Reformed theology into a form of Aristotelian scholasticism is generally thought to have begun with Beza,[2] and represents a significant shift from Calvin's position on a number of matters of importance. The tendency to base theology upon the basis of deductive reasoning from given principles to yield a rationally coherent system had three significant consequences for the development of the doctrine of justification in Reformed theology:[3]

1. The Christological emphasis evident in Calvin's soteriology is replaced by a theocentric emphasis, as the basis of theological speculation shifts from an inductive method based upon the Christ-event to a deductive method based upon the divine decrees of election.[4]

2. A doctrine of limited atonement is unequivocally stated. Although it may be argued that this doctrine is merely the logical conclusion of Calvin's soteriology, the fact remains that Calvin chose not to draw that conclusion.[5]

3. Predestination is considered as an aspect of the doctrine *of God*, rather than as an aspect of the doctrine *of salvation*.

This process of modification of Calvin under Bezan inspiration culminated in the Five Articles of the Synod of Dort (1619). The English-speaking world has paid a curious tribute to the bulb-growers of the Netherlands in the TULIP mnenomic for these five soteriological points summed up in the doctrines of: (T) total depravity; (U) unconditional election; (L) limited atonement; (I) irresistible grace; (P) perseverance of the elect.[6] Against this, the Remonstrants argued that Christ was the saviour of the world, not merely of the elect, having died for each and every man, and obtained for them remission of sins.[7]

One of the most significant features of the doctrines of justification associated with Reformed Orthodoxy, distinguishing them from both that of Calvin on the one hand, and those of Lutheranism on the other, is that of the covenant between God and man. This development can be traced to the Zurich reforming theology of the 1520s (§23), but was restated in terms of a *double* covenant by Gomarus, Polanus and Wollebius.[8] It is this later form of the concept which would become normative within later Reformed Orthodoxy and Puritanism (see §32). So significant a rôle did the federal foundations of justification assume within the Reformed theological tradition that the covenant-concept was frequently defined as the 'marrow (*medula*) of divinity'. The essential features of the concept may be found outlined in the works of Ursinus, who distinguished between the *foedus naturae*, known naturally to man and offering salvation upon condition of absolute obedience to God, and the *foedus gratiae*, known to man by revelation and offering salvation upon condition that he believe in Jesus Christ.[9] Polanus, by redefining Ursinus' *foedus naturae* as the *foedus operum*, established the general outlines of the theology which would become normative within the early Reformed school. The concept of the covenant between God and man eventually came to replace Calvin's Christological solution to the problem of the relationship between the totally gratuitous justification of the sinner and the demands of obedience subsequently laid upon him, without resorting to the moralist solution associated with Zwingli and Bucer. The *foedus gratiae* was grounded Christologically, with Christ as *testator*, thus retaining the emphasis, if not the substance, of Calvin's position.

The general outlines of the pre-Cocceian theology of the double covenant may be studied from Wollebius' *Christianae theologiae compendium* (1626). A fundamental distinction is drawn between God's dealings with man in his innocent and lapsed states. In the former, God entered of his own free and sovereign decision into a covenant of works with man, which promised him eternal life upon condition that he was obedient to God.[10] Man's fall led to a new covenant being established with him, as an expression of the divine graciousness. The *foedus gratiae* must be distinguished from the universal covenant made by God with all creatures, and the *foedus operum* made with Adam: it is the covenant established between God and his elect, by which God promises himself as their father in Christ, provided that they live in filial obedience to him. Although the *foedus gratiae* is offered to all men, the explicit particularism of the later Reformed soteriology permits only the elect to enjoy its benefits.

It is important to appreciate that the *feodus gratiae* is understood to have operated throughout the period of both the Old and the New Testaments. The Old Testament may be considered as the covenant of grace, as it was administered until the time of Christ, and may be divided into three periods. Between Adam and Abraham, the covenant was expressed simply in terms of the promises of God made to all men, unsupported in any external manner, and marked by the ritual of sacrifice. Between Abraham and Moses, the covenant was expressed in terms of the promises of God to the children of Abraham, supplemented by demands of obedience and the ritual of circumcision. Between Moses and Christ, the covenant assumed a more testamentary character, being marked by the ritual of Passover and other types of the death of Christ, who may be regarded as the testator of the *foedus gratiae*, and hence of both the Old and New Testaments. In effect, both the Old and New Testaments may be regarded as the same in substance, in that both contain the promise of grace linked with the demand of obedience: their difference lies primarily in the manner in which the covenant is administered.[11] The dialectic between law and gospel, so characteristic of contemporary Lutheranism, is thus conspicuously absent.

The covenant-theology of Reformed Orthodoxy received a significant development through Cocceius, who emphasised the potential theological significance of the term *testamentum*, which tended to be used interchangeably with *foedus*. Defining the *testamentum Dei* as *libera dispositio Dei Salvatoris de bonis suis ab haerede suo*,[12] Cocceius located the difference between the *foedus operum* and *foedus gratiae* by affirming that the latter alone may be allowed the character of a divine testament (in the sense of a 'will'), ratified beforehand by God to Christ, by which God appointed a heavenly inheritance for his children, to be acquired through the intervening death of Jesus Christ. The contracting parties to this testament are God as Redeemer, man as sinner, and Christ as the federal mediator between them. The testament is actually contracted in eternity between God and Christ, in which God exacted from Christ the condition of perfect obedience to the law in return for the elect as his own inheritance.[13] This development served to distinguish the covenant of works from that of grace, emphasising the novel character of the latter, in that it alone has the status of a testament. Furthermore, the existence of the intratrinitarian pact between Father and Son was held to justify the doctrine of limited atonement, thus further increasing its influence within later Reformed Orthodoxy.

The doctrine of a three-fold covenant between God and man is particularly associated with the Salmurian Academy. In April 1608, John Cameron published *De triplici Dei cum homine foedere theses*,[14] in which he developed an analysis of salvation history based upon three distinct covenants between God and man: the *foedus naturae, foedus gratiae subserviens* and *foedus gratiae*. The *foedus gratiae subserviens* was regarded by Cameron as a preparation for the *foedus gratiae,* and appears to have represented an attempt to incorporate the Lutheran distinction between law and gospel within the context of a federal scheme. Cameron seems to have regarded the harmonisation of law and gospel implicit in the Orthodox Reformed two-fold covenant scheme as compromising the doctrine of justification *sola fide*.[15] The importance of this three-fold scheme derives from its adoption by Moses Amyraut as the basis of his distinctive theology.[16]

Amyraut's 'hypothetical universalism' and his doctrine of the triple covenant between God and man is unquestionably a direct consequence of his emphasis upon the priority of justification over other Christian doctrines.[17] The Pauline dialectic between law and gospel, underlying Cameron's covenant scheme, causes Amyraut to revise the traditional *foedus operum* or *foedus legale* by interpreting the term *lex* in a radically restricted sense. In his disputation *De tribus foederibus divinis*, Amyraut developed a theory of progressive revelation, culminating in the period of the covenant of grace:

Memorantur autem iustismodi *divina foedera tria* in scripturis, *Primum* quod contractum fuit in Paradiso terrestri, et *Naturale* dici solet, *Secundum*, quod Deus pepigit peculiari ratione cum Israelo, et appellatur *Legale. Tertium* denique quod *Gratiae* dicitur, et patefactum est in Evangelio.[18]

It is possible to confuse the Cocceian and Salmurian interpretations of the federal foundations of justification if it is not realised that the Salmurian academicians recognised the three covenants *to be actualised in time*. The Cocceian covenant theology may be restated in the form of three covenants, of which one is made in eternity: the eternal intratrinitarian covenant between Father and Son precedes the temporal covenants of works and grace. The Salmurian academicians recognised no such eternal intratrinitarian covenant, regarding all three covenants as pertaining to human history. The *foedus naturale* was made directly – without a mediator – between God and Adam, promising a continued blessed existence in Eden upon condition of perfect obedience to the law of nature. The *foedus legale* was made through Moses between God and Israel, and promised a blessed existence in the promised land of Canaan upon condition of perfect obedience to the law of nature *as clarified by the written law and ceremonies*. The *foedus gratiae* was made through Christ between God and all mankind, promising salvation and eternal life upon condition of faith. It is at this point that Amyraut's 'hypothetical universalism' becomes evident: Amyraut states that *Christ intended to die for all men*, although he concedes that the will of God which desires universal salvation also specifies that the condition of faith must be met before this is possible.[19]

Seventeenth-century Lutheran Orthodoxy was primarily concerned with the elucidation and defence of the doctrine of justification to be found in the Formula of Concord (§22). Although the concept of forensic justification was maintained with the utmost rigour, attention shifted to the question of the subjective appropriation of justification. As with Reformed Orthodoxy, so Lutheranism came to adopt scholastic terminology and categories in discussions of justification, although the increasing emphasis upon the practical aspect of justification led to its being discussed as a matter of practical theology (*gratia applicatrix*). Although the extrinsic and forensic aspect of justification was thus maintained formally, it is clear that interest in this aspect of the concept was now overshadowed – particularly as the threat posed by Pietism loomed large – by the practical and experiential dimensions of conversion.[20]

The distinctive positions of Lutheran and Reformed Orthodoxy on justification are most easily expounded and compared when considered under three headings: the nature of justification; the objective grounds of justification; the subjective appropriation of justification. We shall consider each of these points individually.

1 The Nature of Justification

Both confessions understand justification to be the forensic declaratory act of God (*actus Dei forensis in foro coeli*), subsequent to vocation and prior to sanctification.[21] Justification consists of two elements: the remission of sins (or the non-imputation of sin, which is treated as identical with the remission of sins), and the imputation of the obedience of Christ. The Augustinian concept of justification as both event and process, still evident in Luther (§20), is rejected by later Lutheranism. Thus the divine judgement implicit in justification is understood to be *synthetic*, rather than *analytic*. The Reformed school are able to justify their emphasis upon the *iudicium Dei secundum veritatem* through the application of the principle of the *unio mystica* between Christ and the believer, as well as the federal relationship between them, so that the alien righteousness of the former may be imputed to the latter.[22] The absence of a corresponding principle or federal basis within Lutheranism leads to a corresponding weakness at this point, with justification tending to be treated as a legal fiction.

The forensic dimension of justification is emphasised by the use of the term *acceptilation* (see §22 for its use in Erasmus). This concept is taken from Roman private law, and refers to the dissolution of an obligation (such as a debt) by a verbal decree on the part of the one to whom the debt was due, without any form of payment having taken place or necessarily being envisaged as taking place in the future. Justification is thus conceived analogically, as the remission of sins and imputation of righteousness by a purely verbal decree *in foro divino*, without any change in the sinner having taken place with reference to which this verdict could be supported. The term *acceptilation*, so frequently used in this context, appears to be misunderstood by several Reformed theologians, such as Alsted, who confuses it with the Scotist concept of *acceptation* (see §§9, 11, 13, 16).

An important distinction is made by the Reformed theologians between active and passive justification. The distinction refers to the act of God by which the sinner is justified (active justification), and the subjective feeling of grace subsequently evoked in the conscience of the justified sinner. God *acts* to justify, and man is *passive* in receiving this justification. The importance of the distinction lies in the fact that God's act of justification, in which the sinner is declared righteous, is perfect, accomplished once and for all, whereas man's realisation of this state of justification is imperfect, in so far as it is based upon the *feeling* of grace evoked in his conscience. While the two coexist simultaneously in the formal act of justification, the extent of the consciousness of justification may vary from one individual to another. The absence of a corresponding distinction within Lutheranism led to considerable confusion concerning the precise causal relationship of faith and justification, whereas the Reformed theologians were able to state that faith was posterior to objective, and prior to subjective, justification.

2 The Objective Grounds of Justification

Both confessions agree that the objective grounds of justification are to be located in the satisfaction offered by Christ as virtue of his fulfilment of the law and his passion. A distinction was drawn between the *obedientia activa Christi* (his obedience to and fulfilment of the law in his life) and the *obedientia Christi passiva* (his obedience in his suffering and death upon the cross). Both Lutheran and Reformed thinking on this question was stimulated by the controversies surrounding the views of Piscator and Socinus. In his *Theses theologicae*, Piscator developed the views of the Lutheran Parsimonius, who had hindered the Stancarist cause somewhat (see §22) by arguing that if man's obedience to the law was still necessary, it followed that the *obedientia activa* had no substitutionary value. Piscator observed that as believers are clearly still under an obligation to fulfil the law, Christ's active obedience cannot be directly imputed to them.[23] *Remissio peccatorum* and *imputatio iustitia* alike are based upon the *iustitia Christi passiva*.

Piscator was refuted in a variety of manners. The Lutheran Johann Gerhard argued that, as justification included both *remissio peccatorum* and *imputatio iustitiae*, the former could be held to be based upon the *obedientia passiva* and the latter upon the *obedientia activa*.[24] However, Gerhard conceded that this suggestion was only valid *secundum rationem*, and did not reflect a theological relationship between the concepts;[25] as Baier pointed out, this would imply – *secundum rationem* – the priority of *imputatio iustitiae* over *remissio peccatorum*.[26] The Reformed reply to Piscator was somewhat different, and requires careful analysis. According to the Lutheran understanding of the *communicatio idiomatum*, the incarnation of the Word may be said to result in the humanity of Christ participating in *all* the divine attributes, including that of superiority to the law (the so-called *exlex*). Thus Christ, as man, is under no positive obligation to fulfil the law, and his subsequent fulfilment of the law must be seen as a vicarious act of exinanition on his part. If this act of exinanition is to have any value, that value must relate to others, rather than to Christ himself. Thus the *obedientia activa* is of purely vicarious satisfactory value.

While insisting that the *obedientia activa* is vicarious (in other words, of value to those for whom Christ became incarnate), the Reformed theologians operated with a significantly different understanding of the *communicatio idiomatum*: the Lutheran understanding of the principle is rejected as practically dissipating the humanity of Christ. The Reformed Christology attempted to preserve the distinction between the human and divine natures at this point, and replaced the Lutheran understanding of the *communicatio idiomatum* with the quite distinct principle of the *unctio spiritus sancti*. The incarnation itself must be seen as an act of exinanition, involving the setting aside of certain divine attributes – including the so-called *exlex* – as a result of which the manhood of Christ retains its primary characteristics, with the exception of its innate sinfulness. Thus Christ, as man, is under obligation to the law,[27] so that the *obedientia activa* is not necessarily vicarious. The vicarious character of the *obedientia activa* arises through the profoundly Christological conception of justi-fication associated with Reformed Orthodoxy, expressed in the doctrine of Christ as *caput et sponsor electorum*, by which the elect may be said to participate in all the benefits of Christ as if they had obtained them through their own efforts. The *obedientia activa*, in that it is of benefit to Christ, is also of benefit to the elect. It is this concept of Christ as *caput et sponsor electorum* – ultimately repre-senting a central element of Luther's soteriology which Lutheranism failed to appropriate – which underlies the Reformed insistence that the verdict of justification is *iudicium Dei secundum veritatem*, and has misled many into concluding that later Reformed Orthodoxy is based upon an *analytical* understanding of the divine judgement in justi-fication. It could thus be argued that the Reformed understanding of the *obedientia activa* involves a concept of derivative or transferred vicariousness.

The two confessions concur in their understanding of the priestly office of Christ, by which he made satisfaction for the sins of mankind, and their mutual opposition to Socinianism. Socinus had denied that God required any form of satisfaction in order to remit sin: God is to be conceived as a private creditor, able to remit debts due to him without the necessity of the imposition of any penalty.[28] Although Socinus retains the traditional three-fold office of Christ as prophet, priest and king, he restricts the office of priest to that of intercession (whereas it had traditionally included satisfaction),[29] shifting the emphasis to the prophetic office, by which Christ revealed the will of God to man. A general statement of the common Protestant understanding of the satisfaction of Christ takes the following form.[30] Man, having fallen into sin, is liable to death, because God, the righteous judge, is under obligation to punish sin. As man cannot provide the necessary satisfaction for sin, this satisfaction is provided by God himself in the form of the God-man, whose sinlessness absolves him from the common human lot of suffering and death. Christ was obedient to the law in his suffering and death on the cross, and this obedience was adequate as a satisfaction for man's sin. The strongly Anselmian basis of this scheme will be evident, although Anselm did not envisage the merit of Christ functioning as a basis for the imputation of righteousness.[31] Both confessions assert the theanthropic nature of the mediation of Christ[32] – in other words, that Christ is mediator as the God-man, and not either as God or as man separately.

The confessions diverge dramatically over the question of the extent of the redeeming work of Christ. The Lutherans asserted that Christ's merit, won by his obedience, was sufficient for all men, although only efficacious in the case of those who, after their regeneration, respond to the Word and are thus justified. The *errores Calvinianorum* are located by Gerhard in their concept of predestination, which underlies their teaching on justification.[33] In effect, Lutheran Orthodoxy interpreted the concept of election as God's affirmation of that which he foreknows will occur within the sphere of his ordained will – in other words, election takes place on the basis of *fides praevisa*. Through man's regeneration, his *liberum arbitrium* is restored, enabling him to respond freely to the Word of the gospel – whether he accepts it or not is up to the individual. This affirmation that *vocatio* is *resistibilis et universalis* is characteristic of later Lutheran Orthodoxy, and raises significant questions to which we shall return in our discussion of the subjective appropriation of justification.

The Reformed divines, while conceding the universal sufficiency of the work of Christ, emphasised the particularity of its efficacy. This opinion represents a development of the views of Calvin, who did not teach limited atonement, but affirmed that the gospel was offered by God for all mankind. Hence, in his critical discussion of the Tridentine decree on justification, Calvin raised no objections to the explicit statement that Christ died for all men.[34] Beza, however, explicitly stated that Christ died only for the elect, and not for all men.[35] As later Orthodoxy would put it, Christ died *sufficienter* for all men, but *efficienter* only for the elect.[36] As Rijssen remarked, a distinction must be drawn between God's general love, exercised towards all men, and his saving love, by which he wills to redeem them.[37] There is thus a clear distinction between the Lutheran concept of the general divine intention to save all, actualised in the case of those who believe, and the Reformed doctrine of an efficacious individual election.

3 *The Subjective Appropriation of Justification*

One of the most significant developments in seventeenth-century Lutheran dogmatics was the affirmation that faith was itself a cause of justification. Although it was emphasised that faith was a *causa impulsiva minus principalis iustificationis*, it was clearly stated that faith was logically prior to justification in the *ordo salutis*. This affirmation was interpreted to mean that justification was dependent upon a change in man, and resulted in justification being placed towards the end of an *ordo salutis* which included elements such as *illuminatio*, *regeneratio* and *conversio*. Although justification is still defined *forensically*, it is understood to be predicated upon a prior alteration within man – namely, that he believes. Where Luther had understood justification to concern the *unbelieving sinner*, Orthodoxy revised this view, referring justification to the *believing sinner*. Thus Calov and Quenstedt defend the following *ordo salutis*:

vocatio → *illuminatio* → *regeneratio* → *conversio* → *iustificatio*

The final Lutheran doctrine of justification, as stated by Hollaz, has the following form: man, in his natural state, is spiritually dead. By the means of grace, especially through the agency of the Word, man receives new powers, the illumination of his understanding, and the excitement of good desires. This brings about the restoration of the *liberum arbitrium*, so that the *arbitrium liberatum* is now enabled, should the individual so wish, to believe. Man thus possesses the *facultas applicandi se ad gratiam* before his justification, and his justification is contingent upon precisely such *applicatio gratiae*. If the individual chooses to do so, he may, although he need not, use these powers consequent to his regeneration to repent and believe, and as a result to be justified.[38] It will be clear that there are thus considerable affinities between later Orthodoxy and Pietism on the relationship between faith and justification.

In part, the later Lutheran insistence on the priority of regeneration and conversion over justification represents a reaction against the Reformed doctrine of irresistible grace, a leading feature of Reformed spirituality in the post-Dort period. In order to avoid such a teaching, it is necessary to develop a theology of justification which simultaneously asserts the inability of man to justify himself *sine gratia* and his ability to reject the possibility of justification once this arises. The assertion of the priority of regeneration over justification thus permits the later Lutheran divines to assert the necessity of grace in justification (in that it is necessary for man's regeneration), while restricting its efficacy (in that man's regeneration is understood to involve the repristination of his volitional faculties, by which he is able to determine whether or not to respond to his call). It will, however, be clear that the result is a theology which places regeneration prior to faith, and faith prior to justification.

The Reformed understanding of the matter is much simpler and more coherent. Man's justification is the temporal execution of the decree of election, effected through grace. The fact that this proceeds through a complex causal sequence does not alter the fact that the entire sequence of events is directly to be attributed to God. Thus Wendelin draws up the following chart for the assistance of his readers.[39]

$$
Acceptatio,\ cuius
\begin{cases}
causa\ instrumentalis = fides\ iustificans \\
\qquad\qquad\qquad\qquad\quad iustificatio \\
effectus\ isque\ triplex
\begin{cases}
iustificatio \\
sanctificatio \\
glorificatio
\end{cases}
\end{cases}
$$

Faith is a divine gift effected within man, functioning as the instrument by which the Holy Spirit may establish the *unio mystica* between Christ and the believer, whose three-fold effect is justification, sanctification and glorification (note how Wendelin includes glorification as an effect of the *insitio in Christum*, where Calvin deferred it within the *ordo salutis*). Man's rôle at each and every stage of the *ordo salutis* is purely passive, in that the elect are called and accepted *efficaciter*. This observation goes some considerable way towards explaining the low status accorded to justification within Reformed dogmatics: justification is merely an aspect of the temporal execution of the eternal decree of election. God exercises his providential rule over creation through the efficacious justification of the elect. It is interesting to observe that although the objective grounds of justification fall under the aegis of the priestly office of Christ in Reformed dogmatics, the subjective appropriation of justification is dealt with under the aegis of the kingly office.

It will be clear that the Lutheran and Reformed understandings of the *nature* of justification are similar, the chief differences between them emerging in relation to the question of the objective grounds and subjective appropriation of justification. The Reformed doctrines of absolute and unconditional predestination and limited atonement, linked with the federal understanding of the basis of justification, distinguish the doctrines of justification associated with that school from those of Lutheranism. Significantly, the Reformed school is considerably closer to Luther (especially the 1525 Luther) than Lutheranism. Given that both confessions adopted a strongly forensic concept of justification, which set them apart from Luther on this point, the strongly predestinarian cast of Reformed theology approximates to that of Luther to a far greater extent than Lutheran Orthodoxy. Similarly, the strongly Christological conception of justification to be found in Luther's writings is carried over into Reformed theology, particularly in the image of Christ as *caput et sponsor electorum*, where it is so evidently lacking in Lutheran Orthodoxy. Both in terms of its substance and emphasis, the teaching of later Lutheran Orthodoxy bears little relation to that of Luther.

The period of Lutheran Orthodoxy was marked by considerable opposition from the increasingly influential Pietist movement, particularly associated with the university of Halle.[40] At its best, the Pietist movement may be regarded as a reaction on the part of a living faith against the empty formulae of a dead Orthodoxy. The term 'Pietism' is particularly applied to the movement within Lutheranism associated with Philipp Jakob Spener, characterised by its insistence upon the active nature of faith, and its critique of the Orthodox doctrine of forensic justification. Such criticism was foreshadowed in many quarters, including sections of the Radical Reformation.[41] The English Quaker Robert Barclay taught that justification is identical with regeneration, whose formal cause is 'the revelation of God in the soul, changing, altering and renewing the mind'.[42] On account of his being made a partaker of the divine nature, man is *made* righteous.[43] A similar, although more extended, critique of the Orthodox doctrine of justification is to be found in the writings of Jakob Böhme.[44]

As Ritschl has observed,[45] Pietism maintained the doctrine of *reconciliation* in a thoroughly orthodox form (in other words, man was understood to be alienated from God through original sin), while subjecting the doctrine of *justification* to extensive modification on the basis of the pastoral concern for personal holiness and devotion.[46] The concept of participation in the divine nature, usually expounded on the basis of 2 Peter 1.4,[47] appears to have become characteristic of Pietist understandings of the nature of justification at an early stage. Five important modifications were made by the Pietists to the Orthodox doctrine of justification.

1. Faith is understood to be active, rather than passive, in justification. The Pietist assertion of the activity of faith in justification was particularly criticised by the Lutheran Valentin Löscher, who appealed to Luther's insistence upon the passivity of justifying

faith.[48] Löscher's criticisms were rejected by Anton and Lange, who argued that faith must be active if it is to lay hold of Christ. Francke himself argued that the activity of faith in justification was not inconsistent with God's being the author of justification.[49]

2. The intense emphasis placed by Pietism upon the necessity for personal piety led to the articulation of the doctrine of Christian perfection, a concept without any counterpart within – indeed, which was excluded by – Orthodoxy.[50]

3. The concept of vicarious satisfaction is rejected as detrimental to personal piety. This criticism of the Orthodox understanding of the objective foundations of justification can be instanced from the writings of Spener, although it is particularly associated with John Wesley.[51] To Wesley, the assertion that Christ had fulfilled the law on man's behalf appeared to imply that man was no longer under any obligation to fulfil it. It is this consideration which underlies Wesley's discussion of the law *sub loco sanctificationis*.

4. The concept of imputed righteousness, which is an essential feature of the Orthodox understanding of justification, is rejected as being destructive of piety.[52] Thus in his *Theses credendorum*, Breithaupt argued for the necessary implication of inherent righteousness in justification.[53] In his sermon *A Blow at the Root, or Christ stabbed in the House of his Friends*, Wesley described the teaching 'that Christ had done as well as suffered all; that his righteousness being imputed to us, we need none of our own' as 'a blow at the root of all holiness, all true religion . . . for wherever this doctrine is cordially received, it leaves no place for holiness'.[54] This criticism was expanded in the Standard Sermon *Justification by Faith*:

Least of all does justification imply that God is deceived in those whom he justifies; that he thinks them to be what, in fact, they are not; that he accounts them to be otherwise than they are. It does by no means imply that God judges concerning us contrary to the real nature of things; that he esteems us better than we really are, or believes us righteous when we are unrighteous . . . [or] . . . judges that I am righteous, because another is so.[55]

5. The Pietist emphasis upon the need for personal holiness appeared to be threatened by the Orthodox doctrine that man might repent at any time of his choosing, which frequently led to 'death-bed conversions' on the part of notorious sinners who had evidently chosen to postpone their conversion until the last possible moment. It was this pastoral consideration which led to the Terminist controversy, particularly associated with Böse's *Terminus peremptorius salutis hominis* (1698).[56] The course of this controversy does not concern us; its

significance lies in its illustrating the Pietist willingness to develop theologies of justification of such a character as to maximise personal piety. In that the Orthodox doctrine of repentance was held to compromise this, it was subjected to modification along the lines indicated. It was for reasons such as this that many regarded Pietists as having *de*formed, rather than *re*formed, the Lutheran church of their day.

Although the early Pietists such as Spener or Francke were more concerned with the promotion of personal piety than with the restructuring of Christian doctrine, it is an inescapable fact that the Pietist emphasis upon regeneration led to a re-evaluation of the received teachings of Lutheran Orthodoxy in terms of their promotion of piety. The emphasis upon the necessity of regeneration led to the assertion of the priority of regeneration over justification – a tendency already evident within Lutheran Orthodoxy itself, which was thus ill prepared to meet this development. The Pietist emphasis upon the priority and necessity of piety, virtue and obedience on the part of believers is significant for another reason, in that it provides a direct link with the moralism of the *Aufklärung*. If an 'active faith' is to be accepted as the arbiter and criterion of justification, in the quasi-Arminian sense often found in the writings of the Pietists, it may be concluded that the practice of piety by an individual is an adequate demonstration of his faith. In other words, the ethical renewal of the individual both causes and demonstrates his justification. This important observation goes some considerable way towards explaining the rise of legalism within the Pietist theological faculty at Halle towards the end of the eighteenth century, and also points to a fundamental affinity with the moralism of the theologians of the *Aufklärung*.

7. The Tridentine decree on justification

Introduction

The Catholic church was ill prepared to meet the challenge posed by the rise of the evangelical faction within Germany and elsewhere in the 1520s and 1530s.[1] Luther's doctrine of justification attracted considerable attention in the 1520s, not all of it unsympathetic. According to Schmidt, three reasons may be suggested to explain the remarkable importance which came to be attached within contemporary Catholicism to the doctrine of justification *sola fide*.[2] First, it required an internalisation of the religious life, thus sharply contrasting with the prevailing external forms of Christian existence.[3] Second, it restored an emphasis upon the priority of the divine rôle in justification, against the prevailing tendency to concentrate upon the human rôle. Third, it amounted to an implicit declaration of war upon the Roman curia. Relatively few works dealing with the doctrine of justification were published within Catholicism in the period 1520–45, with notable exceptions such as Tommaso de Vio Cajetan's *De fide et operibus* (1532).[4] A survey of such works suggests that the Lutheran doctrine of justification was simply not understood by the early opponents of the Reformation,[5] although the rise of polemical theology in the 1530s served to clarify points of importance. Early anti-Lutheran polemic tended to fasten upon points which Luther regarded as trivial – such as Luther's views on the papacy, indulgences or the sacraments, while failing to deal with such crucial questions as the concept of *servum arbitrium* or the nature of justifying righteousness. Indeed, Luther singled out Erasmus alone as identifying the real theological issues involved in his protest.[6]

The task facing the theologians assembled at Trent was thus not merely the clarification of Catholic teaching on justification, but also the definition of Catholic dogma in relation to the perceived errors of Protestantism. In fact, however, views on justification remarkably similar to those associated with the northern European Reformers penetrated deep into the hierarchy of the Italian church in the period 1520–45, and are widely thought to have been espoused by several of those present during the Tridentine debate on justification. What those views were, and whence they originated, are the subject of the following section.

§25 Developments within Catholicism 1490–1545

The late fifteenth and early sixteenth centuries saw the emergence of numerous groups agitating for reform within the church, frequently adopting theologies of justification which foreshadowed the Augustinianism of the Wittenberg Reformation. In the present section, we are particularly concerned with developments in Italy, and the origins and significance of the doctrines of justification associated with Gropper and Contarini, which exercised some influence over evangelical–Catholic attempts at reconciliation in the period 1536–41 and emerged as an issue at the Council of Trent.

The rise of Augustinianism in the late fifteenth and early sixteenth centuries is perhaps best illustrated from developments within Spain.[1] The rise of the *alumbrados* is one of the more remarkable features of the period,[2] and the records of the Spanish Inquisition indicate that radically theocentric views on justification were in circulation within the movement by 1511.[3] Although the marked individualism characteristic of *alumbramiento* distinguishes it from Protestantism,[4] the recognition of affinities between certain *alumbrados* and Luther led to the suppression of the movement in the 1520s.

The most significant figure of the Spanish religious renaissance for our purposes is Juan de Valdés, whose *Diálogo de doctrina cristiana* (1529) developed a radically theocentric doctrine of justification which came to serve as a model for Italian Evangelism in the 1530s.[5] The central problem posed by the doctrine of justification is identified by Valdés in *Las ciento diez divinas consideraciones* as follows:

es útil al honbre que Dios sea omnipotente, liberal, sabio, fiel, vegnino, misericordioso y piadoso, mas no parece que le sea útil que él sea justo: porque, siendo Dios justo y el honbre ynjusto, no alla cómo poderse salvar en el juizo de Dios.[6]

Valdés develops a concept of *la justicia de Dios* based upon the principle 'once in jeopardy' which is markedly different from that of Augustine and the Wittenberg Reformers: God, having punished

Christ, and hence man, for the sins of mankind, may be relied upon not to punish twice for the same offence:

determinando de executar en el su proprio Hijo todoel rigor de la justicia qua avía de executar contra todos los honbres por todas sus ynpiedades y pecados . . . Creamos al Evangelio qual nos certifica que en Christo fuimos castigados, y en esto nos aseguramos, sabiendo que Dios es justo e que fuimos castigados ya en la cruz de Iezu Christo nuestro Señor.[7]

It is therefore necessary for the believer to recognise that he is righteous in Christ, although he is a sinner in himself, in that the penalty for sin has been laid upon Christ:

De manera que, o me debo yo conoscer justo en Christo, bein que yo me conosco pecador en mí; o debo negar aquello que afirmo el Evangelio, que en Christo Dios a castigado las eniquidades y los pecados de todos los honbres y los míos con ellos.[8]

This marks a significant departure from the Erasmian anthropology, although it must be noted that Valdés' statement of the principle *simul iustus et peccator* does not parallel that of either Augustine or Luther exactly.[9] Valdés' arrival in Italy in 1531 led to his considerable influence being subsequently exercised over Italian reforming circles, to which we now turn.

The late fifteenth and early sixteenth centuries witnessed a revival in interest in the theology of Augustine, accompanying extensive publication of editions of his works.[10] In Italy, this Augustinian renaissance was accompanied by a new interest on the part of Italian humanists in the Pauline corpus of the New Testament.[11] It is against this background that the conversion experience of Gasparo Contarini must be seen. A member of a group of Paduan-educated humanists which included Paolo Giustiniani,[12] Contarini shared their common difficulty concerning the means by which salvation might be attained. The contemporary confusion within the Catholic church concerning the doctrine of justification was reflected within this group: some chose to enter a hermitage as the only possible means for expiating their sins, while others – including Contarini – chose to remain in the world. The correspondence between Contarini and Giustiniani indicates the former's concern with problems remarkably similar to those which so preoccupied Luther at the same time.[13] For Contarini, the sacrifice of Christ upon the cross was more than adequate as a satisfaction for human sin, in which man must learn to trust utterly.[14] It is utterly impossible for man to be justified on the basis of his works: man is justified through faith in Christ, as a result of which the righteousness of Christ is made ours.[15] Contarini's theological break-through may be dated in the first half of 1511, thus placing it before that of Luther and even before the alleged 'discovery' by Pietro Speziali of the doctrine of justification by faith in 1512.[16]

The Contarini–Giustiniani correspondence is of importance in that it illustrates the doctrinal confusion of the immediate pre-Tridentine period in relation to the doctrine of justification. Giustiniani was convinced that it was necessary to withdraw from the world and lead a life of the utmost austerity in order to be saved, whereas Contarini came to believe that it was possible to lead a normal life in the world, trusting in the merits of Christ for salvation. But which of these positions represented, or approximated most closely to, the teaching of the Catholic church? The simple fact is that this question could not be answered with any degree of confidence. This doctrinal confusion concerning precisely the issue over which the Reformation was widely held to have begun inevitably meant that the Catholic church was in no position to attempt a coherent systematic refutation of the teaching of the evangelical faction in its crucial initial phase.

The dialectic between *iustitia Christi* and *iustitia hominis* points to an important difference between Luther and Contarini. Although both emphasise the rôle of faith and the 'alien' righteousness of Christ, the exclusivity of Luther's solafideism and extrinsicism is not to be found with Contarini. Contarini's primary concern appears to have been the elimination of human self-confidence, which he regarded as an impediment to justification; he does not exclude the possibility of human cooperation with God, nor does he consider the proper emphasis upon faith to entail the elimination of *caritas* from justification. Nevertheless, Contarini concedes the truth of Luther's insights: pero il fondamento dello aedificio de Luterani e verissimo, ne per alcun modo devemo dirli contra, ma accettarlo come vero et catholico, immo come fondamento della religione christiana.[17]

In respects, Contarini's later views on justification – particularly those dating from 1541 – parallel those of the Cologne theologian Johannes Gropper, whose *Enchiridion* was published in 1538. This work has often been regarded as developing a doctrine of double justification, based on the concept of *duplex iustitia*.[18] In fact, this view appears to rest upon a serious misunderstanding of Gropper's views. It is possible that this misunderstanding derives from Bellarmine's attempt to discredit those present at Regensburg:

Bucerus in libro Concordiae, ut fortasse Catholicos aliquos seduceret, ut fecit, duplicem iustitiam excogitavit, a qua formaliter iustificaremur; unam

244

imperfectam, quae in virtutibus in nobis inhaerentibus sita sit, alteram perfectam, quae est ipsa Christi iustitia nobis imputata. Quoniam enim iustitia nostra nunquam talis esse potest, ut iudicium Dei sustineat, ut ipse dicit, ideo necessarium esse imputationem iustitia Christi, ut illa induti, et quodammodo tecti coram Deo compareamus, et iusti pronunciemur . . . In eandem sententiam sive potius errorem indicit Albertus Pighius in Contr. II et auctores Antididagmatis Coloniensis.[19]

In his influential study on the background to Regensburg, Stupperich appears to follow Bellarmine's analysis of the relation of Bucer, Pighius and Gropper,[20] and concluded that Gropper explicitly taught a doctrine of double justification. This conclusion requires modification. The concept of a 'double righteousness' – but *not* of a double formal cause of justification – is to be found in the earlier medieval discussion of justification, where a clear distinction is drawn (particularly within the early Dominican, and subsequently the Thomist, school) between *iustitia infusa* and *iustitia acquisita* (see §§5, 6). Justification takes place upon the basis of *iustitia infusa*, with the subsequent establishment of *iustitia acquisita*. This is most emphatically *not* a doctrine of double justification! A careful distinction is merely drawn between the righteousness which functions as the formal cause of justification (*iustitia infusa* or *iustitia inhaerens*) and the righteousness which subsequently develops within the believer through his cooperation with grace: in other words, although justification involves *duplex iustitia*, these *iustitiae* are understood to be implicated in totally different manners within the overall scheme of justification. A doctrine of 'double justification', in the strict sense of the term (as it is encountered during the Tridentine proceedings on justification: see §26), is essentially a doctrine of a *double formal cause of justification*: in other words, justification takes place on account of *duplex iustitia*. Stupperich has tended to confuse *iustitia inhaerens* with *iustitia acquisita* in his exposition of the relationship of Gropper's concepts of *iustitia imputata* and *iustitia inhaerens*, with a concomitant misunderstanding both of Gropper's doctrine of justification and its relationship to Melanchthon and Catholicism.[21] The assertion of the inseparability of forgiveness and renewal is most emphatically *not* equivalent to a doctrine of 'double justification', and this confusion over the definition of terms has enormously impeded the proper evaluation of the significance of Gropper. In the *Enchiridion*, it is clear that Gropper merely develops an earlier medieval insight in such a manner as to correct the perceived shortcomings of the Melanchthonian doctrine of justification, while at the same time indicating the common ground between the Lutheran and Catholic doctrines.

The chapter of the *Enchiridion* entitled *de iustificatione hominis* opens with the following definition of justification: iustificatio duo proprie complectitur, nempe remissionem peccatorum et interioris mentis renovationem seu repurgationem.[22] Gropper criticises Melanchthon's concept of forensic justification, which he illustrates with specific reference to the latter's analogy of the people of Rome declaring Scipio to be free: iustificari *plus* apud Paulum significat, quam iustum pronuntiari.[23] Justification is inextricably linked with the internal renewal of the individual: nemo iustificatur, nisi per innovationem voluntatis.[24] Where Gropper so evidently differs from the traditional Catholic account of justification is in his use of the concept of imputed righteousness. It appears, however, that Gropper interprets this concept in a non-Melanchthonian sense, tending to regard it as equivalent to divine acceptation.[25] Justification is not regarded as identical with the forensic pronouncement that the individual is righteous, and Gropper's divergence from Melanchthon at this point is unequivocal. It appears that Gropper regards the divine acceptation of the believer through his renewal (expressed in terms of *remissio peccatorum et renovatio interior voluntatis*) as equivalent to the imputation of righteousness, and thus merely restates the standard later medieval concept of *acceptatio divina* in language which he feels to be more acceptable to his Lutheran opponents. Far from developing a doctrine of 'double justification', Gropper merely states the inseparability of *remissio peccatorum* and *renovatio* in a thoroughly Augustinian sense. Melanchthon's definition of *iustificatio* as *acceptatio*[26] is a passage alluded to be Gropper obviously suggests such an approach.

Those who hold that Gropper develops a doctrine of 'double justification' are obliged to assert that the *Enchiridion* explicitly teaches a *double formal cause of justification*.[27] This is simply not the case. Gropper clearly asserts a single formal cause of justification (*proprie causa formalis iustificationis*), and defines it as *misericordia et gratia Dei nos innovans*.[28] Gropper rigorously excludes the possibility, necessarily associated with a doctrine of 'double justification', that the believer is justified on account of (*propter*) his renewal: iustificationem non assequimur *propter* nostram novitatem, sed *novitas*, quam Deus operatur in nobis, haec *est iustificatio nostra*.[29] It is evident that Gropper is merely restating the traditional medieval teaching that justification *includes*, but does not *take place on account of*, the interior renewal of the believer. Although Gropper's discussion of habitual grace is difficult to follow, it is evident that *gratia Dei nos innovans* – which he defines to be the single formal cause of justification – is functionally identical with the Thomist concept of *iustitia infusa seu inhaerens*, thus establishing the continuity between Gropper and the medieval tradition upon this point. Although Gropper clearly identifies important areas of continuity between the Catholic and Protestant understandings of justification, he cannot be regarded as a pre-Tridentine exponent of 'double justification' in the proper sense of the term.

Views similar to those expressed in Gropper's *Enchiridion* may be found in Contarini's *Epistola de iustificatione*, written from Regensburg on 25 May 1541. For Contarini, justification involves both becoming righteous (*iustum fieri*) and being counted as righteous (*iustum haberi*).[30] Contarini thus develops a theology which, like that of Gropper, has tended to be interpreted as a pre-Tridentine statement of the doctrine of 'double justification', explicitly recognising two types of righteousness implicated in the process of justification:

Attingimus autem ad duplicem iustitiam, alteram nobis inhaerentem, qua incipimus esse iusti et efficimur 'consortes divinae naturae' et habemus charitatem diffusam in cordibus nostris, alteram vero non inhaerentem sed nobis donatam cum Christo, iustitiam inquam Christi et omne eius meritum. Simul tempore utraque nobis donatur et utramque attingimus per fidem.[31]

Which of these *iustitiae* is prior to the other is, according to Contarini, a useless scholastic disputation;[32] the important point is that man's inherent righteousness, which is initially inchoate and imperfect, is supplemented by *iustitia Christi* as a preliminary anticipation of the state which subsequently arises through the agency of *iustitia inhaerens*.[33] The evident similarity between the views of Gropper and Contarini on justification goes some considerable way towards explaining the 'agreement' reached on justification at the Diet of Regensburg (often referred to in its Latinised form 'Ratisbon') in 1541.

Gropper's *Enchiridion* appears to have formed the basis of Article 5 of the *Liber Ratisboniensis* which formed the basis of the discussion between Protestants and Catholics at Regensburg.[34] Although agreement on the matter of justification was reached between those present at the Diet, it is clear that these individuals were simply not regarded as representative by their respective institutions: whatever personal agreement might be found to exist on the matter of justification between men such as Bucer, Contarini and Gropper, this was more than outweighed by the institutional differences between Lutheranism and Catholicism. Furthermore, the agreement appears to have been reached by a process of *zusammenleimen* – 'glueing together' (to use Luther's term), a 'scissors and paste job' (Fenlon) – which merely placed opposing views side by side, without reconciling, or even addressing, the underlying questions. It is clear that Article V *de iustificatione* represented a mere juxtaposition of the Catholic and Protestant positions, with a purely superficial engagement with the serious theological issues at stake.[35] The failure of Regensburg was of considerable political consequence, as it eventually led to the general discrediting of the Italian reforming movement known as 'Evangelism', to which we may now turn.

Evangelism was an undogmatic and transitory movement, originating within Italy itself (and the importance of Contarini's experience of 1511 should not be overlooked), rather than from Protestant currents north of the Alps.[36] The strongly Augustinian and individualist theologies of justification associated with the movement in its early phase paralleled those emerging elsewhere within Catholic Europe at the time. There can, however, be no doubt that the movement rapidly came under Protestant influence through the dissemination of printed works of the Reformers.[37] One of the most intriguing questions concerning this movement relates to the anonymous work *Trattato utilissimo del beneficio di Giesu Cristo crocifisso*, the second edition of which (1543) achieved a significant circulation throughout Europe.[38] Its first four chapters expound the doctrine of justification by faith with some vigour, and it is significant that the mediating position associated with Contarini and the Regensburg delegates appears to have been abandoned in favour of an account of the mode of justification which parallels that associated with Juan de Valdés.[39] The doctrine of justification *sola fide* is constantly interpreted thus: chiunque crede in Cristo è giustificato senza opere e senza merito alcuno.[40] It is through faith that Christ and his righteousness become the believer's, and on the basis of the union of the believer with Christ that God treats the former as righteous:

Così è necessario che noi ci vestiamo de la giustizia di Cristo per la fede, e ci occultiamo sotto la preziosa purità del nostro fratello primogenito, se vogliamo essere ricevuti per giusti nel conspetto di Dio ... Dio ci vedrà ornati della giustizia di Cristo, senza dubbio ci accetterà per giusti e santi e degni della vita eterna.[41]

The strongly personalist understanding of justification associated with both Luther and Calvin is evident throughout the work. Through faith, the believer is united with Christ, clothed with his righteousness, and thence accepted as righteous and worthy of eternal life by God. Although there are unquestionably further recognisable allusions to the writings of northern European Reformers in the work, it is clear that the dominant influence is the form of Augustinian individualism associated with Valdés – evident, for example, in the complete omission of any reference to the implication of the church as an institution in the process of justification. Furthermore, the concept of *imputatio iustitiae* is not to be found in the work in its distinctively Protestant form. Most significant, however, is the outright rejection of the mediating theology of justification by faith *and* works associated with the members of the Viterbo circle, *quelli . . . defendono la giustificazione della fede e delle opere.*[42] This point is important, as it indicates the development of a more radical faction within the Italian reforming movement in the period immediately before its suppression, critical of the mediating Regensburg theology. Although the work develops a doctrine of justification *sola fide*, it is clear that the formula is understood in a sufficiently flexible manner to accommodate those such as Reginald Pole, who retained the verbal formula, while interpreting the concept of faith in an Augustinian sense, as *fides quae per dilectionem operatur*. For Pole, the faith by which man alone was justified was a faith active through love:

Nec enim illos audiendos esse ullo modo censemus, qui sic solam fidem praedicant, ut piis caritatis actionibus detrahant: qui ignavis nihil agendi, impigris ad actiones male agendi occasionem, et licentiam suo perverso loquendi modo praebant: quos non tam perverse quidem, quam impie praedicare fidem existimamus; dum vel parum curare, vel prorsus contemnere leges, et maiorem instituta docent. Nec enim, quam praedicabant Apostoli, per quam iustificantur impii, fides eiusmodi fuit, sed quae caritatem operatur.[43]

This mediating approach appears to have exercised some restraint within the Viterbo circle, restraining its more radical members (such as Flaminio, Priuli and Vittoria) from action which could have proved prejudicial to the future conciliar pronouncement (which Pole appears to have assumed would broadly parallel his own mediating formula).[44]

The period of Italian Evangelism came to a close in 1542. Rather like the 'Prague Spring' of 1968, the period 1520–42 represented a brief interval in which ideas could be freely debated before an external authority intervened to prohibit such discussion. In 1542, Paul III, alarmed by religious unrest in Lucca, Modena and Venice, published the Bull *Licet ab initio*, re-establishing the Roman Inquisition. Whilst the influence of the northern European Reformers upon Evangelism in its later phase is undeniable, there are excellent reasons for suggesting that a form of doctrine of justification *sola fide* initially originated – independent of reforming movements in northern Europe – and subsequently achieved widespread circulation in the highest ecclesiastical circles in Italy. The failure of Regensburg to mediate between Catholicism and Protestantism forced the issue of definition of Catholic dogma upon the church, with the inevitable possibility that the temporary estrangement of the evangelical faction might become permanent schism. The convening of the Council of Trent was intended to provide the definition of Catholic doctrine so urgently required. Before dealing with this crucial period in the development of the doctrine of justification, it is necessary to consider the theologies of justification associated with the main schools of thought represented at the Council, and particularly the question of whether there existed an 'Augustinian' school, represented by Girolamo Seripando.

§26 The theological schools at Trent during the debate on justification

The Council of Trent was faced with a group of formidable problems as it assembled to debate the question of justification in June 1546. The medieval period had witnessed the emergence of a number of quite distinct schools of thought on justification (see §§14–18), clearly incompatible at points, all of which could lay claim to represent the teaching of the Catholic church. The Council of Trent was not concerned with settling long-standing debates between the various Catholic schools of theology, but with attempting a definition of the Catholic consensus on justification in the face of the Protestant challenge. The suggestion of the Bishop of Vaison, that the theologians present at Trent to debate the matter of justification should initially meet as separate Orders under their respective generals,[1] was rejected, presumably because this procedure would merely heighten the differences between the schools of thought present at Trent. In the present section, we are concerned with the identification of the main schools present at Trent, as this has an important bearing upon the relation of the final decree to late medieval Catholic theology in general.

In an important study earlier in the present century, Stakemeier argued for the existence of three theological schools at Trent during the proceedings on justification: the Thomist, Scotist and

Augustinian schools.[2] This division of the theological schools present at Trent has exercised considerable influence over subsequent discussion, and does not appear to have been subjected to critical examination. It is, in fact, quite difficult to establish the precise allegiance of many of the speakers during the proceedings on account of the similarities between the schools in relation to the points under discussion.

It is beyond question that a significant Thomist school was represented at Trent. The revival of the Thomist school had taken place in the fifteenth century under Capreolus,[3] who had established the fundamental principle that Thomas Aquinas' views should be determined on the basis of the *Summa Theologiae*, rather than the earlier *Commentary on the Sentences*. As noted in §7, Thomas' views on justification altered significantly in the intervening period, with the result that Capreolus' maxim led to a more Augustinian understanding of justification being defined as 'Thomist' than would have been regarded as legitimate earlier. It is this presupposition which underlies Cajetan's use of Thomas. In addition, Capreolus appears to have drawn upon the ferociously anti-Pelagian writings of Gregory of Rimini to emphasise the Augustinian elements of Thomas' doctrine of justification,[4] with the result that a theology of justification based jointly upon Augustine and Thomas Aquinas came to be widely current within Catholic circles.[5] The authority with which Thomas was invested may be judged from the fact that he was cited more than any theologian – other than Augustine – during the course of the Tridentine debate on justification, despite the fact that only seven of the fifty-five theologians involved in the debates were Dominicans.[6] The Salamantine school in Imperial Spain, which developed under Francisco de Vitoria, represented a similar approach to Thomas.[7] It is therefore significant that Charles V chose the Thomist Domingo de Soto, who held the chair of theology at Salamanca in the period 1532–45, as the Imperial theologian at Trent.[8] The most significant position associated with the Thomist faction present at Trent is the total and unequivocal rejection of a meritorious disposition towards justification.[9]

The Franciscan theologians were particularly prominent in the Tridentine proceedings on justification. The following analysis indicates the preponderance of the Franciscan contingent:[10]

Table 7.1   Analysis of theologians involved in the Tridentine proceedings

Order	Present at opening session	Present at sixth session
Franciscans	34	29
Dominicans	9	7
Jesuits	2	2
Carmelites	15	4
Servites	19	1
Augustinians	14	4
Secular priests	11	8

As noted earlier (§§15–17), the Franciscans were not unanimous in recognising a single authoritative doctor of their Order, and it is clear that several doctors were treated as authoritative during the course of the Tridentine proceedings, representing the early Franciscan school (such as Alexander of Hales and Bonaventure), the later Franciscan school (Duns Scotus), and even the *via moderna* (such as Gabriel Biel). The obvious reluctance on the part of certain Franciscans to concede the precedence of Scotus over Bonaventure[11] serves to emphasise the importance of this point. The most important Franciscan theologian present at Trent during the proceedings on justification was the Spanish Observant Andrés de Vega, whose *Opusculum de iustificatione* was conveniently published in time for it to be in the hands of those involved in the debate.[12]

In this work, Vega defends the notion of the necessity of a human disposition towards justification which is meritorious *de congruo*. The extreme opinions on this question, according to Vega, are the Pelagian concept of justification *ex meritis*, and the Thomist denial of all merit prior to justification.[13] Vega argues for the *via media*: the denial of merit *de condigno* and recognition of merit *de congruo* prior to grace – a doctrine which he associates with Duns Scotus and Gabriel Biel, among other recent theologians.[14] It is clear that Vega is drawing upon the common teaching of the Franciscan Order, and it is worth recalling that the whole medieval Franciscan tradition taught that the disposition for justification was meritorious *de congruo*.[15] Stakemeier appears to designate the common Franciscan teaching on this question 'Scotist' on the basis of certain presuppositions which more recent scholarship has called into question – for example, Hünermann's restriction of possible theological alternatives within

Catholicism to either Thomism or Scotism.[16] More seriously, he appears to be indirectly dependent upon Carl Stange's essays of 1900 and 1902, in which he argued that the theology of the medieval period was essentially a theology of Orders:[17] the monastic vow was taken as implying obedience to the official doctor of the Order which, according to Stange, implied recognition of the authority of Thomas Aquinas in the case of the Dominicans, and that of Duns Scotus in the case of Franciscans. As both Thomas and Scotus represented the *via antiqua*, Stakemeier was able to suggest that the influence of the *via moderna* at Trent was minimal.[18] However, although Stakemeier notes Hermelink's response to Stange of 1906, he seems to overlook its totally destructive significance, in that it was demonstrated that medieval theology was better designated a theology of *universities* rather than of *Orders*.[19] Thomas Aquinas may well have been regarded as authoritative at the Dominican house in Cologne, where the *via antiqua* was dominant in the local university, but at Erfurt, where the *via moderna* was in the ascendancy in the university faculty of arts, it was to Ockham that the Dominicans looked for guidance. Although Ockham is hardly referred to at Trent by Franciscan theologians – the Avignon condemnation (1326) of his theology as 'Pelagian or worse' doubtless hardly commending him as a reliable theological source[20] – they made frequent reference to two doctors of the Franciscan Order, Bonaventure and Scotus,[21] as well as occasional reference to two others (Alexander of Hales and Gabriel Biel). Since Bonaventure and Scotus represent very different understandings of the doctrine of justification (particularly in relation to the rôle of supernatural habits in justification) it is clear that the Franciscan contingent found itself in difficulty on occasion. In view of this broad theological base upon which the Franciscan contingent based their opinions, it is both unduly restrictive and quite inappropriate to designate this contingent as 'the *Scotist* school'.[22]

The third school which Stakemeier identified at Trent was the 'Augustinian school'. His views on this school, developed in a later study,[23] may be summarised as follows. The General of the Augustinian Order, Girolamo Seripando, defended a doctrine of *duplex iustitia* during the Tridentine proceedings on justification, which represented a theology of justification characteristic of the theologians of the Augustinian Order during the later medieval period. The 'Augustinian school' at Trent could therefore be regarded as adopting a position on justification, exemplified by Seripando, representing a theological tradition within the Augustinian Order since the time of Simon Fidati of Cassia and Hugolino of Orvieto. Stakemeier's thesis has exercised considerable influence upon accounts of the Tridentine debate on justification, and it is therefore necessary to call its foundations into question.

A careful study of Stakemeier's references to the Augustinian theologians whom he adduces as earlier representatives of this theological tradition indicates that he was only familiar with their writings at second hand, his immediate source being the highly controversial study of A. V. Müller on Luther's theological sources.[24] In this study, Müller had argued that Luther was the heir of precisely such a theological tradition within the Augustinian Order – a view which Stakemeier emphatically rejects in the case of Luther, only to attach to the Augustian contingent at Trent.[25] His evidence for this suggestion is quite unconvincing. Not only was this conclusion premature;[26] it has not stood up to subsequent critical examination.[27] The theologians of the Augustinian Order involved in the Tridentine debates on justification[28] appear to have followed the person, rather than the theology, of their General in their voting, making it impossible to suggest that there was a coherent 'school' of thought, characteristic of the Augustinian Order as a whole, represented during the Tridentine proceedings on justification. Thus in the debate of 8 October 1546 Seripando cites the Augustinian Giles of Viterbo as an earlier proponent of the doctrine of 'double justice',[29] also indicating that Jacobus Perez of Valencia is to be associated with the doctrine. However, it is significant that nowhere does he justify this assertion: the only theologian who he cites *verbatim* is Gropper, and Contarini is cited inaccurately.[30] Seripando appears merely to present a version of Gropper's theology, which is not of Augustinian provenance. It is not merely impossible to defend the view that the doctrine of *duplex iustitia* was of Augustinian provenance; it is impossible to provide convincing evidence for an 'Augustinian *school*' at Trent. We therefore see no reason for continuing the discredited practice of reporting the presence of an 'Augustinian school' during the Tridentine proceedings on justification. This is not to deny that the Augustinian contingent at Trent espoused certain specific theological attitudes: it is to call into question the implication that these attitudes were representative of the Augustinian Order as a whole, or that they corresponded to a tradition or school of thought peculiar to that Order.[31]

The Tridentine proceedings on justification suggest that the neo-Thomist school, the early Franciscan school and the later Franciscan school were all represented at Trent, along with a variety of other positions which defy rigid classification. While Trent appears to have taken some care to avoid censuring, or judging between, the traditional teachings associated with the major Orders (a policy particularly evident during the proceedings on original sin), these teachings appear to have exercised considerably less influence upon the proceedings on justification than might be expected. One possible explanation of this observation is that the whole matrix of traditional disputed questions concerning justification was recognised as occasionally having little bearing on the crucial new questions thrown up by the rise of the evangelical faction within Germany. The new questions thus raised demanded new answers, with the result that the appeal to the traditional positions of the theological schools associated with the Orders had to give way to speculation concerning the most appropriate responses to these questions. A further consideration, however, is the rise of an increasingly independent intellectual environment, particularly in Italy, which enabled theologians to break free from the thought patterns of the medieval theological schools.[32]

In the following section, we shall consider the Tridentine debates on certain crucial aspects of the doctrine of justification, with a view to casting further light upon the proper interpretation of the final *decretum de iustificatione* itself.

§27 The Tridentine proceedings on justification

The Council of Trent was the final outcome of a prolonged attempt by the papacy to convene a reforming council. The continuation of the war in Europe between the Emperor and the King of France had led to the postponement of the projected council at Mantua (1537) and the abortive convocation at Trent (1542–3). Only when the Habsburg–Valois conflict was settled by the Peace of Crépy in 1544 was there any real possibility of convening an ecumenical council. Two months after the conclusion of peace, when it became clear that there was a real possibility of a permanent cessation of hostilities, Paul III issued the Bull *Laetare Ierusalem*, announcing his intention to convene a general council for the removal of religious discord, the reform of the church, and the liberation of the faithful from the Turk.[1] Although it had been hoped that the council might open in March, the unsettled relations between the Emperor and the Pope delayed this until 13 December 1545.[2] These difficulties arose partly from the Emperor's wish that the council should discuss the reform of the church, whereas the Pope desired doctrinal clarification. A judicious compromise led to both these questions being considered in parallel.

The initial doctrinal debates concerned the relation of scripture and tradition, and original sin.[3] It was, however, recognised that the doctrine of justification was of peculiar importance. A number of crucial questions required clarification in the light of the Protestant challenge.[4] First, is justification merely *remissio peccatorum*, or does it necessarily include intrinsic sanctification through the action of grace within man? Second, what is the precise relation between faith and good works? This question required a careful response in opposition to the Protestant doctrine of justification *sola fide*. Third, what is the precise nature of the active rôle of the human will in justification, given the general Protestant tendency to assert the passivity of the will? Fourth, what is the relationship between justification and the *sacramenta mortuorum* of baptism and penance? Fifth, can the believer know with any degree of certitude whether he is, in fact, justified? Finally, is it necessary for man to dispose himself towards justification, and if so, is this disposition to be considered meritorious in any sense?

The Council initially set itself the task of dealing with six questions. On 22 June 1546, a commission of theologians laid down the following questions for discussion:[5]

1. What is justification *quoad nomen et quoad rem*; and what is to be understood when it is said that 'man is justified' (*iustificari hominem*)?
2. What are the causes of justification? What part is played by God? And what is required of man?
3. What is to be understood when it is said that 'man is justified by faith' (*iustificari hominem per fidem*)?
4. What rôle do human works and the sacraments play in justification, whether before, during or after it?
5. What precedes, accompanies and follows justification?
6. By what proofs is the Catholic doctrine supported?

Although this approach would eventually prove to be inadequate, in that it omitted important questions such as the certitude of grace, it served as a useful point of departure for the initial discussion leading up to the first draft of the decree on justification.

In the six congregations held in the period 22–28 June 1546, some thirty-four theologians addressed themselves to the questions set for discussion. Although it is far from clear upon what basis the speakers were called, it is clear that their initial concern appears to have been with the question of the *nature* of justification. Most of the speakers addressed themselves to this point, with a variety of concepts of justification being employed. The Conventual Sigismondo Fedrio da Diruta defined the term *iustificatio* as *motus quidam spiritualis de impietate ad pietatem*, and *iustificari* as *ex nocente fieri innocens*.[6] Richard of Le Mans defined *iustificatio* as *adhaesio Dei*, and *iustificari* as *redire in gratiam Dei*.[7] Gregory of Padua defined *iustificatio* in Augustinian terms, as *de impio pium facere vel iniusto iustum*, and *iustificari* as *fieri Deo gratus*.[8] Despite this remarkable variety of definitions,[9] it is clear that there existed a consensus concerning the factitive and transformational character of justification.[10] Two possible exceptions to this consensus may be noted, in the cases of the Dominican Marcus Laureus and the Franciscan Observant Andrés de Vega.

Marcus Laureus defined justification as *remissio peccatorum per gratiam*,[11] omitting any reference to the concomitant transformation of the believer. This might be taken as indicating that Laureus approached the Protestant position at this point. In fact, this conclusion cannot be drawn without further corroborating evidence, which we do not possess. As we indicated in an earlier discussion (§5), Thomas Aquinas had demonstrated, on Aristotelian grounds, that a process could be defined in terms of its *terminus*, with the result that the *processus iustificationis* could be defined simply as *remissio peccatorum*, the final element in this process. Thomas' occasional statements to the effect that *iustificatio* may be defined as *remissio peccatorum* have occasionally been misinterpreted as implying that he did not include *infusio iustitiae* as an element of justification, which is evidently incorrect. Laureus must therefore, in the absence of any evidence to the contrary, be regarded as restating the position of the chief doctor of his Order in the congregation of 23 June 1546.

Andrés de Vega defined justification in a noticeably extrinsicist manner, in terms of three elements: *hominem iustificari est absolutum esse a peccatis et gratiam Dei habere. Et acceptum ad vitam aeternam*.[12] It is evident that Vega's conception of justification parallels that of the later Franciscan school (see §§5, 16), and is reflected in the statements of other Franciscan theologians in these congregations.[13] The weakening of the ontological link between *remissio peccatorum* and *infusio gratiae*, characteristic of both this school and the *via moderna*, places them closest to the extrinsicism of the Reformers at this point. Nevertheless, it is important to appreciate the heterogeneity of the Franciscan contingent at Trent over this point: other Franciscans defined justification in strongly intrinsicist and transformational terms, such as *regeneratio hominis interioris*,[14] or *mutatio quaedam spiritualis in peccatorem a Deo facta per infusionem iustitiae habitualis*,[15] paralleling those of the earlier Franciscan school (see §§5, 15). Although this understanding of justification does not exclude the infusion of grace and the transformation of man, the priority of the extrinsic denomination of the divine acceptation over such intrinsic qualities was rigorously upheld. This observation is of importance in relation to the question of whether there existed a *Scotist* school at Trent: as we suggested earlier (§26), the evidence strongly suggests that the theological tension already present within the Franciscan Order (particularly between the early and later Franciscan schools) is evident during the Tridentine debates on justification.

The general agreement over the nature of justification was summarised by Marcus Laureus as follows:

Omnes igitur theologi in re conveniunt, quamvis in verbis discrepent. Et in sententia dicunt, quod quoad nomen iustificatio idem est quod *iustifactio*, iustificari idem quod *iustum fieri coram Deo*. Quoad rem autem iustifactio est remissio peccatorum a Deo per gratiam. Iustificari idem est quod remitti peccata a Deo per gratiam.[16]

The discussion of the question of the nature of justification was greatly facilitated by the distinction of three stages (*status*) of justification, which permitted three different senses of the term *iustificatio* to be distinguished, thus avoiding some of the confusion evident in the initial discussions. The first *status* concerns the justification of adults, in which the unbeliever is transformed from his state of unbelief and sin to one of faith and grace; the second concerns the increase in righteousness of the justified believer, and his perseverance in the Christian life; the third concerns the justification of lapsed believers.[17]

This general consensus on the nature of justification is reflected in the first draft of the decree on justification, dating from 24 July 1546. Although it was once thought that this draft version was the work of Andrés de Vega, this is now generally regarded as doubtful.[18] The first draft consists of a brief introduction, three chapters, and a series of eighteen canons.[19] No formal definition of justification is given, although it is possible to deduce such a definition from the material appended to the first two canons. The first three canons make the distinction between the Catholic and Protestant understanding of the nature of justification clear in the following manner.

First, the opinion that a sinner may be justified solely as a matter of reputation or imputation, while remaining a sinner in fact, is rejected.

Si quis ergo dixit, impium, qui a Deo per Christum Iesum iustificatur, iniustum quidem esse et manere, sed tantum iustum reputari, non est iustum fieri, ut ipsa iustificatio sit sola imputatio iustitiae: anathema sit.[20]

Justification is thus defined in terms of a man becoming, and not merely being reputed as, righteous (*sic vere non modo reputatur, sed efficitur iustus*). Although this clearly excludes the concept of a 'legal fiction' in justification, it is not clear that it affects mainstream Protestant teaching on the question, in view of the purely notional distinction envisaged between justification and regeneration. It is, however, clear that there was a consensus that the Protestants did, in fact, restrict the meaning of the term *iustificatio* to *iustum reputatio*. This is particularly clear from the comments of the Spanish Jesuit Alfonso Salmeron, who contrasted the Catholic definition of *iustificari* as *recipere donum iustitiae seu habitum, quo ex iniusto evadimus iusti*, with Melanchthon's definition of the same term as *iustum reputari*.[21] Salmeron clearly fails to understand the significance of Melanchthon's distinction between *iustificatio* and *regeneratio*. The fact that Melanchthon understood by 'justification' *and* 'regeneration' what Catholics understood by 'justification' alone does not appear to have been appreciated. As the Catholics understood *iustificatio* to refer to Christian existence in its totality, the Protestant exclusion of *regeneratio* from *iustificatio* appeared to amount to the exclusion of any transformational dimension from Christian existence altogether. A similar difficulty is encountered with the Protestant concept of justification *per solam fidem*, which the Catholics understood to exclude works from Christian existence (whereas the Protestants, working with a quite distinct concept of justification, understood it merely to refer to the exclusion of works from the *initiation* of the Christian life). We shall return to this point below: it is, however, essential to appreciate that the full significance of the new understanding of the nature of justification associated with Melanchthon was not fully grasped by his Catholic opponents, with important consequences for the interpretation of the relevance of the Tridentine pronouncements for Protestant theologies of justification.

Second, the opinion that justification consists solely in the remission of sins, and not in the *donatio iustitiae*, is condemned.[22] Third, the opinion that the righteousness bestowed upon the believer in his justification is the righteousness of Christ won on the cross is condemned.[23] This point is of particular interest, and appears to be directed against the Lutheran doctrine of *imputatio iustitiae alienae Christi*. The righteousness, on the basis of which man is justified, is defined as *habitus divinae gratiae*, which is bestowed *by God through Christ* – in other words, God effects what Christ merited:

Promeruit quidem solus Christus Iesus sua illa magna iustitia, ut homo per eum iustus efficiatur, sed iustitia, quae in illo ipso sit, non in Christo; actus iustitiae illius Christi in eo est, non in nobis. Iustitia, qua iusti sumus, habitus est divinae gratiae, quae in nobis est, quamquam non per nos, sed per eum at a Deo; a Deo ut qui efficit, per eum ut qui meruit. Quomodo et non aliter intelligendum est apud sanctos, iustitiam Dei et Christi fieri nostram iustitiam.[24]

This statement clarifies the relationship between *iustitia Christi* and *iustitia Dei*, indicating that the former is to be understood as the meritorious cause of justification, and the latter the formal cause.

The general consensus concerning the necessity of works subsequent to the first justification evident in the earlier discussions led to the condemnation of solafideism. With the recognition, however, that the phrase *iustificari hominem per fidem* had a legitimate place in the Catholic exposition of the first justification, the condemnation of solafideism was phrased in a slightly unusual manner which made the Catholic objection to the perceived meaning of the concept unambiguous:

Si quis dixerit, quod sola fides omino, sine aliis operibus, iustificat impium, hoc est impetrat illius iustificationem, in quo sensu ab haereticis hac aetate profertur, quasi nihil aliud ad hoc ex parte hominis requiratur quam credere: anathema sit.[25]

It may also be noted that there was a general consensus that Protestants employed the terms *fides* and *credere* in a highly unorthodox sense. Alfonso Salmeron pointed out the manner in which Melanchthon interpreted the term *fides* as *fiducia divinae misericordiae*,[26] thus excluding the Catholic notion of *fides quae per dilectionem operatur*.[27] It is clear that the initial Catholic hostility to the doctrine of justification *per solam fidem* at Trent is thus based upon a quite specific understanding of both the concepts of *fides* and *iustificatio*.

Although the July debate on this draft proved inconclusive,[28] the debate of 17 August made clear the general dissatisfaction concerning it.[29] A document which was to form the basis of a revised draft was presented to the legates by Seripando on 11 August 1546.[30] This document remedied a major deficiency of the first draft – its omission of a formal definition of the term *iustificatio hominis*. Declarat praeterea, hanc de qua loquimur hominis iustificationem nihil aliud esse quam eius translationem per novam quandam et spiritualem nativitatem, ab eo statu, in quo secundum carnem natus est, filius primi Adae, sub ira et inimicitia Dei, in statum adoptionis filiorum Dei per secundum Adam Iesum Christum servatorem nostrum.[31] Of particular interest, in view of subsequent developments, is the draft's unequivocal rejection of the doctrine that the only basis upon which justification may take place is *imputatio iustitiae Christi*.[32] A significantly different approach to this question, however, is found in the draft submitted by Seripando to the legates on 29 August 1546.[33]

The new version of the decree took a radically different form from its predecessors. In its customary form, such a decree consisted of a long series of canons, with a short introduction or introductory chapters. The new draft consisted of fifteen chapters, and a mere eight canons. The significance of the document, however, lies less in its form than in the views on the formal cause of justification expressed in its eighth chapter, entitled *de duplici iustitia*,[34] as well as comparable views implied by the title of the fourth canon.[35] The fourth canon repeats the substance of the second canon of the draft of 11 August, in that it censures the opinion that we are justified *solius Christi iustitiae imputatione cum exclusione omnis iustitiae in cordibus nostris diffusae*.[36] Although the obvious interpretation of this statement is that man is justified on the basis of *donatio seu infusio iustitiae*, it is clear, from the title of this canon, that Seripando intended this merely as the rejection of the opinion that man is justified *solely* on the basis of *imputatio Christi iustitiae*. It is instructive to compare the wording of the condemned opinions in the July drafts with Seripando's versions:[37]

official July draft: ipsa iustificatio sit *sola* imputatio iustitiae
Seripando (11 August): *solius* iustitiae Christi imputatione
Seripando (29 August): *solius* Christi iustitiae imputatione

The substitution of *solius* for *sola* enables Seripando to open the way to a doctrine of justification on the basis of *iustitia duplex* – both *iustitia imputata* and *iustitia inhaerens*. Although the phrase *duplex iustitia* does not occur in the text of Seripando's draft of 29 August, the implications of those drafts were evident.[38]

The September draft of the decree omits any reference to *duplex iustitia*, and develops the teaching of Canon 3 of the July draft in such a manner as to exclude the opinion that the Christian possesses one *iustitia* deriving from God, and another deriving from Christ. Ita non sunt duae iustitiae, quae nobis dantur, Dei et Christi, sed una iustitia Dei per Iesum Christum, hoc est caritas ipsa vel gratia, qua iustificati non modo reputamur, sed vere iusti nominamur et sumus.[39] The careful phrasing of the new chapter appears to exclude the concept of *duplex iustitia* altogether. However, Canon 7 of the September draft follows the wording of Seripando's original version closely, and is clearly intended to permit the doctrine of *duplex iustitia*:

Si quis dixerit, impium iustificari *solius iustitiae Christi imputatione* aut sola peccatorum remissione, cum exclusione omnis iustitiae seu gratiae in cordibus nostris per Spiritum Sanctum diffusae et nobis inhaerentis . . . anathema sit.[40]

The excluded opinion is that the imputed righteousness of Christ *alone* is the basis of man's justification, if this is understood to exclude an inherent righteousness through the action of the Holy Spirit. The opinion that man is justified on the basis of *duplex iustitia* – that is, *iustitia imputata* and *iustitia inhaerens* – is not condemned. It is evident, from the records of the proceedings in the period 27 September–8 October 1546, that many of the delegates found themselves unable to make sense of the phrasing of the seventh chapter.[41] The case for replacing the ambiguous 'non sunt duae iustitiae' with the more explicit 'una est iustitia' was pressed with some force,[42] forcing Seripando and his supporters to make their views on the matter explicit.

In addition to Seripando, the defenders of the doctrine of *duplex iustitia* were the Augustinians Aurelius of Rocca Contrata, Marianus Feltrinus and Stephen of Sestino, the Servite Lorenzo Mazocchi, and the Spanish secular priest Antonio Solis. It is possible that another Spanish secular priest, Pedro Sarra, should be considered a supporter of the doctrine. In his defence of the doctrine, Aurelius merely recapitulates previous statements of his general, Seripando, without developing his arguments in any manner.[43] Stephen of Sestino emphasised the imperfection and inadequacy of human works in a manner which parallels Gropper's argument in the *Enchiridion* to such an extent that dependence upon this source is a probability.[44] The vote of the third Augustinian, Feltrinus, exists only in the outline of Massarelli,[45] and appears to parallel the views of Sestino. It is thus significant, in view of the hypothesis that an authentically Augustinian theology of justification is implicit in these statements, to note the clear priority of the arguments of Gropper over Augustinian theologians such as Jacobus Perez of Valencia.

The remaining supporters of the doctrine appear to have based their views upon considerations so disparate that generalisations are impossible. The vote of Solis survives only in a form which is too brief to permit analysis;[46] that of Sarra, although longer, defies interpretation.[47] Mazocchi's vote is something of an enigma:[48] although Mazocchi appears to have given his fellow-delegates the impression that he supported Seripando, the substance of the vote itself actually renders no support to the doctrine of *duplex iustitia*.[49]

The majority opinion was, however, unequivocal. Although demonstrating a near-total ignorance of the historical origins of the doctrine of *duplex iustitia*,[50] there was a general conviction that the concept of *iustitia imputata* was a theological novelty, unknown to Catholic theology throughout its existence.[51] Furthermore, it was generally agreed that the concept of imputed righteousness was an irrelevance, on account of the renovation of man in justification: non quod tunc nova fiat imputatio, ut quidam falso imaginantur, quia, ut patet sufficienter ex praemissis, ista imputatio nulla ratione requiritur.[52] Although Seripando actually employed the term *imputare* rarely (and never in his votes),[53] it seems that the demand for an explicit condemnation of justification on the basis of *iustitia imputata*[54] was essentially an indirect attack upon his position. There also appears to have been a general consensus that Seripando's appeal to *iustitia Christi* undermined the foundation of human merit.

On 31 October 1546, the September draft of the decree was rewritten in the light of the preceding debate, in which the overwhelming hostility to the concept of *duplex iustitia* (or *duae iustitiae*) had been made clear. The demand for an explicit condemnation of justification on the basis of *iustitia imputata* was met by an unequivocal assertion that man was justified on the basis of an internal righteousness:

Impii autem iustificationis, quae simul in ablutione peccatorum, simul in sanctificatione et in infusione donorum consistit, causae sunt ... formalis iustitia una Dei, qua renovamur spiritu mentis nostrae et non modo reputamur, sed vere iusti nominamur et sumus.[55]

The concept of *iustitia duplex*, incorporated at some length into the September draft, now appeared to be excluded: the formal cause of justification was explicitly identified as *iustitia una Dei*. However, the sense of the statement is clearly as follows: *the formal cause of justification is the one righteousness of God*. In other words, the document is primarily concerned with the emphasis upon the unity of the *iustitia* underlying man's justification. Seripando's position could still be accommodated without difficulty if it were conceded that there was more than one formal cause of justification. It is this ambiguous understanding of the formal cause of justification which became incorporated into the draft of the decree presented on 5 November 1546.[56] However, there were still those who felt that the doctrine of *duplex iustitia*, as defended by Seripando, was not rigorously excluded. In the congregation of 23 November, Claude Le Jay proposed that the phrase 'causa formalis iustitia una Dei' should be replaced with 'causa formalis una iustitia Dei'.[57] This alteration had the effect of defining that the one formal cause of justification was the righteousness of God, in the sense described – in other words, the possibility of a double formal cause of justification (*iustitia imputata* and *iustitia inhaerens*) was excluded. The possibility that this might be interpreted as implying that one formal cause *among others* was *iustitia Dei* required that *una* be altered to *unica* – an alteration which appears to have been agreed upon subsequently. The revised version of the eighth chapter of the decree was drawn up for discussion on 11 December 1546, incorporating this amended version of Le Jay's statement concerning the formal cause of justification: Demum unica formalis causa est iustitia illa Dei, non qua ipse iustus est, sed qua nos coram ipso iustos facit, qua videlicet ab eo donati renovamur spiritu mentis nostrae et non modo reputamur, sed vere iusti nominamur et sumus.[58] This unequivocal statement to the effect that the *single* formal cause of justification was the righteousness of God, in the sense defined, was approved in general congregation the same day,[59] and eventually incorporated into the final version of the decree on justification.[60] It is only at this point that the rejection of Seripando's concept of *duplex iustitia* may be considered to be complete and unequivocal.

The centrality of the concept of assurance of salvation for the Reformers, and particularly for Luther,[61] and the medieval consensus (§8) concerning the impossibility of such assurance, made it impossible for the Council to ignore the matter, despite its absence from the initial agenda. Initially, little interest was shown in the question: the records of the congregations of 22–28 June 1546 demonstrate that only two speakers deemed the matter worthy of consideration. The very different approaches adopted by Andrés de Vega[62] and Antonius Frexius[63] were indicative of the divisions which would subsequently be exposed on this question, and it is significant that these contributions are not included in the *summarium* of Marcus Laureus.[64] Although the Lutheran doctrine of assurance is included among the list of proscribed errors concerning the second *status iustificationis* tabled for discussion on 30 June,[65] little attention was paid to it.[66]

The emergence of the question of assurance as a serious issue dates from the July draft of the decree, which included as its fifteenth canon an explicit condemnation of the Lutheran doctrine of assurance as an assertion contrary to proper Christian humility.[67] It was clear, however, that this canon provoked considerable disquiet. The *notationes theologorum* revealed serious disagreement on the matter among the theologians, as well as a general desire to discuss the matter further.[68] As a result, Costacciaro invited the Conventual Antonio Delfini to prepare an expert opinion *de quaestione illa vehementer dubia, numquid Christianus certitudinem habeat, quod in gratia Dei sit, et quid hac in re opinatus fuerit subtilissimus Ioannes Scotus*.[69] In this document, Delfini interprets Scotus with the aid of Gabriel Biel,[70] indicating that Scotus cannot be regarded as an exponent of the Lutheran doctrine of assurance. Costacciaro himself clearly considered that Scotus upheld the possibility of the certitude of grace on account of the *ex opere operato* character of the sacrament of penance.[71] Zannetino, however, disagreed, and cited John Fisher as an accurate and reliable interpreter of Scotus on this point.[72] By 17 August, it was clear that there was a serious division of opinion on the matter within the council, with the Dominicans implacably opposed to any suggestion that *certitudo gratiae* was possible, and others strongly affirming such a possibility.[73] In view of this difficulty, a general congregation of 28 August 1546 determined to proceed directly merely to the condemnation of the Lutheran position, while leaving unresolved the question of the Catholic position on the matter.[74] This principle was observed in the drawing up of the September draft of the decree.

The September draft refers to the question of the certitude of grace at two points. The seventh chapter rejects the following opinion, which it attributes to 'heretics and schismatics': non omni tamen eam fiduciam et certitudinem acceptae remissionis peccatorum suorum iactanti et in ea sola quiescenti peccata dimitti dicendum est.[75] No clarification on the Catholic teaching is provided. Similarly, Canon 8 explicitly rejects any suggestion that the believer may know with certainty that he is among the predestined, or that he will persevere to the end, apart from special divine revelation.[76] The compromise of 28 August was soon recognised as unsatisfactory, and the debate on the question was resumed on 12 October 1546.[77] On 15 October, the following article was proposed for discussion: Utrum aliquis possit esse certus de sua adepta gratia secundum praesentem iustitiam, et quo genere certitudinis.[78] The discussion of this article over the period 15–26 October 1546 further emphasised the divisions within the council at this point: of the thirty-seven theologians who expressed their opinions, twenty were in favour of the possibility of certitude of grace, fifteen against, and two undecided.[79] Without exception, the Dominican theologians were opposed to the possibility of *certitudo fidei, se esse in gratia* – despite the recent arrival at the Council of the Dominican bishop Ambrogio Catharino, an outspoken supporter of the possibility.[80] The Franciscan contingent, by contrast, was deeply divided, the seven Conventuals supporting the possibility, and the Observants more or less equally divided.

The third draft of the decree was submitted for consideration on 5 November 1546, with a revised statement on the question incorporated into the decree in the form of its ninth chapter.[81] Its substance parallels that of the equivalent statement in the second draft, with an intensification of its opening reference:[82]

September draft: *non omni* tamen eam fiduciam et certitudinem
November draft: *nemini* tamen eam fiduciam et certitudinem

Although this went some way towards meeting the demands of some delegates, that the condemnation of *certitudo fidei, se esse in gratia* be strengthened and made more explicit, the new chapter failed to win their approval through its final statement, which is without parallel in the September draft: Nescit enim homo *communiter*, num divino amore dignus sit.[83] The controversy surrounded the interpretation of the enigmatic term *communiter*, which was also included in the fourteenth canon.[84] Several delegates wished the ambiguity surrounding the term to be removed by the substitution of *communi lege*;[85] others simply wished the term to be dropped altogether,[86] with a clarification of the chapter in question. By 17 December, the issue, although forcefully contested on both sides, was still unresolved. In view of the serious delays this difficulty was occasioning, del Monte proposed that the council should merely condemn the Lutheran position, and leave further discussion of the Catholic position until a future date.[87] Despite opposition from some who did not wish to see the results of months of discussion come to nothing,[88] the procedure was approved.

On 9 January 1547, four days before the final decree was published, a *convocatio praelatorum theologorum* of restricted membership met to attempt to establish a last-minute consensus on the ninth chapter *super certitudine gratiae*.[89] After three hours' debate, a compromise formula was finally agreed: nemo possit esse certus certitudine fidei, cui non potest subesse falsum, se esse in gratia Dei.[90] The formula was immediately incorporated into the fifth draft of the decree, submitted for consideration on the same day,[91] and finally approved.

With the resolution of the questions of the cause of justification and the certitude of grace, the Council of Trent was able to proceed with its extensive pronouncements concerning the Catholic teaching on justification, contained in the chapters of the final decree, as well as its specific condemnation in the canons of the errors of Protestantism. Although, strictly speaking, the decree could not be considered binding upon Catholics until the papal ratification of the Council after its closure in 1563, the decisions were widely regarded as immediately valid – despite Reginald Pole's refusal to seal the document.[92] By 1547, therefore, the teaching of the Catholic church on justification may be regarded as fixed, in the sense that the approved formulae (which permitted a certain degree of latitude of interpretation at crucial points) had been established. In the following section, we shall outline the main features of the decree, before considering the interpretation of the decree in the immediate post-Tridentine period.

§28 The Tridentine decree on justification

The Tridentine decree on justification marks a significant development in conciliar history. Up to that point, conciliar decisions had tended to be framed largely in terms of explicit condemnation, in the form of canons, of specific opinions, without substantial exposition of the Catholic teaching on the matter in question. Perhaps on account of the peculiar importance with which the doctrine of justification was recognised to be invested, the *decretum de iustificatione* devotes sixteen initial chapters to a point-by-point exposition of the Catholic teaching before proceeding to condemn thirty-three specific opinions.[1] As will become clear from the following section, there was considerable disagreement in the immediate post-Tridentine period concerning the precise interpretation of the *decretum de iustificatione*. In the present section, we propose to indicate the broad range of opinions on justification which the Council of Trent recognised as authentically Catholic. In establishing these, the following principles have been employed.

1. In that the Council was primarily concerned with distinguishing Catholic teaching from that of the Reformers, and not to settle disputed matters within the Catholic schools of theology, it follows that the previously professed theological positions of these schools may continue to be held, unless they are explicitly excluded.

2. The final decree is to be interpreted in the light of the debates which led to its formulation, in order to establish what the Tridentine fathers intended particular terms and phrases to mean.[2] Although the attempt to interpret any historical document *e mente auctorum* is notoriously difficult, we possess sufficient documentary evidence to clarify the intended meaning of at least certain otherwise obscure statements.

With these points in mind, we may turn to the analysis of the decree and its canons.

The final arrangement of the decree reflects the three *status iustificationis* which emerged during the proceedings on justification. The first nine chapters discuss the 'first justification', in which man's initial transition from a state of sin to righteousness is described.[3] This is followed by four chapters dealing with the 'second justification' – how man, once justified, may increase in righteousness.[4] The final three chapters deal with the *status tertius*, indicating how a man may forfeit his justification, and subsequently regain it through penance, and clarifying the manner in which this differs from the *status primus*.[5]

The decree opens with an analysis of man's fallen condition, inevitably incorporating certain matters touched upon in the fifth session *de peccato originali*. On account of original sin, which is a condition affecting the entire human race, man is incapable of redeeming himself. Free will is not destroyed, but is weakened and debilitated by the Fall: in eis liberum arbitrium minime exstinctum esset, viribus licet attenuatum et inclinatum.[6] The Council thus reaffirmed the position of Augustine and Orange II on this crucial point, and implicitly rejected Luther's statement: liberum arbitrium post peccatum est res de solo titulo.[7] The particularism implicit in Luther's teaching on election is excluded by the unequivocal assertion that Christ died for all men, granting grace through the merits of his passion in order that man might be born again, and hence justified. (In anticipation of the censure of a purely extrinsic conception of justification in the canons, it is affirmed that no man can be justified unless he has first been born again.)[8] Justification is defined in transformational terms, including reference to necessary alterations in man's status and nature:

Quibus verbis iustificationis impii descriptio insinuatur, ut sit translatio ab eo statu, in quo homo nascitur filius primi Adae, in statum gratiae et adoptionis filiorum Dei, per secundum Adam Iesum Christum Salvatorem nostrum; quae quidem translatio post Evangelium promulgatum sine lavacro regenerationis aut eius voto fieri non potest.[9]

The fifth and sixth chapters deal with the necessity and the mode of preparation towards justification. Man is called through prevenient grace, without reference to his merits, to dispose himself towards justification. As a consequence of man's assenting to and cooperating with this call, God touches man's heart through the illumination of his Holy Spirit.[10] The traditional medieval terminology usually employed in the discussion of the necessity for a disposition towards justification (see §7) is studiously avoided, exemplifying the general tendency to avoid scholastic language wherever possible. Indeed, the *decretum de iustificatione* is notable for its marked preference to appeal directly to scripture, passing over the vocabulary of the medieval period altogether. The preparation for justification is subsequently defined in terms of man's believing the truth of divine revelation and the divine promises (particularly the promise that God will justify the ungodly through his grace), and thence being moved to detest his sins and repent of them. This culminates in the sacrament of baptism, in which the individual declares his intention to lead a new life and observe the divine commandments.[11] Once more, the nature of the disposition towards justification is discussed in terms drawn directly from scripture, rather than from the medieval theological schools.

The seventh chapter presents a careful analysis of the causes of justification.[12] It reaffirms the transformational character of justification (non est sola peccatorum remissio, sed et sanctificatio et renovatio interioris hominis), and the causes of justification are enumerated as follows:

final cause:	the glory of God and eternal life
efficient cause:	the mercy of God
meritorious cause:	the passion of Christ
instrumental cause:	the sacrament of baptism
formal cause:	the righteousness of God.

Although this might appear to be a reversion to scholasticism, the decree is merely clarifying the various contributing factors to man's justification in the most convenient manner possible. The most significant statement concerns the formal cause of justification. The assertion that the *single* formal cause of justification (*unica formalis causa*) is 'iustitia Dei, non qua ipse iustus est, sed qua nos iustos facit'[13] represents a deliberate and conscious attempt to exclude the possibility that there exists more than one formal cause – the opinion particularly associated with Seripando during the proceedings on justification (§27). In effect, the possibility that *iustitia imputata* is a contributing cause to man's justification is intended to be excluded by this statement, despite the absence of any explicit reference to the concept. Perhaps more significantly, the entire medieval debate over whether the formal cause of justification was an intrinsic created habit of grace or the extrinsic denomination of the divine acceptation (see §§13–18) was circumvented by a reversion to the Augustinian concept of *iustitia Dei*. This does not resolve the medieval debate on this matter one way or the other, and represents an attempt to establish the common basis of both medieval understandings of the matter without using the terminology of the period. The linking of the 'first justification' with the sacrament of baptism continues the common medieval tradition of excluding the possibility of extra-sacramental justification, and parallels the subsequent linking of the recovery of justification with the sacrament of penance.

The eighth chapter deals with the concepts of 'to be justified by faith' (*iustificari per fidem*) and 'to be justified freely' (*gratis iustificari*).[14] Both these terms are to be interpreted according to the Catholic tradition: faith is to be seen as the beginning of human salvation, the foundation and root of all justification, without which it is impossible to please God. This gift is given *gratis* in the sense that none of the things which precede justification (including faith, as well as works) can be said to merit justification: gratis autem iustificari ideo dicamur, quia nihil eorum, quae iustificationem praecedunt, sive fides, sive opera, ipsam iustificationis gratiam promereretur. Although this statement clearly excludes the possibility that man may merit justification *de condigno*, it does not – and was not intended to – exclude the possibility that he may merit it *de congruo*. (As the proceedings on justification make clear, this conclusion pertains irrespective of the verb employed, whether *promereri* or *mereri*.)[15] In other words, although the traditional teaching of the Franciscan Order (that man's disposition towards justification is meritorious *de congruo*) is not explicitly permitted, there was a clear intention that it should not be excluded.

The ninth chapter deals with the question of the certitude of faith.[16] This question having been the subject of intense debate at Trent, the chapter is worded with some care. *Fiducia* on the part of the believer concerning the mercy of God, the merit of Christ and the efficacy of the sacraments is certainly appropriate; what is inappropriate is *inana haereticorum fiducia* concerning the individual's justification.

Nemini tamen fiduciam et certitudinem remissionis peccatorum suorum iactanti et in ea sola quiescenti peccata dimitti vel dismissa esse dicendum est … immo nostra tempestate sit et magna contra Ecclesiam catholicam contentione praedicetur vana haec et ab omni pietate remota fiducia.

The tenth chapter opens the section of the *decretum* dealing with the second justification, in which man increases in righteousness. This second justification is seen as a positive duty placed upon man by virtue of the first justification. There are clear connections between the Tridentine concept of the second justification and the Reformed concept of sanctification. Whereas in the first justification, grace operates upon man, in the second, man cooperates with grace. It is thus both possible and necessary to keep the law of God.[17] The opinion that such good works as are involved in the second justification are sinful is rejected.[18] The Augustinian doctrine of final perseverance is reaffirmed: in this mortal life, no one may know whether he is among the number of the predestined, except through special revelation.[19] Although the sacrament of baptism is linked with the first justification, and that of penance with the restoration of justification, it is significant that there is no specific mention of any of the remaining sacraments in connection with the second justification.

The final three chapters deal with those who have fallen from the grace of justification through mortal sin. Those who are moved by grace may regain the grace of justification through the sacrament of penance, on account of the merit of Christ.[20] It is important to appreciate that it is only grace, and not faith, which is lost by mortal sin: the lapsed individual remains a believer. The final chapter deals with the question of merit, and goes some considerable way towards meeting Protestant criticism of the concept.[21] While insisting upon the biblical principle that good works are rewarded by God, Trent emphasises that merit is a divine gift to man, excluding human boasting. Merit remains, however, the result of man's free efforts.

Although the grace of Christ precedes and accompanies man's efforts, those efforts are real nonetheless. The believer, by his cooperation with grace, is entitled to merit and increase in justification. The man who perseveres until the end may be said to receive eternal life as a reward, the crowning gift promised by God to those who persevere. The question of the ultimate foundation of merit (*ratio meriti*), a subject of some controversy in the medieval schools (see §10), is answered in non-scholastic terms (such as the union of the believer with Christ) which permit the traditional views to be retained.

The thirty-three canons appended to the decree condemn specific heretical opinions, by no means restricted to Protestantism.[22] However, it appears that it is certain caricatures of Protestantism which are actually condemned, rather than Protestantism itself. There appears to have been considerable confusion as a consequence of the different understandings of the *nature* of justification associated with Protestants and Catholics. Canon 11 may be singled out as being of particular importance in this respect:

Si quis dixerit, homnes iustificari vel sola imputatione iustitiae Christi, vel sola peccatorum remissione, exclusa gratia et caritate, quae in cordibus eorum per Spiritum Sanctum diffundatur atque illis inhaereat, aut etiam gratiam, qua iustificamur, esse tantum favorem Dei: anathema sit.[23]

It is clear that this condemnation is aimed against a purely extrinsic conception of justification (in the Catholic sense of the term) – in other words, the view that the Christian life may begin and continue without any transformation or inner renewal of the sinner. In fact, the canon does not censure any magisterial Protestant account of *iustificatio hominis*, in that man's initial (extrinsic) justification is either understood (as with Melanchthon) to be inextricably linked with his subsequent (intrinsic) sanctification, so that the concepts are notionally distinct, but nothing more; or else both man's extrinsic justification and intrinsic sanctification are understood (as with Calvin) to be contiguous dimensions of the union of the believer with Christ. Underlying this canon appears to be the view that Protestants denied that transformation and renewal was of the *esse* of Christian existence, an error primarily due to terminological confusion, but compounded by Luther's frequently intemperate (and occasionally obscure) statements on the matter.

The degree of latitude of interpretation incorporated into the Tridentine decree on justification at points of importance makes it impossible to speak of 'the Tridentine doctrine of justification', as if there were *one such doctrine*. In fact, Trent legitimated a range of theologies as catholic, and any one of them may lay claim to be a 'Tridentine doctrine of justification'. Trent may be regarded as endorsing the medieval Catholic heritage on justification, while eliminating much of its technical vocabulary, substituting biblical or Augustinian phrases in its place. Trent thus marks a point of transition in our study, in that it marks the deliberate and systematic rejection of much of the *terminology* of the medieval schools, while retaining the *theology* which it expressed. It is possible to argue that Trent marks the end of the medieval discussion of justification, in the sense that it established a new framework within which subsequent discussion of the matter was increasingly obliged to proceed.

It will, however, be clear that the degree of latitude of interpretation implicitly endorsed by Trent did more than permit the traditional teaching of the medieval schools to be considered Catholic: it also caused uncertainty concerning the precise interpretation of the decree. The result of this uncertainty may be seen in the immediate post-Tridentine period, in which it transpired that the debate on justification within Catholicism was renewed, rather than settled. It is to this period that we now turn.

§29 The post-Tridentine debates on justification

There can be no doubt that the Tridentine decree on justification was the most significant statement on the matter ever to have been made by the Christian church. The question of its correct interpretation is therefore of the utmost importance. In his still influential account of the Tridentine debate on justification, Rückert argued that the final decree, particularly in relation to its statements concerning the meritorious nature of the disposition towards justification, represented a victory for Thomism.[1] This judgement was not universally accepted in the immediate aftermath of Trent, nor is it accepted today. In the following section, we propose to consider the interpretation of the Tridentine statement on the meritorious nature of the disposition towards justification to illustrate the difficulties associated with interpreting the decree, before proceeding to a discussion of Baianism, Molinism and Jansenism.

The eighth chapter of the Tridentine decree on justification makes the following statement:

gratis autem iustificari ideo dicamur, quia nihil eorum, quae iustificationem praecedunt, sive fides, sive opera, ipsam iustificationis gratiam promeretur.[2]

As noted earlier (§§14–18), there was a substantial body of opinion within the Franciscan Order which held that man could merit justification *de congruo*. Is this opinion excluded by this statement?

An emphatically negative answer to this question was given in the present century by Heiko A. Oberman, who drew attention to the use of the verb *promereri* in the place of the more usual *mereri* in the above statement.[3] Oberman suggests that a contrast between *mereri* and *promereri* had become well established within Catholicism by the time of the Council of Trent, the latter meaning 'merit in the full sense of the term'.[4] He thus asserts that, during the Tridentine proceedings on justification, the verb *mereri* was associated with *meritum de congruo*, and *promereri* with *meritum de condigno*.[5] The statement cited above should therefore be interpreted as follows: none of the acts which precede justification, whether faith or works, merit the grace of justification *de condigno*. The possibility of a disposition towards justification which is meritorious *de congruo* is thus not excluded by the decree.

This distinction between *promereri* and *mereri* has been rejected by subsequent commentators. Rückert drew attention to the fact that the Council of Trent was anxious to break away from the vocabulary of medieval theology, including such terms as *meritum de congruo* and *meritum de condigno*.[6] Phrases such as *mereri ex debitum* or *proprie et vere mereri* were used extensively in lieu of *mereri de condigno*. Thus the following form was used in the September draft of Canon 3:

Si quis impium quibuscumque suis operibus praecedentibus dixerit posse proprie et vere iustificationem mereri coram Deo, ita ut illis debeatur gratia ipsa iustificationis: anathema sit.[7]

It is clear that this was intended as an unequivocal rejection of the Pelagian doctrine of justification *ex meritis* – in other words, the doctrine that an individual may merit his justification in the strict sense of the term (*de condigno*). Oberman suggests that *promereri* was understood by the Tridentine fathers to mean *proprie et vere mereri*, and that its use in place of the usual term *mereri* was intended to emphasise this hardening in meaning. This suggestion rests upon inadequate documentary evidence. There are no grounds for supporting that such a distinction was current in the later medieval period, or that it was recognised or employed by those present at Trent. Indeed, the supplementation of *promereri* with *vere* at points during the Tridentine proceedings suggests that the verbs *mereri* and *promereri* were regarded as synonymous.[8] Elsewhere, ample evidence is to be had that the terms were not distinguished in the manner Oberman suggests.[9] Oberman himself notes that Domingo de Soto does not distinguish the two terms,[10] and his suggestion that such a distinction is made by Andrés de Vega has been shown to be untenable.[11] In fact, this debate is quite irrelevant to the point of interpretation in question, as will become clear from the following discussion.

In what follows, we shall consider several interpretations of the Tridentine decree on justification dating from the period, including two from the pens of Tridentine *periti*. In his 1547 *de natura et gratia*, the Dominican theologian Domingo de Soto argued that Trent denied that man's disposition towards justification was meritorious *de congruo*. Conceding the necessity of a disposition towards justi-fication,[12] Soto argues that man cannot dispose himself towards grace without the *auxilium speciale Dei*.[13] Although a purely natural disposition towards justification is conceivable, Soto insists that this is merely *dispositio impropria seu remota*.[14] Merit prior to justification is rigorously excluded, even in the weak sense of merit *de congruo*.[15] Soto thus understands Trent to have rejected explicitly the doctrine of a congruously meritorious disposition towards justification. In this, he was followed by the English Catholic émigré Thomas Stapleton, who rejected the concept of congruous merit as long since discredited.[16] The Tridentine decree is unequivocal on this matter: merit can only exist in the case of the regenerate.[17]

A very different interpretation of the Tridentine decree is associ-ated with the Franciscan Andrés de Vega. Although Vega emphati-cally denied that man could merit prevenient grace,[18] it is clear that he understands this to refer to merit *de condigno*.[19] He thus expounds the eighth chapter of the Tridentine decree as follows:

Et ita hic Patres asseverant neque fidem neque *aliqua opera bona praecedentia iustificationem promereri ipsam iustificationis gratiam*. Nullus enim peccator iustificatur ex debito, nullus ex rigore iustitiae, nullus ex condignitate suorum operum, sed omnes qui iustificantur gratis a Deo iustificantur et ex gratia et misericordia et absque meritis et condignitate suorum operum.[20]

It is clear that Vega understands Trent to have excluded the opinion that man can make a claim on God *ex debito* or *ex rigore iustitiae* – but not that he may rely upon the divine benevolence and generosity. Manifesta igitur luce constat nihil repugnare opinionem asserentium meritum ex congruo verbis nostri Concilii.[21] Vega understands the terms *meritum* and *mereri* to refer solely to merit in the strictest sense of the term, but does not extend the use of the term to *congruous* merit. In other words, the Tridentine rejection of merit prior to justification is merely a rejection of the Pelagian doctrine of justification *ex meritis* – that is, justification on the basis of condign merit. The Franciscan doctrine of a congruously meritorious disposition towards justification is thus unaffected by the Tridentine statements, whether these employ the verb *promereri* or *mereri* – Vega understands *both* to mean 'merit in the strict and proper sense of the term'.

In fact, there are excellent reasons for suggesting that the Tridentine fathers intended this latitude of interpretation. The Council was concerned to exclude the possibility that man could merit – in the strict sense of the term – his own justification: it was not concerned with resolving the long-standing debate within the Catholic schools of theology on whether the immediate disposition towards justification could be deemed meritorious in a weaker sense of the term. The presence of so large a contingent of Franciscan theologians at Trent, and particularly the prominent position which they assumed during the proceedings on justification, made it improbable that the traditional teaching of their own order would be censured. In effect, both the Thomist and the Franciscan (whether inclined to accept Bonaventure or Scotus as mentor) could claim that Trent condoned their characteristic views on this matter.

The success enjoyed by early Protestant catechisms, such as Luther's *Kleiner Catchismus* of 1529, made a Catholic catechetical response imperative. Two such unofficial responses appeared soon after the Tridentine decree on justification. Peter Canisius produced his *Catechismus Major* in 1555,[22] while his work in Germany was paralleled by that of Edmund Augerius in France.[23] Work on an official catechetical response to the Reformers began in 1547, but does not appear to have been taken seriously until 1563[24] – the year which saw both the closure of the Council of Trent, and the publication of the great Reformed *Heidelberger Katechismus*. The definitive catechism of the Catholic church, the *Catechismus Romanus*, appeared in October 1566, with a subtitle (*Catechismus ex decreto Tridentini*) clearly implying that it provided an exposition of the Tridentine decrees. In fact, however, the work is an exposition of the creed, the sacraments, the decalogue and the Lord's Prayer, rather than of the Council of Trent. It is, however, possible to determine the work's teaching on justification by correlating its various elements as they are found at various points in its course.[25]

Grace always precedes, accompanies and follows man's works, and merit is impossible apart from grace.[26] The Catechism makes no distinction between condign and congruous merit, however, and its statements on merit are thus open to precisely the same latitude of interpretation as the Tridentine decree itself: once more, this appears to be deliberate.

The Council of Trent did not produce a definitive and exhaustive account of the Catholic doctrine of justification, and must be regarded as a response to past errors, rather than an anticipation of those of the future. In particular, the Council was content to affirm the reality of the human free will and the universal necessity of grace, without specifying the precise manner in which these notions might be reconciled. As with the Council's teaching on congruous merit, it seems that a certain degree of latitude of interpretations was envisaged by the Tridentine fathers in regard to their statements on these matters. A general feature of the post-Tridentine period was its patristic positivism, particularly the renewed interest in the writings of Augustine of Hippo. That the reality of the human *liberum arbitrium* and the necessity of divine grace had been reconciled by Augustine was generally accepted – but the African bishop had many post-Tridentine interpreters, eventually forcing the church to determine which represented the closest approximation to his thought.

The first major post-Tridentine controversy to arise concerning the doctrine of justification was Baianism, characterised by its rejection of *supernaturale quoad essentiam*, and the cognate distinction between 'natural' and 'supernatural'.[27] The main features of Baius' theology may be deduced from his basic assertion that man was created *rectus* by God, and that this defines his natural state.[28] Abandoning the concept of *natura pura* (whose characteristics, particularly concerning the grace with which it had been endowed, had been the subject of a long-standing debate between the Dominican and Franciscan schools: §§14–17), Baius lays down three principles upon the basis of which the characteristics and qualities of man's natural state may be established.[29] First, the quality involved must not compromise the exigencies of human nature. Second, any quality which is necessarily implicated in the specific elements of human nature must be considered as 'natural' to man. Third, a quality must be considered 'natural' to man when his nature requires it as its necessary complement, so that without it his nature suffers privative evil. Thus Adam's innocence was not a supernatural gift, but the essential complement of his human nature. These principles may be illustrated with reference to Baius' assertion that Adam was given the Holy Spirit at his creation.

As it is part of man's nature that he should be alive, Baius argues that he is necessarily endowed with whatever is necessary to life – and includes the Holy Spirit among such endowments on basic theological presuppositions. The absence of the Holy Spirit would have resulted in a privation, and hence in evil. Furthermore, those powers and faculties which lead to the completion of nature must, according to Baius, be considered as part of nature itself. The subjection of man's lower nature to his higher spiritual nature, and of the *totus homo* to God, is immediately dependent upon the inhabitation of the Holy Spirit in man *ex natura rei*. As it is unthinkable that God would deny to Adam anything essential to the completion of his being, it may be concluded that he was endowed with the Holy Spirit at creation.

This approach to the 'natural' state of man has a number of important consequences. Adam's perseverance would have resulted in his receiving beatitude as a reward: there is no need to involve divine grace in this matter, because man has certain rights over God *ex natura rei*. Thus 'natural' man receives eternal life as a reward, not as a gift. 'Natural' man has certain rights before God: the divine assistance which man requires must be considered to arise from an obligation on God's part, rather than from his generosity, in that this assistance must be regarded as an integral aspect of his 'natural' state. It is instructive to compare Augustine and Baius on this point. Both agree that man is created in such a manner as to require divine assistance, and reject the possibility that he may attain his destiny unaided, by virtue of his own powers and abilities. Augustine, however, affirms that this divine assistance is bestowed gratuitously, in order that he may obtain his *supernatural* destiny (although Augustine does not use this precise term), where Baius insists that God is under an obligation to bestow such assistance, in order that man may attain his *natural* state. The comparison with Pelagius is also instructive. Where Pelagius asserted the total autonomy of human nature, Baius simultaneously asserted its *impotence apart from grace* and the *divine obligation to bestow grace as and when required*. Where Pelagius affirms man's independence of God, Baius affirms his total dependence upon God, and thus – in the manner of a litigant rather than a beggar – demands his due assistance from God.

Baius' definition of Adam's original state carries with it the implication that Adam possessed nothing other than that which was essential to his nature, so that the deprivation of any quality of this state could only result in its vitiation. As a consequence of the Fall, man now exists in an 'unnatural' state, in that his innocence is destroyed through the privation of essential natural qualities, to be replaced with 'viciousness'.[30] Original sin is defined in terms of a *habitus concupiscentiae*, which prevents man from breaking free from sin unaided.[31] Indeed, Baius' radical dichotomy between *concupiscentia* and *caritas* leads to his asserting that all works prior to justification are sinful – far exceeding the more cautious statements of Augustine on this point, and tending to approach the more radical views of the Reformers. The problem of justification, as stated by Baius, thus comes to concern the means by which the transition from a state of concupiscence to a state of charity may be effected. However, it must be emphasised that justification is conceived in purely natural terms: it is essentially a restoration of the state of innocence and natural faculties, by which man is enabled to lead a moral existence. It is this principle which underlies the proposition, subsequently condemned by Pius V, that the *ratio meriti* is not the Holy Spirit, but obedience to the law.[32]

It is clear that Baius' theology of justification is radically different from that of Augustine, despite his attempt to recover the latter's views from the adumbrations of the medieval period. This departure from Augustine appears to arise from the rejection of the concept of *supernaturale quoad essentiam*, from which most of Baius' views ultimately derive. Although Augustine does not employ the *term* 'supernatural', this cannot be taken as an indication that the *concept* is not implicitly present in his theology of justification. The medieval development of Augustine's theology of grace (see §9) may be regarded as making this concept explicit within, rather than imposing it as an alien concept upon, this theology. By rejecting the concept of the supernatural altogether, Baius inevitably reduced Augustine's theology to pure naturalism.

Seventy-nine propositions culled from Baius' works were condemned by Pius V in the Bull *Ex omnis afflictionibus* (1 October 1567).[33] This Bull, however, was itself to prove the source of considerable controversy, which has passed into history as the affair of the *Comma Pianum*. The Bull concludes as follows:

Quas quidem sententias stricto coram nobis examine ponderatas, quamquam nonnullae aliquo pacto sustineri possent in rigore et proprio verborum sensu ab assertoribus intento *haereticas, erroneas, suspectas, temerarias, scandalosas* et *in pias aures offensionem immittentes* respective ... damnamus.[34]

The Bull was not punctuated in its original form. The affair of the *Comma Pianum* arose from the fact that the sense of the Bull was totally determined by the placing of a single comma. The Louvain theologians, and after them the Jansenists, placed the comma after 'intento', whilst their Jesuit opponents placed it after 'sustineri possent'. The former punctuation yields the following interpretation: the preceding list contains some heretical propositions, but others which are orthodox, in the sense intended by the authors. The latter punctuation yields a rather different interpretation: the list of propositions includes some which are open to an orthodox interpretation, but which are heretical as interpreted by the authors. The *magisterium* subsequently made it clear that the placing of the comma after 'intento' was unacceptable.[35]

Further controversy developed between the Dominican and Jesuit Orders in Spain, such as the acrimonious Valladolid confrontation of 1582 between Prudentius Montemayor and Domingo Báñez. This controversy entered a new phase with the publication of Luis de Molina's *Concordia* in 1588.[36] This work takes the form of a commentary upon certain sections of Thomas Aquinas' *Summa Theologiae*, and reconciles human freedom and grace by denying the efficacy of *gratia ab intrinseco*, and substituting the efficacy of grace in the divine foreknowledge *de scientia media* of human cooperation with the gift of grace.

Rejecting Thomas Aquinas' teaching on the causal relation of grace and free will,[37] Molina develops a theory of the relation between primary and secondary causes which has important consequences for his discussion of the concord between grace and the human free will in justification. This theory may be illustrated from an example Molina provides.[38] Consider the reproduction of a horse or a man. The freedom of the horse, or man, to reproduce is not in any way affected by the fact that the universal and general influence of the sun is required for that production. The sun provides a general and universal *influxus*, which forms one cause with the *influxus* of the secondary cause itself, and which derives its specific determination (that is, horse or man) from that secondary cause. As the effect proceeds from the total cause, both primary and secondary cause are necessary for the production of that effect, although they are involved in quite distinct manners. These two *influxus* do not interact directly: the interaction takes place through the *influxus* of the primary cause into the *effectus* of the secondary cause. As the secondary cause receives its *influxus* passively, its freedom is not in any sense restricted or compromised. Furthermore, the primary cause cannot be regarded as being prior to the secondary. Applying this metaphysics of causality to the question of the relation of grace and the free will, Molina draws the following conclusions: first, that the free will is responsible for its own actions; and second, that God cannot be said to be responsible for the actions of the free will.

The relationship between divine foreknowledge and human free will is resolved through an analysis of the concepts of contingency and eternity. God foreknows all that comes to pass, freely and contingently, through secondary causes.[39] This foreknowledge compromises neither the contingency of the present order of things, nor the autonomy of the human free will. Molina defines the knowledge of the behaviour of every autonomous secondary cause in all circumstances as *scientia media*.[40] This *scientia media* relates to the hypothetical and the contingent – which includes the decisions of an individual free will under a given set of circumstances.

God thus knows infallibly how each individual will respond to the grace which is offered to him, without compromising the autonomy of that individual. Molina uses this concept of the *scientia media* to reconcile the two propositions:

1.   God decreed from all eternity that Paul should go to Macedonia.
2.   Paul went to Macedonia of his own free will.

God knew infallibly, by his *scientia media*, that if Paul went to Troas, and thence received a call to go to Macedonia, he would obey this call. Therefore, Molina argues, God created the world with such circumstances that Paul would find himself in Troas at an opportune moment, and thence proceed to Macedonia – thus maintaining both the divine sovereignty and human freedom. The efficacy of grace is thus maintained, but is understood to arise on account of something extrinsic to grace (the consent of the human will) rather than the intrinsic nature of grace itself.[41]

This view was sharply attacked by Spanish Thomists, particularly Báñez, who upheld the notion of intrinsically efficacious grace. In contrast to sufficient grace, which confers upon man a capacity to act, efficacious grace moves man's will to action. Báñez and his supporters were particularly critical of Molina's assertion that God foreknew something because it would happen contingently through free will, and his rejection of the opinion that something happened on account of the divine foreknowledge.[42] The doctrine of *scientia media* was thus rejected in favour of the Báñezian *praemotio physica*. It is interesting to note that the term 'semi-Pelagian' was introduced during the course of this dispute by the followers of Báñez to describe the teachings of their Molinist opponents. The controversy between Jesuits and Dominicans at Valladolid in 1594 eventually became so heated that the papal nuncio at Madrid was obliged to impose silence upon the disputing parties, and referred the matter to Rome for resolution. A commission was appointed in November 1597 to consider the matter.

The celebrated *Congregatio de auxiliis* began at Rome in 1598, and continued over two pontificates until 1607.[43] Although the commission was initially in favour of censuring Molinism, pressure from representatives of both the King of Spain and the Society of Jesus led to a widening of the commission's membership and terms of reference, and the eventual declaration on 5 September 1607 that the Báñezian teaching was not Calvinist, nor the Molinist Pelagian. The Jesuit and Dominican Orders were permitted to defend their own teachings on the matter, but were forbidden to criticise each other, pending a final settlement of the question.[44] No such settlement has been made, to this day.

This deficiency was, however, overshadowed by the rise of Jansenism and the political threat which this posed to the papal influence in France.[45] Jansen's *Augustinus*, published posthumously in 1640, shows strong affinities with Baianism, particularly in its rejection of the concept of 'pure nature', and the corresponding distinction between 'nature' and 'supernature'. Jansen defines the grace conferred upon Adam at his creation as *adiutorium sine quo non*, which he distinguishes from *adiutorium quo*.[46] The former, bestowed upon Adam at his creation, is the divine grace without which he could do nothing, *tanquam lumen sanis oculis*, despite the fact that he is *sanus*. Just as a healthy man still requires light before he can see, despite his perfect vision, so man requires *adiutorium sine quo non* if he is to function properly. Just as human eyes require illumination if they are to function correctly, so man's *liberum arbitrium* requires *adiutorium sine quo non* before it too can function correctly. This *adiutorium* is thus an essential part of man's original nature.[47]

The Fall robbed man of *adiutorium sine quo non*, with a resulting radical vitiation of his nature. However, on account of the radical effects of the Fall on his faculties, which are now reduced from the natural to the subnatural level, man now requires more than light to restore his vision: he requires a cure for his blindness. By his sin,

Adam passed from a state of health to a state of decay. The grace required to free man from this *necessitas peccandi* is thus *adiutorium quo* – an *adiutorium* which is not merely necessary for good action, but which is itself intrinsically efficacious in producing such action.

Jansen thus rejects the Molinist concept of *gratia sufficiens* as an absurdity: on account of man's radically vitiated nature arising through the Fall, such grace would only be sufficient if it actually and effectually cured man's will, thereby restoring his health and permitting him to do good. Such grace was adequate in the case of Adam's natural state – but in the case of fallen man, medicinal grace (*gratia sanans*) was required in the form of *adiutorium quo*.[48] Jansen then proceeds to demonstrate that *gratia sanans* is necessary, efficacious and non-universal.[49] The second and third points are of particular importance. Jansen argues that Augustine never uses the term 'grace' unless he intends it to mean 'efficacious grace': if grace is given, the performance of the work for which it was given necessarily follows; if no such grace is given, no corresponding work results. Jansen's rejection of the universality of grace leads to his criticism of certain accounts of the effects of Christ's death, particularly those which suggested that Christ died for all men. According to Jansen, Augustine never concedes that Christ died for all men without exception, but only for those who benefited by his death.[50] When Christ is said to have died for all men in certain scriptural passages, this should be understood to mean that he died for all *types* of men (such as kings and subjects, nobles and peasants; or men of all nations or languages).[51] Augustine does not speak of Christ as being a redemption for all men, unless this is interpreted as meaning all *the faithful*. In all the writings of Augustine, Jansen stated that he found no reference to Christ dying for the sins of those unbelievers who remain in unbelief.[52] Although Christ's work is sufficient for all men, it is efficacious only for some. Jansen thus rejects the opinion that God must confer his grace upon the man who does *quod in se est*, claiming the support of Augustine in doing so.[53]

It was clear, in the light of the rise of Jansenism, that the Tridentine decree on justification required supplementation. On 31 May 1653, Innocent X condemned five Jansenist propositions in the Bull *Cum occasione*,[54] to be followed by more extensive condemnation of Jansenist positions (as stated by Pasquier Quesnel) in the 1713 papal constitution *Unigenitus filius Dei*.[55] The strongly political overtones to the condemnation of Jansenism, particularly evident in the association of the movement with Gallicanism,[56] lend weight to the suggestion that *Unigenitus* should be seen as a political, rather than a theological, document.

The post-Tridentine debates on justification ended with the magisterial toleration of the various forms of Thomism and Molinism, and the rejection of Jansenism and Baianism. Although individual Catholic theologians have subsequently written extensively on the question of justification,[57] the broad outlines of the Catholic teaching on the matter may be regarded as having been finally fixed by 1713.

Two points may be noted in closing this chapter. First, it may be emphasised that, despite the considerable degree of convergence evident at points between Jansenism and Protestantism, the entire post-Tridentine Catholic tradition (including those otherwise considered heterodox, such as Baianists and Jansenists) continued to regard justification as a process in which man was made righteous, involving the actualisation rather than the imputation of righteousness. The Protestant conception of justification was not adopted even by those who came closest to Protestant understandings of the mode in which justification came about. The continuity within the western tradition concerning the nature of justification was upheld by its post-Tridentine representatives. Second, the very term 'justification' itself appears to have been gradually eliminated from the homiletical and catechetical literature of Catholicism. Although the term is employed extensively in the polemical works of the sixteenth century, and may still be encountered in sermons of the seventeenth,[58] it seems that the associations of the term led to an increased reluctance to employ it from the late seventeenth century onwards – despite the extensive use of the concept by the Council of Trent. The dating of this elimination suggests that it may have been a reaction to Jansenism, rather than Protestantism. The general reintroduction of the term into the vocabulary of Catholicism appears to date from the Second Vatican Council.

8. The legacy of the English Reformation

§30 The English Reformation: Tyndale to Hooker

The Reformation in England drew its inspiration primarily from its continental counterpart, although the Lollard movement had done much to instil the anti-clerical and anti-sacramental attitudes upon which the English Reformers would base their appeal to the doctrine of justification *sola fide*.[1] The strongly political cast of the English Reformation tended to result in theological issues having a secondary and derivative importance, which goes some way towards accounting for the theological mediocrity of the movement. Furthermore, the English Reformers appear to have busied themselves chiefly with eucharistic controversies – unnecessarily drawing attention to their differences in doing so[2] – rather than with the doctrine of justification. It is, however, clear that the doctrines of justification circulating in English reforming circles in the 1520s and early 1530s were quite distinct from those of the mainstream continental Reformation, thus raising the question of the sources of these doctrines. Although the Cambridge 'White Horse circle' met to discuss the works of Luther in the 1520s, it is clear that few of the Reformer's distinctive ideas became generally accepted in England.[3]

There are excellent reasons for supposing that essentially Augustinian doctrines of justification were in circulation in England independently of the influence of Luther, and that the doctrines of justification which developed as an indirect consequence of such influence appear to have omitted the idea of the *reputatio iustitiae Christi alienae* – a central feature of Luther's conception of justification – altogether. Thomas Bilney, for example, a leading figure of the 'White Horse circle', developed a concept of justification framed solely in terms of the non-imputation of sin, omitting any reference to the concept of the 'imputation of righteousness'.[4] Similarly, William Tyndale, although making extensive use of Luther in his early polemical works,[5] tends to interpret justification as 'making righteous'.[6] Tyndale's emphasis upon the renewing and transforming work of the Holy Spirit within man is quite distinct from Luther's emphasis upon faith, and clearly parallels Augustine's transformational concept of justification. John Frith reproduces a sanative concept of justification, clearly Augustinian in its structure.[7] Frith's most characteristic definition of justification is that it consists of the non-imputation of sin,[8] omitting any references to the imputation of righteousness. The first clear and unambiguous statement of the concept of the imputation of righteousness to be found in the writings of an English Reformer may be found in the 1534 edition of Robert Barnes' *Supplication unto King Henry VIII*. The vague statements of the 1531 edition on this matter[9] are expanded to yield an unequivocal statement of the concept of imputed righteousness.[10] Barnes, however, was exceptional in his understanding of, and affinity with, Lutheranism: the early English Reformation as a whole appears to have been characterised by theologies of justification which demonstrate many points of contact with their continental counterparts, except in their understanding of the *nature* of justification. In 1531, George Joye defined justification thus:

To be justified, or to be made righteous before God by this faith, is nothing else but to be absolved from sin of God, to be forgiven, or to have no sin imputed of him by God.[11]

The assertion that justification is the forgiveness or non-imputation of sin *without* the simultaneous assertion that righteousness is imputed to the believer, or *with* the assertion that justification is to be understood as *making* righteous, appears to be characteristic of the English Reformation until the late 1530s.

The years between Henry VIII's break with Rome and his death saw the publication of a series of formularies of faith, which attempted to define the theological position of the new national church: the Ten Articles (July 1536); the Bishops' Book (August 1537); the Six Articles (statute enacted June 1539); and the King's Book (published May 1543). While these formularies of faith give insights perhaps more into the political, rather than the theological, concerns of the period, their statements on justification are particularly interesting to the extent that they refer to the *nature* of that concept.

The Ten Articles of July 1536 deal with justification and the three sacraments, amongst other matters. Although the influence of Lutheranism upon these Articles, mediated through the Wittenberg Articles of the same year,[12] is well established, this influence appears to have been minimal in relation to their statements on justification. Justification is defined in an Augustinian manner:

Justification signifieth remission of our sins, and our acceptation or reconciliation into the grace and favour of God, that is to say, our perfect renovation in Christ.[13]

Although grace is clearly conceived extrinsically as the *favor Dei*, justification continues to be defined non-forensically. This definition of justification is, in fact, based upon that of Philip Melanchthon's 1535 *Loci communes*:[14]

Iustificatio significat remissionem peccatorum et reconciliationem seu acceptationem personae ad vitam aeternam. Nam Hebraeis iustificare est forense verbum; ut si dicam, populus Romanus iustificavit Scipionem accusatum a tribunis, id est, absolvit seu iustum pronuntiavit.[15]

It is clearly significant that the entire second sentence, which contains an unequivocal assertion of the *forensic* character of justification, has been omitted, and a final phrase ('perfect renovation in Christ') substituted which completely eliminates any possibility of a distinction between *iustificatio* and *regeneratio*. This Article was incorporated *verbatim* into the Bishops' Book of the following year.[16] Elsewhere, the Bishops' Book emphasised the *communication* – and not the *imputation* – of the righteousness of Christ to the believer:

He hath planted and grafted me into his own body, and made me a member of the same, and he hath communicated and made me participant of his justice, his power, his life, his felicity, and all of his goods.[17]

Although this Book contains extracts from William Marshall's 1535 *Primer*, which is held to be based upon Luther's 1523 *Betbuchlein*,[18] the influence of Lutheranism upon the work is not marked.

The King's Book of 1543 contained an entirely new article on justification, abandoning the previous definition, based partly on Melanchthon, in favour of a definition which could be taken directly from the works of Augustine himself:

Justification ... signifieth the making of us rightous afore God, where before we were unrighteous.[19]

The phrase 'afore God' here appears to reflect the Augustinian and medieval *apud Deum*, rather than the Lutheran *coram Deo*. Elsewhere in the Book, the teachings of baptism as the first justification, and of 'restoration to justification' through penance, may be found – clearly indicative of a concept of justification continuous with the medieval Catholic tradition.

A work of particular importance in establishing the position of the early English national church on the nature of justification is the *Homily of Salvation*, usually regarded as the work of Thomas Cranmer himself.[20] In many respects, the *Homily* is Melanchthonian. For example, the obvious similarity between the explanations of Cranmer and Melanchthon concerning the correct interpretation of the phrase *sola fide* have often been noted.[21] The *Homily* is, in fact, a fine exposition of the Melanchthonian doctrine of justification *per solam fidem*. The verbal similarity between Melanchthon and Cranmer on the rôle of the law is also striking,[22] as is their similarity in relation to the fiduciary character of faith and the Anselmian approach to the death of Christ. However, Melanchthon's influence is conspicuously absent in Cranmer's discussion of the nature of justification. Cranmer interprets justification to mean 'making righteous',[23] which clearly reflects the strongly factitive Augustinian concept of justification evident in the collection of patristic texts assembled by Cranmer in support of the position he develops in the *Homily*.[24] Although Cranmer rejects Augustine's doctrine of justification on the basis of *fides quae per dilectionem operatur*, excluding charity from his account of man's justification, he does not extend this criticism to Augustine's understanding of the *nature* of justification.

This raises an important point. The English Reformers appear to have understood that their continental colleagues developed a doctrine of justification *by fayth onely*, and that its leading feature was the total exclusion of human works from man's justification. Several of them also appear to have understood that this faith was 'reputed' as righteousness, possibly drawing on the use of this term in the *Apology* for the Augsburg Confession. They do not, however, appear to have realised precisely what was meant by the very different concept of the imputation of righteousness, or its potential theological significance. In general, the English Reformers appear to have worked with a doctrine of justification in which man was understood to be *made* righteous *by fayth onely*, with good works being the natural consequence of justifying faith – a possible interpretation of the Lutheran teaching, as stated in the important confessional documents of 1530, but not the most reliable such interpretation.

The year 1547 marked the beginning of the reign of Edward VII, and the dawning of new possibilities for the English Reformers to consolidate the Protestantism of the national church. 'Since these churches of ours are in great want of learned men',[25] Cranmer wrote to various continental Reformers, inviting them to England to supervise the religious developments which he envisaged – including the clarification of points of doctrine. Of these points, the most important was the following: does justification make a man really righteous, or does it merely make him acceptable to God as though he were really righteous?[26] By 1549, Bucer and Fagius felt able to write to their colleagues in Strasbourg to the effect that 'the doctrine of justification is purely and soundly taught' in England.[27] It is not clear what moved them to this judgement: even as late as 1571, the teaching of the English church on this matter was unclear. The 1552 Article *de hominis iustificatione* affirms that 'justification *ex sola fide Iesu Christi*, in the sense in which it is explained in the *Homelia de iustificatione*', is the most important and healthy doctrine of Christians.[28] The fact that this Article refers interested readers to the *Homily of Justification* (almost certainly Cranmer's *Homily of Salvation*) for further details, when this Homily simultaneously develops an Augustinian concept of justification and a Melanchthonian doctrine of justification *per solam fidem*, further indicates that, at least in this respect, the English Reformation had yet to assimilate the teaching of its continental counterpart. It is, of course, possible that the English Reformers were misled through the occasional references in the *Apology* of the Augsburg Confession which do indeed refer to justification as 'making righteous', and which use the term 'repute', rather than 'impute'.[29] Although the *Homily* clearly states the doctrine of justification *per solam fidem* in an orthodox Melanchthonian sense (apparently with extracts from the *Loci* being worked into the text), it is significant that the crucial concept of imputed righteousness is absent. The 1563 Articles, however, contain an important addition. The reader is referred to the *Homily* merely for details of *the manner in which faith justifies*;[30] justification itself is defined as follows:

Tantum propter meritum Domini ac Servatoris nostri Iesu Christi, per fidem, non propter opera et merita nostra, iusti coram Deo reputamur.[31]

This is clearly a much more precise statement of the Melanchthonian doctrine of justification *per solam fidem*; indeed, this entire sentence could be constructed from Melanchthon's statements in the 1530 *Apologia*. Four phrases or terms may be singled out for particular comment. The use of the Melanchthonian term *per fidem* – rather than *propter fidem* or simply *fide* – makes it clear that faith is the *instrument* of justification, as explained by Melanchthon in the *Apologia* and in the *Loci*. 'Propter opera et merita nostra', with the possessive pronoun present where it is absent in the earlier reference to faith, makes it clear that man is not justified on account of any quality which he may possess, and implies that *fides* is not to be understood as such a quality. Once more, the technical expressions of the *Confessio Augustana* and its associated *Apologia* found their way into this Article – a point confirmed by the use of the crucial phrase *coram Deo*, characteristic of the forensic language of the Melanchthonian sources upon which it is so closely dependent. Finally, the use of the term *reputamur* is significant, in that it is the term used most frequently by Melanchthon in the 1530 *Apology* to describe the forensic aspect of justification: 'reputentur esse iusti coram Deo;[32] fide propter Christum coram Deum [sic] iusti reputemur'.[33] Although the term *reputatio* was displaced at a relatively early stage by *imputatio*, the fact remains that it was the former which was employed by Melanchthon in the documents which appear to have exercised so significant an influence over the English Reformers at this point. It is therefore evident that the 1563 Article on justification is intended to clarify the somewhat vague statement of 1552 along Lutheran lines. It will, nevertheless, be clear that the Article does not distinguish between the idea of *the imputation of faith for righteousness* and the quite distinct idea of the *the imputation of the righteousness of Christ*. The former expresses the notion that God accepts, reckons or 'reputes' the faith of the believer to be 'righteousness'; the latter, which corresponds to the teaching characteristic of the continental Reformation by this stage, expresses the notion that faith is the means by which the extrinsic righteousness of Christ is appropriated by the individual believer. The importance of the distinction may be seen from the later seventeenth-century controversy among Independent and Presbyterian divines, in which Thomas Gataker, John Graile, John Owen and Joshua Watson held the latter, and Richard Baxter, Christopher Cartwright, John Goodwin and Benjamin Woodbridge the former, to be the formal cause of justification (see §32). Although there are reasons for supposing that the early English Reformers actually inclined towards the former position, the latter became established as normative within the English national church by the end of the sixteenth century.

Despite this clear alignment with the Lutheran Reformation, rather than the Swiss Reformations of Zurich or Geneva, the Elizabethan period witnessed a general decline in the fortunes of Lutheranism in England. The returning Marian exiles, many of whom were promptly elevated to the episcopacy in the aftermath of the deprivations of 1559, had generally spent their time of exile in cities (such as Zurich, Strasbourg and Geneva) strongly influenced by the Reformed, rather than Lutheran, theology.[34] Although Elizabeth herself had read Melanchthon's *Loci* as a girl (the 1538 edition was dedicated to her father), and in 1559 expressed the wish that the 'Augustanean Confession' be maintained in the realm, it is clear that the Reformed theology made considerable headway in England during the final decades of the sixteenth century. The tension between Episcopalians and Presbyterians (both of whom were obliged to consider themselves members of the same church as a result of the Act of Uniformity) led to a number of important apologetic works appearing justifying the existence and teachings of the Episcopal national church. The most important of these for our purposes are Richard Hooker's sermons on the book of Habakkuk, preached in 1586, although not published until 1612.[35] In these sermons, Hooker addresses himself to issues such as the 'grand question which hangeth yet in controversy between us and the Church of Rome, about the matter of justifying righteousness'.[36] In his response, it is clear that Hooker attempts to construct a mediating doctrine of justification between Catholicism and Protestantism, which avoids the discredited eirenicon of double justification. Hooker considers that the chief error of his Catholic opponents is their teaching that a habit of grace is infused into man at his first justification to produce an inherent and real righteousness within man, which may subsequently be increased, by merit acquired through good works, in the second justification.[37] For Hooker, God bestows upon man justifying and sanctifying righteousness in his justification at one and the same time: the distinction between the two lies in the fact that the former is external to man, and imputed to him, while the latter is worked within him by the Holy Spirit.[38] Hooker distinguishes habitual and *actual* sanctifying righteousness, the former being the righteousness with which the soul is endowed through the indwelling of the Holy Spirit, and the latter the righteousness which results from the action of that Spirit.[39] At the instant of his justification, man is simultaneously accepted as righteous in Christ and given the Holy Spirit, which is the formal cause of his subsequent actual sanctifying righteousness. Hooker interprets the phrase 'justification by faith alone' as follows:

We teach that faith alone justifieth: whereas we by this speech never meant to exclude either hope and charity from being always joined as inseparable mates with faith in the man that is justified; or works from being added as necessary duties, required at the hands of every justified man: but to shew that faith is the only hand that putteth on Christ unto justification; and Christ the only garment, which being so put on, covereth the shame of our defiled natures, hideth the imperfections of our works, preserveth us blameless in the sight of God, before whom otherwise the very weakness of our faith were cause sufficient to make us culpable.[40]

As Hooker concedes, however, faith is itself a work of the Holy Spirit within man,[41] so that faith is both the prerequisite and consequence of justification.[42]

It will thus be clear that Hooker's understanding of the nature of justification is similar to that of Calvin. Man is justified *per fidem propter Christum*.[43] Justification is to be conceived Christologically, in terms of the appropriation of the personal presence of Christ within the believer through the Holy Spirit, on account of which he is declared righteous and the process of sanctification initiated. A clear distinction is thus drawn between justification through imputed righteousness, and sanctification through inherent righteousness. The importance of this distinction will become clear in the section which follows.

§31 Anglicanism: the Caroline Divines

Just as the seventeenth century witnessed the consolidation of the two main theological streams of the Continental Reformation in the shape of Lutheran and Reformed Orthodoxy, so the theological developments initiated by the English Reformation may be regarded as having been consolidated in the century which followed. The 'golden age of Anglican divinity' took place in a century which witnessed considerable change in England, including the turmoil and the uncertainty occasioned by the Civil War and Interregnum, and the theological and ecclesiological changes introduced by the Westminster Assembly. Despite the political revolution of 1688, and the no less significant, and practically simultaneous, revolution in the world of ideas accompanying the publication of Newton's *Principia mathematica* and Locke's *Essay concerning Human Understanding*, the Church of England appeared to remain relatively unaltered, retaining both her episcopal system of church government, and the reigning monarch as her head. Nevertheless, significant alterations had taken place within Anglican theology: for example, the origins of Deism may be detected in the writings of certain post-Reformation divines.

In the present section, we propose to illustrate an important discontinuity in Anglican thinking on justification over the period 1600–
1700, and assess its significance.[1]

The seventeenth-century churchmen collectively known as the
Caroline Divines may, in general, be regarded as exponents of an
Arminianism which immediately distinguishes them from their
Puritan opponents. In May 1595, William Barrett, a fellow of Caius
College, Cambridge, preached a sermon which touched off the
predestinarian controversy ultimately leading to the nine Lambeth
Articles of 1595.[2] These strongly predestinarian Articles never had
any force, other than as the private judgement of those who drafted
them. The seventeenth century saw their failing to achieve any
authority within the Church of England, particularly when John
Reynolds failed to persuade the Hampton Court Conference of 1604
to append them to the Thirty-Nine Articles of Religion. This left
Article XVII – easily harmonised with an Arminian doctrine of
election – as the sole authoritative pronouncement of the Church of
England on the matter.

Although there can be little doubt that the Reformed doctrine of
election continued to be widely held, particularly within Puritan
circles, increasing opposition to the doctrine, largely from academic
sources, was evident in the early seventeenth century. Thus Richard
Hooker at Oxford, and Launcelot Andrewes at Cambridge, developed an 'Arminianism before Arminius', which received considerable
impetus through the influence of William Laud, subsequently translated to Canterbury. Like Vincent of Lérins, Andrewes declined to
support the latest continental speculation on predestination precisely
because he felt it to be an evident innovation. The Arminianism of the
leading divines of the period – and the intense hostility towards them
from Puritans[3] – is perhaps best illustrated from the controversy
surrounding the publication of Henry Hammond's *Practical Catechism* in 1644.[4] This work may be regarded as a classic statement of
the soteriological convictions of the Laudian party, asserting unequivocally that Christ died for all men.[5] This view was variously
described by his opponents: Cheynell accused him of subscribing to
the doctrine of universal salvation; others charged him with Arminianism. The response of Clement Barksdale to this latter charge is
particularly significant:

You are mistaken when you think the Doctrine of Universall Redemption
Arminianisme. It was the Doctrine of the Church of England before
Arminius was borne. We learne it out of the old Church-Catechisme. I

believe in Iesus Christ, Who hath redeemed mee and all mankind. And the Church hath learned it out of the plaine Scripture, where Christ is the Lamb of God that taketh away the sinnes of the world.[6]

In this, Barksdale must be regarded as substantially correct. The Bezan doctrine of limited atonement was somewhat late in arriving in England, by which time the older Melanchthonian view had become incorporated into the confessional material of the English national church – such as the catechism of 1549. This evidently poses a nice problem in relation to terminology: should one style men such as Peter Baro (d. 1599) as an 'Arminian *avant la lettre*',[7] or accept that their teaching was typical of the period before the Arminian controversy brought the matter to a head and a new theological term into existence? Most Anglican divines in the late sixteenth and early seventeenth centuries appear to have based their soteriology on the dialectic between universal redemption and universal salvation, declining to accept the Bezan solution of their Puritan opponents.[8] More significantly, the early Caroline Divines appear to have been unanimous in their rejection of the doctrine of justification by inherent righteousness.

In 1701, two letters of Thomas Barlow (1607–71), sometime Bishop of Lincoln, were published.[9] Addressed to a priest in his diocese, the letters condemn the tendency to harmonise Paul and James to yield a doctrine of justification by faith *and* works, particularly on account of its associated denial of the imputation of the righteousness of Christ in justification. As we shall indicate later in the present section, this doctrine is characteristic of the post-Reformation Caroline Divines. The real significance of the letters, however, lies in their historical insight. Barlow states that Anglican divines

who have writ of our justification *coram Deo* before the late unhappy rebellion, such as Bishop Jewel, Hooker, Reynolds, Whittaker, Field, Downham, John White, etc., do constantly prove and vindicate the imputation of our blessed Saviour's Righteousness against the contrary doctrine of Racovia and Rome, Papists and Socinians. So that in truth it is only you, and some Neotericks who (since the year 1640) deny such imputation.[10]

In this respect, Barlow must be judged correct. In the case of every divine which he mentions, the doctrine of justification by imputed righteousness is defended, reflecting the general theological consensus upon this point in the Caroline church up to 1640. Had he so desired, Barlow could have added Ussher, Hall, Jackson, Davenant,

Cosin, and Andrewes to his list.[11] Thus George Downham defined justification as 'a most gracious and righteous action of God whereby he, imputing the righteousness of Christ to a believing sinner, absolveth him from his sinnes and accepteth him as righteous in Christ'.[12] In common with his contemporaries, Downham distinguished between the *imputation* of the righteousness of Christ, as the formal cause of man's justification, and the *infusion* of righteousness in his subsequent sanctification. The Tridentine doctrine of justification by inherent righteousness (or, more strictly, the doctrine that the formal cause of justification was inherent righteousness) was criticised on six counts,[13] closely paralleling similar criticisms made of the Tridentine teaching – particularly as presented in the writings of Bellarmine – by Lutheran and Reformed apologists. Indeed, in the period 1590–1640, the Caroline Divines may be regarded as developing an understanding of justification which parallels that of Lutheran Orthodoxy, and criticising both Rome (on the formal cause of justification) and Geneva (on the nature of predestination) on grounds similar to those by then well established within Lutheranism.

Isolated traces of an emerging discontinuity may be detected in the final years of the troubled reign of Charles I. Henry Hammond reverted to the more Augustinian definition of justification associated with the earlier period of the English Reformation, including the non-imputation of sin, but *not* the imputation of righteousness, among its elements. In his *Practical Catechism*, Hammond defines justification as:

God's accepting our persons, and not imputing our sins, His covering or pardoning our iniquities, His being so reconciled unto us sinners, that He determines not to punish us eternally.[14]

A similar understanding of justification may be found in the works of William Forbes, particularly his posthumously published *Considerationes*. In this work, Forbes reverts to the Augustinian understanding of justification as 'an entity, one by aggregation, and compounded of two, which by necessary conjunction and co-ordination are one only' – in other words, justification subsumes both the forgiveness of sins and the regeneration of man through inherent righteousness.[15] The 'whole sanctification or renewal of man ought to be comprehended in the expression "forgiveness of sins"'.[16]

The idea of justification *sola fide* is also criticised by the same authors. Hammond agrees that regeneration must be regarded as a precondition of justification,[17] while Forbes, conceding that faith justifies 'in a singular manner', denies that it is faith, *and faith alone* which justifies. Works cannot be excluded from justification, precisely because faith is itself a work.[18] This understanding of the implication of both faith and works in justification is, of course, a necessary consequence of the reversion to the Augustinian concept of justification, which subsumes the new life of the believer under the aegis of justification, rather than sanctification.

The leading features of the doctrines of justification characteristic of the leading Anglican divines in the period of the Restoration may thus be shown to have been anticipated in the earlier part of the century. These leading features are:[19]

1. Justification is treated as both an event and a process, subsuming regeneration or sanctification.

2. The formal cause of justification is held to be *either* imputed righteousness, *or* inherent and imputed righteousness – but *not* inherent righteousness alone.

3. The teachings of Paul and James are harmonised in such a manner that both faith and works are held to be involved in man's justification, frequently on the basis of the explicitly stated presupposition that faith is itself a work.

The most significant expositions of this understanding of justification are Jeremy Taylor's Dublin sermons of 1662,[20] and George Bull's *Harmonia Apostolica* (1669–70) – the 'apostles' in question being, of course, Paul and James.[21] Of particular interest is Bull's apparent awareness that his views on justification are at variance with those of an earlier generation of Anglican divines: he acknowledges significant points of disagreement with Hooker on the question of justifying righteousness.[22] Nevertheless, whatever its relationship with the earlier Caroline divinity may have been, it is clear that the 'theology of holy living' came to exercise a profound influence over later Caroline theology in general, and particularly its moral theology. This is not to say that there were no critics of this new theology of justification among the later Caroline Divines: Barlow, Barrow and Beveridge, for example, argued that Paul was referring to justification *coram Deo* and James to justification *coram hominibus*,[23] thus challenging the *harmonia apostolica* of the 'holy living' school. Similarly, many of the earlier Caroline Divines – such as Bramhall and Sanderson – survived until the period of the post-Restoration Caroline church, maintaining the older view of the nature of the formal causes of justification.[24]

In his *Learned Discourse of Justification*, delivered towards the end of the sixteenth century, Richard Hooker spoke of 'that grand question, which hangeth yet in controversy between us and the Church of Rome, about the matter of justifying righteousness'.[25] The following century saw disagreement concerning precisely this 'grand question' arise within the Church of England itself. Whereas the Anglican tradition had been virtually unanimous upon this, and related, questions until about 1640 (the earlier Caroline divines following Hooker himself in insisting that justifying righteousness was imputed to man; that faith was not a work of man; that justification and sanctification were to be distinguished), the later period of Caroline divinity came to be dominated by the theology of 'holy living', with a quite distinct – indeed, one might go so far as to say totally different – understanding of justification (justifying right-eousness is inherent to man; faith is a work of man; justification subsumes sanctification). Although the intervention of the Common-wealth between these two periods of Caroline divinity suggests that the new directions within the Anglican theology of justification may have arisen as a conscious reaction against that of the Westminster divines, the origins of these new directions may be found in the earlier Caroline period. Even in the later period, however, significant support for the older view persisted.

These observations are clearly of significance in relation to John Henry Newman's attempt to construct a *via media* doctrine of justification on the basis of the teachings of the later Caroline Divines, such as Bull and Taylor (see §33). Newman's own doctrine of justification, as expounded in the 1837 *Lectures on Justification*, is essentially coterminous with that of the later Caroline Divines just mentioned. However, Newman appears to appreciate that his own teaching on justification is at variance with some of the pre-Common-wealth divines. Thus Newman appeals to 'the three who have sometimes been considered the special lights of our later church, Hooker, Taylor and Barrow':[26] while he feels able to claim the support of the latter two for his own teaching, he is obliged to report that Hooker 'decides the contrary way, declaring not only for one special view of justification ... but that the opposite opinion is a virtual denial of gospel truth'.[27] This 'opposite opinion' bears a remarkable resemblance to the position carefully established by Newman himself. Furthermore, it is questionable, to say the least, whether Barrow may be cited as an antecedent of Newman's position, on account of his strong affinities with the earlier Caroline theology of justification: Newman merely cites Barrow to demonstrate the latter's awareness of the confusion and uncertainty concerning the terminology of justification, and his cautionary comments arising as a consequence;[28] this does not, however, inhibit Barrow from unequivocally affirming the earlier Anglican teaching of justification by imputed, rather than inherent, righteousness, and by faith, rather than by works.[29] Newman's claim to present an 'Anglican' theology of justification appears to involve the unwarranted restriction of 'Anglican' sources to the 'holy living' divines, with the total exclusion of several earlier generations of Anglican divines – men such as Andrewes, Beveridge, Davenant, Downham, Hooker, Jewel, Reynolds, Ussher and Whittaker. The case for the 'Anglican' provenance of Newman's *via media* doctrine of justification thus rests upon the teachings of a small, and unrepresentative, group of theologians operating over a period of a mere thirty or so years, which immediately followed the greatest discontinuity within English history – the period of the Commonwealth. It is therefore nothing less than absurd to regard certain divines of the Restoration period as in any way representing a classic statement of the essence of 'Anglican' thinking on justification, in that it represents an arbitrary historical positivism. Anglicanism cannot be defined with reference to the teachings of such a small group of theologians, operating over so short a period of time, contradicting a previously well-established tradition, and subject to considerable contemporary criticism. If any such group *could* be singled out in this manner, it is the group of *earlier* Anglican theologians, operating in the period immediately following the Elizabethan Settlement – for whom Hooker is generally regarded as spokesman.

We shall return to consider Newman's teaching later (§33). Our attention is now claimed by what is probably the most significant contribution of the English Reformation to Christendom: Puritanism.

§32 Puritanism: from the Old World to the New

The term 'Puritan' is notoriously difficult to define,[1] this difficulty unquestionably reflecting the fact that it was a term of stigmatisation used uncritically in a wide variety of social contexts over a long period of time. As early as 1565, Catholic exiles from Elizabethan England were complaining of the 'hot puritans of the new clergy',[2] and it is possible that Shakespeare's Malvolio (1600) exemplifies the stereotyped puritan of the new 'character' literature, particularly in the aftermath of the Marprelate Tracts. For the purposes of the present study, the term 'Puritanism' may be regarded as the English manifestation, especially during the period 1564–1640, of Reformed theology which laid particular emphasis upon both the experimental basis of faith and the divine sovereignty in election.[3] In this period, Puritans may be regarded as those members of the English national church who, although critical of its theology, church polity and liturgy, chose to remain within it; terms such as 'Brownist', 'Separatist' or 'Barrowist' were used to refer to those who, though criticising the same church for substantially the same reasons, did so from without its bounds.[4] Although some historians have suggested that Puritanism is the 'earlier and English form of that mutation from the Protestantism of the Reformation which on the Continent is called Pietism',[5] it must be emphasised that the Arminianism which is so characteristic a feature of Pietism is rejected by Puritan theologians in favour of the *decretum absolutum*. Indeed, the term is recorded as being used in 1622 to refer specifically to anti-Arminian elements.[6] More recently, the particular form of predestinarianism associated with Puritanism has been characterised as 'experimental predestinarianism',[7] thus capturing the twin elements of the characteristic Puritan understanding of justification. It is perfectly legitimate to suggest that perhaps the most important feature of Puritan spirituality – the quest for assurance – results from the tension inherent between the emphasis simultaneously placed upon an emotional searching for communion with God (unquestionably paralleling later Pietism in this respect) and upon the divine sovereignty in election.

The tension between Anglicanism and Puritanism led to the great exodus of pilgrim fathers from the old England to the new. The early American Puritans were refugees from an intolerant England. An old theology thus came to be planted in the New World, where it developed unhindered. The legacy of Puritanism is to be sought chiefly in American, where its influence upon the piety and culture of a new nation, with no indigenous theology or culture to oppose it, was incalculable. Just as no student of European history can neglect the Reformation, so no student of American history can neglect the Puritans, who shaped a nation in the image of their God.

One of the most important features of Puritan theologies of justification is the federal foundation upon which they are based. The concept of a covenant between God and man underlies the soteriology of the *via moderna* (§17), the young Luther (§§11, 20) and Reformed Orthodoxy (§24). It is the version of this federal theology initially associated with the Reformed theologian Heinrich Bullinger and subsequently with the Heidelberg theologians Zacharias Ursinus, Kaspar Olevianus and Girolamo Zanchius which appears to underlie that of Puritanism. The concept of a covenant between God and man, on the basis of which the justification of the latter may proceed, appears to have been introduced to the English Reformation by William Tyndale. Tyndale's covenant theology is only evident in his writings subsequent to 1530, and is probably best seen in the 1534 Genesis prologue:

Seek, therefore, in the scripture, as thou readest it, chiefly and above all, the covenants made between God and us; that is to say, the law and commandments which God commandeth us to do; and then the mercy promised unto all them that submit themselves unto the law. For all the promises throughout the whole scripture do include a covenant: that is, God binding himself to fulfil that mercy unto thee only if thou wilt endeavour thyself to keep his laws.[8]

It must be pointed out, however, that the covenant theology which established itself within English Puritanism was significantly different from that of Tyndale: for example, Tyndale recognises but *one* covenant between God and man, whereas Reformed Orthodoxy and Puritanism recognised *two*. Tyndale's influence upon the theology of the English church appears to have been ephemeral: while martyrs had their uses, the later sixteenth century saw the recognition of an even greater need – a systematic exposition of the theological foundations of the English Reformation.

The introduction of the covenant concept into the English church appears to have been largely due to the influence of Bullinger, whose *Decades* were published in English translation in 1577, and subsequently commended by Archbishop Whitgift. In the same year, John Knewstub delivered a series of lectures in London, in which he expounded the soteriological benefits of the 'league' between God and man.[9] The first clear statement of the concept of the *double* covenant may be found in Dudley Fenner's highly influential *Theologia sacra* (1585), but passed into general circulation through William Perkins' *Armilla aurea* (1590). Although Perkins' theology is essentially Bezan, his piety is overwhelmingly Puritan, demonstrating the intense concern with casuistry and personal election so characteristic of Cambridge Puritanism at the time. The *Armilla*, based largely upon Beza's *Summa totius theologiae*, did much to promote the Bezan doctrines of election and limited atonement in the period before the Synod of Dort, and its perhaps most famous feature – the 'chart of salvation', resembling an early map of the London Underground[10] –

permitted those who found theologising difficult to follow the course of their election along well-established Bezan paths with the minimum of effort. Perkins declared that the outward means of election is the covenant, which is God's

> contract with men concerning the obtaining life eternall upon a certain condition. This covenant consisteth of two parts: God's promise to man, man's promise to God. God's promise to man is that whereby he bindeth himself to man to be his God, if he perform the condition. Man's promise to God is that whereby he voweth his allegiance unto his Lord and to perform the condition betweene them.[11]

Following the Heidelberg theologians, he distinguishes between a covenant of works and a covenant of grace, this latter being 'that whereby God, freely promising Christ and his benefits, exacteth againe of man that he would by faith receive Christ and repent of his sinnes'.[12]

We shall return to consider the federal foundations of the Puritan soteriology later. A second aspect of this theology which claims our attention is the concept of 'temporary faith', intimately linked with the Puritan quest for assurance of election. Perkins' discussion of the question: how may I know that I am among the elect? exemplifies both the Puritan preoccupation with, and response to, this issue.[13] The earlier Reformed appeal to the present existence of faith as the basis of assurance was negated by the rise of the Bezan doctrine of limited atonement. The reprobate may seem to have a faith at every point identical with that of the elect, but it is merely a 'temporarie faith', which fails to apply the promises of God to the believer. The individual believer is therefore prevented from knowing whether his is a true or a temporary faith, and thus from knowing whether he is among the elect or reprobate. Perkins produces the following syllogism for troubled consciences:[14]

Everyone that beleeves is the childe of God.
But I doe beleeve.
Therefore I am the childe of God.

Unfortunately, as Perkins himself appears to have appreciated (in that he died in the conflict of a troubled conscience, uncertain as to whether he was among the elect), the similarity between the faith of the elect and reprobate excluded such an appeal as the basis of assurance. Similarly, Miles Mosse argued that the fact that the reprobate were able to recognise the divine mercy, and thus trust in the gospel promises, was to no avail, in that they were unable to be 'ingrafted into Christ'.[15] It is precisely this difficulty which led to the later shift in emphasis away from faith to *personal sanctification* as the basis of assurance. As Samuel Clarke put it: 'Kings may pardon traytours, but they cannot change their hearts; but Christ pardons none, but he makes them new creatures.'[16] Thus man has grounds for assurance in the stirrings of the new creature within him:

> As a woman that hath felt her childe stirre, concludes that she hath conceived, though she does not always feel it stirre; so if upon good grounds we have found God's grace and favour, by the powerful work of God upon our souls, we may be assured of spiritual life, although we find it not so sensibly at work in us at all times.[17]

This particular approach to the question may also be shown to have been common among Perkins' contemporaries. Thus William Bradshaw appealed to personal holiness as the proper ground of assurance; Richard Rogers argued that man could clinch his election by purity of heart: George Webb followed the earlier medieval tradition in suggesting that an earnest desire for godliness constituted reasonable grounds for assurance; John Dod even developed an existentialist approach paralleling Luther's concept of *Anfechtung* – only the elect *are* troubled in conscience concerning their election, the reprobate being exempt from any such anxiety.[18]

It is of interest to note that the Westminster Confession (1647), while explicitly following Beza in teaching limited atonement,[19] is somewhat vague concerning the pastoral consequence of such a teaching. Perkins' doctrine of temporary faith, by which the reprobate believe but are not saved, is passed over in discrete silence.[20] The Confession concedes that believers may have their assurance shaken,[21] but stipulates that it is the 'duty of every man to give all diligences to make his calling and election sure'.[22] *Si non es praedestinatus, fac ut praedestineris?*

In general, the English Puritans may be regarded as following Reformed Orthodoxy in their teaching on justification, particularly in relation to the doctrines of election and the imputation of the righteousness of Christ. The strongly anti-Arminian character of English Puritanism is best illustrated from the writings of John Owen, evident in his first work, *A Display of Arminianism*.[23] In this work, Owen reduced the Arminian teaching to two points: first, the precise object of Christ's death; second, the efficacy and end of his death.[24] The controversy was thus defined in terms of the identity of those on whose behalf Christ died, and what he merited or otherwise obtained on their behalf. Both these points were developed at greater length in *Salus electorum, sanguis Jesu* (1647). Although Owen displays the usual Puritan veneration for scripture, it is significant that this work is essentially a logical analysis of the Arminian doctrine of universal redemption. Owen argues that the Arminian proposition 'Christ died for all men' contains within itself the further proposition 'Christ died for nobody', in that no men are actually and effectively saved by his death. For Owen, it is beyond dispute that all men are not saved: therefore, if Christ died to save all men, he has failed in his mission – which is unthinkable.[25] For Owen, the Arminians subscribe to a doctrine of conditional redemption, so that God may be said to have given Christ to obtain peace, reconciliation and forgiveness of sins for all men, 'provided that they do believe'.[26] Thus the Arminians treat the 'blood of Christ'

as a medicine in a box, laid up for all that shall come to have any of it, and so applied now to one, then to the other, without any respect or difference, as though it should be intended no more for one than for another; so that although he hath obtained all the good that he hath purchased for us, yet it is left indifferent and uncertain whether it shall ever be ours or no.[27]

For Owen, 'salvation indeed is bestowed conditionally, but faith, which is the condition is absolutely procured'.[28]

Although Owen himself taught that the formal cause of justification was the imputation of the righteousness of Christ, the controversy surrounding Baxter's *Aphorisms of Justification* (1649) served to demonstrate the remarkable variety of opinions within Puritanism on this question. For Baxter himself, the formal cause of justification was the faith of the believing individual, imputed or reputed as righteousness on account of the righteousness of Christ.[29] Underlying this doctrine is a federal scheme characteristic of Puritanism, in which a distinction is drawn between the old and new covenants. According to Baxter, Christ has fulfilled the old covenant, and therefore made it possible for man to be justified on the basis of the somewhat more lenient terms of the new.[30] The righteousness of Christ in fulfilling the old covenant is thus the meritorious cause of justification, in that it is on account of this fulfilment that the faith of the believer may be the formal cause of justification under the new covenant. A similar teaching may be found in John Goodwin's *Imputatio fidei* and George Walker's *Defence*, although these two writers differed on the grounds on which man's faith could be treated as righteousness: for Walker, man's faith is reckoned as righteousness only because it apprehends Christ as its object,[31] whereas Goodwin argued that the remission of sin implied that the sinner was 'compleately and perfectly righteous',[32] and thus did not require the imputation of the righteousness of Christ. In many respects, the disagreements over the formal cause of justification within seventeenth-century Puritanism parallel those within contemporary Anglicanism (see §31). Nevertheless, it is clear that the most favoured view was unquestionably that adopted by John Owen and others – that the formal cause of justification was none other than the imputed righteousness of Christ,[33] thus aligning the English movement with continental Reformed Orthodoxy.

In the year 1633, the *Griffin* set sail from Holland for the New World, carrying with her two refugees from Laudian England: Thomas Hooker and John Cotton. Both were to prove of considerable significance in the establishment of Puritanism in New England. It was not, however, merely English Puritanism, but also the tensions within English Puritanism, which sailed with the *Griffin* to America, there to flare up once more with renewed vigour. Of particular significance was the issue of 'preparationism', to which we now turn.

We have already noted the importance of assurance as both a theological and a practical aspect of Puritan spirituality, and the tendency to treat the experimental aspects of the Christian life (such as faith or regeneration) as grounds of assurance. During his period as a preacher in the Surrey parish of Esher, Hooker was called to counsel one Mrs Joan Drake, who was convinced that she was beyond salvation. Although we have no record of Hooker's advice to her – which succeeded where that of others had failed – it is probable that it is incorporated into the 1629 sermon *Poor Doubting Christian drawne unto Christ.*[34] In this sermon, Hooker rejected the experimental basis of assurance:

A man's faith may be somewhat strong, when his feeling is nothing at all. David was justified and sanctified, and yet wanted this joy; and so Job rested upon God, when he had but little feeling ... Therefore away with your feeling, and go to the promise.[35]

Having rejected experience as the foundation and criterion of assurance, Hooker substituted the process of preparation in its place. It is within man's natural powers to be sufficiently contrite to permit God to justify him: 'when the heart is fitted and prepared, the Lord Jesus comes immediately into it'.[36] The absence of Christian experience is therefore of secondary importance in relation to the matter of assurance: developing an argument which parallels the federal theology of the *via moderna* (see §§7, 11, 17), Hooker argues that, once man has satisfied the minimum precondition for justification, he may rely upon God's faithfulness to his promises of mercy to ensure his subsequent justification and assurance of the same. Man's preparation for justification (the 'fitting of the sinner for his being in Christ'), in which the heart is 'fitted and prepared for Christ', thus constitutes the grounds of assurance.

A similar understanding of the relation of man's preparation for grace and his assurance of the same may be found in the early writings of John Cotton. In an early discussion of Revelation 3.20, he argued that conversion consists of an act of God, knocking at the door of man's heart, followed by an act of man, opening the door in order that God may enter.[37] Once man has performed this necessary act, he may rest assured that God will do the rest – which he, and only he, may do. In an intriguing exposition of Isaiah 40.3–4, he declares: 'if we smooth the way for him, then he will come into our hearts'.[38] Before his departure from England, however, Cotton's theology appears to have undergone a significant alteration. Prior to this point, Cotton and Hooker had assumed that man was naturally capable of preparing himself for justification (once more, it is necessary to point out the similarity with the soteriology of the *via moderna* on this point). But what if man's depravity was such that he could not prepare himself? In a development which parallels that of Luther over the period 1513–16, Cotton appears to have arrived at the insight that there is no saving preparation for grace prior to union with Christ: Christ is offered in a promise of free grace without any previous gracious qualification stipulated.[39] In other words, man cannot turn to God of his own volition: he requires God to take hold of him. Christ is given to the sinner upon the basis of an absolute, rather than a conditional, promise.[40] As a result, Cotton makes faith itself the basis of man's assurance, rather than preparation or sanctification. Cotton's rejection of sanctification as the basis of assurance was based upon his conviction that this was to revert to the covenant of works from the covenant of grace. Unfortunately for him, his views appear to have been misunderstood by some of his more intimate circle, most notably by Mrs Anne Hutchinson. Prior to her demise at the hands of the Indians in late 1643, Mrs Hutchinson suggested that every minister in Massachusetts Bay – with the exception of Cotton – was preaching nothing more and nothing less than a covenant of works.[41] The resulting controversy did not seriously damage his reputation. More significant, however, was his evasion of the crucial question which Hooker had addressed so directly: although Cotton implies that the believer knows that he has faith, he has nothing to say concerning how that faith may be obtained in the first place.

The controversy over 'the heart prepared' is of importance in a number of respects, particularly as it indicates the manner in which Puritan thinking on justification and assurance were related. Although Hooker and Cotton adopt very different theologies of justification (the former asserting the activity, the latter the passivity, of man prior to his justification), they share a common desire to establish the grounds of assurance within the context of that theology. It is therefore of importance to note that the grounds of assurance are the consequence of a prior understanding of the mode in which man is justified.

The later seventeenth and early eighteenth century saw New England Puritanism in decline.[42] The emphasis upon human impotence in the face of the divine omnipotence, a cornerstone of mainstream Puritan thought, tended to induce religious paralysis rather than renewal. As a consequence, subsequent generations of New Englanders were largely unconverted, obliging the churches to introduce the 'Half-Way Covenant', by which baptised persons of moral character would be treated as church members, save in certain respects.[43] The emphasis on the 'means of grace' – apparently peculiar to New England – permitted pastors to admit the unregenerate to church services on the basis of the principle that the public reading of the Bible, the preaching of the Word (and, in the Stoddardean system, the attending of the Lord's Supper) were means by which divine grace could be bestowed upon man.

This situation was radically altered through the 'Great Awakening', particularly associated with Jonathan Edwards.[44] In 1734, Edwards preached a series of sermons on the theme of 'justification by faith'.[45] Although these sermons contained nothing which could be described as radical innovations, the earnestness with which they were preached appears to have proved decisive in achieving their astonishing and celebrated effects. The intense emphasis placed by Edwards and others upon the need for spiritual rebirth was such that it became the criterion of church membership, thus ensuring the demise of the Half-Way Covenant.

The Great Awakening was based upon a covenant theology similar to that which had long been accepted in New England. God is understood to have entered into an agreement with man, by which he promised to pardon those who have faith in him, upon condition that man promises to work towards his sanctification. Edwards' discussion of the covenant of grace parallels that of Reformed Orthodoxy: God has made a covenant of redemption with Christ from all eternity, by which man would be redeemed, and the covenant of grace is the temporal manifestation of this eternal covenant.[46] Just as the imputation of the sin of Adam to his posterity is the consequence of his being the federal representative of all mankind in the covenant of works,[47] so the imputation of the righteousness of Christ to the elect is the consequence of his being their federal representative in the covenant of redemption, actualised in the covenant of grace.[48]

Edwards' somewhat traditional presentation of the federal basis of justification was developed and modified by his followers. Joseph Bellamy modified the Bezan foundations of the 'New England Theology'[49] by following Grotius in insisting that Christ's sufferings were a penal example stipulated by God as the moral governor of the universe, rather than a satisfaction rendered to God as the offended party. Samuel Hopkins explicitly rejected the 'Old Calvinist' emphasis upon the 'means of grace' – the principle upon which the Half-Way Covenant was based – although his chief contribution to the development of the movement was his understanding of the positive rôle of sin within the economy of salvation.[50]

Of particular significance was the rise of federal Arminianism within New England Puritanism. Recognising that the federal condition required of man for justification was faith (which the 'Old Calvinists' regarded as a divine gift to man), the Arminians regarded faith as a condition, equivalent to obedience, capable of being met by all men. In many respects, the Arminian party within the Puritan movement may be regarded as the direct equivalent of European Pietism, the one significant difference between Puritanism and Pietism (the doctrine of election) having been abandoned. Indeed, there are excellent grounds for suggesting a direct link between the two movements through the correspondence between Cotton Mather and the Halle Pietists.[51] The Arminians thus followed the 'Old Calvinists' in relation to the principle of the 'means of grace': grace was understood to be available to all men, particularly through 'means' such as reading the Bible, attending public worship and hearing the proclamation of the Word. As Jonathan Mayhew stated this principle: 'Tho' God is omnipotent, yet he seldom or never works wholly without means.'[52] The Arminians thus sided with the 'Old Calvinists' over the question of unregenerate church membership, proclaiming the universality of grace:

The Gospel takes no Notice of different Kinds or Sorts of Grace – Sorts of Grace specifically different, – one of which may be call'd *special* and the other not so; – one of which, from the peculiar and distinguishing Nature of it, shall prove converting and saving, and the other not.[53]

The emphasis upon the necessity of both faith and works in justification was usually justified with reference to the need to harmonise the opinions of Paul and James,[54] with both faith and works being understood 'as the *gracious Terms* and *Conditions*, appointed by the Redeemer, without which we shall not be *pardon'd* and *accepted*'.[55]

Although the effects of the Great Awakening in New England were to extend far beyond the purely religious sphere, the revival in preaching and intense interest in personal conversion and religious experience thus resulted in a number of differences on the question of justification becoming evident within New England Puritanism, in many respects paralleling similar developments within continental Protestant theology.

It is now necessary to return to England in order to consider one of the most significant discussions of the doctrine of justification to emerge within the Anglican church: John Henry Newman's *Lectures on Justification*.

§33 John Henry Newman's *Lectures on Justification*

As noted in §31, the Restoration of Charles II in 1660 appears to have been the occasion for the introduction of a new Anglican theology of justification, which asserted the positive rôle of inherent righteousness in justification, with faith being understood as a human work. If these later Anglican divines believed in justification *sola fide*, it was in the sense that faith justifies *in its own particular manner*. These features of the later Caroline understanding of justification were emphasised by the 'High Churchmen'[1] of the later eighteenth century in their polemic against the possibility that their Evangelical counterparts might cause the faithful to become complacent or negligent of good works through their preaching of the doctrine of justification *sola fide*. The nineteenth century saw the theological differences between High Churchmen and Evangelicals on this matter fairly well established, and not the subject of major controversy. Indeed, both parties to the debate emphasised the need for personal holiness as a result of justification, showing a remarkable uniformity in their respective teachings on piety. It is a fact which is often overlooked, that many Evangelicals – such as C. R. Sumner –

followed the early stages of the Oxford Movement with great sympathy.

This relative calm was shattered through the publication (1834–7) of the *Remains* of Alexander Knox, a lay theologian of some considerable talent. The *Remains* included his 1810 essay *On Justification*,[2] in which Knox argued that the Church of England, far from teaching a doctrine of *forensic* justification in her Homilies and Articles, was actually committed to a doctrine of *moral* justification. 'In the judgement of the Church of England justification by faith contains in it the vitalisation which vera et viva fides (true and lively faith) produces in the subject; as well as the reputation of righteousness, which follows coram Deo (before God).'[3] Noting Cranmer's frequent references to patristic writers in the *Homily of Salvation*, and the failure of the church historian Joseph Milner to demonstrate that such writers taught a forensic doctrine of justification, Knox suggested that the patristic consensus favoured a doctrine of moral justification.[4] The editor of Knox's *Remains*, John Henry Newman, subsequently (1837) delivered a course of lectures at Oxford in which he defended and enlarged upon Knox's essay of 1810. It is with these *Lectures on Justification*, easily the most significant theological writing to emerge from the Oxford Movement, that we are concerned in the present section. In these lectures, Newman defined what he took to be a *via media* understanding of justification, which allowed an authentically *Anglican* concept of justification to be defended in the face of the distortions of both Protestantism and Roman Catholicism.[5] Newman thus declared his intention to 'build up a system of theology out of the Anglican divines', and indicated that the lectures were a 'tentative inquiry' towards that end.[6]

Newman's theology of justification rests primarily upon an historical analysis of the doctrines of justification associated with Luther (and to a much lesser extent, with Melanchthon), with Roman Catholic theologians such as Bellarmine and Vásquez, and with the Caroline Divines. It is therefore of the utmost importance to appreciate that in every case, and supremely in the case of Luther himself, Newman's historico-theological analysis appears to be seriously and irredeemably inaccurate. In other words, Newman's construction of a *via media* doctrine of justification appears to rest upon a fallacious interpretation of both the extremes to which he was opposed, as well as of the Caroline divinity of the seventeenth century, which he regarded as a prototype of his own position. We shall develop these criticisms at the appropriate point in the present section.

The essential feature of Newman's understanding of the nature of justification is his insistence upon the real presence of the Trinity within the soul of the justified believer, conceived in broadly realist terms which undoubtedly reflect his interest in and positive evaluation of the Greek fathers, such as Athanasius.[7] It is this understanding of the nature of justification which underlies the most difficult stanza of his most famous hymn:

> And that a higher gift than grace,
> Should flesh and blood refine;
> God's presence and his very self,
> And essence all-divine.[8]

It is God himself, the 'essence all-divine', who dwells within and thus 'refines' sinful man, in the process of justification. '*This* is to be justified, to receive the Divine Presence within us, and be made a Temple of the Holy Ghost.'[9] Justification thus refers to a present reality, the 'indwelling in us of God the Father and the Word Incarnate through the Holy Ghost'.[10] Although this divine presence is to be understood in Trinitarian terms, Newman makes it clear that it is most appropriately understood as the presence of Christ himself. 'If to justify be to impart a certain inward token of our personal redemption, and if the presence of God within us is such a token, our justification must consist in God's coming to us and dwelling in us.'[11] This real presence of the Trinity within the soul of the believer has certain associated and necessary consequences, which Newman identifies as being *counted righteous* and being *made righteous*. Both justification and sanctification are bestowed simultaneously with the gift of the divine presence within the souls of the justified. In other words, Newman understands the primary and fundamental sense of the term 'justification' to be the indwelling of the Trinity within the soul of the believer, which has as its necessary consequence those aspects of his conversion which are traditionally (although Newman feels *inappropriately*) termed 'justification' (that is, being counted as righteous) and 'sanctification' (that is, being made righteous).[12] This is made clear in what is probably the most important passage in the *Lectures*:

We now may see what the connection really is between justification and renewal. They are both included in that one great gift of God, the indwelling of Christ in the Christian soul. That dwelling is *ipso facto* our sanctification and justification, as its necessary results. It is the divine presence which justifies us, not faith, as say the Protestant schools, not renewal, as say the Roman. The word of justification is the substantive and living Word of God, entering the soul, illuminating and cleansing it, as fire brightens and purifies material substances. He who justifies also sanctifies, because it is He. The first blessing runs into the second as its necessary limit; and the second being rejected, carries away with it the first. And the one cannot be separated from the other except in idea, unless the sun's rays can be separated from the sun, or the power of purifying from fire or water.[13]

Justification is therefore *notionally distinct* from sanctification, although inseparable from it, in that they are both aspects of one and the same thing – the indwelling of the Holy Trinity within the soul of the believer. This distinction between justification and renewal allows Newman to maintain a proleptic relation between them: 'Justification is at first what renewal could but be at last; and therefore is by no means a mere result or consequence of renewal, but a real, though not a separate act of God's mercy.'[14] The distinction between justification and sanctification is thus 'purely mental',[15] relating to the single act of divine mercy, and does not necessitate the division of that act itself.

In his tenth lecture, Newman turns his attention to the vexed question of the precise rôle of faith in justification. Newman rejects a purely fiduciary interpretation of faith as excluding other Christian virtues, such as love or obedience. Whilst Newman would not go so far as to state 'that there is no such thing as a trusting in Christ's mercy for salvation, and a comfort resulting from it',[16] he insists that this is inadequate to characterise true Christian faith. The evil and good alike can trust in God's mercy, whereas the good and the evil are distinguished on account of the former's charity, love and obedience. The Protestant understanding of faith, as Newman perceives it, is thus not so much wrong, as incomplete.[17] Following Bull and Taylor (see §31), Newman argues that faith and works must both be said to justify, although in different manners.[18] Thus the fact that all acknowledge that it is Christ who justifies does not prevent the simultaneous assertion that faith justifies, nor does the fact that faith justifies exclude works from justifying:

It seems then, that whereas faith on our part fitly corresponds, or is the correlative, as it is called, to grace on God's part, sacraments are but the manifestation of grace, and good works are but the manifestation of faith; so that, whether we say we are justified by faith, or by works or by sacraments, all these but mean this one doctrine, that we are justified by grace, which is given through sacraments, impetrated by faith, manifested in works.[19]

The importance of Newman's *Lectures* lies in their representing an attempt to construct an authentically *Anglican* doctrine of justification representing the *via media* between Protestantism and Roman Catholicism, on the basis of the following understanding of the spectrum of theologies of justification:[20]

Luther	Gerhard	Melanchthon	*Via Media*	Pighius	Bellarmine	Vasquez

Protestant Roman Catholic

This evaluation is essentially correct. It may, however, be noted that Newman tends to direct his invective chiefly against the Protestant, rather than the Roman Catholic region, of this spectrum, and that the Protestant divines whom he singles out for discussion are Lutheran, rather than Reformed. In view of the fact that Newman was addressing himself to the contemporary situation within the Church of England in the context of the predominantly Protestant theological climate of England, it is understandable that he should wish to direct particular attention to his Protestant opponents. His failure to deal at any length with Reformed theologians is, however, unjustified: Lutheranism has exerted a minimal influence over English theology since 1600,[21] although a Melanchthonian influence upon the Homilies and Articles may be conceded. From 1600 onwards, the main Protestant influence upon English theology was *Reformed*, rather than *Lutheran* – in other words, due to Calvin and Beza (in an equally great variety of manners and refractions), rather than Luther. Newman, presumably on account of the intimate association between Luther and the doctrines of justification, appears to assume unconsciously that contemporary Protestant opinions on this matter were essentially those of Luther himself – which is clearly not the case.

The construction of the *via media* upon dialectical principles inevitably means that its validity is dependent upon the accuracy with which the extremes are represented and analysed. Furthermore, as Newman appears to regard the Caroline Divines as precursors or representatives of the *via media*, it will be clear that the accuracy of his understanding of their position is crucial in ascertaining the 'Anglican' character of the resulting doctrine. In what follows, we propose to examine the accuracy of Newman's presentation of two of the three elements upon whose basis the *via media* is constructed: Luther and the Caroline Divines.

1 *Luther*[22]

Newman's critique of Luther in the *Lectures* appears to rest upon the quite fallacious assumption that the Reformer regards faith as a human work. His criticism of Luther for his insistence upon the fiduciary aspects of faith, while neglecting hope, love and obedience, reflects his basic conviction that Luther singled out the *human activity of trust in God* as the defining characteristic of justifying faith. This criticism is inept.[23] For Luther, man is passive towards his justification; he takes no part in his own justification, which is totally the work of God. Faith itself, however it may be defined, is a work of God within man. God operates upon man in justification, and man contributes nothing to the process apart from being the inert material upon which God operates – a view which, as noted earlier (§30), coincides with that of Richard Hooker.[24] The misunderstanding of Luther which Newman reproduces coincides with that of George Bull (see §31), and it appears that Newman merely projected the Caroline caricature of Luther on to what little of the Reformer he troubled to read. Newman understood Luther to teach that man is *active* in justification, and that the nature of this human activity is defined in terms of fiduciary apprehension of the benefits of Christ, without reference to such *desiderata* as hope, love and obedience. In fact, of course, Luther rarely uses the phrase *sola fide*, and where he does use it, it is clear that the reference is to *fides Christi* – a *Christological* concept, with the emphasis placed upon the real and redeeming presence of Christ in the believer, rather than the faith which procured this in the first place. The 1521 treatise *Rationis Latomianae confutatio* makes it clear that *Christ and faith* are *given simultaneously* to the sinner in his justification. The distinguishing mark of faith is not its 'fiduciary' character – and how influential Newman's caricature has become in English-speaking circles! – but the real and redeeming presence of Christ in the soul of the believer. For Luther, *fides Christi*, upon the basis of which alone justification takes place, is the real presence of Christ in the believer, brought about by the gracious working of the Holy Spirit – in fact, something remarkably close to Newman's own position. Luther does not understand 'justification by faith' to mean that man puts his trust in God, and is justified on that account: indeed, such an understanding of the phrase was rigorously excluded by the confessional material of both the Lutheran and Reformed churches – rather, it means that God bestows upon that man faith and grace, without his cooperation, effecting within him the real and redeeming presence of Christ as the 'righteousness of God' within him, and justifying him on *this* account. In effect, the phrase *sola fide* is merely a convenient statement of the justification of man upon Christological grounds without his cooperation. Luther does not understand the 'righteousness of God' to be some impersonal attribute of God fictitiously ascribed to man – it is none other than Christ himself. 'The Christ who is grasped by faith and lives in the heart of the true Christian righteousness, on account of which God counts us righteous, and grants us eternal life.'[25] Similar statements are made frequently in the course of the work from which this citation is taken. Newman's own statement concerning this point should be compared with this: 'This indwelling [of the divine presence] accurately answers ... to what the righteousness which justifies has already been shown to consist in.'[26] These statements clearly presuppose precisely the same understanding of the basis and nature of justification. Luther's statement noted immediately above is, however, taken from the 1535 Galatians commentary, from which most of Newman's citations from Luther are drawn. Why did Newman not notice it, or the many others in the same work which express substantially the same idea? It seems to us that Newman did not read Luther at first hand. If this conclusion can be shown to be false, then, reluctantly, we are forced to draw the more serious conclusion that Newman deliberately misrepresents Luther. We shall indicate the grounds for this suggestion in what follows.

In his discussion of the relation between faith and works, Newman takes the remarkable step of citing Luther in support of his own opinion that justification is to be ascribed to 'believing deeds' (that is, both faith and works, as taught by Bull and Taylor). Newman prefaces his citation of Luther on this point with the caustic remark that this opinion might appear unusual, coming from Luther, but that the Reformer was obliged to concede this point 'in consequence of the stress of texts urged against him'.[27] He then quotes, in English translation, Luther's comments on Galatians 3.10 as they appear in the 1535 Galatians commentary:

'It is usual with us', he says, 'to view faith, sometimes apart from its work, sometimes with it. For as an artist speaks variously of his materials, and a gardener of a tree, as in bearing or not, so also the Holy Ghost speaks variously in Scripture concerning faith; at one time of what may be called abstract faith, faith as such: at another of concrete faith, faith in composition, or embodied. Faith as such, or abstract, is meant when Scripture speaks of justification, as such, or of the justified. (Vid. Rom. and Gal.) But when it speaks of rewards and works, then it speaks of faith in composition, concrete or embodied. For instance: 'Faith which worketh by love'; 'This do and thou shalt live'; 'If thou wilt enter into life, keep the commandments'; 'Whoso doeth these things, shall live in them'; 'Cease to do evil, learn to do well.' In these and similar texts, which occur without number, in which mention is made of doing, believing doings are always meant; as, when it says, 'This do, and thou shalt live', it means, 'First see that thou art believing, that thy reason is right and thy will good, that thou hast faith in Christ; that being secured, work.' Then he proceeds:– 'How is it wonderful, that to that embodied faith, that is, faith working, as was Abel's, in other words, to believing works, are annexed merits and rewards? Why should not Scripture speak thus variously of faith, considering it so speaks even of Christ, God and man; sometimes of His entire person, sometimes of one or other of His two natures, the Divine or human? When it speaks of one or other of these, it speaks of Christ in the abstract; when of the Divine made one with the human in the one person, of Christ as if in composition and incarnate. There is a well-known rule in the schools concerning the 'communicatio idiomatum', when the attributes of His divinity are ascribed to His humanity, as is frequent in Scripture; for instance, in Luke ii. the Angel calls the infant born of the Virgin Mary, 'the Saviour' of men, and 'the Lord' both of Angels and men, and in the preceding chapter, 'the Son of God'. Hence I may say with literal truth, That Infant who is lying in a manger and in the Virgin's bosom, created heaven and earth, and is the Lord of Angels.... As it is truly said, Jesus the Son of Mary created all things, so is justification ascribed to faith incarnate or to believing deeds.'[28]

As it stands, this citation is quite astonishing, in that the final sentence appears to state unequivocally the principle of justification by 'believing deeds' – an excellent description of the teaching both of Newman and certain later Caroline Divines. The argument of the passage is clear, if not entirely persuasive: just as it is possible to employ the standard principle of the communication of attributes to Christ, so that attributes of his divinity may be applied to his humanity, so justification may be ascribed to believing deeds. The essential point which Newman wishes us to grasp is that even Luther is obliged to concede a positive rôle for works in justification.

Astonishment, however, gives way to intense irritation when the sections of this passage which have been omitted are considered. Thus the final dramatic sentence of this citation is preceded by four periods, suggesting that a sentence or portion of a sentence irrelevant for Newman's purposes, but not significant in determining the meaning of the passage, has been omitted. In view of the great length of the citation up to this point, this might appear quite unnecessary: omission of portions of previous sentences would have done little detrimental to the sense of the passage. Why this verbal economy at this stage? In fact, Newman has omitted not a portion of a sentence, or still a single, or even a couple of sentences. An *entire section* has been omitted, which so qualifies the final sentence as to exclude Newman's interpretation of it. The omitted section is so long that we ourselves have been forced to omit the list of scriptural citations given by Luther, indicated by three periods. The section which Newman chose to omit is here reproduced, with the parts Newman did include printed in italics:

That Infant who is lying in a manger and the Virgin's bosom, created heaven and earth, and is the Lord of Angels. I am indeed speaking about a man here. But 'man' in this proposition is obviously a new term, and, as the sophists say, stands for the divinity; that is, this God who became man created all things. Here creation is attributed to the divinity alone, since the humanity does not create. Nevertheless, it is correct to say that 'the man created', because the divinity, which alone creates, is incarnate with the humanity, and therefore the humanity participates in the attributes of both predicates ... Therefore the meaning of the passage: 'This do, and thou shalt live', is, 'You will live on account of this faithful doing; this doing will give you life solely on account of faith.' Thus justification belongs to faith alone, just as creation belongs to the divinity. *As it is truly said, Jesus the Son of Mary created all things, so is justification ascribed to faith incarnate or to believing deeds.*[29]

The significance of the omitted section lies in the fact that it unequivocally qualifies the final sentence as a statement of the principle that justification is by faith alone, and indicates that scriptural passages which indicate the necessary implication of works in salvation are to be understood primarily and fundamentally as an assertion of the necessity of *faith*. The statement 'Jesus the Son of Mary created all things' is a statement that God alone is creator, just as the statement 'Justification is ascribed to ... believing deeds' remains a statement that faith alone justifies.

We are thus confronted with two possibilities. Either Newman encountered this passage at second hand, already in its mutilated form; or else he deliberately chose to omit a section on account of its evident significance. We incline towards the former, not merely out of respect for Newman, but on account of a further consideration: where Newman cites Luther elsewhere in Latin, it frequently appears as a garbled version of the original. For example, he cites Luther's 'paradox of justification' as follows: sola fides, non fides formata charitate, iustificat: fides justificat sine et ante charitem.[30] The closest approximation to this we have been able to find is: sola fide, non fide formata charitate iustificat ... haec fides sine et ante charitatem iustificat.[31] As Newman normally cites his sources with some care, it is probable that his references derive from an inaccurate secondary source, accurately cited.

It will be clear that Newman has failed to grasp the essence of Luther's understanding of justification, and to appreciate the similarities between his own position and that of the Reformer. A similar critique could be made of his totally inadequate references to Calvin. Had Newman studied Calvin seriously, he could hardly have failed to notice the remarkable similarities between them on the nature of justification. Thus Calvin regards both justification and sanctification as notionally distinct yet inseparable aspects of the believer's incorporation into Christ through the Holy Spirit in a mystical union. 'Christ, when he enlightens us with faith by the power of the Spirit, simultaneously grafts us into his body, that we may become partakers of all his benefits.'[32] This corresponds exactly to Newman's view, that justification and renewal 'are both included in that one great gift of God, the indwelling of Christ in the Christian soul'.[33] The similarity between Newman and Calvin may arise through their common respect for, and use of, the works of Athanasius. Newman's purely superficial engagement with the thought of the Reformation prevents him from even observing, let alone evaluating, their evident similarity on the Christological conception of justification.

2 The Caroline Divines

As we noted in §31, a distinction may be drawn between the pre-Commonwealth divines up to 1640, and certain of the divines writing in the post-Restoration period. The latter were essentially unanimous in asserting that the formal cause of justification was imputed, rather than inherent, righteousness, and excluded the idea of justification by 'believing deeds'. Newman, however, develops a theology of justification which corresponds, in many respects, to that of certain of the post-Restoration divines, such as Bull and Taylor. As we indicated in §31, this view by no means represented the unanimous, and probably not even the *majority*, opinion within contemporary Anglicanism. Yet Newman appears to suggest that this understanding of the formal cause of justification is characteristic of Anglicanism, and may be taken to define the *via media* between Protestant and Roman Catholic. Put crudely, but nonetheless accurately, Newman appears to believe that Protestants taught that man was justified on account of faith (which, as we have seen, is an Arminian, rather than an Orthodox view) and that Roman Catholics taught that man was justified on account of his works or renewal – and therefore that the *via media* consisted in the affirmation that man is justified on account of both faith and works. This view corresponds with that of the 'holy living' school within later Caroline divinity, which appears to establish the 'Anglican' character of this mediating doctrine. However, as we have seen, the discontinuity within Anglicanism over the period 1550–1700 on precisely this point is sufficient to negate any attempt to characterise such a position as 'Anglican'.

It is interesting to consider, in concluding, Newman's understanding of the Roman Catholic position on justification. Newman nowhere attempts a detailed analysis of the teaching of Bellarmine and Vásquez, forcing us to base our tentative conclusions upon the few passing statements made in the *Lectures* concerning Roman Catholicism in general. Newman clearly believes the Roman Catholic teaching to be that man is justified on account of his renewal.[34] Like many contemporary Evangelicals, Newman appears to have assumed that the notion of factitive justification implies that the analytic divine verdict of justification is based upon the inherent righteousness of the individual, *achieved through moral renewal* – whereas the reference is, of course, to the *infusion* of *divine* righteousness which is the *cause* of subsequent moral renewal, and is not identical with that renewal itself. The evidence contained within the body of the *Lectures* is suggestive, but not conclusive, that Newman simply did not understand the Tridentine doctrine of justification.

There is thus every reason to state that Newman's construction of a *via media* doctrine of justification unquestionably rests upon an historico-theological analysis of the dialectic between Protestantism and Roman Catholicism which is seriously inaccurate in the case of Luther, and may well be, although conclusive evidence may never be forthcoming, equally inaccurate in the case of Roman Catholicism. The demonstration of a serious misrepresentation of one extreme is, however, adequate, given Newman's dialectical construction of the *via media*, to invalidate its results. Furthermore, there are excellent reasons for calling into question the 'Anglican' character and provenance of the *via media* which Newman thus constructs. This is not necessarily to say that a *via media* cannot be constructed, although its possibility is remote, to say the least; rather, it is to say that, if such a possibility is conceded, Newman failed in his attempt to construct one.

The publication of *Tract 90* on 27 February 1841 effectively ended Newman's usefulness to the Oxford Movement. The purpose of the *Tract* was to demonstrate that the Thirty-Nine Articles, 'the offspring of an uncatholic age, are, through God's good providence, to say the least, not uncatholic, and may be subscribed to by those who aim at being Catholic in heart and doctrine'.[35] For many of its readers, however, the *Tract* merely confirmed what they had long suspected – that Newman was closer to Rome than to Canterbury on most issues of substance. In fact, the *Tract* merely restates, rather than develops, the views on justification expressed in the *Lectures*, and the greatest offence appears to have been caused by the passages relating to purgatory (Article 22) and the sacrifice of the mass (Article 31). The publication of the *Tract*, however, marked the beginning of the decline of the Oxford Movement's interest in justification as other, more pressing, theological considerations came to the fore. As with the Reformation, the ecclesiological was never far behind the soteriological question. The Tractarian interest in justification as a theological issue appears to have been entirely due to Newman's personal influence, and it declined accordingly during the remainder of the nineteenth century, never to be revived.[36]

In the present section, we have been concerned with Newman's conception of the *via media* on justification, which it has proved necessary to reject as untenable. The *dialectical* approach to the *via media* adopted by Newman is immediately invalidated if the thesis and antithesis are misunderstood or misrepresented. Furthermore, it will be clear that, in the case of Newman's *Lectures on Justification*, the *via media* thus established is identified with reference to the later Caroline Divines, which Newman regarded as encapsulating the essence of Anglicanism, at least in this respect. This presupposition must be considered to represent an arbitrary historical positivism, for the following reasons. First, Anglicanism cannot be defined with reference to what such a small group of theologians, operating over so short a period of time, taught. Second, if any such group *can* be singled out, the first generation of Anglican theologians (including Cranmer, Jewel and Hooker) have a far greater claim to merit the distinction, rather than the later Caroline Divines. Third, as our analysis of the development of Anglican theology on justification in the seventeenth century indicated (see §31), the later divines of the period were associated with a doctrine of justification which marked a reversal of the accepted teaching of the earlier Caroline Divines, as well as that of the divines of the Elizabethan Settlement, concerning a crucial element of Newman's doctrine of justification (namely, the nature of justifying righteousness). Newman's appeal to the post-Restoration Caroline Divines as the embodiment of an 'Anglican' theology of justification must therefore be regarded as inept.

The fact that Newman's attempt to construct a *via media* doctrine of justification is irredeemably discredited does not, however, invalidate the general principle of such a mediating doctrine of justification. Clearly, if it were possible to establish, in the light of the best possible scholarship available, the leading characteristics of Protestant and Catholic theologies of justification, it should, in principle, be possible to construct a *via media* doctrine on the basis of a dialectical approach such as that employed by Newman. In the remainder of this section, we propose to demonstrate that this is an impossibility, on account of the *naïveté* of its historical and theological presuppositions.

To illustrate this point, let us consider how the essence of Protestant doctrines of justification might be determined. The simplest solution is to select a leading theologian of Protestant inclination, and establish with the utmost impartiality precisely what his teaching on justification is.[37] Simple solutions, however, are notoriously seductive. How, it may reasonably be asked, may such a theologian be selected in the first place? For example, should that theologian be Lutheran or Reformed? And should he be selected from the early sixteenth, or the later seventeenth, century? In effect, the very process of selection itself dictates the resulting profile of a 'typically Protestant' theology of justification. This conclusion is given added weight through the observation that Protestant doctrines of justification have been subject to a process of continual modification from the time of the Reformation onwards, with the result that what may have been 'typical' of Lutheranism in 1525 was not so in 1725. Furthermore, there is a serious theological problem associated with establishing whether movements such as Pietism or the *Aufklärung* can be regarded as Protestant in their teachings on justification. The direct appeal to the confessional material of Protestantism (such as the Formula of Concord) is also of questionable value, as it is not clear what force such material has today. In general, it may be pointed out that the spirit of free inquiry and emphasis upon scripture, rather than tradition, which is so characteristic of Protestantism militates against the historical approach to the *via media*.

In the case of Catholicism, it might be thought that the emphasis upon tradition, coupled with the authority of the *magisterium* in matters of doctrine, facilitates the establishment of the essence of its theology of justification. This is clearly not, however, the case. We have already drawn attention to the fact that Trent legitimated a *range* of theologies of justification, rather than a single, well-defined, doctrine of justification (see §28). Furthermore, the post-Tridentine debates on justification, culminating in the disputes *de auxilius* (see

§29), indicate the variety of opinions subsequently associated with Catholic theologians.[38] The fact that neo-Thomist and Molinist alike may claim to represent Catholic thinking on justification indicates the difficulty in identifying a *single, well-defined* doctrine of justification which is characteristic of Catholicism – yet the dialectical approach necessitates precisely such an identification.

Finally, it may be pointed out that the dialectical approach to the *via media* has a disquieting tendency to lead to a theology of justification which is already discredited – the 'Regensburg theology' of 1541 (see §25), rejected by Protestant and Catholic alike.[39]

An attempt to construct a *via media* theology of justification is thus not merely artificial, but rests upon unacceptable historical and theological presuppositions. If Protestant and Catholic held theologies of justification which were rigidly defined and mutually exclusive at points of importance, there would clearly be considerable value in attempting to mediate between the two. This is, however, evidently not the case. The fact that the Council of Trent legitimates a *range* of theologies of justification, and that this range is contiguous with certain Protestant theologies of justification at crucial points, suggests that the pursuit of the *via media* is one of the less significant of theological activities. The common heritage of Protestant and Catholic alike may be explored without reference to the obsolete concept of the *via media*.

9. The modern period

Introduction

Practically every period in human history since the time of the Italian Renaissance of the *Quattrocento* may lay at least some claim to having initiated the 'modern' period. For instance, Renaissance Italy may be regarded as having laid the foundations of modern political theory,[1] and may thus be regarded as marking the transition to the 'modern' understanding of this particular matter. Similarly, the theologians of the *via moderna* designated themselves as 'modern' in their rejection of the reality of universals.[2] In the case of the development of Christology, it is clear that the Enlightenment marks the opening of the 'modern' period.[3] The question thus arises: when may the transition to the 'modern' understanding of the theology of justification be deemed to have taken place?

The answer traditionally given to this question is that the modern discussion of the question dates from the period of the Reformation.[4] While it is certainly true that the Reformation marked an irreversible change in many aspects of man's self-understanding,[5] it is clear, not merely that the Reformers discussed the question of man's justification *coram Deo* within the same general framework as their medieval counterparts,[6] but also that there existed a substantial number of uncontroverted presuppositions relating to the doctrine – such as the presupposition of the necessity of the reconciliation of man to God, traditionally expressed in the dogma of original sin. The growing recognition of the medieval character of the Reformation in general[7] must be extended to include its theologies of justification. The theocentricity underlying Luther's so-called 'Copernican Revolution' was a well-established feature of certain schools of thought in the late medieval period,[8] and cannot be considered to represent a permanent universal alteration in theological outlook which parallels that attending the recognition of the heliocentricity of the solar system. The rise of anthropocentric theologies of justification within both the Lutheran and Reformed traditions in the late seventeenth century, apparently to attain a dominant position in the eighteenth and nineteenth centuries, effectively calls into question the suggestion that Luther's theocentricity can be deemed quintessentially 'modern'.

If there is a 'modern' period in the development of the doctrine of justification, that period must be regarded as having been initiated by the Enlightenment in England, France and Germany in the eighteenth century. It was this movement which called into question the presuppositions (such as the dogma of original sin) upon which theologies of justification, whether Protestant or Catholic, had until then been based, and which dictated the means by which such presuppositions might be defended. We therefore begin our discussion of the 'modern period' with an analysis of the significance of the Enlightenment for the development of the doctrine.

§34 The Enlightenment critique of Orthodox doctrines of justification

The origins of the Enlightenment critique of Orthodox doctrines of justification may be located in the new emphasis upon the autonomy of man as a moral agent so characteristic of the movement. The new optimism concerning the capacity of the natural human faculties to understand and master the world led to those moral and religious systems which called into question the autonomy of man being held in suspicion. The particular hostility demonstrated by the theologians and philosophers of the Enlightenment towards the Orthodox dogma of original sin was ultimately a rejection of the implied heteronomous conditioning and moral inadequacy of the individual. In that the Orthodox theology of justification – whether Lutheran, Reformed or Catholic – presupposed the essential natural alienation of the individual from God (in other words, that an individual enters the world already alienated from God, rather than that he becomes alienated from God through his subsequent actions), it will be evident that a serious challenge was posed to such theologies by the rise of the moral optimism and rationalism of the Enlightenment. In the present section, we are particularly concerned with the critique of Orthodox Protestant theologies of justification associated initially with English Deism, and subsequently with the German *Aufklärung*.[1]

The founder of English Deism is usually, although incorrectly, considered to be Edward Herbert, Lord Cherbury.[2] Deeply influenced by Bodinus' *Colloquium* of 1588, he subsequently published his highly influential treatise *De veritate religionis* (1624). This work was essentially an attack on empiricism, arguing for the existence of *notitiae communes* or *ideae innatae* within every man upon which a system of eudaemonistic ethics might be constructed.[3] The strongly religious orientation of Cherbury's thought is indicated by the central position occupied by the *quinque notitiae communes circa religionem*, given to all men by nature in such a manner that they could function as the basis of human moral action (and thence as the means by which eternal life might ultimately be gained), without the necessity of a special revelation. These *notitiae* were originally stated in the following form:

1. Esse Supremum aliquod Numen.
2. Istud Numen debere coli.
3. Probam facultatum conformationem praecipuam partem cultus divini semper habitam fuisse.
4. Vitia et scelera quaecumque expiari debere ex poenitentia.
5. Esse praemium vel poenam post hanc vitam.[4]

The third *notitia* immediately identifies the moral emphasis which distinguished Herbert even from Christian humanists, in that the real aim of religion is identified to be the promotion of morality. The fourth sets him apart from Orthodoxy in relation to the question of forgiveness (note how the term *scelera* is adopted in preference to *peccata*). Where Orthodoxy held that man is justified *per fidem propter Christum*, Herbert asserted that forgiveness takes place *propter poenitentiam*. In this, he is not merely adopting the characteristically Arminian doctrine of justification *propter fidem* (that is, that forgiveness is contingent upon a human, rather than a divine, act);[5] any reference to the implication of Christ in divine forgiveness is omitted.

The Stoicism evident in Herbert's concept of *notitia communes* is also evident in his concept of the self-determination of the will (αὐτεξουσία) which stands in diametrical opposition to even the most modest Augustinian view of the corruption or compromise of the human will through original sin (see §4). Such views were developed and modified in the later seventeenth century. Thus John Toland's *Christianity not Mysterious* rejects the view that human reason is corrupted through original sin to such an extent that it is unable to recognise the truths of the gospel.[6] Similarly, John Locke (upon whom Toland is clearly dependent) earlier rejected the idea of original sin as unworthy of God.[7] The man who is totally obedient to

God is the man who attains eternal life. Locke, however, concedes the weakness of human nature, and permits any deficiencies in human obedience to the law of God to be supplemented:

The rule therefore, of right, is the same that ever it was; the obligation to observe it is also the same: the difference between the law of works, and the law of faith, is only this: that the law of works makes no allowance for failing on any occasion . . . But by the law of faith, faith is allowed to supply the defect of full obedience: and so the believers are admitted to life and immortality, as if they were righteous.[8]

Although Locke defines the *theological* element of faith to be belief that 'Jesus is the Messiah',[9] it must be emphasised that Locke insists upon the necessity of a *moral* element in faith. The theological element of faith is itself inadequate to justify, and must be supplemented with the moral element.[10] 'These two, faith and repentance, i.e., believing Jesus to be the Messiah, and a good life, are the indispensable conditions of the new covenant, to be performed by all those who would obtain eternal life.'[11] It is clear that Locke reduces the dogmatic content of Christianity to a single statement, in order to permit the believer to lead a moral life untroubled by intricate matters of doctrine.[12] Thus the work of Christ may be defined in terms of the 'great encouragement he brought to a virtuous and pious life'.[13]

The moralist understanding of the divine nature so characteristic of Latitudinarianism and the later Deism may be regarded as being substantiated by the theological method which Locke developed in his *Essay concerning Human Understanding* (1690).[14] The emphasis this essay laid upon the necessity of the universalisation of method had profound consequences for Anglican theological method in the eighteenth century, in that it lent weight to two significant developments. First, the Lockean insistence upon the necessity of demonstration in the establishment of positive knowledge paralleled the rise in interest in natural theology on the part of Anglican theologians at the time, with a concomitant decline in interest in the concept of supernatural revelation.[15] Second, the moralism so characteristic of seventeenth-century Anglicanism[16] became transformed into the rationalism of the eighteenth, assisted by the Lockean 'construction' of the concept of God by the projection of human moral values *ad infinitum*.

The basic features of Locke's epistemology may be summarised as follows: all knowledge, whether sensitive, intuitive or demonstrative, derives from experience.[17] Demonstrative knowledge, characterised by generality and certainty, must begin from and be based upon experience, as the abstract ideas which are linked in the mind are the result of the 'resolution' or 'abstraction' of the 'materials' given to the mind in experience.[18] The abstract ideas, upon which knowledge is based, are obtained through the analysis (Locke prefers the term 'decomposition') of the complexity of sentient states. On the basis of this assumption, Locke denies the existence of innate ideas, and innate speculative or moral principles. The theological significance of this empiricist presupposition lies in the fact that the existence of an innate idea of God is denied: 'though the knowledge of a God, be the most natural discovery of humane reason, yet the *idea of him*, is *not innate*'.[19]

The essential question which thus arises is the following: given that 'God' is not an innate idea, but one which can only be derived from experience, how can God's character be determined *empirically*?[20] Having established that there indeed exists 'an eternal, most powerful, and most knowing Being; which whether anyone will please to call God, it matters not',[21] Locke turns to the question of the character of this being. Having demonstrated that complex ideas are 'composed' by the association of simple ideas, Locke argues that the complex idea of 'God' is 'composed' by the association of certain simple ideas with the idea of *infinity*:

If we examine the *Idea* we have of the incomprehensible supreme Being, we shall find, that we come by it the same way; and that the complex *Ideas* we have both of God, and separate Spirits, are made up of the simple *Ideas* we receive from *Reflection*; *v.g.* having from what we experiment in our selves, got the *Ideas* of Existence and Duration; of Knowledge and Power; of Pleasure and Happiness; and of several other Qualities and Powers, which it is better to have than to be without; when we would frame an *Idea* the most suitable we can to the supreme Being, we enlarge every one of these with our *Idea* of Infinity; and so putting them together, make our complex *Idea of God*.[22]

For Locke, 'there is no *Idea* we attribute to God, bating Infinity, which is not also a part of our complex *Idea* of other Spirits'.[23] The concept of 'God' is therefore constructed through the mind's infinite enlargement of its ideas, received from sensation and reflection, of 'Qualities and Powers, which it is better to have than to be without'.

The egocentricity of Locke's account of experience thus inevitably leads to the moral character of God being constructed in terms of the moral value-judgements of the individual. If moral ideas were capable of being established demonstratively, on the basis of the analysis of experience, this difficulty could be avoided: however, Locke's statements on the grounds of morality are inconsistent.[24] The basic theological method employed by him in the *Essay* leads to the establishment of the moral character of God by the projection of human ideas of good, justice, and so forth, *ad infinitum* – and thus inevitably leads to the endorsement, rather than the critique, of human concepts of morality. In an age increasingly dominated by rationalism, it was inevitable that God should be deemed to act according to precisely such concepts, and be modelled upon the institution which was increasingly being recognised as the ultimate arbiter of justice – the state.

According to Thomas Hobbes, the state imposes certain restrictions upon man in order that he may benefit as a consequence. The ultimate reality to be reckoned with is the claim of the individual to self-preservation and happiness. As all men have a natural claim to all things, the only restraining factor which can be brought into operation to prevent universal war is the rational acceptance of certain self-imposed restrictions. The subjective right of the individual is therefore transposed into an objective right by a *translatio iuris*, by which each individual transfers to the state a portion of his individual rights.[25] In effect, the state may be regarded as representing the general will of the individuals which compose it, offering them protection and promising to each his due. 'For Justice, that is to say, Performance of Covenant, and giving to every man his due, is a Dictate of the Law of Nature.'[26] The state is thus conceived as *persona civilis*, whose function is to promote the happiness and well-being of man.[27] The application of such insights leads to an empirically derived concept of God modelled on the state as the philanthropic preserver of mankind, and the rejection of theological notions (such as that of eternal punishment)[28] which cannot be justified on the basis of this criterion of preservation.

Precisely such a eudaemonistic concept of God is to be found in the Deist writings, such as Tindal's *Christianity as Old as the Creation*. God's commands are given purely in order to benefit mankind:

Nothing can be a Part of the Divine Law, but what tends to promote the common Interest, and mutual Happiness of his rational Creatures . . . As God can require nothing of us, but what makes for our Happiness; so he . . . can forbid us those Things only, which tend to our Hurt.[29]

The later phase of Deism involved not merely the rejection of the concept of original sin and an emphasis upon the moral character of Christianity, but a sustained attack upon central dogmas of the

Christian faith which were held to be at variance with reason. Significantly, most of these dogmas related to the Christological dimension of the doctrine of justification. In *The True Gospel of Jesus Christ* (1738), Thomas Chubb asserted the identity of the *lex Christi* with the law of reason, which has always been in existence.[30] Chubb thus summarised the 'Gospel of Jesus Christ, or the Christian revelation', in three propositions:[31]

1. Man must ground his life and actions on the eternal and unchangeable rule of action which is grounded in the reason of things.
2. God requires repentance and reformation of the man who departs from this rule of life if he is to be forgiven.
3. God will judge man on the basis of whether he has lived in accordance with this rule.

Christ has a place in this soteriological scheme only in so far as he established the laws with reference to which man must live – laws which may be established equally well on the basis of unaided reason. 'Christ preached his own life, if I may so speak, and lived his own doctrine.'[32] Thus Chubb argues that the essential moral simplicity of Christianity has been compromised by certain unjustifiable theological beliefs – such as the doctrine of imputed righteousness, and the vicarious significance of the death of Christ. The only manner in which Christ could effect the salvation of man was by summoning him to repentance and conversion.[33] Thus Paul's statement that the 'blood of Christ takes away sin' is to be understood in the sense that the moral example of the death of Christ moves the sinner to repentance, and hence leads to his forgiveness on this account.[34] Christ saves men 'by his working a personal change in them', in that this alteration leads to their becoming worthy of divine forgiveness and salvation. The basis upon which God favours one man rather than another lies in man himself.[35]

The strongly naturalist and rationalist cast of Chubb's analysis parallels the general outlook of later Deism. Thus Thomas Morgan argued that Christianity represented the 'best rendering' of the law of nature,[36] and that Christ was a superior moral legislator to Moses, Zarathustra, Confucius or Mahomet.[37] For Morgan, it is axiomatic that God acts and legislates only in such a manner as is 'necessary to the Wellbeing and Happiness of Mankind throughout the whole period of their existence'.[38] The essential feature of the Deist soteriology was the rejection of the concept of the *mediatorship* of Christ in favour of the 'republication' by Christ of the eudaemonistic laws of nature. Although the notion of the mediation of Christ between God and man was defended with some vigour, particularly in Joseph Butler's influential *Analogy of Religion* (1736),[39] the Deist critique of this and related ideas was received with some sympathy, initially in England, and subsequently in France[40] and Germany. The traditional structure of the Christian doctrine of justification was discarded, occasionally on the basis of criticism paralleling those made earlier by Socinus, in favour of a purely moral conception of the matter. Man is justified *propter fidem*, in the Arminian sense – in other words, he is justified on the basis of his unaided act of repentance, inspired by the moral example and teaching of Christ, and motivated by the knowledge of the good which this repentance will bring him. The strongly eudaemonistic cast of Deist ethics lent weight to the assertion that morality was the foundation and criterion of religion, thus inverting the traditional understanding of the relation of the two.

The period 1690–1750 may be characterised as the period in which rationalism dominated English theology. The great Evangelical Awakening of England under the influence of the particular form of Pietism known as Methodism followed this period, and may be regarded as bringing its popular appeal to an end.[41] In Germany, by contrast, rationalism followed the rise of Pietism, and was deeply influenced by this movement[42] – despite the evident and considerable influence of English Deism upon its German counterpart at points. Many of the *Aufklärer* were of Pietist origins. The Pietist critique of the theologies of justification of Protestant (especially Lutheran) Orthodoxy was based upon the conviction that they did not encourage moral regeneration (see §24). For the Pietist, the object of justification was the potentially or actually morally regenerate man, whose moral regeneration both caused and demonstrated his justification. This emphasis upon the moral dimension of justification, and the rejection of the view that justification entailed a synthetic, rather than an analytic, judgement, is also characteristic of the early *Aufklärung*. Thus Johann Franz Budde makes no reference to the concept of *iustificatio impii* where it might be expected, and insists that it is the regenerate alone who may be justified: certum enim est, in homine, qui iustificatur, mutationem quamdam contingere.[43] It is necessary that the object of the divine justification possesses an inherent quality, or undergoes a transformation (*mutatio*) in order that such a quality may come about, which legitimates this pronouncement: 'illa [mutatio] tamen, quae per regenerationem exsistit, in iustificatione supponitur, cum nemo iustificetur nisi regenitus'.[44] Although justification is understood as a forensic divine declaration, it is presupposed that this declaration is based upon an inherent quality within man. Thus Christoph Matthaeus Pfaff defines justification as 'actus ille iudicalis, quo Deus ex mera gratia, intuitu redemptionis a Christo facta, quae vera fide iam a nobis apprehenditur, a reatu et poena peccati nos absolvit nosque perfectae sic iustos pronunciat atque declarat,'[45] while developing a moralist understanding of the *ratio iustificationis*. In his *Elementa theologiae dogmaticae* (1758), Lorenz von Mosheim explicitly stated the transformational concept of justification underlying his moralist soteriology: generatim iustificatio est actio Dei, per quam iniustus ita mutatur, ut iustus fiat.[46] Although clearly developing a theology of *iustificatio regenerati*, Mosheim still feels able to retain the forensic structure of the *actus iustificationis* inherited from Lutheran Orthodoxy:

Actus ... Dei, qui iustificatio nominatur, tametsi simplex et unus est, in tres tamen actus secari et dividi potest:
I.   in imputationem iustitiae Christi
II.   in absolutionem a culpa et poena et
III. in attributionem iuris ad gratiam et gloriam.[47]

These three aspects of the believer's justification are, however, contingent upon his already having been converted, possessing faith, and being regenerate.[48] The divine judgement implicit in the process of justification is necessarily *iudicium secundum veritatem*, and is thus grounded in the qualities which such a judgement presupposes already being present in the object of justification.

In many respects, the early *Aufklärung* paralleled later Pietism in its theology of justification, retaining the concept of justification as *actus forensis Dei*, whilst substituting an analytical concept of the divine judgement in place of Orthodoxy's synthetic equivalent. While Pietism and Orthodoxy shared a common understanding of the work of Christ, on the other hand, it was, however, clear that a major assault upon precisely such an understanding by the theologians of the *Aufklärung* was not far removed. In the earlier part of this section, the theological significance of emerging theories of the nature and function of the state (such as that of Hobbes) was noted. Such theories represented the state as the means towards the end of the welfare of the individual, and this understanding of the *persona civilis* had been extended to include God as the moral governor of the universe, working towards the end of its welfare. Hobbes had extended this teleological understanding of the state to include a rationale for the state punishment of individuals: given that the state exists as a means towards the end of the welfare of the individual, the function of punishment is essentially to deter the individual from committing acts which are detrimental to his own welfare, or reforming him, should such deterrence fail.[49] The *Aufklärung* is particularly significant, in that this understanding of the basis of punishment came to be applied to God, with important consequences for the Christian doctrine of justification.[50] The explicit transfer of Hobbes' understanding of the basis of punishment from the theory of the state to the theology of justification is particularly associated with Johann Konrad Dippel, and we propose to consider it in some detail.[51]

Dippel transferred to God the function of the state – that is, the well-being of the individual, along with the understanding of the rationale of punishment within this context. On this basis, Dippel argued that God could not conceivably wish to destroy a sinner, since this is at variance with his understanding of the divine purpose, but merely to eradicate his sin and reform him. For Dippel, the consequences of sin relate solely to man, in that his well-being is affected by its existence. In marked contrast to Anselm of Canterbury and Protestant Orthodoxy, Dippel argued that sin has no effect upon God whatsoever, except indirectly, in that his love for mankind is grieved by the disadvantages which sin is perceived to bring to them. There is no need for God to punish sin, in that sin brings its own natural punishment with it, on account of its dysteleological character. If God does threaten man with punishment – as Dippel reluctantly concedes to be the case – it is solely with the object of deterring man from sin. God's threats against man do not arise from sin being committed *against* God, but on account of the potential frustration of the divine purposes in creating man in the first place. God, in his love for man, works actively towards his well-being – and is therefore obliged, as is the state, to discourage inherently self-destructive actions, which pose a threat to man's well-being. Thus Dippel prefers not to speak of 'retributive' or 'vindictive justice',[52] and is reluctant to speak of the divine 'wrath', lest this be misunderstood as divine wrath against *sinners*, rather than *sin*.

The consequences of this understanding of the nature of God for Dippel's understanding of the doctrine of reconciliation are considerable. First, Dippel departs from the Orthodox understanding of the scheme of reconciliation, in that he declines to allow a divine wrath directed against sinners, which the death of Christ can be said to appease or satisfy. Second, as sin is accompanied by its own natural punishments, it is clear that there is no sense in which Dippel may speak of Christ having removed man's punishment for sin. Dippel understands Christ's passion and death as a model for human conquest of sin, which has no soteriological significance until it is successfully imitated. Christ's death cannot be said to remit the divine punishment of man's sins, in that sin has its own natural punishment, which God cannot remove, save by abrogating the natural order.[53]

Although Dippel's criticisms of the Orthodox doctrine of reconciliation made relatively little impact at the time of their publication, similar criticisms made later were to have considerable effect. An excellent example of the latter is to be found in Johann Gottlieb Töllner's celebrated criticism of the satisfactory value of the active obedience of Christ. In his celebrated monograph *Der thätige Gehorsam Christi untersucht* (1768), Töllner rejected the thesis of the independent satisfactory value of the active obedience of Christ (see §24) with a rigour never before encountered. Earlier, Piscator had argued that Christ's active obedience (that is, his obedience to the law) was essentially a presupposition of his passive obedience (that is, his suffering and death upon the cross). Töllner's thesis is far more radical, and is based upon the analysis of the concepts of the person and office of Christ, and the nature of vicarious satisfaction itself.

Töllner argues that Christ, as man, was under the common human obligation to obey the law.[54] As such, he was only able to fulfil the law for himself, and not for others. This thesis thus calls into question the Lutheran doctrine of *exlex*, according to which Christ was under no such obligation whatsoever (see §24). The possibility of the *obedientia Christi activa* possessing any independent vicarious satisfactory value can thus only be maintained if it can be shown that one of two conditions has been satisfied. Either Christ must be the authorised federal representative of mankind, so that the actions which he performs on behalf of mankind may be duly accredited to them; or else Christ's obedience must be accepted by God as if it were performed on behalf of those whom he represents. Although Töllner gives no indication that he is familiar with the Reformed teaching on this question, it will be clear that the specified conditions correspond to the Reformed understanding of Christ as *caput et sponsor electorum* (see §24), by which the union between Christ and the believer in justification permits a *commercium admirabile* between them, as a result of which Christ's righteousness and merit become the believer's, and the latter's sin and guilt Christ's. Töllner, however, rejects the first condition as unproven, and the second as unprovable, and accordingly feels able to deny the notion of Christ's active obedience being of benefit to man.

On the basis of this conclusion, Töllner argues that the concept of vicarious satisfaction for sin may be rejected: 'nun ist es augenscheinlich, wie ohne den ganzen thätigen Gehorsam Christi die vertretende Genugthuung desselben unmöglich gewesen wäre'.[55] Töllner then argues, in the manner noted above, that it is the renewal (*Heiligung*) of the individual which leads to the bestowal of grace (*Begnadigung*), rather than the satisfaction of Christ. The obedience of Christ is an essentially moral quality, which inspires a corresponding moral quality within man – upon the basis of which man is forgiven and justified. Thus Töllner explicitly appeals to the Socinian critique of the satisfaction-doctrine of Orthodoxy, arguing that Socinus 'übersah richtig, daß das Wesentliche in der Religion auf die Tugend ankomme'.[56] The man who is justified is the morally regenerate man, whose justification does not depend upon the allegedly 'objective' value of the death of Christ, but upon the subjective moral influence which it exerts upon him. Töllner draws the conclusion that all explanations of the significance of the death of Christ (*alle Erklärungsarten vom versöhnenden Tode Christi*) actually reduce to one essential point: that Christ's death is the grounds of our assurance of God's graciousness towards us, and confirms the reliability of previous divine promises concerning the bestowal of divine grace.[57] This single point, it may be emphasised, pertains to man's perception of God, rather than the divine relationship with or attitude towards man. Christ represents God to man, and not man to God.

These insights were developed by Gotthelf Samuel Steinbart in his strongly moralist *Glückseligkeitslehre* (1778). For Steinbart, the divine dispensation towards mankind was totally concerned with the promotion of 'a supremely excellent and complete morality',[58] which finds its personification in Jesus Christ. God demands nothing of man which is not directly and totally beneficial to man himself. Steinbart thus insists that God asks nothing of his children other than that which leads immediately to their increased happiness and perfection.[59] Steinbart's tendency to employ the term *Besserung* where *Heiligung* had traditionally been used serves to emphasise the moral cast of his theology.[60] The essential simplicity of this moral gospel has, however, become obscured, according to Steinbart, by the intrusion of 'arbitrary hypotheses', of which the most significant are the following:[61]

1. The Augustinian doctrine of original sin.
2. The Augustinian doctrine of predestination.
3. The Anselmian doctrine of the satisfaction of Christ.
4. The Protestant doctrine of the imputation of the righteousness of Christ.

It will be evident that all these 'arbitrary hypotheses' are of direct relevance to our study. On the basis of extensive historical arguments,[62] Steinbart concludes that the origins of these concepts are such as to call their continued use into question. Thus Augustine's doctrines of original sin and predestination represent vestiges of his Manichaeism, which should be eliminated in order that the teaching of the Greek fathers and Pelagius might be recognised as the older and authentic Christian teaching on the matter. Similarly, Anselm's concept of vicarious satisfaction represents a further distortion, based upon Augustinian presuppositions, of the original moral interpretation of Christ's death. The concept arises through the union of the Manichaean good and evil principles in one God, so that they constitute a permanent and internally irreconcilable tension which must be resolved from outside the Godhead.[63] No such tension may be found in the teaching of Jesus.[64] Furthermore, Steinbart appeals to Töllner's critique of the *obedientia Christi activa* as a devastating theological critique of a concept already virtually discredited on the grounds of its questionable historical origins.[65]

What, then, does Steinbart understand to be the objective grounds of man's justification? According to Steinbart, Christ redeemed man from false understandings of God – such as the idea of God as wrathful, as a tyrant, or as one who imposed arbitrary penalties or conditions upon man.[66] Following the view – ultimately due to Hobbes – which we noted above, Steinbart insists that the only penalties due to man are those which are the immediate natural consequences of his sins, or which are necessary to reform man, in order that he may avoid such natural penalties in future. Steinbart dismisses questions such as the necessity and significance of Christ's passion and death as beyond meaningful discussion,[67] and irrelevant to human happiness and moral perfection. The concept of vicarious satisfaction is both impossible theologically, and unnecessary practically.[68]

It will be clear that the general position of the *Aufklärung* in relation to the objective grounds of justification leads to the total disintegration of the Orthodox doctrine of reconciliation. The emphasis upon the intellectual and moral autonomy of man, particularly evident in the writings of Töllner,[69] calls into question the crucial Orthodox assertion that man was *naturally* alienated from God. For the *Aufklärer*, man is not naturally alienated from God, although he may impose such an alienation upon himself by his acts of sin. These acts of sin, however, are conceived dysteleologically – in other words, they work against man's own interests, defined in terms of his happiness and moral perfection. Sin is defined with reference to the injury it causes to man: God is only affected by sin indirectly, in so far as he is concerned with man's destiny. Sin is most emphatically *not* understood as an offence against God, for which an appropriate satisfaction is required. If Christ's death has any significance for man, this significance is to be located in the effect which it has on man himself. This important conclusion finds its expression in the 'moral' or 'exemplarist' interpretation of the death of Christ,[70] characteristic of the theologians of the later *Aufklärung*. Christ's death is understood to serve as a supreme example or inspiration to man, motivating and encouraging him to emulate the outstanding moral character of Christ, in order that he may become *der wirkliche gute Mensch*.[71] The strong moralism and naturalism of the *Aufklärung* is evident in this moralist reduction of the Christian understanding of the nature of salvation, and the manner in which it is related to the death of Christ.[72] If Christ may be said to redeem man, it is in the restricted sense of 'redeeming man from false concepts of God'. Thus Steinbart declares that Christ has redeemed man from the *idea* of God as a tyrant, and from the *idea* of Satan, illustrating with some clarity the notion of 'redemption' as 'intellectual liberation' so characteristic of the rationalism of the movement.

By the year 1780, therefore, the foundations of the Christian doctrine of justification had been subjected to such destructive criticism by the Enlightenment in England, France and Germany that it appeared impossible that they could ever be restored. In fact, however, the period which lay ahead saw the Enlightenment criticism of Orthodoxy itself subjected to destructive criticism, with significant results for the development of the doctrine. We thus turn to consider the distinctive contributions of Kant and Schleiermacher to the re-establishment of the doctrine of reconciliation.

§35 The critique of the *Aufklärung* soteriology: Kant and Schleiermacher

The soteriologies of the later *Aufklärung* can be characterised in terms of their rationalism, moralism and naturalism (see §34). Religion, and most religious categories (particularly those relating to soteriology), were regarded as essentially ethical in character, expressing general universal moral truths in a particular (though not necessarily the most appropriate) manner. Whatever conditions might be conceded to be attached to man's justification were regarded as essentially moral in character. Furthermore, fundamental to the *Aufklärung* soteriologies was the axiom of the soteriological autonomy of the individual: each individual must be regarded as possessing whatever soteriological resources were necessary for his justification. In the present section, we are concerned with two critiques of the soteriologies of the *Aufklärung* which emerged in the period 1790–1830. Both concerned the relation between religion and morality, Kant demonstrating that the traditional Enlightenment account of this relationship was inadequate, and Schleiermacher developing a purely religious account of the Christian faith, thus severing this relationship altogether. In addition, Schleiermacher's critique of the adequacy of the soteriological resources of the individual posed a significant challenge to the fundamental axiom upon which the soteriologies of the *Aufklärung* were based.

The modern era in European thought, particularly epistemology, is frequently regarded as having been initiated by Kant.[1] Kant has rightly been compared with Copernicus in relation to the ideological revolution which he occasioned, particularly in relation to his concept of the synthetic *a priori* judgement. Although the Kantian proclamation of the inalienable subjectivity of judgements has important consequences for Christian theology, it must be emphasised that Kant's significance in relation to the development of the doctrine of justification lies in his insistence upon the autonomy and absoluteness of the moral consciousness, which has profound implications for the doctrine of reconciliation. Indeed, Kant's significance to the development of the doctrine lies in his analysis of the presuppositions of the concept of reconciliation which lies in the consciousness of moral freedom and moral guilt,[2] which led him to criticise the moral and exemplarist soteriologies of the *Aufklärung*.[3]

Although Kant's exposition of the relationship between morality and religion is to be found in his *Kritik*, his most lucid and sustained discussion of the matter may be found in the important essay of 1793, *Religion innerhalb der Grenzen der bloßen Vernunft*.[4] This work appeared some eleven years after the appearance of the *Kritik der reinen Vernunft*, and has as its presuppositions certain of the fundamental doctrines of this earlier work – for example, the unconditional authority of the moral law, the autonomy of the rational human subject, the critical evaluation of the transcendent metaphysical impulse, and the assertion of the primacy of practical reason. It is the first of these presuppositions which is of particular importance, especially when Kant is viewed in relation to his context within the later *Aufklärung*.

The cornerstone of Kant's theology in general is the priority of the apprehension of moral obligation over anything else. For Kant, it is a fundamental axiom of theology, that all which man believes himself to be capable of doing to please God, apart from a moral way of life, is mere 'religious delusion' (*Religionswahn*) and 'pseudo-worship' (*Afterdienst*) of God:

Ich nehme erstlich folgenden Satz als einen keines Beweises benötigten Grundsatz an: alles, was außer dem guten Lebenswandel der Mensch noch thun zu können vermeint, um Gott wohlgefällig zu werden, ist bloßer Religionswahn und Afterdienst Gottes.[5]

Kant's emphasis upon the moral basis of the Christian religion, with the concomitant rejection of 'arbitrary demands' made by God of man, clearly parallels that of the *Aufklärung*. However, Kant diverges from the movement at two significant points. First, the essentially utilitarian or eudaemonistic approach to morality is replaced with an emphasis upon the concept of moral obligation as an end in itself (rather than as a means towards the end of man's perfection or happiness), expressed in terms of the concept of the 'highest good'.[6] Second, Kant argues that to base morality upon the known commands of God would be to concede the heteronomous character of ethics: rather, morality must be held to be based upon the self-imposed 'categorical (or unconditional) imperative' (*unbedingte Forderung*) of the autonomous human will. Man's sense of moral obligation (*das Sollen*) is prior to the correlation of virtue and happiness. Furthermore, Kant insists that the apprehension of the categorical imperative is quite independent of the idea of 'another Being above man' (in other words, God): however, Kant allows that the *idea* of such a Being may subsequently arise, through an act of faith which correlates the apprehension of *das Sollen* with the existence of God as a 'moral legislator apart from man'. The religiously disposed individual will interpret *das Sollen* as an expression of divine obligations laid upon him, an interpretation which Kant's critical philosophy places beyond the scope of pure reason, even if it does not involve conceding that religion is essentially a postulate of practical reason.

Kant notes that the presupposition of man's duty to pursue the highest good has as its necessary presupposition the possibility of moral perfection. For Kant, the denial of the possibility of moral perfection has as its corollary the denial of the possibility of the highest good, in that the former is the unconditioned component of the latter. Therefore the rejection of the possibility of the highest good entails the rejection of the moral law, which Kant dismisses as an *absurdum practicum*. For Kant, the apprehension of *das Sollen* has as its fundamental and necessary presupposition the possibility of moral perfection. It is of the utmost importance to appreciate that this presupposition forces him to break with the *Aufklärung* on several crucial points. The reasons for this will become clear when his concept of 'radical evil' is considered.[7]

It is to Kant's credit that he recognised that man is a free creature, with an ability to misuse precisely that freedom. His account of moral obligation is able to take account of the possibility that man will ignore his apprehension of *das Sollen*. (It may be noted that he excludes the suggestion that a man may deliberately choose to do evil, knowing it to be evil.) The moral qualities of the will, both good and evil, are the consequences of human freedom. Man himself must determine whether he is morally good or evil; if he does not, or is unable to, he cannot be held responsible for his moral condition, and thus cannot be considered to be good or evil *morally*.[8] The consciousness of moral obligation leads Kant to conclude that man must be free to exercise or decline to exercise that obligation – otherwise the concept of 'obligation' becomes evacuated of its moral content. For Kant, as for the *Aufklärung* as a whole, the notion of original sin is to be rejected – and hence the origin of human evil is to be sought within the human will. But why should the human will choose evil? If there is no evil within man until he himself causes it, how does the will come to be corrupted in such a manner?

Kant answers this crucial question by developing the concept of the dispositional aspect of the human will (*Willkur*) to account for this fundamental ambivalence within human volition. While he defines evil in terms of a lesser good, so that the evil man is the man who subordinates the demands of *das Sollen* to the demands of his sensible nature, it is clear that even this approach to the existence of evil calls into question the possibility of moral perfection. The thesis of 'radical evil' excludes the essential presupposition upon which Kant's ethics are based, in that it indicates that the most which can realistically be expected is progress towards, rather than attainment of, the end of moral perfection. Kant thus (re)defines moral perfection in terms of a 'disposition' (*Gesinnung*) towards this (unattainable) objective, which is now recognised as an *Urbild*, which man recognises as good, and towards which he actively works.

Having defined a 'good disposition' as the intention to work towards the *Urbild* of moral perfection, Kant takes the remarkable step of asserting that God treats the man who possesses an *intention* to work towards moral perfection *as if he were already in full possession of that perfection*. Although he concedes that man has no right to expect God to treat him in this remarkable manner, he insists that God gratuitously (*aus Gnaden*) reckons the *Gesinnung* as the *Urbild*:

Hier ist nun derjenige Überschuß über das Verdienst der Werke, der oben vermißt wurde, und ein Verdienst, das uns aus Gnaden zugerechnet wird. Denn damit das, was bei uns in Erdenleben (vielleicht auch in allen künftigen Zeiten und allen Welten) immer nur im bloßen Werden ist (nämlich ein Gott wohlgefälliger Mensch zu sein), uns, gleich *als ob* wir schon hier in vollen Besitz desselben wären, zugerechnet werde, dazu haben wir doch wohl keinen Rechtsanspruch (nach der empirischen Selbsterkenntnis), so weit wir uns selbst kennen (unsere Gesinnung nicht unmittelbar, sondern nur nach unseren Thaten ermessen).[9]

The reappearance of an *als-ob-Theologie*, or 'legal fiction', so vigorously rejected by Pietism and the *Aufklärung*, in the works of Kant is of considerable importance. As we noted earlier, the later *Aufklärer* had stressed that *Begnadigung* was contingent upon *Verbesserung*: for Kant, it is clear that grace is implicated at the earliest phase of justification. The 'man who is pleasing to God' (*der wohlgefällige Mensch*) is only 'pleasing' on the basis of a gratuitous act by which God overlooks his deficiencies. As he puts this elsewhere, the man who attempts to be pleasing to God 'in so far as it lies within his ability' (*so viel in seinem Vermögen ist*)[10] may rely upon God to 'supplement' (*ergänzen*) his deficiencies:

Man muß mit allen Kräften der heiligen Gesinnung eines Gott wohlgefälligen Lebenswandels nachstreben, um glauben zu können, daß die (uns schon durch die Vernunft versicherte) Liebe desselben zur Menschheit, sofern sie seinem Willen nach allem ihrem Vermögen nachstrebt, in Rücksicht auf die redliche Gesinnung den Mangel der That, auf welche Art es auch sei, ergänzen werde.[11]

The obvious parallels between Kant and the *via moderna* at this point will be evident (see §17), particularly in their mutual presupposition that the man who does his best (*quod in se est – so viel in seinem*

Vermögen ist) will become pleasing to, or accepted by, God *as an act of grace, rather than strict justice.*

The divergence between Kant and the *Aufklärung* becomes increasingly evident from Kant's discussion of how God may justify an individual leading an immoral life who subsequently decides to repent. Kant insists that this is a *real* possibility – as, indeed, it must be, if the practical possibility of the unconditioned component of the highest good is to be maintained, even in the weakest of senses. However, Kant notes three difficulties raised by this possibility, of which the third is of particular significance.[12] The individual who alters his evil disposition to the good is nevertheless the same individual who formerly committed evil acts, and as a result is burdened with the guilt associated with that evil.[13] How can God justify such an individual? Kant actually merely demonstrates that it is acceptable for God to permit guilt to go unpunished, and defers his solution of how such an individual may be justified (in the strict sense) until a later section of the work. This solution is, however, of enormous significance.

Kant's solution to this difficulty is, in fact, apparently irreconcilable with the general principles upon which his moral philosophy is based, particularly the axiom that an individual is responsible for *his own* moral actions. No individual can be good on behalf of another, nor can the goodness of a morally outstanding individual be permitted to remove the guilt of another. The basis of Kant's rejection of the concept of vicarious satisfaction (*stellvertretende Genugthuung*) is the principle that guilt, like merit, is strictly non-transferable. It is therefore remarkable that Kant's solution to the difficulty noted above is based upon the assertion that the individual who turns away from his evil disposition to adopt a good disposition may be regarded as having become a different person: the old disposition *ist moralisch ein anderer* from the new.[14] The discontinuity between the old and the new disposition is such that Kant denies that they may be predicated of the same moral individual. This conclusion appears to rest upon the assumption that the disposition itself is the only acceptable basis of establishing the identity of the moral agent. Having established this point, Kant takes the remarkable step of asserting that the new disposition 'takes the place' (*vertritt*) of the old in respect of the guilt which is rightly attached to the latter disposition.[15] It is on account of the new disposition that man's former guilt is cancelled, and that he is justified before God. On the basis of these assumptions, Kant asserts that the man who attempts to be pleasing to God may rest assured of the truth expressed by the doctrine of reconciliation, which represents his former sins as abolished (*abgetan*):

Dieser Muth, auf eigenen Fußen zu stehen, wird nun selbst durch die darauf folgende Versöhnungslehre gestärkt, indem sie, was nicht zu ändern ist, als abgethan vorstellt und nun den Pfad zu einem neuen Lebenswandel für uns eröffnet.[16]

In effect, Kant interprets the doctrine of reconciliation to mean that the man who determines to keep the moral law, whatever his previous history may have been, has the right to hope that his moral past may be abolished, and present moral deficiencies supplemented, through divine grace. The relation between *Begnadigung* and *Verbesserung* is thus demonstrated to be considerably more complex than the *Aufklärer* recognised.

The significance of Kant's *Religion* lies in the deduction of the necessity of divine grace *as a postulate of practical reason*. The deep pessimism of his doctrine of 'radical evil' is counteracted by his optimism concerning the rôle of divine grace in the supplementation of a good disposition, and the abolition of the moral guilt of a prior evil disposition (by a process of vicarious satisfaction). Although Kant cannot be said to have advanced the Orthodox doctrine of reconciliation (or, indeed, to have intended to), it is clear that the doctrines of justification and reconciliation were shown to have their proper and necessary place within moral philosophy, even if stated in forms quite distinct from their Orthodox equivalents. The naïve moralism of the *Aufklärung* was thus called into question through the Kantian analysis of the moral dimension of reconciliation.[17]

The remarkable rise of German Romanticism in the closing years of the eighteenth century is generally regarded as a reaction of 'spirit' against 'reason', in that the latter was regarded as quite inadequate to analyse the depths of human feeling (*Gefühl*).[18] Although Schleiermacher was not himself a *Romantiker*, it is clear that the new significance attached to human *Gefühl* permitted him to develop an account of Christian faith which dissociated it from the hitherto prevailing rationalist reductions of the concept. The fundamental fact (*Grundtatsache*) of Christian dogmatics is the existence of the individual's faith or 'piety' (*Frömmigkeit*), and it is the task of Christian dogmatics to give an account of the content of this *datum*, rather than to establish it in the first place.[19] Thus Schleiermacher distinguishes between Christian dogmatics (which begins from an inward perception), historical sciences (which begin from an outward perception), and deductive sciences (which begin from a fundamental principle (*Grundsatz*)).[20] The essence of 'piety', which Schleiermacher holds to be the irreducible element in every religion, is not some rational or moral principle, but 'feeling' (*Gefühl*), the immediate self-consciousness.[21] Thus Christian doctrines are, in essence, individually accounts of Christian religious feelings.[22] Schleiermacher constructs his dogmatics upon the basis of the fact of redemption in Christ, and thence upon the antithesis of sin and grace.[23] In Part I of *Der christliche Glaube*, Schleiermacher discussed the human religious consciousness (*Bewußtsein*) in isolation from this antithesis. Although this consciousness is presupposed by Christian piety, the specifically Christian consciousness is to be distinguished from it, in that it is the 'feeling of absolute dependence (*das Gefühl schlechthinniger Abhängigkeit*)', which faith interprets as a consciousness of God.[24]

Having established Christian piety, and particularly the 'feeling of absolute dependence', as the starting point for Christian theology, Schleiermacher argues that the origins of this piety are to be explained soteriologically in terms of the perceived effects of Christ upon the collective consciousness of the Christian community. It must be emphasised that this represents a purely *religious* approach to the matter, which sharply distinguishes it from the moralism of the *Aufklärung*. Schleiermacher attributes to Christ an 'absolutely powerful God-consciousness (*schlechthin kräftiges Gottesbewußtsein*)', charged with such assimilative power that it is able to effect the redemption of mankind.[25] The essence of redemption is that the God-consciousness already present in human nature, although feeble and repressed, becomes stimulated and elevated through the 'entrance of the living influence of Christ'.[26] As the redeemer (*Erlöser*), Christ is distinguished from all other men both in degree and kind by the uninterrupted power of his God-consciousness. The redemptive activity of Christ consists in his assuming individuals into the power of his God-consciousness. On the basis of this presupposition, Schleiermacher criticises the soteriologies of both the *Aufklärung* and Orthodoxy.[27]

For Schleiermacher, the *Aufklärer* treated Christ solely as a prophet, regarding him primarily as the teacher of an *idea* of God, or the exemplar of a religious or moral principle. This view – which Schleiermacher designates the 'empirical' understanding of the work of Christ – 'attributes a redemptive activity on the part of Christ, but one which is held to consist only in bringing about an increasing perfection in us, and which cannot take place other than by teaching and example'.[28] If this account of the significance of Christ is correct, Schleiermacher argues that belief in redemption *im eigentlichen Sinne* becomes an impossibility. The Orthodox understanding of the work of Christ – which Schleiermacher designates as 'magical' – attributes to Christ a purely objective transaction which is 'not mediated by anything natural'. This approach, which Schleiermacher considers to approximate to Docetism, is incapable of doing justice to the historical figure of Jesus of Nazareth: if Christ were able to exert his influence in this supernaturalist manner, it would have been possible for him to work in precisely the same way at any time, so that his personal appearance in history would have been superfluous.[29] Underlying this observation is Schleiermacher's conviction that the supranaturalist approach involves a non-natural concept of divine causality. For Schleiermacher, divine causality operates through natural means – and at this point, his affinity with the *Aufklärung* is evident. The assimilative power of Christ's dominant God-consciousness is mediated to man through natural channels.

Having discussed how the individual believer enters into fellowship with Christ, Schleiermacher moves on to consider how this expresses itself in the life of the believer.[30] It is clear that Schleiermacher is obliged to follow the arguments of the *Aufklärung*, and hold that justification is contingent upon a real change in man:

Rechtfertigung sezt etwas voraus in Beziehung worauf jemand gerechtfertigt wird; und da in dem höchsten Wesen kein Irrthum möglich ist, so wird angenommen, zwischen dem vorher und jezt sei dem Menschen etwas begegnet, wodurch das frühere göttliche Mißfallen aufgehoben wird, und ohne welches er nicht habe können ein Gegenstand des göttlichen Wohlgefallens werden.[31]

The same emphasis is to be found here as in the writings of Töllner, Steinbart and Teller: justification is contingent upon a prior alteration within man. Where Schleiermacher diverges so radically from the *Aufklärung* in this respect is the nature of the alteration. For the *Aufklärer*, the alteration was to be conceived morally (note the tendency to refer to the condition as *Besserung*, rather than *Heiligung*: see §34). For Schleiermacher, the alteration was to be conceived *religiously* as 'laying hold of Christ in a believing manner (*Christum gläubig ergreifen*)'.[32] Although conceding that this might appear to suggest that man is capable of justifying himself, Schleiermacher states that justification actually derives from the assumption of man into fellowship with Christ,[33] and adopts an understanding of man's rôle in justification which is sharply distinguished from that of the *Aufklärung*.

343

Schleiermacher, developing the Kantian concept of radical evil, argues that man is unable to attain a dominant God-consciousness unaided. There is an inherent disposition within man towards sin, understood as a 'total incapacity for the good',[34] which leads man to recognise his need for external assistance (*Hülfe*).[35] This point is also developed in Schleiermacher's important discussion of the four 'natural heresies' of Christianity – the Docetic and Ebionite interpretations of the person of Christ, and the Pelagian and Manichaean interpretations of man's soteriological resources.[36] As Schleiermacher observes, the understanding of man's soteriological resources must be such that it can account for the necessity of redemption from outside humanity itself – in other words, that it can explain why all men cannot be redeemers. The understanding of the object of redemption – man – must be such that it can accommodate the two presuppositions fundamental to Schleiermacher's soteriology: that man requires redemption from outside humanity; and that he is capable of receiving or accepting that redemption, once it is offered to him: 'wenn die Menschen sollen erlöst werden, so müssen sie eben sowohl der Erlösung bedürftig sein, als auch fähig sie anzunehmen'.[37] If man's need for redemption is conceded, and yet his impotence to provide such redemption is denied, the conclusion must be drawn, that man himself could be the agent of his own redemption. Redemption could then be effected, either by the soteriologically sufficient individual, or by one individual for another: and if not by all men, then at least by some, to varying degrees. If man's impotence to redeem himself is conceded, and yet his ability to appropriate that redemption, once offered, is denied, it will be clear that redemption is an impossibility. Broadly speaking, these two positions correspond to the Pelagian and Manichaean heresies, although the specific historical forms taken by these heresies differ somewhat from Schleiermacher's characterisations of them.

The importance of this discussion relates to Schleiermacher's definition of the distinctive feature of Christianity being the principle that 'all religious emotions are related to redemption in Christ'.[38] The *Aufklärung* axiom of the soteriological autonomy of man eliminated this distinctive element, in that the principle of redemption from outside humanity was regarded as violating human autonomy. Schleiermacher's careful statement of the heteronomous character of human soteriological resources leads to the position of the *Aufklärung* on this question being recognised as Pelagian (by Schleiermacher's definition).

A further point at which Schleiermacher criticises the soteriologies of the *Aufklärung* relates to the concept of sin. Schleiermacher, as is well known, subordinates sin to the divine purpose of redemption, regarding the human recognition of sin as the necessary prelude to his redemption. The first consciousness of the actuality of sin is effectively the first presentiment of the possibility of redemption.[39] Schleiermacher rejects the *Aufklärung* axiom of the reformatory character of punishment,[40] as well as the distinction between natural and arbitrary punishments (see §34).[41] For him, a positive correlation is established by the divine righteousness between sin and penalty for sin *as a means of generating the consciousness of redemption*.[42] The view – which assumes the status of an axiom in the soteriologies of the *Aufklärung* – that the divine righteousness recognises a positive correlation between human good (such as moral action) and divine reward (such as justification) is rejected. Defining the 'righteousness of God' as 'the divine causality by which a connection is established between evil and actual sin in the state of universal sinfulness', Schleiermacher concedes that this represents a considerable restriction upon the term, in that no correlation between good and reward is recognised.[43] However, he defends this restriction by observing that the Christian consciousness recognises no such positive correlation between human good and divine reward, save in the specific and unique case of Christ.[44] Consciousness of the divine righteousness is thus consciousness of the divine punitive justice (*strafende Gerechtigkeit*) alone,[45] thus leading to the realisation of the possibility of redemption. It is therefore evident that Schleiermacher has replaced the moral understandings of divine punishment and the divine righteousness, characteristic of the *Aufklärung*, with *religious* understandings of the concepts, and that these are subordinated to a *religious* concept of salvation.

It is thus clear that the essential presuppositions of the soteriologies of the *Aufklärung* were called into question by developments during the period 1790–1830. The following are of particular importance:

1. The Kantian analysis of the concept of moral autonomy in the light of the principle of radical evil, which demonstrated the superficiality of the moralism of the Enlightenment.

2. Schleiermacher's rejection of the equation of religion and morality, and the associated moral interpretation of soteriological concepts (such as the preconditions of justification, the righteousness of God, or the work of Christ).

3. Schleiermacher's demonstration of the heteronomous character of man's soteriological resources.

Although the rationalist spirit of the *Aufklärung* remained influential for some considerable time thereafter, it exercised a steadily diminishing influence over the articulation of the doctrine of justification in the remainder of the period 1830–1914. While the rise of rationalism in England had been checked through the great Evangelical revival of the late eighteenth century, thus largely obviating the necessity for such critiques of rationalist soteriologies, the situation in Germany demanded that rationalism be refuted on different grounds. The very different character of the English and German discussions of justification in the period 1780–1914 ultimately reflects the different relationship of Pietism and rationalism in the two countries. In England, the rise of Pietism subsequent to rationalism led to the critical questions raised by the Deists being largely ignored, so that the discussion of justification within the English church over the period 1780–1914 is essentially a continuation, and occasionally an extension, of the debate between Anglican and Puritan (see §§ 30–3), rather than a new development in its own right. The German situation, in contrast, demanded the development of new theological methods and insights, in order that rationalism might be defeated – and thus the period 1780–1914 witnessed significant and genuine *developments* in the theology of justification, as rationalism was initially checked, to be followed by a sustained period of consolidation. It is to the developments which are associated with this period of consolidation that we now turn.

§36 The consolidation of the doctrine 1820–1914: Ritschl

Although Schleiermacher's soteriology was subjected to considerable criticism in the period 1820–70,[1] it is clear that it made a permanent impact upon the German theological consciousness. The purely rationalist or moralist account of the justification of man before God was subjected to a significant reversal. If this reversal was to become permanent, however, it was necessary that the anti-rationalist offensive should be consolidated, particularly through the reintroduction of an objective dimension to the doctrine of justification. Initially, it was not clear whether this was a real possibility, let alone how this might be attained. In his influential study of the development of the doctrine of reconciliation, published in 1838, Ferdinand Christian Baur asserted, on the basis of his Hegelian understanding of the nature of historical development,[2] that an element of this doctrine, once eliminated, could no longer be restored. Baur's Hegelianism led him to suggest that objective soteriological concepts had been permanently eliminated from the doctrine of reconciliation. The use of Hegelian speculative categories was widespread within theological circles, and is particularly evident in the first work of one of Baur's most promising pupils: Albrecht Ritschl's *Die Entstehung des altkatholischen Kirche* (1850). As most of Baur's contemporaries were sympathetic to his Hegelian presuppositions, and thus to his views on the development of the doctrine of reconciliation, it was thus far from clear how this consolidation might take place, in that the objective elements of the doctrine rejected by the *Aufklärung* were generally regarded as irretrievably lost.

The sudden collapse of Hegelianism in the fifth decade of the nineteenth century led to a general rejection of the Hegelian understanding of the nature of historical development. The consequences of this development are immediately evident from the second edition of Ritschl's *Entstehung* (1857), in which a break with both Baur and Hegelianism is evident. More significant, from the standpoint of the present study, was Ritschl's decision to reinvestigate the development of the Christian doctrine of justification without the restrictions of the Hegelian interpretative framework imposed upon it by Baur. After a series of preparatory articles in *Jahrbuch für deutsche Theologie*, the first volume of his *Christliche Lehre von der Rechtfertigung und Versöhnung* was published in 1870. The full importance of this historical analysis in consolidating the doctrine of justification has not been fully appreciated. In this work, Ritschl was able to demonstrate that, contrary to Baur's axiom, elements eliminated from the doctrine of reconciliation by one generation had subsequently been reappropriated by another. The closing sentences of this important study merit consideration:

I may now appeal to the delineation of the history of the doctrines of reconciliation and justification, which here closes, to test whether or not [Baur's] belief in the progress of knowledge in a direct line is one to which we are of necessity driven by the facts. At all events, the last link recognised by my predecessor in the history unfolded by him . . . has been so surpassed that an older position has again been taken up.[3]

Having thus demonstrated that Baur's *a priori* imposition of the speculative and unempirical categories of Hegel's philosophy of history was incapable of accounting for the objectively given historical data pertaining to the development of the doctrine of reconciliation, Ritschl was able to move towards the positive restatement of the doctrine through the reappropriation of *objective* soteriological concepts (such as sin) without being impeded by the constraints imposed upon such a restatement by Baur's understanding of the nature of historical development. It is this positive restatement which forms the subject of the third volume of his *Christliche Lehre von der Rechtfertigung und Versöhnung*.[4]

For Ritschl, all religion is exclusively soteriological in character, seeking a resolution of the contradiction in which man finds himself, in that he is at one and the same time a part of the world of nature, dependent upon and confined to the natural order, and yet also a spiritual entity motivated by his determination to maintain his independence of nature.[5] Religion is therefore essentially an interpretation of man's relation to God and the world, based upon the belief that God may effect the redemption of man.[6] Ritschl's theology in its entirety is based upon the centrality of God's redemptive action in history, with its associated (and subsequent) human response and obligations. In the second edition of *Die Entstehung der altkatholischen Kirche*, Ritschl drew an important, and highly influential, distinction between early authentic Christianity, and its later inauthentic form, which resulted from the intrusion of elements essentially alien to the gospel itself. According to Ritschl, Christianity was essentially soteriologically orientated, but became corrupted through the intrusion of Hellenistic metaphysics into a Christologically orientated religion. Ritschl's intense suspicion of the rôle of metaphysics in theology reflects his fundamental conviction that man has no true knowledge of God outside the sphere of his redemptive activity, and that even then, this knowledge takes the form of value-judgements (*Werthurtheile*), which cannot be allowed to be equivalent to disinterested and impartial knowledge.

In his polemic against the claims of idealistic rationalism, Ritschl argues that the specifically Christian knowledge of God takes the form of *Werthurtheile* evoked by divine revelation.[7] For him, we know the nature of God and Christ only in terms of their perceived significance for us. Thus he makes frequent approving reference to Melanchthon's celebrated dictum: Hoc est Christum cognoscere, beneficia eius cognoscere.[8] Ritschl's theological method is based upon the assumption that faith is grounded in the saving revelation of God in Christ, so that the actual justification of man is defined as the point of departure for all Christian statements concerning God. All the believer's statements concerning God and Christ reflect the importance which he personally attaches to them, and cannot be divorced from his faith. Thus for Ritschl, the question: who is Christ? must reduce to the more pertinent and radical question: who is Christ *for me*? this latter constituting a *Werthurtheil* upon which theology is based. Exploiting the Kantian insistence upon the inalienable subjectivity of value-judgements, Ritschl insists that the *Bild* cannot be separated from the *Ding-an-sich*. Thus man cannot consider the person of Christ (the *Ding-an-sich*) in isolation from the work of Christ (the *Bild*). This point is made with particular clarity in the first edition of Ritschl's *Hauptwerk*, where the Christological consequences of the phenomenalist thesis that *Dinge-an-sich* escape our perception altogether (except in the form in which they are perceived and evaluated) are analysed.[9] Ritschl thus argues that our knowledge of the person of Christ, in so far as this represents a genuine possibility, derives from our knowledge of the work of Christ – in other words, that soteriology is prior to Christology in the theological *ordo cognoscendi*. Ritschl's celebrated reluctance to avert his gaze from the phenomenal aspects of reality to their ontological foundation inevitably leads to a certain lack of interest in the *Christusbild* which underlies his soteriological concentration.

This point is brought out with particular importance by Ritschl in his introduction to his historical study of the development of the doctrines of justification and reconciliation:

The Christian doctrine of justification and reconciliation . . . constitutes the real centre of the theological system. In it is developed the determinate and direct result of the historical revelation of God's purpose of grace through Christ.[10]

Of course, it may be emphasised that the affirmation of the subjectivity of religious value-judgements does not entail the denial of their objective foundation: faith, in making its value-judgements, bases them upon the objective reality of the saving revelation of God in Jesus Christ. It is clear that Ritschl regards man's justification as the fundamental datum from which all theological discussion must proceed, and upon which it is ultimately grounded.[11] This conviction expresses itself in the manner in which Ritschl's systematic exposition of Christian theology proceeds. An initial examination of the concept of justification (§§5–26) is followed by an analysis of the presuppositions of man's justification, such as the doctrines of sin and the work and person of Christ (§§27–50). After a discussion of the difficulties which might be thought to arise from the doctrine (§§51–61), the work ends with an analysis of the consequences of man's justification (§§62–8).

Ritschl's initial definition of justification is of immediate significance, in that it represents the reintroduction of objective concepts into the systematic discussion of the doctrine. 'Justification, or the forgiveness of sins (as the religious operation of God upon men, fundamental within Christianity), is the acceptance of sinners into that fellowship with God within which their salvation will be effected and developed into eternal life.'[12] Ritschl's explicit identification of justification and the remission of sins indicates his concern to emphasise the objective dimension of justification, and represents a reappropriation of certain aspects of the concept associated with the Reformation in general, and Luther in particular.[13] Thus Ritschl identifies Luther's statement in the 1518 sermon on the sacrament of penance, 'alßo sihestu, das die gantz Kirch voll ist vogebung der sund',[14] as the key to the reformer's theology of justification,[15] and hence incorporated it into his own positive exposition of the doctrine. For Ritschl, sin separates man from God, effecting the withdrawal of God's presence from the sinner; justification is therefore the divine operation through which the sinner is restored to fellowship with God. The objective dimension of justification is therefore prior to, although inseparable from, the subjective consciousness of this forgiveness.[16] Ritschl thus criticises an earlier generation of Lutheran theologians for their excessive objectivism, which led to justification becoming divorced from personal experience and practice.[17] Of considerably greater importance, however, is Ritschl's critique of the axiom of the *Aufklärung*, that God enters into no real relationship with man, unless the man in question is morally regenerate. This principle amounts to the destruction of the central and fundamental presupposition of Christianity which, according to Ritschl, is that God justifies *sinners*. Ritschl stresses that justification necessarily finds its expression in the lifestyle of the individual:[18] justification (*Rechtfertigung*), which is concerned with the restoration of man's fellowship with God, necessarily finds its concrete expression in reconciliation (*Versöhnung*), the lifestyle of the reconciled community. In so far as the moral implications of justification and reconciliation derive from and are grounded in man's new relationship to God, established in justification, it may be said that reconciliation is the ethical complement of justification – in other words, that the *moral* aspects of this fellowship with God are secondary to its specifically *religious* character.

It will be evident that Ritschl has reinterpreted the concept of 'reconciliation' (*Versöhnung*). For Orthodoxy, 'reconciliation' referred to the objective basis of justification, especially the historical work of Christ. Ritschl inverted the traditional frame of reference, so that God is now understood as the *subject*, rather than the *object*, of reconciliation.[19] Indeed, Ritschl appears to regard the terms *Rechtfertigung* and *Versöhnung* as being essentially synonymous, their difference lying in the aspects of the God–man relationship to which they referred. *Rechtfertigung* refers to the divine judgement, understood as an unconditional act of will, independent of whether an individual or a community appropriates it. *Versöhnung* refers to the same basic concept of a synthetic divine judgement, as it is appropriated by an individual or community. In other words, *Versöhnung* expresses as an actual result the effect which is intended in *Rechtfertigung* – that the individual or community who is justified actually enters into the intended relationship.

For Ritschl, God's gracious gift of justification is inextricably and irrevocably linked with the ethical consequences of this divine act: 'Christianity, so to speak, resembles not a circle described from a single centre, but an ellipse which is determined by two *foci*.'[20] The first *focus* is 'redemption through Christ', and the second 'the ethical interpretation of Christianity through the idea of the Kingdom of God'. His conviction that Lutheran Orthodoxy had tended to concentrate upon redemption without correlating it with Christian existence led to his insistence upon the necessity of correlating the divine and human elements in justification and reconciliation. However, it is evident that Ritschl had some difficulty in establishing the relative weighting to be given to the two *foci* of his theology: in the first edition of the work (1870), it seems that the ethical *focus* is regarded as the more significant, whereas the second (1883) and third (1888) editions gave the *focus* of redemption greater weight.[21]

Ritschl's statement that justification involves a *synthetic* judgement on the part of God represents a decisive break with the soteriologies of the *Aufklärung* and their precursors within Pietism, which even Schleiermacher had not felt able to make. In making this assertion, Ritschl clearly considers himself to be reappropriating a vital element of the Reformation and Orthodox soteriologies rejected by the 'Age of Reason'. If justification involves an *analytic* judgement on the part of God, God is understood to 'analyse' the righteousness which is already present in the *objectum iustificationis*, and on the basis of this analysis, to pronounce the sentence of justification. This pronouncement is thus based upon a quality already present within man, prior to his justification, which God recognises and proclaims in the subsequent verdict of justification. 'Righteousness' is already predicated of man – the function of the pronouncement of justification is to endorse man's present status *coram Deo*. It will be evident that this corresponds to the moralist soteriology of the *Aufklärung*. If, on the other hand, justification involves a *synthetic* judgement, God is understood to act in a creative manner, adding something to man which was not his previously. God 'synthesises' the righteousness upon the basis of which the divine verdict of justification proceeds: in justification, a predicate is added to man which is not already included in the notion of 'sinner' ('ein Prädicat gesetzt wird, welches nicht schon in dem Begriffe des Sünders eingeschlossen ist').[22] Ritschl declares his intention to break free from the moralism of Catholicism[23] and the *Aufklärung* (the latter he considers to be Socinian in character) by affirming that justification is a creative act of the divine will which, in declaring the sinner to be righteous, *effects* rather than *endorses* the righteousness of man. It will be evident that Ritschl's insistence upon the synthetic character of the divine judgement of justification eliminates any claim by the morally renewed man to be justified on that account.[24] Ritschl thus argues that Pietism (and, by inference, the *Aufklärung*) represent an 'inversion of the Reformation point of view'.

Although Ritschl is severely critical of the soteriologies of the *Aufklärung*, it is also clear that he regards the theologies of justification associated with Orthodoxy as open to criticism, singling out the judicial approach to justification and the concept of original sin for particular comment.

Fundamental to Ritschl's critique of an analytic understanding of the divine judgement of justification is the question of the positive laws or principles by which such a judgement may be undertaken. 'Every judicial judgement is an analytic judgement of knowledge. The subsequent decree of punishment or acquittal is also an analytic judgement, in that it is a conclusion based upon the prohibitive or permissive law [*Schluß aus dem verbietenden oder erlaubenden Gesetz*] and the knowledge of the guilt or innocence of the person involved.'[25] If God's justifying verdict is based upon *law*, the question of God's status in regard to that law must be positively established. This question is, of course, particularly associated with the Arminian theologian Hugo Grotius,[26] and Ritschl may be regarded as extending the critique of the Orthodox doctrine of justification associated with this Arminian divine to exclude totally a judicial interpretation of justification.

'The attribute of God on the basis of which the older theology attempts to understand justification is that of lawgiver [*Gesetzgeber*] and judge [*Richter*].'[27] By these terms, Ritschl intends to convey the quite distinct concepts of God as *rector* and *iudex* (underlying Grotius' critique of Orthodox theologies of justification). Ritschl points out how the divine pardon of the sinner in justification was generally treated by Orthodoxy as analogous to the bestowal of pardon upon a guilty individual by a head of state. On the basis of this analogy, it was argued that justification could be interpreted as a judicial act of God, by which the individual was found guilty of sin, and yet pardoned through precisely the same legal process. Any apparent contradiction between the divine justice and the divine grace could be resolved by developing a theory of penal substitution, so that any hint of injustice in relation to the pardoning of the guilty individual could be remedied.

Ritschl, however, argued that the exercise of the head of state's right to pardon is not comparable to the divine justification of the sinner. The head of state is obliged to act in accord with the best interests of the individual members of the state, and the established law is merely a means towards that end. As such, the law is subordinate to the greater good of the state:

The right of granting pardon [*Begnadigung*] . . . follows from the fact that the legal order is merely a means to the moral ends of the people, and that consequences of legal action are conceivable, which are incongruous with the respect which is due to public morality, as well as to the moral position of guilty persons.[28]

The ability of the head of state to take certain moral liberties with the established law is a direct consequence of the fact that the moral good of the people is to be considered as being of greater importance than the strict observance of the law, which is merely a means to that end. As such, the question of whether a guilty individual should be pardoned is not one of *law*, but one of *public moral interests*. The state may thus relax a law with this end in view, without its action being deemed to be improper.[29] The reason why the state is able to take such liberties with the established law is that it maintains two potentially conflicting principles at one and the same time – the need to obey the law, and the need to act towards the greatest good of the people. Although these principles are usually reconcilable, situations inevitably must arise when they cannot be maintained simultaneously – and Ritschl argues that, on such occasions, it is the latter which must be upheld. It is therefore, according to Ritschl, impossible to model God upon the institution of the state and assert that his action in justification is *judicial*, in that it is clearly *extra-judicial*. Ritschl thus notes with approval Tieftrunk's emphasis upon the subordination of God's rôle as lawgiver to that of public benefactor.[30] It is clear that Ritschl regards this extra-judicial approach to justification as avoiding the impasse of the Orthodox doctrine of God as the righteous God who justifies men, despite their being sinners, in order to develop an understanding of justification based upon a teleological principle of paralleling that of the state as public benefactor.

Ritschl locates this teleological element of Christianity in the concept of the 'Kingdom of God' (*Reich Gottes*). In adopting this position, Ritschl was following a general trend among the theologians of his time.[31] Ritschl's innovation lay in the significance he attached to the concept in connection with his doctrines of justification and reconciliation. His biblical investigations had led him to the conclusion that the concept of the Kingdom of God was both the key to the preaching of Jesus, and the unifying principle of the Old and New Testaments.[32] Ritschl thus rejects the 'Scotist' principle of God as *dominium absolutum* and the juristic concept of God, modelled upon the state, in favour of the concept of God as the originator and ground of the teleological principle of the Kingdom of God.[33] All else in Christian theology is to be regarded as subordinated to this goal. This general principle is of particular importance in connection with Ritschl's discussion of the divine attributes. Thus God's eternity may be taken to refer to the fact that God 'remains the same, and maintains the same purpose and plan by which he creates and directs the world'.[34] Similarly, the divine attribute of 'righteousness' (*Gerechtigkeit*) is defined teleologically, in terms of the Kingdom of God:

Omnipotence receives the particular character of *righteousness* in the particular revelation of the old and new covenants. By 'righteousness', the Old Testament signifies the consistency of the divine direction towards salvation [*die Folgerichtigkeit der göttlichen Leitung zum Heil*] ... In so far as the righteousness of God achieves his dominion in accordance with its dominant purpose of salvation ... it is *faithfulness*. Thus in the New Testament the righteousness of God is also recognised as the criterion of the special actions by which the community of Christ is brought into existence and led on to perfection. Such righteousness therefore cannot be distinguished from the grace of God.[35]

Ritschl regards this deobjectified teleological understanding of the 'righteousness of God' as having circumvented the difficulties of the Orthodox concept, and to amount to a recovery of the teaching of the

Old and New Testaments,[36] as well as of Luther.[37] The concept clearly marks a break with the concept of *iustitia distributiva* (whether in the form associated with Orthodoxy, Pietism or the *Aufklärung*), and permits Ritschl to avoid discussion of the question of how God *can* justify sinful man (in that his understanding of the divine righteousness relates solely to the manner in which God *does* justify sinners).

On the basis of this teleological understanding of the economy of salvation, Ritschl mounts a sustained critique of the soteriology of Lutheran Orthodoxy. He characterises the Orthodox approach to the *locus iustificationis* as follows:[38]

1.　A doctrine of original sin is developed on the basis of texts such as Romans 5.12, by which original sin is deduced from the actual sin of Adam and Eve.
2.　The fact of this universally inherited sin of the human race is then used as the basis of the demonstration of the necessity of redemption. The mode of this redemption is determined by comparing sin with the divine attribute of retributive righteousness, following the general method of Anselm of Canterbury.
3.　From this, the doctrine of the person and work of Christ is deduced, as is its application to the individual and community of believers.

Ritschl argues that this approach is based upon purely rational ideas of God, sin and redemption, and is quite unsuited either to the positive exposition of the doctrine, or to its defence against its rationalist critics. In particular, Ritschl objects to the Augustinian doctrine of original sin as implying a false hypostasisation of mankind over and against the individuals who are its members, and as failing to account for the fact that all men are sinful to different degrees. Ritschl is at his closest to the soteriologies of the *Aufklärung* at this point.

It will, however, be clear that Ritschl's exposition of the doctrine of justification represents a significant consolidation of the doctrine in the face of earlier rationalist criticism. Three points may be singled out as being of particular importance:

1. The demonstration, on the basis of an historical analysis of the development of the doctrine of justification, that elements of the doctrine rejected in one cultural situation might subsequently be reappropriated in another. Thus the Enlightenment critique of the Orthodox doctrine, and particularly its elimination of any objective dimension to justification, was not of permanent significance. It is difficult for the modern reader to appreciate the full force of this

point, in that he is unlikely to share the Hegelian framework within which theologians such as F. C. Baur constructed their thesis of the irreversibility of theological development.

2. The reappropriation of objective elements in the discussion of justification. Schleiermacher, although providing a strongly anti-rationalist foundation for his soteriology, had not taken this crucial step in re-establishing the traditional framework of the doctrine of justification.

3. The explicit statement that justification involves a *synthetic*, rather than an *analytic* judgement, which eliminated the theological foundation of the moral soteriologies of the *Aufklärung*.

It is also clear that Ritschl's analysis of the distinction between *rector* and *iudex* has considerable implications for certain Enlightenment soteriologies: indeed, it is significant that the *Aufklärer* (Tieftrunk) singled out by Ritschl for approval in his exposition of this matter was one of the few who had responded to the Kantian critique of the moralism of the Enlightenment (see §35).

Nevertheless, a strong degree of affinity may still be detected between the *Aufklärung*, Schleiermacher and Ritschl in relation to their discussion of the work of Christ. The subjectivism of the earlier period is still evident in Ritschl's exposition of the work of Christ. Christ is the revealer of certain significant (and not necessarily rational) insights concerning an unchangeable situation between God and man, rather than the founder of a new relationship between God and man.[39] For Martin Kähler, there remained an essential continuity between Ritschl and the *Aufklärung* at precisely this point.[40] According to Kähler, such a subjective approach to the meaning of the death of Christ represented a radical devaluation of its significance (*eine Entwertung des Werkes Christi*), in that Christ tends to be reduced to a mere symbol of the grace of God, without having any essential connection with that grace. It is this point which underlies his criticism of Ritschl's interpretation of the concepts of *Rechtfertigung* and *Versöhnung*: for Kähler, the latter corresponds to the objectively altered situation between God and man, arising through the historic work of Christ, while *Rechtfertigung* refers to a specific aspect of this situation – the individual's appropriation of this reconciliation through faith. The objective reality of reconciliation is necessarily prior to the subjective consciousness of this reconciliation.

Despite Kähler's strictures, the period 1880–1914 was characterised by the emergence of a significant degree of broad consensus relating to the question of justification. Drawing heavily upon the theme of the 'religious personality' of the historical Jesus, it was generally assumed that man's justification came about through the influence of this supremely powerful religious personality as it impinged upon his existence. The anti-rationalist character of this view may be judged by the general concession of an objective dimension to justification, and the non-rational character of the 'religious personality'. Although the development of critical biblical studies was gradually undermining this theology,[41] it would remain dominant until the year 1914, when the outbreak of the First World War posed a radical, and ultimately irresistible, challenge to its foundations. It is to that challenge which we now turn.

§37 The dialectical theology of justification: Barth

The outbreak of the First World War ushered in a new period in European theology, as the bourgeois optimism of the dawn of the century gave way to the sombre realism of the immediate post-war period. The impact of the war upon German theology, and particularly preaching, was momentous.[1] The link between Christianity and culture, one of the most significant achievements of Ritschl's theological synthesis, was widely regarded as discredited through the Kaiser's war policies.[2] The growing sense of the 'otherness' of God is reflected in many developments of the period, particularly Karl Holl's famous lecture of 31 October 1917, delivered before the University of Berlin, which inaugurated the Luther renaissance by demonstrating how radically Luther's concept of God differed from the somewhat emasculated deity of liberal Protestantism.[3] Such radical developments in the world of religious ideas could not fail to have an impact upon the doctrine of justification. To illustrate this impact, we turn to consider Karl Barth's lecture of 16 January 1916 in the Aarau Stadtkirche, on the theme of 'the righteousness of God'.[4]

Even today, the rhetorical power of this lecture may still be felt, and the passage of time has done nothing to diminish the force of Barth's sustained critique of man's self-assertion in the face of God, which he links with the question of the true meaning of the 'righteousness of God'. For Barth, the 'deepest, inmost and most certain fact of life, is that "God is righteous"'.[5] This fact is brought home to man by his conscience, which affirms the existence of a righteous God in the midst of human unrighteousness, which Barth recognised in the forces of capitalism as much as in the war which was raging over the face of Europe as he spoke.[6] Deep within man's

357

inmost being lies the desire for the righteousness of God – and yet paradoxically, just when this divine righteousness appears to be on the verge of altering man's nature and conduct, man asserts his own self-righteousness. He is unable to contemplate the concept of a 'righteousness' which lies beyond his own control. Man welcomes the intervention of divine righteousness if it puts an end to wars or general strikes – but feels threatened by it when he realises that behind the *results* of human unrighteousness lies the unfathomable reality of *human righteousness* itself. The abolition of the consequences of human unrighteousness necessarily entails the abolition of human unrighteousness itself, and hence an entirely new existence.[7] Unable to accept this, man deforms the 'righteousness of God' into various forms of human righteousness, of which Barth singles out three types for particular criticism.

1. Moral righteousness (*die Gerechtigkeit unserer Moral*).[8] Barth rejects those spheres of human existence within which *Kulturprotestantismus* had located the locus of human morality (such as the family, or the state), on the grounds that, by restricting moral action to these spheres, man is simply ignoring the obvious fact that his action is immoral in others. For Barth, the existence of the capitalist system and the war demonstrated the invalidity of this thesis, as *both* were perpetrated in the name of morality.

2. Legal righteousness (*die Gerechtigkeit des Staates und der Juristen*).[9] Barth emphasises (prophetically, as the Third Reich was to demonstrate)[10] that human law is essentially orientated towards the ends specified by the state itself. At best, law could be regarded as an attempt to restrict the effect of human unrighteousness; at worst, it resulted in the establishment and perpetuation of human unrighteousness by the agencies of the state itself. Once more, Barth cites the war as exemplifying the defection of human ideas of 'righteousness' from those which conscience dictated should be recognised as divine.

3. Religious righteousness (*die religiöse Gerechtigkeit*).[11] Foreshadowing his mature critique of religion, Barth argues that man's religion, like his morality, is a tower of Babel, erected by man in the face of, and in defiance of, what his conscience tells him to be right.

In these three ways, Barth argues that man is failing to take the 'righteousness of God' seriously, lest it overwhelm and transform him: 'wir haben es nicht weiter gebracht als bis zu einem schlaftrunkenen Spiel mit den Schattenbildern der göttlichen Gerechtigkeit'.[12]

For Barth, the First World War both questions and demonstrates the righteousness of God. It *questions* that righteousness, in that man is unable to understand how a 'righteous' God could permit such an outrage; it *demonstrates* that same righteousness, in that it shows up human caricatures of divine righteousness for what they really are. Man has made his own concepts of righteousness into a God, so that God is simply the 'great personal or impersonal, mystical, philosophical or naïve Profundity and patron saint of our human righteousness, morality, state, civilisation, or religion'.[13] For Barth, the war has destroyed this image of God for ever, exposing it as an idol. By asserting his own concept of righteousness in the face of God, man constructed a 'righteous' God who was the first and least mourned casualty of the war.[14] The 'death' of this God has forced man to recognise that the 'righteousness of God' is qualitatively different from, and stands over and against, human concepts of righteousness.

This lecture is of considerable significance in a number of respects. Of particular importance is the dialectic between human and divine righteousness, which marks an unequivocal break with the 'liberal' understanding of the nature of history, progress and civilisation. 'God's will is not a superior projection of our own will: it stands in opposition to our will as one that is totally distinct [*als ein gänzlich anderer*].'[15] It is this infinite qualitative distinction between human and divine righteousness which forms the basis of Barth's repeated assertion that God is, and must be recognised as, God.

The radical emphasis upon the 'otherness' of God so evident in Barth's programmatic critique of concepts of the 'righteousness of God' clearly parallels the theological concerns of the young Luther.[16] It might therefore be thought that Barth's early dialectical theology, or mature 'theology of the Word of God', might represent a recovery of the Reformer's insights into the significance of the *articulus iustificationis*. In fact, this is not the case, and Barth actually remains within the framework established by the *Aufklärer*, Schleiermacher and Ritschl for the discussion of the justification of man before God.

Barth's mature theology may be regarded as extended reflection upon the fact that God has spoken to man – *Deus dixit* – abrogating the epistemological chasm separating them in doing so. God has spoken, in the fullness of time, and it is this event – or these events – which stand at the heart of Barth's theological concerns. It is the task of any authentic and responsible *Christian* theology to attempt to unfold the nature and identity of the God who had spoken to sinners in the man-ward movement envisaged in the *Deus dixit*. The structures and the inner nexus of relationships presupposed by the fact –

not the *idea* – of the *Deus dixit* determine what Christian theology has to say concerning the God who thus speaks. Barth thus abandons his earlier attempt, in the *Christliche Dogmatik*, to construct a 'grammatical' doctrine of the Trinity, based upon the idea or notion of revelation, in terms of the logical analysis of the event of the *Deus dixit* in terms of its implied subject, object and predicate: it is now the *fact*, rather than the *idea*, of revelation which claims Barth's attention. In effect, Barth develops an *Offenbarungspositivismus* in which the concrete structure of revelation as it has happened, and as it still happens, is interpreted theologically. To interpret the idea of revelation would, in effect, be to reduce theology to anthropology, in that a prior human model with its attending epistemological presuppositions is required for an analysis of the idea in question. Although revelation is a unitary act, it nevertheless possesses a divinely grounded unity in that diversity, which Barth formulates as 'Das Wort Gottes in seiner dreifachen Gestalt'. God speaks in history, but is not bound by its categories: the divine event of revelation can be actualised in every human circumstance, and is not confined to any given historical form under which he may speak (although Barth concedes that revelation demands historical predicates). The *function* of Barth's concept of the three-fold form of the Word of God is therefore to provide a secure theological foundation for Barth's insistence that God, who has spoken his final and supreme Word in Jesus Christ, still speaks to man today – and in every conceivable historical human circumstance. The single assumption, which alone can be recognised as a leading principle in Christian theology, is that God has spoken: *Dominus dixit*.

It is clear that Barth's theological system is, in essence, the unfolding of the inner structures and relationships which characterise the *fact* that God has spoken. The theological enterprise could thus be characterised as an exercise in *Nach-Denken*, following out the order of revelation in the man-ward movement of God in history. God has spoken to man across the epistemological chasm which separates them, and by so speaking to him, discloses both the reality of that separation and also the possibility of its abrogation. Barth confronts us with the paradox that man's inability to hear the Word of God is disclosed to him by that very Word. It is the reality of this divine abrogation of this epistemological chasm between God and man, and hence of the axiom *homo peccator non capax verbi Dei*, which stands at the heart of Barth's theological system.

But is the fact that God has spoken to man really what the gospel is all about? For Luther, the gospel was primarily concerned with the forgiveness of sins, whereas for Barth it is primarily concerned with the possibility of the right knowledge of God. Barth has placed the *divine revelation to sinful man* at the point where Luther placed the *divine justification of sinful man*. Although there are clearly points of contact between Luther and Barth, it is equally clear that Barth cannot share Luther's high estimation for the *articulus iustificationis*. In what follows, we propose to indicate why this is the case.

In the course of his exposition of the doctrine of justification,[17] Barth finds himself obliged to disagree with Ernst Wolf's analysis of the significance of the *articulus iustificationis* for the Reformers in general, and Luther in particular.[18] Wolf locates the significance of the *articulus iustificationis* in terms of its function, which he conveniently finds expressed in the celebrated dictum of Luther: 'articulus iustificationis est magister et princeps, dominus, rector et iudex super omnia genera doctrinarum, qui conservat et gubernat omnem doctrinam ecclesiasticam et erigit conscientiam nostram coram Deo'.[19] Wolf summarises Luther's understanding of the function of the *articulus iustificationis* in terms of its defining the 'centre and limits of Reformation theology' (*Mitte und Grenze reformatorischer Theologie*), which he elaborates as follows:

Mitte – das heißt: alles in reformatorischer Theologie ist auf sie bezogen; in ihr wird ja das *subiectum theologiae* zentral erfaßt.
Grenze – das heißt: alles, was außerhalb des durch diese Mitte Bestimmten und Zusammengefaßten liegt, ist *'error et venenum' in theologia.*[20]

Wolf illustrates this interpretation of the function of the *articulus iustificationis* with reference to Luther's anthropology and ecclesiology, with convincing results, and thus establishes two important principles concerning this function. First, the *articulus iustificationis* is established as the leading principle of Luther's theology, as is the priority of soteriological considerations within the same context. Second, the *subiectum theologiae* is defined as God's salvific activity towards sinful man. The modesty of Barth's soteriological interests is emphasised when compared with Luther's insistence upon their dominating rôle in positive theological speculation. Furthermore, the secondary and derivative rôle of revelation within the context of Luther's theology will be evident,[21] although Barth does not seem to appreciate this point.

Barth is thus clearly obliged to dispute Wolf's analysis,[22] which he does in an important discussion of the *temporary* significance of the *articulus iustificationis.* He acknowledges the peculiar importance which Luther attached to the doctrine, and further concedes that Luther did not regard the *articulus iustificationis* as the *primus et principalis articulus* merely in the polemic against Rome, but against all form of sectarianism. However, he notes that no evangelical theologian – with the possible exception of Martin Kähler – ever dared to construct a dogmatics with the *articulus* at its centre. This observation leads Barth to his critique of such a procedure. Conceding that the *articulus iustificationis* has been regarded as being *the* Word of the gospel on several occasions in the history of the church, he points out that these occasions represented instances where the gospel, understood as the free grace of God, was under threat – such as the Pelagian controversy. Barth then argues that it is necessary to free the theological enterprise from the contingencies of such controversies.[23] Barth then asserts that the *articulus iustificationis* is not central to the Christian proclamation:

Sie war nun einmal auch in der Kirche Jesu Christi nicht immer und nicht überall das Wort des Evangeliums, und es würde einen Akt allzu krampfhafter und ungerechter Ausschließlichkeit bedeuten, wenn man sie als solches ausgeben und behandeln würde.[24]

In one sense, this is clearly correct: it is true that the *articulus iustificationis* has not always been regarded as the centre of theological speculation. However, in that the *lex orandi* continually proclaims the centrality of the soteriological dimension of Christianity to Christian prayer, adoration and worship, in that the community of faith is understood to be based upon a soteriological foundation, it is possible that Barth has not represented the situation accurately. Furthermore, the fundamentally soteriological orientation of the patristic Trinitarian and Christological debates[25] leads to the conclusion that the Trinitarian and Christological dogmas are ultimately an expression of the soteriological convictions of the early church, whatever reinterpretation Barth may choose to place upon them. If the *articulus iustificationis* is taken to represent an assertion of the priority of soteriological considerations within the sphere of the church, Barth's statement must be regarded as seriously misleading.

It is, however clear that Barth's chief reason for relegating the *articulus iustificationis* to a secondary position is that it poses a serious and comprehensive threat to his own theological method. It is for this reason that he singles out Wolf's study of the function of the *articulus iustificationis* within the theology of the early Reformers for particular criticism. He therefore argues that the *articulus stantis et cadentis ecclesiae*, properly understood, is not the doctrine of justification as such, but its 'basis and culmination' in the 'confession of Jesus Christ'. This point is, however, hardly disputed, and is made by Wolf himself. The *articulus iustificationis* is merely a convenient statement of the salvific activity of God towards man, concentrated in Jesus Christ. While Barth is prepared to retain the traditional designation of the *articulus iustificationis* as the *articulus stantis et cadentis ecclesiae*, it is only on account of the community of faith's need to know of the objective basis of its existence: 'ohne die Wahrheit der Rechtfertigungslehre gäbe und gibt es gewiß keine wahre christliche Kirche'.[26] Nevertheless, so long as the essential truth of this article is not denied, Barth argues that it may withdraw into the background:

Gerade des Menschen Rechtfertigung und gerade das Vertrauen auf die objecktive Wahrheit der Rechtfertigungslehre verbietet uns das Postulat, daß ihr theologischer Vollzug in der wahren Kirche *semper, ubique et ab omnibus* als das *unum necessarium*, als die ganze Mitte oder als die einzige Spitze der christliche Botschaft und Lehre angesehen und behandelt werden müsse.[27]

In fact, it is clear that Barth's criticism of those who see in the *articulus iustificationis* the centre of the Christian faith is merely a consequence of his theological method. Soteriology is necessarily secondary to the fact of revelation, *Deus dixit*. As we noted earlier, Barth's own theology may be regarded as a reaction against the anthropocentricity of the liberal school – a reaction particularly evident in his inversion of the liberal understanding of God and man as epistemic object and subject respectively.[28] It will therefore be clear that Barth's theology is subject to precisely the same charge as that levelled by him against those who made the *articulus iustificationis* the centre of their theology. Barth has merely inverted the liberal theology, without fundamentally altering its frame of reference.[29] As such, he may be regarded as perpetuating the theological interests and concerns of the liberal school – particularly the question of how God may be known. The theologians of the liberal school were simply not concerned with the question of 'guilt' or of 'righteousness *coram Deo*', in that they possessed no sense of human bondage or slavery to sin. Thus Albrecht Ritschl regarded Luther's *de servo arbitrio* (1525), which develops the notion of man's bondage to sin in some depth (see §21), as 'an unfortunate botch' (*unglückliches Machwerk*) – although it was precisely this work which Rudolf Otto singled out as the 'psychological key' to understanding Luther. Similarly, Karl Holl's celebrated 1917 lecture on Luther was primarily concerned with the correct *knowledge* of God, rather than the soteriological dimension of his thought.[30] It is significant that the Luther renaissance initially served to emphasise the Reformer's emphasis upon the deity and 'otherness' of God, rather than the importance of the *articulus iustificationis* within the context of his theology. Dialectical theology was initially passionately concerned with the question of the right knowledge of God, inspired by a conviction of man's ignorance of God and the impossibility of any theologically significant natural knowledge of God. There is no means by which the yawning chasm (which Barth designates a 'crevasse') between God and man may be bridged from man's side – hence the news that God has bridged this chasm from his side must be taken with the utmost seriousness.

Early dialectical theology thus took up one aspect of Luther's theology (the 'otherness' of God) and abandoned the other (man's bondage to sin). Hence for the young Barth, as we have seen, the significance of the 'righteousness of God' lay in the fact that it was diametrically opposed to human concepts of righteousness. The lack of interest in man's bondage to sin, so characteristic of the liberal school and nineteenth-century theology in general, thus passed into the dialectical theology of the early twentieth century. The theological drama which constitutes the Christian faith is thus held to concern man and his knowledge of God, rather than the salvation of sinful man, caught up in the cosmic conflict between God and sin, the world and the devil.[31] Such a conflict is an impossibility within the context of Barth's theology, in that Barth shares with Hegel the difficulty of accommodating sin within an essentially monistic system. Barth has simply no concept of a divine engagement with the forces of sin or evil (unless these are understood in the epistemically reduced sense of 'ignorance' or 'misunderstanding'): instead, we find only talk about God making himself *known* to man. Barth even reduces the cross – traditionally the *locus* of precisely such a conflict – into a monologue between God the Father and God the Son.[32] The impartation of knowledge is no substitute for a direct confrontation with sin, death and evil.

The most significant aspect of Barth's criticism of the rôle allocated by Wolf to the *articulus iustificationis* lies in the different theological methods which they presuppose. For the later Barth, the concept of 'Christomonism' (Althaus) or 'Christological concentration' (von Balthasar) becomes of increasing importance. This Christological concentration finds its expression not in the history of Jesus of

Nazareth in general, or even in the crucifixion or resurrection in particular, but in the pre-existence of Christ, before all eternity.[33] The reason for this lies in Barth's understanding of the divine freedom to reveal, or not to reveal, himself, and is particularly well expressed in his critique of Hegel.[34] The antecedence of the doctrine of the eternal generation of the Son preserves the divine freedom in revelation. As a result, Barth now finds himself obliged to assert that Christ is equally present at every stage of the history of salvation. That redemption presupposes sin is a difficulty which cannot really be accommodated within Barth's essentially supralapsarian understanding of the Fall. It is simply impossible to accommodate the existence of sin and evil in a convincing manner within the context of a theology which presupposes that the historical process is absolutely determined by what is already perfected at the beginning of time. For Paul, sin 'entered into the world'; Barth cannot convincingly speak of sin 'entering into' such a Christologically determined historical process.[35]

Setting aside for a moment Barth's general lack of interest in soteriology, it will be clear that his emphasis upon what has been Christologically determined from all eternity leads to a certain lack of interest in what pertains here and now. The *articulus iustificationis* deals with man's predicament here and now, as he is enslaved by sin and unable to redeem himself. Barth's interests clearly lie elsewhere than with sinful man, even if it is possible to argue that his theology ultimately represents the outcome of anthropological and epistemological considerations.

A further point of importance relates to theological method in general. If the starting point for theological speculation is defined to be the *articulus iustificationis*, it is clear that an analytic and inductive method must be followed, arguing from the particular event of the divine justification of the sinner to the context in which it is set (such as the decrees of election). It can be shown that this methodology characterised the first period of Reformed theology, and is also characteristic of Arminius.[36] However, the onset of Reformed Orthodoxy (see §24) saw the starting point for theological speculation shifted from the concrete event of the justification of the sinner in Christ to the divine decrees of election and reprobation. Instead of an analytic and inductive method, a synthetic and deductive method was employed, involving the appeal from general principles (such as the divine decree to elect) to particular events (such as the justification of the elect in Christ). As a result, justification is accorded a place of low priority in the *ordo salutis*, in that it is merely the concrete actuali-sation of the prior divine decision of election. It will be clear that Barth approximates more closely to the theological method of Refor-med Orthodoxy than to that of Calvin. The synthetic and deductive approach necessitated by his insistence upon the antecedence of the doctrine of the eternal generation of the Son leads to the incarnation, death and resurrection of Christ being placed low in the order of priorities within the context of his theological method. In that it is the application of a synthetic and deductive theological method by the theologians of Reformed Orthodoxy (such as Beza) which leads to the abstract *decretum absolutum*, so heavily criticised by Barth, it is somewhat ironical that his own theological method approximates so closely to this method.

Barth's modest soteriological concerns also express themselves in his doctrine of the work of Christ, in which a remarkable degree of continuity is evident with the *Aufklärung*, Schleiermacher and Ritschl,[37] demonstrating once more Barth's close affinity with the theological framework of the liberal school, despite substantial differences in substance. At first glance, Barth's theology of the work of Christ appears to be irreconcilably opposed to that of the *Aufklärung*. In his study of Protestant theology in the eighteenth and nineteenth centuries, Barth frequently displays his contempt for the theology of the *Aufklärung*.[38] Yet, as an analysis of the relation of his doctrine of the work of Christ, the passive nature of justifying faith and the related doctrine of the *servum arbitrium*, and the doctrine of election makes clear, Barth reproduces the main features of the *Aufklärung* soteriology. To make this point, we must begin with an analysis of Barth's Christological concentration of man's knowledge of God.

For Barth, theology is essentially an exposition of the identity and significance of Jesus Christ.[39] In effect, Barth turns the whole of theology into Christology, in that the doctrines of creation, election and redemption are considered in so far as they are determined by Christological considerations. Thus in the exposition of his doctrine of election, Barth insists that the concept must not be regarded as a theological abstraction which bears witness to the divine omni-potence. He consciously distances himself from the pronouncements of the Synod of Dort (see §24) by reinterpreting Calvin's concept of the *speculum electionis* to mean that Jesus Christ is at one and the same time the electing God and the elected man. If Christ were not the former, it would be necessary to look for the basis of election outside of Christ, and thus be driven to the doctrine of the *decretum absolutum* – which Barth considers unthinkable. Furthermore, in Jesus Christ the divine decision to become man is expressed tangibly. As there is a duality in this election, Barth feels himself able to retain the term *praedestinatio gemina*, while totally altering its traditional meaning.[40] Whereas Reformed Orthodoxy had interpreted the term to mean that God irresistibly wills some to eternal life and others to eternal death (§24), Barth argues that it refers to the divine decision to will *man* to election, salvation and life, and *God himself* to reprobation, perdition and death.[41] It is God himself who is condemned and rejected by his own judgement, and not those whom he elected in Christ. God thus chose as his own portion the negative element of the divine predestination, so that the positive element alone might be man's: in so far as predestination involves a negative verdict, that verdict is not pronounced against man.[42] In other words, although Barth concedes that predestination includes a negative element, this has no bearing upon man whatsoever.[43]

It is clear that God has elected man unilaterally (*einseitig*) and autocratically (*selbstherrlich*),[44] without any cooperation upon man's part.[45] Christ took man's place as his federal representative and substitute, so that whatever needed to be done for our salvation has been done, without man's consent or cooperation. Indeed, Barth insists upon the total inability of man to justify himself, or to cooperate with God in a significant manner with God in bringing about his salvation. For Barth, it is necessary to take a positive stand against the delusion (*Wahn*) of man's *liberum arbitrium* and cooperation with God, and to recognise that the Word of God includes a 'knowledge of the *servum arbitrium*, and the inability of man to give God his due and thus justify himself'.[46] If man is to have any say in his own justification – as the Catholic tradition within western Christianity has insisted to be the case – he must have the freedom to respond to divine grace. Barth follows the 1525 Luther (§21) and Calvin in asserting that man possesses no such freedom.[47] The freedom of man's will is totally and irreparably compromised by sin.[48] Barth's insistence upon the bondage of the human will, and his evident agreement with Calvin that faith is *res mere passiva*,[49] serve to emphasise further that man is absolutely and totally unable to make any response whatsoever to the divine initiative in justification. When this doctrine of the soteriological impotence of man is related with Barth's theology of election, an astonishing situation results.

For Barth, it is impossible for God to select man to reprobation, as we have noted above. God has already elected this element of *praedes-tinatio gemina* for himself. In so far as predestination includes a 'No!', this 'No!' is not spoken against man.[50] Man is totally unable to reject whatever God may have elected for him. This point is made by Barth repeatedly, as he emphasises the ultimate impotence of unbelief in the face of divine grace. Unbelief does not cancel God's decision to elect man. God's judgement has been executed against Christ, and will never be executed against man himself, in whose place Christ stood. Man may believe, or he may not believe – but whether he believes or not is quite irrelevant to his election. It may seem impossible for man to be elected, on account of his sin and unbelief – but in fact, precisely the opposite is the case. It is impossible for man not to be elected. As is well known, this aspect of Barth's theology has been criticised for its apocatastasian tendencies.[51] His doctrine of election, when linked with his understanding of the capacities of fallen man, necessarily leads to a doctrine of universal restoration: all men are saved, whether they know it or not, and whether they care for it or not.

With this point in mind, it will be clear that the crucial question now concerns man's knowledge of this election. Barth frequently emphasises that Christ is the *locus* of man's self-knowledge as a theological entity. Thus man only knows himself to be a sinner, and what this implies for his theological existence and status, in the light of Jesus Christ.[52] Similarly, Barth insists that man's election is disclosed to him through the *speculum electionis*, Jesus Christ. In his discussion of both the positive and negative dimensions of the death and resurrection of Christ, Barth reveals an overriding concern for the *knowledge* which results:

Im Spiegel des für uns dahingegebenen und als dieser Dahingegebene gehorsamen Jesus Christus *wird offenbar*, wer wir sind: wir als die, für die er dahingegebenen wurde, sich selbst gehorsam dahingegeben hat. Im Licht der Demut, in deren Bewährung er als wahrer Gott für uns gehandelt, d.h. gelitten hat und gestorben ist, sind wir *durchschaut, erkannt und haben wir uns selbst zu erkennen* als die Hochmütigen, die sich selbst Gott, Herr, Richter, Helfer sein wollen, die als solche von Gott abgewichen und also Sünder sind ... Und so ist und bleibt die *Erkenntnis* der Gnade Gottes und des aus ihr fließenden Trostes in diesem Urteil und also die *Erkenntnis* seines positiven Sinnes gebunden daran, daß wir nicht aufhören, uns auch als in Ihm Verurteilten *zu erkennen*.[53]

It is on the basis of the Christologically disclosed knowledge of the reconciliation of the world to God that the community of faith stands or falls:

Und gäbe es keine Erkenntnis der hier waltenden Gerechtigkeit Gottes oder Erkenntnis nur in Form von Verkennung, getrübt und entstellt durch teilweise oder gänzliche Mißverständnisse, wie könnte dann die Gemeinde dem Irrtum und Zerfall und der Glaube dem Zweifel, der Auflösung in allerlei Unglauben und Aberglauben entrinnen?[54]

The astonishingly frequent references to *Erkenntnis* and its cognates, where one might expect to find reference to *Heil* or *Versöhnung*, is one of the more remarkable aspects of Barth's discussion of man's justification *coram Deo*, suggesting that Barth regards man's knowledge and insight, rather than God's activity, as forming the centre of theological reflection. Barth's entire discussion of the justification of man appears to refer to man's epistemic situation – in other words, to his *Christologically disclosed knowledge of the Christologically determined situation*.

Barth's frequently observed emphasis upon salvation as *Erkenntnis* is easily understood: given that all men are saved eventually – which is the inevitable conclusion which must be drawn from his doctrines of election and *servum arbitrium* – the *present knowledge* of this situation is clearly of enormous importance. As all men will be saved eventually, it becomes of some importance that this salvation be actualised in the present – for such is the basic presupposition of Christian dogmatics and ethics alike. Both these disciplines are totally and absolutely dependent upon the presupposition that *man knows that he is saved*. Furthermore, in that dogmatics is a discipline which is carried out within the community of faith, it must reflect the basic presupposition upon which that community is grounded – in other words, the knowledge of its present salvation. Barth's repeated emphasis upon the cognitive character of salvation is perfectly consistent with this theology of election, in that, whatever salvation may be ultimately, it is certainly a deliverance from false thinking at present. Man may feel that all is lost, that there is no hope of salvation in a world permeated by sin and unbelief – and yet precisely the opposite is, in fact, the case. As Brunner has pointed out,[55] Barth's doctrine of election may be compared to a group of men who think that they are about to drown in a stormy sea, whereas the water is actually so shallow that there is no possibility whatsoever of drowning – this knowledge has, however, been withheld from them. What is necessary is that they be informed of the *true* situation which underlies the *apparent* situation. Thus Barth's doctrine of faith permits the believer to see beyond the sinful world of unbelief to the triumph of divine grace which lies behind it, and is disclosed in

Christ, the *speculum electionis*. As all men will be saved eventually, apparently quite independently of their inclinations or interest, it is quite natural that Barth's attention should be concentrated upon the resolution of the epistemological confusion with which the believer is faced. Christ is thus the mirror, or *locus*, in which the Christologically determined situation is disclosed to man.

With this point in mind, let us return to Martin Kähler's criticism of the soteriologies of the *Aufklärung*, Schleiermacher and the liberal school (see §35). For Kähler, a theology of the work of Christ could be classified under one of two types: the first, which corresponds to that of the *Aufklärung*, understands Christ to have communicated certain significant insights concerning an unchangeable situation; the second, which corresponds to his own view, understands Christ to be the founder of an altered situation.[56] Kähler's distinction allows two quite different approaches to the death of Christ to be identified:

1. Those which regard man's predicament as being *ignorance of the true situation*. Man *is* saved, but does not realise it: upon being informed of the true situation, he is enabled to act upon the basis of this knowledge, and adjust and reorientate his existence to what he now realises to be the true state of affairs. In so far as any alteration takes place in the situation, it is in man's subjective awareness; indeed, one could argue that the true situation is irrelevant, unless man recognises it as such – thus emphasising the necessity of being informed of it.

2. Those which regard man's predicament as being *bondage to sin or evil*. Man is enslaved, and may not realise it: upon being informed of the true situation, he still requires liberation. The knowledge of man's bondage may well lead to a recognition of the possibility of liberation, and hence the search for the means of that liberation – but such liberation is not identical with, or given simultaneously with, or even a necessary consequence of, the knowledge of man's true situation. A victory of good over evil, of grace over sin, is required, which man may appropriate and make his own, if he is to break free from the hegemony of sin – and precisely such a victory is to be had in the death of Christ upon the cross.

It is clear that Barth's understanding of the work of Christ falls into the first of these categories. For Barth and the *Aufklärer* (see §34), Christ is supremely the revealer of the knowledge of man's true situation, by which man is liberated from false understandings of his situation. For Barth, the death of Christ does not in any sense change the soteriological situation, in that this has been determined from all eternity – rather, he discloses the Christologically determined situation to man. Man's dilemma concerns his knowledge of God, rather than his bondage to sin or evil (unless these are understood in the epistemically reduced sense of 'ignorance' or 'confusion').[57]

It will therefore be clear that Barth's new emphasis upon the theocentricity of theology, and particularly his recognition of the divinity of God, is not associated with a revival in interest in the *articulus iustificationis*. Indeed, Barth operates within the same theological framework as the *Aufklärer*, Schleiermacher and the liberal school at this point, despite their evident differences at others.

§38 Justification as a hermeneutical principle

Barth is the last major theologian to be discussed in the present study. This is not to say that justification has ceased to be of theological significance in the last decades, but reflects the fact that sufficient time has not elapsed to establish a proper historical perspective, with reference to which the significance of more recent developments may be judged. In this concluding section, we propose merely to indicate the general features of more recent developments, which are particularly associated with the recognition of the doctrine of justification as a hermeneutical principle. Another generation will have to pass judgement upon their significance, in the light of subsequent developments.

The development of the doctrine of justification within the Christian tradition may be regarded as a systematic engagement with four major questions concerning the church's proclamation of the justification of sinful man.

1. How is the concept of the 'justification of the ungodly' to be understood?
2. How is the 'justification of the ungodly' possible?
3. In what sense is the proclamation of the 'justification of the ungodly' relevant?
4. How may the proclamation of the 'justification of the ungodly' be established as a legitimate and necessary interpretation of the history of Jesus of Nazareth?

The development of the doctrine in the pre-modern period (that is, to about 1700) may be regarded as a systematic engagement with the first two such questions.[1] As the present chapter has indicated, the modern period was not totally unconcerned with these questions (see §34), but nevertheless found itself increasingly forced to consider the two latter such questions. The rise of increasingly sophisticated methods of biblical criticism led to the suggestion, increasingly voiced during the later nineteenth century, that there existed a radical disjuncture between the preaching of Jesus and Paul, so that the doctrine of justification represented a gross distortion of the essentially simple message of Jesus.[2] In the late nineteenth century, liberal theologians such as Schweitzer, Wernle and Wrede argued that the Pauline doctrine of justification by faith was of purely historical interest, being an aspect of Paul's anti-Jewish polemic rather than the positive proclamation of a universal theology of redemption. The rise of European secularism in the aftermath of the First World War led to increased scepticism concerning the relevance of God to 'modern emancipated man',[3] with a consequent decline in the perceived significance of Luther's celebrated question concerning the quest for a gracious God.[4] Whereas earlier generations of theologians were primarily concerned with the exposition and analysis of the church's proclamation of the divine justification of sinful man, Western theologians of the present century have found themselves increasingly obliged to defend its relevance and legitimacy in the face of fundamental challenges to both.

In response to the first challenge, the present century has witnessed a growing tendency to relate the doctrine of justification to the question of the meaning of human existence, rather than the more restricted sphere of man's justification *coram Deo*.[5] It is this trend which underlies the existentialist reinterpretation of the doctrine, associated with Bultmann, Tillich and Ebeling, to which we now turn.

In his highly influential *Sein und Zeit* (1927), Martin Heidegger employed the phenomenological method of Husserl to develop an existential understanding of the structures of human existence.[6] Arguing that the basic meaning of *Existenz* derives from *ex-sistere*, 'to stand outside', Heidegger characterised man's existence in terms of his ability to stand outside the world of things. What is it that distinguishes the existence of man from that of inanimate objects? Heidegger argues that there are three fundamental senses in which man's peculiar way of being (*Dasein*) may be distinguished from that of things (*Vorhandenheit*).[7]

1. Man transcends the subject–object relationship, in that he is at one and the same time both subject and object to himself. He has the unique ability to reflect upon his nature, to understand himself, and to be open to himself in his being. He may properly be said to be at

one with himself, or at war with himself, in that his relation to *Dasein* is open and alterable.

2. Human existence must be regarded as open-ended, in that man is never fixed or complete in his being. In other words, it is to be understood in terms of possibility, rather than actuality.

3. Human existence must be regarded as individual. Heidegger lays emphasis upon the 'individuality' (*Jemeinigkeit*) of exitence, which cannot be separated from the individual in question.

Like Kierkegaard, Heidegger is concerned with man in his subjectivity.[8] Whereas the traditional approach to questions of existence involved an ontic inquiry concerning entities (*das Seiende*), Heidegger argues that the question should be approached from an ontological perspective, inquiring concerning 'Being' (*Sein*) itself.

Although it is clear that Heidegger's analysis of human existence in general is of considerable potential theological significance,[9] the aspect of his analysis which is of particular relevance to our study is his distinction between authentic (*eigentlich*) and inauthentic (*ineigentlich*) existence.[10] Man exists in the world, which defines the arena within which he is confronted with the various possibilities open to him. Man is in the world, and is bound up with its existence, even though he is quite distinct from its way of being. The possibility that man will be overwhelmed by the way of being which the world represents, and thus 'fall' from an authentic to an inauthentic mode of existence, is an essential element of Heidegger's analysis of existence. Man may fall away (*abfallen*) from himself, obliterating his awareness of the essential distinction from the world by becoming absorbed in it, and thus becoming 'uprooted' (*entwurzelt*) from his proper way of being.[11] Man thus becomes alienated from his true existence through his fall into the world.[12] Although it is tempting to equate *Verfallenheit* directly with the theological concept of original sin, it is clear that Heidegger maintains that fallenness and alienation are merely existential *possibilities open to man*, rather than a normative definition of human existence.

The relevance of this existential analysis of human existence to the Christian theology of justification was indicated by Heidegger himself, who pointed out that Luther's doctrine of justification, especially when considered in relation to the question of the assurance of salvation, could be interpreted in existentialist categories.[13] Although critics have subsequently pointed out that Luther is primarily concerned with the justification of man *coram Deo*, rather than the self-justification of man in his particular existential situation,[14] it is this understanding of the significance of the doctrine of justification which achieved considerable influence through the works of Bultmann and Tillich.

For Bultmann, the New Testament is concerned with the fundamental question of the nature of human existence. The Christian kerygma, expressed in mythical form in the New Testament, is a divine word addressed directly to man, revealing that his present state of existence is inauthentic, and making known the possibility of authentic existence through the Christ-event, upon condition of the decision (*Entscheidung*) of faith.[15] Man is a 'potentiality to be' (*ein Sein-Können*), whose innate potentiality for authentic existence is exposed and developed by the kerygma. The Pauline concept of justification by faith thus concerns a fundamental aspect of human existence. In man's decision of faith, in response to the kerygma, he attains his authentic self (*sein eigentliches Sein*).[16] Although Bultmann was criticised for his use of Heidegger's analysis of human existence, in that it appeared to reduce the gospel to an analysis of the condition of natural man,[17] Bultmann argued that the specifically Christian answer to the question of how authentic existence might be attained served to distinguish the gospel from secular understandings of human existence.[18]

A similar existential interpretation of the doctrine of justification is associated with Paul Tillich. In an important essay of 1924, Tillich noted that the doctrine of justification applied not merely to the religious aspects of moral life, but also to the intellectual life of religion, in that it is not merely the *sinner*, but also the *doubter*, who is justified by faith.[19] Tillich thus extends the scope of the doctrine to the universal human situation of despair and doubt concerning the meaning of existence. Tillich thus argues that the doctrine of justification, when rightly understood, lies at the heart of the Christian faith.[20] While nineteenth-century man was characterised by his idealism, his twentieth-century counterpart is characterised by existential despair and anxiety – and it is to this latter man that the Christian message must be made relevant. Tillich attempts this task by the 'method of correlation', by which the Christian proclamation is 'correlated' with the existential questions arising from human existence.[21] For Tillich, the doctrine of justification addresses a genuine human need: man must learn to accept that he is accepted, despite being unacceptable.[22]

Similarly, Gerhard Ebeling argues that the concept of 'justification' is as strange to modern man 'as an Egyptian sphinx', and argues that the concept must be demythologised and interpreted in order that it may be shown to have an essential connection with human existence and its problems.[23] For Ebeling, in the event of justification, a fundamental change in man's situation takes place, by which he is transferred from the state of non-existence (*Nichtsein*) to that of authentic existence (*Sein*).[24] Although Ebeling's approach to the doctrine may appear to parallel that of Bultmann or Tillich, Ebeling has gone far beyond them in drawing attention to the hermeneutical insights which lay at the basis of Luther's doctrine of justification *sola fide*, thus clarifying the nature of the doctrine as a critical principle in judging thought and practice. According to Ebeling, the central point of the Christian faith is that the proclamation of the grace of God in word and sacrament is itself the saving event, in that it proclaims the death and resurrection of Christ, and thence effects what it proclaims.

On the basis of this analysis, it will be clear that there has been a growing tendency to treat the doctrine of justification as an hermeneutical principle for interpreting, and subsequently transforming, human existence. As a result, there has been a corresponding increased emphasis upon both the subjective or anthropological dimension of the doctrine, as well as upon the proclamation which brings about this existential transformation of the human situation.[25] This increased emphasis upon the rôle of the kerygma, or the Word of God, evidently raises the question of the legitimation of the kerygma – in other words, whether the soteriological or existential interpretation placed upon the history of Jesus of Nazareth by the Christian church, and expressed in the doctrine of justification, is justifiable. Lying behind the kerygma of the justification of the ungodly is the problem of the justification of the kerygma itself.

This problem is particularly linked with the question of the relation between the preaching of Jesus and the proclamation of Paul – in other words, the question of how a legitimate and theologically coherent account may be given of the transition from the preaching of Jesus to the proclamation about Jesus. The *Aufklärer* suggested that the Pauline interpretation of Jesus (expressed in the doctrine of justification) was an improper and unnecessary dogmatic transformation of what was originally an essentially ethical proclamation. The rise of the 'New Quest of the Historical Jesus' since 1953 has, however, been based upon the explicitly acknowledged presupposition that there is an essential continuity between the history of Jesus of Nazareth and the proclamation of Christ.[26] In the Christian proclamation, the proclaimer himself becomes the proclaimed, as the one who calls to faith becomes the one who is believed. It may therefore be argued that the proclamation of the justification of the ungodly is an historically and theologically legitimate interpretation of the significance of the history of Jesus of Nazareth.[27] A further refinement of this development is the argument that it is axiomatic that there is an essential continuity between the 'Jesus of history' and the 'Christ of faith', so that the *articulus iustificationis* is treated as the axiomatic foundation of the Christian faith.[28]

It will thus be evident that the twentieth century has not witnessed a general abandonment of the doctrine of justification, but rather the discussion of aspects of the doctrine which were taken for granted by earlier generations. The difficulties which contemporary western theologians have been obliged to consider were not envisaged in the pre-modern period. Although the church continues to proclaim the justification of man through the free grace of God, and although this message continues to find a response in those to whom it is addressed, there has been growing recognition of the need to establish and defend the relevance and legitimacy of this proclamation in the first place.

Our attention now turns to the development of the 'new perspective on Paul', which has called into question some of the traditional notions concerning justification, especially those inherited from the Lutheran wing of the Reformation.

§39 Justification in recent Pauline scholarship

Since the time of the Reformation in the sixteenth century, considerable attention has been paid to the theme of justification as it is stated in the writings of Paul. For Martin Luther, as we have seen, the doctrine of justification was not merely the centre and focus of Paul's thought; it was the 'article by which the church stands or falls', the touchstone and heartbeat of all Christian theology and spirituality (§21). That judgement has, however, been subject to intense scrutiny over the last two centuries. Recent discussion of Paul's understanding of justification have tended to focus on a number of major themes, each of which merits careful attention. These issues are:

1. The meaning of the term 'justification' within the Pauline corpus.
2. The relation of Paul's thought to that of contemporary Judaism,

centring on the issues raised by the leading Pauline scholar E. P. Sanders.

3. Paul's understanding of the term 'the righteousness of God'.
4. The relation between faith and works in Paul's thought.
5. The significance of the concept of justification within Paul's thought.

In this present section of the work, we shall explore and explain the present state of scholarly research on these questions. We begin by considering recent discussions of what Paul means by the term 'justification', and how this differs from related terms such as 'sanctification' and 'salvation'.

1 The meaning of the term 'justification'

The Pauline vocabulary relating to justification is grounded in the Old Testament, and seems to express the notion of 'rightness' or 'rectitude' rather than 'righteousness'. The Old Testament prefers the verb, rather than the noun, presumably thereby indicating that justification results from an action of God, whereby an individual is set in a right relationship with God – that is, vindicated, or declared to be in the right. Paul echoes this emphasis, using the verb 'to justify' relatively often, but generally avoiding using the noun 'justification' (Romans 4.25). The verb denotes God's powerful, cosmic and universal action in effecting a change in the situation between sinful humanity and God, by which God is able to acquit and vindicate believers, setting them in a right and faithful relation to him.

One recent interpretation (K. Donfried) has suggested that the key Pauline concepts of justification, sanctification and salvation may be accommodated within a neat past-present-future framework, as follows:[1]

justification:	a past event, with present implications (sanctification);
sanctification:	a present event, dependent upon a past event (justification), which has future implications (salvation);
salvation:	a future event, already anticipated and partially experienced in the past event of justification and the present event of sanctification, and dependent upon them.

Despite its neatness, this approach seems inadequate. For

example, within the Pauline corpus, justification has future, as well as past, reference (Romans 2.13; 8.33; Galatians 5.4–5), and appears to relate to both the beginning of the Christian life and its final consummation. Similarly, sanctification can also refer to a past event (1 Corinthians 6.11), or a future event (1 Thessalonians 5.23). And salvation is an exceptionally complex idea, embracing not simply a future event, but something which has happened in the past (Romans 8.24; 1 Corinthians 15.2), or which is taking place now (1 Corinthians 1.18).

It is important to note that not all Paul's statements regarding justification are specifically linked with the theme of faith. A. J. Hultgen has pointed out that the statements appear to fall into two general categories:[2] those set in strongly theocentric contexts, referring to God's cosmic and universal action in relation to human sin; and those making reference to faith, which identify the identity of the people of God. This is perhaps best regarded as a difference of emphasis, rather than substance. In its universal sense, justification seems to underlie Paul's argument for the universality of the gospel; there is no distinction between Jews and Gentiles. But in its more restricted sense, justification is concerned with the identification of the Christian church, and the basis of its membership.

Justification language appears in Paul with reference to both the inauguration of the life of faith, and also its final consummation. It is a complex and all-embracing notion, which anticipates the verdict of the final judgement (Romans 8:30–4), declaring in advance the verdict of ultimate acquittal. The believer's present justified Christian existence is thus an anticipation and advance participation of deliverance from the wrath to come, and an assurance in the present of the final eschatological verdict of acquittal (Romans 5.9–10).

2 The relation of Paul's thought to that of contemporary Judaism

In recent years, a considerable debate on the relation of Paul's views on justification to those of first-century Judaism has developed, centring upon the writings of E. P. Sanders. The 'new perspective' on Paul can be argued to have been stated earlier in the writings of G. F. Moore; nevertheless, its full development is particularly associated with Sanders, especially his major work *Paul and Palestinian Judaism* (1977), which was followed several years later by the more important *Paul, the Law and the Jewish People* (1983). Sanders' work represents a demand for a complete reappraisal of existing understandings of Paul's relation to the Judaism of his time. Sanders noted that Paul has too often been read through Lutheran eyes. According to the Lutheran interpretation of Paul (which, in marked contrast to the reformed standpoint, linked with Bullinger and Calvin, stresses the divergence between the law and the gospel), Luther argued that Paul criticised a totally misguided attempt on the part of Jewish legalists to find favour and acceptance in the sight of God, by earning righteousness through performing works of the law. This view, Sanders argued, coloured the analysis of such Lutheran writings as Käsemann and Bultmann. These scholars, perhaps unwittingly, read Paul through Lutheran spectacles, and thus failed to realise that Paul had to be read against his proper historical context in first-century Judaism.[3]

According to Sanders, Palestinian Judaism at the time of Paul could be characterised as a form of 'covenantal nomism'. The law is to be regarded as an expression of the covenant between God and Israel, and is intended to spell out as clearly and precisely as possible what forms of human conduct are appropriate within the context of this covenant. Righteousness is thus defined as behaviour or attitudes which are consistent with being the historical covenant people of God. 'Works of the law' are thus not understood (as Luther suggested) as the means by which Jews believed they could gain access to the covenant; for they already stood within it. Rather, these works are an expression of the fact that the Jews already belonged to the covenant people of God, and were living out their obligations to that covenant.

Sanders rejects the opinion that 'the righteousness which comes from the law' is 'a meritorious achievement which allows one to demand reward from God and is thus a denial of grace'. 'Works of the law' were understood as the basis not of entry to the covenant, but of maintaining that covenant. As Sanders puts it, 'works are the condition of remaining "in", but they do not earn salvation'. If Sanders is right, the basic features of Luther's interpretation of Paul are incorrect, and require radical revision.

So what, then, is Paul's understanding of the difference between Judaism and Christianity, according to Sanders? Having argued that Jews never believed in salvation on account of works or unaided human effort, what does Sanders see as providing the distinctive advantage of Christianity over and against Judaism? Having argued that it is not correct to see Judaism as a religion of merit and Christianity as a religion of grace, Sanders argues that Judaism sees the hope of the Jewish people for salvation as resting upon 'their status as God's covenant people who possess the law', whereas Christians believe in 'a better righteousness based solely upon believing participation in Christ'. Paul, like Judaism, was concerned with the issue of entering into and remaining within the covenant. The basic difference is Paul's declaration that the Jews have no national charter of privilege; membership of the covenant is open to all who have faith in Christ, and who thus stand in continuity with Abraham (Romans 4).

Sanders' analysis is important, not least in that it forces us to ask hard questions about Paul's relation to his Jewish background, and the relation between the idea of participating in Christ and justification. (Interestingly, both Martin Luther and John Calvin made the notion of participating in Christ of central importance to their doctrines of justification, Calvin to the point of making justification the consequence of such participation.) But is he right? The debate over this matter continues, and is likely to go on for some time. But the following points seem to be sufficiently well established to note here.

First, Sanders is rather vague about why Paul is convinced of the superiority of Christianity over Judaism. Judaism is presented as being wrong, simply because it is not Christianity. They are different dispensations of the same covenant. But, for many of Sanders' critics (e.g., R. Gundry), Paul seems to regard Christianity as far more than some kind of dispensational shift within Judaism; salvation-history does not account for all that Paul says, much less for the passion with which he says it.[4]

Second, Sanders suggests that both Paul and Judaism regard works as the principle of continuing in salvation through the covenant. Yet Paul appears to regard good works as evidential, rather than instrumental. In other words, they are demonstration of the fact that the believer stands within the covenant, rather than instrumental in maintaining him within that covenant. One enters within the sphere of the covenant through faith. There is a radical new element here, which does not fit in as easily with existing Jewish ideas as Sanders seems to imply. Sanders may well be right in suggesting that good works are both a *condition for* and a *sign of* remaining within the covenant. Paul, however, sees faith as the necessary and sufficient condition for and sign of being in the covenant, with works (at best) a sign of remaining within its bounds.

Third, Sanders tends to regard Paul's doctrine of justification in a slightly negative light, as posing a challenge to the notion of a national ethic election. In other words, Paul's doctrine of justification is a subtle challenge to the notion that Israel has special religious rights on account of its national identity. However, N. T. Wright has argued that Paul's doctrine of justification should be viewed positively, as an attempt to redefine who comes within the ambit of the promises made by God to Abraham (see the related idea in J. D. G. Dunn). Paul's teaching on justification by faith is thus seen as Paul's redefinition of how the inheritance of Abraham genuinely embraces the Gentiles apart from the law.

3 Paul's understanding of the 'righteousness of God'

There is a close semantic connection between the terms 'justification (*dikaiosis*)' and 'righteousness (*dikaiosune*)' in Paul's thought. The idea of the revelation of the righteousness of God is obviously of major importance to Paul's conception of the gospel (e.g., Romans 1.16–17). As we have seen (§6), there is a distinguished history of interpretation of this term within the western Christian tradition. Augustine of Hippo argued that 'the righteousness of God' did not refer to the personal righteousness of God (in other words, the righteousness by which God is himself righteous), but to the righteousness which he bestows upon sinners, in order to justify them (in other words, the righteousness which comes from God). This interpretation of the phrase seems to have dominated the western theological tradition until the fourteenth century, when writers such as Gabriel Biel began to reinterpret it in terms of 'the righteousness by which God is himself righteous' – an interpretation which led to Luther's sustained engagement with the issue around 1515 (§20). Such an understanding of the nature of the righteousness of God has continued to find service in the modern period, especially on the part of Lutheran interpreters of Paul. Two such interpreters may be considered in detail – R. Bultmann and E. Käsemann.

Bultmann, basing himself especially on Romans 10.3 and Philippians 3.9, argued that the 'righteousness of God' was not a moral, but a relational, term. The believer is counted as being righteous, on account of his or her faith. The term 'righteousness of God' represents a genitive of authorship. Whereas Judaism regarded the bestowal of this righteousness as part and parcel of the future eschatological hope, something which would happen at the end of history, Bultmann argues that Paul is declaring that this righteousness is imputed to believers in the present time, through faith.

E. Käsemann subjected Bultmann's interpretation to a penetrating criticism, on a number of grounds. First, he argued that Bultmann had fallen into the trap of a radical individualism, based on his anthropocentric approach to theology. Bultmann was mainly concerned with questions of human existence; he ought, according to Käsemann, to have concentrated on the purpose of God. Furthermore, by interpreting 'the righteousness of God' as a genitive of authorship, Bultmann had managed to drive a wedge between the God who gives and the gift which is given. Bultmann's approach isolates the gift from the giver, and concentrates upon the gift itself, rather than God himself. Käsemann comments thus: 'The Gift can never be separated from the Giver; it participates in the power of God, since God steps on to the scene in the gift.'

This lack of balance could be recovered by understanding 'righteousness' as referring to God himself, rather than to that which he gives. Käsemann then argues that the 'righteousness of God' refers to God in action. It refers to both his power, and to his gift. (Strictly speaking, then, Käsemann is not treating the 'righteousness of God' as a statement about God's attributes, but as a reference to God in action.) A cluster of phrases may help convey the sort of things that Käsemann has in mind here: 'salvation-creating power'; 'a transformation of [our] existence'; 'the power-character of the Gift'; 'a change of Lordship'. The basic theme that recurs throughout Käsemann's discussion is that of God's saving power and action, revealed eschatologically in Jesus Christ. It merges a number of central Pauline themes, including those of victory through Christ, God's faithfulness to his covenant, and his giving of himself in power and action.[5]

Käsemann's approach has been very influential in recent years, both positively and negatively. Basing himself on Käsemann, P. Stuhlmacher argues that it is unacceptable to treat the 'righteousness of God' as if it were a purely theocentric notion or an exclusively anthropocentric idea. It brings together elements of both, as the embodiment of the saving action of God in Christ, which brings new life for believers in its wake. The righteousness of

God is both demonstrated and seen in action in the redemptive event of Christ – both in terms of God's faithfulness to his covenant, and in terms of the salvific transformation of the believer.[6]

A much more critical approach is adopted by the Swedish writer K. Stendahl,[7] who argued that Käsemann had neglected the importance of salvation-history (often referred to in its German form, *Heilsgeschichte*) in his analysis. In fact, Stendahl suggests that Käsemann has virtually lost sight of the fact that Paul locates the event of justification in a specific historical context – namely, the history of God's dealings with his people, Israel. There is every danger that Käsemann's approach could lead to some kind of unhistorical mysticism, by failing to see that Paul discusses justification within the context of 'reflection on God's plan for the world'. Drawing on a series of passages (most significantly, Romans 9–11), Stendahl argues that Paul seems far more interested in the way in which God enables salvation to come about through history (above all, through the history of Israel), rather than with the abstract idea of justification by faith.

Once more, an important debate is still under way, and has yet to be resolved. J. Reumann suggests that four main lines of interpretation of the 'righteousness of God' may be discerned, along with their respective champions, as follows:[8]

1. An objective genitive: 'a righteousness which is valid before God' (Luther).

2. A subjective genitive: 'righteousness as an attribute or quality of God' (Käsemann).

3. A genitive of authorship: 'a righteousness that goes forth from God' (Bultmann).

4. A genitive of origin: 'man's righteous status which is the result of God's action of justifying' (Cranfield).

However, there is a general consensus on one point of major importance, which needs to be emphasized. *The 'righteousness of God' is not a moral concept.* Rather, it represents a profound statement about the relevance of God for the human situation. Especially in popular circles, there is often a disturbing tendency to use Pauline texts to construct a picture of God as some kind of moral rigorist, and thus impose human conceptions of righteousness upon God. If Pauline exegesis has achieved anything, it is to remind us of the need to interpret Pauline phrases within their proper context, rather than impose 'self-evident' interpretations upon them.

4 The relation between faith and works

A long and distinguished tradition of interpretation within Protestant Pauline scholarship, drawing its inspiration largely from Martin Luther in the sixteenth century (§§21–2), has argued for an absolute contradiction between justification by faith and human works in the Pauline corpus. These are to be seen as mutually exclusive entities, designating two radically opposed ways of thinking about, and responding to, God. The way of works is seen as orientated towards human achievement, centred upon human righteousness, and based upon human merit. The way of faith is seen as radically opposed, orientated towards God's achievement in Christ, centred upon the righteousness of God, and based upon divine grace.

Yet this is now generally recognised to be an inadequate understanding of a complex aspect of Paul's understanding of justification, which fails to do justice to the highly nuanced understanding of the relation of faith and works within Paul's thought, most notably expressed in the terse statement that 'not the hearers, but the doers of the law will be justified' (Romans 2.13). Some (e.g., R. Bultmann) have sought to dismiss this as a vestige of Paul's Jewish phase. But this just will not work.

Perhaps the most important issue to emerge from recent Pauline interpretation concerning their relation centres on clarifying the relation between Paul's theme of 'justification by faith' and 'judgement by works'. There seems to be an apparent contradiction here, the resolution of which is made considerably more difficult by the fact that Paul can speak of this future judgement both negatively (as a warning against disobedience) and positively (as an encouragement for obedience). E. P. Sanders argues that Paul reproduces a characteristic first-century Jewish attitude, which could be summarised in the words 'God judges according to their deeds those whom he saves by his grace.' Justification by faith resonates with the theme of grace – so why are believers going to be judged on the basis of our works (e.g., Romans 2.12; 14.10; 1 Corinthians 3.15; 2 Corinthians 5.10), which resonates with the theme of human achievement? But this statement of the problem fails to deal with the fact that justification is not seen as something in the past, but as something with future reference (Romans 2.13, 8.33; Galatians 5.4–5). It is not simply a case of being justified in the past, and judged in the future; there is a 'not yet' element to

Paul's teaching on justification, which Sanders cannot quite explain.

One possible explanation of the way in which justification and future judgement are related involves an enhanced sensitivity towards the different contexts which the Pauline letters presuppose (N. M. Watson).[9] Paul's message of justification is directed towards audiences with very different backgrounds. The one doctrine finds itself applied practically for very different ends. The Corinthians appeared to be living in a state of delusion and spiritual arrogance; Paul's objective is to break down their arrogance by warning them of judgement. Paul does not intend the message of judgement to be his last word, but rather the word they need to hear so long as they remain unaware of the full implications of the gospel. On the other hand, those who exist in a state of spiritual dejection or discouragement need reassurance of the unconditionality of grace. If this approach is correct, it implies that the theme of judgement by works is not Paul's final word to his audience; it is his penultimate word, determined by the pastoral situation of his audience, and intended to shake up those who exploit (and thus distort) the gospel proclamation of grace. Yet the idea of a 'penultimate' word raises certain difficulties, not least over how one might be reassured that it is indeed God's penultimate (and not final) word.

Perhaps the simplest approach to the problem has the most to commend it. In one of his earliest writings, Paul uses the enormously important phrase 'works of faith' (1 Thessalonians 1.3). This would most naturally be understood as implying a genitive of origin – that is, 'works which come from faith'. Faith is such that it does not produce merely obedience (Romans 1.5 speaks of the 'obedience of faith' – that is, assuming a genitive of origin, the obedience which comes from faith), but also activity. Believers are thus justified on the basis of faith, seen not as a human work or merit, but as an expression and result of the grace of God. And believers are judged on the basis of our works, seen as the natural outcome, result and expression of justifying faith. Believers are justified by faith, and judged by its fruit. There is thus a strong connection between the past and future elements of justification – embracing faith and its outworking. Works are the visible demonstration of a real and justifying faith – not the dead faith of which James complained (James 2.14–24). And so these two moments of justification coinhere.

5 The importance of justification to Paul's thought

The question of the precise rôle of the concept of justification to Paul's understanding of the gospel remains intensely controversial within modern Pauline scholarship. Luther, as is well known, regarded it as central. While some modern writers have endorsed Luther's judgement, others have been more critical, seeing the centre of gravity of Paul's thought as lying elsewhere. It is actually quite difficult to identify a centre to Paul's thought, not least because there is disagreement among scholars as to what the idea of a 'centre' actually means. A principle of coherence? A summarising principle? A criterion of authenticity? These difficulties stand in the path of any attempt to reach agreement on the importance of justification to Paul's thought.

Nevertheless, three broad positions may be discerned within recent scholarship on this question.[10]

(a) Justification by faith is of central importance to Paul's conception of Christianity (H. Bornkamm, E. Conzelmann, E. Käsemann and K. Kertelge). As noted above, this position has strong historical associations with Martin Luther, and it is perhaps not surprising that it is echoed by many modern German Lutheran New Testament scholars. This school of thought tends to regard justification as the real theological centre of gravity within Paul's thought, and is critical of any attempt to treat it as being of lesser importance. Justification by faith is not simply concerned with clarifying the Christian gospel in relation to first-century Judaism; it addresses the fundamental question of how sinful human beings can find favour or acceptance in the sight of a righteous God.

Nevertheless, differences can be discerned within this broad approach. For example, Bultmann adopts what is recognisably a Lutheran position, stressing the positive importance of faith, while at the same time interpreting Paul's 'justification' language in existentialist terms. On the other hand, C. E. B. Cranfield takes a more Reformed position on this matter, noting the continuing importance of the law for Paul.[11]

(b) Justification by faith is a 'subsidiary crater' (A. Schweitzer) in Paul's overall presentation and understanding of the Christian gospel. The origins of this view may be traced back to the nineteenth century, especially the writings of W. Wrede. Wrede argued that justification by faith was simply a polemical doctrine, designed to neutralise the theological threat posed by Judaism. Having neutralised this threat, Paul was then able to develop the positive aspects of his own thought (which, for Wrede, centred on the idea of redemption in Christ). The real emphasis of Paul's thought thus lies elsewhere than justification. Among those who adopt this position, the following may be noted (along with their views on where the centre of Paul's thought really lies): A. Schweitzer (the rising and dying of the believer with Christ), R. P. Martin (reconciliation with God), and E. P. Sanders (believing participation in Christ).

(c) A third view may be regarded as a compromise between these two views. Justification by faith is regarded as one of a number of ways of thinking about, or visualising, what God has achieved for believers in and through Christ (J. Jeremias). The centre of Paul's thought does not lie with justification as such; rather it lies with the grace of God. But justification is one of a number of ways of describing this grace (in juridical terms of unconditional pardon and forgiveness). It is thus central in one sense (in that it is a way of expressing the core of the gospel), and not central in another (in that it is only one way, among others, of expressing this core).

This debate seems set to continue, and it is not clear whether there is any hope of a genuine consensus. It is perhaps worth noting that it is genuinely difficult to classify some approaches to Paul's theology in terms of this neat framework. Nevertheless, both the first and second positions continue to attract supporters, and this debate is likely to continue, and be both productive and interesting, for some considerable time to come. The last word has yet to be spoken on this issue.

Much the same can be said about the ecumenical dialogue between Protestants and Roman Catholics on the issue of justification, to which we now turn.

§40 Justification in recent ecumenical debates

It will be clear from the analysis set out earlier in this volume that the doctrine of justification is of major importance to the fissures which opened up within the western church during the sixteenth century. The question of whether the historical divisions which are associated with the doctrine can be overcome is of more than theoretical importance, and has come to the fore in the last few decades. One of the most important developments within Christianity since the Second World War has been the rise of the ecumenical movement, with its willingness to discuss past divisions with a view to overcoming them, to whatever extent this may be possible. The new open relationship between the Roman Catholic and Protestant churches may partly be explained on the basis of the progressive attitudes adopted at the Second Vatican Council (1962–5), although it is likely that the social factors which lessened the tension between the churches in western liberal democracies must be taken into consideration in this matter as well.

The new willingness on the part of Roman Catholic theologians to discuss the controverted issue of justification is widely thought to have been stimulated by an early work of the Swiss theologian Hans Küng. In his major study *Justification*[1] (German edition, 1957; English translation, 1964), Küng compared the views of Karl Barth with those of the Council of Trent, and argued that there was fundamental agreement between the position of Barth and that of the Roman Catholic church, seen in its totality.[2] This conclusion was the cause of some surprise at the time (1957), as well as a certain degree of uncritical optimism concerning its significance. A more reliable judgement of the significance of Küng's work would be that he demonstrates that, if the Council of Trent is interpreted in a Thomist sense (rather than a Franciscan sense), and if certain aspects of Barth's doctrine of justification are overlooked, a significant degree of convergence between Trent and Barth emerges.[3]

As has been indicated, Küng's work is open to criticism on a number of points. For example, Küng is perhaps somewhat unduly selective in those aspects of Barth's theology of justification which he chooses to expound. The obvious differences between Barth and Trent on the question of the freedom of the will and the nature of election are not touched upon by Küng, whereas they clearly require attention. Furthermore, Küng does not interpret the Tridentine decree on justification in terms of its historical context, and thus presents one interpretation of Trent – not surprisingly, that approximating most closely to the views of Barth – as *the* Tridentine doctrine of justification. This point is of particular importance in relation to Trent's teaching on merit, as we noted earlier (§28). Küng represents Trent as teaching 'no merit whatsoever prior to justification', which is questionable (in that it overlooks the role played by the concept of congruous merit). Additionally, Küng fails to consider the implications of the post-Tridentine debates on justification for a contemporary Roman Catholic understanding of justification (§29).

Despite such criticisms, Küng's book may be regarded as having initiated the ecumenical discussion of justification, indicating that at least some degree of agreement on the doctrine of justification could be reached between Roman Catholics and Protestants. It is, of course, true that Küng deals primarily with sixteenth-century *misunderstandings* rather than with sixteenth-century *disagreements*, with the result that he does little more than demonstrate that Roman Catholics and Protestants share a common Christocentric anti-Pelagian theology of justification: this achievement, however, did much to highlight the misconceptions which abounded on both the Protestant and Roman Catholic sides concerning the other's teachings on the matter, and pointed ahead to the possibility of a sustained discussion of the doctrine by ecumenical commissions. It is no exaggeration to suggest that Küng's book marked the dawn of a new era of positive ecumenical discussion of a doctrine which had hitherto been seen largely as an insuperable obstacle to such dialogue. In a period of two decades (1970–89), a significant number of such dialogues took place, of which we shall note only two: the dialogue between Roman Catholics and Lutherans on the one hand, and between Roman Catholics and Anglicans on the other.

In 1972 the Joint Study Commission of the Lutheran World Federation and the Vatican Secretariat for Promoting Christian Unity published the document now generally known as the 'Malta Report'.[4] This Commission noted a developing ecumenical consensus on the doctrine of justification. This development underlies the important discussion, begun in 1978, between Lutheran and Roman Catholic theologians in the United States, which led to the publication of the most significant ecumenical document to date on the doctrine of justification.

On 30 September 1983, the US Lutheran–Roman Catholic dialogue group released a 24,000 word document which represented the fruit of six years of discussions on the doctrine of justification. This document, entitled *Justification by Faith*,[5] is by far the most important ecumenical document to deal with the theme of justification to date, and represents a landmark in ecumenical discussions. Anyone who wishes to deal with the dialogue between Protestant and Roman Catholic theologians on justification will have to make this document his point of departure. Its 218 footnotes, which distil the learning underlying this document and its associated volume *Righteousness in the New Testament*,[6] serve two purposes: first, to allow the most recent scholarly insights to be brought into the service of ecumenical dialogue; second, to convince the critical reader of the theological and historical competence of the dialogue group. In both these objectives, a notable degree of success is achieved. The document consists of a thorough analysis of the historical development of the doctrine, along with a careful assessment of the nature and significance of the controverted issues between Lutherans and Roman Catholics.

The document begins by dealing with the history of the question. A careful study of the development of the doctrine prior to the sixteenth century allows the most recent scholarly insights into crucial historico-theological questions (such as the nature of the Pelagian controversy) to be brought to bear on their discussions. This is followed by a particularly comprehensive, competent and insightful account of the sixteenth-century debates on justification, in which the points at issue between Lutheranism and the Council of Trent are identified and analysed. 'Lutheranism' tends to be defined with reference to the Formula of Concord, facilitating the harmonisation of Lutheran and Tridentine views: Luther was perhaps too close to Calvin and Reformed Orthodoxy in his teaching on justification to function as a basis of such harmonisation. Nevertheless, the document's treatment of Luther is fair, in relation both to his thought and the historical context in which his reforming programme was set.

This is followed by an analysis of developments after the sixteenth century, including excellent summaries of the relevance of Jansenism, Baianism, Pietism, Vatican II, and the particularly important discussions of the Helsinki Assembly of the Lutheran World Federation (1963). By the end of this historical analysis, the critical reader will almost certainly be persuaded that the contributors to this document are competent and informed, so that it is with some confidence that he turns to the crucial section dealing with theological reflections and interpretation, in which the contemporary relevance of the historical course of the great Reformation controversies is evaluated. This is a particularly fine attempt to come to terms with the historical memories of these two great traditions, and, indeed, ought to serve as a model for contemporary ecumenical theological reflection on past differences. Six areas of *convergence* (note the decision not to use the term 'agreement') are noted, concerning the forensic nature of justification, the sinfulness of the justified, the sufficiency of faith, the concepts of merit and satisfaction, and criteria of authenticity. In these areas, the dialogue group notes that, despite differing theological perspectives and structures of thought, similar concerns and foundational beliefs can be discerned as lying beneath the specific doctrinal formulations of each church. The final section of the document then considers perspectives for reconstruction. It affirms a 'fundamental consensus on the gospel', which is reached through extensive engagement with the appropriate texts in the light of the best New Testament scholarship, both Lutheran and Roman Catholic – and the convergences which have become evident in this scholarship of late are thus harnessed to considerable ecumenical advantage.

It is important to note that the sixteenth-century controversies between Protestants and Roman Catholics over the issue of justification were of two broad types: those which rested upon *misunderstandings* (most notably, those reflecting different understandings of what the term 'justification' meant) and those which reflected *genuine disagreements* (especially over issues such as assurance and the formal cause of justification). This document addresses both these matters. Misunderstandings are resolved through positive statements of common beliefs along the following lines.[7]

1. Christians have no hope of final salvation and basis for justification before God other than through God's free gift of grace in Christ, offered to them through the Holy Spirit. Our entire hope of justification and salvation rests upon the promises of God and the saving work of Jesus Christ, expressed in the gospel.

2. As a result of original sin, all human beings – whoever they are and whenever and wherever they live – stand in need of justification.

3. Justification is a completely free act of God's grace, and nothing which we can do can be said to be the basis or ground of our own justification. Even faith itself must be recognised as a divine gift and work within us. We cannot turn to God unless God turns us first. The priority of God's redeeming will and action over our own actions in bringing about our salvation is expressed (and its mystery safeguarded) by the doctrine of predestination.

4. In justification we are declared righteous before God, and the process of making us righteous in his sight through the renewing action of the Holy Spirit is begun. In that justification, we receive by faith the effects of the death and resurrection of Jesus Christ as we respond personally to the gospel, the power of God for salvation, as we encounter the gospel through scripture, the

proclamation of the word of God, and the sacraments, and as it initially awakens and subsequently strengthens faith in us.

5. Whoever is justified is subsequently renewed by the Holy Spirit, and motivated and enabled to perform good works. This is not to say that individuals may rely upon these works for their salvation, in that eternal life remains a gift offered to us through the grace and mercy of God.

The document goes further than this, however, by dealing at some length with real questions of disagreement. The question of the nature of justifying righteousness is dealt with in detail, and no attempt is made to disguise the fact that real differences between the churches remain on this issue. It is recognised that the concepts of justification by an external and intrinsic righteousness are totally different: although neither excludes the other, they are not identical. The dialogue group expresses the hope that they may be *complementary*, but the gross error of suggesting that they are substantially the same, reflecting only verbal differences, is avoided. The fact that there are 'remaining differences' between the two churches on a number of important aspects of the doctrine is explicitly acknowledged; this is *interpreted*, however, in terms of *complementary* rather than *contradictory* approaches to the doctrine. In this way, the document recognises the quite distinct approaches to the doctrine associated with the two churches, arguing that they are complementary and convergent, rather than contradictory and divergent.

This elimination or resolution of misunderstandings and disagreements allows the dialogue group to make the following affirmation, in which the tension between the two ways of understanding justification is maintained:[8]

Our entire hope of justification and salvation rests on Jesus Christ and on the gospel whereby the good news of God's merciful action in Christ is made known; we do not place our ultimate trust in anything other than God's promise and saving work in Christ. Such as [sic] affirmation is not fully equivalent to the Reformation teaching on justification according to which God accepts sinners as righteous for Christ's sake on the basis of faith alone; but by its insistence that reliance for salvation should be placed entirely on God, it expresses a central concern of that doctrine. Yet it does not exclude the traditional Catholic position that the grace-wrought transformation of sinners is a necessary preparation for final salvation.

The document thus affirms that the quite distinct ideas of forensic justification and justification by inherent righteousness are two ways of conceptualising essentially the same theological principle:[9]

It must be emphasised that our common affirmation that it is God in Christ alone whom believers ultimately trust does not necessitate any one particular way of conceptualising or picturing God's saving work. That work can be expressed in the imagery of God as judge who pronounces sinners innocent and righteous (cf. no. 90), and also in a transformist view which emphasises the change wrought in sinners by infused grace.

The crucial question of the formal cause of justification – the *real* crux of division in the sixteenth century – is thus resolved by suggesting that both positions (justification by an alien righteousness and justification by an intrinsic righteousness) are appropriate (but not *identical*) ways of conceptualising the ultimate foundation of our justification in the action of God in Jesus Christ. The document recognises that this is no mere difference of words – it amounts to quite distinct theological frameworks, vocabularies, hermeneutics, emphases and manners of conceptualising the divine action. The fundamental point which the document wishes to affirm is that both positions are legitimate ways of attempting to safeguard the same crucial insight.

Justification by Faith represents a milestone in the ecumenical discussion of justification, laying a significant theological foundation for all such subsequent discussions to the extent that it is the standard by which they will be judged. However, it is clear that even this document has difficulty in dealing with some aspects of the sixteenth-century debates. For example, the assertion that 'the Tridentine decree on justification . . . is not necessarily incompatible with the Lutheran doctrine of justification *sola fide*, even though Trent excluded this phrase',[10] points to a fundamental difficulty facing such discussions: doctrines which *were* regarded as unacceptable by Trent in the sixteenth century are now treated as 'not necessarily' unacceptable. Does this mean that Trent was wrong? Or that Trent has been misunderstood by Roman Catholic theologians since 1547, and is only now being interpreted in the correct manner? It is also significant that the question of congruous merit is not addressed with the precision and seriousness one might expect.

The issue of justification was also discussed by the Second Anglican–Roman Catholic International Commission (ARCIC II), whose conclusions were set out in the document *Salvation and the Church* (1987).[11] *Salvation and the Church* greatly assists contemporary dialogue between Anglicans and Roman Catholics by summarising the main points of agreement between the churches, which were often obscured by controversy in the sixteenth and early seventeenth centuries. It is very helpful to have these misunderstandings clarified. It is shown that both churches are agreed that 'even the very first movements which lead to justification, such as repentance, the desire for forgiveness and even faith itself, are the work of God'; that justification is an 'unmerited' gift of God; that our justification leads to our recreation and hence to good works as the fruit of our new freedom in Christ; and that justification involves being incorporated into the community of the church, rather than a solitary life of faith.

The document, however, appears somewhat reluctant to address the disagreements which classical Anglican theologians of the late sixteenth and early seventeenth centuries perceived to exist between themselves and Rome, such as the Caroline emphasis upon the formal cause of justification as the central issue, even the 'grand question which hangeth yet in controversy', between Rome and the Church of England (see §§30, 31). The Commission is evidently aware of the difficulties raised by this difference, but appears to address it rather circumspectly. It is far from clear as to whether we are to regard the question of the formal cause of justification as having been *resolved*, or having been declared to be *irrelevant*. The impression gained is that it is quietly being marginalised. The document concedes the forensic nature of justification, but argues that this image must be complemented by 'other biblical ideas and images of salvation', so that other dimensions of salvation (such as renewal, sanctification, and so forth) might be included.

In contrast, *Justification by Faith* was not prepared to adopt this approach; rather, it chose to engage with this problem by conceding that there exist two quite distinct ways of talking about and conceptualising justification, and asserting that both represent permissible, but different, ways of representing what God has done for us in Christ. It is clear that this is a much more satisfactory approach, which maintains confessional integrity while attempting to discern underlying convergences. The theological perceptivity and sophistication of this dialogue group is evident from the careful attention paid to the nature of theological language and doctrinal statements – for example, in the assertion of the need to 'acknowledge the legitimacy of the contrasting theological perspectives and structures of thought' associated with each church.

The ecumenical discussion of justification in the second half of the twentieth century has seen a welcome advance in understanding between the churches, with at least some of the confusions resulting from the sixteenth-century debates being clarified. Nevertheless, difference and difficulties remain. This point is made clearly by *Justification by Faith*, which noted:[12]

Further study will be needed to determine whether and how far Lutherans and Catholics can agree on these points, which have far-reaching ramifications for traditionally disputed doctrines such as the sacrament of penance, Masses for special intentions, indulgences and purgatory. These questions demand more thorough exploration than they have yet received in this or other dialogues.

There can be no doubt that such dialogues are of major importance, and that discussions between Roman Catholics and Protestants will continue in the future. It is also clear that such discussions need to be based upon a full knowledge of the complex evolution of the western Christian tradition on justification. By setting out this development in some detail, it is hoped that the present volume may be of some value to assisting such dialogues in the future, as well as evaluating those which have already taken place.

Conclusion

It is customary for volumes which have surveyed the history of a specific Christian teaching to conclude by setting out the author's views on how the doctrine should be restated or redeveloped in the situation faced by the churches today. The history of the doctrine thus forms merely the prolegomenon to the real purpose of the work, and is often subservient to that end. No such intention underlies this work. The history of the development of the Christian doctrine of justification is here set out as an enormously interesting and complex subject, worthy of careful consideration. There is no doubt that the material set out in this work will be of major interest to all concerned with ecumenical discussions, the history of the theology of the Protestant and Catholic Reformations, and the development of Christian doctrine, to name but three obvious categories.

But the real purpose of the work has been, quite simply and unashamedly, to allow its author to spend ten years of his life researching a fascinating subject, in the hope that it will encourage others to do the same.

A glossary of medieval soteriological terms

acceptatio divina
The divine act by which God grants man eternal life. In later medieval theology, the term is used to emphasise the fact that man's salvation is ultimately dependent upon the divine decision to accept him, rather than any quality (such as a created habit) which man himself may possess. See §13. It should be emphasised that *acceptatio divina* should not be confused with *acceptio personarum*: this latter term is used by Julian of Eclanum and others to refer to the idea of divine favouritism, which is rejected in favour of the divine *aequitas*. See §6.

amor amicitiae
The pure love of another for the sake of love itself, without any ulterior motive. The term is frequently employed by the theologians of the *via moderna* in discussing the preconditions of justification.

attritio
An imperfect natural form of repentance for sin, which arises out of fear of divine punishment. See §§7, 8. To be distinguished from *contritio*.

concursus generalis
The natural influence of God upon his creation, also referred to as the *influentia generalis*. The concept is usually discussed in terms of Aristotelian physics, where the general *concursus* of the first cause (i.e., God) is understood to be essential if the potentiality of second causes is to be actualised. See §7.

contritio
A perfect form of repentance for sin arising out of love for God (*amor amicitiae*), to be distinguished from *attritio*. *Contritio* is usually regarded as being possible only with the assistance of divine grace. See §§7, 8.

ex natura rei – ex pacto divino
Two fundamentally different concepts of causality underlying the medieval discussion of justification. Ontological, or *ex natura rei*, causality is based upon the presupposition that an inherent connection exists between the

causally related entities or processes which necessitates their causal relationship; covenantal, or *ex pacto divino*, causality is based upon the presupposition that whatever connection exists between the causally related entities or processes exists solely on account of a divine ordination that such a relationship shall exist. See §§7, 11, 13.

ex puris naturalibus
The abilities of man in his purely natural state, without any special assistance of God, except the *concursus generalis*. This should not be confused with the concept of *natura pura* introduced later by Cajetan.

facere quod in se est
The requirement laid upon man by God if he is to dispose himself towards the reception of the gift of grace. See §7.

gratia gratis data
A transitory gift of grace to the *viator* which may coexist with a state of sin. See §9.

gratia gratum faciens
A habitual gift of grace which renders the *viator* acceptable to God, and which may not coexist with a state of mortal sin. See §9.

habitus
A permanent state or disposition within the *viator*, to be distinguished from a transitory act. The habit of grace is understood to be a created form within the soul of the *viator*, intermediate between the divine and human natures, through whose influence the *viator* is changed to become more like God. See §9. The *habitus gratiae* is often referred to as *gratia creata*, to distinguish it from the uncreated grace (*gratia increata*) of the Holy Spirit himself. See further §13.

meritum de condigno
Merit in the strict sense of the term – i.e., a moral act performed in a state of grace, and worthy of divine acceptation on that account. See §10.

meritum de congruo
Merit in a weak sense of the term – i.e., a moral act performed outside a state of grace which, although not meritorious in the strict sense of the term, is considered an 'appropriate' ground for the infusion of justifying grace (*gratia prima*). See §10. The concept is generally discussed in relation to the axiom *facienti quod in se est Deus non denegat gratiam*: see §7.

pactum
The 'covenant' between God and man which governs the theology of the *via moderna*. See §§7, 11, 17.

Appendix: medieval soteriological terms

potentia Dei absoluta

The absolute power of God – i.e., the possibilities open to God before he entered into any decisions concerning his course of action which led him to establish the ordained order through creation and subsequently redemption. It refers primarily to God's ability to do anything, subject solely to the condition that the outcome should not involve logical contradiction. See §11.

potentia Dei ordinata

The ordained power of God – i.e., the established order of salvation, which although contingent, is totally reliable. See §11. The dialectic between the absolute and ordained powers of God was used by the theologians of the later Franciscan school, the *via moderna* and the *schola Augustiniana moderna* to demonstrate the contingency of the implication of created habits of grace in justification. See §13.

viator

Literally, 'wayfarer' or 'pilgrim'. The traditional medieval term used to refer to the believer on his way to the heavenly Jerusalem.

Abbreviations

Bibliographical abbreviations follow the guidelines provided by S. Schwertner, *Internationales Abkurzungsverzeichnis für Theologie und Grenzgebiete* (Berlin, 1974).

ARG	*Archiv für Reformationsgeschichte*
AThA	*Année théologique augustinienne*
BSLK	*Bekenntnisschriften der evangelisch- lutherischen Kirche*
BSRK	*Bekenntnisschriften der reformierten Kirche*
CChr	Corpus Christianorum Series Latina
CFr	*Collectanea Franciscana*
ChH	*Church History*
CR	Corpus Reformatorum
CSEL	Corpus Scriptorum Ecclesiasticorum Latinorum
CT	Concilium Tridentinum: diariorum, actorum, epistolarum, tractatuum nova collectio
D	*Enchiridion Symbolorum*
DThC	*Dictionnaire de théologie catholique*
EE	*Estudios eclesiásticos*
EThL	*Ephemerides Theologicae Lovanienses*
FS	*Franziskanische Studien*
FrS	*Franciscan Studies*
HThR	*Harvard Theological Review*
JEH	*Journal of Ecclesiastical History*
KuD	*Kerygma und Dogma*
MGH.Ep	*Monumenta Germaniae historica: Epistolae*
MGH.SRG	*Monumenta Germaniae historica: Scriptores rerum Germanicarum*
OS	*Calvini Opera Selecta*
PG	Patrologiae cursus completus, Series Graeca
PL	Patrologiae cursus completus, Series Latina
REAug	*Revue des études augustiniennes*
RET	*Revista española de teología*

List of abbreviations

RSPhTh	*Revue des sciences philosophiques et théologiques*
RSR	*Revue des sciences religieuses*
RThAM	*Recherches de théologie ancienne et médiévale*
SJTh	*Scottish Journal of Theology*
StA	*Melanchthons Werke in Auswahl: Studienausgabe*
StTh	*Studia Theologica*
WA	D. Martin Luthers Werke: Kritische Gesamtausgabe
ZKG	*Zeitschrift für Kirchengeschichte*
ZKTh	*Zeitschrift für katholische Theologie*
ZSTh	*Zeitschrift für Systematische Theologie*
ZThK	*Zeitschrift für Theologie und Kirche*

Notes

Notes to §1

1 F. Loofs, 'Der articulus stantis et cadentis ecclesiae', *Theologische Studien und Kritiken* 90 (1917) 323–400; A. E. McGrath, 'Der articulus iustificationis als axiomatischer Grundsatz des christlichen Glaubens', *ZThK* 81 (1984) 383–94.

2 J. Gross, *La divinisation du chrétien*; H. Merki, *Homoiosis Theoi von der platonischen Angleichung an Gott zur Gottähnlichkeit bei Gregor von Nyssa* (Freiburg, 1952).

3 V. N. Lossky, 'Rédemption et déification', in *A l'image et ressemblance de Dieu* (Paris, 1967) 95–108.

4 H. F. Dondaine, *La corpus dionysien de l'Université de Paris au XIIIᵉ siècle* (Rome, 1953).

5 See G. A. Hadjiantoniou, *Protestant Patriarch. The Life of Cyril Lucaris, Patriarch of Constantinople* (Richmond, Va., 1961).

Notes to §2

1 P. Stuhlmacher, *Gerechtigkeit Gottes bei Paulus* (Göttingen, 1966); G. Herold, *Zorn und Gerechtigkeit Gottes. Eine Untersuchung zu Röm. 1, 16–18* (Bern/Frankfurt, 1973). A detailed discussion of the findings of contemporary scholarship on the Pauline doctrine of justification is beyond the scope of the present study: for excellent introductions and further references, see E. Käsemann, 'Gottesgerechtigkeit bei Paulus', *ZThK* 58 (1961) 367–78; E. Jüngel, *Paulus und Jesus* (Tübingen, 1962); K. Kertelge, *Rechtfertigung bei Paulus. Studien zur Struktur und zum Bedeutungsgehalt des paulinischen Rechtfertigungsbegriffs* (Tübingen, 1966); Käsemann, *An die Römer*, 2nd edn (Tübingen, 1974) 84–240; U. Wilkens, *Rechtfertigung als Freiheit: Paulusstudien* (Neukirchen, 1974); Subilia, *La giustificazione per fede*, 7–29.

2 McGrath, 'Justice and Justification'; idem, '"The Righteousness of God"'.

3 M. Cohen, *Essai comparatif sur le vocabulaire et la phonétique du Chamito-Sémitique* (Paris, 1947).

4 For example, the use of the Canaanite *saduk* in the Tel el-Amarna texts to indicate that the king had acted 'correctly' when dealing with the 'Kasi'

(= Cushite?) people. See D. Hill, *Greek Words and Hebrew Meanings. Studies in the Semantics of Soteriological Terms* (Cambridge, 1967) 82–98, esp. 82–6. The following studies should be consulted: H. Cazelles, 'A propos de quelques textes difficiles relatifs à la justice de Dieu dans l'Ancien Testament', *Revue Biblique* 58 (1951) 169–88; A. Dünner, *Die Gerechtigkeit nach dem Alten Testament* (Bonn, 1963); O. Kaiser, 'Dike und Sedaqa. Zur Frage nach der sittlichen Weltordnung. Ein theologische Präludium', *Neue Zeitschrift für systematische Theologie und Religionsphilosophie* 7 (1965) 251–75; H. H. Schmid, *Gerechtigkeit als Weltordnung. Hintergrund und Geschichte des alttestamentlichen Gerechtigkeitsbegriffs* (Tübingen, 1968). It is significant that the findings of these modern studies were foreshadowed in the study of Ludwig Diestel, 'Die Idee der Gerechtigkeit, vorzüglich im Alten Testament, biblisch-theologisch dargestellt', *Jahrbuch für deutsche Theologie* 5 (1860) 173–204, and thence in the seminal study of Albrecht Ritschl, *Die christliche Lehre von der Rechtfertigung und Versöhnung* (3 vols: Bonn, 1870–74) 2.102 n.1.

5 W. Eichrodt, *Theology of the Old Testament* (2 vols: Philadelphia, 1975) 1.239–49; G. von Rad, *Old Testament Theology* (2 vols: London, 1975) 1.370–83. It may be noted that there are two Hebrew words usually translated as 'righteousness', the masculine ṣedeq and the feminine ṣᵉdāqâ. Until recently, it was assumed that these were synonymous. The recent study of A. Jepsen, '*sdq* und *sdqh* im Alten Testament', in *Gottes Word und Gottes Land*, ed. H. G. Reventloh (München, 1965) 78–89, calls this into question, for two reasons. First, it is philologically improbable that two different words should bear exactly the same meaning at the same time. Second, ṣedeq is used as a characterising genitive, especially for weights and measures, as in Leviticus 19.36. ṣᵉdāqâ is not used in this manner.

6 On ṛtá, see Heinrich Lüders, *Varuṇa* I: *Varuṇa und die Wasser* (Göttingen, 1951) 13–27, especially 27 (on the relation between the Vedic ṛtá and the Avestic aša); idem, *Varuṇa* II: *Varuṇa und das Ṛta* (Göttingen, 1959) 402–654. The complex nuances of the Iranian term aša are well brought out by Christian Bartholomae, *Altiranisches Wörterbuch* (Strassburg, 1905) 229–38. The Caucasian term äcäg, deriving from the Iranian, should also be noted in this context: see H. Hommel, 'Wahrheit und Gerechtigkeit. Zur Geschichte und Deutung eines Begriffspaars', *Antike und Abendland* 15 (1969) 159–86; 182–3 n.86. Note also the functions of the Egyptian deity *Maʿat* (ibid., 165 n.24) and the relationship of the Babylonian *kittu* and *mesaru* (ibid., 165 n.25).

7 J. Barr, *The Semantics of Biblical Language* (Oxford, 1961) 107–60; 107. The studies of G. Weiler, 'A Note on Meaning and Use', *Mind* 76 (1967) 424–7, and J. M. E. Moravcsik, 'How do Words get their Meanings?', *Journal of Philosophy* 78 (1981) 5–24, are of relevance here.

8 G. Wildeboer, 'Die älteste Bedeutung des Stammes *sdq*', *Zeitschrift für die alttestamentliche Wissenschaft* 22 (1902) 167–9.

9 e.g., I Samuel 12.7; Micah 6.5.

10 Judges 5.11.

11 e.g., Judges 11.27; cf. also II Samuel 18.31.

12 Schmid, op. cit., 67; Cf. von Rad, op. cit., 1.370.

13 H. Cremer, *Die paulinische Rechtfertigungslehre im Zusammenhang ihrer geschichtlichen Voraussetzungen* (Gütersloh, 1899). The German term 'Gemeinschaftstreue' has subsequently become increasingly used as a translation of ṣᵉdāqâ.

14 Isaiah 46.13; cf. 56.1. See C. F. Whitley, 'Deutero-Isaiah's Interpretation of *sedeq*', *Vetus Testamentum* 22 (1972) 469–75.

15 Thus J. F. A. Sawyer, *Semantics in Biblical Research. New Methods of Defining Hebrew Words for Salvation* (London, 1972) 50. For a penetrating criticism of Sawyer's work, see the review by P. Wernberg-Møller, *Journal of Theological Studies* 24 (1973) 215–17.

16 S. Öhmann, 'Theories of the "Linguistic Field"', *Word* 9 (1953) 123–34; N. C. W. Spence, 'Linguistic Fields, Conceptual Spheres and the *Weltbild*', *Transactions of the Philological Society* (1961) 87–106.

17 P. Guiraud, 'Les champs morpho-sémantiques', *Bulletin de la Societé Linguistique de Paris* 52 (1956) 265–88.

18 e.g., H. Chadwick, *Early Christian Thought and the Classical Tradition* (Oxford, 1984).

19 See R. A. Kraft, 'Jewish Greek Scriptures and Related Topics', *New Testament Studies* 16 (1970) 384–96; 17 (1971) 488–90.

20 M. Salomon, *Der Begriff der Gerechtigkeit bei Aristoteles* (Leiden, 1927); P. Trude, *Der Begriff der Gerechtigkeit in der aristotelischen Rechts- und Staatsphilosophie* (Berlin, 1955). For a useful general survey, see E. A. Havelock, 'DIKAIOSUNE. An Essay in Greek Intellectual History', *Phoenix* 23 (1969) 49–70.

21 For the difficulties they faced, see H. S. Gehman, 'The Hebraic Character of LXX Greek', *Vetus Testamentum* 1 (1951) 81–90; H. M. Orlinsky, 'The Treatment of Anthropomorphisms and Anthropopathisms in the Septuagint of Isaiah', *Hebrew Union College Annual* 27 (1956) 193–200; C. Rabin, 'The Translation Process and the Character of the Septuagint', *Textus* 6 (1968) 1–26.

22 e.g., Psalm 24.5; 33.5; 103.6. The problem is evident in Deutero-Isaiah: see J. W. Olley, *'Righteousness' in the Septuagint of Isaiah: A Contextual Study* (Missoula, Mont. 1979) 65–78.

23 For a survey of the knowledge of Hebrew in the Middle Ages, see B. Smalley, 'Andrew of St Victor, Abbot of Wigmore: A Twelfth Century Hebraist', *RThAM* 10 (1938) 358–74; idem, *The Study of the Bible in the Middle Ages*, 2nd edn (Notre Dame, 1970) 112–95.

24 Cicero, *Rhetoricum libro duo* II, 53. Cf. Justinian, *Institutio* I, 1 'Iustitia est constans et perpetua voluntas suum unicuique tribuens'.

25 For details of the two translations, see J. N. D. Kelly, *Jerome: his Life, Writings and Controversies* (London, 1975).

26 H. Bornkamm, 'Iustitia Dei in der Scholastik und bei Luther', *ARG* 39 (1942) 1–46.

27 See N. M. Watson, 'Some observations concerning the use of δικαιόω in the Septuagint', *Journal of Biblical Literature* 79 (1960) 255–66.

28 e.g., Polybius III.xxxi.9; cited Olley, op. cit., 38.
29 In apocryphal works, the secular Greek sense of the term is usually
    encountered, as at Ecclesiasticus 42.2. Here the term 'justification of the
    ungodly' (δικαιοῦσθαι τοῦ ἀσηβῆ), so profound in its Pauline sense,
    merely means 'the punishment of the wicked'.
30 *Nicomachean Ethics* V 1136ᵃ30.
31 *de civ. Dei* VII, 14; CSEL 40.322.10–17.
32 For what follows, see McGrath, 'Justice and Justification', 412–13.
33 *de Trin.* xi, 19; CChr 62A.549.16–17 'Mereri enim eius est, qui sibi ipse
    meriti adquierendi auctor existat'. See further Peñamaria de Llano, *La
    salvación por la fe*, 191–7.

Notes to §3

1 B. Gerhardsson, *Tradition and Transmission in Early Christianity* (Lund/
   Copenhagen, 1964).
2 J. K. Mozley, *The Impassibility of God* (Cambridge, 1926); R. B.
   Edwards, 'The Pagan Doctrine of the Absolute Unchangeableness of
   God', *Religious Studies* 14 (1978) 305–13. For a criticism of this doctrine,
   see J. Moltmann, *Der gekreuzigte Gott. Das Kreuz Christi als Grund und
   Kritik christlicher Theologie* (München, 1981⁴) especially 256–8; W.
   McWilliams, 'Divine Suffering in Contemporary Theology', *SJTh*
   33–54; K. Surin, 'The Impassibility of God and the Problem of Evil',
   SJTh 35 (1982) 97–119.
3 For its classic statements, see A. von Harnack, *History of Dogma*; idem,
   Grundriß der Dogmengeschichte (Freiburg, 1889). See also J. Rivière, *La
   propagation du christianisme dans les trois premiers siècles d'après les conclusions de M. Harnack* (Paris, 1908); A. Grillmeier, 'Hellenisierung-
   Judaisierung des Christentums als Deuteprinzipien der Geschichte des
   kirchlichen Dogmas', *Scholastik* 33 (1958) 321–55; 528–58; W. Panne-
   berg, 'Die Aufnahme des philosophischen Gottesbegriffs als dogmatisches Problem der frühchristlichen Theologie', *ZKG* 70 (1959) 1–45.
4 Oberman, *Werden und Wertung*, 133–4 n. 179.
5 Loofs, *Leitfaden*, 229–32; M. F. Wiles, *The Making of Christian Doctrine.
   A Study in the Principles of early Doctrinal Development* (Cambridge, 1978)
   94–113.
6 Beck, *Vorsehung und Vorherbestimmung*.
7 Wörter, *Verhältnis von Gnade und Freiheit*.
8 For an introduction to the questions involved, see S. Lyonnet, 'Le sens de
   ἐφ' ᾧ en Rom v.12 et l'exégèse des pères grecs', *Biblica* 36 (1955) 436–57;
   idem, 'Le péché originel et l'exégèse de Rom v.12–14', *RSR* 44 (1956)
   63–84; idem, 'Le péché originel en Rom v.12–14', *RSR* 44 (1956) 63–84;
   idem, 'Le péché originel en Rom v.12. L'exégèse des pères grecs et les
   décrets du Concile de Trente', *Biblica* 41 (1960) 325–55.
9 K. Stendahl, *Paul among Jews and Gentiles* (Philadelphia, 1983) 83.
10 A. von Harnack, *Marcion. Das Evangelium von fremden Gott* (Leipzig,
   1924) is useful here.

11 Thus O. Cullmann, *The Early Church* (London, 1956) 96.

12 Edition in PG 65.929–66. It is possible that this tract is part of the larger work *de lege spirituali*: see J. Quasten, *Patrology* (3 vols: Philadelphia, 1963) 3.505–6.

13 See Wörter, op. cit.; T. F. Torrance, *The Doctrine of Grace in the Apostolic Fathers* (Edinburgh, 1948).

14 e.g., see *LThK* 4.984–8.

15 *I Apol.* 43–4.

16 D. Amand, *Fatalisme et liberté dans l'antiquité grecque* (Louvain, 1945) 195–207.

17 ibid., 86–7; J. Daniélou, *Philon d'Alexandria* (Paris, 1958) 175–81.

18 H. Jonas, *The Gnostic Religion* (Boston, 1958) 46–7; 270–7.

19 Theophilus of Antioch, *Epist. ad Autol.* ii, 27. For a discussion of the use of the term αὐτεξουσία in early Pauline exegesis, see Schelkle, *Paulus Lehrer der Väter*, 439–40.

20 The controversy is particularly associated with Macarius the Egyptian: see Davids, *Bild vom neuen Menschen*. See also I. Hausherr, 'L'erreur fondamentale et la logique de la messalianisme', *Orientalia Christiana Periodica* I (1935) 326–60; F. Dorr, *Diadochus von Photike und die Messalianer* (Freiburg, 1937); H. Dörries, *Symeon von Mesopotamia. Die Überlieferung der messalianischen 'Makarios' Schriften* (Leipzig, 1941). The relationship between Gregory of Nyssa and the movement is intriguing: R. Staats, *Gregor von Nyssa und die Messalianer* (Berlin, 1968).

21 Macarius of Egypt, *de custodia cordis* xii; PG 34.836A.

22 ibid.; PG 34.834D.

23 John of Damascus, *de fide orthodoxa* ii, 30.

24 John Chrysostom, *In epist. ad Rom.*, Hom. xix, 6. It is significant that the Latin translations of Chrysostom's sermons were the work of the Pelagian Anianus of Celeda: see B. Altaner, 'Altlateinische Übersetzungen von Chrysostomusschriften', *Kleine patristische Schriften*, Texte und Untersuchungen 83 (1967) 416–36. Cf. PL 48.626–30.

25 Schelkle, op. cit., 248–52.

26 J. Gaïth, *La conception de la liberté chez Grégoire de Nysse* (Paris, 1953) 79–81.

27 E. Dobler, *Nemesius von Emesa und die Psychologie des menschlichen Aktes bei Thomas von Aquin* (Freiburg, 1950).

28 See C. C. J. Webb, *God and Personality* (London, 1919) 44–5.

29 *de anima* 21; CSEL 20.334.27–9 'Haec erit vis divinae gratiae, potentior utique natura, habens in nobis subiacentem sibi liberam arbitrii potestatem, quod αὐτεξούσιον dicitur.'

30 See F. Ricken, 'Nikaia als Krisis des altchristlichen Platonismus', *Theologie und Philosophie* 44 (1969) 333–9.

31 Text in PL 17.45–508. See A. Souter, *The Earliest Latin Commentaries on the Epistles of St Paul* (Oxford, 1927).

32 Souter, op. cit., 65; 72–3; 80.

33 e.g., H. von Campenhausen, *Fathers of the Latin Church* (London, 1964).

34 e.g., A. Nygren, *Agape and Eros* (Philadelphia, 1953) 343–8.

35 *de paenitentia* 2; CChr 1.323.44–6.
36 *de paenitentia* 5; CChr 1.328.32–329.25. It may, of course, be argued that there are grounds for suggesting the 'ingenuous use of *mereri* and *meritum*' in the pre-Augustinian tradition: see Bakhuizen van den Brink, 'Mereo(r) and meritum'. For an excellent study of Hilary of Poitiers' understanding of the relationship between merit and faith, see Peñamaria de Llano, *La salvación por la fe*, 191–247.
37 A. Beck, *Römisches Recht bei Tertullian. Eine Studie zur frühen Kirchenrechtslehre* (Aalen, 1967); P. Vitton, *I concetti giuridici nelle opere di Tertulliano* (Roma, 1971) 50–4.

Notes to §4

1 *Carmina S. Isidora ascripta* 5; PL 83.1109A.
2 *Monologion*, praefatio; ed. Schmitt, 1.8.9.
3 *de praed. sanct.* iii, 7; *Retractiones* I, xxiii, 3–4.
4 *de praed. sanct.* iv, 8; PL 44.966A 'Nam si curassent, invenissent istam quaestionem secundum veritatem divinarum scripturarum solutam in primo libro duorum, quos ad beatae memoriae Simplicianum scripsi episcopum Mediolanensis ecclesiae ... in ipso exordio episcopatus mei.'
5 See Salguerio, *Doctrine de Saint Augustin*, for an excellent analysis.
6 P. Brown, *Augustine of Hippo* (London, 1967) 151. It is perhaps misleading for Brown to suggest that Augustine 'interpreted Paul as a Platonist' in his early period: to his dying day, Augustine never ceased to interpret Paul as a Platonist, and even died with a quotation from Plotinus on his lips. Presumably Brown intends us to understand that Augustine approached Paul with *different* Platonist presuppositions in his later period. (Thus it could be argued, for example, that his development of the doctrine of predestination reflects *Platonic* determinism as much as Pauline, in that the neo-Platonic tradition was never lacking in sympathy for determinist turns of thought, or for the attribution of human actions to transcendent forces and powers.)
7 e.g., *de serm. Dom. in monte* I, xviii, 55; *Expos. quar. prop. ex Epist. ad Rom.* 44.
8 *ad Simpl.* I, ii, 6.
9 *ad Simpl.* I, ii, 12. Augustine here remarks that Paul 'ostendit etiam ipsam bonam voluntatem in nobis operante Deo fieri': CChr 44.36.324–5.
10 *ad Simpl.* I, ii, 21. 'Liberum voluntatis arbitrium plurimum valet, immo vero est quidem, sed in venundatis sub peccato, quid valet?' CChr 44.53.740–2.
11 Nygren, *Das Prädestinationsproblem*, 47–8. This is not to exclude further development of significance prior to 396: thus, for example, his initial opinion that Paul was referring to unbelievers in Romans 7 later gave way to the insight that he was referring to believers.
12 For a chronological list, see E. TeSelle, *Augustine the Theologian* (London, 1970) 11–14.

13 Others in Augustine's circle of acquaintances held 'Augustinian' views before Augustine himself – see *de lib. arb.* III, iii, 7, where Evodius is mentioned as linking the divine will and necessity.

14 *contra Iul.* II, viii, 23 'Sed vos festinatis et praesumptionem vestram festinando praecipitatis. Hic enim vultis hominem perfici, atque utinam Dei dono et non libero, vel potius servo proprie voluntatis arbitrio.'

15 An important exception, noted by Nygren, op. cit., 41, is his rejection of the opinion that the initiative to respond to God's offer of salvation belongs to man's *liberum arbitrium* – compare *de lib. arb.* III, xvi, 45 with *Retractiones* I, 9, or *Epist.* 143.

16 *de spir. et litt.* v, 7 '... homini Deus dedit liberum arbitrium sine quo nec male nec bene vivitur' CSEL 60.159.12–13. For a more detailed analysis of Augustine's doctrine of *liberum arbitrium*, see Ball, 'Libre arbitre et liberté'; idem., 'Développements de la doctrine de la liberté'; G. R. Evans, *Augustine on Evil* (Cambridge, 1982) 112–49.

17 *de spir. et litt.* xxxiii, 58 '... (omnibus) adimat liberum arbitrium, quo vel bene vel male utentes iustissime iudicentur' CSEL 60.216.20–1.

18 *de spir. et litt.* xxx, 52 'Liberum ergo arbitrium evacuamus per gratiam? Absit; sed magis liberum arbitrium statuimus ... quia gratia sanat voluntatem, qua iustitia libere diligatur' CSEL 60.208.16–27.

19 *de nat. et grat.* lxvi, 77. See E. Gilson, *Introduction à l'étude de S. Augustin,* 3rd edn (Paris, 1949) 185–216; M. T. Clark, *Augustine Philosopher of Freedom* (New York, 1958), especially 45 n.1; Gilson, *History of Christian Philosophy in the Middle Ages* (London, 1978) 78–9. It may be noted that Gilson tends to over-systematise Augustine's thought, and that it is possible that the distinction he here detects is less significant than might at first appear to be the case.

20 *contra duas epist. Pelag.* III, viii, 24 'Et liberum arbitrium captivatum non nisi ad peccatum valet, ad iustitiam vero nisi divinitus liberatum adiutumque non valet' CSEL 60.516.24–6.

21 e.g., see the medical image employed in *de nat. et grat.* iii, 3. Cf. n.18.

22 *de grat. et lib. arb.* ii, 4.

23 *Epist.* 214, 2.

24 *Serm.* 169, 13.

25 e.g., the somewhat unperceptive discussion in N. P. Williams, *The Grace of God* (London, 1930) 19–43.

26 *de grat. et lib. arb.* xvii, 33 'Ut ergo velimus, sine nobis operatur; cum autem volumus, et sic volumus ut faciamus, nobiscum cooperatur.' For an earlier distinction between 'operation' and 'cooperation', see *ad Simpl.* I, ii, 10 'ut velimus enim et suum esse voluit et nostrum: suum vocando, nostrum sequendo. Quod autem voluerimus, solus praestat, id est, posse bene agere et semper beate vivere' CChr 44.35.298–301.

27 See the seriously inaccurate statements of J. I. Packer and O. R. Johnston, *The Bondage of the Will* (London, 1957) 49.

28 See J. Rivière, art. 'Mérite', *DThC* 10.642–51.

29 e.g., *Epist.* 194, 19. On this, see Bakhuizen van den Brink, 'Mereo(r) and Meritum'.

30 See §1.

31 For an excellent discussion, see Burnaby, *Amor Dei*, 219–52.

32 *Enarr. in Ps. 109,1*; CChr 40.1601.11–13. Cf. *Sermo* 110, iv, 4 'Promissorum suorum nobis chirographum fecit. Non debendo enim sed promittendo debitorum se deus fecit, id est non mutuo accipiendo' PL 38.641A. For an excellent discussion of this concept of self-obligation, see Hamm, *Promissio, pactum, ordinatio*, 8–25.

33 *Epist.* 194, 5, 19; CSEL 57.190 'cum Deus coronat merita nostra, nihil aliud coronat quam munera sua'.

34 As suggested by R.-C. Dhont, *Le problème de la préparation à la grâce* (Paris, 1946), on the basis of texts such as *de div. quaest. lxxxiii* 68, 4 'Praecedit ergo aliquid in peccatoribus, quo, quamvis nondum sint iustificati, digni efficiantur iustificatione: et item praecedit in aliis peccatoribus quod digni sunt obtunsione' CChr 44A.180.126–9.

35 K. Holl, 'Die iustitia dei in der vorlutherischen Bibelauslegung des Abendlandes', in *Gesammelte Aufsätze zur Kirchengeschichte* (Tübingen, 1928) 3. 171–88; McGrath, '"The Righteousness of God"'.

36 Studer, 'Jesucristo, nuestra justicia', 266–70.

37 *de spir. et litt.* xi, 18.

38 The fullest discussion is *de Trin.* XIII. See J. Rivière, *Le dogme de la rédemption chez Saint Augustin*, 3rd edn (Paris, 1933). The later dogmatic distinction between the 'person' and 'work' of Christ is unknown to Augustine.

39 Burnaby, op. cit., 168–72.

40 e.g., *de grat. Christi et pecc. orig.* II, xxviii, 33.

41 e.g., *Serm.* 152, 9.

42 e.g., *Serm.* 163, 1.

43 Particularly in relation to the virtue of humility: e.g., *Enarr. in Ps. 31, 18*; CChr 38.239.41–54.

44 *de corr. et grat.* viii, 18. See Nygren, op. cit.; F.-J. Thonnard, 'La prédestination augustinienne. Sa place en philosophie augustinienne', *REAug* 10 (1964) 97–123.

45 e.g., *Epist.* 98, 2. Elsewhere, Augustine criticised the Pelagians for making the grace of Christ consist solely in his example, and asserting that men are justified by imitating him, where they are in fact justified by the Holy Spirit who *subsequently* leads them to imitate him: *Opus imp. contra Iul.* II, 46.

46 Burnaby, op. cit., 173.

47 *Serm.* 297, 1.

48 *de Trin.* XV, xvii, 31.

49 *de Trin.* XV, xviii, 32.

50 Augustine frequently treats *dilectio* and *caritas* as synonymous – e.g., *de Trin.* XV, xviii, 32; xix, 33–7.

51 *de Trin.* XV, xviii, 32.

52 *in Johan. tr.* xxix, 6; xxv, 12; *Serm.* 164, 2; *Enarr. in Ps. 31.1–8*. The Vulgate translates the verse as '. . . per fidem, quae per caritatem operatur'.

53 For Augustine's concept of faith as intellectual adherence to revealed truth, see A. Dorner, *Augustinus. Sein theologisches System und seine religions-philosophische Anschauung* (Berlin, 1873) 194–7; M. Löhrer, *Der Glaubensbegriff des hl. Augustinus in seiner ersten Schriften* (Einsiedeln, 1955). J. Hessen, *Augustins Metaphysik der Erkenntnis* (Leiden, 1960) provides useful background material.

54 *in ep. Johan. tr.* v, 7; *Serm.* 90, 6; 93, 5; 165, 4; *Epist.* 183, i, 3; *de spir. et litt.* xxxii, 56.

55 Burnaby, op. cit., 78 'It cannot be denied that faith, in Augustine's general usage of the term, has the predominantly intellectual connotation of the definition which he gave at the end of his life – to believe means simply to affirm in thought, *cum assensione cogitare*'. The reference is to *de praed. sanct.* ii, 5. See also n.53.

56 Bavaud, 'La doctrine de la justification d'après Saint Augustin', 31–2.

57 Burnaby, op. cit., 78.

58 e.g., *Exp. quar. prop. ex Ep. ad Rom* 22; *ad Simpl.* I, ii, 3; *Serm.* 131, 9; 292, 6; *Epist.* 160, xxi, 52; *de grat. et lib. arb.* vi, 13. Other expressions used include *efficitur iustus* (e.g., *de spir. et litt.* xxxii, 56) and *fit pius* (e.g., *Serm.* 160, 7; *in John. tr.* iii, 9).

59 *de grat. et lib. arb.* xvii, 33.

60 *Ench.* I, 44.

61 See the important conclusions reached by J. Henninger, *S. Augustinus et doctrina de duplici iustitia* (Mödling, 1935) 79 'i. Existit aliqua iustitia, qua homo vere, intrinsecus, coram Deo iustus est; ii. Haec iustitia consistit in aliquo dono permanenti, quo homo elevatur ad aliquem statum, altiorem, ita ut sit particeps Dei, deificatus.'

62 J. A. Stoopio, *Die deificatio hominis in die Sermones en Epistulae van Augustins* (Leiden, 1952); Capánaga, 'La deificación en la soteriología agustiniana'. The theme appears to be more pronounced in Augustine's sermons than in his specifically doctrinal works.

63 Burnaby, op. cit., 141–53; 168–77.

64 G. Philips, 'Saint Augustin a-t-il connu une "grâce créée"?', *EThL* 47 (1971) 97–116; P. G. Riga, 'Created Grace in St. Augustine', *Augustinian Studies* 3 (1972) 113–30.

65 *Serm.* 192, 1 – possibly a direct citation from the Cappadocians. For Augustine's relation to the Cappadocians, see B. Altaner, 'Augustinus, Gregor von Nazianz und Gregor von Nyssa', *Revue Bénédictine* 61 (1951) 54–62; idem, 'Augustinus und die griechische Patristik. Eine Zusammenfassung und Nachlese zu den quellenkritischen Untersuchungen', *Revue Bénédictine* 62 (1952) 201–15.

66 *de Trin.* XIV, xii, 15.

67 *Enarr. in Ps.* 49, 2; *Serm.* 192, 1.

68 *contra Iul.* I, ix, 45.

69 *de spir. et litt.* xxix, 50.

70 *contra duas epist. Pelag.* III, v, 14. The entire section at III, v, 14–vii, 23 merits careful study.

71 *Serm.* 349, i, 1.

72 *de grat. et lib. arb.* xvii, 36; *de spir. et. litt.* xxvii, 48. The excellent study of J. Wang Tch'ang-Tche, *Saint Augustin et les vertus des païens* (Paris, 1938) should be noted.

73 *contra Iul.* IV, iii, 19.

74 *contra Iul.* IV, iii, 31.

75 *de civ. Dei* II, 21. On the theme of the 'two cities', see A. Lauras and H. Rondet, 'Le thème des deux cités dans l'œuvre de saint Augustin', *Etudes Augustiniennes* 28 (1953) 99–160; Y. Congar, '"Civitas Dei" et "Ecclesia" chez S. Augustin', *REAug* 3 (1957) 1–14.

76 *de civ. Dei* XI, 17. See also *de lib. arb.* I, v, 11 '... iustum est, ut omnia sint ordinatissima'. The Platonic conception of justice as the right ordering of the parts of the soul is also evident in Augustine's definition of justice as *amor amato serviens et propterea recte dominans: de moribus ecclesiae* xv, 25.

77 Gilson, op. cit., 77–81.

78 R. A. Markus, *Saeculum: History and Society in the Theology of St. Augustine* (Cambridge, 1970) 72–104.

79 On this see McGrath, 'Justice and Justification'; idem., '"The Righteousness of God"'.

80 e.g., *de lib. arb.* xviii, 27; *Enarr. in Ps.* 83, *11*. For Augustine's relation to Cicero, see M. Testard, *Saint Augustin et Cicéron* (2 vols: Paris, 1958).

81 See McGrath, 'Divine Justice and Divine Equity' for a more detailed analysis.

82 Lactantius, *Divinae Institutiones* V, vii, 2; CSEL 19.419.12–14.

83 Cicero, *de rep.* I, 39 'Est igitur, inquit Africanus, res publica, res populi; populus autem non omnis hominim coetus quoquo modo congregatus, sed coetus multitudinis iuris consensu et utilitatis communione societatis.' See Testard, op. cit., 2.39–43.

84 *de civ. Dei* XIX, 23. Cf. XIX, 21.

85 *de lib. arb.* I, vi, 15.

86 On this whole question, see P. A. Schubert, *Augustins Lex-Aeterna-Lehre nach Inhalt und Quellen* (Münster, 1924). See also J. Rief, *Der Ordobegriff des jungen Augustinus* (Paderborn, 1962).

87 *de div. quaest. lxxxiii* 83, 2 '... quia omnis ista hominum iustitia, quam et tenere animus humanus recte faciendo potest et peccando amittere, non imprimeretur animae, nisi esset aliqua incommutabilis iustitia, quae integra inveniretur a iustis, cum ad eam converterenter, integra relinqueretur a peccantibus, cum ab eius lumine averterentur' CChr 46A.245.31–6. See also *ad Simpl.* I, ii, 16. Cf. F. J. Thonnard, 'Justice de Dieu et justice humaine selon Saint Augustin', *Augustinus* 12 (1967) 387–402.

88 *de spir. et. litt.* xxvi, 45.

Notes to introduction to chapter 3

1 Julian of Toledo, *Antikeimenon* II, 69; PL 96.697C. Cf. Augustine, *de civ. Dei* XI, 1, where he refers to living 'in an intermediate age' (*in hoc interim*

saeculo) in a similar context. See further H.-I. Marrou, *L'ambivalence du temps de l'histoire chez saint Augustin* (Montréal, 1950); idem, 'Civitas Dei, civitas terrena: num tertium quid?', *Studia Patristica* 2 (Berlin, 1957) 342–50.

2 See J. J. Contreni, *The Cathedral School of Laon from c. 850–c. 1000* (Munich, 1978); J. Marenbon, *From the Circle of Alcuin to the School of Auxerre. Logic, Theology and Philosophy in the Early Middle Ages* (Cambridge, 1981) and references therein.

3 D. M. Cappuyns, 'Le premier représentant de l'augustinisme médiévale', *RThAM* 1 (1929) 309–37.

4 G. R. Evans, *The Language and Logic of the Bible. The Earlier Middle Ages* (Cambridge, 1984) 133–9.

5 e.g., Isidore of Seville, *Sententiae*: PL 83.537–738; Burchard of Worms, *Decretum*: PL 140.338–1058.

6 Grabmann, *Geschichte der scholastischen Methode*, 2.385–6.

7 Oberman, *Werden und Wertung der Reformation*, 82–140.

8 G. Aulén, *Christus Victor* (London, 1934). On the development of the idea of the 'Harrowing of Hell', see J. M. Usteri, *Hinabgefahren zur Hölle* (Zürich, 1886).

9 D. M. de Clerk, 'Droits du démon et nécessité de la rédemption. Les écoles d'Abélard et de Pierre Lombard', *RThAM* 14 (1947) 32–64.

10 Thus A. B. Ritschl, *Die christliche Lehre von der Rechtfertigung und Versöhnung* (Bonn, 1870) §4, begins his discussion of the doctrine with reference to Anselm of Canterbury.

11 Landgraf, *Einführung in die Geschichte* 29; 39–40.

12 C. Spicq, *Esquisse d'une histoire de l'exégèse latine au moyen âge* (Paris, 1944).

13 W. Affeld, 'Verzeichnis der Römerbriefkommentare der lateinischen Kirche', *Traditio* 12 (1957) 396–406. For an exhaustive list of medieval biblical commentaries, see F. Stegmüller, *Reportorium Biblicum Medii Aevii* (7 vols: Barcelona, 1950–61).

14 e.g., Robert of Melun, *Questiones de epistolis ad Romanos*, ed. Martin, 80.14–81.20.

15 e.g., Hervaeus of Bourg Dieu, *Comm. in ep. divi Pauli*, PL 181.644B–47A.

16 See H. Cloes, 'La systématisation théologique pendant la première moitié du XIIe siècle', *EThL* 34 (1958) 277–329, who illustrates this point with particular reference to Hugh of St Victor's *de sacramentis*. See also H. Köster, *Die Heilslehre des Hugo von Sankt Viktor* (Emsdetten, 1940); V. Marcolino, *Das alte Testament in der Heilsgeschichte. Untersuchung zum dogmatischen Verständnis des alten Testaments als heilsgeschichtliche Periode nach Alexander von Hales* (Münster, 1970).

Notes to §5

1 On the medieval theories of signification, see G. R. Evans, *The Language and Logic of the Bible. The Earlier Middle Ages* (Cambridge, 1984) 72–122.

2 e.g., Luke 1.6.

3 e.g., Atto of Vercelli, *Exp. epist. Pauli*, PL 134.149C; Haimo of Auxerre, *Expos. in divi Pauli epist.*, PL 119.381A.

4 e.g., Sedulius Scotus, *Coll. in omnes Pauli epist.*, PL 103.41C '. . . aliud est iustificari coram Deo, aliud coram hominibus'.

5 See McGrath, 'Forerunners of the Reformation?'.

6 See E. Dietrich, 'Die Lehren der angelsächsischen Kirchen, nack Ælfriks Schriften', *Zeitschrift für die historische Theologie* 25 (1855) 550–94; M. M. Gatch, *Preaching and Theology in Anglo-Saxon England* (Toronto, 1977) for further details.

7 See H. MacGillivray, *The Influence of Christianity on the Vocabulary of Old English* (Studien zur englischen Philologie 8: Halle, 1902) 148–58; N. O. Halvorsen, *Doctrinal Terms in Ælfric's Homilies* (University of Iowa Studies: Humanistic Studies 5/1: 1932) 56–7; M.-M. Dubois, *Ælfric sermonnaire, docteur et grammarien* (Paris, 1943). It may be noted that Wulfstan's vocabulary is limited compared with Ælfric's: see L. H. Dodd, *A Glossary of Wulfstan's Homilies* (New York, 1908).

8 *The Pearl*, ed. E. V. Gordon (Oxford, 1953) ll. 699–700.

9 See his translation of Romans 8.30: B. Thorpe, *The Homilies of the Anglo-Saxon Church* (2 vols: London, 1864–6) 2.367.1–3.

10 e.g., see *The Gothic and Anglo-Saxon Gospels, with the Versions of Wycliffe and Tyndale* ed. J. Bosworth (London, 1865) 10.29; *Libri Psalmorum versio antiqua Latina cum paraphrasi Anglo-Saxonica* ed. B. Thorpe (Oxford, 1835) 18.8, where '. . . iustificati sunt . . .' is translated 'Hi synt gerihtwisode . . .'. See also *Homilies* 2.430.2; 472.2–3.

11 *Homilies* 2.286.2–5.

12 *Die gotische Bibel*, ed. W. Streitberg (2 vols: Heidelberg, 1965).

13 Thus Romans 1.1–6.22 are missing, as well as other important sections.

14 See Streitberg's edition for full notes on the manuscript giving this translation.

15 The best translation of *wairthan* in modern German is *werden*, which can be justified on philological grounds. The Gothic term is frequently used to translate γίνεσθαι – see Streitberg, op. cit., 2.167.

16 *contra Iul.* II, viii, 23; PL 44.689B.

17 *Exp. in Psalmos*, PL 152.1087A 'Notandum quod haec beneficia non narrat ordine; prius enim fuit a captivitate per fidem averti, postea vero peccata operiri, et sic post iniquitatem remitti; et ad ultimum in bonis operibus et virtutibus benedici.'

18 *Comm. in epist. Pauli*, PL 181.642D.

19 For an excellent discussion of the *processus iustificationis* in the early medieval period, see Landgraf, *Dogmengeschichte der Frühscholastik*, I/1 287–302. The reference is to Cod. Paris Nat. lat. 15269 fol. 44, cited Landgraf, op. cit., 291 n.11.

20 Peter Comestor, *Sermo* 17; PL 198.1769B 'Iustificatio etiam in tribus consistit, vel notatur; in gratia infusione, in liberi arbitrii cooperatione, tandem in consummatione; primum est incipientium, secundum proficientium, tertium pervenientium.'

21 Cod. Vat. lat. 1174 fol. 83v; Cod. Vat. lat. 1098 fol. 151v, 157; cited Landgraf, op. cit., 299. Cf. 298 n.41 and 299 n.45.

22 *Sententiarum libri quinque* III, 2; PL 211.1044A–B. Peter of Poitiers was a pupil of Peter Lombard, upon whose *Sentences* his own work was modelled: see P. S. Moore, *The works of Peter of Poitiers* (Notre Dame, 1936) 1–24. He must not be confused with Peter of Poitiers of St Victor or Peter of Poitiers of Cluny: see J. W. Baldwin, *Masters, Princes and Merchants* (2 vols: Princeton, 1970) 1.32–4; J. Kritzeck, *Peter the Venerable and Islam* (Princeton, 1964) 31–4.

23 *Summa Aurea* lib. III tr. ii q.1; fol. 121v.

24 Alexander of Hales, *In IV Sent.* dist. xvii n.7; Albertus Magnus, *In IV sent.* dist. xviiA a. 10; ed. Borgnet, 29.673 'Dicitur ab omnibus, quod quattuor exiguntur ad iustificationem impii, scilicet infusio gratiae, motus liberi arbitrii in peccatum sive contritio, quod idem est, motus liberi arbitrii in Deum, et remissio peccati'; Bonaventure, *In II Sent.* dist. xxvi a.1 dub. 3; Thomas Aquinas, *In IV Sent.* dist. xvii q.1 a.4; ed. Mandonnet, 4.843; idem, *Summa Theologiae* IaIIae q.113 a.6; Odo Rigaldi, *In II Sent.* dist xxvi membr. 1 q.2 a.3 (ed. Bouvy, 331.48–32.68). Matthew of Aquasparta redefines the four elements as *satisfactio, conversio, reformatio, vivificatio*: *In II Sent.* dist. xxviii a.1 q.1.

25 See McGrath, 'The Influence of Aristotelian Physics upon St Thomas Aquinas' Discussion of the "Processus Iustificationis" '. See also Flick, *L'attimo della giustificazione*, 104–54.

26 *In IV Sent.* dist. xviiA a.15.

27 G. Grunwald, *Geschichte der Gottesbeweise im Mittelalter* (Münster, 1907) 107–10.

28 IaIIae q.113 a.8.

29 IaIIae q.113 a.6.

30 IaIIae q.113 a.6 ad 1um.

31 IaIIae q.113 a.8 ad 2um.

32 IaIIae q.113 a.5.

33 IaIIae q.113 a.6 3um.

34 IaIIae q.113 a.8 ad 3um 'Philosophus dicit, in *II Physic.*, in motibus animi omnino praecedit motus in principium speculationis, vel in finem actionis ... Et quia motus liberi arbitrii est motus animi, prius naturae ordine movetur in Deum sicut in finem, quam ad removendum impedimentum peccati.'

35 IaIIae q.113 a.8.

36 *de veritate* q.28 a.8; ed. Spiazzi, 1.549 'et ideo inter gratiae infusionem et culpae remissionem nihil cadet medium'. An identical opinion is encountered earlier: *In IV Sent.* dist. xvii q.1 a.4; ed. cit., 4.847.

37 IaIIae q.113 aa.1, 2.

38 IaIIae q.63 a.4.

39 IIaIIae q.58 a.5.

40 IaIIae q.113 a.1.

41 IaIIae q.100 a.12.

42 IaIIae q.100 a.12 ad 3um.

43 IaIIae q.83 a.4.

44 IaIIae q.113 a.1 ad 2um 'Iustitia importat generaliter totam rectitudinem ordinis. Et ideo magis denominatur huiusmodi transmutatio a iustitia quam a caritate vel fide.' On the significance of 'rectitude', see McGrath, 'Rectitude: The Foundations of Anselm of Canterbury's Soteriology'. Thomas is aware of Anselm's definition of *iustitia* as 'rectitudo voluntatis propter se servata', and cites it with approval on occasion. For the relation between *rectitudo* and *iustitia* according to Thomas, see IaIIae q.21 a.3; q.46 a.7 ad 2um; q.55 a.4 ad 4um; q.100 a.2 ad 2um; q.113 a.1. The essential distinction being made is between *iustitia proprie* as *rectitudo actus* and *iustitia metaphorice* as *rectitudo ordinis in partibus hominis*.

45 IaIIae q.109 a.8.

46 IaIIae q.113 a.1 ad 2um.

47 See McGrath, 'The Influence of Aristotelian Physics'.

48 *Itinerarium mentis in Deum* IV, 3.

49 On this, see the brilliant study of R. Guardini, *Systembildende Elemente in der Theologie Bonaventuras. Die Lehren vom Lumen Mentis, von der Gradatio Entium and der Influentia Sensus et Motus* (Leiden, 1964).

50 *Quaestiones disputatae de gratia* q.2; ed. Doucet, 45–9.

51 *Quaestiones disputatae de gratia* q.7; ed. Hödl, 63.

52 e.g., *Glossa in Decretum Gratianis*, Cod. Bamberg Can. 13, cited Landgraf, op. cit., I/1 210 'Talis est gratia, quia nec virtus nec opus vel motus mentis. Et secundum hoc nichil ponit.' See Alszeghy, *Nova Creatura*, for further references and discussion.

53 *Alexandri de Hales Summa Theologica* pars I inq. I tr. ii q.3 tit.3 membr. 2 cap. 1. sol; ed. Quaracchi, 2.77 'Dicendum quod "Deus esse per gratiam" ponit necessario gratiam creatam in creatura.'

54 *I Sent* dist. xxxvii cap. 1.

55 See Oberman, 'Wir sind pettler'; Courtenay, 'Covenant and Causality'; Hamm, *Promissio, pactum, ordinatio*; McGrath, 'Anti-Pelagian Structure'.

56 *Opus Oxoniense* IV dist. xvi q.2.

57 Thomas Aquinas, *Summa Theologiae*, IIIa 1.56 a.2 ad 4um.

58 e.g., IaIIae q.113 a.1 'Remissio peccatorum est iustificatio'.

59 McGrath, 'Forerunners of the Reformation?'.

60 *Canonis Missae Expositio* 31B; ed. Oberman/Courtenay, 1.314–5.

61 See McGrath, op. cit., for details.

Notes to §6

1 See H. Denifle, *Luther und Luthertum. Die abendländischen Schriftausleger bis Luther über iustitia Dei und iustificatio* (Mainz, 1905); Holl, *Iustitia Dei in der vorlutherischen Bibelauslegung*; H. Bornkamm, 'Iustitia Dei in der Scholastik und bei Luther', *ARG* 39 (1942) 1–46; McGrath, '"The Righteousness of God"'.

2 Ambrosiaster, *Comm. in epist. Pauli*, PL 17.56B. See also 17.74B; 80A–B.

3 e.g., Atto of Vercelli, *Expos. epist. Pauli*, PL 134.160B. See also 134.161B; 162A. On Augustine himself, see §4.

4 'Hieronymus', *Brev. in Psalm. 70.2*, PL 26.1025D.

5 *Brev. in Psalm. 30.1*; PL 26.906B 'Quia nisi a Deo iustificemur, per nos non possumus iustificari.'

6 On this, see McGrath, 'Divine Justice and Divine Equity in the Controversy between Augustine and Julian of Eclanum'.

7 Augustine, *Opus imperf. contra Iul.* III, 2; CSEL 85/1.352.6–7.

8 Augustine, *Opus imperf. contra Iul* I, 38; CSEL 85/1.28.10–35.

9 PL 131.291D 'Mea iustitia est malum pro malo reddere. Tu solus iustus, quam circa nos ostendisti, reddens bonum pro malo, qua de impio facis bonum.'

10 Atto of Vercelli, *Exp. epist. Pauli*, PL 134.137A–8B.

11 e.g., Sedulius Scotus, *Coll. in omnes Pauli epist.*, PL 103.18D 'Iustitia Dei est, quia quod promisit, dedit'; Haimo of Auxerre, *Expl. in Psalmos* PL 116.295A; Bruno of Würzburg, *Expos. Psalm.*, PL 140.132D; 265C. This understanding of *iustitia Dei* is reproduced in the 14th century vernacular poem *The Pearl*: see A. D. Horgan, 'Justice in *The Pearl*', *Review of English Studies* 32 (1981) 173–80; McGrath, 'Divine Justice and Divine Equity' 317–18; idem. '"The Righteousness of God"', 70–1.

12 See G. Paré, A. Brunet and P. Tremblay, *La renaissance du XIIe siècle* (Paris, 1933).

13 A. von Harnack, *History of Dogma*, 3.310. Cf. H. Rashdall, *The Idea of Atonement in Christian Theology* (London, 1920) 355 'Anselm appeals to justice ... but his notions of justice are the barbaric ideals of an ancient Lombard king or the technicalities of a Lombard lawyer rather than the ideas which would have satisfied such a man as Anselm in ordinary human life.' For a similar misunderstanding, see G. Aulén, *Christus Victor* (London, 1934) 100–9.

14 On this, see McGrath, 'Rectitude. The Moral Foundations of Anselm of Canterbury's Soteriology'.

15 *Proslogion*, 9; ed. Schmitt, 1.106.18–107.3.

16 *Proslogion*, 10; ed. cit., 1.109.4–5.

17 *Cur Deus homo* I, 12.

18 For this concept as developed by the medieval canonists, see E. Wohl-hauper, *Aequitas Canonica. Eine Studie aus dem kanonischen Recht* (Paderborn, 1931); H. Lange, 'Die Wörter aequitas und iustitia auf römischen Münzen', *Zeitschrift der Savigny-Stiftung für Rechtsgeschichte*, Romanistische Abteilung, 52 (1932) 296–314.

19 *Cur Deus homo* I, 23.

20 *de veritate* 12; *de casu diaboli* 9.

21 *de veritate* 4; ed. cit., 1.181.6–8.

22 *de veritate* 12; ed. cit., 1.192.6–8. Our interpretation is supported at this point by the study of G. Söhngen, 'Rectitudo bei Anselm von Canterbury als Oberbegriff von Wahrheit und Gerechtigkeit', in *Sola Ratione* ed. H. Kohlenberger (Stuttgart, 1970) 71–7.

23 See H. Hommel, 'Wahrheit und Gerechtigkeit. Zur Geschichte und
Deutung eines Begriffspaares', *Antike und Abendland* 15 (1969) 159–86.
24 *Cur Deus homo* I, 11.
25 *de casu diaboli* 16; *de conceptu virginali et originali peccato* II, 22–3. On this,
see Blomme, *La doctrine du péché*. The earlier work of R. M. Martin, *La
controverse sur le péché originel au début du XIVe siècle* (Louvain, 1930) is
also useful. It may be noted that the influence of Anselm's concept of
original sin appears to have been insignificant until Albertus Magnus
defined the formal element of original sin as *privatio iustitiae*, although the
same concept may be found in Odo of Cambrai, *de peccato originali*, PL
160.1071–1102. In particular, the school of Laon maintained the older
Augustinian understanding of original sin as concupiscence: William of St
Thierry, *Disp. adv. Abael.* 7; PL 180.275A; Robert Pullen, *Sententiarum
libri octo* II, 27; PL 186.754B–5C.
26 *Cur Deus homo* I, 12.
27 *Aliquot quaestionum liber XV*, PL 93.471–8. On this, and other aspects of
the *ius diaboli*, see Rivière, *Le dogme de la rédemption*.
28 Gregory, *Moralium libri XXXIII*, xv, 31; PL 76.692D–3C.
29 For an excellent analysis, see F. Hammer, *Genugtuung und Heil. Absicht,
Sinn und Grenzen der Erlösungslehre Anselms von Canterbury* (Wien, 1966).
30 Anselm of Laon, *Sententiae* 47; ed. Lottin, *Psychologie et Morale* 5.144;
Sententiae Atrebatenses, ed. Lottin, 5.414; *Sententie divine pagine*, ed.
Bliemetzrieder, 41. See also note 25.
31 Anselm of Laon, *Sententiae* 47–8, ed. Lottin, 5.44–7; the School of Laon,
Sententiae 354–5, ed. Lottin, 5.269–70. Cf. Peter Lombard, *III Sent.*
dist. xviii, 5.
32 Abailard, *Exp. in Epist. ad Rom.*, PL 178.834D. See de Clerck, *Droits du
démon*; R. E. Weingart, *The Logic of Divine Love. A Critical Analysis of the
Soteriology of Peter Abailard* (Oxford, 1970) 84–8.
33 Hugh of St Victor, *de sacramentis* I, viii, 4; PL 176.308A–B.
34 De Clerk, op. cit., 39–45. It must be conceded that the *Epitome theologiae
Christianae* departs considerably from the 'received view' when it denies
that man was *ever* subject to the power of the devil: *Epitome* 23; PL
178.1730D–31A 'constat hominem sub potestate diaboli non fuisse, nec
de eius servitute redemptum esse'.
35 *de erroribus Abaelardi* V, 13–14; PL 182.1063D–65B.
36 *Sententiarum libri quinque* IV, 19; PL 211.1212A. See also de Clerck, op.
cit., 56–7.
37 *Exp. in epist. ad Rom*, PL 178.864A; 868B; *Sermo* 30; PL 178.567D;
Dialogus, PL 178.1653A; 1654C; 1656D–57A. See Weingart, op. cit.,
141–2.
38 e.g., *Epitome theologiae Christianae* 32; PL 178.1750C. See Lottin, *Le
concept de justice*, 512–13. A similar definition is due to Stephen Langton:
ibid., 513–14.
39 Lottin, op. cit., 514 n. 1.
40 Lottin, op. cit., 514 n. 2.

41 Lottin, op. cit., 515 nn. 1–2.

42 Text as established by Lottin, op. cit., 517.13–18, from Paris Nat. lat. 14891 and 15952, and Brussels Bibl. roy. 12042–9.

43 *de sacramentis* I, viii, 8; PL 176.310D.

44 *de sacramentis* I, viii, 8–9; PL 176.311A–D.

45 Lottin, op. cit., 521 n. 1. See also A. H. Chroust, 'The Philosophy of Law from St. Augustine to St. Thomas Aquinas', *New Scholasticism* 20 (1946) 26–71; 64–70, esp. 64 n.141.

46 Lottin, op. cit., 521 n. 2.

47 Thomas Aquinas, *de veritate* q.23 a.6; ed. Spiazzi, 1.426 'Dicero autem quod ex simplici voluntate dependeat iustitia, est dicere quod divina voluntas non procedat secundum ordinem sapientiae, quod est blasphemum.'

48 O. Lottin, *L'ordre morale et l'ordre logique d'après St. Thomas* (Louvain, 1924); idem, 'L'intellecturalisme de la morale Thomiste', *Xenia Thomistica* I (1925) 411–27.

49 *Summa Theologiae* IIIa q.46 a.3.

50 IIIa q.46 a.2 ad 3um.

51 See G. Stratenwerth, *Die Naturrechtslehre des Johannes Duns Scotus* (Göttingen, 1951), where it is argued that Scotus thereby drove a conceptual wedge between the realms of natural and divine law. On Ockham, see W. Kölmel, 'Das Naturrecht bei Wilhelm Ockham', *FS* 35 (1953) 39–85; for Biel's in relation to Ockham's, see idem, 'Von Ockham zu Gabriel Biel. Zur Naturrechtslehre des 14. und 15. Jahrhunderts', *FS* 37 (1955) 218–59.

52 Biel, *Canonis missae expositio* 23 E; ed. Oberman/Courtenay 1.212. Cf. *In I Sent.* dist. xliii q.1 a.4 cor.; ed. Werbeck/Hoffmann 1.746.5–7 'Deus potest aliquid facere, quod non est iustum fieri a deo; si tamen faceret, iustum esset fieri. Unde sola voluntas divina est prima regula omnis iustitiae, et eo quod vult aliquid fieri, iustum est fieri.'

53 *Opus Oxoniense* III dist. xix q.1 n.7.

54 See M. M. Menges, *The Concept of Univocity regarding the Predication of God and Creatures according to William of Ockham* (New York/Louvain, 1952).

55 e.g., *Alexandri de Hales Summa Theologica*, pars I inq.1 tr.4 q.1 membr.2 cap.2 ad 4um; ed. Quaracchi, 1.207 'Dicendum quod iustitia dicitur dupliciter. Uno modo retributio unicuique secundum merita: et sic non omnia facit de iustitia; Alio modo condecentia bonitatis; et sic omnia facit de iustitia nec aliquid facit nisi quod condecet iustitiae'; Thomas Aquinas, *In IV Sent.* dist. xlvi q.1 a.1 sol.1; idem, *Summa Theologiae* Ia q.21 a.1 ad 3um. Philip the Chancellor, *Summa*, cited Lottin, op. cit., 518–19; Odo Rigaldi, cited Lottin, op. cit., 518–19; Albertus Magnus, *Summa de bono*, cited Lottin, op. cit., 519–21.

56 *Summa Theologiae* Ia q.21 a.3 ad 2um; cf. idem, *In IV Sent.* dist. xlvi q.2 a.2 sol.2.

57 *Opus Oxoniense* IV dist. xlvi q.1 n.7.

58 *Opus Oxoniense* IV dist. xlvi q.1 nn.2–4. It must be pointed out that

Scotus elsewhere notes that it is not *contrary* to justice to forgive sin: *Opus Oxoniense* IV dist. xlvi q.4 n.17 'dare bonum indebitum non est contra iustitiam, quia est liberalitatis et actus unius virtutis non repugnat alteri'.

59 Bornkamm, op. cit., 20.

60 See McGrath, 'Mira et nova diffinitio iustitiae'; idem, *Luther's Theology of the Cross* (Oxford, 1985) 95–113.

61 *In I Sent.* dist. xli q.1 a.3 dub.3 summ.3; ed. Werbeck/Hoffmann, 1.732.16–18.

62 *In II Sent.* dist. xxvii q.1 a.3 dub.4; ed. cit., 2.253.7–9.

63 Hamm, *Promissio, Pactum, Ordinatio*, 462–6.

64 *Missae canonis expositio* 59S; ed. Oberman/Courtenay, 2.446. For the possibility that *iustitia Dei* is thus understood to be purely arbitrary, see McGrath, '"The Righteousness of God"', 72; idem, 'Some Observations concerning the Soteriology of the *Via Moderna*', *RThAM* 52 (1985) 182–93.

65 *In II Sent.* dist. xxxvi q. unica a.1 nota 3; ed. cit., 2.622.5–3.10.

66 WA 55 II.108.15–109.11 for the full text; for the gloss, see WA 55 I.70.9–11.

67 WA 4.262.4–5. For Luther's concept of covenantal causality, see McGrath, *Luther's Theology of the Cross*, 85–90.

68 On this, see McGrath, op. cit., 93–161.

69 See G. R. Evans, *The Language and Logic of the Bible. The Earlier Middle Ages* (Cambridge, 1984) 101–22.

70 *Theologia Christiana* I, 7.

71 *Theologicae Regulae* 26; PL 210.633D. See G. R. Evans, *Alan of Lille. The Frontiers of Theology in the Later Twelfth Century* (Cambridge, 1983) 29–33.

72 G. R. Evans, 'The Borrowed Meaning. Grammar, Logic and the Problems of Theological Language in Twelfth-Century Schools', *Downside Review* 96 (1978) 165–75.

73 See Evans, *Alan of Lille*, 41–51.

74 *Tract. in Hexam.* I, 12; PL 192.1252B.

75 See McGrath, '"The Righteousness of God"'. What follows is based on Ockham, *In I Sent.*, dist. ii q.3; *Opera Theologica* 2.50–74.

76 See Menges, op. cit.; G. Leff, *William of Ockham. The Metamorphosis of Scholastic Discourse* (Manchester, 1977) 400–11.

77 Ockham, *In I Sent.* dist. ii q.3; *Opera Theologica*, 2.61–2.

Notes to §7

1 Augustine, *Sermo* 169, 13.

2 The term 'axiom' is, of course, being used in a loose sense, rather than in the Euclidean or Boethian senses of the term: see G. R. Evans, 'Boethian and Euclidian Axiomatic Method in the Theology of the Later Twelfth Century', *Archives Internationales d'Histoire des Sciences* 103 (1980) 13–29.

3 Recent studies have emphasised Pelagius' orthodox intentions: R. F. Evans, *Pelagius: Inquiries and Reappraisals* (New York, 1968); G. Greschat, *Gnade als konkrete Freiheit. Eine Untersuchung zur Gnadenlehre des Pelagius* (Mainz, 1972). The older study of G. de Plinval, *Pélage, ses écrits*,

sa vie et sa réforme (Lausanne, 1943) is still helpful. On the reforming nature of Pelagianism, see the two excellent studies of Peter Brown: 'Pelagius and His Supporters: Aims and Environment', *Journal of Theological Studies* 19 (1968) 93–114; 'The Patrons of Pelagius: The Roman Aristocracy between East and West', *Journal of Theological Studies* 21 (1970) 56–72. Particular attention is drawn to the fact that the ascetic discipline and aims of Pelagianism are now regarded as the *least* original aspects of the movement, being regarded as part of the general western reception of oriental monastic traditions through the translations of Rufinus in the late fourth century (on which see F. Winkelmann, 'Spätantike lateinische Übersetzungen christlicher griechischer Literatur', *Theologische Literaturzeitung* 95 (1967) 229–40).

4 *de dono persev.* xx, 53. Cf. *Confessiones* X, xxix, 40 'da quod iubes et iube quod vis'.

5 Cf. Harnack, *History of Dogma* 5.245 n.3. The alternative 'synergism' is similarly unacceptable: Williams, *Grace of God*, 44.

6 *de praed. sanct.* i, 2.

7 *Commonitorium* 2; Pl 50.640B 'In ipsa item catholica ecclesia magnopere curandum est, ut id teneamus, quod ubique, quod semper, quod ad omnibus creditum est; hoc est etenim vere proprieque catholicum.'

8 D. J. MacQueen, 'John Cassian on Grace and Free Will'. Cf. A. Hoch, *Die Lehre des Johannes Cassianus von Natur und Gnade* (Freiburg, 1894). The two general studies of Chéné, 'Que significiaent "initium fidei"' and 'Le sémipelagianisme du Midi de la Gaule' provide valuable background material.

9 *de incarnat.* VII, i, 2.

10 Both this council and Orange II (q.v.) were *local*, rather than ecumenical. For the difficulties this raises, see *Problems of Authority. An Anglo-French Symposium* ed. J. M. Todd (London, 1964), 63–4.

11 D. 105.

12 C. Gore, 'Our Lord's Human Example', *Church Quarterly Review* 16 (1883) 298. A similar link between Nestorius and Pelagius is identified by John Cassian (*de incarnat.* I, iii, 5). See also the somewhat scurrilous poem of Prosper of Aquitaine, *Epitaphium Nestorianae et Pelagianae haeresos*, PL 51.153.

13 Cap. 1; D. 130.

14 Cap. 3; D. 132.

15 Cap. 9; D. 141 'Non aufertur liberum arbitrium, sed liberatur.'

16 Can. 1; D. 174. The reference here appears to be to freedom from sin, rather than *liberum arbitrium*. See also n.10.

17 Can. 5; D. 178. For the terms *initium fidei* and *affectus credulitatis*, as they occur in this canon, see the studies of Chéné cited in n.8.

18 Can. 8; D. 181 '... per liberum arbitrium, quod in omnibus, qui de praevaricatione primi hominis nati sunt, constat esse vitiatum ... omnium liberum arbitrium per peccatum primi hominis asserit infirmatum'. This is made especially clear in the 'profession of faith' appended to the canons (D. 199).

19 This remarkable fact appears first to have been noticed by Bouillard, *Conversion et grâce chez Thomas d'Aquin*, 98–102; 114–21. See also M. Seckler, *Instinkt und Glaubenswille nach Thomas von Aquin* (Mainz, 1961) 90–133.

20 *II Sent.* dist. xxviii 4. See further J. N. D. Kelly, *Jerome* (London, 1975) 309–23. The attitude of Thomas Bradwardine and Gregory of Rimini to the *Epistula ad Demetriadem*, allegedly due to Jerome, is significant: Oberman, *Werden und Wertung*, 87.

21 M. de Kroon, 'Pseudo-Augustin im Mittelalter', *Augustiniana* 22 (1972) 511–30. For the problems this raises, see McGrath, '"Augustinianism"?' 253–4.

22 D. 348 'Gratiam Dei praevenire et subsequi hominem credo et profiteor, ita tamen, ut liberum arbitrium rationali creaturae non denegem.'

23 Anselm, *de lib. arb.* 3. Cf. F. Bäumker, *Die Lehre Anselms von Canterbury über dem Willen und seine Wahlfreiheit* (Münster, 1912).

24 See Mitzka, 'Anfänge einer Konkurslehre'. For this concept in the early Augustinian school, see Trapè, *Il concorso divino del pensiero di Egidio Romano*. On the development of the concept in High Scholasticism, see Auer, *Entwicklung der Gnadenlehre*, 2.113–45.

25 Mitzka, op. cit., 175.

26 *II Sent.* dist. xxv 8–9.

27 See L. Grane, *Contra Gabrielem. Luthers Auseinandersetzung mit Gabriel Biel in der Disputatio contra scholasticam theologiam (1517)* (Gyldendal, 1972); Ernst, *Gott und Mensch am Vorabend der Reformation*.

28 For an analysis of these theses, see Grane, op. cit., 369–73.

29 *In II Sent.* dist xxv q. unica a.3 dub.2.

30 *In II Sent.* dist. xxv q. unica a.1 not.1.

31 For an excellent analysis, see Ernst, op. cit., 325–8.

32 e.g., *In II Sent.* dist. xxviii q. unica a.2 concl.1.

33 *In II Sent.* dist. xxviii q. unica a.2 conc.3.

34 *In II Sent.* dist. xxviii q. unica a.2 conc.2.

35 *In II Sent.* dist. xxvii q. unica a.3 dub.2 prop.1.

36 *In II Sent.* dist. xxviii q. unica a.2 conc.1.

37 Thus Oberman, *Harvest of Medieval Theology*, 176–7; H. J. McSorley, 'Was Gabriel Biel a Semi-Pelagian?', in *Wahrheit und Verkündigung* ed. L. Scheffczyk *et al.* (2 vols: München, 1967) 2.1109–20; J. E. Biechler, 'Gabriel Biel on "liberum arbitrium"', *The Thomist* 34 (1970) 114–27. For replies, see F. Clark, 'A New Appraisal of Late Medieval Nominalism', *Gregorianum* 46 (1965) 733–65; Ernst, op. cit.; McGrath, 'The Anti-Pelagian Structure of "Nominalist" Doctrines of Justification'.

38 e.g., Biechler, op. cit., 125 'Biel's own doctrine of justification, clearly Pelagian though it was, apparently provoked little or no pre-Lutheran opposition.' It may be pointed out that the list of forbidden books published after Trent makes no reference to Biel or other theologians of the *via moderna*: indeed, Biel was still highly regarded by the German Roman Catholic church in the late sixteenth century: Oberman, op. cit., 427.

39 For an excellent study of Biel's attitude to tradition, see Oberman, op. cit., 365–408.
40 The conciliar collections of the period, however, generally attributed the canons of the Council of Carthage (418) to the Council of Mileve (416).
41 *Sententiarum libri quinque* III, 2; PL 211.1047A–B.
42 *Quaestiones disputatae 'antequam esset frater'* q.53 membr.3; ed. Quaracchi, 2.1020.24–22.7.
43 *Quaestiones disputatae de gratia* q.7; ed. Hödl, 64; cf. *Tractatus de gratia* q.2 membr.1 a.2; ed. Hödl, 72.
44 *In II Sent.* dist. xxvi membr.1 q.1; ed. Bouvy, 308.89–92. See also B. Pergamo, 'Il desiderio innato del soprannaturále nelli questioni inediti di Oddone Rigaldo', *Studi Francescani* 32 (1935) 414–46; 33 (1936) 76–108.
45 *In II Sent.* dist. xxvi membr.1 q.1 ad 1um; ed. cit., 308.95–105. It may be noted at this point that Thomas Aquinas never seems to use the term *gratia creata* at all, although he appears to demonstrate familiarity with the term at one point (*In II Sent.* dist. xxvi q.1 a.1).
46 See E. Gössmann, *Metaphysik und Heilsgeschichte. Eine theologische Untersuchung der Summa Halensis* (München, 1964); G. Philips, 'La théologie de la grâce dans la "Summa Fratris Alexandri"', *EThL* 49 (1973) 100–23. This work is composite, and does not stem from Alexander of Hales: J. Auer, 'Textkritische Studien zur Gnadenlehre des Alexander von Hales', *Scholastik* 15 (1940) 63–75. For the origins of the distinction between *gratia creata* and *gratia increata*, see Auer, *Entwicklung der Gnadenlehre*, 1.86–123.
47 *Summa Fratris Alexandri* pars III inq.1 tract.2 q.1 cap.1 and the following sections; *Alexandri de Hales Summa Theologica*, 4.1023–60.
48 *Summa Fratris Alexandri* pars III inq.1 tract.1 q.2 cap. 1 a.2 sol.; ed. cit., 4.959. On this whole question, see Dhont, *Le problème de la préparation à la grâce*.
49 *Summa Fratris Alexandri* pars II inq.2 tract.3 sect.2 q.2 tit.3 cap.4 a.1 ad 3um; ed. cit., 1.729. For a more detailed study of this question, see G. Philips, *L'Union personnelle avec le Dieu vivant*.
50 See Mitzka, *Die Lehre des hl. Bonaventura von der Vorbereitung auf die heiligmachenden Gnade*.
51 *Breviloquium* V, ii, 2.
52 *In IV Sent.* dist. xvii pars 1 a.2 q.2 ad 1.2.3um.
53 On this point, see Mitzka, op. cit., 64.
54 *Quaestiones disputatae de gratia* q.3; ed. Douchet, 69–72. The argument is based on the maxim 'naturaliter est anima gratiae capax', which will be shown to be characteristic of the early Dominican school.
55 *Quaestiones* q.4; ed. cit., 94–6.
56 *Quaestiones* q.4; ed. cit., 97.
57 *Quaestiones* q.4; ed. cit., 98–9 'Gratia enim gratis data quasi medium tenet inter naturam vel voluntatem et gratiam gratum facientem.'
58 *In II Sent.* dist. xxix a.1 q.1. The important study of Heynck, 'Die aktuelle Gnade bei Richard von Mediavilla', should be consulted.

59 *In II Sent.* dist. xxviii a.1 q.2.

60 Hocedez, *Richard de Middleton*, 277.

61 *Quaestiones disputatae de statu naturae lapsae* q.2; ed. cit., 178.

62 See M. Grabmann, *Die philosophische und theologische Erkenntnislehre des Kardinals Matthaeus ab Aquasparta* (Wien, 1906); E. Gilson, 'Roger Marston, un cas d'Augustinisme avicennisant', *Archives d'histoire doctrinale et littéraire du moyen âge* 8 (1952) 37–42.

63 Thomas Aquinas, *Summa Theologiae* IaIIae q.113 a.10. It is interesting to compare this with Tertullian's assertion that the soul is 'anima naturaliter Christiana': see H. Chadwick, *Early Christian Thought and the Classical Tradition* (Oxford, 1984) 3.

64 See McGrath, 'Influence of Aristotelian Physics'.

65 Doms, *Die Gnadenlehre des Albertus Magnus*, 163–8.

66 *In II Sent.* dist. xxviii q.1 a.4, ed. Mandonnet, 2.726–30.

67 *In II Sent.* dist. xxviii q.1 a.4, ed. Mandonnet, 2.728.

68 *Summa Theologiae* IaIIae q.109 a.6.

69 loc. cit.: Cf. J. Stufler, *Gott der erste Beweger aller Dinge* (Innsbruck, 1936).

70 *In II Sent.* dist. xxviii q.1 a.4, ed. Mandonnet, 2.728. See Stufler, 'Die entfernte Vorbereitung auf die Rechtfertigung nach dem hl. Thomas'.

71 *de veritate* q.24 a.15, ed. Spiazzi, 1.467.

72 For details of this work, which is actually an extract from the *Eudemian Ethics*, see A. Pelzer, 'Les versions des ouvrages de morale conservés sous le nom d'Aristote en usage au XIIIe siècle', *Revue néo-scholastique de philosophie* 23 (1921) 37–9; T. Deman, 'Le "Liber de bona fortuna" dans la théologie de S. Thomas d'Aquin', *RSPhTh* 17 (1928) 41–50.

73 See Bouillard, *Conversion et grâce*, 114–21.

74 *Summa contra Gentiles* III, 149, 8.

75 *Summa contra Gentiles* III, 149, 1. For a discussion of the axiom which so influenced Thomas, see Stufler, 'Der hl. Thomas und das Axiom "omne quod movetur ab alio movetur"'.

76 *Summa contra Gentiles* III, 149. 1.

77 *Quodl.* q.1 a.7. A similar opinion may be found in the Romans *Reportatio* cap. 10 lect. 3.

78 *Summa Theologiae* IaIIae q.112 a.2 ad 3um 'nulla praeparatio exigitur quam ipse non faciat'.

79 IaIIae q.112 a.3.

80 IaIIae q.112 a.2 ad 2um. See J. Stufler, 'Zur Kontroverse über die praemotio physica', *ZKTh* 47 (1927) 533–64.

81 See Steinmetz, *Misericordia Dei*, 93–5.

82 Literally, 'God does not deny grace to the man who does what is in him.'

83 Irenaeus, *adv. haer.* IV, xxxix, 2. Cf. Origen, *contra Celsum* VII, 42. See J. Rivière, 'Quelques antécédents patristiques de la formule "facienti quod in se est"', *RSR* 7 (1927) 93–7.

84 For an excellent discussion of the axiom in this period, see Landgraf, *Dogmengeschichte* I/1 249–64.

85 *Homiliae de sanctis* 2; PL 155.1496B.

86 e.g., in his Romans commentary, cited Landgraf, op. cit., 251 nn.14, 15. Cf. n.16 'Facite, quod vestrum est, quia Deus faciet, quod suum est.' On his concept of merit, which is closely related, see Hamm, *Promissio, pactum, ordinatio*, 109–18.

87 Cod. Erlangen lat. 353 fol. 84; cited Landgraf, op. cit., 252.

88 *Sententiarum libri octo* VI, 49; PL 186.893B. See Courtney, *Robert Pullen*, 226–33.

89 *contra Hereticos* I, 51; PL 210.356B. Cf. 356A 'Nec poenitentia est causa efficiens remissionis peccati, sed tantum gratuita Dei voluntas.' See also *Theologicae Regulae* 87; PL 210.666A–C.

90 Cod. Vat. lat. 1098 fol. 155v; cited Landgraf, op. cit., 260.

91 *Quaestiones de gratia* q.6; ed. Hödl, 55–6. See also *Tractatus de gratia* q.3 membr.2 a.2 sol.; ed. Hödl, 61.

92 *Tractatus de gratia* q.3 membr.2 a.2 sol.; ed. cit., 60 'Concedo igitur quod si homo faciat quod in se est, Deus necessario, id est immutabiliter dat ei gratiam.'

93 *In II Sent.* dist. xxvi membr.1 q.2 a.3; ed. Bouvy, 331.48–332.68.

94 *In II Sent.* dist. xxviii membr.1 q.4 a.2 ad 3um; ed. cit., 86.49–52.

95 *Summa Halensis* Inq.4 tr.3 q.3 tit.1; ed. Quaracchi, 2.730–1.

96 *Summa Halensis* Inq.4 tr.3 q.3 tit.1; ed. cit., 2.731.

97 *In IV Sent.* dist. xiv pars 1 a.2 q.2; dist. xvii pars 1 a.1 q.2. This point is emphasised by G. Božitkovič, *S. Bonaventurae doctrina de gratia et libero arbitrio* (Marienbad, 1919).

98 e.g., *Breviloquium* V, iii, 4 'Rursus, quoniam Deus sic reformat, quod leges naturae inditas non infirmat; ideo sic hanc gratiam tribuit libero arbitrio, ut tamen ipsum non cogat, sed eius consensus liber maneat.'

99 *In II Sent.* dist. xxviii q.1 a.4.

100 *In II Sent.* dist. xxviii q.1 a.4 ad 4um.

101 *In IV Sent.* dist. xvii q.1 aa.3–4.

102 Thus Roger of Marston, *Quaestiones disputatae de statu naturae lapsae* q.1 ad 11um; ed. cit., 195.

103 Cod. Paris Nat. lat. 14551 fol. 103r; Cod. Paris Nat. lat. 15690 fol. 228v; Klosterneuburg Cod. 322; cited Grabmann, *Mittelalterliches Geistesleben* 2.453–5.

104 *Summa Theologiae* IaIIae q.112 a.3 'Praeparatio ad hominis gratiam est a Deo sicut a movente, a libero autem arbitrio sicut a moto.'

105 IaIIae q. 109 a.6 ad 2um. See also *in Hebr.* cap. 12 lect. 3 nn. 688–0.

106 Dhont, op. cit., 267–8. See also L. Capéran, *Le problème du salut des infidèles* (2 vols: Toulouse, 1934) 2.49–57.

107 *In II Sent.* dist. xxvii q.2 a.4 ad 3um. Peter allows that man may dispose himself remotely, but not proximately, to justification through his unaided powers: *In II Sent.* dist. xxviii q.1 aa.2, 3.

108 *In II Sent.* dist. xxviii q.1 a.4; ed. cit., 2.728–9.

109 *de veritate* q.29 a.6; ed. cit., 1.564.

110 *Summa Theologiae* IaIIae q.114 a.6.

111 IaIIae q.114.a.5 Cf. IaIIae q.112 aa.2, 3; q.114 aa.3, 5.

112 *In II Sent.* dist. xxvii q.2 a.2. 'Meritum impetrativum' is synonymus with 'meritum de congruo'.

113 *In II Sent.* dist. xxviii, xxix q.1 a.4.

114 *Textbeilage* 119; cited Zumkeller, 'Der Wiener Theologieprofessor Johannes von Retz'.

115 *In II Sent.* dist. xxvi, xxvii q.1 a.3, conc.2.

116 *Textbeilage* 117. Here, as above, Retz is heavily dependent upon Thomas of Strasbourg – cf. *In II Sent.* dist. xxviii, xxix q.1.

117 Oberman, *Archbishop Thomas Bradwardine*, 155–9; Gregory of Rimini, *In II Sent.* dist. xxvi q.1 aa.1, 2; Zumkeller, 'Johannes Klenkok', 240–52; idem, 'Erfurter Augustinertheologen' 46–8; idem, 'Johannes von Dorsten', 32–6; 44–8; 184–6. On the role of the *auxilium speciale Dei* in Gregory's theology of justification, see Burger, 'Das auxilium speciale Dei in der Gnadenlehre Gregors von Rimini'.

118 Steinmetz, op. cit., 94–97; 114–22.

119 Zumkeller, 'Erfurter Augustinertheologen', 54–5. For a fuller study of his theology, see M. Ferdigg, 'De vita et operibus et doctrina Ioannis de Palz', *Analecta Augustiniana* 30 (1967) 210–321; 31 (1968) 155–318. See also Steinmetz, op. cit., 94–7; 114–22.

120 On this, see Courtenay, 'Covenant and Causality'; idem., 'The King and the Leaden Coin'; Oberman, *Werden und Wertung*, 161–200. On token coins, see W. J. Courtenay, 'Token Coinage and the Administration of Poor Relief during the Late Middle Ages', *Journal of Interdisciplinary History* 3 (1972–3) 275–95.

121 *In IV Sent.* dist. q.1 C 'Sicut si rex ordinaret quod quicumque acciperet denarium plumbeum haberet certum donum, et tunc denarius plumbeus esset causa sine qua non respectu illius doni.'

122 *Super libros Sapientiae* III, 35.

123 See McGrath, '"The Righteousness of God"', 113–17.

124 *In II Sent.* dist. xxvii q. unica a.3 dub.4.

125 *In II Sent.* dist. xxvii q. unica a.2 conc.4; ed. Werbeck/Hoffmann, 2.517.1–8.

126 *In II Sent.* dist. xxvii q. unica a.3 dub.4.

127 On Geiler, see Douglass, *Justification in Late Medieval Preaching*.

128 *Orat. Domini* 9B; cited Douglass, op. cit., 144 n.2.

129 *Nav. fat.* 22S; cited Douglass, op. cit., 145 n.1.

130 *Nav. pen.* 28v 1, cited Douglass, op. cit., 139 n.3.

131 *Nav. pen.* 18r 1; cited Douglass, op. cit., 143 n.1.

132 See McGrath, *Luther's Theology of the Cross*, 72–92.

133 WA 4.262.4–7. Cf. WA 3.288.37–289.4. See further L. Grane, *Contra Gabrielem. Luthers Auseinandersetzung mit Gabriel Biel in der Disputatio contra scholasticam theologiam 1517* (Gyldendal, 1968), 296–301; R. Schwarz, *Vorgeschichte der reformatorischen Bußtheologie* (Berlin, 1968), 249–59; O. Bayer, *Promissio. Geschichte der reformatorischen Wende in Luthers Theologie* (Göttingen, 1971), 115–43.

Notes to §8

1 J. de Ghellinck, 'Un chapitre dans l'histoire de la définition des sacrements au XIIe siècle', in *Mélanges Mandonnet* (Paris, 1930) 2.79–96; N. M. Haring, 'Berengar's Definitions of *Sacramentum* and Their Influence upon Medieval Sacramentology', *Medieval Studies* 10 (1948) 109–46; D. van den Eynde, 'Les définitions des sacrements pendant la première période de la théologie scolastique (1050–1235)', *Antonianum* 24 (1949) 183–228; 439–88; 25 (1950) 3–78.

2 Cassiodorus, *Exp. S. Pauli epist. ad Rom.*; PL 68.417B; Sedulius Scotus, *Coll. in omnes B. Pauli epist.*; PL 103.42D. The central significance of baptism to the Pelagian soteriology should be noted here: see T. Böhlin, *Die Theologie des Pelagius und ihre Genesis* (Uppsala, 1957), especially 29–43. The controversy surrounding the views of Jovinian on the relationship between baptism and membership of the church called this theology into question (e.g., Jerome, *Dialog. contra Pelag.* III, 1; PL 23.595B) – but see S. Prete, 'Lo scritto pelagiano "de castitate" è di Pelagio?', *Aevum* 35 (1961), 315–22.

3 Jerome, *Epist.* 130, 9; CSEL 56.189.4–5.

4 *Regula canonicorum* 14; PL 89.1104A–05B.

5 O. D. Watkins, *A History of Penance* (2 vols: London, 1920). Cf. B. Poschmann, *Penance and the Anointing of the Sick* (New York, 1954).

6 Harnack, *History of Dogma* 5.325.

7 See J. F. McNeill and H. M. Gamer, *Medieval Handbooks of Penance* (New York, 1938). The older edition of H. J. Schmitz, *Die Bußbücher und die Bußdisziplin der Kirche. Die Bußbücher und das kanonische Bußverfahren* (2 vols: Düsseldorf, 1883–98) is still invaluable.

8 L. Wallach, *Alcuin and Charlemagne. Studies in Carolingian History and Literature* (Ithica, NY, 1959); J. Marenbon, *From the Circle of Alcuin to the School of Auxerre. Logic, Theology and Philosophy in the Early Middle Ages* (Cambridge, 1981).

9 *Liber de divinis officiis* 55; PL 101.1284B. See also *de virtutibus et vitiis* 12; PL 101.622A; *de confessione peccatorum*, PL 101.652B 'Dic tu prior iniustitias tuas, ut iustificeris.'

10 It occurs, in various forms, throughout the period: see Alcuin, *de virtutibus et vitiis* 13; PL 101.623A; Eadmer, *Liber de S. Anselmi similitudinibus* 175; PL 159.695A; Ivo of Chartres, *Decretum* XV, 26; PL 161.862D; Bruno of Asti, *Comm. in Ioannem* II, 11; PL 165.545A; Honorius of Autun, *Speculum ecclesiae*; PL 172.881C; *Summa Sententiarum* V, 7; PL 176.133A; Hugh of St Victor, *de sacramentis* II, xiv, 8; PL 176.567A; Werner of St Blasien, *Deflorationes* 2; PL 157.1184A; Zacharias Chrysopolitanus, *In unum ex quattuor* III, 99–100; PL 186.315D; Richard of St Victor, *de potestate ligandi* 19; PL 196.1171C; Ermengaudus, *contra Waldenses* 13; PL 204.1261A; Alan of Lille, *contra Hereticos* I, 55; PL 210.358B; Peter Lombard, *IV Sent.* dist. xx 1, 5.

11 In fact, Rabanus quotes Alcuin at some length, without acknowledge-

ment: compare Alcuin, PL 101.621D–22B with Rabanus, PL 101.102D–3A; and Alcuin, PL 101.622B–3A with Rabanus, PL 101.103A–4A.

12 *Exp. in epist. S. Pauli*; PL 117.391C.

13 *Exp. in omnes epist. Pauli*; PL 153.55B–C.

14 e.g., that of Hugh of St Cher, cited Landgraf, *Dogmengeschichte*, I/1 298 n.41, where the fifth element is *peccati remissio quoad penam temporalem*.

15 For an excellent discussion, see Landgraf, op. cit., III/1 279–345.

16 *de conceptu virginali* 29; ed. Schmitt, 2.173.1–3 'Quare si sic moriuntur: quia non sunt iniusti, non damnantur, sed et iustitia Christi qui se dedit pro illis, et iustitia fidei matris ecclesiae quae pro illis credit quasi iusti salvantur.'

17 *Tractatus de baptismo* II, 9; PL 182.1037D.

18 Cod. Paris Nat. lat. 15269 fol. 151v; cited Landgraf, op. cit., III/1 289 n.22.

19 *Exp. in epist. ad Rom.* II, 3; PL 178.838B.

20 Leipzig Universitätsbibliothek Cod. lat. 427, cited Landgraf, op. cit., I/2 50.

21 *Theologiae Regulae* 86; PL 210.667B 'Habentur ergo virtutes in habitu, quando homo per illas potentias quamdam habet habilitatem, et pronitatem ad utendum eis, si tempus exigerit.'

22 D. 410.

23 A. Landgraf, 'Die frühscholastischen Definition der Taufe', *Gregorianum* 27 (1946) 200–19; 353–83. See also Haring, op. cit., 131–8.

24 *de sacramentis* I, ix, 2; PL 176.317D 'Sacramentum est corporale vel materiale elementum foris sensibiliter propositum ex similitudine repraesentans, et ex institutione significans, et ex sanctificatione continens aliquam invisibilem et spiritualem gratiam.'

25 *IV Sent.* dist. i 1–4. See E. F. Rogers, *Peter Lombard and the Sacramental System* (New York, 1917); van den Eynde, op. cit., 222–8. On the significance of the number seven, see B. Geyer, 'Die Siebenzahl der Sakramente in ihrer historischen Entwicklung', *Theologie und Glaube* 10 (1918) 324–48.

26 *Speculum ecclesiae*; PL 172.1061C.

27 *Homilia* 13; PL 158.622B–C.

28 *Comm. in Lucam*; PL 165.427C–D.

29 Honorius of Autun, *Elucidarum* II, 20; PL 172.1050C–D.

30 e.g., Anselm of Canterbury, *de concordia praescientiae* III, 6.

31 Anciaux, *La théologie du sacrement du pénance* 164–274. For the necessity of penance in justification, see Alger of Liège, *Liber de misericordia et iustitia*; PL 180.888D; Richard of St Victor, *Sermo* 53; PL 177.1051C; Bernard of Clairvaux, *Tractatus de interiori domo*; PL 184.509B; Peter of Blois, *Liber de confessione*; PL 207.1081D; Philip of Harvengt, *In cantica canticorum*; PL 203.552B; Peter Lombard, *IV Sent.* dist. xiv 1. In his *Decretum*, Gratian appears to leave open the question of the necessity of confession in justification, although he notes the strong case which can be made in its favour: e.g., PL 187.1532A.

32 Cap. 21; D. 437.
33 On this, see G. J. Spykman, *Attrition and Contrition at the Council of Trent* (Kampen, 1955) 17–89.
34 See McGrath, 'Rectitude', 211–12.
35 *Ethica* 18; PL 178.661A.
36 *Ethica* 24–26; PL 178.668C–74A.
37 *I Sent.* dist. xviii 6.
38 *Sententiarum libri quinque* III, 2; PL 201.1047C.
39 *Quaestio* 78; ed. Warichez, 205.
40 *contra Hereticos* I, 51; PL 210.356A–C.
41 *contra Hereticos* I, 51; PL 210.354A–B.
42 Thomas Aquinas, *Summa Theologiae* IIIa q.90 a.2.
43 *Purgatori* IX.94–102.
44 *Opus Oxoniense* IV dist. i q.6 nn.10–11.
45 *Opus Oxoniense* IV dist. xiv q.4 n.14.
46 e.g., N. Krautwig, *Der Grundlagen der Bußlehre des Joh. Duns Scotus* (Freiburg, 1938). For a reply, see J. Klein, 'Zur Bußlehre des seligen Joh. Duns Scotus', *FS* 27 (1940) 104–13; 191–6, especially 108.
47 *Opus Oxoniense* IV dist. xiv q.4 n.14.
48 *Opus Oxoniense* IV dist. xiv q.4 n.14.
49 This point has been well brought out by V. Heynck, 'A Controversy at the Council of Trent concerning the Doctrine of Duns Scotus', *FrS* 9 (1949) 181–258.
50 Feckes, *Rechtfertigungslehre des Gabriel Biel*, 66 n.189.
51 *In IV Sent.* dist. xiv q.2 a.2 concl.4.
52 See Oberman, *Harvest of Medieval Theology*, 146–60.
53 *In IV Sent.* dist. xiv q.2 a.2 concl.4. Biel uses the traditional appeal to the leper-cleansing ritual (Luke 17.14 – cf. Leviticus 14) to illustrate the need for confession; see *Sermones dominicales de tempore* (Hagenau, 1510) 76.
54 *In IV Sent.* dist. xiv q.2 a.1 nota. 2.
55 *In IV Sent.* dist. xiv q.2 a.1 nota. 2; cf. *Canonis Missae expositio* 26F.
56 *Canonis Missae expositio* 31C.
57 Valla, *Adnotationes*; in *Monumenta politica et philosophica rariora* (Torino, 1959–) 5.807 (on Matthew 3.2); 5.824 (on Mark 1.14); 5.872 (on II Corinthians 7.9–10). It is interesting to note that the opinion of Isidore of Seville, that there exists an etymological connection between *punire* and *poenitere* (*Etymologiae* VI, xix, 71; PL 82.258C), was generally rejected during the twelfth century. However, a close link between *poenitentia* and fear of punishment was presupposed by certain theologians, such as Anselm of Laon, possibly on the basis of this alleged etymological association: see Anciaux, op. cit., 155–7.
58 Biel's linking of justification and the eucharist should be noted here: Oberman, op. cit., 271–80.
59 Cf. Augustine, *de baptismo* IV, xvii, 24 'Salus extra ecclesiam non est.'
60 e.g., see the use made of this text by Astesanus of Asti: Schmitz, op. cit., 1.800.

Notes to §9

1 See Alszeghy, *Nova Creatura*; Auer, *Entwicklung der Gnadenlehre*; Beumer, *Gratia supponit naturam*; Doms, *Die Gnadenlehre des sel. Albertus Magnus*; Gillon, *La grâce incréée*; Hervé de l'Incarnation O.C.D., 'La grâce dans l'œuvre de S. Léon le grand', *RThAM* 22 (1955) 193–212; Heynck, *Die aktuelle Gnade bei Richard von Mediavilla*; R. Javelet, *Image et ressemblance au XIIe siècle de S. Anselme à Alain de Lille* (2 vols: Paris, 1967); Landgraf, *Dogmengeschichte* I/1 51–140; 141–201; Molteni, *Roberto Holcot*; Philips, 'La théologie de la grâce chez les préscolastiques'; idem, 'La théologie de la grâce dans la "Summa Fratris Alexandri"'; Schupp, *Die Gnadenlehre des Petrus Lombardus*; Stoeckle, '*Gratia supponit naturam*'; Vanneste, 'Nature et grâce dans la théologie du XIIe siècle'; idem, 'Nature et grâce dans la théologie de Saint Augustin'.
2 Cf. H. de Lubac, *Surnaturel: Etude historique* (Paris, 1946).
3 See Vanneste, op. cit.
4 *Comm. in Iohan.*, PL 122.325C; *de divisione naturae* III.3, PL 122.631D.
5 *de divisione naturae* V.23, PL 122.904B.
6 *de divisione naturae* V.30, PL 122.939A.
7 e.g., Hervaeus of Bourg Dieu, *Comm. in epist. divi Pauli*, PL 181.1446C–D; Hugh of St Victor, *de sacramentis* I, vi, 17; PL 176.237D–8A; Hugh of Amiens, *Dialogi* IV, 6; PL 192.1184A.
8 *Quaestio* 64; ed. Warichez, 179.
9 *Sententiarum libri quinque* II, 20; PL 211.1025A. Cf. also here the anonymous Cod. Paris Nat. lat. 686 fol. 40v, cited Landgraf, op. cit., I/1 180 n.76 'quod dicitur natura quantum ad creationem, dicitur gratia quantum ad recreationem vel reformationem'.
10 *Summa*, Cod. Erlangen 353 fol. 32, cited Landgraf, op. cit., 180 'Fides mea est supra rationem et ratione nullum naturale bonum est homine excellentius. Ergo fides supra omnia naturalia.' Praepositinus was associated with a group of scholars upon whom the strongest influence was Peter Lombard, including Peter of Poitiers, Peter of Capua and Stephen Langton: see J. W. Baldwin, *Masters, Princes and Merchants* (2 vols: Princeton, 1970).
11 *Summa Aurea* lib. II tr. xiv cap 2; fol. 69.
12 *Summa de bono*, Cod. Vat. lat. 7669 fol. 12, cited Landgraf, op. cit., I/1 198–99 n.84.
13 *Summa Theologiae* IaIIae q.110 a.1 'Sic igitur per hoc quod dicitur homo gratiam Dei habere, significatur quiddam supernaturale in homine a Deo proveniens.' For the relation between grace and supernature in High Scholasticism, see Auer, *Entwicklung der Gnadenlehre*, 2.219–50.
14 *II Sent.* dist. xxvii 7.
15 Bonaventure, *In II Sent.* dist. xxvii dub.1; ed. Quaracchi, 2.669 'Accipitur enim gratia uno modo largissime, et sic comprehendit dona naturalia et dona gratuita … Alio modo accipitur gratia minus communiter, et sic comprehendit gratiam gratis datam et gratum facientem.'
16 Doms, op. cit., 167–8.

17 *In II Sent.* dist. xxviii a.2 q.3; ed. cit., 2.689.
18 *In II Sent.* dist. xxviii a.2 q.1; ed. cit., 2.682.
19 Thomas, *In II Sent.* dist. xxviii q.1 a.4; ed. Mandonnet, 2.728. See
    Stufler, 'Die entfernte Vorbereitung auf die Rechtfertigung nach dem hl.
    Thomas'; P. de Vooght, 'A propos de la grâce actuelle dans la théologie de
    Saint Thomas', *Divus Thomas* (Piacenza) 31 (1928) 386–416. Thomas
    elsewhere appears to regard it as a *charism* – i.e., a gift to help *others*:
    Summa Theologiae IaIIae q.111 a.1.
20 e.g., Bonaventure, *In II Sent.* dist. xxvii a.1 qq.1–5; Thomas, *In II Sent.*
    dist. xxvi q.1 aa.1–6. The systematic use of the term *habitus* in this
    context appears to be due to the influence of Philip the Chancellor: see
    P. Fransen, 'Dogmengeschichtlichen Entfaltung der Gnadenlehre', in
    Mysterium Salutis ed. J. Feiner and M. Löhrer (Einsiedeln, 1973)
    4/2.631–722; 672–9. The first magisterial reference to grace as a *habitus* is
    encountered in the decisions of the Council of Vienne of 1312 (D 483: 'et
    virtutes ac informans gratia infunduntur quoad habitum'), although the
    term is used earlier (1201) in relation to the virtues (D 410 'et virtutes
    infundi . . . quoad habitum').
21 See Albertus Magnus, *In II Sent.* dist. xxvi aa.6–7.
22 *In II Sent.* dist. xxvi q.1 a.6; ed. cit., 2.682–6. For what follows, see the
    excellent study of Lonergan, *Grace and Reason*.
23 *de veritate* q.27 a.5; ed. Spiazzi, 1.524–8.
24 *Summa Theologiae* IaIIae q.111 a.2.
25 Ia q.62 a.2 ad 3um; *Quodl.* I a.7.
26 *In II Sent.* dist. xxvi q.1 a.6 ad 2um; ed. cit., 2.685.
27 Cited in *In III Sent.* dist. xxiii q.1 a.1; ed. cit., 3.698.
28 *de veritate* q.27 a.5 ad 3um; ed. Spiazzi, 1.526.
29 *de veritate* q.27 a.5 ad 3um; ed. cit., 1.526–7. Thomas emphasises that
    this arises 'non quidem propter defectum gratiae, sed propter infirmi-
    tatem naturae'. Cf. q.24 a.7.
30 For an introduction to the problem, see D. Janz, 'A Reinterpretation of
    Gabriel Biel on Nature and Grace', *Sixteenth Century Journal* 8 (1977)
    104–8.

Notes to §10

1 Augustine, *de grat. et lib. arb.* vi, 15. See also *Epist.* 194. 19.
2 Bakhuizen van den Brink, 'Mereo(r) and meritum in some Latin
   Fathers'; Peñamaria de Llano, *La salvación por la fe*, 191–211. See also the
   earlier study of K. H. Wirth, *Der 'Verdienst'-Begriff in der christlichen
   Kirche* I. *Der 'Verdienst'-Begriff bei Tertullian* (Leipzig, 1892); II. *Der
   'Verdienst'-Begriff bei Cyprian* (Leipzig, 1901).
3 Augustine, *Sermo* 111, iv, 4; PL 38.641A. For an excellent discussion of
   this aspect of Augustine's theology, see Hamm, *Promissio, pactum,
   ordinatio*, 11–18.
4 Augustine, *Epist.* 130, 14.
5 e.g., Hervaeus of Bourg-Dieu, *Comm. in epist. Pauli*; PL 181.1052B–D;

Anselm of Canterbury, *de casu diaboli* 17; *de veritate* 12; Peter Abailard, *Exp. in Epist. ad Rom.*, PL 178.903A, 919B, 920A–B; Bernard of Clairvaux, *de grat. et lib. arb.* vi, 16; PL 182.1010C; Honorius of Autun, *Elucidarum* II, 3; PL 172.1135D; Robert Pullen, *Sententiarum libri octo* V, 9; PL 186.837B–C; Peter of Poitiers, *Sententiarum libri quinque* III, 2; PL 211.1045A–D; Alan of Lille, *Theologicae Regulae* 86; PL 210.665C–6A; Hugh of St Victor, *de sacramentis* I, vi, 17; PL 176.247C–D; Richard of St Victor, *In apoc. Ioann.* VII, 8; PL 196.883C–D; Peter Lombard, *II Sent.* dist. xxvii, 7.

6 The remark of Magister Martinus is typical of many: 'Cum Deus coronat nostra merita, quid aliud coronat quam sua munera.' Cod. Paris Nat. lat. 14556 fol. 314, cited Landgraf, *Dogmengeschichte* I/1 185. 'Master Martin' (i.e., Martin of Fougères) was one of the theologians, such as Alan of Lille and Simon of Tournai, who owed a particular debt to Gilbert de la Porrée: see J. W. Baldwin, *Masters, Princes and Merchants* (2 vols: Princeton, 1970) 1.44. Cf. the Augustinian *loci* referred to in note 1.

7 See Landgraf, 'Untersuchungen zu den Eigenlehren Gilberts de la Porrée'; idem, 'Mitteilungen zur Schule Gilberts de la Porrée'; idem, 'Neue Funde zur Porretanerschule'; idem, 'Der Porretanismus der Homilien des Radulphus Ardens'.

8 e.g., Alan of Lille, *Theologicae Regulae* 82; PL 210.663C 'Solus Christus proprie nobis meruit vitam aeternam': cf. Hamm, op. cit., 32–4. Cardinal Laborans' critique of the theological application of *civil* concepts of merit should be noted here (Hamm, op. cit., 47–66), along with Hamm's excellent discussion of the general teaching of the *Porretani*: op. cit., 26–40.

9 Cod. British Museum Harley 957 fol. 179v; cited Landgraf, op. cit., I/1 271.

10 e.g., Cod. British Museum Royal 9 E XII fol. 95v; Cod. Vat. lat. 4297 fol. 24; cited Landgraf, op. cit., I/1 272 nn.17, 18.

11 e.g., as used in Geoffrey of Poitiers' *Summa*: Brugge Bibliothèque de la Ville Cod. lat. 220 fol. 114v; cited Landgraf, op. cit., 276 n.35 'Et ita patet, quod non meretur de congruo. Et certum est, quod nec de condigno.'

12 Landgraf, op. cit., I/1 238–302.

13 Most notably by Harnack, *History of Dogma*, 6.275–317.

14 *In II Sent.* dist. xxvii q.2.

15 Auer, *Entwicklung der Gnadenlehre*, 2.85 'Es war das religiöse und vielleicht seelsorgliche Bedürfnis, aus der Güte Gottes die Möglichkeit einer wirksamen Vorbereitung auf die Gnade zu erweisen.'

16 Auer, op. cit., 2.86 'Daß diese Lehre nichts mit den von Harnack aus tiefem innerem Unverständnis für die Hochscholastik geborenen Vorwürfen eines Neosemipelagianismus zu tun hat, ist ganz selbstverständlich, wenn man das ganz auf Gottes Barmherzigkeit gebaute interpretative Verdienst (das mit Harnacks menschlich-bürgerlichem Verdienstbegriff nichts zu tun hat) und die ganz in Gottes Gnade gesetzte Betätigung des Menschen überhaupt und die eigens vorausgesetzten

aktuellen göttlichen Anregungen für diese Bereitung des Menschen für Gott ins Auge faßt.'

17 *De tropis loquendi*, Cod. Vat. lat. 1283 fol. 38r, cited Landgraf, op. cit., I/1 270 n.5. On this work, see G. Evans, 'Peter the Chanter's *De Tropis Loquendi*: The Problem of the Text', *New Scholasticism* 55 (1981) 95–103.

18 *Theologicae Regulae* 82; PL 210.663B–C.

19 Cod. Salzburg St Peter a. X 19 fol. 25; cited Landgraf, 'Untersuchungen zu den Eigenlehre Gilberts de la Porrée', 201–2 n.7.

20 *Summa*, Cod. Paris Nat. lat. 15747 fol. 42v; cited Landgraf, *Dogmengeschichte* I/1 276 n.37.

21 *De meritis*; in *Opera Omnia* 1.310 aF.

22 This point is emphasised by Hamm, who distinguishes two distinct senses in which the concept of self-limitation was understood: an *absolute* sense (Hamm, op. cit., 41–103) and a *restricted* sense (ibid., 104–249). This useful distinction permits much of the earlier confusion on this matter to be resolved.

23 *In II Sent.* dist. xxviii q.4 a.1 arg.1; ed. Bouvy, 82.10.

24 *In III Sent.* dist. xviii a.1 q.2 resp.

25 *Summa Aurea* lib. III tr.2 q.6 arg.1; fol. 136d 'Mereri ex condigno est facere de indebito debitum vel de debito magis debitum.'

26 *Summa* 35, 2; ed. Cortesi, 117.

27 cf. Thomas Aquinas, *In II Sent.* dist. xxvi q.1 a.3.

28 Roland of Cremona, *Summa* 347, 66; ed. Cortesi, 1050.

29 Auer's distinction between *Würdigkeit* (i.e., 'worth') and *Verdienst* (i.e., 'merit') is valuable here: Auer, op. cit., 2.150.

30 *In II Sent.* dist. xxvii a.2 q.2.

31 *Summa Aurea* lib. III tr.16 q.2 arg.7; fol. 221c.

32 *Summa Theologiae* IaIIae q.114 a.1. Cf. *In II Sent.* dist. xxvii q.1 a.3; *In III Sent.* dist. xviii a.2.

33 IaIIae q.114 a.1.

34 IaIIae q.114 a.1 ad 3um. This important section is frequently overlooked by Thomas' critics.

35 *Opus Oxoniense* III dist. xix q.1, 7. This view should be contrasted with that of Peter Aureoli, *In I Sent.* dist. xvii q.1 a.2 'ex quo patet quod ex divino amore debetur actibus nostris ut habeant meriti rationem *intrinsice et ex natura rei*'. (Our italics: note the assertion of *ex natura rei* causality.)

36 e.g., Iserloh, *Gnade und Eucharistie* 64–7.

37 It may be noted that Ockham actually notes two solutions to the problem of the relation between grace and merit, without actually committing himself to either: see Leff, *William of Ockham*, 498–9.

38 Iserloh, op. cit., 111.

39 *In III Sent.* q.12.

40 *In IV Sent.* q.9.

41 *In IV Sent.* q.9 'Et dico quod respectu gratie nullus actus est meritorius de condigno nisi ille qui est respectu eterne beatitudinis.'

42 An excellent example of this is provided by Leff's early study of Bradwardine, in which he seriously misrepresents Ockham: G. Leff,

Bradwardine and the Pelagians: A Study of 'De Causa Dei' and its Opponents (Cambridge, 1957) 188–210. His later *William of Ockham* acknowledges and corrects these misunderstandings: see especially *William of Ockham*, 470 n.85.

43 *De Causa Dei* I, 39. Cf. Oberman, *Archbishop Thomas Bradwardine*, 155–9; Leff, *Bradwardine and the Pelagians*, 75–7. Leff is incorrect when he states that Bradwardine denied congruous merit *totally*.

44 *In II Sent*. dist. xxvi, xxvii, xxviii q.1 a.1.

45 e.g., Robert Holcot, *In IV Sent*. q.1 a.8 'Nam peccator meretur de congruo iustificationem per motum contritionis.'

46 For the relation between the two theologians, see Laun, 'Die Prädestination bei Wiclif und Bradwardine'.

47 *De sciencia Dei*, cited J. A. Robson, *Wyclif and the Oxford Schools* (Cambridge, 1961) 209 n.1. It is, of course, possible that Wycliffe means that congruous merit results from God's prevenient grace *prior to* justification.

48 *In II Sent*. dist. xxvii q.5; ed. Flajshans, 2.308–9.

49 *In II Sent*. dist. xxvii q.5; ed. cit., 307.

50 *In II Sent*. dist. xxvii q.5; ed. cit., 308.

51 Even Durandus of St Pourçain's discussion of the questions appears innocent of this assumption: *In II Sent*. dist. xxvii q.2; fol. 177r–8r.

52 *In II Sent*. dist. xxvii q.1 a.1 nota 3.

53 Steinbach, *Opera exegetica* 1.136.4–6.

54 On this, see A. E. McGrath, 'John Calvin and Late Medieval Thought: A Study in Late Medieval Influences upon Calvin's Theological Development', *ARG* 77 (1986) 58–78.

55 The replies are incorporated into the 1559 edition of the *Institutio* at the following points: II.17.1–5; III.2.11–12. See the marginal notes in *Ioannis Calvini Opera Selecta* ed. P. Barth and G. Niesel (München, 1926–36) 3.509; 4.20–22.

56 e.g., A. Gordon, 'The Sozzini and their School', *Theological Review* 16 (1879) 293–322.

57 *Institutio* II.17.1; ed. cit., 3.509.

Notes to §11

1 For the best study of this concept, see Hamm, *Promissio, pactum, ordinatio*. See also §§7, 10.

2 *Sermo* 110, iv, 4; PL 38.641A.

3 Hamm, op. cit., 15 'Der promissio-Begriff hat somit im Zusammenhang der Vorstellung von Gott als Schuldner die spezifische Funktion, Gottes Selbstverpflichtung als Ausdruck seiner Souveränität zu interpretieren.'

4 *Summa Theologiae* Ia q.25 a.5 ad 1um.

5 For a useful discussion, see E. Gilson, *History of Christian Philosophy in the Middle Ages* (London, 1978) 406–8.

6 For the thesis in question, see P. Mandonnet, *Siger de Brabant de*

l'Averroisme latin au XIIIe siècle (2 vols: Louvain, 1908–11) 2.195. The example noted is the twentieth on the published list.

7 See M. A. Pernoud, 'Innovation in William of Ockham's References to the *Potentia Dei*', *Antonianum* 65 (1970) 65–97; Bannach, *Die Lehre von der doppelten Macht Gottes bei Wilhelm von Ockham*.

8 *Quodl.* VI q.6; *Opera Theologica* 9.604.13–16 'Credo in deum patrem omnipotentem. Quem sic intelligo quod quodlibet est divine potentiae attribuendum quod non includit manifestam contradictionem.'

9 *Quodl.* VI q.1; ed. cit., 9.585.14–586.24.

10 See A. Pelzer, 'Les 51 articles de Guillaume d'Occam censurés en Avignon en 1326', *Revue d'histoire ecclésiastique* 18 (1922) 240–70. A second, briefer version of the list of articles is now known: J. Koch, 'Neue Aktenstücke zu dem gegen Wilhelm von Ockham in Avignon geführten Prozess', *RThAM* 8 (1936) 168–97. The list of 56 articles drawn up by John Lutterell, along with his appended comments, has been edited by F. Hoffmann, *Die Schriften des Oxforder Kanzlers Johannes Lutterell* (Leipzig, 1959) 3–102.

11 Pelzer, op. cit., 250–1.

12 ibid., 251 'Dicimus quod iste longus processus in predicto articulo contentus est erroneus et sapit heresim Pelagianam vel peius.'

13 ibid., 253.

14 ibid., 253.

15 ibid., 252 'Nec potest excusari per illam addicionem, quam ponit: de potentia Dei absoluta, quia argumentum suum eque procedit absque illa condicione sicut cum illa. Propositio autem, quam assumit, est heretica et conclusio heretica.'

16 Gregory of Rimini, *In I Sent.* dist. xvii q.1 a.2.

17 See Courtenay, 'Covenant and Causality in Pierre d'Ailly', 107–9.

18 Feckes, *Rechtfertigungslehre des Gabriel Biel*, 12 'Darum retten sich die Nominalisten gern auf das Gebiet der potentia absoluta hinüber, wenn die Konsequenzen ihrer Prinzipien mit der Kirchenlehre in Konflikt zu geraten drohen.' On the basis of this presupposition, Feckes argues that Biel developed two essentially independent doctrines of justification, one according to God's absolute power (which represents Biel's own teaching), and one according to God's ordained power (which represents the teaching of the church): ibid., 22.

19 On the question of Luther's relationship to the theology of the *via moderna*, see McGrath, *Luther's Theology of the Cross*, 72–147.

20 Vignaux, *Justification et prédestination*.

21 ibid., 127–40. Particular attention should be paid to the comments made concerning Seeberg and Feckes: 132 n.1.

22 Vignaux, *Luther Commentateur des Sentences*.

23 ibid., 78 'La *potentia absoluta* ne représente pas la raison et le droit, ni la *potentia ordinata*, une pure donnée de fait: toute interprétation de ce genre trahirait la pensée de Gabriel Biel ... (L'ordre établi) est un ordre fait de libéralité à la fois et de la justice.'

24 e.g., R. Weijenborg, 'La charité dans la première théologie de Luther', *Revue d'histoire ecclésiastique*, 45 (1950) 615–69; 617.

25 Iserloh, *Gnade und Eucharistie*, 137–46. It may be noted that Oberman's early emphasis upon the priority of the *potentia absoluta* (e.g., see H. A. Oberman, 'Some Notes on the Theology of Nominalism with Attention to its Relation to the Renaissance', *HThR* 53 (1960) 47–76 is later replaced by a much more balanced approach in *The Harvest of Medieval Theology*, 30–47.

26 Erasmus, *Opera Omnia*, 6.927B.

27 Erasmus, *Opera Omnia*, 6.927B–C.

28 See W. J. Courtenay, 'John of Mirecourt and Gregory of Rimini on whether God can undo the past', *RThAM* 39 (1972) 244–56; 40 (1973) 147–74; A. E. McGrath, '*Homo assumptus*? A Study in the Christology of the *Via Moderna*, with Particular Reference to William of Ockham', *EThL* 61 (1985) 283–97.

29 On this, see Oberman, 'Wir sind pettler'; Courtenay, 'The King and the Leaden Coin'; McGrath, 'The Anti-Pelagian Structure of "Nominalist" Doctrines of Justification'.

30 *Summa Theologiae* IIIa q.62 a.1. See W. Lampen, *De causalitate sacramentorum iuxta scholam Franciscanum* (Bonn, 1931).

31 WA 3.289.1–5. Cf. WA 4.261.32–39; 4.262.2–7. See McGrath, *Luther's Theology of the Cross*, 72–92.

Notes to §12

1 We follow Nygren, *Das Prädestinationsproblem in der Theologie Augustins*, 294, in distinguishing between the *doctrine* and the *problem* of predestination. While the former is stated in the Pauline corpus, the latter is first recognised in the writings of Augustine.

2 e.g., Schelkle, *Paulus Lehrer der Väter*, 336–53; 436–40.

3 See §3 for a consideration of the issues involved.

4 For a careful analysis, see Nygren, op. cit., 41–8.

5 Ambrose, *Epist.* 37, 1.

6 *ad Simplic.* I, ii, 6; CChr 44.30.165–31.198.

7 *de grat. et lib. arb.* xxi, 42–3.

8 *de grat. et lib. arb.* xx, 41; xxi, 43; xxiii, 45.

9 *de grat. et lib. arb.* xxiii, 45 'et deus induravit per iustum iudicium, et ipse Pharao per liberum arbitrium'.

10 *de grat. et lib. arb.* xx, 41 'sicut ipse iudicat, occultissimo quidem iudicio, sed sine ullo dubitatione iustissimo'. Augustine's tendency to refer to the reprobate as *non praedestinati* appears to result from his reluctance to make God the author of sin. This is clearly stated in *de praed. sanct.* x, 19 'Praedestinatione quippe Deus ea praescivit quae fuerat ipse facturus . . . Praescire autem potens est etiam quae ipse non facit, sicut quaecumque peccata; quia etsi sunt quaedam quae ita peccata sunt ut poena sint etiam peccatorum, unde dictum est "Tradidit illos Deus in reprobam mentem

ut faciant quae non conveniunt", non ibi peccatum est, sed iudicium. Quocirca praedestinatio Dei quae in bono est, gratiae est, ut dixi, praeparatio; gratia vero est ipsius praedestinationis effectus.' This tendency to use the term *praedestinatio* solely *in bono* represents, in our opinion, the final position of Augustine on this matter. However, it is possible to point to earlier phases in his thinking on the question. Initially, Augustine appears to have regarded predestination simply as an aspect of the doctrine of justification, and refers to the operation of grace upon man in a purely positive sense. There appears, however, to have been a middle period, corresponding broadly to the greater part of the Pelagian controversy, in which Augustine occasionally speaks of *praedestinatio ad aeternam mortem* – e.g., *de an. et orig.* IV.xi.16 'qui est et illis quos praedestinavit ad aeternam mortem iustissimus supplicii retributor'; *Ench.* 100, 26 '. . . bene utens et malis, tamquam summe bonus, ad eorum damnationem quos iuste praedestinavit ad poenam, et ad eorum salutem quos benigne praedestinavit ad gratiam'. Augustine appears to have later realised the difficulties attending such a concept, not least in the realm of theodicy, and abandoned it. Although it is clearly possible to argue that the concept logically follows from Augustine's doctrine of grace, the fact remains that Augustine chose to exercise a terminological reserve at this point in order to avoid compromising other aspects of his theology.

11 Augustine makes it clear that wisdom is to be understood as the antithesis of fate: *Epist.* 194, ii, 5. It is interesting to note Ælfric's rejection of the fatalist associations of the Old English term *wyrd* in precisely the same context: *The Homilies of the Anglo-Saxon Church* ed. B. Thorpe (2 vols: London, 1864–6) 1.114.13; cf. N. O. Halvorsen, *Doctrinal Terms in Ælfric's Homilies* (University of Iowa Studies: Humanistic Studies 5/1, 1932) 11; 52–3.

12 e.g., *Epist.* 194, ii, 3–4. Cf. A. Sage, 'Praeparatur voluntas a Deo', *REAug* 10 (1964) 1–20.

13 See McGrath, 'Divine Justice and Divine Equity in the Controversy between Augustine and Julian of Eclanum'.

14 D. 160a. Cf. E. Amman, art. 'Lucidus', *DThC* 9.1020–40. Both the date and the status of this council are open to question: it may date from 475, and it appears to represent the private judgement of a group of individuals, rather than that of the church.

15 D. 200. See also the confirmation of the pronouncements of Orange II on this matter by Boniface II in 531: D. 200a–b.

16 The best study is that of K. Vielhaber, *Gottschalk der Sachse* (Bonn, 1956), especially 68–82. For useful studies of the intellectual spirit of the period, see L. M. de Rijk, 'On the Curriculum of the Arts of the Trivium at St. Gall from c.850–c.1000', *Vivarium* 1 (1963) 35–86; J. J. Contreni, *The Cathedral School of Laon from 850–930* (Munich, 1978).

17 G. Morin, 'Gottschalk retrouvé', *Revue Bénédictine* 43 (1931) 302–12. The contents of MS Berne 83 were published by Lambot, *Œuvres théologiques et grammaticales de Godescalc d'Orbais*.

18 *de praedestinatione* 13; ed. Lambot, 234.

19 *Responsa de diversis* 6; ed. cit., 148.
20 *de praedestinatione* 15; ed. cit., 242.
21 *Confessio brevior*; ed. cit., 52.
22 *Responsa de diversis* 7; ed. cit., 157. Cf. *Confessio prolixior*; ed. cit., 56.
23 Isidore of Seville, *Sent.* II, vi, 1; PL 65.656A.
24 e.g., Godescalc, *Confessio brevior*; ed. cit., 54 'Unde dicit et sanctus Isidorus: Gemina est praedestinatio sive electorum ad requiem, sive reproborum ad mortem'; *Responsa de diversis* 7; ed. cit., 154–5.
25 *Opuscula theologica* 20; ed. cit., 279–82.
26 *de praedestinatione* 14; ed. cit., 238. The same conclusion was expressed more forcefully by Servatus Lupus, *Quaest.*, PL 119.646A–B.
27 See G. R. Evans, 'The Grammar of Predestination in the Ninth Century', *Journal of Theological Studies* 33 (1982) 134–45; idem, *The Language and Logic of the Bible: The Earlier Middle Ages* (Cambridge, 1984), 111–13.
28 *de praedestinatione* 26; PL 125.270B.
29 *de praedestinatione* 23; PL 125.209C.
30 The work is also known as *Hypomnesticon* or *Commonitorium contra Pelagianos et Coelestianos*, probably written by Marius Mercator. For the impact of pseudo-Augustinian literature in the Middle Ages, see M. de Kroon, 'Pseudo-Augustin im Mittelalter', *Augustiniana* 22 (1972) 511–30.
31 *Hypognosticon* VI, ii, 2; PL 45.1657D. Hincmar cites this work in *Epist.* 37b; *MGH.Ep* 8.17–18.
32 *Liber de tribus epistolis* 34; PL 121.1043C.
33 *Liber de tribus epistolis* 35; PL 121.1044–47. The *Liber de tribus epistolis* is of considerable importance in connection with our knowledge of the Synod of Quiercy.
34 D. 316–19.
35 Hincmar, *Epist.* 37b; *MGH.Ep* 8.19.
36 D. 317.
37 D. 316 'Deus omnipotens hominem sine peccato rectum cum libero arbitrio condidit.'
38 Florus of Lyons, *de tenenda scriptura veritate* 3; PL 121.1087C–D.
39 *de tenenda scriptura veritate* 4; PL 121.1091B–92B.
40 D. 318. This point was never seriously questioned.
41 D. 319.
42 Hincmar, *Recl.*; ed. Gundlach, 290–1.
43 Hincmar, *de praedestinatione* 32; PL 125.309B.
44 *de praedestinatione* 34; PL 125.350A.
45 Florus of Lyons, *Liber de tribus epistolis* 16; PL 121.1015C.
46 *Liber de tribus epistolis*; PL 121.1129A.
47 *Liber de tribus epistolis* 1–6; PL 121.989–98.
48 Ratramnus, *de praedestinatione* 2; PL 121.54D; 69B–C.
49 Servatus, *Epist. Add.* 3, 4; *MGH.Ep* 6.110–12.
50 D. 320–5.
51 Can. 3; D. 322.
52 Can. 3; D. 322.

53 The report may be found in the *Annals of Saint-Berlin* 859, as cited in *MGH.SRG* 31.53.

54 Hincmar, *Epist.* 187; *MGH.Ep* 8.196.

55 M. Grabmann, *Die Geschichte der katholischen Theologie* (Darmstadt, 1961) 28.

56 *I Sent.* dist. xl, xli.

57 *de veritate* q.6 a.1; ed. Spiazzi, 1.114 'Praeexigitur etiam et electio, per quam ille qui in finem infallibiliter dirigitur ab aliis separatur qui non hoc modo in finem diriguntur. Haec autem separatio non est propter diversitatem aliquam inventam in his qui separantur quae possit ad amorem incitare: quia antequam nati essent aut aliquid boni aut mali fecissent, dictum est: Iacob dilexi, Ezau odio habui.' However, predestination includes *propositum*, *praeparatio* and *praescientia exitus* (*In I Sent.* dist. xl q.1 a.2; ed. Mandonnet, 1.945), whereas reprobation is merely *praescientia culpae et praeparatio poenae* (*In I Sent.* dist. xl q.4 a.1; ed. cit., 1.954). Cf. *de veritate* q.6 a.3; *Summa Theologiae* Ia q.23 aa.3, 5.

58 Pannenberg, *Die Prädestinationslehre des Duns Skotus*, 30–3, 77–9. For a reliable summary of the two main medieval traditions on the *ratio praedestinationis*, see Johannes Eck, *Chrysopassus Praedestinationis* I, 2.

59 *Opus Oxoniense* I dist. xl q. unica n.2. For an excellent analysis of Scotus' doctrine of predestination, see Pannenberg, op. cit., 54–68; 90–119; 125–39.

60 Lennerz, 'De historia applicationis principii "omnis ordinate volens prius vult finem quam ea quae sunt ad finem"'. As Lennerz notes (op. cit., 245), there is no hint in the text (*Opus Oxoniense* I dist. xli q. unica n.11) to suggest that Scotus accepted this on the basis of an earlier authority.

61 Pannenberg, op. cit., 90–3.

62 Pannenberg, op. cit., 95–100. The discussion of the question in the later Paris *Reportata* is significantly different: ibid., 103–11.

63 *Opus Oxoniense* I dist. xli q. unica n.12.

64 *Opux Oxoniense* III dist. xix q. unica n.6.

65 *Tractatus de praedestinatione* q.1 N; ed. Boehner, 13 'Quarta suppositio: Quod omnes propositiones in ista materia, quantumcumque sint vocaliter de praesenti vel de praeterito, sunt tamen aequivalenter de futuro, quia earum veritas dependet ex veritate propositionum formaliter de futuro.' Cf. Boehner's analysis of this text: ed. cit., 49.

66 *Tractatus de praedestinatione* q.1 M; ed. cit., 12–13.

67 op. cit., 50–1 for the argument, which is rather obscure. A better statement of the same principle may be found elsewhere: *In I Sent.* dist. xli q.1 F.

68 *Tractatus* q.4 B; ed. cit., 36.

69 Oberman, *Harvest of Medieval Theology*, 211. In taking this stand, Oberman finds himself in conflict with Seeberg and Vignaux, both of whom correctly find a concept of predestination in the strict sense in Ockham's thought: op. cit., 206–11.

70 McGrath, 'The Anti-Pelagian Structure of "Nominalist" Doctrines of Justification', 108–10.

71 On Biel's relation to Ockham, see M. L. Picascia, *Un Occamista quattrocentesco Gabriel Biel* (Firenze, 1971) 37–41. Cf. *In I Sent.* dist. xli q. unica a.2 conc.3.

72 As pointed out by F. Clark, 'A New Appraisal of Late Medieval Nominalism', *Gregorianum* 46 (1965) 733–65. Oberman appears to be dependent upon Feckes at this point: cf. Feckes, *Die Rechtfertigungslehre des Gabriel Biel*, 88 n. 268.

73 *In II Sent.* dist. xxvii q. unica a.3 dub. 4; ed. Werbeck/Hoffmann, 2.523.11–16.

74 Oberman, op. cit., 196.

75 *In II Sent.* dist. xxvii q. unica a.1 nota. 1.

76 See Oberman, *Werden und Wertung*, 81–90; M. Schulze, '"Via Gregorii" in Forschung und Quellen', in *Gregor von Rimini. Werk und Wirkung bis zur Reformation* ed. H. A. Oberman (Berlin, 1981) 1–126; 25–64.

77 As W. von Loewenich points out, doctrines such as double predestination or irresistible grace are 'tätsachlich bedenkliche Elemente in Augustins Gnadenlehre': *Von Augustin zu Luther* (Witten, 1959) 111. Oberman labours under the mistaken apprehension that Augustine's most characteristic teaching on predestination is *praedestinatio gemina*, which goes some considerable way towards explaining his simplistic designation of Bradwardine's theology as 'Augustinian': Oberman, *Archbishop Thomas Bradwardine*, 145 n.1.

78 *The Nonne Preestes Tale* 421–2; Group B 4431–2.

79 For details of this important group based on Merton, see W. J. Courtenay, *Adam Wodeham: An Introduction to his Life and Writings* (Leiden, 1978).

80 *De causa Dei* I, 35.

81 *De causa Dei* I, 35.

82 *De causa Dei* II, 31.

83 For an excellent discussion, see Oberman, op. cit., 65–70.

84 e.g., Harnack, *History of Dogma* 6.169–70. Harnack is totally dependent upon the earlier study of G. Lechler, *Johann von Wiclif und die Vorgeschichte der Reformation* (Leipzig, 1873).

85 See Laun, 'Die Prädestination bei Wiclif und Bradwardin'.

86 *de domino divino* I, 14, apparently making reference to *de causa Dei* III, 1 '... omnia quae eveniunt de necessitate eveniunt'. This thesis, however, is condemned by Bradwardine as heretical: *de causa Dei* III, 12. For the important distinction between *antecedent* and *absolute* necessity, as used by Bradwardine, see Oberman, op. cit., 70–5. Wycliffe's thesis, that everything happens by absolute necessity, was condemned by the Council of Constance on 4 May 1415, and again in papal bulls of 22 February 1418: D. 607.

87 S. H. Thomson, 'The Philosophical Basis of Wyclif's Theology', *Journal of Religion* 11 (1931) 86–116; 113.

88 See M. Schüler, *Prädestination, Sünde und Freiheit bei Gregor von Rimini* (Stuttgart, 1934) 39–69; Vignaux, *Justification et prédestination*, 141–75.

89 *In I Sent.* dist. xl, xli q.1 a.2.

90 *In I Sent.* dist. xl, xli q.1 a.2; ed. Trapp, 3.326.17–26.

91 See Zumkeller, 'Hugolin von Orvieto'.

92 See Zumkeller, *Dionysius de Montina*, 77–8.

93 See Zumkeller, 'Johannes Hiltalingen von Basel', 81–98.

94 See Zumkeller, 'Johannes Klenkok', 259–66.

95 See Zumkeller, 'Angelus Dobelinus', 77–91.

96 Eck, *Chrysopassus praedestinationis* I, 66. On the circumstances surrounding the composition of this work, see J. Greving, *Johann Eck als junger Gelehrter. Eine literatur- und dogmengeschichtlich Untersuchung über seinen Chrysopassus praedestinationis aus dem Jahr 1514* (Münster, 1906) 16–19.

97 Eck, *Chrysopassus praedestinationis* IV, 13 'nam multis flectibus et undosis ventis agita carina nostra, doctoribus hincinde in diversa euntibus, tandem ad divi Eustachii Bonaventureae portum applicuimus'.

98 Cf. Eck, *Chrysopassus praedestinationis* III, 51. This point is made especially clear in the later *annotatiunculae* on the first book of the Sentences; *In I Sent.* dist. xli; ed. Moore, 120.27–8 'Deus nunquam deest homini facienti quod in se est. Et haec est ratio praedestinationis.' It is, however, clear that Eck is aware of a different interpretation of the axiom *facienti quod in se est* which excludes it being the *ratio praedestinationis*: *In I Sent.* dist. xli; ed. cit., 120.19–24 '... Hoc modo facere quod in se est est malum et damnabile.'

99 Johannes Altenstaig, *Vocabularius theologiae* (Hagenau, 1517), art. 'Praedestinatio'.

100 The sermons were preached during Advent 1516, and were published in Latin and in German translation the following year. See Steinmetz, *Misericordia Dei*, 79–97.

101 As first demonstrated by P. Minges, *Die Gnadenlehre des Johannes Duns Scotus auf ihren angeblichen Pelagianismus und Semipelagianismus geprüft* (Münster, 1906). See further W. Dettloff, 'Die antipelagianische Grundstruktur der scotischen Rechtfertigungslehre.'

102 e.g. Oberman, *Harvest of Medieval Theology*, 196.

Notes to §13

1 *I Sent.* dist xvii 6.

2 Thomas Aquinas, *In I Sent.* dist. xvii q.1 a.1.

3 See Iserloh, *Gnade und Eucharistie*, 81 'Besonders Thomas hatte noch betont, daß das Prinzip des übernatürlichen Handelns dem Menschen innerlich zu eigen sein muß, damit die Handlung freiwillig und verdienstlich ist. Deshalb könne sie nicht vom Heiligen Geist unmittelbar hervorgebracht sein, sondern müße einer dem Menschen inhärierenden Form entspringen.' Cf. T. Bonhoeffer, *Die Gotteslehre des Thomas von Aquin* (Tübingen, 1961) 87–97.

4 *In II Sent.* dist. xvii q.1 a.1.

5 *In II Sent.* dist. xvii q.1 a.1.

6 *In II Sent.* dist. xvii q.1 a.1 'Quantum ad primum ponam duas conclusiones. Prima est, quod gratia gratificans nos Deo, vel per quam nos grati sumus Deo, est aliquid creatum in anima. Secunda est, quod naturali cognitione nullus potest certitudinaliter in se cognoscere huiusmodi, quamviscunque realiter creatus sit in anima sua.'

7 We here follow Dettloff, *Die Lehre von der acceptatio divina bei Johannes Duns Skotus.*

8 Dettloff, op. cit., 3 nn.6–21 for examples.

9 *Reportata Parisiensis* I dist. xvii q.2 n.4.

10 *Reportata Parisiensis* I dist. xvii q.1 n.3.

11 *Reportata Parisiensis* I dist. xvii q.1 n.3.

12 *Reportata Parisiensis* I dist. xvii q.1 n.4.

13 For the full text, see Dettloff, op. cit., 56 n.204. A fuller version of the previous argument may also be found at n.202.

14 *Reportata Parisiensis* I dist. xvii q.1 n.4.

15 *Reportata Parisiensis* I dist. xvii q.1 n.7.

16 *Reportata Parisiensis* I dist. xvii q.2 n.2 'sed per solam caritatem distinguitur acceptus Deo a non accepto'.

17 *Reportata Parisiensis* I dist. xvii q.2 n.5.

18 *Reportata Parisiensis* I dist. xvii q.2 n.6.

19 Dettloff, op. cit., 159.

20 ibid., 160.

21 See Vignaux, *Justification et prédestination*, 43–95.

22 R. Schmücker, *Propositio per se nota. Gottesbeweise und ihr Verhältnis nach Petrus Aureoli* (Werl, 1941).

23 A. Maier, 'Literarhistorische Notizen über Petrus Aureoli, Durandus und den "Cancellarius"', *Gregorianum* 29 (1948) 213–51.

24 R. Dreiling, *Der Konzeptualismus in der Universalienlehre des Franziskanerbischofs Petrus Aureoli* (Münster, 1913).

25 For an excellent analysis, see Dettloff, *Die Entwicklung der Akzeptations- und Vedienstlehre*, 29–36.

26 *In I Sent.* dist. xvii p.1 a.2; 408 bD 'Quod est aliqua forma creata a Deo quae ex natura rei et de necessitate cadit sub Dei complacentia et cuius existentiam in anima ipsa gratificetur et sit Deo accepta et dilecta aut cara.'

27 *In I Sent.* dist. xvii p.1 a.2; 410 aD 'Quod huiusmodi forma qua ex natura rei redditur anima Deo grata non profluit ex divina acceptatione in anima.'

28 *In I Sent.* dist. xvii p.1 a.2; 410 bG 'Quod forma qua anima sit accepta est quaedam habitualis dilectio, quae ab ipso infunditur nec ex puris naturalibus generatur.'

29 *In I Sent.* dist. xl a.1.

30 *In I Sent.* dist. xvii q.1; *Opera Theologica* 3.445.13. For what follows, see 445.13–466.21.

31 *In I Sent.* dist. xvii q.1. On this, see Vignaux, op. cit., 99–118.

32 *In I Sent.* dist. xvii q.2; *Opera Theologica* 3.471.15–472.5.

33 On this, see Vignaux, *Luther Commentateur des Sentences*, 45–86; Oberman, *Harvest of Medieval Theology*, 160–84.

34 *In I Sent.* dist. xvii q.3 a.3 dub.2; ed. Werbeck/Hoffmann, 1.433.5.
35 *In II Sent.* dist. xxvii q. unica a.1 nota 1.
36 Zumkeller, 'Johannes von Retz', Textbeilage 48. Cf. Thomas of Strasbourg, *In II Sent.* dist. xxvi, xxvii q.1 a.1.
37 *In I Sent.* dist. xvii q.1 a.2. On this, see Vignaux, *Justification et prédestination*, 142–53.
38 *In I Sent.* dist. xvii q.1 a.2 'alioquin . . . caritas creata natura sua aliquam dignitatem in respectu ad vitam aeternam tribueret animae quam nullo modo posset sibi per seipsum tribuere Spiritus sanctus'.
39 Zumkeller refers to him as 'der Vertreter eines ausgesprochenen Augustinianismus': Zumkeller, 'Hugolin von Orvieto', 110.
40 Zumkeller, op. cit., 120–1.
41 ibid., 144.
42 Zumkeller, *Dionysius de Montina*, 76–81.
43 Zumkeller, 'Johannes Klenkok', 256.
44 ibid., 255 n.8.
45 Zumkeller, 'Johannes Hiltalingen', 136 n.246.
46 Zumkeller, 'Angelus Dobelinus', 118–19.
47 Steinmetz, *Misericordia Dei*, 106.
48 ibid., 106–7.
49 See Vignaux, *Luther Commentateur des Sentences*; R. Schwarz, *Fides, Spes und Caritas beim jungen Luther* (Berlin, 1962); 13–40 McGrath, *Luther's Theology of the Cross*, 81–5.
50 WA 9.44.1–4; cf. WA 9.43.2–8.

Notes to introduction to chapter 4

1 M. D. Chenu, *La théologie au XIIe siècle* (Paris, 1957); J. de Ghellinck, *Le mouvement théologique du XIIe siècle* (Bruxelles, 1969²). For more general studies, see C. Haskins, *The Renaissance of the Twelfth Century* (Cambridge, Mass., 1927); G. Paré, A. Brunet and P. Tremblay, *La renaissance du XIIe siècle* (Paris, 1933); W. A. Nitze, 'The so-called Twelfth Century Renaissance', *Speculum* 23 (1948) 464–71; E. M. Sandford, 'The Twelfth Century: Renaissance or Proto-Renaissance?', *Speculum* 26 (1951) 635–42.
2 MS 45, Pembroke College, Cambridge; cited B. Smalley, *The Study of the Bible in the Middle Ages* (Notre Dame, Ind., 1970²) 116 n.1.
3 On this, see A. Fliche, *La querelle des investitures* (Paris, 1946).
4 See J. J. Contreni, *The Cathedral School of Laon from c.850–c.1000* (Munich, 1978); J. Marenbon, *From the Circle of Alcuin to the School of Auxerre* (Cambridge, 1981).
5 'Ut omnes episcopi artes litterarum in suis ecclesiis docere faciant': cited P. Delhaye, 'L'organisation des écoles au XIIe siècle', *Traditio* 5 (1947) 240.
6 See A. Clerval, *Les écoles de Chartres au Moyen-Age* (Chartres, 1895); F. Bliemetzrieder, 'Robert von Melun und die Schule Anselms von Laon', *ZKG* 53 (1934) 117–70; R. Klibansky, 'The School of Chartres',

in *Twelfth Century Europe and the Foundations of Modern Society* ed. M. Clagett *et al.* (Wisconsin, 1961) 3–14; J. W. Baldwin, *Masters, Princes and Merchants. The Social Views of Peter the Chanter and his Circle* (2 vols: Princeton, 1970).

7 *Chartularium Universitatis Parisiensis* ed. H. Denifle and E. Chatelain (4 vols: Paris, 1889–97) 1.65 n.5.

8 *Chartularium Universitatis Parisiensis* 1.85 n.27. The number of chairs over the period were as follows: 1200–1218 – 8; 1218–19 – 10; 1219–21 – 11; 1221 onwards – 12. For details, see P. Glorieux, *Répertoire des Maîtres en théologie de Paris au XIIIᵉ siècle* (2 vols: Paris, 1933).

9 H. Rashdall, *The Universities of Europe in the Middle Ages*, ed. F. M. Powicke and A. B. Emden (3 vols: London, 1935) 1.370–6; P. R. McKeon, 'The Status of the University of Paris as *Parens Scientiarum*: An Episode in the Development of its Autonomy', *Speculum* 39 (1964) 651–75; M.-M. Dufeil, *Guillaume de Saint-Amour et la polémique universitaire parisienne 1250–1259* (Paris, 1972) 146–282.

10 For the text, see R. Paqué, *Das Pariser Nominalistenstatut. Zur Entstehung des Realitätsbegriffs der neuzeitlichen Naturwissenschaft* (Berlin, 1970) 8–12.

11 C. E. du Boulay, *Historia Universitatis Parisiensis* (6 vols: Paris, 1665–75) 4.273–4. A minimum age of thirty-five was specified elsewhere: *Chartularium Universitatis Parisiensis* 1.79.

12 d'Ailly was granted his *magisterium* in theology at Paris on 11 April 1381, being then four years under the minimum age laid down by statute: *Chartularium Universitatis Parisienses* 3.259 n.33.

13 For a list of the doctors of this school, see A. Zumkeller, 'Die Augustinerschule des Mittelalters: Vertreter und philosophisch-theologische Lehre', *Analecta Augustiniana* 27 (1964) 167–262; 174–6. The close association of the school with Paris will be evident.

14 See McGrath, *Luther's Theology of the Cross*, 27–40; 53–71.

15 Of course, Calvin's period of study at Paris raises the fascinating question of the influence of these schools upon his thought: see A. E. McGrath, 'John Calvin and Late Medieval Thought. A Study in Late Medieval Influences upon Calvin's Theological Thought', *ARG* 77 (1986) 58–78.

Notes to §14

1 *Fontes vitae Sancti Thomae Aquinatis* ed. M.-H. Laurent (Toulouse, 1934) Fasc. 6 *Documenta* c.52; 662.

2 *Acta capitulorum generalium Ordinis Praedicatorum* ed. B. M. Riecherd (Romae, 1898) 2.64.

3 See M. Grabmann, 'Johannes Capreolus O.P. der "Princeps Thomistarum" und seine Stellung in der Geschichte der Thomistenschule', in *Mittelalterliches Geistesleben* ed. L. Ott (München, 1955) 3.370–410.

4 E. Gilson, *History of Christian Philosophy in the Middle Ages* (London, 1978) 260. The study of F. J. Roensch, *Early Thomistic School* (Dubuque,

Iowa, 1964) contains an invaluable discussion of the early English and French followers of Thomas' noetic.

5 This is the position of Peter Lombard, Alexander of Hales, Albertus Magnus and Bonaventure: see R. Garrigou-Lagrange, *La synthèse Thomiste* (Paris, 1947) 305–11.

6 *In II Sent.* dist. xx q.1 a.3 appears to avoid any firm statement on the matter. A more definite statement may be found later: *In II Sent.* dist. xxix q.1 a.2.

7 Dating from 1268(?).

8 *de malo* q.4 a.2 ad 17um.

9 *Summa Theologiae* Ia q.95 a.1.

10 Ia q.100 a.1 ad 2um.

11 IaIIae q.83 a.2 ad 2um.

12 Ia q.100 a.1 ad 2um.

13 IaIIae q.112 a.5. This article is of considerable importance. Thomas elsewhere teaches that the grace of final perseverance is a further gift of God to the elect, which cannot be merited: IaIIae q.114 a.9.

14 IIIa q.27 a.2 ad 3um. This question is discussed further in §16.

Notes to §15

1 J. Auer, 'Textkritische Studien zur Gnadenlehre des Alexander von Hales', *Scholastik* 15 (1940) 63–75.

2 Published as *Glossa in Quatuor Libros Sententiarum Petri Lombardi*. For an excellent introduction, see *Glossa* 4.18*–44*. Alexander is of particular significance in that it was through him that Peter Lombard's *Sentences* was divided into its present divisions, and became the standard text in the schools: see I. Brady, 'The Distinctions of the Lombard's Book of Sentences and Alexander of Hales', *FrS* 25 (1965) 90–116.

3 *In II Sent.* dist. xxiv n.1; ed. cit., 2.206.9–11.

4 *In II Sent.* dist. xxiv n.1; ed. cit., 2.207.14–19.

5 *In II Sent.* dist. xxix q.1; ed. Bouvy, 90.57–88.

6 *In II Sent.* dist. xxxiv pars 2 a.3 q.2 ad 3um. For a useful summary of the differences between Bonaventure and Thomas, see Bruch, 'Die Urgerechtigkeit als Rechtheit des Willens nach der Lehre des hl. Bonaventuras', especially 193–4. See further Kaup, 'Zum Begriff der iustitia originalis in der älteren Franziskanerschule'.

7 See M. Grabmann, 'Zur Erkenntnislehre des älteren Franziskanerschule', *FS* 4 (1917) 105–18; E. Gilson, 'Sur quelques difficultés de l'illumination augustinienne', *Revue néoscolastique de philosophie* 36 (1934) 321–31; idem., 'Roger Marston, un cas d'Augustinisme avincennisant', *Archives d'histoire doctrinale et littéraire du moyen âge* 8 (1952) 37–42; P. A. Faustino Prezioza, 'L'attività del soggeto pensante della gnoseologia di Matteo d'Acquasparte e di Ruggerio Marston', *Antonianum* 25 (1950) 259–326.

8 *Opus Oxoniense* I dist. iii q.4 aa.1–3. For an outstanding study of Scotus' critique of Henry of Ghent's illuminationism, see P. C. Vier, *Evidence*

and Its Function According to John Duns Scotus (New York, 1951). The early Dominican school, it may be noted, was also critical of Augustine's illuminationism: see the classic study of E. Gilson, 'Pourquoi S. Thomas a critiqué S. Augustin', *Archives d'histoire doctrinale et littéraire du moyen âge* I (1926–7) 5–127.

Notes to §16

1 See V. Heynck, 'A Controversy at the Council of Trent concerning the Doctrine of Duns Scotus', *FrS* 9 (1949) 181–258.
2 *Opus Oxoniense* IV dist. xvii q.3 n.21.
3 *Reportata Parisiensis* IV dist. ix q. única n.2.
4 See H. Ameri, *Doctrina theologorum de Immaculata B.V.M. Conceptione tempore Concili Basiliensis* (Roma, 1954); I. Brady, 'The Development of the Doctrine of the Immaculate Conception in the Fourteenth Century after Aureoli', *FrS* 15 (1955) 175–202; K. Balic, 'Die Corredemptrixfrage innerhalb der franziskanischen Theologie', *FS* 39 (1957) 218–87; M. Mückshoff, 'Die mariologische Prädestination im Denken der franziskanischen Theologie', *FS* 39 (1957) 288–502.
5 *In III Sent.* dist. iii q.1 ad 2um. Cf. *Summa Theologiae* IIIa q.27 a.2 ad 3um.
6 *Opus Oxoniense* III dist. iii q.1 n.4. Cf. K. Balic, *Duns Scoti Theologiae Marianae elementa* (Sibenici, 1933).
7 *Opus Oxoniense* III dist. iii. q.1 n.10.
8 For a survey of opinions, see F. de Guimarens, 'La doctrine des théologiens sur l'Immaculée Conception de 1250 à 1350', *Etudes Franciscains* 3 (1952) 181–203; 4 (1953) 23–51; 167–87; A. di Lella, 'The Immaculate Conception in the Writings of Peter Aureoli', *FrS* 15 (1955) 146–58; E. M. Buytaert, 'The Immaculate Conception in the Writings of Ockham', *FrS* 10 (1950) 149–63.
9 *Super libros Sapientiae* lect. 160C.

Notes to §17

1 e.g., G. H. Tavard, *Protestantism* (London, 1950) 20. For similar understandings of 'Nominalism' as that of Tavard, see R. M. Torelló, 'El Ockhamismo y la decadencia escolástica en el siglo XIV', *Pensamiento* 9 (1953) 199–228; J. R. Gironella, 'Para la historia del nominalismo y de la reacción antinominalista de Suárez', *Pensamiento* 17 (1961) 279–310.
2 See H. Grisar, *Luther* (6 vols: London, 1913–17) 1.130.
3 Ritter, *Marsilius von Inghen und die okkamistische Schule in Deutschland*; Feckes, *Die Rechtfertigungslehre des Gabriel Biel*; A. Lang, *Heinrich Totting von Oyta. Ein Beitrag zur Entstehungsgeschichte der ersten deutschen Universitäten und zur Problemsgeschichte der Spätscholastik* (Münster, 1937); N. Häring, *Die Theologie der Erfurter Augustiner-Eremiten Bartholomäus Arnoldi von Usingen* (Limburg, 1939).

4 Ehrle, *Der Sentenzenkommentar Peters von Candia*, 106–7. For his discussion of 'Nominalist' diversity, see ibid., 108–251.

5 A. Lang, *Die Wege der Glaubensbegründung bei den Scholastikern des 14. Jahrhunderts* (Münster, 1931) 131.

6 Hochstetter, 'Nominalismus?'.

7 P. Vignaux, art. 'Nominalisme', *DThC* 11.717–18. On 'Terminism', see L. M. de Rijk, *Logica Modernorum. A Contribution to the History of Early Terminist Logic* (2 vols: Assen, 1962–7).

8 Cited Ehrle, op. cit., 323.

9 See D. M. Armstrong, *Nominalism and Realism. Universals and Scientific Realism* (2 vols: Cambridge, 1978) 1.12–57.

10 A. E. McGrath, *'Homo Assumptus?* A Study in the Christology of the *Via Moderna*, with Particular Reference to William of Ockham', *EThL* 61 (1984) 283–97.

11 WATr 5.633.1–18; cited Oberman, *Werden und Wertung*, 425.

12 J. Würsdorfer, *Erkennen und Wissen nach Gregor von Rimini* (Münster, 1917).

13 A. Zumkeller, *Hugolino von Orvieto und seine theologische Erkenntnislehre* (Würzburg, 1941) 257–61.

14 Thus P. Vignaux, *Nominalisme au XIVe siècle* (Paris, 1948).

15 M. Schepers, 'Holkot contra Crathorn', *Philosophisches Jahrbuch* 77 (1970) 320–54; 79 (1972) 106–36.

16 On the latter, see G. Gál, 'Gaulteri de Chatton de Guillelmi de Ockham controversia de natura conceptus universalis', *FrS* 27 (1967) 191–212; N. Fitzpatrick, 'Walter Chatton on the Univocity of Being. A Reaction to Peter Aureoli and William Ockham', *FrS* 31 (1971) 88–177.

17 See Ritter, *Via antiqua und via moderna auf deutschen Universitäten des XV. Jahrhunderts*; R. R. Post, *De via antiqua en de via moderna bij vijftiende eeuwse Nederlandse theologen* (Nijmegen, 1964); K.-H. Gerschmann, '"Antiqui-Novi-Moderni" in den "Epistolae obscurorum Virorum"', *Archiv für Begriffsgeschichte* 11 (1967) 23–36; A. G. Weiler, art. 'Antiqui/moderni (via antiqua/via moderna)', in *Historisches Wörterbuch der Philosophie* ed. J. Ritter (Basel, 1971) 1.407–10; A. L. Gabriel, '"Via antiqua" and "via moderna" and the Migration of Paris Students and Masters to the German Universities in the Fifteenth Century', in *Antiqui und Moderni. Traditionsbewußtsein und Fortschrittsbewußtsein im späten Mittelalter* ed. A. Zimmermann (Berlin/New York, 1974) 439–83; Oberman, *Werden und Wertung der Reformation*, 28–55; W. Urban, 'Die "via moderna" an der Universität Erfurt am Vorabend der Reformation', in *Gregor von Rimini. Werk und Wirkung bis zur Reformation* ed. H. A. Oberman (Berlin/New York, 1981) 311–30. It may be noted that the *via moderna* was known by various names at different universities; at Paris, it was referred to as the *via nominalium* (R. G. Villoslada, *La Universidad de Paris durante los estudios de Francisco de Vitorio O.P. 1507–1522* (Roma, 1938) 76; 118); at Heidelberg, as the *via Marsiliana* (after Marsilius of Inghen: Ritter, *Marsilius von Inghens*, 46); at Wittenberg, as the *via*

Gregorii (apparently after Gregory of Rimini: McGrath, *Luther's Theology of the Cross*, 31–4).

18 See McGrath, *'Homo Assumptus?'*; idem., 'Some Observations concerning the Soteriology of the *Via Moderna*', *RThAM* 52 (1986) 182–93.

19 e.g., Oberman, *Harvest of Medieval Theology*, 108–11; McGrath, *Luther's Theology of the Cross*, 110–11.

20 Oberman, op. cit., 112–13.

21 Biel, *In III Sent.* dist. xl q. unica a.2 conc.

22 Oberman, op. cit., 118 n.92. It is this understanding of Christ's function which appears to underlie Luther's early theological difficulties: see WA 38.148.12; 40 I.298.9; 40.I.326.1; 41.653.41; 45.482.16; 47.590.1.

23 Biel, *In III Sent.* dist. xl q. unica a.3 dub.3; ed. Werbeck/Hoffmann, 3.704.18–19.

24 *Sermones Dominicales de tempore* 32D.

25 Biel, *In II Sent.* dist. xxvii q. unica a.3 dub.5; ed. cit., 2.525.11–14 'Homo non potest evidenter scire se facere quod in se est, quia hoc facere includit in se proponere oboedire Deo propter Deum tamquam ultimum et principalem finem, quod exigit dilectionem Dei super omnia, quam ex naturalis suis homo potest elicere.'

26 Biel, *In II Sent.* dist. xxviii q. unica a.1 nota.2; ed. cit., 2.536.1–537.9 'Secundo notandum quod, cum loquimur de puris naturalibus, non excluditur generalis Dei influentia ... Sed per "pura naturalia" intelligitur animae natura seu substantia cum qualitatibus et actionibus consequentibus naturam, exclusis habitibus ac donis supernaturaliter a solo Deo infusis.'

Notes to §18

1 e.g., Zumkeller, 'Hugolin von Orvieto'; Toner, 'The Doctrine of Justification according to Augustine of Rome'; Werbeck, *Jacobus Perez von Valencia*; Ferdigg, 'De vita et operibus et doctrina Joannis de Paltz'; Steinmetz, *Misericordia Dei*; Zumkeller, 'Johannes von Retz'; idem, 'Johannes Klenkok'; idem, 'Johannes von Dorsten'; idem, 'Johannes Hiltalingen von Basel'; idem, 'Erbsünde, Gnade und Rechtfertigung im Verständnis der Erfurter Augustinertheologen des Spätmittelalters'; idem, 'Angelus Dobelinus'; McGrath, '"Augustinianism"? A Critical Assessment of the so-called "Medieval Augustinian Tradition" on Justification'.

2 Cf. D. C. Steinmetz, *Luther and Staupitz. An Essay in the Intellectual Origins of the Protestant Reformation* (Durham, N.C., 1980) 13–16. Steinmetz distinguishes five senses of the term.

3 A. V. Müller, *Luthers theologische Quellen. Seine Verteidigung gegen Denifle und Grisar* (Giessen, 1912).

4 idem, 'Agostino Favorini e la teologia di Lutero', *Bilychnis* 3 (1914) 373–87; idem, 'Giacomo Pérez di Valenza, O.S. Aug., Vescovo di Chrysopoli e la teologia di Lutero', *Bilychnis* 9 (1920) 391–403; idem,

'Una fonte ignota del sistema di Lutero. Il beato Fidati da Cascia e la sua teologia', *Bilychnis* 10 (1921) fasc. 2; idem, 'Il Dr. Paulus di Monaco, il beato Fidati e Lutero', *Bilychnis* 12 (1922) 247-57.

5 E. Stakemeier, *Der Kampf um Augustin. Augustinus und die Augustiner auf dem Tridentinum* (Paderborn, 1937).

6 H. Jedin, *History of the Council of Trent* (2 vols: Edinburgh, 1957-61) 2.258.

7 W. von Loewenich, *Duplex Iustitia. Luthers Stellung zu seiner Unionsformel des 16. Jahrhunderts* (Wiesbaden, 1972).

8 J. Henniger, *S. Augustinus et doctrina de duplici iustitia* (Mödling, 1935).

9 Auer, *Entwicklung der Gnadenlehre in der Hochscholastik* 2.200, with reference to Scotus, *Lectura Prima* I, 17; Oberman, *Harvest of Medieval Theology*, 160-5, with reference to Biel, *Canonis Missae Expositio* 59L.

10 B. Warfield, *Calvin and Augustine* (Philadelphia, 1956), 322.

11 *de causa Dei*, 174.

12 Gregory refers critically to (an unnamed) *unus modernus doctor* in this context: *In II Sent.* dist. xxxix q.1 a.1. The name 'Bradwardine' is inserted in the margins to two manuscripts (Paris Nat. lat. 15891 and Mazarin 914).

13 Zumkeller, 'Johannes Klenkok', 266-90.

14 Zumkeller, 'Hugolin von Orvieto über Urstand und Erbsünde', 175-82.

15 Zumkeller, 'Johannes Hiltalingen von Basel', 115-18.

16 Zumkeller, 'Angelus Dobelinus', 97-103.

17 K. Werner, *Der Augustinismus in der Scholastik des später Mittelalters* (Wien, 1883) 234-300; Zumkeller, 'Die Augustinerschule des Mittelalters'.

18 C. Stange, 'Über Luthers Beziehungen zur Theologie seines Ordens', *Neue kirchliche Zeitschrift* 11 (1900) 574-85; especially 578. For the refutation of this opinion, see McGrath, *Luther's Theology of the Cross*, 36-8.

19 A. V. La Valle, *La giustizia di Adamo e il peccato originale secondo Egidio Romano* (Palermo, 1939); G. Díaz, *De peccati originalis essentia in schola Augustiniana praetridentina* (El Escorial, 1961); idem, 'La escuela agustiniana pretridetina y el problemo de la concupiscencia', *La Ciudad de Dios* 174 (1961) 309-56.

20 Trapp, 'Augustinian Theology of the Fourteenth Century', especially 156-7.

21 e.g., *In I Sent.* dist. xvii q.2.

22 e.g., see Zumkeller's edition of Retz, in *Augustiniana* 22 (1972) 540-82; Textbeilage 126, citing Thomas of Strasbourg *In II Sent.* dist. xxviii, xxix q.1 a.3.

23 Trapp, op. cit., 248.

24 J. Beumer, 'Augustinismus und Thomismus in der theologischen Prinzipienlehre des Aegidius Romanus', *Scholastik* 32 (1957) 542-60.

25 Zumkeller, 'Augustinerschule des Mittelalters', 193-5.

26 Oberman, *Harvest of Medieval Theology*, 286-92.

27 Werbeck, *Jacobus Perez von Valencia*, 214-15, n.1.

28 R. Weijenborg, 'Doctrina de immaculata conceptione apud Ioannem de Paltz O.E.S.A., magistrum Lutheri novitii', *Virgo Immaculata* (Roma, 1957) 160–83.

29 Steinmetz, op. cit., 146–7.

30 e.g., compare Johannes Hiltalingen of Basel with Thomas of Strasbourg: Zumkeller, 'Johannes Hiltalingen von Basel', 68–9.

31 As documented by Trapp, op. cit., *passim*.

32 Trapp makes the important point that no theologian of the Augustinian Order uses the dialectic between the two powers of God in the unorthodox manner associated with *moderni* such as John of Mirecourt and Nicholas of Autrecourt: Trapp, op. cit., 265.

33 For documentation of this transition, see McGrath, '"Augustinian-ism"?'.

34 This does not, of course, imply that the *schola Augustiniana moderna* derived these methods from the *via moderna*: it seems that both schools ultimately derived them from Duns Scotus, the former *via* Gregory of Rimini and the latter *via* William of Ockham.

35 See McGrath, *Luther's Theology of the Cross*, 81–5.

Notes to §19

1 On this, see G. Aulén, *Reformation och Katolicitet* (Stockholm, 1959).

2 See E. Wolf, 'Die Rechtfertigungslehre als Mitte und Grenze reformator-scher Theologie', *Evangelische Theologie* 9 (1949–50) 298–308. There is, of course, a genuine difficulty in establishing the precise causal relation-ship between the origins of Luther's own theology and that of the Reformation as a whole: see H. A. Oberman, 'Headwaters of the Reformation: *Initia Lutheri – Initia Reformationis*', in *Luther and the Dawn of the Modern Era* ed. H. A. Oberman (Leiden, 1974) 40–88; McGrath, *Luther's Theology of the Cross*, 24 n.45; 52–3; 142.

3 For the sense and origins of this celebrated phrase, see F. Loofs, 'Der articulus stantis et cadentis ecclesiae', *Theologische Studien und Kritiken* 90 (1917) 323–400. It is necessary to challenge Loofs upon several points, particularly his suggestion that the phrase is first used in the eighteenth century by the Lutheran theologian Valentin Löscher in his famous anti-Pietist essay *Timotheus Verinus* (Wittenberg, 1718). For example, the *Reformed* theologian Johann Heinrich Alsted uses the phrase a century earlier, opening his discussion of man's justification *coram Deo* as follows: 'articulus iustificationis dicitur articulus stantis et cadentis ecclesiae' (*Theologia scholastica didacta* (Hanoviae, 1618) 711). Precursors of the phrase may, of course, be found in the writings of Luther himself – e.g., WA 40 III.352.3 '... quia isto articulo stante stat Ecclesia, ruente ruit Ecclesia'.

4 Bossuet, *Première Instruction pastorale* xxvii; cited O. Chadwick, *From Bossuet to Newman. The Idea of Doctrinal Development* (Cambridge, 1957) 17.

5 Thus Philip Melanchthon, *Corpus Reformatorum (Melanchthon)* 2.884

448

'So man nun fragt, warum sondert ich euch denn von der vorigen Kirchen? Antwort: wir sondern uns nicht von der vorigen rechten Kirchen. Ich halte es eben das, welches Ambrosius und Augustinus gelehret haben.' For the early Protestant understanding of history entailed in such statements, see the suggestive study of H. Rückert, 'Das evangelische Geschichtsbewußtsein und das Mittelalter', in *Mittelalterliches Erbe – Evangelische Verantwortung. Vorträge und Ansprachen zum Gedenken der Gründung des Tübinger Augustinerklosters 1262* (Tübingen, 1962) 13–23.

6 Thus Flacius Illyricus, initially in his *Catalogus testium veritatis* (1556), and subsequently in his celebrated *Magdeburg Centuries* (1559–74).

7 The most important interpretation of the 'Forerunners' is due to Karl H. Ullmann, *Reformatoren vor der Reformation vornehmlich in Deutschland und den Niederlanden* (2 vols: Hamburg, 1841–2). For a critical assessment of this work, see H. A. Oberman, *Forerunners of the Reformation. The Shape of Late Medieval Thought* (Philadelphia, 1981) 3–49, especially 32–43.

8 H. A. Oberman, 'Fourteenth Century Religious Thought. A Premature Profile', *Speculum* 53 (1978) 80–93.

9 See H. A. Oberman, 'Das tridentinische Rechtfertigungsdekret im Lichte spätmittelalterlichen Theologie', *ZThK* 61 (1964) 251–82; idem, 'Duns Scotus, Nominalism and the Council of Trent', in *John Duns Scotus 1265–1965* ed. J. K. Ryan and B. M. Bonansea (New York, 1965), 311–44.

10 See McGrath, 'Forerunners of the Reformation?', 223–8.

11 See McGrath, *Luther's Theology of the Cross*, 133–6.

12 WA 56.270.9–11; 343.16–23; 351.23–352.7. It is this principle which underlies Luther's maxim *simul iustus et peccator*: see R. Hermann, *Luthers These 'Gerecht und Sünder zugleich'* (Gütersloh, 1930).

13 As pointed out by Oberman, *Werden und Wertung*, 110–12.

14 Oberman, op. cit., 82–140, especially 83–92.

15 McGrath, *Luther's Theology of the Cross*, 36–40; 63–71; idem, 'John Calvin and Late Medieval Thought. A Study in Late Medieval Influences upon Calvin's Theological Development', *ARG* 77 (1986) 58–78.

16 P. Vignaux, *Luther Commentateur des Sentences* (Paris, 1934) 5–44; McGrath, *Luther's Theology of the Cross*, 81–5.

17 A. B. Ritschl, *The Christian Doctrine of Justification and Reconciliation* (Edinburgh, 1872) 90–1.

18 See W. Niesel, 'Calvin wider Osianders Rechtfertigungslehre', *ZKG* 46 (1928) 410–30; W. Koehler, *Dogmengeschichte als Geschichte des christlichen Selbstbewusstseins* (Zürich, 1951) 354. Cf. the celebrated statement of Richard Hooker, *Works* ed. J. Keble (3 vols: Oxford, 1845³) 3.486 '... that grand question, which hangeth yet in controversy between us and the Church of Rome, about the matter of justifying righteousness'.

19 See McGrath, 'Forerunners of the Reformation?', 228–36.

20 Latomus, *Duae Epistolae* (Antwerp, 1544) 38.

21 J. Buchanan, *The Doctrine of Justification. An Outline of Its History in the*

Church and of Its Exposition from Scripture (Edinburgh, 1867; reprinted Edinburgh, 1961) 94.

22 ibid., 104. In common with many nineteenth-century polemicists, Buchanan appears to confuse 'justification by inherent righteousness' with 'justification by works'. This fact alone is sufficient to indicate the poverty of their understanding of Augustine's teaching on the matter.

23 It is interesting to note that Oberman's case for 'Forerunners' of the Reformation doctrines of justification is nowhere stated explicitly, but appears to rest upon certain writings pertaining to predestination: Oberman, *Forerunners of the Reformation*, 121–41.

24 H. A. Oberman, '"Iustitia Christi" and "Iustitia Dei". Luther and the Scholastic Doctrines of Justification', *HThR* 59 (1966) 1–26; 4. Cf. idem, *Harvest of Medieval Theology*, 185–7, especially 185 'It is a reliable rule of interpretation for the historian of Christian thought that the position taken with respect to the doctrine of predestination is a most revealing indicator of the understanding of the doctrine of justification'.

Notes to introduction to chapter 6

1 See Wolf, 'Die Rechtfertigungslehre als Mitte und Grenze reformatorischer Theologie'. For a useful (if purely descriptive) general survey of the thought of the Reformers on this matter, see Henry Strohl, *La pensée de la Réforme* (Neuchâtel, 1951), 29–45 (on 'faith'); 85–120 (on 'justification by faith').

2 e.g., see WA 25.332.12–13; 39 I.205.2–5; 40 I.72.20–1; *BSLK* 416.22–3.

3 On the basis of his analysis of Valentin Löscher's *Timotheus Verinus* (Wittenberg, 1714), Loofs argued that this celebrated phrase actually dates from the eighteenth century, and is characteristic of Lutheran theologians alone: 'Der articulus stantis et cadentis ecclesiae', 345. In fact, it appears to have been in use at least a century earlier. Thus the Reformed theologian J. H. Alsted begins his discussion (1618) of the justification of man before God with the following assertion: 'articulus iustificationis dicitur articulus stantis et cadentis ecclesiae' (*Theologia scholastica didactica*, 711). Precursors of the phrase may, of course, be found in the writings of Luther himself: e.g., WA 40 III.352.3, 'quia isto articulo stante stat Ecclesia, ruente ruit Ecclesia'.

4 See Heiko A. Oberman, 'Headwaters of the Reformation: *Initia Lutheri – Initia Reformationis*', in *Luther and the Dawn of the Modern Era*, ed. H. A. Oberman (Leiden, 1974), 40–88.

5 e.g., see Benjamin B. Warfield, *Calvin and Augustine* (Philadelphia, 1956), 322: 'The Reformation, inwardly considered, was just the triumph of Augustine's doctrine of grace over Augustine's doctrine of the church.'

6 On the late medieval Augustinian renaissance, see H. A. Oberman, *Werden und Wertung der Reformation* (Tübingen, 1977), 82–140; on the Amorbach edition of Augustine, see J. de Ghellinck, 'La première édition imprimée des "opera omnia S. Augustini"', in *Miscellanea J.*

Gessler I (Antwerp, 1948), 530–47. For useful insights into the Reformers' use of patristic sources, see Peter Fraenkel, *Testimonia Patrum: The Function of the Patristic Argument in the Theology of Philip Melanchthon* (Genève, 1961); Alfred Schindler, *Zwingli und die Kirchenväter* (Zürich, 1984).

7 See §19 and McGrath, 'Forerunners of the Reformation? A Critical Examination of the Evidence for Precursors of the Reformation Doctrines of Justification', *HThR* 75 (1982), 219–42 for further discussion.

8 See A. J. Beachy, *The Concept of Grace in the Radical Reformers* (Nieuwkoop, 1977), for a discussion of the tendency of the radical Reformers to supplement or replace the notion of *imputatio iustitiae* with that of an essential ontological change within man (often conceived realistically, as 'deification').

Notes to §20

1 WA 9.42.35–43.6; 44.1–4. Cf. McGrath, *Luther's Theology of the Cross*, 82–5.

2 WA 3.289.1–5; 4.261.32–9; 262.2–7. Cf. O. Bayer, *Promissio: Geschichte der reformatorischen Wende in Luthers Theologie* (Göttingen, 1971), 119–23; 128–43; 313–17; McGrath, *Luther's Theology of the Cross*, 85–92.

3 Note especially WA 4.262.2–7. Cf. §7 of the present study.

4 WA 54.185.12–186.21. English translations in Rupp, *The Righteousness of God*, 121–2; McGrath, *Luther's Theology of the Cross*, 95–8. For the debate in the literature, see Gerhard Pfeiffer, 'Das Ringen des jungen Luthers um die Gerechtigkeit Gottes', *Luther-Jahrbuch* 26 (1959), 25–55; Regin Prenter, *Der barmherzige Richter: Iustitia Dei passiva in Luthers Dictata super Psalterium 1513–1515* (København, 1961); Albrecht Peters, 'Luthers Turmerlebnis', *ZSTh* 3 (1961), 203–36; Bornkamm, 'Zur Frage der Iustitia Dei beim jungen Luther'; Kurt Aland, *Der Weg zur Reformation: Zeitpunkt und Charakter des reformatorischen Erlebnisses Martin Luthers* (München, 1965); Oberman, '"Iustitia Christi" and "Iustitia Dei"'; McGrath, *Luther's Theology of the Cross*.

5 WA 54.185.12–20.

6 Heinrich Denifle, *Luther and Luthertum in der ersten Entwickelung, quellenmäßig dargestellt* (2 vols: Mainz, 1904), especially 392–5; 404–15.

7 *Die abendländischen Schriftausleger bis Luther über Iustitia Dei (Röm. 1.17) und Iustificatio* (Mainz, 1905).

8 Biel, *In II Sent.* dist. xxvii q. unica a. 3 dub. 5; ed. Werbeck/Hoffmann, 2.525.11–526.17: 'Homo non potest evidenter scire se facere quod in se est . . .'

9 For a detailed analysis of the nature, date and theological significance of this 'discovery', see McGrath, *Luther's Theology of the Cross*, 95–147; 153–61.

10 These *lectures* (now published in WA 57.5–108) should not be confused with the Galatians *commentary* of 1519 (WA 2.436–618). Although the

commentary is clearly based upon the lectures, there are significant differences.

11 For this important phrase, see WA 3.588.8; 4.127.10; 231.7; 56.282.9–13. Bizer asserts that *fides* and *humilitas* are synonymous over the period 1513–18, with excellent reasons for doing so: *Fides ex auditu*, 19–21.

12 WA 3.124.12–14; 4.91.4–5; 111.33–7; 262.2–7. Cf. Bayer, *Promissio: Geschichte der reformatorische Werde in Luthers Theologie*, 128; McGrath, *Luther's Theology of the Cross*, 89–92.

13 For the argument, see McGrath, *Luther's Theology of the Cross*, 113–19.

14 Most notably by Vogelsang, *Die Anfänge von Luthers Christologie*.

15 For the argument, see McGrath, *Luther's Theology of the Cross*, 119–28.

16 WA 56.379.1–15.

17 It is possible that Luther has come to this conclusion toward the end of the *Dictata*: WA 4.309.6–11 is highly suggestive.

18 WA 56.385.15–22. Note the occurrence of the term *servum arbitrium*.

19 WA 56.382.26–7; 502.32–503.5.

20 Luther's marginal comments on Biel are of importance here: unfortunately, their date remains uncertain: H. Volz, 'Luthers Randbemerkungen zu zwei Schriften Gabriel Biels: Kritische Anmerkungen zu Hermann Degerings Publikation', *ZKG* 81 (1970), 207–19.

21 McGrath, *Luther's Theology of the Cross*, 100–13. See also §6.

22 McGrath, 'Mira et nova diffinitio iustitiae'.

23 McGrath, *Luther's Theology of the Cross*, 153–61.

24 Scholion to Galatians 2.16; WA 57.69.14–16; cf. WA 2.503.34–6. Note also the 1516 statement: 'Iustitia autem ista non est ea, de qua Aristoteles 5. Ethicorum vel iurisperiti agunt, sed fides seu gratia Christ iustificans' (WA 31 1.456.36). (We have taken the liberty of correcting the clearly incorrect '3. Ethicorum'.) It is Luther's critique of the concept of *iustitia* underlying the soteriology of the *via moderna* which lies at the heart of his later critique of Aristotle: see McGrath, *Luther's Theology of the Cross*, 136–41.

25 For the reasons, see McGrath, *Luther's Theology of the Cross*, 141–2.

26 e.g., see Rich, *Anfänge*, 73–95. Cf. CR (Zwingli) 1.224.11–2: 'Hat der Luter da getruncken, da wir getruncken habend, so hatt er mit uns gemein die euangelisch leer.' Recently, however, Neuser has suggested that, in his reminiscences, Zwingli tends defensively to minimise his debts to both Luther and Erasmus: Wilhelm H. Neuser, *Die reformatorische Wende bei Zwingli* (Neukirchen, 1977). However, Zwingli's dependence upon Luther is still to be dated from the 1520s.

Notes to §21

1 WA 56.502.32–503.5 is particularly significant here.

2 WA 40 1.357.18–22.

3 The historical background to this question is complex: see McGrath, *Luther's Theology of the Cross*, 27–71.

4 For this suggestion, see McGrath, 'John Calvin and Late Medieval Thought'.

5 Holl, 'Die Rechtfertigungslehre in Luthers Vorlesung über den Römerbrief mit besonderer Rücksicht auf die Frage der Heilsgewißheit', in *Gesammelte Aufsätze*, I.111–54.

6 Holl, 'Rechtfertigungslehre', 117.

7 Holl, 'Rechtfertigungslehre', 123.

8 Holl, 'Rechtfertigungslehre', 128.

9 e.g., Regin Prenter, *Spiritus Creator: Studien zu Luthers Theologie* (München, 1954).

10 See E. Schott, *Fleisch und Geist nach Luthers Lehre* (Leipzig, 1930); W. Joest, *Ontologie der Person bei Luther* (Göttingen, 1967); Gerhard Ebeling, *Lutherstudien* II: *Disputatio de homine 1. Teil. Text und Traditionshintergrund* (Tübingen, 1977); H.-M. Barth, 'Martin Luther disputiert über den Menschen: Ein Beitrag zu Luthers Anthropologie', *KuD* 27 (1981), 154–66.

11 WA 56.347.2–11.

12 WA 56.343.16–19.

13 WA 56.270.9–11; 343.16–23; 351.23–352.7. Cf. Hermann, *Luthers These 'Gerecht und Sünder zugleich'*.

14 WA 56.268.27–269.2. Cf. 269.25–30.

15 WA 56.442.17, 20–3.

16 e.g., see P. S. Schubert, *Augustins Lex-Aeterna-Lehre nach Inhalt und Quellen* (Münster, 1924). See §4 for further discussion.

17 WA 56.3.6; 157.2.

18 WA 40 I.229.28; cf. 229.4.

19 WA 5.608.16.

20 e.g., *WA* 56.259.14.

21 Walter von Loewenich, 'Zur Gnadenlehre bei Augustin und Luther', in *idem, Von Augustine zu Luther* (Witten, 1959), 75–87; 83.

22 WA 56.442.3.

23 WA 40 II.24.2–3.

24 WA 56.347.11–13.

25 WA 57.232.26. Cf. Schwarz, *Fides, spes und caritas beim jungen Luther*, 50, where Luther is shown to have employed the traditional understanding of *fides* in 1509–10.

26 WA 57.215.16–20. On the existential dimension of Luther's concept of faith, see L. Pinomaa, *Der existenzielle Charakter der Theologie Luthers* (Helsinki, 1940).

27 On this important concept, see P. T. Bühler, *Die Anfechtung bei Luther* (Zürich, 1942); H. Beintker, *Die Überwindung der Anfechtung bei Luther* (Berlin, 1954).

28 WA 57.233.16–19.

29 WA 8.106.10–13.

30 e.g., *WA* 8.106.18–22; 107.21.

31 e.g., *WA* 56.279.22: 'Ideo recte dixi, quod extrinsecum nobis est omne bonum nostrum, quod est Christus.'

32 WA 56.287.23–4.

33 The best study of this aspect of Luther's theology is Harry J. McSorley, *Luther – Right or Wrong?*, 217–73; 297–366.

34 WA 1.224 Thesis 4. On Luther's attack on the *via moderna*, personified by Gabriel Biel, see Grane, *Contra Gabrielem*, 369–85.

35 WA 1.354 Thesis 13. Cf. D. 776. See further H. Roos, 'Die Quellen der Bulle "Exsurge Domine"', in *Geschichte und Gegenwart: Festschrift für Michael Schmaus*, ed. J. Auer and H. Volk (3 vols: München, 1957), 3.909–26.

36 See D. 781, and compare with the *in globo* condemnation of D. 484–90 and 690. See McSorley, *Luther: Right or Wrong?*, 251–3. Luther was, of course, condemned at the end of the Diet of Worms (25 May 1525) for teaching a pagan determinism which denied free will: see *Deutsche Reichstagakten unter Karl V* (2 vols: Göttingen, 1962), 2.647.1–3. More generally, see *Lutherprozess und Lutherbann*, ed. Remigius Bäumer (Münster, 1972).

37 WA 7.146.6–12; 18.615.12–17.

38 WA 7.144.34–145.4; 18.709.28–36.

39 WA 18.709.28–36 should be read carefully here.

40 WA 18.615.13–16 leaves no room whatsoever for contingency on the part of any created being, including man, whether he is a sinner or not.

41 e.g., G. L. Plitt, 'Luthers Streit mit Erasmus über den freien Willen in den Jahren 1525–25', *Studien der evangelisch-protestantischen Geistlichen des Grossherzogthums Baden* 2 (1876), 205–14.

42 See B. Lohse, *Ratio und Fides: Eine Untersuchung über die Ratio in der Theologie Luthers* (Göttingen, 1958), 82–6; B. A. Gerrish, *Grace and Reason: A Study in the Theology of Martin Luther* (Oxford, 1962), 84–99; McGrath, *Luther's Theology of the Cross*, 136–41.

43 WA 40 1.347.27.

44 WA 40 1.204.11–14.

45 See T. M. McDonough, *The Law and the Gospel in Luther: A Study of Martin Luther's Confessional Writings* (Oxford, 1963); Modalsi, *Das Gericht nach den Werken: Ein Beitrag zu Luthers Lehre vom Gesetz*; Peters, *Glaube und Werk: Luthers Rechtfertigungslehre im Lichte der Heiligen Schrift*.

46 WA 39 1.96.6–8.

47 WA 39 1.254.27–30.

48 WA 39 1.208.9–10.

49 WA 39 1.96.9–14.

50 It is clear that Luther owed little to mysticism: H. A. Oberman, 'Simul gemitus et raptus: Luther und die Mystik', in *Kirche, Mystik, Heiligung und das Natürliche bei Luther*, ed. I. Asheim (Göttingen, 1967), 20–59; K.-H. zur Mühlen, *Nos extra nos: Luthers Theologie zwischen Mystik und Scholastik* (Tübingen, 1972); S. E. Ozment, *Homo Spiritualis: A Comparative Study of the Anthropology of Johannes Tauler, Jean Gerson and Martin Luther (1509–15) in the Context of their Theological Thought* (Leiden, 1969). It is also probable that Luther owed little to the *schola Augustiniana moderna*, although further discussion of this point is required: McGrath, *Luther's Theology of the Cross*, 27–40; 63–71. See further below.

51 See McGrath, *Luther's Theology of the Cross*, 95–147, especially 113–19.

52 F. de Lagarde, *Naissance de l'esprit laïque au déclin du Moyen Age* (6 vols: Paris, 1948), 6.86–8.

53 C. Feckes, *Die Rechtfertigungslehre des Gabriel Biels und seine Stellung innerhalb der nominalistischen Schule* (Münster, 1925), 12.

54 H. A. Oberman, *The Harvest of Medieval Theology: Gabriel Biel and Late Medieval Nominalism* (Cambridge, Mass., 1963).

55 Vignaux, 'Sur Luther et Ockham'.

56 See McGrath, *Luther's Theology of the Cross*, 27–40; 63–71. It is significant that Staupitz cites older Augustinian theologians (i.e., members of the *schola Aegidiana*, rather than the *schola Augustiniana moderna*) as theological sources: Ernst Wolf, *Staupitz und Luther: Ein Beitrag zur Theologie des Johannes von Staupitz und deren Bedeutung für Luthers theologischen Werdegang* (Leipzig, 1929), 23–5.

57 As established by Leif Grane, 'Gregor von Rimini und Luthers Leipziger Disputation', *StTh* 22 (1968), 29–49. The crucial text is *Resolutiones Lutherianae super propositionibus suis Lipsiae disputatis*: *WA* 2.394.31–395.6: 'Certum est enim, Modernos (quos vocant) cum Schotistis et Thomistis in hac re (id est libero arbitrio et gratia) consentire, excepto uno Gregorio Ariminense, quem omnes damnant, qui et ipse eos Pelagianis deteriores esse et recte et efficaciter convincit. Is enim solus inter scholasticos contra omnes scholasticos recentiores cum Carolostadio, id est Augustino et Apostolo Paulo, consentit. Nam Pelagiani, etsi sine gratia opus bonum fieri posse asseruerint, non tamen sine gratia coelum obtineri dixerunt. Idem certe dicunt Scholastici, dum sine gratia opus bonum, sed non meritorium fieri docent. Deinde super Pelagianos addunt, hominem habere dictamen naturale rectae rationis, cui se possit naturaliter conformare voluntas, ubi Pelagiani hominem adiuvari per legem dei dixerunt.'

58 See Oberman, *Werden und Wertung der Reformation*, 110–12.

59 e.g., A. V. Müller, *Luther und Tauler auf ihren theologischen Zusammenhang neu untersucht* (Bern, 1918), 25.

60 The best study remains Ozment's *Homo Spiritualis*.

61 Ozment, *Homo Spiritualis*, 215.

62 e.g., see S. E. Ozment, 'Homo Viator: Luther and Late Medieval Theology', *HThR* 62 (1969), 275–87.

Notes to §22

1 See Gordon Rupp, *Patterns of Reformation* (London, 1969), 55–63; McGrath, *Luther's Theology of the Cross*, 44–6. For Karlstadt's own account, see Karlstadt, *De spiritu et litera*, ed. Kähler, 4.13–28.

2 *De spiritu et litera*, 5.4–10.3.

3 For the text of these theses, see *De spiritu et litera*, 11*–37*. He also published 405 theses partly directed against Eck: *Vollständige Reformations-Acta und Documenta*, ed. V. E. Löscher (3 vols: Leipzig, 1720–3), 2.79–104.

4 e.g., *De spiritu et litera*, 28*, Theses 103–5. Karlstadt actually uses the term 'gospel' infrequently over the period 1516–21, and it is somewhat misleading for Kriechbaum to devote an important section of her work to the antithesis of 'law and gospel': Kriechbaum, *Grundzüge der Theologie Karlstadts*, 39–76.

5 *De spiritu et litera*, 71.14–15: 'Sola igitur gratia Dei per Iesum Christum dominum nostrum nos adiuvat'; 91.17–20; 16* Theses 21–2. On the basis of Theses 106 and 109, Kähler suggests that Karlstadt appears to have modified Augustine's concept of *litera occidens* slightly: *De spiritu et litera*, 29*.

6 *De spiritu et litera*, 69.27–31. Cf. 55.32–56.2.

7 Cf. Oberman, *Werden und Wertung der Reformation* (Tübingen, 1977), 110–12.

8 *De spiritu et litera*, 43*. Cf. Kriechbaum, *Grundzüge der Theologie Karlstadts*, 42–5.

9 In his study of Karlstadt, Sider appears to misunderstand the term 'forensic justification', apparently regarding it as synonymous with 'the merciful pardoning of sins': Sider, *Andreas Bodenstein von Karlstadt*, 67–8; 122–5; 258–9. Although Sider frequently refers to the concept of 'imputed righteousness' the texts which he adduces do not support his interpretation of the concept. Furthermore, he recognises that Karlstadt continues to emphasise the interior regeneration implicit in justification: e.g., see 126–9; 258. Karlstadt's doctrine of justification is no more forensic than that of Augustine, which he reproduces remarkably faithfully. The term 'forensic' derives from the Latin *forum* – the place in which judicial and other business was transacted – and in relation to the doctrine of justification, refers to a purely legal declaration that the sinner is righteous, *without or prior to* the concomitant actualisation of righteousness in the sinner.

10 *De spiritu et litera*, 32* Thesis 138.

11 Augustine, *Enn. in Psalm.* 140.15. See further Nygren, 'Simul iustus et peccator bei Augustin und Luther'.

12 Holfelder, *Ausbildung von Bugenhagens Rechtfertigungslehre*, 24–42. For the concept of the non-imputation of sin in his commentary on the Psalter, see Holfelder, *Tentatio et consolatio*, 173–98.

13 As pointed out, with documentation, by Holfelder, *Ausbildung von Bugenhagens Rechtfertigungslehre*, 23 n. 25.

14 Cf. *ibid.*, 59n. 6.

15 *ibid.*, 41n. 74.

16 Bugenhagen, *Annotationes im epistolas Pauli* (1525); cited in Holfelder, *Ausbildung von Bugenhagens Rechtfertigungslehre*, 24.

17 Cf. Melanchthon, *Locus de gratia* (1521); StA 2.85.16–88.4.

18 H. Bornkamm, 'Humanismus und Reform im Menschenbild Melanchthons' in *idem*, *Das Jahrhundert der Reformation* (Göttingen, 1961), 69–87.

19 StA 1.24 Thesis 9, 'Ergo Christi beneficium est iustitia'; Thesis 10, 'Omnis iustitia nostra est gratuita dei imputatio.'

20 *Annotationes in Evangelium Matthaei*; StA 4.173.5–6. But see Bizer, *Theologie der Verheißung*, 123–8.

21 StA 2.86.23–5; cf. 2.86.26–8; 106.20–2. See W. Maurer, *Der junge Melanchthon zwischen Humanismus und Reformation* 2. *Der Theologe* (Göttingen, 1969), 361–8.

Notes to pages 210–14

22 See Bizer, *Theologie der Verheißung*, 82–5.
23 e.g., see CR (Melanchthon) 14.1068; 1080. Cf. Bornkamm, 'Menschenbild Melanchthons'.
24 The analogy first appears in the 1533 edition of the *Loci*: CR (Melanchthon) 21.421. For the 1555 edition, see *StA* 2.359.10–18. On the case of Scipio, see *Realencyclopädie der classischen Alterthumswissenschaft*, ed. August Pauly, IV/I (Leipzig, 1900), 1475–83. For the differences between Luther and Melanchthon at this point, see H. Lindroth, *Försoningen: En dogmhistorisk och systematisk undetsökning* (Uppsala, 1935), 242–3; Josefson, *Ödmjukhet och tro: En studie i den unge Luthers teologi* (Stockholm, 1939), 127; 179; Robert Stupperich, 'Die Rechtfertigungslehre bei Luther und Melanchthon 1530–1536', in *Luther und Melanchthon: Referate und Berichte des Zweitens Internationalen Kongresses für Lutherforschung* (Göttingen, 1961), 73–88; L. Haikola, 'Melanchthons und Luthers Lehre von der Rechtfertigung', in *Luther und Melanchthon*, 89–103; Greschat, *Melanchthon neben Luther*.
25 *BSLK* 56.1–10.
26 *Apologia* art. 21 para. 19; *BSLK* 320.40–6: 'Ut si quis amicus pro amico solvis aes alienum, debitor alieno merito tamquam proprio liberatur. Ita Christi merita nobis donantur, ut iusti reputemur fiducia meritorum Christi, cum in eum credimus, tamquam propria merita haberemus.'
27 *Apologia*, art. 4 para. 305; *BSLK* 219.43–5.
28 *Apologia*, art. 4 para. 252; *BSLK* 209.32–4.
29 *Apologia*, art. 4 para. 214; *BSLK* 201.23.
30 *Apologia*, art. 4 para. 72; *BSLK* 174.37–40. Note also the continuation of this citation (41–4): 'Ideo primum volumus hoc ostendere, quod sola fides ex iniusto iustum efficiat, hoc est, accipiat remissionem peccatorum.' See also art. 4 para 78; *BSLK* 175.37–9: 'Igitur sola fide iustificamur, intelligendo iustificationem, ex iniusto iustum effici seu regenerari'; art. 4 para. 117; *BSLK* 184.9–11: '. . . quod sola fide iustificemur, hoc est, ex iniustis iusti efficiamur seu regeneremur'.
31 e.g., see Loofs, *Leitfaden*, 825–6 n. 16. For a careful study and an attempt to resolve the ambiguity, see Pfnür, *Einig in der Rechtfertigungslehre?*, 155–81, especially 157–68; 178–81.
32 See F. C. Baur, *Brevis disquisitio in Andreae Osiandi de iustificatione doctrinam* (Berlin, 1831). Niesel, 'Calvin wider Osianders Rechtfertigungslehre', while dealing primarily with Calvin's critique of Osiander, gives a useful exposition of the latter's views. Cf. Osiander, *Von dem einigen Mittler* G iiij: 'a solche irren all sehr grewlich, Erstlich das sie das wortlein Rechtfertigen verstehen und auslegen allein fur gerecht halten und sprechen, und nicht der that und in der wahrheit gerecht machen'.
33 These are chiefly to be found in the Fourth Gospel: note the texts cited in *Von dem einigen Mittler*, E iib and following.
34 Perhaps the best account of the views and influence of Stancari may be found in C. A. Selig, *Vollständige Historie des Augsburger Confession* (3 vols: Halle, 1730), 2.714–947.
35 WA 1.96.6–8: 'Opera sunt necessaria ad salutem, sed non causant

457

salutem, quia fides sola dat vitam.' Cf. WA 30 II.663.3–5; 39 I.254.27–30. For an excellent study, see Modalsi, *Gericht nach den Werken*, 83–9.

36 WA 39 I.46.20.

37 WA 6.204.25–6; 206.36.

38 *StA* 4.153–4.

39 *StA* 2.148.22–4; 149.19–21.

40 Amsdorf, *Das die propositio (Gute werck sind sur Seligkeit schedlich) eine rechte ware christliche propositio sey* (Magdeburg, 1559). In his preface to Luther's sermons on John 18–20, published in 1557, Amsdorf represented Luther as teaching that good works were unnecessary and harmful: WA 28.765–7. See further Kolb, *Nikolaus von Amsdorf*, 123–80, especially 158–62.

41 Cf. W. Joest, *Gesetz und Freiheit: Das Problem des tertius usus legis bei Luther und neutestamentliche Parainese*, 3rd edn (Göttingen, 1961); J. Seehawer, *Zur Lehre vom Gebrauch des Gesetzes und zur Geschichte des späteren Antinomianismus* (Rostok, 1887).

42 Melanchthon cites Chrysostom's gloss on John 6.44 in this connection: see N. P. Williams, *The Grace of God* (London, 1930), 81.

43 A. Evard, *Etude sur les variations du dogme de la prédestination et·du libre arbitrie dans la théologie de Melanchthon* (Laval, 1901).

44 See the letter to Brenz of 30 September 1531 (No. 1010): CR (Melanchthon) 2.547.

45 Strigel, *Loci theologici*, ed. Petzel (4 vols: Neustadt, 1581–4). These volumes are very heavily dependent upon Melanchthon. The best study remains that of H. Merz, *Historia vitae et controversiae V. Strigelii* (Tübingen, 1732).

46 Both Amsdorf and Flacius were strident defenders of the 'Gnesio-Lutheran' principle of absolute predestination, which they held to be compromised by Pfeffinger: Kolb, *Nikolaus von Amsdorf*, 188–201. Curiously, Amsdorf accused Pfeffinger of Scotism (Kolb, *Nikolaus von Amsdorf*, 196–7), although Amsdorf's predestinarianism is often thought to reflect his own Scotist background.

47 Chemnitz, *Examen*, 129.a 7–16.

48 *Ibid.*, 130.b 15–18.

49 Chemnitz, *Loci Theologici*, Pars II, 626. Examen, 130.b 24–48; 131.b 18–23; 132.b 1–3.

50 *Loci*, Pars II, 642 '[Augustinus] involvit et obscurat mentem Pauli.'

51 *Examen*, 131.a 39–41.

52 *BSLK*, 913–36.

53 *BSLK* III.9; 917.15–33. Note, however, III.54 (932.45–933.17), where the indwelling of the essential righteousness of God in the believer is conceded, but distinguished from *iustitia fidei*, the righteousness on the basis of which man is justified.

54 *BSLK* III.17; 919.24–9.

55 *BSLK* III.60; 935.14–19.

56 *BSLK* III.4; 914.19–916.3; III.12; 918.10–12; III.56; 933.36–934.11.

57 *BSLK* Epitome IV.6; 787.19–22; IV.18; 789.30–2.

58 *BSLK* Epitome IV.16; 789.15–20. The exact phrases condemned are due to Georg Major.

59 *BSLK* Epitome II.11; 779.1–17. Note also the assertion 'homo nihil agit aut operatur, sed tantum patitur': II.89; 910.16–18.

60 *BSLK* Epitome I.15; 773.28 'cum magnes allii succo illinitur'.

61 *BSLK* Epitome II.6; 778.4–14.

62 *BSLK* XI.5; 1065.23–7.

63 *BSLK* XI.4; 1065.2–6.

64 *BSLK* XI.81; 1086.26–41: 'enim Deus non est causa peccati'. Cf. XI.41 (1076.4–16), where the possibility that the reprobate's contempt for the Word of God as a consequence of divine predestination is also rejected.

65 *BSLK* Epitome II.18; 780.30–781.3. Cf. II.83; 906.5–24.

66 *BSLK* II.44; 889.11–41. On this, see McSorley, *Luther – Right or Wrong?*, 360–2.

67 See Werner Elert, 'Deutschrechtliche Züge in Luthers Rechtfertigungs-slehre', *ZSTh* 12 (1935), 22–35.

68 Erasmus, *Novum Instrumentum omne* (Basileae, 1516), 429: 'Accepto fert: λογίζηται, id est, imputat sive acceptum fert. Est autem acceptum fere, debere, sive pro accepto habere, quod non acceperis, *quae apud iure consultos vocatur acceptilatio*'.

Notes to §23

1 See Bernd Moeller, 'Die deutschen Humanisten und die Anfänge der Reformation', *ZKG* 70 (1959), 46–61; *idem*, 'Die Ursprünge der reformierten Kirche', *Theologische Literaturzeitung* 100 (1975), 642–53.

2 See E.-W. Kohls, *Die Theologie des Erasmus* (2 vols: Basel, 1966), I.143–58.

3 Cf. Kohls, 'Die Bedeutung literarischer Überlieferung bei Erasmus', *Archiv für Kulturgeschichte* 48 (1966), 291–33, especially 226–7.

4 For a useful discussion of Erasmus' moralist exegesis of scripture, see Henning Graf Reventloh, *The Authority of the Bible and the Rise of the Modern World* (London, 1984), 39–48.

5 e.g., see Richard Stauffer, 'Einfluß und Kritik des Humanismus in Zwinglis "Commentarius de vera et falsa religione"', *Zwingliana* 16 (1983), 97–110 (which should be compared with the older study of J. F. Gerhard Goeters, 'Zwinglis Werdegang als Erasmianer', in *Reformation und Humanismus: Robert Stupperich zum 65. Geburtstag*, ed. M. Greschat and J. F. G. Goeters (Witten, 1969), 225–71); Christine Christ, 'Das Schriftverständnis von Zwingli und Erasmus im Jahre 1522', *Zwingliana* 16 (1983), 111–25; F. Krüger, *Bucer and Erasmus: Eine Untersuchung zum Einfluß des Erasmus auf die Theologie Martin Bucers* (Wiesbaden, 1970). The strong emphasis upon personal responsibility for sin which causes Zwingli to abandon the traditional Augustinian understanding of original sin (and which underlies his moralist theology of justification) may be due to Erasmian influence: see Rudolf Pfister, *Das Problem der Erbsünde bei Zwingli* (Leipzig, 1939). Zwingli's discussion of the relation of original sin

and baptism suggests that he regards the former to be insignificant theologically until it is actualised as a conscious and deliberate act of sin, in knowledge of the demands of the law: CR (Zwingli) 3.760.

6 CR (Zwingli) 1.67.17–20. For a useful analysis of this *Pestlied*, see Rich, *Anfänge*, 112–19.

7 e.g., Beatus Rhenanus: see CR 7.115.10–4.

8 e.g., see CR 7.328.17–20. See Rich, *Anfänge*, 56–70.

9 CR 2.649.19–21. Note the emphasis upon doing God's will at CR 3.29.25–7. For further discussion, see Heinrich Schmid, *Zwinglis Lehre von der göttlichen und menschlichen Gerechtigkeit* (Zürich, 1959).

10 CR 2.6434.2.5. See further McGrath, 'Humanist Elements in the Early Reformed Doctrine of Justification'.

11 CR 2.76.18–21.

12 CR 1.178.1; 2.496.22.

13 Cited in Zwingli, *Opera*, ed. M. Schuler and J. Schulthess (8 vols: Zürich, 1929–42), 4.185. Zwingli's tendency to identify *lex* and *evangelium* leads to a similar conclusion: Rich, *Anfänge*, 64–7.

14 Henri Strohl, *La pensée de la Réforme* (Neuchâtel, 1951), 107. Cf. E. Staehelin, *Das theologische Lebenswerk Johannes Oecolampadius* (Leipzig, 1939); E. G. Rupp, *Patterns of Salvation* (London, 1969), 3–48; 17: 'His was always the faith of a moralist.'

15 Strohl, *La pensée de la Réforme*, 108.

16 Bullinger, *Sermonum decades quinque*, 157b. Note also the emphasis upon the consonance of Paul and James, also evident in *De gratia dei iustificante*, 65–7.

17 This is clearly seen from his early preoccupation with the works of Erasmus: Martin Greschat, 'Martin Bucers Bücherverzeichnis', *Archiv für Kulturgeschichte* 57 (1975), 162–85.

18 This is well brought out by Karl Koch, *Studium Pietatis: Martin Bucer als Ethiker* (Neukirchen, 1962), 10–15, on the basis of his correspondence with Beatus Rhenanus.

19 *Enarrationes in sacra quattuor evangelia* (1530), 48 B-C; 49 C. Cf. Koch, *Studium Pietatis*, 67.

20 *Metaphrasis et enarratio in epist. D. Pauli ad Romanos*, 231 A-B; 232 D-E. Elsewhere in the same work, he notes a three-fold scheme, which includes the final glorification of the sinner as its third element: 119 A-B. See Johannes Müller, *Martin Bucers Hermeneutik* (Heidelberg, 1965), 122 n. 184.

21 Robert Stupperich, 'Der Ursprung des Regensburger Buches von 1541 und seine Rechtfertigungslehre', *ARG* 36 (1939), 88–116.

22 *Metaphrasis et enarratio in epist. D. Pauli ad Romanos*, 11–14. Cf. W. P. Stephens, *The Holy Spirit in the Theology of Martin Bucer* (Cambridge, 1970), 48–100, especially 55–61.

23 August Lang, *Der Evangelienkommentar Martin Butzers und die Grundzüge seiner Theologie* (Leipzig, 1900), 8; 137; 377–8; *idem, Puritanismus und Pietismus: Studien zu ihrer Entwicklung vom M. Butzer bis zum Methodismus* (Gütersloh, 1941), 13–71. Unfortunately, Lang's assertion that Bucer

was devoid of humanist influence has not stood up to critical evaluation. For further comment see Eduard Ellwein, *Vom neuen Leben: de novitate vitae* (München, 1932), *passim*. However, Bucer's ideological flexibility may go some way towards explaining difficulties in interpretation at such points: see Martin Greschat, 'Der Ansatz der Theologie Martin Bucers', *Theologische Literaturzeitung* 103 (1978), 81–96.

24 e.g., *Metaphrasis et enarratio in epist. D. Pauli ad Romanos*, 405 C. It is not clear whether this should be understood as a logical or a chronological sequence: Stephens, *Martin Bucer*, 30, suggests it is logical, although the more careful analysis of Müller, *Martin Bucers Hermeneutik*, 24 n. 38 suggests it is chronological.

25 Stephens, *Martin Bucer*, 99, states that 'there is an unbreakable link holding together predestination, vocation, justification, *sanctification* and glorification' (our italics): the reference given makes no mention of sanctification (99 n. 2). Similarly, Stephens' entire section on 'sanctification' (71–98) represents the imposition of an alien structure upon Bucer's thought, and cannot be supported on the basis of the texts cited. Bucer must be allowed to speak for himself rather than having a later structure imposed upon him.

26 See Emmanuel Graf von Korff, *Die Anfänge der Föderaltheologie und ihre erste Ausgestaltung in Zürich und Holland* (Bonn, 1908).

27 Schrenk, *Gottesreich und Bund*, 36–7, argues that Zwingli derived the concept from the Radical Reformers. Zwingli's covenantal theology is undoubtedly closely linked with his theology of baptism: see David C. Steinmetz, 'The Baptism of John and the Baptism of Jesus in Huldrych Zwingli, Balthasar Hubmeier and Late Medieval Theology', in *Continuity and Discontinuity in Church History*, ed. F. F. Church and Timothy George (Leiden, 1979), 169–81; Timothy George, 'The Presuppositions of Zwingli's Baptismal Theology', in *Prophet, Pastor, Protestant: The Work of Huldrych Zwingli after Five Hundred Years*, ed. E. J. Furcha and H. Wayne Pipkin (Allinson Park, Pennsylvania, 1984), 71–87. On Bullinger, see Peter Walser, *Die Prädestination bei Heinrich Bullinger im Zusammenhang mit seiner Gotteslehre* (Zürich, 1957), 234–49. On the differences between Bullinger and Zwingli, see J. Wayne Baker, *Heinrich Bullinger and the Covenant: The Other Reformed Tradition* (Athens, Ohio, 1980), 1–25.

28 e.g., see Hans H. Wolff, *Die Einheit des Bundes: Das Verhältnis von Altem und Neuem Bund bei Calvin* (Neukirchen, 1958).

29 On the distinction between 'testament' and 'covenant', and its importance for the development of the later Reformed federal soteriologies, see Kenneth L. Hagen, 'From Testament to Covenant in the Early Sixteenth Century', *Sixteenth Century Journal* 3 (1972), 1–24.

30 Although the main features of Calvin's theology of justification may be found in his exegetical works (e.g., see H. P. Santmire, 'Justification in Calvin's 1540 Romans Commentary', *ChH* 33 (1963), 294–313), we propose to develop our analysis upon the basis of the 1559 *Institutio*. It is only in this later work that the distinction between Calvin and

Osiander on the nature of the believer's relation to Christ is fully clarified. Furthermore, the propagation of Reformed theology in the later sixteenth century was largely due to the 1559 *Institutio*, either in translation or in a condensed edition, rather than his biblical commentaries.

31 *Christianae religionis institutio* (Basileae, 1536), 111; *OS* 1.73. For the differences between the 1536 and 1539 editions, see A. Autin, *L'Institution chrétienne de Calvin* (Paris, 1929), 47–83; *OS* 3.vi–xv. The 1539 edition contains a chapter (*VI. de iustificatione fidei et meritis operum*) which represents a massive expansion of the brief comments of the first edition.

32 *Institutio* (1559), III.xi.2; *OS* 4.183.7–10.

33 *Institutio*, III.xi.11; *OS* 4.193.2–5; 193.17–194.21.

34 See McGrath, 'John Calvin and Late Medieval Thought', for an analysis. Calvin's doctrine of the *meritum Christi* – of importance in this respect – is discussed in relation to the late medieval doctrine of merit (§10).

35 *Institutio*, III.xi.23; *OS* 4.206.29–32. Thus Calvin criticises Augustine's intrinsic concept of justifying righteousness: *Institutio*, III.xi.15; *OS* 4.199.25–200.6.

36 For Calvin's attitude to the Augsburg Confession, see Willem Nijenhuis, 'Calvin en de Augsburgse Confessie', *Nederlands Theologisch Tijdschrift* 15 (1960–1), 416–33.

37 *Institutio*, III.xi.10; *OS* 4.191.31–192.4. This section should be read with some care.

38 See Niesel, 'Calvin wider Osianders Rechtfertigungslehre'. Also of relevance here is Calvin's attitude to the Regensburg article of justification (1541): see W. H. Neuser, 'Calvins Urteil über den Rechtfertigungsartikel des Regensburger Buches', in *Reformation und Humanismus: Robert Stupperich zum 65. Geburtstag*, ed. M. Greschat and J. F. G. Goeters (Witten, 1969), 176–94.

39 *Institutio*, III.xi.1, 6. For further discussion and references, see Boisset, 'Justification et sanctification chez Calvin'; Stadtland, *Rechtfertigung und Heiligung*; McGrath, 'Humanist Elements in the Early Reformed Doctrine of Justification', 14–16.

40 For the phrase, see CR (Calvin) 50.437–8.

41 *Institutio*, III.xi.7; *OS* 4.188.24–5: 'Quod obiicit, vim iustificandi non inesse fidei ex seipsa, se quatenus Christum recipit, libenter admitto.' For Calvin's definition of faith, see *Institutio*, III.ii.7.

42 *Institutio*, IV.xvii.42; III.xvii.11; III.xviii.10.

43 *Institutio*, III.xi.7.

44 CR (Calvin) 49.61; *Institutio*, III.xi.7.

45 Thus J. R. Packer, in *John Calvin*, ed. G. E. Duffield (Abingdon, 1966), 157. Cf. W. Niesel, *The Theology of Calvin* (London, 1956), 130. Göhler suggests that there is *no* central doctrine in the theology of Calvin: *Calvins Lehre von der Heiligung*, 81. It must also be noted that the circumstances of Calvin's 'conversion' were quite different from those attending Luther's theological breakthrough, in that soteriological questions do not appear to have been pre-eminent: see P. Sprenger, *Das Rätsel um die Bekehrung Calvins* (Neukirchen, 1960); A. Ganoczy, *Le jeune Calvin:*

Genèse et évolution de sa vocation réformatrice (Wiesbaden, 1966), 286–304;
Harro Höpfl, *The Christian Polity of John Calvin* (Cambridge, 1985),
219–26.

46 That this is also the case with early Scottish Reformed theology (e.g., that
of John Knox or the *Scots Confession* of 1560) has been brought out by
T. F. Torrance, 'Justification: Its Radical Nature and Place in Reformed
Doctrine and Life', *SJTh* 13 (1960), 225–46, especially 225–7.

47 See Alexander Schweizer, *Die protestantischen Centraldogmen in ihrer
Entwicklung innerhalb der reformirten Kirche* (2 vols: Zürich, 1854–6).
Schweizer, however, argues that Calvin treats the doctrine of predestination as central – a conclusion which modern Calvin scholarship has not
endorsed.

Notes to §24

1 See Alister E. McGrath, 'Reformation to Enlightenment', in *The Science
of Theology*, ed. P. D. L. Avis (London, 1986), for a discussion. The
parallels between Protestant and medieval Catholic scholasticism are well
brought out by Robert Scharlemann, *Aquinas and Gerhard: Theological
Controversy and Construction in Medieval and Protestant Scholasticism* (New
Haven, 1964). The scholasticism of Gerhard's soteriology is best seen
from his Aristotelian analysis of the causes of justification: see Richard
Schröder, *Johann Gerhards lutherische Christologie und die aristotelische
Metaphysik* (Tübingen, 1983), 69–97.

2 See E. Bizer, *Frühorthodoxie und Rationalismus* (Zürich, 1963), 5–15.

3 See Otto Gründler, *Die Gotteslehre Giralmo Zanchis* (Neukirchen, 1965);
Walter Kickel, *Vernunft und Offenbarung bei Theodor Beza* (Neukirchen,
1967); J. S. Bray, *Theodore Beza's Doctrine of Predestination* (Nieuwkoop,
1975); J. P. Donnelly, *Calvinism and Scholasticism in Vermigli's Doctrine
of Man and Grace* (Leiden, 1976).

4 See Kickel, *Vernunft und Offenbarung*, 167–8, for an excellent discussion
of this point. While Calvin regarded Christ as the *speculum electionis* (see
CR (Calvin) 35.479), Beza regarded the decrees of election and reprobation as the *speculum* in which the glory of God was reflected (*Tractationes
theologicae*, 3.403).

5 For the reasons why, see the second of the *Treze Sermons*: CR (Calvin)
58.31–44. These points are also emphasised by Basil Hall, 'Calvin against
the Calvinists', in *John Calvin*, ed. G. E. Duffield (Abingdon, 1966),
19–37, especially 25–8. Unfortunately, Hall is incorrect in his assertion
(27) that Beza altered Calvin's teaching on the *nature* of justification by
including both remission of sin and acceptance of the sinner as righteous,
where Calvin included only the former element: it is clear (see §22) that
Calvin included both – e.g., *Institutio*, III.11.2; *OS* 4.183.7–10.

6 *BSRK* 843.15–861.8 On the final point, see Jürgen Moltmann, *Prädestination und Perseveranz: Geschichte und Bedeutung der reformierten Lehre 'de
perseverantia sanctorum'* (Neukirchen, 1961), especially 110–62. For
details of the Arminian controversy over the decisions of the Synod of

Dort, see A. W. Harrison, *The Beginnings of Arminianism to the Synod of Dort* (London, 1926). On the background to Dort, see Gustav Adolf Benrath, 'Die hessische Kirche und die Synode in Dordrecht', *Jahrbuch der Hessischen Kirchengeschichtlichen Vereinigung* 20 (1969), 56–81.

7 See *Acta et scripta synodalia Dodrecena ministrorum remonstrantium* (Harderwijk, 1622), 1.71–4.

8 Schrenk, *Gottesreich und Bund*, 63. On the theological significance of the covenant-motif in later Reformed and Puritan theology, see Perry Miller, 'The Marrow of Puritan Divinity', in *Errand into the Wilderness* (Cambridge, Mass., 1956), 48–98.

9 Especially his *Summa religionis Christianae* (Nystadt, 1584). The study of F. A. Lampe, *Einleitung zu dem Geheimnis des Gnadenbundes* (Marburg/Frankfurt, 1782), is still useful as a source.

10 *Christianae theologiae compendium* 1, 7. Man's obligations to God under the *foedus operum* may be defined as the general obligation to love God and one's neighbour, and the specific obligation to eat of the tree of the knowledge of good and evil: Lampe, *Einleitung*, 25. For a well-documented discussion of the *foedus operum* within Reformed theology, see H. Heppe, *Die Dogmatik der evangelisch-reformierten Kirche*, ed. E. Bizer (Neukirchen, 1958), 224–54. On the pre-Cocceian covenant in Scotland, see S. A. Burrell, 'The Covenant Ideas as a Revolutionary Symbol: Scotland, 1596–1637', *ChH* 27 (1958), 338–50; R. L. Greaves, 'John Knox and the Covenant Tradition', *Journal of Ecclesiastical History* 24 (1973), 23–32; J. B. Torrance, 'Covenant or Contract? A Study of the Theological Background of Worship in Seventeenth Century Scotland', *SJTh* 23 (1970), 51–76; *idem*, 'The Covenant Concept in Scottish Theology', *SJTh* 34 (1981), 225–43.

11 *Compendium* 1, 21. For a general survey, see Heppe, *Dogmatik*, 295–322.

12 *Summa doctrinae de foedere et testamento Dei* IV, 6. See further Heiner Faulenbach, *Weg und Ziel der Erkenntnis Christi: Eine Untersuchung zur Theologie des Johannes Coccejus* (Neukirchen, 1973).

13 e.g., see Burmann, *Synopsis Theologiae*, II.xv.2.

14 *Opera* (Genevae, 1642), 544–52.

15 Thesis 46 is particularly important: 'in foedere subserviente Deus ius suum non alio fine exigit, quam ut homines convicti imbecilitatis suae ad Christum confugiant' (*Opera*, 548).

16 See Moltmann, 'Prädestination und Heilsgeschichte bei Moyse Amyraut'; Laplanche, *Orthodoxie et prédication*; Armstrong, *Calvinism and the Amyraut Heresy*.

17 Armstrong, *Calvinism and the Amyraut Heresy*, 222–40.

18 Thesis 2; in *Syntagma thesium theologicarum* (2 vols: Saumur, 1641), 1.212.

19 *Defense de la doctrine de Calvin sur le sujet de l'election* (Saumur, 1644), 544. The whole of this chapter (512–68) should be studied. Note also 312–13, where Amyraut makes it clear that he regards the doctrine of election to function as an *ex post facto* explanation of why some believe and others do not, rather than as a speculative principle of deductive theology. For the manner in which Amyraut reconciles the universality of the offer of

salvation and the particularity of faith, see *Brief traitté de la prédestination* (Saumur, 1634), 89–90; Laplanche, *Orthodoxie et prédication*, 87–108.

20 See Wilhelm Dantine, *Die Gerechtmachung der Gottlosen: Eine dogmatische Untersuchung* (München, 1959), 15–29; H. E. Weber, *Reformation, Orthodoxie und Rationalismus*, 2nd edn (2 vols: Gütersloh, 1940–51), I/1.126.

21 On the Lutheran side, see Hafenreffer, *Loci theologici*, 664; Koenig, *Theologia positiva acroamatica*, §562; 208; Brochmand, *Universae theologiae systema*, 1.471. On the Reformed, see Heidegger, *Medulla*, XXII, 4; 169; XXI, 6; 169; XXII, 26; 183; Wollebius, *Christianae theologiae compendium*, 1.xxx.2; 234; Bucanus, *Institutiones theologicae*, XXXI, 6; 332; Alsted, *Theologia scholastica didactica*, IV.xxv.1; 709; Musculus, *Loci communes*, 262–3. Note the explicit criticism of Augustine evident in certain of these citations (e.g., Musculus).

For an analysis of the Aristotelian foundations of Johann Gerhard's understanding of the causality of justification, see Richard Schröder, *Johann Gerhards lutherische Christologie und die aristotelische Metaphysik* (Tübingen, 1983), 69–96. For a description of Quenstedt's doctrine of justification, which illustrates Lutheran Orthodoxy at its best, see R. D. Preuss, 'The Justification of a Sinner before God as taught in Later Lutheran Orthodoxy', *SJTh* 13 (1960), 262–77. On the forensic character of justification, see 270–7. For the general character of Quenstedt's theology, see Jörg Baur, *Die Vernunft zwischen Ontologie und Evangelium: Eine Untersuchung zur Theologie Johann Andreas Quenstedt* (Gütersloh, 1962),.

22 See Bucanus, *Institutiones theologicae* XXXI, 27; 341: 'Iustitia Christi aliena est, quatenus extra nos est . . . sed aliena non est, quatenus nobis destinata est . . . Est etiam nostra illa iustitia, quatenus illud ipsum eius subjectum, nempe Christus, noster est adeoque spiritualiter per fidem factus est unus nobiscum.' Cf. Polanus, *Syntagma* IV, 27; 781. For an excellent introduction to the thought of Polanus, see Heiner Faulenbach, *Die Struktur der Theologie des Amandus Polanus von Polansdorf* (Zürich, 1967), which remedies the theological deficiencies of the older study of Ernst Staehelin, *Amandus Polanus von Polansdorf* (Basel, 1955).

23 It is not strictly correct to suggest that Piscator denied that Christ's active obedience was totally devoid of satisfactory value. Piscator asserted that the active obedience of Christ affected the satisfactory value of his death, in that without Christ's sinless and obedient life, his passion could not have had any satisfactory value. Thus the *obedientia activa* may be said to possess *indirect* satisfactory value.

24 *Loci theologici*, ed. Cotta, loc. xvii cap. 4; 7.260.

25 *Loci theologici* 7.261.

26 See the important discussion in Ritschl, *The Christian Doctrine of Justification and Reconciliation* (Edinburgh, 1872), 248–67, especially 256.

27 It may be noted that federal theologians, such as Burmann, discussed the *obedientia activa* in terms of Christ's *natural* submission to the law as on account of his *being* a man, and his *federal* submission to the law by virtue of his *becoming* man on behalf of the elect.

28 The best study of Socinianism remains O. Fock, *Der Socianismus nach seiner Stellung* (Kiel, 1847). A useful analysis in English is to be found in R. S. Franks, *The Work of Christ* (London, 1962), 362–77.

29 Fock, *Der Socianismus*, 552; 615–39.

30 For an excellent description of the Lutheran and Reformed teaching on the work of Christ, exemplified by Quenstedt and Heidegger respectively, see Franks, *The Work of Christ*, 410–47.

31 There appears to have been considerable confusion within Lutheranism upon the relation of Christ's merits and satisfaction. Gerhard appears to treat the concepts as identical, although a distinction between them emerges later: see Koenig, *Theologia positiva acroamatica*, §§219–20; §§150–1. See also Ritschl, *Justification and Reconciliation*, 261.

32 On the Lutheran side, see Koenig, *Theologia positiva acroamatica*, §217; 150; §232; 153; Brochmand, *Universae theologiae systema*, 1.709–11; Gerhard, *Loci theologici*; in *Opera* 7.70. On the Reformed, see Heidegger, *Medulla*, XIX, 15; 53; Wollebius, *Christianae theologiae compendium*, I.xvii.4; 117; Polanus, *Syntagma*, VI, 27; 266–82.

33 *Loci theologici* locus xvii, *de iustificatione per fidem, prooemium*; ed. Cotta, 7.1: 'Calviniani errant in articulo praedestinationis; ergo et in articulo iustificationis, quia iustificatio est praedestinationis executio.'

34 To the Tridentine assertion (*decretum de iustificatione*, cap. 6) of the universality of the passion and benefits of Christ, cited at CR (Calvin) 7.431, Calvin replies (435) 'Tertium et quartum caput non attingo.' For the background to this work, see T. W. Casteel, 'Calvin and Trent: Calvin's Reaction to the Council of Trent in the Context of His Conciliar Thought', *HThR* 63 (1970), 91–117.

35 Beza, *Tractationes theologicae*, 1.344; 363; 418. See Hall, 'Calvin against the Calvinists', 27; Bray, *Beza's Doctrine of Predestination*, *passim*.

36 Heidegger, *Medulla*, XIXI, 56; 77–8.

37 *Compendium theologiae*, VI.xviii.2.

38 Interestingly, Koenig does not even include *iustificatio* in his *ordo salutis*: *Theologia positiva acroamatica*, §426; 184 (although it is possible that he intends to subsume it under *regeneratio* – cf. §447; 188). See further Bengt Hägglund, 'Rechtfertigung – Wiedergeburt – Erneuerung in der nachreformatorischen Theologie', *KuD* 5 (1959), 318–37; Carl E. Braaten, 'The Correlation between Justification and Faith in Classical Lutheran Dogmatics', in *Symposium on Seventeenth Century Lutheranism* (St Louis, 1962), 77–90.

39 *Christianae theologiae libri II*, facing prolegomena at beginning of work. Only a small part of a complex chart is reproduced. The inclusion of glorification as a consequence of the *unio mystica* between Christ and the believer can be illustrated from many Reformed works of the period, including those otherwise deemed heterodox – e.g., Amyraut, *Brief traitté*, 86–7.

40 See A. B. Ritschl, *Geschichte des Pietismus* (3 vols: Bonn, 1880–6); M. Schian, *Orthodoxie und Pietismus in Kampf um die Predigt* (Giessen, 1912); Martin Schmidt, *Wiedergeburt und neuer Mensch: Gesammelte Studien zur*

Geschichte des Pietismus (Witten, 1969); McGrath, 'Reformation to Enlightenment'.

41 See A. J. Beachy, *The Concept of Grace in the Radical Reformers* (Nieuwkoop, 1977), especially 28–9, who demonstrates the transformational concept of justification widely employed within the movement, generally articulated in terms of the concept of 'deification'.

42 Robert Barclay, *An Apologie for the True Christian Divinity*, 13th edn (Manchester, 1869), 136.

43 *Apologie*, 131.

44 E. Hirsch, *Geschichte der neuern evangelischen Theologie* (5 vols: Gütersloh, 1949–51), 2.245–9.

45 Ritschl, *Justification and Reconciliation*, 515.

46 See Schian, *Orthodoxie und Pietismus*, 86–97; Jörg Baur, *Salus Christiana: Die Rechtfertigungslehre in der Geschichte des christlichen Heilsverständnisses* (Gütersloh, 1969), 87–110; Erhard Peschke, 'Speners Wiederburtslehre und ihr Verhältnis zu Franckes Lehre von der Bekehrung', in *Traditio – Krisis – Renovatio aus theologische Sicht* (Marburg, 1976), 206–24; Dietrich Meyer, 'Zinzendorfs Sehnsucht nach der "naturellen Heiligkeit"', in *Traditio – Krisis – Renovatio*, 284–97; Horst Weigelt, *Pietismus-Studien* I (Stuttgart, 1965), 105–18. The Methodist movement may be regarded as the English manifestation of Pietism: see E. von Eicken, *Rechtfertigung und Heiligung bei John Wesley* (Heidelburg, 1934); D. Lerch, *Heil und Heiligung bei John Wesley* (Zürich, 1941); H. Lindström, *Wesley and Sanctification: A Study in the Doctrine of Salvation* (London, 1956).

47 Schmidt, *Wiedergeburt und neuer Mensch*, 273.

48 On this controversy, see H.-M. Rotermund, *Orthodoxie und Pietismus: Valentin Ernst Löschers 'Timotheus Verinus' in der Auseinandersetzung mit der Schule August Hermann Franckes* (Berlin, 1960), 48–51.

49 E. Peschke, *Studien zur Theologie August Hermann Franckes* I (Berlin, 1964), 47.

50 The concept is first encountered in the writings of Spener: Hirsch, *Geschichte*, 2.148. In England, the doctrine is particularly associated with Wesley, who expressed it in his concept of 'entire sanctification'.

51 See the criticism of Wesley on this point by the Reformed divine James Buchanan, *The Doctrine of Justification* (1867; reprinted London, 1961), 192–4.

52 See Baur, *Salus Christiana*, 91–5; Buchanan, *Doctrine of Justification*, 193–4.

53 Rotermund, *Orthodoxie und Pietismus*, 56–7. Löscher saw in this the spectre of Osiandrism.

54 Wesley, *Works*, 10.366.

55 Wesley, *Standard Sermons*, 1.120. Baur notes the general Pietist hostility towards the *als-ob-Theologie* of Lutheran Orthodoxy: *Salus Christiana*, 94.

56 Cf. Spener, *Das Gericht der Verstockung* (Frankfurt, 1701), 24–7. Traces of the idea may be found in Dannhauer's *Hodosophia Christiana sive theologia positiva* (Strasbourg, 1649).

Notes to introduction to chapter 7

1 See Jedin, *Geschichte des Konzils von Trientes*, 2.140–2. The earlier (and somewhat impressionistic) study of Catholic responses to the Lutheran doctrine of justification in the period 1520–45 of H. Laemmer, *Die vortridentinisch-katholische Theologie des Reformationszeitalter* (Berlin, 1858), 137–99, has now given way to the detailed study of Pfnür, *Einig in der Rechtfertigungslehre?*, 273–378.

2 H. Schmidt, *Bruckenschlag zwischen den Konfessionen* (Paderborn, 1951), 162.

3 For useful studies of the late medieval religious outlook, see J. Toussaert, *Le Sentiment religieux en Flandre à la fin du Moyen Age* (Paris, 1963); P. Heath, *The English Parish Clergy on the Eve of the Reformation* (London/Toronto, 1969); M. Bowker, *The Secular Clergy in the Diocese of Lincoln* (Cambridge, 1968).

4 Pfnür, *Einig in der Rechtfertigungslehre?*, 369–78.

5 The full implications of the forensic dimension of the Melanchthonian concept of justification occasionally appear to have been recognised – e.g., in the case of Johannes Dietenberger, *Phimostoms Scripturariorum* (1530), and Johannes Mensing, *Antapologie* (1535): see Pfnür, *Einig in der Rechtfertigungslehre?*, 280 n. 66; 359–60.

6 See *WA* 18.786.26–8.

Notes to §25

1 The renaissance within the late medieval Spanish church is particularly associated with Francisco Ximénez de Cisneros: see J. Garcia Oro, *Cisneros y la reforma del clero español en tiempo de los reyes católicos* (Madrid, 1971). On the reforming synods of Alcalá and Talavera, see L. Fernández de Retana, *Cisneros y su siglo: Estudio histórico de la vida y actuación pública del Cardenal Ximénez de Cisneros* (2 vols: Madrid, 1929–30), 1.497–8.

2 See Nieto, *Juan de Valdés and the Origins of the Spanish and Italian Reformation* (Geneva, 1970), 13–88 for a discussion.

3 The relevant portions of the confessions of Pedro Ruiz de Alcaraz and Isabella de la Cruz should be noted: e.g., see Nieto, *Juan de Valdés*, 62 n. 49; 64 nn. 55–6. See further M. Serrano y Sanz, 'Pedro Ruiz de Alcaraz, illuminado alcarreno del siglo XVI', *Revista de archivos, bibliotecas y museos* 8 (1903), 1–16; 126–39; A. Selke de Sánchez, 'Alguno datos nuevos sobre los primeros alumbrados: El edicto de 1525 y su relación con el proceso de Alcaraz', *Bulletin Hispanique* 54 (1952), 125–52; Nieto, *Juan de Valdés*, 60–88.

4 The parallels with Quakerism have often been noted: e.g., R. M. Jones, 'A Quaker Forerunner', *Friends' Quarterly Examiner* 66 (1932), 47–57. For the question of the nature and extent of Protestant influence upon the later Spanish Reformation, see J. I. Tellechea Idígoras, *Melanchton y Carranza: Préstamos y afinados* (Salamanca, 1979), 36–201.

5 See Ortolani, *Pietro Carnesecchi*, 172. For further discussion, see Fr.

Domingo de Sta. Teresa, *Juan de Valdés 1498(?)–1541: su pensamiento religioso y las corrientes espirituales de su tiempo* (Roma, 1957), 284–316; M. J. Montsérin, 'La andadura humana de Juan de Valdés', in *Dialogo de doctrina cristiana* (Biblioteca de visionarios, heterodoxos y marginados: Madrid, 1979), 161–89.

6 *Las ciento diez divinas consideraciones*, ed. Idígoras, 85.

7 *Las ciento diez divinas consideraciones*, 85–6.

8 *Las ciento diez divinas consideraciones*, 291.

9 For a discussion of the Lutheran works which may have been available in Spain at the time, see Nieto, *Juan de Valdés*, 66 n. 1. Of course, it must be remembered that the Luther known in Spain was a vague and distant figure, quite unlike the reality: see J. I. Tellechea Idígoras, 'Lutero desde España', *Revista de Occidente* 29 (1983), 5–32.

10 See P. O. Kristeller, 'Augustine and the Early Renaissance', in *Studies in Renaissance Thought and Letters* (Rome, 1956), 355–72 for details of such works. On the first printed edition of Augustine, see J. de Ghellinck, 'La première édition imprimée des "Opera omnia S. Augustina"', in *Miscellanea J. Gessler* 1 (Antwerp, 1948), 530–47. A pronounced Augustinianism may be found in Jacques Lefèvre d'Etaples' 1512 Pauline commentaries: A. Renaudet, *Préréforme et humanisme à Paris pendant les premières guerres d'Italie 1494–1517*, 2nd ed (Paris, 1953), 622–34; R. M. Cameron, 'The Charges of Lutheranism brought against Jacques Lefèvre d'Etaples', *HThR* 63 (1970), 119–49.

11 For a careful study, see R. Cessi, 'Paolinismo preluterano', *Rendiconti dell' Academia nazionale dei Lincei*, Classe di scienze morali, storiche e filologe Ser. VIII, 12 (1957), 3–30. Note also that Valdés was regarded as *iuvenis divi Pauli studiosissimus*: J. N. Bakhuizen van den Brink, *Juan de Valdés réformateur en Espagne et en Italie* (Genève, 1969), 16.

12 On whom see J. Leclerq, *Un humaniste érémite: le bienheureux P. Giustiniani (1476–1528)* (Rome, 1951).

13 For the correspondence, discovered in 1957, see Hubert Jedin, 'Contarini und Camaldoli', *Archivio italiano per la storia della pietà* 2 (1959), 51–117. For the comparison with Luther, see *idem*, 'Ein Turmerlebnis des jungen Contarini', in *Kirche des Glaubens – Kirche des Geschichte* (2 vols: Freiburg, 1966), 1.167–80.

14 The episode of Easter Eve 1511, which he recounts to Giustiniani in a letter of 24 April 1511 (Jedin, 'Contarini und Camaldoli', 64), should be studied in full.

15 Jedin, 'Contarini und Camaldoli', 117. This letter, dated 7 February 1523, is the last surviving letter in the collection discovered by Jedin.

16 Supporting text, as cited by Peter McNair, *The Anatomy of Apostasy: Peter Martyr in Italy* (Oxford, 1967), 8 n. 1: 'Ego iampridem antequam insigne Lutheri nomen esset, abhinc triginta et eo amplius fortasse annis, cum adhuc Martinus se non aperuisset, et pro veritate scribebam, ea dicebam, ut quidam veritatis inimici famosos libellos, nominatim appellato me, templi ualuis affigerent, quod scilicet depressum hominem, Deus exaltatum uolebam.' The influence of Luther in Italy dates from the mid

1520s: see D. Cantimori, *Eretici Italiani del Cinquecento* (Firenze, 1939), 24; E. G. Gleason, 'Sixteenth Century Italian Interpretations of Luther', *ARG* 60 (1969), 160–73.

17 *Regesten und Briefe des Kardinals Gasparo Contarinis*, ed. Dittrich, No. 90; 358. A similar view appears to have been expressed at the time by Reginald Pole: see C. Corviersi, 'Compendio di Processi del Santo Uffizio', *Archivio della Società Romana di Storia Patria* 3 (1880), 261–91; 449–73; 284: 'Polus defendit et nititur probare doctrinam Lutheranam de iustificatione esse veram.' However, Pole appears to have interpreted justifying faith as *fides quae per dilectionem operatur*, a view to which Luther was radically opposed: see Pole, *De Concilio* (Romae/Venetiis, 1562), 24v–25v. (On the basis of internal evidence, this work may be deduced to have been written in April 1545: see 1r–v; 58v.) See further n. 43 below.

18 e.g., see S. Ehses, 'Johannes Groppers Rechtfertigungslehre auf dem Konzil von Trient', *Römische Quartalschrift* 20 (1906), 175–88; 184; Hanns Rückert, *Die theologische Entwicklung Gasparo Contarinis* (Bonn, 1926), 97 n. 1. The suggestion that Kaspar Schatzgeyer developed a doctrine of *duplex iustitia* rests upon a misunderstanding of the significance of the Scotist analysis of the elements of justification: see Valens Heynck, 'Bemerkungen zu dem Buche von O. Müller, *Die Rechtfertigungslehre nominalistischer Reformationsgegner*', *FS* 28 (1941), 129–51, especially 145–50. There is no convincing evidence that Contarini's views on justification derive from Gropper's *Enchiridion*: see Rückert, *Die theologische Entwicklung Gasparo Contarinis*, 102–4, where it is shown that there are excellent reasons for supposing that Contarini reflects theological currents prevalent in Italy in the 1530s. The discovery of the Contarini–Giustiniani correspondence some thirty years after Rückert's investigation has enormously strengthened his conclusions.

The movement to which Rückert refers is now generally known as 'Evangelism': see E. M. Jung, 'On the Nature of Evangelism in Sixteenth Century Italy', *Journal of the History of Ideas* 14 (1953), 511–27.

19 Bellarmine, *Disputationum . . . de controversiis Christianae fidei* (Ingolstadt, 1601), 1028. Cf. 1096–7. Bellarmine may base his views upon the vote of Seripando at Trent, in which Contarini, Cajetan, Pighius, Julius Pflug and Gropper are identified with the doctrine of 'double justification': CT 5.487.33–4.

20 Robert Stupperich, *Der Humanismus und die Wiedervereinigung der Konfession* (Leipzig, 1936), 11–36. Cf. Walter Lipgens, *Kardinal Johannes Gropper (1503–1559) und die Anfänge der katholischen Reform in Deutschland* (Münster, 1951), 100–8; 192–203.

21 As pointed out by Braunisch, *Die Theologie der Rechtfertigung im 'Enchiridion' (1538) des Johannes Gropper*, especially 419–38.

22 *Enchiridion Christianae institutiones* (Coloniae, 1538), fol. 163r. Cf. fol. 163v: 'Nam quis iustificatum dixerit eum, cui tantum sunt remissa peccata, non autem voluntas etiam commutata, nempe ex mala facta bona? Quemadmodum nemo servum nequam, ob id tantum, quod ei

indulgens dominus noxam clementer remiserit iustificatum dixerit, nisi is bonam quoque voluntatem (qua posthac servus non inutilis sed frugi esse contendat) ceperit?'

23 *Enchiridion*, fol. 163r (Marg). The Melanchthonian text to which Gropper alludes is cited as n. 24 of §21 of the present study.

24 *Enchiridion*, fol. 163v (Marg).

25 e.g., *Enchiridion*, fol. 129v treats *imputatio iustitiae* and *acceptatio* as synonymous.

26 CR (Melanchthon) 21.421: 'Sumpsit igitur Paulus verbum iustificandi ex consuetudine Hebraici sermonis pro acceptatione, id est, pro reconciliatione et remissione peccatorum.' On this, see Braunisch, *Die Theologie der Rechtfertigung im 'Enchiridion'*, 367: 'Die melanchthonische "imputatio iustitiae Christi" als positives Pendant der Sündenvergebung kennt das "Enchiridion" nicht. Um der Begriffsverwirrung bezüglich der Lehre von der "doppelten Gerechtigkeit" vorzubeugen, muß klar unterscheiden werden: Wo Melanchthon "remissio" und "imputatio" einander zuordnet und in beiden Momenten primär das Rechtfertigungsereignis erblickt ... betont Gropper die Einheit von Vergebung und Erneuerung.'

27 e.g., W. van Gulik, *Johannes Gropper (1503–1559): Ein Beitrag zur Kirchengeschichte Deutschlands* (Freiburg, 1906), 54 n. 5.

28 *Enchiridion*, fol. 167v. For an excellent critical analysis, see Braunisch, *Die Theologie der Rechtfertigung im 'Enchiridion'*, 360–72; 381–98, especially 394–6.

29 *Enchiridion*, fol. 167v (Marg).

30 Contarini, *Epistola de iustificatione*; in Corpus Catholicorum VII, ed. F. Hünermann (Münster, 1923), 24.1–2. See also n. 33 below. Those at Rome who read the letter were sceptical concerning its catholicity: see *Epistolae Reginaldi Poli Cardinalis* (5 vols: Bresciae, 1744–57), 3.ccxxxi–xl.

31 *Epistola de iustificatione*, 28.12–18.

32 *Epistola de iustificatione*, 26.18–19.

33 *Epistola de iustificatione*, 29.19–38; see further Rückert, *Die theologische Entwicklung Gasparo Contarinis*, 93. Rückert's suggestion (86 n. 2) that Contarini affirms that *iustitia inhaerens* and *iustitia imputata* function as the double formal cause of justification cannot be sustained on the basis of the text cited in its support: the adverb *formaliter* is transferred from its proper clause to one subsequent, from which it does not appear to have been elided.

34 Text of the article in CR (Melanchthon) 4.198–201. The parallels between the two documents have been brought out by Stupperich, 'Der Ursprung des "Regensburger Buches" von 1541 und seine Rechtfertigungslehre'. For the background to the discussion at Regensburg, see Peter Matheson, *Cardinal Contarini at Regensburg* (Oxford, 1972) 101–7. It may be noted that three of the five major theological figures present were amenable to this doctrine of *duplex iustitia* – Bucer, Contarini and Gropper. Eck was critical of the document, and Melanchthon more favourably disposed towards it. For Luther's attitude to Regensburg on

justification, see von Loewenich, *Duplex Iustitia*, 48–55; for Calvin's, see W. H. Neuser, 'Calvins Urteil über den Rechtfertigungsartikel des Regensburger Buches', in *Reformation und Humanismus: Robert Stupperich zum 65. Geburstag*, ed. M. Greschat and J. F. G. Goeters (Witten, 1969), 176–94.

35 See Peter Matheson, *Cardinal Contarini at Regensburg* (Oxford, 1972), 181: 'The dialogue between Protestantism and Catholicism at the Diet of Regensburg in 1541 did not fail. It never took place'; von Loewenich, *Duplex Iustitia*, 34–8; Dermot Fenlon, *Heresy and Obedience in Tridentine Italy* (Cambridge, 1972), 45–68; V. Pfnür, *Die Einigung bei den Religionsgesprächen von Worms und Regensburg (1540–41)* (Gütersloh, 1980). For a more positive (although now generally discredited) assessment, see Stupperich, *Humanismus und die Wiedervereinigung der Konfession*, 120–4.

36 *Contra* McNair, *Anatomy of Apostasy*, 1–50, especially 8. See further n. 18 above.

37 See Carlo de Frede, 'La stampa nel Cinquecento e la diffusione della Riforma in Italia', *Atti della Accademia Pontiniana* (Napoli) 13 (1963–64), 87–91; *idem*, 'Per la storia della stampa nel Cinquecento in rapporto con la diffusione della Riforma in Italia', in *Gutenberger Jahrbuch 1964* (Mainz, 1964), 175–84; E. G. Gleason, 'Sixteenth Century Italian Interpretations of Luther', *ARG* 60 (1969), 160–73. The Viterbo Circle appears to have been of particular importance in this respect in the 1530s and early 1540s: see Fenlon, *Heresy and Obedience*, 69–99, for an excellent introduction.

38 See *Il Beneficio di Cristo*, ed. Caponetto, 469–96, for details of the work. Note particularly the suggestion that Giulio Contarini's *sententia* on justification at Trent may reflect the direct influence of this work: see Domingo de Sta. Teresa, *Juan de Valdés*, 297–301.

39 See Caponetto, *loc. cit.* For the suggestion that the work is Lutheran in inspiration, see A. C. Politi, *Compendio d'errori et inganni luterani contenuti in un libretto intitolato Trattato utilissimo del beneficio di Cristo crocifisso* (Roma, 1544). However, the influence of Calvin's 1539 *Institutio* is much more evident: see Tomasso Bozza, *Il Beneficio di Cristo e la Istituzione della religione cristiana di Calvino* (Roma, 1961), 4–5. An examination of the critical apparatus of Caponetto's critical edition makes evident the dependence upon Valdés in the first four chapters at points of crucial significance. Bozza's thesis that the work is essentially a summary of the 1539 *Institutio* raises a number of difficulties, of which we here note three. First, chapter 1 does not develop the anthropological pessimism characteristic of Calvin where it would be expected; second, chapter 6 develops a doctrine of the eucharist based directly upon Augustine, rather than Calvin; third, the 1539 *Institutio* is unlikely to have penetrated sufficiently far south in the time necessary to exercise so significant an influence upon the work.

For a more recent survey of the influence of Juan de Valdés in Italy, see Salvatore Caponetto, 'Richerche recenti su Juan de Valdés e il valdesianismo in Italia', *Bullettino della Società di Storia valdesi* 150 (1981), 50–7.

40 Beneficio di Cristo, cap. 4; 37.261–2; cf. 37.272–4. On the phrase *sola fide* as used by Grimaldi at the time, see M. W. Anderson, *Peter Martyr: A Reformer in Exile* (Nieuwkoop, 1975), 271–2.

41 *Il Beneficio di Cristo*, cap. 4; 38.281–9.

42 *Il Beneficio di Cristo*, cap. 4; 46.514–47.515.

43 Pole, *De Concilio*, 24r–v.

44 See Fenlon, *Heresy and Obedience*, 203–4.

Notes to §26

1 CT 5.259.3–6.

2 Stakemeier, 'Die theologische Schulen'. The older study of H. Lennerz, 'Das Konzil von Trient und die theologischen Schulmeinungen', *Scholastick* 4 (1929), 38–53, should also be noted. A major deficiency of Stakemeier's study is the implicit implication that the proceedings on justification were of interest only to academic theologians, whereas it is clear that many bishops regarded the matter as of practical and spiritual importance: see Giuseppe Alberigo, *I vescovi italiani at Concilio di Trento (1545–7)* (Firenze, 1959), 337–94.

3 M. Grabmann, 'Johannes Capreolus O.P., der "princeps Thomistarum", und seine Stellung in der Geschichte der Thomistenschule', in *Mittelalterliches Geistesleben: Abhandlungen zur Geschichte der Scholastik und Mystik* III, ed. L. Ott (München, 1956), 370–410.

4 This was first pointed out by Friedrich Stegmüller, 'Gratia sanans: Zur Schicksal des Augustinismus in der Salmantizienerschule', in *Aurelius Augustinus: Festschrift der Görres-Gesellschaft zum 1500. Tod des heiligen Augustinus*, ed. M. Grabmann and J. Mausbach (Köln, 1930), 395–409; 402–3.

5 See Joseph Hefner, *Die Entstehungsgeschichte des Trienter Rechtfertigungsdekretes* (Paderborn, 1909), 68. It is important to appreciate the significance of the pre-Tridentine Dominican polemic in ensuring the ascendancy of the views of Thomas: see A. Walz, 'La polemica domenicana pre-tridentina', *Sapientia* 9 (1956), 469–87.

6 See the *Index nominum et rerum* of CT 5.1053–72. On the Thomist school at Trent, see Stakemeier, 'Die theologischen Schulen', 199–207; 322–31.

7 See Stegmüller, *Francisco de Vitoria y la doctrina de gracia en la escuela salmantina*. The most significant product of this school was the massive *Cursus theologicus Summam D. Thomae complectens*, written in the period 1631–1701: see O. Merl, *Theologia Salmanticensis: Untersuchung über Entstehung, Lehrrichtung und Quellen des theologischen Kurzus der spanischen Karmeliten* (Regensburg, 1947).

8 See Stegmüller, 'Zur Gnadenlehre des spanischen Konzilstheologen Domingo de Soto'; Becker, *Rechtfgertigungslehre*.

9 See Becker, *Rechtfertigungslehre*, 141–53. On this question, with particular reference to Francisco de Vitoria, see Xiberta, 'La causa meritoria de la justificación'.

10 Those present at the opening session were ascertained from the list

published in CT 5.1041–4. The list published at CT 5.819–20 is misleading, as it notes only those present at the closing session on 13 January 1547: the numbers given for the sixth session are based upon an analysis of those actually taking part in the debate.

11 See the comments of Bonaventura Pius de Costacciaro, dated 28 December 1546: CT 5.741.28–32. The quite distinct positions of Bonaventure and Scotus noted here made a Franciscan consensus upon the matter difficult.

12 Sagués, 'Un libro pretridentino de Andrés de Vega sobre la justificación'.

13 *Opusculum de iustificatione*, fol. 146–8. Perhaps with Capreolus in mind, Vega links Thomas Aquinas and Gregory of Rimini together as exponents of the 'no merit whatsoever prior to justification' school.

14 *Opusculum de iustificatione*, fol. 148: 'theologi recentiores, Gabriel, Maiores, Almanyus et similes; et ante illos, ne adeo nova existemetur, videtur iam tempore doctoris subtilis fuisse haec opinio communis in scholis'.

15 Heynck, 'Der Anteil des Konzilstheologen Andreas de Vega O.F.M. an dem ersten amtlichen Entwurf des Trienter Rechtfertigungsdekretes', 57. We have confirmed this conclusion for all three phases of Franciscan theology (i.e., the early and later Franciscan schools, and the *via moderna*, which is contiguous with the later school): see §§15–17.

16 e.g., Hünermann, *Wesen und Notwendigkeit der aktuellen Gnade nach dem Konzil von Trient*, 5 n. 1; cf. Stakemeier, 'Die theologischen Schulen', 341.

17 Carl Stange, 'Über Luthers Beziehungen zur Theologie seines Ordens', *Neue kirchliche Zeitschrift* 11 (1900), 574–85; *idem*, 'Luther über Gregor von Rimini', *Neue kirchliche Zeitschrift* 13 (1902), 721–7.

18 Stakemeier, 'Die theologischen Schulen', 342–3.

19 Heinrich Hermelink, *Die theologische Fakultät in Tübingen vor der Reformation* (Stuttgart, 1906). Stakemeier merely notes this study: Stakemeier, 'Die theologischen Schulen', 342 n. 3.

20 For the incompetence of the theologians who censured Ockham's doctrine of justification as 'Pelagian', see McGrath, *Luther's Theology of the Cross*, 53–8.

21 As noted by Stakemeier himself: e.g., 'Die theologischen Schulen', 344–5.

22 The controversy at Trent over Scotus' views on the certitude of grace raises further questions over the 'Scotism' of the Franciscan contingent: see Heynck, 'A Controversy at the Council of Trent'. Heynck correctly notes (257) the much greater faithfulness of the Conventuals than the Observants to the earlier Franciscan tradition.

23 See Stakemeier, *Augustinus und die Augustiner*.

24 A. V. Müller, *Luthers theologische Quellen: Seine Verteidigung gegen Denifle und Grisar* (Giessen, 1912); cf. Wilfred Werbeck, *Jacobus Perez von Valencia: Untersuchungen zu seinem Psalmenkommentar* (Tübingen, 1959), 212 n. 6. See also §18 of the present work.

25 Stakemeier, *Augustinus und die Augustiner*, 21–2.

26 As Jedin pointed out, the sources required for such a conclusion were not available in 1937: H. Jedin, in *Theologische Revue* 37 (1938), 425–30.

27 See §18; McGrath, '"Augustinianism?" A critical assessment of the so-called "Medieval Augustinian Tradition" on Justification', *Augustiniana* 31 (1981), 247–67, *passim*. The study of Anselm Forster, *Gesetz und Evangelium bei Girolamo Seripando* (Paderborn, 1963), indicates the conventional character of much of Seripando's views.

28 See D. Gutiérrez, *Los Agustinos en el Concilio de Trento* (El Escorial, 1947); A. Zumkeller, 'Die Augustiner-Eremiten und das Konzil von Trient', in *Das Weltkonzil von Trient*, 2.523–40.

29 Seripando appears to have derived his Platonism from Giles: H. Jedin, *Girolamo Seripando* (2 vols: Wurzburg, 1937), 1.68–9; 80–2.

30 CT 12.668.16–18. Cf. 12.313.26–9. Seripando also links Cajetan and Pighius with the idea elsewhere: CT 12.665.16–667.43.

31 It should not be overlooked that this also involves the rejection of the suggestion that Luther and Seripando represent equally possible outcomes of an 'Augustinian' theology. However, there were prelates present at Trent, associated with the Viterbo circle, who unquestionably approximated to Luther on several matters of importance: see Dermot Fenlon, *Heresy and Obedience in Tridentine Italy* (Cambridge, 1972), 116–60.

32 See Alberigo, *I vescovi italiani*, 388–9. Alberigo is primarily concerned with the intellectual climate in Italy, from which most of those involved in the Tridentine proceedings on justification were drawn. His conclusions, however, would appear to have a wider validity.

Notes to §27

1 See Jedin, *Geschichte des Konzils*, vol. 1, for details.

2 CT 2.409.

3 The importance and inseparability of the doctrines of original sin and justification had been stressed in the Legates' report of 15 April 1546 (CT 10.548–60). However, the two doctrines were eventually discussed in isolation.

4 For a slightly different list, see Jedin, *Geschichte des Konzils*, 2.142–4. It should be borne in mind that the council was committed to the simultaneous discussion of the questions of residence and of translation.

5 CT 5.261.26–35. For background information to such congregations, see H. Lennerz, 'De congregationibus theologorum in Concilio Tridentino', *Gregorianum* 26 (1945), 7–21. For similar information in relation to votes, see *idem*, 'Voten auf dem Konzil von Trient', *Gregorianum* 15 (1934), 577–88.

6 CT 5.262.18–19.

7 CT 5.262.20–1.

8 CT 5.262.31–5.

9 See the opinions noted by Marcus Laureus: CT 5.279.6–26.

10 See the following: CT 5.263.9–10; 22–3; 27–9; 31–2; 264.1–5; 264.43–265.2; 265.12–14; 272.40–1; 273.11–12; 45–6; 274.35–6; 275.25–6.

11 CT 5.264.31–2.

12 CT 5.275.9–11.

13 e.g., Antonio Delfini: CT 5.274.21–30. Note particularly the reference to *tectio seu non imputatio peccatorum* (274.24). See further Santoro, 'La giustificazione in Giovanni Antonio Delfini, teologo del Concilio di Trento'.

14 CT 5.278.20–1.

15 CT 5.278.1–2.

16 CT 5.279.27–31 (our italics).

17 See the list of errors noted at CT 5.281–2. The subsequent discussion follows this division, with interest particularly concerning the *primus status*: e.g., see CT 5.287–96; 298–310.

18 See the careful study of Valens Heynck, 'Der Anteil des Konzilstheologen Andreas de Vega an dem ersten amtlichen Entwurf des Trienter Rechtfertigungsdekretes', *FS* 33 (1951), 49–81.

19 CT 5.384–91. The numeration of the canons is confusing, and errors of reference are frequent in the secondary literature. The Görres edition numbers the chapters and canons consecutively, without distinguishing them, so that the paragraph numbered '4' is actually Canon 1, that numbered '18' is Canon 15, etc. It is clear from the *notationes theologorum* (CT 5.392.1–394.6) that the first three chapters were actually treated *as canons*. Thus a reference to 'Canon 18' (CT 5.393.36) refers to the section numbered '18' (CT 5.390.22–40), even though, strictly speaking, this is actually the *fifteenth* canon.

20 Canon 1: CT 5.386.12–14.

21 CT 5.266.3–28. The full text cited from Melanchthon's Romans prologue reads: 'Iustificari proprie est iustum reputari, quia iustus significat relative acceptum Deo. Et sic iustitiam in Pauli disputationibus non esse qua iusti sumus, sed relative qua iusti habemur etiam non existentes, quia accepti sumus Deo propter fidem, id est fiduciam divinae misericordiae.'

22 Canon 2: CT 5.386.18–20.

23 Canon 3: CT 5.386.25–7.

24 CT 5.386.28–33.

25 Canon 9: CT 5.387.40–2.

26 CT 5.268.43–4.

27 It was on the basis of this concept of faith that Pole had hoped a compromise might be possible between Protestants and Catholics: see §24.

28 CT 5.392–4. An exception may be noted: objections were raised to Canon 11, dealing with the certitude of grace in its present form (396.36–41).

29 CT 5.408–14. The postponement of the debate occurred on account of political considerations.

30 Seripando's draft is to be found in CT 5.821–8.

31 Cap. 4: CT 5.823.6–9.

32 Canon 3: CT 5.824.33–5. This canon also condemns the doctrine of justification *sola fide*.

33 CT 5.828–3. The first four chapters correspond to those of the draft of 11

August. The date given in the Görres edition (19 August) is incorrect, and should be amended to 29 August.

34 CT 5.829.40–9.

35 Canon 4: CT 5.832.25–6.

36 CT 5.832.27–8; cf. 5.824.33–4.

37 CT 5.386.13–14; 824.33–4; 832.27–8.

38 The phrase does, of course, occur in the titles of the respective chapter and canon, as noted above. See further P. Pas, 'La doctrine de la double justice au Concile de Trente', *EThL* 30 (1954), 5–53.

39 Cap. 7: CT 5.423.34–6.

40 Canon 7: CT 5.427.1–7 (our italics).

41 e.g., see Pas, 'La doctrine de la double justice', 20–3.

42 e.g., CT 5.492.10–11; 496.2 'Tenet quod una sit iustitia tantum, qua iustificamur, videlicet nobis inhaerens.' The objections noted at CT 5.505.26–7 should be noted. To the twenty-two votes recorded in the Görres edition of the *Acta* should be added those of Salmeron and Hervet: see J. Olazarán, 'En el IV centenario de un voto tridentino del jesuito Alfonso Salmerón sobre la doble justicia', *EE* 20 (1946), 211–40; *idem*, 'Voto tridentino de Gentian Hervet sobre la certeza de la gracia y la doble justicia', *Archivio Teologico Granadino* 9 (1946), 127–59.

43 See Aurelius' vote of 19 October 1546: CT 5.561.47–564.12. For the similarities, compare CT 5.563.4–13 with 12.665.2–12; 5.563.35–6 with 12.667.46–668.9; 5.563.37–42 with 12.635.37–42 and 5.374.10–15.

44 e.g., compare CT 5.609.22–7 with Gropper, *Enchiridion*, fol. 132v; 5.611.17–24 with *Enchiridion*, fol. 168r–v.

45 CT 5.599.4–10.

46 CT 5.576.31–5.

47 CT 5.547.8–549.43.

48 CT 5.581.17–590.19.

49 It is possible that certain statements made (e.g., 5.584.29–30: 'quo ad hunc actum nihil absurdi de nova nostra imputatione ad vitam, si novo actu resurgimus') may have aroused the suspicions of his more critical hearers.

50 Thus there is to be found no reference to Gropper or his *Enchiridion*, or to the Diet of Regensburg, throughout the entire debate. However, the personal association of Reginald Pole with similar views was known to many delegates: see Dermot Fenlon, *Heresy and Obedience in Tridentine Italy* (Cambridge, 1972), 161–95.

51 e.g., see CT 5.564.38–9; 569.8; 579.5–6; 602.37–42; 617.27–9.

52 CT 5.541.45–6. For a full study of the main lines of criticism directed against Seripando's position, see Pas, 'La doctrine de la double justice', 31–43.

53 e.g., see CT 5.489.31–2; 12.671.16, 32.

54 e.g., CT 5.643.31–2; 644.34; 644.31–2; 647.12–15; 649.10–11.

55 CT 5.512.12–20.

56 CT 5.636.30–637.11. Note especially 35–6: 'formalis iustitia una Dei'.

57 CT 5.658.24–6.

58 CT 5.700.25–8.

59 CT 5.701.14–704.14.

60 Cap. 7; D. 799. There is a slight alteration in the wording, which does not affect the sense of the statement in question.

61 e.g., see H. J. Iwand, *Nachgelassene Werke: 5. Luthers Theologie* (München, 1974), 64–104, especially 90–104. For the general problem at Trent, see Guérard des Lauriers, 'Saint Augustin et la question de la certitude de la grâce au Concile de Trente'; Heynck, 'Zur Kontroverse über die Gnadengewissheit auf dem Konzil von Trient'; Huthmacher, 'La certitude de la grâce au Concile de Trente'; Schierse, 'Das Trienterkonzil und die Frage nach der christliche Gewissheit'; Stakemeier, *Das Konzil von Trient über die Heilsgewissheit.*

62 CT 5.275.14–16, rejecting the possibility, apart from special divine revelation.

63 CT 5.277.42–3, in which the possibility is upheld.

64 CT 5.279.6–281.15.

65 CT 5.282.24–5: '9. Quod iustificatus tenetur credere, se esse in gratia et sibi non imputari peccata, et se esse praedestinatum'.

66 It is discussed, in passing, at CT 5.324.34–42. Seripando noted the point (CT 12.634.31–635.11), but did not permit his views to be included in the general discussion.

67 CT 5.390.22–40, especially 37–40. On the numeration of the canons, see n. 19 above.

68 CT 5.393.36–41. On the numeration of the canon, see n. 19.

69 CT 5.410 n. 1. The reference to Scotus is significant: as Heynck has shown, there was considerable confusion among the delegates (particularly the Franciscans) concerning Scotus' views on the certitude of grace; Heynck, 'A Controversy at the Council of Trent', *passim*. On Delfini, see Friedrich Lauchert, *Die italienischen literarischen Gegner Luthers* (Freiburg, 1912), 487–536; Santoro, 'La giustificazione in Giovanni Antonio Delfini'.

70 For the document, see CT 12.651.22–658.14. For the appeal to Biel's interpretation of Scotus, see CT 12.657.53–658.11.

71 CT 5.404.41–3. He appears to have been supported in this assertion by the General of the Carmelites (CT 5.404.50) and Martellus of Fiessole (CT 5.406.16–18).

72 CT 10.586.22–587.20.

73 Thus the Generals of both the Conventuals and Observants spoke in favour of the latter: CT 5.410.1–2; 5.410.5–6. The English bishop Richard Pate, himself suspected by many of Lutheranism, also spoke in support of this latter position on 28 August 1546: CT 5.419.18–19. His views were expressed even more forcefully on 13 November: CT 5.648.4–5: 'Homo iustificatus secundum praesentem iustitiam potest esse certus certitudine fidei, se esse in gratia Dei.'

74 CT 5.418.1–9; 419.44.

75 Cap. 7; CT 5.424.12–13.

76 Canon 8; CT 5.427.8–11. It should be recalled that the term *praedestinatio* is used in the positive sense of 'predestination to life'.

478

77 Note the comments of del Monte: CT 5.497.3–4; cf. 497.12–15. For some comments of the theologians on the respective chapter and canon, see CT 5.505.46–51; 5.508.40–2.
78 CT 5.523.17–19.
79 For the names of the theologians in each group, see Massarelli's lists at CT 5.632.31–633.10. We have taken the liberty of transferring the secular priest Andrés de Navarra from the list of supporters of *certitudo fidei, se esse in gratia* to that of its opponents. His vote (CT 5.559.14–561.46) clearly opposes the concept; we are unable to account for Massarelli's error.
80 See J. Olazarán, 'La controversia Soto–Caterino–Vega sobre la certeza de la gracia', *EE* 19 (1942), 145–83; Beltrán de Heredia, 'Controversia de certitudine gratiae entre Domingo de Soto y Ambrosio Catarino'; Oltra, *Die Gewissheit des Gnadenstandes bei Andres de Vega*. His vote of 22 November 1546 is of particular importance: CT 5.655.34–657.18.
81 Cap. 9; CT 5.637.12–21. The contents of Canon 8 of the September draft are to be found in Canons 12 and 13; CT 5.649.39–42. A new canon on the subject follows: Canon 14: CT 5.649.43–4.
82 September draft, cap. 7: CT 5.424.13; November draft, cap. 9: CT 5.637.14–15.
83 CT 5.637.20–1 (our italics).
84 Canon 14: CT 5.649.43–4: 'Si quis dixerit, omnes renatos et iustificatos teneri ad hoc, ut certo credant, se esse in gratia Dei, aut iustificatos *communiter* certo scire, se esse in gratia Dei: anathema sit.'
85 e.g., CT 5.643.4–5; 643.43; 644.39; 645.11–12; 647.37–8; 653.21.
86 e.g., CT 5.655.36–7; 5.662.9–11.
87 CT 5.727.1–11.
88 The objection of Pachecco should be noted (CT 5.727.12–17), as well as del Monte's reply (CT 5.727.18–27). Pachecco's final rejoinder makes his hostility to this proposal evident: CT 5.727.28–30.
89 CT 5.772.10–773.5.
90 CT 5.773.4–5. Their evident relief is recorded: 773.5.
91 CT 5.777.1–10.
92 Ehses notes the absence of Pole's seal from the volume of the Bologna edition of 1548 specially reserved to receive it: CT 5.xxv.10–xxvi.40.

Notes to §28

1 D. 729a–843. The unusual structure of the *decretum de iustificatione* is best seen by comparing it with the *decretum super peccato originali*, which immediately precedes it (D. 787–92). See further Brunner, 'Die Rechtfertigungslehre des Konzils von Trient'; Buuck, 'Zum Rechtfertigungsdekret'; Joest, 'Die tridentinische Rechtfertigungslehre'; Walz, 'La giustificazione tridentina'.
2 One of the most significant shortcomings of Hans Küng's analysis of the Tridentine decree (*Rechtfertigung: Die Lehre Karl Barths und eine katholische Besinnung*) is his failure to deal with the decree in its proper historical

perspective. We have discussed Küng's analysis of Trent critically elsewhere: 'ARCIC II and Justification', 27–42, especially 34–9.

3 D. 793–802.

4 D. 803–6.

5 D. 807–10.

6 Cap. 1; D. 793.

7 Proposition 36, as condemned in *Exsurge Domine* (15 June 1520): D. 776.

8 Cap. 3; D. 795.

9 Cap. 4; D. 796.

10 Cap. 5; D. 797.

11 Cap. 6; D. 798. The charge of 'neo-semipelagianism' levelled against the decree at this point is quite absurd: F. Loofs, *Leitfaden zum Studium der Dogmengeschichte*, 4th edn (Halle, 1906), 668–9. A similar criticism must be levelled at the study of A. Th. Jörgenssen, 'Was verstand man in der Reformationszeit unter Pelagianismus?', *ThStK* 83 (1910), 63–82, in which any theology of justification which recognises the necessity of a preparation for justification is treated as 'semi-Pelagian'.

12 Cap. 7; D. 799.

13 The reference is to Augustine, *de Trinitate*, XIV.xii.15: cf. §§3, 5.

14 Cap. 8; D. 801.

15 The dispute concerning the sense of the verb *promereri* is considered in §28.

16 Cap. 9; D. 802.

17 Cap. 11; D. 804.

18 Cap. 11; D. 804.

19 Cap. 12; D. 805. Cf. Cap. 13; D. 806.

20 Cap. 14; D. 807.

21 Cap. 16; D. 809–10.

22 The specific condemnation of Pelagianism in the opening canons is significant, as it represents a much-needed magisterial clarification in this area.

23 Canon 11; D. 821.

Notes to §29

1 Rückert, *Die Rechtfertigungslehre auf dem Tridentinischen Konzil*, 185. Cf. Gonzáles Rivas, 'Los teólogos salmantinos y el decreto de la justificación'.

2 D. 801.

3 Oberman, 'Das tridentinische Rechtfertigungsdekret'. The verb *promereri* also occurs at one additional point in the decree itself (chapter 16; D. 809: 'consequendum vere promeruisse censeantur'), and in canon 2 (D.812: 'vitam aeternam promereri possit'). The supplementation of *promereri* with *vere* in chapter 16 is itself sufficient to raise doubts concerning Oberman's thesis.

4 Oberman, 'Das tridentinische Rechtfertigungsdekret', 268–78.

5 Oberman, 'Das tridentinische Rechtfertigungsdekret', 278.

6 Rückert, 'Promereri: Eine Studie zum tridentinischen Rechtfertigungs-

dekret als Antwort an H. A. Oberman'.

7 CT 5.426.35–7.
8 See the proceedings of 2 January 1547; CT 5.753.17–20; 9 January 1547: CT 5.777.16–19.
9 CT 5.737.15–16; 20–1.
10 Oberman, 'Das tridentinische Rechtfertigungsdekret', 278–9.
11 See Heynck, 'Die Bedeutung von "mereri" und "promereri" bei dem Konzilstheologen Andreas de Vega O.F.M.'.
12 De natura et gratia, ii.1; fol. 96r.
13 De natura et gratia, ii.3; fol. 102r.
14 De natura et gratia, ii.3; fol. 101r–v.
15 De natura et gratia, ii.4; fol. 109r–111v. Soto's views on congruous merit prior to justification were defended by Suaréz (although the latter was reluctant to concede any form of disposition, however remote, towards justification): de gratia, VIII.vii.9; Opera, ed. Vivés (28 vols: Paris, 1856–61), 9.339–42.
16 De universa iustificationis doctrina, viii.16; in Opera, 2.265B. See further Seybold, Glaube und Rechtfertigung.
17 See the references collected by Seybold, Glaube und Rechtfertigung, 89 n. 189.
18 De iustificatione doctrina universa, vi.10; fol. 86.
19 De iustificatione doctrina universa, vii.8; fol. 137.
20 De iustificatione doctrina universa, viii.10; fol. 192. We have italicised the allusion to the text of the decree.
21 De iustificatione doctrina universa, viii.10; fol. 194.
22 Summa doctrina Christianae (Vienna, 1555); modern edition in S. Petri Canisii . . . catechismi Latini et Germanici, ed. F. Streicher (Romae, 1933), 1.1–75; a shorter version appeared the following year: Streicher, 1.263–71. For further details, see O. Braunsberger, Entstehung und erste Entwicklung der Katechismen des seligen Petrus Canisius (Freiburg, 1893).
23 See F. J. Brand, Die Katechismen des Edmundus Augerius in historischer, dogmatisch-moralischer und katechetischer Bearbeitung (Freiburg, 1917). The demand for such works appears to have been greatest in northern Europe.
24 P. Paschini, 'Il Catechismo Romano del Concilio di Trento: sua originali e sua prima diffusione', in Cinquecento Romano e riforma cattolico (Roma, 1958), 67–91.
25 See G. Bellinger, Der Catechismus Romanus und die Reformation (Paderborn, 1958), 95–8. Bellinger's suggestion (97–8) that the Catechism teaches the necessity of a disposition for justification, based on faith and penitence, does not appear to be borne out by the evidence.
26 Catechismus Romanus (Leipzig, 1852), II.v.68; 247.
27 For the general background, see J. B. du Chesne, Histoire du Baïanisme (Douai, 1731); F. X. Linsenmann, Michael Baius und die Grundlegung des Jansenismus (Tübingen, 1867); F.-X. Jansens, Baius et le Baïanisme (Louvain, 1927); N. Abercrombie, The Origins of Jansenism, 87–93; 137–42. On the theological issues, see Alfaro, 'Sobrenatural y pecado

original en Bayo'; Kaiser, *Natur und Gnade im Urstand*; Henri de Lubac, *Augustinisme et théologie moderne* (Paris, 1965), 15–48.

28 *de prima hominis iustitia*, 1; *Opera*, 49.

29 *de prima hominis iustitia*, 9; *Opera*, 62–3. Cf. Kaiser, *Natur und Gnade im Urstand*, 69–157.

30 *de peccato originis*, 2–13; *Opera*, 3–13.

31 *de peccato originis*, 11; *Opera*, 12.

32 Proposition 13; *Opera*, 51; cf. D. 1013: 'Opera bona, a filiis adoptionis facta, non accipiunt rationem meriti ex eo, quod fiunt per spiritum adoptionis inhabitantem corda filiorum Dei, sed tantum ex eo, quod sunt conformia legi, quodque per ea praestatur oboedientia legi.'

33 D. 1001–80.

34 D. 1080. See further E. van Eijl, 'L'Interprétation de la Bulle de Pie V portant condamnation de Baius', *Revue d'Histoire Ecclésiastique* 1 (1955), 499–542.

35 See the footnote to D. 1080.

36 The best study remains G. Schneemann, *Die Entstehung und Entwickelung der thomistisch–molinistischen Kontroverse* (2 vols: Freiburg, 1879–80). More recently, see F. Stegmüller, *Geschichte des Molinismus* (Münster, 1935).

37 As stated in *Summa Theologiae*, Ia q. 105 a. 5; Molina, *Concordia liberi arbitrii cum gratiae donis* (Lisbon, 1588), disp. 26; 167–71.

38 *Concordia*, disp. 26; 170–1. This may be compared with Suaréz' opinion, that justification is to be attributed to grace rather than to the free will, despite the latter being a proximate cause of justification: *de gratia* v.xxxi.3–4; *Opera*, 8.544–5.

39 *Concordia*, disp. 47; 298.

40 *Concordia*, disp. 50; 329–30. Molina distinguishes this *scientia media* from *scientia visionis* (by which God knows realities) and *scientia simplicis intelligentiae* (by which God contemplates the realm of the unreal). The objects apprehended by the *scientia media* thus fall between the categories of the real and unreal – i.e., *futurabilia*, which exist only if certain preconditions are realised.

41 Molinism is paralleled at this point by Congruism, particularly associated with Roberto Bellarmine and Francisco de Suaréz: see F. Stegmüller, *Zur Gnadenlehre des jungen Suaréz* (Freiburg, 1933). This teaching should be distinguished from that of Gabriel Vásquez: see J. A. de Aldama, 'Un perecer inédito del P. Gabriel Vásquez sobre la doctrina agustiniana de la gracia eficaz', *EE* 23 (1949), 515–20.

42 Báñez, *Apologia*, I.xxiii.1; in V. Beltrán de Heredia, *Domingo Báñez y las controversias sobre la gracia: textos y documentos* (Madrid, 1968), 210–11.

43 The classic account of the congregation remains J. H. Serry, *Historia congregationum de auxiliis divinae gratiae* (Antwerp, 1709).

44 D. 1090.

45 For the history of the controversy, see L. Ceyssens, *Sources relatives aux débuts du jansénisme et de l'antijansénisme 1640–1643* (Paris, 1957); Abercrombie, *The Origins of Jansenism*. *Augustinus* is divided into three parts,

and reference will be made to the part by name, rather than number. The edition used in the present study is that published at Paris in 1641. For a convenient synopsis of the work in English, see Abercrombie, *The Origins of Jansenism*, 126–53.

46 *de gratia primi hominis*, 10–12; 51A–59A.
47 To all intents and purposes, Jansen's *adiutorium sine quo non* appears to correspond to the general medieval concept of *concursus generalis*.
48 *de gratia Christi salvatoris*, ii.5; 36bE.
49 *de gratia Christi salvatoris*, i–iii.
50 *de gratia Christi salvatoris*, iii.20; 161bC-D; 161bE-162aA.
51 *de gratia Christi salvatoris*, iii.20; 162aE.
52 *de gratia Christi salvatoris*, iii.20; 162bD.
53 This interpretation of Augustine goes back to Baius, and had been challenged by Suaréz: Suaréz, *de gratia*, I.xxi.1; *Opera*, 1.468–9.
54 D. 1092–6. For the background, see L. Ceyssens, *La première Bulle contre Jansénius: sources relatives à son histoire (1644–53)* (2 vols: Rome, 1961–2).
55 D. 1351–1451. See further J. D. Thomas, *La querelle de l'Unigenitus* (Paris, 1950); J. A. G. Tans, *Pasquier Quesnel et les Pays-Bas* (Gronigen, 1960).
56 V. Martin, *Les Origines du Gallicanisme* (2 vols: Paris, 1939).
57 Most notably, *Die katholische Lehre von der Rechtfertigung und von der Gnade*, ed. Wilfried Joest (Lüneburg, 1954); Hans Küng, *Rechtfertigung: Die Lehre Karl Barths und eine katholische Besinnung* (Einsiedeln, 1957); Karl Rahner, 'Fragen der Kontroverstheologie über die Rechtfertigung', in *Schriften zur Theologie* IV (Einsiedeln, 1960), 237–71.
58 A study of sermons preached in seventeenth-century Spain on the theme of justification indicates the considerable difficulties encountered in explaining the Council's pronouncements on the matter to the laity: see H. D. Smith, *Preaching in the Spanish Golden Age: A Study in Some Preachers of the Reign of Philip III* (Oxford, 1978), especially 140–5.

Notes to §29

1 J. F. Davis, 'Lollardy and the Reformation in England', *ARG* 73 (1982), 217–37.
2 Thus Thomas More was quick to point out the difference between the eucharistic views of Barnes, Frith and the anonymous *Souper of the Lorde*: W. A. Clebsch, *England's Earliest Protestants 1520–35* (New Haven, 1964), 293. For the argument that the author of the *Souper* was George Joye, see W. D. J. Cargill Thompson, 'Who wrote the "Supper of the Lord"?', in *Studies in the Reformation: Luther to Hooker* (London, 1980), 83–93.
3 For a careful study of the decline in Luther's influence, see Basil Hall, 'The Early Rise and Gradual Decline of Lutheranism in England (1520–1600)' in *Reform and Reformation: England and the Continent c. 1500–c. 1750*, ed. Derek Baker (Oxford, 1979), 103–31.
4 Rupp, *English Protestant Tradition*, 161; Knox, *Doctrine of Faith*, 106–9.

5 His *Parable of the Wicked Mammon* (1528: incipit *That fayth the mother of all good workes iustifyeth us*) is generally thought to be based upon Luther's 1522 sermon for the ninth Sunday after Trinity: WA 10 III.283–92. Note the conclusions of Clebsch, *England's Earliest Protestants*, 153, on Tyndale's general conformity to Luther's positions. L. J. Trinterud, 'A Reappraisal of William Tyndale's Debt to Martin Luther', *ChH* 31 (1962), 24–45, argues that Tyndale owed more to humanism and the Rhineland Reformers than to Luther; this suggestion was clarified and criticised by Jens G. Møller, 'The Beginnings of Puritan Covenant Theology', *JEH* 14 (1963), 46–67.

6 e.g., see the *Prologue to Romans: Works*, 493–4, which emphasises that faith 'altereth a man, and changeth him into a new spiritual nature'. See further *Mammon: Works*, 53–5. In his later works, such as his *Exposition of Matthew V VI VII*, he appears to reproduce the basic features of the concept of the *imputatio iustitiae*.

7 His statement that, although the believer is righteous in Christ, he continues to be a sinner in fact, is based upon a proleptic understanding of justification: 'Bulwark against Rastell': *Workes*, 72.

8 See Knox, *Doctrine of Faith*, 43–51; 44. There is one isolated passage in which Frith refers to Christ's righteousness being 'reputed unto us for our own': *Workes*, 49. The parallelism between Adam's sin and Christ's righteousness is evidently constructed on the basis of Augustinian presuppositions, rather than those of later Lutheranism.

9 e.g., *Supplication* (1531), fol. liiir: 'the faith of Christ Jesus which is imputed unto them for justice'. For an incomplete list of the differences between the two editions, see W. D. J. Cargill Thompson, 'The Sixteenth Century Editions of *A Supplication unto King Henry VIII* by Robert Barnes D.D.', *Transactions of the Cambridge Bibliographical Society* 3 (1960), 133–42.

10 e.g., *Supplication* (1534); *Workes*, 242A: 'Wherefore we say with S. Paul, that faith only justifies *imputative*; that is, all the merits and goodness, grace and favour, and all that is in Christ, to our salvation, is imputed and reckoned unto us.'

11 George Joye, *Answer to Ashwell* (London, 1531), B3.

12 Rupp, *English Protestant Tradition*, 109–14. See further Jasper Ridley, *Thomas Cranmer* (Oxford, 1962), 113–15; Philip Hughes, *The Reformation in England* (3 vols: London, 5th edn, 1963), 1.348–55.

13 Hardwick, *Articles of Religion*, 250; Lloyd, *Formularies of Faith*, xxvi.

14 R. W. Dixon, *History of the Church of England* (6 vols: London, 3rd edn, 1895–1902) 1.415; Hughes, *Reformation in England*, 2.29 n. 2. It may also be noted that the scriptural citations (Romans 8.12 – note that Lloyd wrongly attributes it to the tenth chapter – and Matthew 19.17) in Article Five are taken from Melanchthon's 1535 *locus de bonis operibus*, which follows immediately after the *locus de gratia et de iustificatione*. Tyndale's definition of justification parallels Melanchthon's closely, but omits any reference to its forensic dimension: *Prologue to Romans: Works*, 508: 'By justifying, understand no other thing than to be recon-

ciled to God, and to be restored unto his favour, and to have thy sins forgiven thee.'

15 CR (Melanchthon) 21.421. See also §22.

16 Lloyd, *Formularies of Faith*, 209–10.

17 Lloyd, *Formularies of Faith*, 35.

18 See E. Burton, *Three Primers put forth in the Reign of Henry VIII* (Oxford, 1834): Rupp, *English Protestant Tradition*, 133.

19 Lloyd, *Formularies of Faith*, 364. For full text of the article, see 363–9.

20 The Gardiner–Somerset correspondence makes it clear that Cranmer was the author of this anonymous work: see John Foxe, *Acts and Monuments*, ed. J. Pratt (8 vols: London, 1877), 4.45–55. For the text of the *Homily*, see *The Two Books of Homilies appointed to be read in Churches* (Oxford, 1859), 24–35.

21 cf. *Homily*, 29.6–18, with the *locus de vocabulo gratiae* of the 1543 edition of the *Loci communes*, CR (Melanchthon) 21.755. See W. Fitzgerald, *Lectures on Ecclesiastical History* (2 vols; London, 1885), 2.214–5. Fitzgerald suggests that it is beyond doubt that Cranmer had Melanchthon's *locus* open before him as he wrote: however, as Cranmer began work on the *Homily* in 1539, and the Melanchthonian passage he cites is only to be found in editions of the *Loci* subsequent to 1543, he must be challenged on this point. Fitzgerald is, however, positively convincing in comparison with the ridiculous suggestion of R. C. Jenkins, *Pre-Tridentine Doctrine: A Review of the Commentary on the Scriptures of Thomas de Vio* (London, 1891), 70–2, that the *Homily* is dependent upon Cajetan. Both Cajetan and Cranmer represent refractions of Augustine's thought, and in so far as they share this common source, a certain degree of similarity is inevitable.

22 Cranmer: 'no man can fulfil the law, and therefore by the law all men are condemned' (*Homily*, 32.3–5); Melanchthon: 'nemo legem satisfaciet; lex accusat omnes' (CR 21.426).

23 *Homily*, 30.30–2.

24 See 'Notes on Justification', in *Works*, 2.203–8. Included among these patristic gobbets are such as: 'nos iustificari, hoc est, iustos fieri' (203); 'impius accepit Spiritum Dei et factus est iustus' (206). Note also the important reference to the 'continuation and increase' of justification (208). These texts appear to underlie passages such as *Homily*, 28.7–22.

25 Letter of Cranmer to Paul Fagius, dated 24 March 1549; *Original Letters relative to the English Reformation* (2 vols: Cambridge, 1846–7), 1.329. Peter Martyr arrived in 1547; Bucer and Fagius in 1549.

26 As noted by Hughes, *Reformation in England*, 2.97 n. 1.

27 Letter of 26 April 1549; *Original Letters*, 2.535–6.

28 *BSRK* 509.24–8 (left-hand column).

29 e.g., *BSLK* 174.34–44; 175.37–9. For the significance of these passages in relation to the doctrine of the *Apology* as a whole, see Pfnür, *Einig in der Rechtfertigungslehre*, 155–81.

30 *BSRK* 509.24–8 (right-hand column).

31 *BSRK* 509.20–4 (right-hand column).

32 *BSLK* 165.12–13.

33 *BSLK* 201.23. See also 200.25–6; 298.45; 299.29.
34 Hughes, *Reformation in England*, 3.16–47. All but six of the new bishops were Marian exiles; only one (Richard Cheney) was a Lutheran.
35 *Works*, 3.469–81; 483–547. For an analysis of these sermons, see Gibbs, 'Richard Hooker's *Via Media* Doctrine of Justification'.
36 *Works*, 3.486.
37 *Works*, 3.487–9.
38 *Works*, 3.507.
39 *Works*, 3.485–6; 531–2.
40 *Works*, 3.530.
41 *Works*, 3.515. Note the reference to man's passivity in his justification, 'working no more than dead and senseless matter, wood or stone or iron': *Works*, 3.531.
42 For a discussion of this paradox, see *Works*, 3.508.
43 Hooker is careful to exclude the doctrine of justification *propter fidem*: 'God doth justify the believing man, yet not for the worthiness of his belief, but for his worthiness which is believed' (*Works*, 3.538).

Notes to §31

1 See Charles F. Allison, *The Rise of Moralism: The Proclamation of the Gospel from Hooker to Baxter* (London, 1966); McGrath, 'Anglican Tradition on Justification'. For useful background material, see R. Buick Knox, 'Bishops in the Pulpit in the Seventeenth Century: Continuity amid Change', in *Reformation, Conformity and Dissent : Essays in Honour of Geoffrey Nuttall* (London, 1977), 92–114.
2 *BSRK*, 532.15–526.5. Cf. Philip Hughes, *The Reformation in England* (3 vols: London, 5th edn, 1963), 3.232–4. Barrett's sermon was sharply critical of Calvin, Beza, Bullinger and Peter Martyr.
3 Charles I appears to have elevated known Arminians, such as Richard Montagu, to the episcopacy largely on account of their anti-Puritan attitudes, thus occasioning the famous, and largely justified, jibe concerning the tenets of Arminianism:
   Q. What do the Arminians hold?
   A. All the best bishoprics and deaneries in England.
4 J. W. Packer, *The Transformation of Anglicanism 1643–1660* (Manchester, 1969), 26–8.
5 *A Practical Catechism*, 2nd edn (London, 1646), 9.
6 Packer, *Transformation of Anglicanism*, 53–6; 56. Cf. *BSRK* 523.3.
7 Thus H. C. Porter, *Reformation and Reaction in Tudor Cambridge* (Cambridge, 1958), 281.
8 But see James Ussher's more predestinarian views: *Works*, 11.203.
9 *Two Letters written by the Rt Rev. Thomas Barlow* (London, 1701).
10 *Two Letters*, 139. Cf. 102.
11 Ussher, *Works*, 13.250–1; 264; Hall, *Works*, 9.322; Jackson, *Works*, 5.118; Davenant, *Treatise on Justification*, 164–5; Cosin, *Works*, 2.49; Andrewes, *Works*, 5.104–26, especially 116–17.

12 *A Treatise of Justification* (London, 1639), 2.

13 See Allison, *Rise of Moralism*, 181-2.

14 Hammond, *Practical Catechism*, 78. Note also his criticism of the priority of justification over sanctification (78-83).

15 Forbes, *Considerationes*, 1.174; 204. His appeal to the support of Augustine is significant.

16 *Considerationes*, 1.216. Cf. McGrath, 'Anglican Tradition on Justification', 33-6.

17 See Allison, *Rise of Moralism*, 98-106.

18 *Considerationes*, 1.54.

19 See McGrath, 'Anglican Tradition on Justification', 33.

20 *Works*, 8.247-302; especially 284-90 (on the relation between Paul and James). See H. R. McAdoo, *The Structure of Caroline Moral Theology* (London, 1949); Allison, *Rise of Moralism*, 64-95; McGrath, 'Anglican Tradition on Justification', 38-9.

21 See Allison, *Rise of Moralism*, 118-37.

22 *Harmonia Apostolica*, 279-80.

23 Barlow, *Two Letters*, 82; Barrow, *Works*, 5.162; 168-70; Beveridge, *Works*, 7.292.

24 Bramhall, *Works*, 1.56; Sanderson, *Sermons*, 1.543.

25 Hooker, *Works*, 3.486.

26 Newman, *Lectures on Justification*, 400.

27 Newman, *Lectures on Justification*, 402.

28 Newman, *Lectures on Justification*, 400-1.

29 See Barrow, *Works*, 162-79.

Notes to §32

1 See C. H. and K. George, *The Protestant Mind of the English Reformation 1570-1640* (Princeton, 1961); J. F. H. New, *Anglican and Puritan. The Basis of Their Opposition 1558-1640* (London, 1964); Basil Hall, 'Puritanism: The Problems of Definition', in *Studies in Church History* II, ed., G. J. Cuming (London, 1965), 283-96; C. H. George, 'Puritanism as History and Historiography', *Past and Present* (1968), 77-104; J. S. Coolidge, *The Pauline Renaissance in England: Puritanism and the Bible* (Oxford, 1970); J. Sears McGee, *The Godly Man in Stuart England: Anglicans, Puritans and the Two Tables* (New Haven, 1976); R. L. Greaves, *Society and Religion in Elizabethan England* (Minneapolis, 1981).

2 *Elizabethan Puritanism*, ed. L. J. Trinterud (New York, 1971), 6-7.

3 See J. van der Berg, 'Het puriteinse ethos en zijn bronnen', *Vox Theologica* 33 (1963), 161-71; 34 (1964), 1-8.

4 On the 'grey area' between Puritan and Separatist, see M. I. Tolmie, *The Triumph of the Saints: The Separate Churches of London 1616-1649* (Cambridge, 1977).

5 Hall, 'Puritanism', 296.

6 Hall, 'Puritanism', 288-9.

7 R. T. Kendall, *Calvin and English Calvinism to 1649* (Oxford, 1979), 8-9.

8 Tyndale, *Works*, 1.403. Cf. *Works*, 1.469: 'God hath made a covenant with us, to be merciful unto us, if we will be merciful one to another'; 2.90. For further references, see Trinterud, 'The Origins of Puritanism'; Møller, 'The Beginnings of Puritan Covenant Theology'; Clebsch, *England's Earliest Protestant*, 182–95.

9 Knewstub, *Lectures*, 5–6.

10 The 'chart' may be found in later editions: see *Works* (3 vols: Cambridge, 1608–9), 2.689 (printed facing the page). The chart is not contained in the 1590 or 1600 editions although its contents may be deduced from the work itself. For modern facsimiles, see H. C. Porter, *Puritanism in Tudor England* (London, 1970), 296–7; I. Breward, *The Work of William Perkins* (Abingdon, 1970),169.

11 *Workes*, 1.32.

12 *Workes*, 1.71.

13 See Kendall, *Calvin and English Calvinism*, 51–76.

14 *Workes*, 1.541. This 'practical syllogism' should be compared with the 'murtherer'-syllogism employed earlier: *Workes*, 1.529. Cf. *Workes*, 1.290; 2.322. The comparison with Richard Sibbes on this point is instructive: Kendall, *Calvin and English Calvinism*, 102–9.

15 Mosse, *Iustifying and Saving Faith*, 17. The distinction is further illustrated later: 29–35.

16 Clarke, *Saints Nosegay*, 242 (Spiritual Flower No. 688).

17 Clarke, *Saints Nosegay*, 53 (Spiritual Flower No. 134).

18 Kendall, *Calvin and English Calvinism*, 79–93.

19 *BSRK* 562.40–563.10; 563.23–9.

20 Kendall, *Calvin and English Calvinism*, 202–5.

21 *BSRK* 580.30–42.

22 *BSRK* 580.12–14.

23 *Works*, ed. Russell, 5.41–204.

24 *Works*, 5.145–59, especially 145.

25 *Works*, 5.284–90.

26 *Works*, 5.308. Owen's distinction between *impetration* and *application* should be noted: *Works*, 5.307–8.

27 *Works*, 5.320–1. Owen thus styles the Arminian Christ 'but a half-mediator' (323), in that he procures the end, but not the means thereto. Similarly, he ridicules the Arminian condition of salvation (i.e., faith) as an impossibility: it is 'as if a man should promise a blind man a thousand pounds upon condition that he will see' (323).

28 *Works*, 5.324.

29 Baxter, *Treatise of Justifying Righteousness*, 29; 88; 129–30.

30 Baxter, *Aphorisms on Justification*, 70.

31 *Defence of the True Sence*, 15.

32 *Imputatio fidei*, 3–4. Cf. 212.

33 e.g., John Eedes, *The Orthodox Doctrine concerning Justification* (London, 1642), 56–62; William Eyre, *Vindiciae Iustificationis Gratuitae* (London, 1654), 7; Thomas Gataker, *An Antidote against Error* (London, 1670), 37–8; Owen, *Works*, 11.214–15; 258–60.

34 Hooker, *Writings*, 152–86. Cf. Norman Pettit, *The Heart Prepared* (New Haven, 1966); Kendall, *Calvin and English Calvinism*, 125–38.

35 *Writings*, 160–2.

36 *The Soules Humiliation*, 170. Cf. *Unbeleevers Preparing* 1; 104; *The Soules Preparation*, 165. Note also the important statement to the effect that not every *saving* work is a *sanctifying* work: *Writings*, 145.

37 Cotton, *Gods Mercie mixed with his Iustice*, 10–12. See also Pettit, *The Heart Prepared*, 129–79; Kendall, *Calvin and English Calvinism*, 110–17; 167–83.

38 *Christ the Fountaine*, 40–1.

39 Pettit, *The Heart Prepared*, 137; Kendall, *Calvin and English Calvinism*, 169–77. Kendall indicates (170 n. 1) the reasons for supposing that Cotton arrived at his new insights while still in England.

40 *A Treatise of the Covenant of Grace*, 39–42.

41 A contemporary source which summarises the chief points of her teaching is E. Pagitt, *Heresiography* (London, 1662), 124–6. This work also provides a useful general summary of English Antinomianism (122), based on Thomas Gataker, *Antinomianism Discovered and Confuted* (London, 1642).

42 See Perry Miller, *The New England Mind: The Seventeenth Century* (New York, 1939); A. Simpson, *Puritanism in Old and New England* (Chicago, 1955).

43 See A. E. Dunning, *Congregationalists in America* (New York, 1894), 186–8; W. Walker, *Ten New England Leaders* (New York, 1901), 126–34; 244–7. The later defence of this 'Half-Way Covenant' by William Hart, Moses Hemmenway and Moses Mather is important: see W. Walker, *Creeds and Platforms of Congregationalism* (New York, 1893), 283–7.

44 See P. J. Tracy, *Jonathan Edwards, Pastor: Religion and Society in Eighteenth Century Northampton* (New York, 1979), 109–22, and references therein. For an excellent analysis of Edwards' reaction to Stoddardeanism, see John F. Jamieson, 'Jonathan Edwards' Change of Position on Stoddardeanism', *HThR* 74 (1981), 79–99.

45 For the emphasis upon justification by faith, characteristic of the period, see E. B. Lowrie, *The Shape of the Puritan Mind: The Thought of Samuel Willard* (New Haven, 1974); R. F. Lovelace, *The American Pietism of Cotton Mather: Origins of American Evangelicalism* (Grand Rapids, 1979), 73–109.

46 *Works*, 2.950b. For Samuel Willard's views on the covenant, see Lowrie, *Shape of the Puritan Mind*, 160–85. For the importance of the covenant-concept to Puritan theology in the period, see the classic study of Perry Miller, 'The Marrow of Puritan Divinity', in *Errand into the Wilderness* (Cambridge, Mass., 1956), 48–98.

47 On the federal doctrine of original sin, of particular importance in this respect, see H. S. Smith, *Changing Concepts of Original Sin: A Study in American Theology since 1750* (New York, 1955), 1–9.

48 *Works*, 2.983b.

49 See F. H. Forster, *A Genetic History of the New England Theology* (Chicago, 1907).

50 Hopkins, *The Wisdom of God in the Permission of Sin* (Boston, 1759).

51 K. Francke, 'The Beginning of Cotton Mather's Correspondence with August Hermann Franke', *Philological Quarterly* 5 (1926), 193–5. See also Lovelace, *Cotton Mather, passim*.

52 Mayhew, *Practical Discourses* (Boston, 1760), 5.

53 John Tucker, *Observations on the Doctrines and Uncharitableness of the Rev Mr Jonathan Parsons of Newbury* (Boston, 1757), 5.

54 e.g., William Balch, *The Apostles Paul and James Reconciled with Respect to Faith and Works* (Boston, 1743).

55 Samuel Webster, *Justification by the Free Grace of God* (Boston, 1765), 27. It will be obvious that this opened the Arminians to the charge that they were preaching justification by works – a charge which they vigorously denied: Lemuel Briant, *Some Friendly Remarks upon a Sermon Lately Preached at Braintree* (Boston, 1750), 10; Charles Chauncy, *Twelve Sermons* (Boston, 1765). 12; Jonathan Mayhew, *Striving to enter in at the Strait Gate* (Boston, 1761), 19–20.

Notes to §33

1 On the sense of the term 'High Church', see Owen Chadwick, *The Mind of the Oxford Movement* (London, 1960), 14–15.

2 Originally a letter to D. Parker, dated 16 April 1810, entitled 'On Justification': *Remains*, 1.281–317.

3 *Remains*, 1.308. Note the deliberate avoidance of the term 'imputation'. Cf. 1.298–9.

4 G. S. Faber's *Primitive Doctrine of Justification investigated* (London, 1837) attempted to disprove Knox on this point, while at the same time suggesting that Knox was Tridentine, rather than Anglican, in his personal view on justification.

5 For a useful introduction, see Thomas Sheridan, *Newman on Justification* (New York, 1967).

6 Newman, *Apologia pro vita sua* (London, 1964), 86. Note the statement that the 'essay on Justification' was 'aimed at the Lutheran dictum that justification by faith only was the cardinal doctrine of Christianity'.

7 C. S. Dessain, 'Cardinal Newman and the Eastern Tradition', *Downside Review* 94 (1976), 83–98.

8 *English Hymnal* No. 471; *Hymns Ancient and Modern Revised* No. 185. The hymn first appeared in 1865, as part of the *Dream of Gerontius*.

9 *Lectures on Justification*, 144. Cf. 150–1.

10 *Lectures on Justification*, 144.

11 *Lectures on Justification*, 149.

12 Newman here distances himself from Knox, who suggested that justification concerned being *made righteous*, and sanctification being *made holy*: Knox, *Remains*, 1.307–9.

13 *Lectures on Justification*, 154.

14 *Lectures on Justification*, 74. This also permits the earlier statement (63) to be understood correctly: 'justification and sanctification [are] in fact substantially one and the same thing; ... in order of ideas, viewed relatively to each other, justification followed upon sanctification.'

15 *Lectures on Justification*, 112.

16 *Lectures on Justification*, 263.

17 *Lectures on Justification*, 262.

18 *Lectures on Justification*, 275–6.

19 *Lectures on Justification*, 303.

20 *Lectures on Justification*, 343–404.

21 See Basil Hall, 'The Early Rise and Gradual Decline of Lutheranism in England (1520–1600)', in *Reform and Reformation: England and the Continent c. 1500–c. 1750*, ed. Derek Baker (Oxford, 1979), 103–31.

22 See McGrath, 'High Church Misrepresentation of Luther'. It is possible that Newman bases his evaluation of Luther upon the Tübingen Roman Catholic Johann Adam Möhler's *Symbolik* (1832). There is evidence to suggest that Newman read his work (in French translation) while preparing for his *Lectures*: Henry Tristram, 'J. A. Moehler et J. H. Newman et la renaissance catholique en Angleterre', *RSPhTh* 27 (1938), 184–204. It is known to have been in E. B. Pusey's library: Y. Brilioth, *The Anglican Revival* (London, 1933), 329 n. 2. There are certainly strong similarities between Newman and Möhler at points of importance – for example, in their common assertion that Luther excluded love, hope and obedience from justification. Möhler's criticism of Luther also underlies N. P. Williams' hostile and inaccurate assessment of the Reformer: *The Idea of the Fall and of Original Sin* (London, 1927), 427–31. Note especially the references to Möhler at 428 n. 1; 429 n. 3.

23 See M. Schloenbach, *Glaube als Geschenk Gottes* (Stuttgart, 1962) for documentation.

24 Luther, WA 40 1.41.2; Hooker, *Works*, 3.531.

25 WA 40 1.229.28–9.

26 *Lectures on Justification*, 148. Cf. 149: 'Whatever blessings in detail we ascribe to justification, are ascribed in Scripture to this sacred indwelling.'

27 *Lectures on Justification*, 300.

28 *Lectures on Justification*, 300–1.

29 Cf. *Luther's Works* (56 vols: St Louis, 1955–76), 26.265–6.

30 *Lectures on Justification*, 343 n. 1.

31 WA 40 1.239.31–240.2.

32 *Institutio*, III.iii.35. See §22 for further details.

33 *Lectures on Justification*, 154.

34 *Lectures on Justification*, 154.

35 *Remarks on Certain Passages*, 4.

36 An exception may be noted in the case of N. P. Williams' unpublished commentary on Romans (MS in library of Christ Church, Oxford). For a brief survey of its features, see A. E. McGrath, 'Justification; "Making Just" or "Declaring Just"?', *Churchman* 96 (1982), 44–52. A totally inept

account of the teaching of the Anglican Reformers on justification was given by A. H. Rees, *The Doctrine of Justification in the Anglican Reformers* (London, 1939), and convincingly refuted by E. G. Rupp, *English Protestant Tradition*, 172–85. An uncritical appraisal of Rees' work underlies the serious inaccuracies and misunderstandings which litter Gregory Dix's *Question of Anglican Orders: Letters to a Layman* (London, 1944), 21–8 (note especially the appeal to Rees: 27).

37 This is the somewhat simplistic approach adopted by Hans Küng (*Rechtfertigung: Die Lehre Karl Barths und eine katholische Besinnung*), who identifies Karl Barth as such a 'typical' theologian.

38 Once more, it is necessary to point out the deficiencies of Küng's study, which tends to adopt a Thomist interpretation of Trent, overlooking alternative interpretations less congenial to his attempt to harmonise Barth and Trent.

39 Thus the Council of Trent's explicit statement that there is only a single formal cause of justification is directed against Seripando's version of the mediating Regensburg theology: see §§27, 28.

Notes to introduction to chapter 9

1 e.g., see Hans Baron, 'Towards a More Positive Evaluation of the Fifteenth Century Renaissance', *Journal of the History of Ideas* 4 (1943), 22–49; Karl Dannhauer, *The Renaissance: Medieval or Modern?* (Boston, 1959), 35–48; 64–75. For a careful evaluation of the 'Burckhardtian thesis' – that the Renaissance was the first-born among the sons of modern Europe – see Wallace K. Ferguson, *The Renaissance in Historical Thought: Five Centuries of Interpretation* (Boston, 1948), 195–252; 290–385.

2 See Ruprecht Paqué, *Das Pariser Nominalistenstatut: Zur Entstehung des Realitätsbegriff der neuzeitlichen Naturwissenschaft* (Berlin, 1970).

3 See Alister E. McGrath, *The Making of Modern German Christology: From the Enlightenment to Pannenberg* (Oxford, 1986), for a discussion.

4 e.g., see James Buchanan, *The Doctrine of Justification: An Outline of its History in the Church and of its Exposition from Scripture* (1867: reprinted London, 1961), 114–40.

5 Gerhard Ebeling, 'Luther und der Anbruch der Neuzeit', *ZThK* 69 (1972), 185–213.

6 The continuity between the late medieval period and the Reformation has been emphasised throughout the present study. For the specific case of Luther, see McGrath, *Luther's Theology of the Cross*, 72–128.

7 See the essay of Ernst Troeltsch, 'Renaissance und Reformation', in *Gesammelte Schriften* (4 vols: Tübingen, 1912–25), 4.261–96. The thesis of the medieval and non-modern character of the Reformation was developed at greater length – against Hegel and his disciples – in two of Troeltsch's more important works: *Vernunft und Offenbarung bei Johann Gerhard und Melanchthon: Untersuchungen zur Geschichte der altprotestantischen Theologie* (Göttingen, 1891); and *Die Bedeutung des Protestantismus für die Entstehung der modernen Welt* (München/Berlin, 1911). For a more

scholarly exposition of this point, see Heiko A. Oberman, *Forerunners of the Reformation: The Shape of Late Medieval Thought illustrated by Key Documents* (Philadelphia, 1981), 3–66. Oberman's later study *Werden und Wertung der Reformation* explores this theme in some depth.

8 Although Althaus, 'Gottes Gottheit als Sinn der Rechtfertigungslehre Luthers', emphasises the theocentric dimension of Luther's theology of justification, it must be noted that it is quite inadequate as a leading characteristic.

Notes to §34

1 For an introduction, see A. O. Dyson, 'Theological Legacies of the Enlightenment: England and Germany', in *England and Germany: Studies in Theological Diplomacy*, ed. S. W. Sykes (Frankfurt, 1982), 45–62. For the influence of Deism upon the *Aufklärung*, see G. Gawlick, 'Deismus als Grundzug der Religionsphilosophie der Aufklärung', in *Hermann Samuel Reimarus (1694–1768), ein 'bekannter Unbekannter' der Aufklärung* (Hamburg, 1973), 15–43.

For the Enlightenment in general, see the important studies of Paul Hazard, *La crise de la conscience européenne (1680–1715)* (3 vols: Paris, 1935); *idem, La pensée européenne au XVIIᵉ siècle de Montesquieu à Lessing* (3 vols: Paris, 1946).

2 Herbert was treated as a precursor of Deism by its exponents: Blount's *Religio Laici* is clearly dependent upon an earlier draft of Herbert's work of the same name. See further M. Rossi, *La vita, le opere i tempi di Eduardo Herbert di Chirbury* (3 vols: Roma, 1947).

3 The Stoicism underlying the concept of *notitiae communes* derives from Cicero: see G. Gawlick, 'Cicero and the Enlightenment', *Studies on Voltaire and the Eighteenth Century* 25 (1963), 657–62. Rossi suggests an Aristotelian basis for Herbert's epistemology, but concedes the influence of Stoicism: Rossi, *Eduardo Chirbury*, 1.291.

4 Rossi, *Eduardo Chirbury*, 1.535 n. 1.

5 On this distinction see M. Schneckenburger, *Vorlesungen über die Lehrbegriffe der kleineren protestantischen Kirchenparteien* (Frankfurt, 1863), 22.

6 Toland, *Christianity not Mysterious*, ed. Gawlick, 58–63. See further F. Heinemann, 'John Toland and the Age of Reason', *Archiv für Philosophie* 4 (1950), 35–66.

7 Locke, *Reasonableness of Christianity: Works*, 7.6.

8 *Reasonableness of Christianity: Works*, 7.14. Cf. 7.112.

9 *Reasonableness of Christianity: Works*, 7.101; 110. Cf. Leslie Stephen, *History of English Thought in the Eighteenth Century* 3rd edn (2 vols: London, 1902), 1.95–6.

10 *Reasonableness of Christianity: Works*, 7.101–3.

11 *Reasonableness of Christianity: Works*, 7.105.

12 Locke treats the New Testament epistles as occasional writings, rather than as sources of fundamental Christian truths, being intended to strengthen Christians rather than proclaim basic truths to outsiders:

Reasonableness of Christianity: Works, 7.151–5. A further point which Locke emphasises is that only fundamentals – i.e., the belief that Jesus is the Christ, and repentance – can be necessary to salvation, on account of the obscurity which the Bible, as an ancient text, displays: see J. T. Moore, 'Locke's Analysis of Language and the Assent to Scripture', *Journal of the History of Ideas* 36 (1976), 707–14.

13 *Reasonableness of Christianity: Works*, 7.148.

14 On this work, see J. W. Yolton, *Locke and the Compass of Human Understanding* (Cambridge, 1970); R. I. Aaron, *John Locke* (Oxford, 1971); J. L. Mackie, *Problems from Locke* (Oxford, 1976); P. A. Schouls, *The Imposition of Method: A Study of Descartes and Locke* (Oxford, 1980), 149–85.

15 See H. R. McAdoo, *The Spirit of Anglicanism: A Survey of Anglican Theological Method in the Seventeenth Century* (London, 1965), 240–315.

16 See H. R. McAdoo, *The Structure of Caroline Moral Theology* (London, 1949).

17 *Essay*, II.23–25; ed. Nidditch, 117.24–118.31.

18 See L. Krüger, 'The Concept of Experience in John Locke', in *John Locke: Symposium Wolfenbüttel*, ed. R. Brandt (Berlin/New York, 1981), 74–89.

19 *Essay*, I.iv.17; 95.10–11. Cf. I.iv.9; I.iv.16; IV.x.1.

20 The question of how God's existence may be determined empirically is also significant: see M. R. Ayers, 'Mechanism, Superaddition and the Proof of God's Existence in Locke's *Essay*', *Philosophical Review* 90 (1981), 210–51.

21 *Essay*, IV.x.6; 621.6–8.

22 *Essay*, II.xxiii.33; 314.25–35. See also II.xxiii.35. It is important to note that Locke has avoided applying moral epithets (such as 'good' or 'righteous') to the 'Supreme Being' until this point.

23 *Essay*, II.xxiii.36; 315.34–6.

24 See the analysis of G. A. J. Rogers, 'Locke, Law and the Laws of Nature', in *Symposium Wolfenbüttel*, 146–62.

25 See G. Schedler, 'Hobbes on the Basis of Political Obligation', *Journal of the History of Philosophy* 15 (1977), 165–70. On the concept of 'contract' in Hobbes' theory of cession, see M. T. Delgano, 'Analysing Hobbes' Contract', *Proceedings of the Aristotelian Society* 76 (1975–6), 209–26.

26 Hobbes, *Leviathan* (London, 1651), II.xxvi.4; 138. For the concept of 'covenant' employed, see Delgano, 'Hobbes' Contract'; for the concept of the 'Law of Nature', see P. E. Moreau, 'Loi divine et loi naturelle selon Hobbes', *Revue Internationale de Philosophie* 33 (1979), 443–51.

27 For the development of the theory of the state from Hobbes to Locke, see C. B. Macpherson, *The Political Theory of Possessive Individualism: Hobbes to Locke* (Oxford, 1962).

28 See D. P. Walker, *The Decline of Hell: Seventeenth-Century Discussions of Eternal Torment* (London, 1964). The chief argument advanced against the notion was that it appeared to serve no useful preservatory function.

29 *Christianity as Old as the Creation*, ed. Gawlick, 14–15. Gawlick suggests

that Tindal was the first to reverse the traditional relationship of morality and religion (17*): it seems to us that this development is implicit in the writings of Locke.

30 Chubb, *True Gospel of Jesus Christ*, in *Posthumous Works* (2 vols: London, 1748), 2.20. For a useful discussion of Chubb's doctrine of the work of Christ, see R. S. Franks, *The Work of Christ* (London, 1962), 485–91.

31 *Posthumous Works*, 2.18; 104–5; 140–1. Note that these correspond to the final three *notitiae communes*, as defined by Cherbury.

32 *Posthumous Works*, 2.55.

33 *Posthumous Works*, 2.32. Cf. 2.43–9; 112–20. For his critique of the doctrine of original sin, see 2.164.

34 *Posthumous Works*, 2.150.

35 *Posthumous Works*, 2.115–16.

36 Morgan, *The Moral Philosopher*, 1.439. Cf. 1.412.

37 *The Moral Philosopher*, 1.411–12.

38 *The Moral Philosopher*, 3.150.

39 See Franks, *The Work of Christ*, 492–7.

40 For the critique of the doctrine of original sin associated with the French Enlightenment, see Ernst Cassirer, *The Philosophy of the Enlightenment* (Boston, 1960), 137–60.

41 See Herbert Butterfield, 'England in the Eighteenth Century', in *A History of the Methodist Church in Great Britain*, eds. Rupert Davies and Gordon Rupp (4 vols: London, 1965–   ), 1.1–33. On the relation of John Wesley to German Pietism, see Jean Orcibal, 'The Theological Originality of John Wesley and Continental Spirituality', in *A History of the Methodist Church*, ed. Davies and Rupp, 1.81–111.

42 See A. C. McGiffert, *Protestant Thought before Kant* (London, 1919), 251. On the soteriologies of the *Aufklärung*, see F. C. Baur, *Die christliche Lehre von der Versöhnung in ihrer geschichtlichen Entwicklung* (Tübingen, 1838), 478–530; Baur, *Salus Christiana*, 111–79.

43 *Institutiones theologiae dogmaticae*, IV.iv.4; 956. Cf. IV.iv.12; 978; 'neminem nisi regenitum iustificari'.

44 *Institutiones theologiae dogmaticae*, IV.iv.4; 956. As Stolzenburg emphasises, both Budde and Pfaff presuppose that man is naturally capable of receiving grace without the necessity of *satisfactio Christi* (in the Orthodox sense): A. F. Stolzenburg, *Die Theologie des J. Fr. Buddeus und des Chr. M. Pfaff* (Berlin, 1926), 211.

45 *Institutiones theologiae*, 487. See further Stolzenburg, *Theologie*, 207–20.

46 *Elementa theologiae dogmaticae*, 819.

47 *Elementa theologiae dogmaticae*, 822.

48 'Ponendo scilicet tres salutis conditiones, conversionem, fidem, renovationem': *Elementa theologiae dogmaticae*, 713. Cf. 829: 'Nemo negat, pios motus antecedere iustificationem et adesse in actu iustificationis.' For similar views in the writings of a noted later *Aufklärer*, see Henke, *Lineamenta*, §116; 165–6. The theme is important in the preaching of the later *Aufklärung*: see R. Krause, *Die Predigt der späten deutschen Aufklärung* (Stuttgart, 1965).

49 Hobbes, *Leviathan*, II.xxvii; 161–7.
50 The impact of Hobbes' theory of punishment upon German theology was delayed through the influence of Leibniz' *Théodicée* (1710), in which he developed the view that the *civitas Dei*, the moral world, is an end in itself, rather than the means to some other end.
51 See Ritschl, *Justification and Reconciliation*, 337–41.
52 A similar critique of the concept of vindictive justice underlies the contemporary critique of the notion of eternal punishment, particularly in early eighteenth-century France: see Walker, *The Decline of Hell*, 40–51.
53 It is of interest to note that the most penetrating contemporary criticism of Dippel's views was due to the Wolffian I. G. Kanz. Unlike Dippel, who regarded the divine government of mankind as the means towards man's well-being, Kanz retained the Leibnizian concept of the *civitas Dei* as an end in itself. The establishment of moral order among mankind is thus an end in itself, rather than a means to an eudaemonistic end. Kanz is thus able to follow Leibniz in retaining the concept of the retributive justice of God, in addition to the purely natural punishment for sin which Dippel allowed.
54 *Der thätige Gehorsam*, 419–21. For a useful analysis, see Ritschl, *Justification and Reconciliation*, 346–55; Baur, *Salus Christiana*, 132–44. Ritschl's suggestion that Töllner adopts an Abailardian understanding of the significance of the death of Christ rests upon his improper exposition of Abailard's soteriology: see R. E. Weingart, *The Logic of Divine Love* (Oxford, 1970), 120–50. In part, the success of Töllner's critique of the significance of the *obedientia activa Christi* was due to the astonishingly poor quality of his opponents. Thus J. A. Ernesti, finding himself obliged to concede that it was impossible to conceive of a man who was not under an obligation to obey the law, laboured under the misapprehension that the denial of the obligation of Christ's obedience to the law was equivalent to the denial of the humanity of Christ. For a consideration of some of the responses to Töllner, see I. A. Dorner, *History of the Development of the Doctrine of the Person of Christ* (5 vols: Edinburgh, 1863), 5.263–5.
55 *Der thätige Gehorsam*, 42. Cf. 631–2, especially 632: 'Ich stelle mich vor, daß Gott zur Begnadigung an sich niemals eine Genugtuung gefordert oder veranstaltet haben würde: und daß wir daher gar nicht auf dem rechten Wege sind, wenn wir sie als eine zur Begnadigung der Menschen nöthig befundne Veranstaltung betrachten.'
56 *Der thätige Gehorsam*, 685.
57 See his important essay 'Alle Erklärungsarten vom versöhnenden Tode Christi laufen auf Eins heraus', in *Theologische Untersuchungen*, 2.316–35.
58 *Glückseligkeitslehre*, 78.
59 *Glückseligkeitslehre*, 73.
60 Cf. *Glückseligkeitslehre*, 83.
61 *Glückseligkeitslehre*, 93–162.
62 It is worth recalling Loofs' famous remark, 'Die Dogmengeschichte ist ein Kind der deutschen Aufklärungszeit': Friedrich Loofs, *Leitfaden zum Studium der Dogmengeschichte*, 4th edn (Halle, 1904), 1. The original

purpose of *Dogmengeschichte* was the *criticism* of dogma through an historical investigation of its origins, rather than a mere scientific documentation of its historical forms. This point is of particular importance in relation to our study, in that the early studies of the development of the doctrine of justification (such as those of F. C. Baur and A. B. Ritschl) were undertaken for polemical, rather than purely scholarly, motives.

63 *Glückseligkeitslehre*, 146. Note also his criticism of the Christological application of the concept of 'sacrifice': *Glückseligkeitslehre*, 288.
64 *Glückseligkeitslehre*, 149.
65 *Glückseligkeitslehre*, 130.
66 *Glückseligkeitslehre*, 161–2.
67 *Glückseligkeitslehre*, 162.
68 *Glückseligkeitslehre*, 180: 'Gott fordert so wenig, als irgends ein menschlicher Vater von schwachen unmündigen Kindern mehr als aufrichtigen Willen und treuen Gebrauch der vorhandnen Kräfte.'
69 See Baur, *Salus Christiana*, 134–8.
70 See McGrath, 'The Moral Theory of the Atonement'.
71 See Teller, *Religion der Vollkommnern*, 9–12; especially 12.
72 For further discussion of the Christology of the *Aufklärung*, see Alister E. McGrath, *The Making of Modern German Christology: From the Enlightenment to Pannenberg* (Oxford, 1986), 9–18.

Notes to §35

1 For the remarkable influence of Kant upon the nineteenth-century Göttingen theological faculty, and particularly Albrecht Ritschl, see J. Meyer, 'Geschichte der Göttinger theologischen Fakultät 1737–1937', *Zeitschrift für niedersächsische Kirchengeschichte* 42 (1937), 7–107; P. Wrzecionko, *Die philosophischen Wurzeln der Theologie Albrecht Ritschls: Ein Beitrag zum Problem des Verhältnisses von Theologie und Philosophie im 19. Jahrhundert* (Berlin, 1964).
2 See Ritschl's careful analysis of Kant's significance in this respect: *Justification and Reconciliation*, 320–86.
3 See McGrath, 'The Moral Theory of the Atonement'.
4 The brilliant study of A. Schweitzer, *Die Religionphilosophie Kants in der Kritik der reinen Vernunft bis zur Religion innherhalb der Grenzen der bloßen Vernunft* (Freiburg, 1899), is still invaluable. See further W. Reinhart, *Über das Verhältnis von Sittlichkeit und Religion bei Kant* (Bern, 1927); A. Messer, *Kommentar zu Kants ethischen und religionsphilosophischen Hauptschriften* (Leipzig, 1929); and especially the richly documented study of J. Bohatec, *Die Religionsphilosophie Kants in der 'Religion innherhalb der Grenzen der bloßen Vernunft'* (Hildesheim, 1966). The best study of the question of the translation of human finitude from the cognitive to the moral realm remains G. Krüger, *Philosophie und Moral in der Kantischen Kritik* (Tübingen, 1931).
5 *Schriften*, 6.170.15–19.

6 See the classic study of A. Döring, 'Kants Lehre vom höchsten Gut', *Kantstudien* 4 (1898), 94–101. The more recent studies of J. R. Silber should be noted, especially his essay 'The Importance of the Highest Good in Kant's Ethics', *Ethics* 73 (1963), 179–97.

7 For a useful introduction to this concept, see E. L. Fackenheim, 'Kant and Radical Evil', *University of Toronto Quarterly* 23 (1953), 339–52.

8 See the argument of H. J. Paton, *The Categorical Imperative* (London, 1946).

9 *Schriften*, 6.75.1–76.6 (our italics). For the background to this remarkable statement, see *Werke*, 6.62.14–66.18. Elsewhere in this work, Kant asserts that a lenient judge who relaxes the moral law represents a contradiction in terms: *Werke*, 6.141.9–142.3. The apparent discrepancy between such statements is not discussed.

10 *Schriften*, 6.117.14–15.

11 *Schriften*, 6.120.10–16.

12 The first difficulty concerns the relationship between moral acts and the moral disposition, and forces Kant to discuss how God can accept a good moral disposition as equivalent to perfectly good moral acts: *Schriften*, 6.66.21–67.16. The second difficulty concerns how an individual may know with certainty that his new disposition is, in fact, good: *Schriften*, 6.67.17–71.20.

13 *Schriften*, 6.71.21–78.2.

14 *Schriften*, 6.74.16–17.

15 For the argument, see *Schriften*, 6.74.1–75.1.

16 *Schriften*, 6.183.37–184.3.

17 For the influence of Kant upon contemporary discussion of the theology of reconciliation, see J. H. Tieftrunk, *Censur des christlichen Lehrebegriffs nach den Prinzipien der Religionskritik* (3 vols: Berlin, 1791–95) (the first volume of which appeared in a second edition in 1796). Note the explicit reference to the theological significance of radical evil (e.g., 3.122), and the concept of grace as *die Ergänzung unseres Unvermögens zum Übergange aus dem Bösen zum Guten* (2.228).

18 For further details, see Jack Forstman, *A Romantic Triangle: Schleiermacher and Early German Romanticism* (Missoula, Mont., 1977). On 'Romanticism' in general, see F. Schulz, 'Romantik und Romantiker als literarhistorische Terminologien und Begriffsbildungen', *Deutsche Vierteljahrschrift für Literaturwissenschaft und Geistesgeschichte* 2 (1924), 349–66; B. M. G. Reardon, *Religion in the Age of Romanticism* (Cambridge, 1985), *passim*. On the rôle of *Gefühl* in Schleiermacher's theology, see W. Schutz, 'Schleiermachers Theorie des Gefühls und ihre religiöse Bedeutung', *ZThK* (1956), 75–103; F. W. Graf, 'Ursprüngliches Gefühl unmittelbarer Koinzidenz des Differenten: Zur Modifikation des Religionsbegriffs in der verschiedenen Auflagen von Schleiermachers "Reden über Religion"', *ZThK* 75 (1978), 147–86.

19 *Der christliche Glaube*, §33, 3; 1.174–6.

20 *Der christliche Glaube*, §28, 2; 1.154–6.

21 *Der christliche Glaube*, §3, 2–4; 1.7–13.

22 *Der christliche Glaube*, §15, 1; 1.99–100. It should be noted that Schleiermacher emphasises the communal dimension of such experience, and does not lapse into a form of solipsism: for Schleiermacher, Christian faith is essentially and primarily faith in Christ as grounded in the community of faith. See further D. Offermann, *Schleiermachers Einleitung in die Glaubenslehre* (Berlin, 1969), 293–321.

23 See Graß, 'Die durch Jesum von Nazareth vollbrachte Erlösung', for an excellent analysis. Schleiermacher's definition of Christianity is significant in this respect, in that it makes explicit that the distinguishing feature of Christianity lies in the total subordination of its content to the redemption accomplished by Jesus of Nazareth: *Der christliche Glaube*, §11 (title); 1.67.

24 *Der christliche Glaube*, §4, 4; 1.20–2. Cf. F. Beisser, *Schleiermachers Lehre von Gott* (Göttingen, 1970), 57–68; Offermann, *Einleitung*, 47–65.

25 *Der christliche Glaube*, §94, 1–3; 2.40–5. On the use of the term *Urbild*, see P. Seifert, *Die Theologie des jungen Schleiermacher* (Gütersloh, 1960), 141–2.

26 *Der christliche Glaube*, §106, 1; 2.162.

27 *Der christliche Glaube*, §102, 1; 2.112–13. Schleiermacher notes the traditional interpretation of the *munus Christi triplex*, as prophet, priest and king, and argues that any attempt to reduce Christ to a single one of these 'offices' results in serious distortion. His (inaccurate) criticism of the Roman Catholic position is not relevant to our purpose.

28 *Der christliche Glaube*, §100, 3; 2.101.

29 *Der christliche Glaube*, §100, 3; 2.101.

30 See H. Pieter, *Theologische Ideologiekritik: Die praktische Konsequenzen der Rechtfertigungslehre bei Schleiermacher* (Göttingen, 1977).

31 *Der christliche Glaube*, §107, 2; 2.167–8.

32 *Der christliche Glaube*, §109, 4; 2.201. But note the emphatic rejection of the suggestion that faith is the instrumental cause of justification: §109, 4; 2.202.

33 *Der christliche Glaube*, §107, 1; 2.165–7.

34 *Der christliche Glaube*, §70; 1.376 '[eine] aufzuhebende vollkommne Unfähigkeit zum Guten'.

35 *Der christliche Glaube*, §71, 3; 1.386–8. Note how Schleiermacher thus correlates the first consciousness of sin with the first presentiment of redemption.

36 *Der christliche Glaube*, §22, 1–3; 1.124–9. See further K.-M. Beckmann, *Der Begriff der Häresie bei Schleiermacher* (München, 1959), 36–62. For consideration of the four heresies in more detail, see 85–114.

37 *Der christliche Glaube*, §22, 2; 1.125.

38 *Der christliche Glaube*, §22, 2; 1.125.

39 *Der christliche Glaube*, §109, 4; 2.201.

40 *Der christliche Glaube*, §84, 3; 1.471.

41 *Der christliche Glaube*, §84, 3; 1.470.

42 *Der christliche Glaube*, §84, 3; 1.471–3.

43 *Der christliche Glaube*, §84, 1; 1.465–6.

44 *Der christliche Glaube*, §84, 1; 1.466–7.
45 *Der christliche Glaube*, §84. 1; 1.467.

Notes to §36

1 See Alister E. McGrath, *The Making of Modern German Christology* (Oxford, 1986), 32–52 for details. Of particular importance is F. C. Baur's critique of Schleiermacher's inference of the Christ-event from the collective Christian consciousness: 38–9.

2 F. C. Baur, *Die christliche Lehre von der Versöhnung in ihrer geschichtlichen Entwicklung* (Tübingen, 1838), 748. It may be noted that Baur minimised the distinction between the soteriologies of the *Aufklärung* and both Kant and Schleiermacher, presumably to achieve consistency with his Hegelian theory of historical development.

3 Ritschl, *Justification and Reconciliation*, §76; 605.

4 The third edition of this work (1888) has been used in the present study: for the differences between the various editions, see C. Fabricius, *Die Entwicklung in Albrecht Ritschls Theologie von 1874 bis 1889 nach der verschiedene Auflagen seiner Hauptwerke dargestellt und beurteilt* (Tübingen, 1909).

5 *Rechtfertigung und Versöhnung*, §27; 189–90.

6 *Rechtfertigung und Versöhnung*, §27; 185.

7 *Rechtfertigung und Versöhnung*, §28; 195–200.

8 *Loci communes* (1521), preface. It should, of course, be noted that Melanchthon was not defining the basis of a theological programme with this statement, but merely explaining the omission of a *locus* concerning Christology from this work, which was primarily concerned with soteriology. Melanchthon's theological criticisms were directed against the medieval soteriologies, not the Christologies of the period. In subsequent editions, in which a Christological *locus* is included, this dictum is omitted.

9 *Rechtfertigung und Versöhnung*, (Bonn, 1st edn, 1874) §44; 343: 'Wir erkennen nämlich die Art und die Eigenschaften, d.h. die Bestimmtheit des Seins, nur an dem Wirken eines Dinges auf uns, und wir denken die Art und den Umfang seines Wirkens auf uns als sein Wesen.'

10 *Justification and Reconciliation*, §1; 1.

11 See Hermann Timm, *Theorie und Praxis in der Theologie Albrecht Ritschls und Wilhelm Herrmanns* (Gütersloh, 1967); James Richmond, *Ritschl: A Reappraisal* (London, 1978), 124–67.

12 *Rechtfertigung und Versöhnung*, §16; 83. The other two definitions of justification offered by Ritschl represent an extension of this basic definition.

13 See Schäfer, 'Rechtfertigungslehre bei Ritschl und Kähler', 69–70.

14 *WA* 2.722.24–5.

15 *Rechtfertigung und Versöhnung*, §56; 517.

16 *Rechtfertigung und Versöhnung*, §31; 58–9.

17 *Rechtfertigung und Versöhnung*, §15; 72.

18 *Rechtfertigung und Versöhnung*, §15; 75–7.
19 See W. von Loewenich, *Luther und der Neuprotestantismus* (Witten, 1963), 105; Schäfer, 'Rechtfertigungslehre bei Ritschl und Kälher', 73–4.
20 *Rechtfertigung und Versöhnung*, §1; 11. For a helpful analysis of this structure, see G. Hök, *Die elliptische Theologie Albrecht Ritschls nach Ursprung und innerem Zusammenhang* (Uppsala, 1941).
21 See Fabricius, *Entwicklung in Albrecht Ritschls Theologie*, 75–88.
22 *Rechtfertigung und Versöhnung*, §16; 78.
23 Ritschl has clearly misunderstood the theological significance of the concept of *gratia gratum faciens* within the context of Roman Catholic theologies of justification: *Rechtfertigung und Versöhnung*, §16; 78. His criticisms directed against the *Aufklärung* are considerably more accurate.
24 *Rechtfertigung und Versöhnung*, §16; 77–83, especially 82–3. Note particularly Ritschl's criticism of Pietism, which would be developed in his *Geschichte des Pietismus* (3 vols: Bonn, 1880–6).
25 *Rechtfertigung und Versöhnung*, §17; 90.
26 For a discussion of Grotius, see R. S. Franks, *The Work of Christ* (London, 1962), 389–409. The point with which Ritschl is concerned is developed in A. E. McGrath, 'Justice and Justification: Semantic and Juristic Aspects of the Christian Doctrine of Justification', *SJTh* 35 (1982), 403–18, *in fine*.
27 *Rechtfertigung und Versöhnung*, §17; 84.
28 *Rechtfertigung und Versöhnung*, §17; 86.
29 *Rechtfertigung und Versöhnung*, §17; 87–9.
30 *Rechtfertigung und Versöhnung*, §17; 89–90.
31 See C. Walther, 'Der Reich-Gottes-Begriff in der Theologie Richard Rothes und Albrecht Ritschls', *KuD* 2 (1956), 115–38; R. Schäfer, 'Das Reich Gottes bei Albrecht Ritschl und Johannes Weiß', *ZThK* (1964), 68–88. The older study of R. Wegener, *Albrecht Ritschls Idee des Reich Gottes* (Leipzig, 1897), is intensely hostile.
32 Schäfer, 'Das Reich Gottes', 82–5.
33 Some earlier commentators suggested that Ritschl confuses the abstract concept of the destiny of the universe with that of God: see James Orr, *The Ritschlian Theology and the Evangelical Faith* (London, 1897), 255–6; A. E. Garvey, *The Ritschlian Theology* (Edinburgh, 1902), 237–63.
34 *Unterricht in der christlichen Religion* (Bonn, 1875), §14. Cf. *Rechtfertigung und Versöhnung*, §37; 284.
35 *Unterricht in der christlichen Religion*, §16.
36 Particular attention should be paid to §§14 and 15 of the second volume of *Rechtfertigung und Versöhnung* (Bonn, 1874). Note particularly the reference to the study of Ludwig Diestel, 'Die Idee der Gerechtigkeit, vorzüglich im Alten Testament, biblisch-theologisch dargestellt', *Jahrbuch für deutsche Theologie* 5 (1860), 173–204: *Rechtfertigung und Versöhnung* II, §14; 102 n. 1.
Cf. *WA* 2.504.25: 'iustitia Dei in scripturis fere semper pro fide et gratia accipitur'.
38 *Rechtfertigung und Versöhnung*, §1; 5.

39 Note the question raised by Martin Kähler, *Zur Lehre von der Versöhnung* (Leipzig, 1898), 337: 'Hat Christus bloß irrige Ansichten über eine unwandelbare Sachlage berichtigt, oder ist er der Begründer einer veränderten Sachlage?' For the Christology of Ritschl and Harnack, of relevance here, see Alister E. McGrath, *The Making of Modern German Christology: From the Enlightenment to Pannenberg* (Oxford, 1986), 53–68.

40 See Schäfer, 'Rechtfertigungslehre bei Ritschl und Kähler', 77–85.

41 See McGrath, *The Making of Modern German Christology*, 69–93.

Notes to §37

1 See W. Pressel, *Die Kriegspredigt 1914–1918 in der evangelischen Kirche Deutschlands* (Göttingen, 1967); K. Hammer, *Deutsche Kriegstheologie (1870–1918)* (München, 1971).

2 The 'Manifesto of the Intellectuals' is particularly significant in this respect: see W. Härle, 'Der Aufruf der 93 Intellektuellen und Karl Barths Bruch mit der liberalen Theologie', *ZThK* 72 (1975), 207–24.

3 Karl Holl, 'Was verstand Luther unter Religion?', in *Gesammelte Aufsätze zur Kirchengeschichte* (3 vols: Tübingen, 1928), I.1–110.

4 'Die Gerechtigkeit Gottes', in *Das Wort Gottes und die Theologie*, 5–17.

5 'Die Gerechtigkeit Gottes', 5.

6 'Die Gerechtigkeit Gottes', 7.

7 'Die Gerechtigkeit Gottes', 10.

8 'Die Gerechtigkeit Gottes', 11.

9 'Die Gerechtigkeit Gottes', 11–12.

10 For some useful reflections upon the impact of the *Rechtswillkür* of The Third Reich upon Protestant understanding of law, see Ernst Wolf, 'Zum protestantischen Rechtsdenken', in *Peregrinatio* II: *Studien zur reformatorischen Theologie, zum Kirchenrecht und zur Sozialethik* (München, 1965), 191–206.

11 'Die Gerechtigkeit Gottes', 12–13.

12 'Die Gerechtigkeit Gottes', 13.

13 'Die Gerechtigkeit Gottes', 13.

14 'Die Gerechtigkeit Gottes', 14.

15 'Die Gerechtigkeit Gottes', 15.

16 See Althaus, 'Gottes Gottheit als Sinn der Rechtfertigungslehre Luthers'.

17 *Kirchliche Dogmatik*, IV/1 §61, 1; 573–89. On Barth's doctrine of justification in general, see Küng, *Rechtfertigung*; G. C. Berkouwer, *The Triumph of Grace in the Theology of Karl Barth* (London, 1956); McGrath, 'Justification: Barth, Trent and Küng'.

18 *Kirchliche Dogmatik*, IV/1 §61, 1; 581. See McGrath, 'Karl Barth and the Articulus Iustificationis'.

19 WA 39 1.205.2–5. Barth refers to this dictum: *Kirchliche Dogmatik*, IV/1 §61, 1; 582.

20 Wolf, 'Die Rechtfertigungslehre als Mitte und Grenze reformatorischer Theologie', 14. The reference to the *subjectum theologiae* derives from WA 40 II.328.17–21: 'Theologiae proprium subiectum est homo peccati reus

ac perditus et Deus iustificans ac salvator hominis peccatoris. Quicquid extra hoc subiectum in theologia queritur aut disputatur, est error et venenum.'

21 Thus Luther's celebrated distinction between *Deus absconditus* and *Deus revelatus* arises within the context of his soteriology: see H. Bandt, *Luthers Lehre vom verborgenen Gott: Eine Untersuchung zu dem offenbarungsgeschichtlichen Ansatz seiner Theologie* (Berlin, 1958). Note the reference to Barth in the preface.

22 Note the reference at *Kirchliche Dogmatik*, IV/1 §61, 1; 581.

23 *Kirchliche Dogmatik*, IV/1 §61, 1; 583: 'Man tut aber in der Theologie gut, über die Bedürfnisse und Notwendigkeiten des Tages hinaus immer auch auf weitere Sicht zu denken, sich in allem noch so berechtigten Reagieren Maß zu auferlegen, sich der Grenzen der jeweils herrschenden "Anliegen" (mögen diese noch so echt und begründet sein!) bewußt zu bleiben.' Perhaps Barth has forgotten that his own theology is essentially a reaction against a particular theological position (that of the liberal school), and might therefore be subject to precisely the same criticism.

24 *Kirchliche Dogmatik*, IV/1 §61, 1; 583.

25 See M. F. Wiles, *The Making of Christian Doctrine: A Study in the Principles of Early Doctrinal Development* (Cambridge, 1978), 94–112.

26 *Kirchliche Dogmatik*, IV/1 §61, 1; 583. Cf. *Kirchliche Dogmatik*, IV/1 §61, 1; 578.

27 *Kirchliche Dogmatik*, IV/1 §61, 1; 584. Note also Barth's suggestion that a preoccupation with the question of how a gracious God may be found leads to a 'certain narcissism': *Kirchliche Dogmatik*, IV/1 §61, 1; 588: 'Die Frage: Wie kriege ich einen gnädigen Gott? in höchsten Ehren! Sie ist aber dem Protestantismus – jedenfalls dem europäischen und inbesondere dem deutschen Protestantismus – allzu lange Anlaß und Versuchung gewesen, einem gewissen Narzismus zu huldigen und gerade nach der nun zuletzt angedeuteten Seite auf der Stelle zu treten.' More generally, see Eberhard Leppin, 'Luthers Frage nach dem gnädigen Gott – heute', *ZThK* 61 (1964), 89–102.

28 For a comparison of the liberals, Brunner and Barth on this point, see Alister E. McGrath, *The Making of Modern German Christology: From the Enlightenment to Pannenberg* (Oxford, 1986), 105–6.

29 See the analysis of Hans Urs von Balthasar, *Karl Barth: Darstellung und Deutung seiner Theologie* (Köln, 1961), 210, who argues that Schleiermacher (as a typical representative of this school) determines Barth's theological concerns and methods as 'der Prägstock, der ein nicht mehr auszulöschendes Zeichen aufdrückt, die Form, aus der man bei aller materiellen Entgegensetzung, sich nicht mehr befreit'.

30 Holl, 'Was verstand Luther unter Religion?'. Holl appears to treat Luther's doctrine of justification as an aspect of his *Gewissensreligion*.

31 On this theme in Luther's theology, see G. Aulén, 'Die drei Haupttypen des christlichen Versöhnungslehre', *ZSTh* 7 (1930), 301–38; M. Leinhard, *Luther témoin de Jésus Christ* (Paris, 1968).

32 A monologue which von Balthasar derides as 'ein gespenstischer Spuk ohne Wirklichkeit': von Balthasar, *Karl Barth*, 225–6; 380.
33 See the important essay of Jacques de Senarclens, 'La concentration christologique', in *Antwort: Karl Barth zum 70. Geburtstag* (Zürich, 1956), 190–207.
34 Karl Barth, *Die protestantische Theologie im 19. Kahrhundert* (Zürich, 1952), 375–7.
35 On this, and especially Barth's concept of *das Nichtige*, see Wolf Krötke, *Sünde und Nichtiges bei Karl Barth* (Berlin, 1971).
36 See Alister E. McGrath, 'From the Reformation to the Enlightenment', in *The Science of Theology*, ed. P. D. L. Avis (London, 1986), for further details.
37 We first demonstrated this point recently: McGrath, 'Karl Barth als Aufklärer?'. Cf. G. Ebeling, *Lutherstudien* III (Tübingen, 1985), 492–573.
38 Barth, *Die protestantische Theologie*, 16–21.
39 *Kirchliche Dogmatik*, IV/1 §57, 1; 16: 'Wir müssens uns jetzt vergegenwärtigen, daß die christliche Botschaft in ihrer Mitte keinen Begriff und keine Idee ausspricht und auch nicht von einer anonymen, in Begriffen und Ideen als Wahrheit und Wirklichkeit aufzufangenden Geschichte Bericht erstattet ... Aber eben von dieser Geschichte und ihrer inkludierenden Kraft und Bedeutung berichtet sie in der Weise, daß sie einen Namen ausspricht ... Sie können gerade nur der Umschreibung dieses Namens dienen: des Namens Jesu Christi.' See further H. J. Iwand, 'Vom Primat der Christologie', in *Antwort: Karl Barth zum 70. Geburtstag* (Zürich, 1956), 172–89. S. W. Sykes, 'Barth on the Centre of Theology', in *Karl Barth: Studies of his Theological Method* (Oxford, 1979), 17–54. For Barth's Christology, see McGrath, *The Making of Modern German Christology*, 94–126.
40 See H. Vogel, 'Praedestinatio gemina: Die Lehre von der ewigen Gnadenwahl', in *Theologische Aufsätze: Karl Barth zum 50. Geburtstag* (München, 1936), 222–42; Konrad Stock, *Anthropologie der Verheißung: Karl Barths Lehre vom Menschen als dogmatisches Problem* (München, 1980), 65–72.
41 *Kirchliche Dogmatik*, II/2 §33, 2; 176–8.
42 *Kirchliche Dogmatik*, II/2 §33, 2; 181.
43 *Kirchliche Dogmatik*, II/2 §33, 2; 183: 'Prädestination heißt: der von Gott von Ewigkeit her beschlossene Freispruch des Menschen von der Verwerfung zu Gottes eigenen Ungusten, der Freispruch des Menschen, in welchem Gott sich selbst ... zum Verworfenen an Stelle des Freigesprochenen bestimmt.'
44 *Kirchliche Dogmatik*, IV/1 §57, 3; 72–3: 'Gottes Gnade triumphiert also – und das ist das Geschehen der Erfüllung des Bundes in Jesus Christus – über den Menschen und seine Sünde. Aber sie bekommt und hat nun den Charakter jenes "Dennoch" und "Trotzdem". Sie triumphiert nun – mitten im Gegensatz des Menschen zu ihr – erst recht wunderbar, einseitig, selbstherrlich.'
45 *Kirchliche Dogmatik*, IV/1 §59, 2; 252.
46 *Kirchliche Dogmatik*, IV/1 §60, 1; 458.

47 *Kirchliche Dogmatik*, III/2 §43, 2; 43: 'Die Lehre vom *liberum arbitrium* des sündigen Menschen ist ein Spottgebilde, das in alle Winde verwehen muß, wenn es von Erkenntnis der Güte Gottes auch nur von Ferne berührt wird.'

48 *Kirchliche Dogmatik*, III/2 §43, 2; 31: 'jene Verkehrtheit und Verderbnis ist radikal und total'. Cf. Stock, *Anthropologie der Verheißung*, 102–11.

49 *Kirchliche Dogmatik*, IV/1 §61, 4; 679–718, especially 701.

50 *Kirchliche Dogmatik*, II/2 §33, 2; 183: 'und heißt Prädestination Nicht-Verwerfung des Menschen'.

51 e.g., Berkouwer, *Triumph of Grace*, 262–96.

52 *Kirchliche Dogmatik*, IV/1 §60, 1; 410, where the following thesis is established: 'Daß der Mensch der Mensch der Sünde ist, was seine Sünde ist und was sie für ihn bedeutet, das wird erkannt, indem Jesus Christus erkannt wird, nur so, so wirklich'.

53 *Kirchliche Dogmatik*, IV/1 §61, 1; 574–5 (our italics).

54 *Kirchliche Dogmatik*, IV/1 §60, 1; 578.

55 E. Brunner, *Dogmatik* I: *Die christliche Lehre von Gott* (Zürich, 1946), 375–9. See further E. Buess, 'Zur Prädestinationslehre Karl Barths', in *Heilsgeschehen und Welt: Theologische Traktate* I (Göttingen, 1965), 77–132; Stock, *Anthropologie der Verheißung*, 44–61.

56 M. Kähler, *Zur Lehre von der Versöhnung* (Leipzig, 1898), 337.

57 For further discussion, see McGrath, 'Karl Barth als Aufklärer?', 280–3.

Notes to §38

1 The question of how it is possible for God to justify the sinner was, of course, by far the more important, raising questions concerning the nature of the 'righteousness of God', the work of Christ, and such. The question of the nature of justification, once settled by Augustine, only became an issue once more at the time of the Reformation itself.

2 See Jürgen Moltmann, 'Justification and New Creation', in *The Future of Creation* (London, 1979), 149–71, especially 151–2; 157–64.

3 See Walter Kern, 'Atheismus – Christentum – emanzipierte Gesellschaft', *ZKTh* 91 (1969), 289–321. Cf. C. Villa-Vicencio, 'Protestantism, Modernity and Justification by Faith', *SJTh* 38 (1985), 369–82. Subilia notes that contemporary interest lies in the question of the justification of *God*, rather than of man: *La giustificazione per fede*, 343–51.

4 See Eberhard Leppin, 'Luthers Frage nach dem gnädigen Gott – heute', *ZThK* 61 (1964), 89–102.

5 The trend is well illustrated by the first four statements of the document *Justification Today*, issued by the Helsinki Assembly of the Lutheran World Federation (1963): see '"Justification Today": Document 75 – Assembly and Final Versions', *Lutheran World* 12/1 Supplement (1965), 1–11. On the background to this document, see Peter Kjeseth and Paul Hoffmann, 'Document 75', *Lutheran World* 11 (1964), 83–6. For further comment, see Albrecht Peters, 'Systematische Besinnung zu einer Neuinterpretation der reformatorischen Rechtfertigungslehre', in *Rechtfertigung im neuzeitlichen Lebenszusammenhang: Studien zur Neuinterpretation*

der Rechtfertigungslehre, ed. W. Lohff and C. Walther (Gütersloh, 1974), 107–25.

6 T. Langan, *The Meaning of Heidegger: A Critical Study of an Existentialist Phenomenology* (London, 1959); A. Chapell, *L'Ontologie phénoménologique de Heidegger: un commentaire de 'Sein und Zeit'* (Paris, 1962). On Heidegger's divergence from Husserl at points, see J. McGinley, 'Heidegger's Concern for the Lived-World in his Dasein Analysis', *Philosophy Today* 16 (1972), 92–116.

7 Heidegger, *Sein und Zeit* (Tübingen, 1927), 41–2.

8 See H. Diem, *Die Existenzdialektik von Sören Kierkegaard* (Zürich, 1950); K. E. Lögstrup, *Kierkegaarde und Heideggers Existenzanalyse und ihr Verhältnis zur Verkündigung* (Berlin, 1950).

9 See Jean Beaufret, 'Heidegger et la théologie', in *Heidegger et la question de Dieu*, ed. R. Kearny and J. S. O'Leary (Paris, 1980), 19–36.

10 See J. A. Macquarrie, *An Existentialist Theology* (London, 1973), 29–105; 127–49, for an excellent analysis.

11 *Sein und Zeit*, 177.

12 *Sein und Zeit*, 179. Cf. Macquarrie, *Existentialist Theology*, 78–97.

13 R. Lorenz, *Die unvollendete Befreiung vom Nominalismus: Martin Luther und die Grenzen hermeneutischer Theologie bei Gerhard Ebeling* (Gütersloh, 1973), 131–44. A similar point is made by H. Blumenberg, *Die Legitimät der Neuzeit* (Frankfurt, 1966).

14 See G. Ebeling, 'Gewißheit und Zweifel: Die Situation des Glaubens im Zeitalter nach Luther und Descartes', *ZThK* 64 (1967), 282–324.

15 On this, see Alister E. McGrath, *The Making of Modern German Christology: from the Enlightenment to Pannenberg* (Oxford, 1986), 127–43.

16 Bultmann, *Glauben und Verstehen* (4 vols: Tübingen, 1964–5), 2.111.

17 Gerhardt Kuhlmann, 'Zum theologischen Problem der Existenz: Fragen an Rudolf Bultmann', *ZThK* 10 (1929), 28–57.

18 Bultmann, 'Die Geschichtlichkeit des Daseins und der Glaube: Antwort an Gerhardt Kuhlmann', *ZThK* 11 (1930), 339–64.

19 The original essay, 'Rechtfertigung und Zweifel', was published in the 1924 *Vorträge der theologischen Konferenz zu Gießen*. Cf. Tillich, *The Protestant Era* (London, 1951), xxix.

20 For what follows, see 'The Protestant Message and the Man of Today', in *The Protestant Era*, 189–204.

21 See John P. Clayton, *The Concept of Correlation: Paul Tillich and the Possibility of a Mediating Theology* (Berlin, 1980).

22 See Tillich, 'You are Accepted', in *The Shaking of the Foundations* (New York, 1948), 153–63. Despite the verbal parallels with the concept of *acceptatio Dei*, it is difficult to see quite how Tillich understands man to be accepted *by God*.

23 Ebeling, *Dogmatik des christlichen Glaubens* (3 vols: Tübingen, 1979), 3.205–6, 218. On the concept of 'relational ontology', which underlies Ebeling's statements, see Miikka Ruokanen, *Hermeneutics as an Ecumenical Method in the Theology of Gerhard Ebeling* (Helsinki, 1982), 72–100.

24 *Dogmatik des christlichen Glaubens*, 3.195–200.

25 For the relation of anthropology, the Word of God, and justification according to Eberhard Jüngel, see J. B. Webster, *Eberhard Jüngel: An Introduction to His Theology* (Cambridge, 1986), 93–103.
26 See J. M. Robinson, *A New Quest of the Historical Jesus* (London, 1959); McGrath, *The Making of Modern German Christology*, 161–85.
27 The contribution of Eberhard Jüngel is particularly significant: Jüngel, *Paulus und Jesus: Eine Untersuchung zur Präzisierung der Frage nach dem Ursprung der Christologie* (Tübingen, 1962).
28 McGrath, 'Justification and Christology'; *idem*, 'Der articulus iustificationis als axiomatischer Grundsatz des christlichen Glaubens'.

Notes to §39

1 Donfried, 'Justification and Last Judgement in Paul'. See also Cosgrove, 'Justification in Paul'; Seifrid, *Justification by faith*.
2 Hultgren, *Paul's Gospel and Mission*.
3 Sanders, *Paul and Palestinian Judaism*; idem, *Paul, The Law, and the Jewish People*. See further Dunn, 'The New Perspective on Paul'; Westerholm, *Israel's Law and the Church's Faith*; Wright, *The Climax of the Covenant*.
4 Gundry, 'Grace, Works and Staying Saved in Paul'.
5 Käsemann, *New Testament Questions of Today*; idem, *Commentary on Romans*. See also S. K. Williams, 'The "Righteousness of God" in Romans', *Journal of Biblical Literature* 99 (1980), 241–90.
6 Stuhlmacher, *Gerechtigkeit Gottes bei Paulus*; see also J. Reumann, *Righteousness in the New Testament* (Philadelphia, 1982); J. A. Ziesler, *The Meaning of Righteousness in Paul* (Cambridge, 1972).
7 K. Stendahl, *Paul among Jews and Gentiles* (Philadelphia, 1976).
8 Reumann, *Righteousness in the New Testament*, passim.
9 N. M. Watson, 'Justified by faith, judged by works: an antimony?', *New Testament Studies* 29 (1983), 209–21.
10 C. J. A. Hickling, 'Centre and Periphery in the Thought of St Paul', *Studia Biblica 3* (Sheffield, 1978*)*, 199–214. See also Sanders, *Paul and Palestinian Judaism*; idem, *Paul, The Law, and the Jewish People*; Stendahl, *Paul among Jews and Gentiles*; D. V. Way, *The Lordship of Christ: Ernst Käsemann's Interpretation of Paul's Theology* (Oxford, 1991).
11 C. E. B. Cranfield, *The Epistle to the Romans* (2 vols: Edinburgh, 1975).

Notes to §40

1 Hans Küng, *Justification: The Doctrine of Karl Barth and a Catholic Reflection* (London, 1964).
2 Küng, *Justification*, 264.
3 See McGrath, 'Justification: Barth, Trent and Küng'; idem, 'ARCIC

II and Justification: Some Difficulties and Obscurities relating to Anglican and Roman Catholic Teaching on Justification'.

4 'The Gospel and the Church', published jointly in *Lutheran World* 19 (1972), 259–73, and *Worship* 46 (1972), 326–51. The discussion documents underlying this statement, as well as the statement itself, may be found in *Evangelium - Welt - Kirche: Schlußbericht und Referate der römisch-katholisch/evangelisch-lutherischen Studienkommission 'Das Evangelium und die Kirchen' 1967-71* (Frankfurt, 1975).

5 'Justification by Faith', *Origins: NC Documentary Service*, 6 October 1983, 13/17, 277–304.

6 J. Reumann, *Righteousness in the New Testament: 'Justification' in Lutheran-Catholic Dialogue* (Philadelphia/New York, 1982). This document should be read as background material to 'Justification by Faith'.

7 'Justification by Faith', §156, pp. 297–8, which we have paraphrased.

8 'Justification by Faith' §157; p. 298.

9 'Justification by Faith', §158; p. 298.

10 'Justification by Faith', §56; p. 286.

11 *Salvation and the Church: An Agreed Statement by the Second Anglican - Roman Catholic International Commission* (London, 1987).

12 'Justification by Faith', §116; p. 292.

Bibliography

1. Primary literature

a. Collected works

Die Bekenntnisschriften der reformierten Kirche, ed. E. F. K. Müller (Leipzig, 1903)

Die Bekenntnisschriften der evangelisch-lutherischen Kirche, 2nd edn (Göttingen, 1952)

Concilium Tridentinum diarorum, actorum, epistularum, tractatuum nova collectio, ed. Societas Goeresiana (Freiburg, 1901–)

Corpus Christianorum Series Latina (Turnholt, 1953–)

Corpus scriptorum ecclesiasticorum Latinorum (Vienna, 1886–)

Denzinger, H., *Enchiridion Symbolorum Definitionum et Declarationum de Rebus Fidei et Morum*, 24–25th edn (Barcelona, 1948)

Hardwick, C., *A History of the Articles of Religion*, 3rd edn (London, 1890)

Lloyd, C., *Formularies of Faith put forth by Authority during the Reign of Henry VIII* (Oxford, 1825)

Migne, J. P., *Patrologia cursus completus series Latina* (221 vols.: Paris, 1844–64)

Patrologia cursus completus series Graeca (162 vols.: Paris, 1857–66)

b. Biblical

Biblia Hebraica, ed. R. Kittel, 17th edn (Stuttgart, 1972)

Septuaginta, ed. A. Rahlfs, 9th edn (Stuttgart, 1975)

Biblia Sacra iuxta Vulgatam versionem (Stuttgart, 1975)

c. Primary sources

Aegidius Romanus *Commentarius in secundum librum sententiarum* (2 vols.: Venice, 1581)

Albertus Magnus *Opera Omnia*, ed. S. C. A. Borgnet (38 vols.: Paris, 1890–9)

Bibliography

Alexander of Hales, *Glossa in IV. libros ententiarum* (4 vols.: Quaracchi, 1951–7)

Quaestiones disputatae 'antequam esset frater' (3 vols.: Quaracchi, 1960)

Alexander of Hales (attributed), *Summa Theologica* (4 vols.: Quaracchi, 1924–48)

Alsted, Johann Heinrich, *Theologia scholastica didactica* (Hanover, 1618)

Andrewes, Launcelot, *Works* (11 vols.: London, 1841–52)

Anselm of Canterbury, *Opera Omnia*, ed. F. S. Schmitt (6 vols.: Stuttgart, 1968)

Anselm of Laon, *Anselms von Laon systematische Sentenzen*, ed. F. P. Bliemetzrieder (Münster, 1919)

Arminius, Jakobus, *Works* (3 vols.: London, 1825–75)

Baius, Michel, *Opera* (Cologne, 1696)

Barlow, Thomas, *Two Letters written by the Rt Rev. Thomas Barlow* (London, 1701)

Barrow, Isaac, *Theological Works*, ed. A. Napier (9 vols.: Cambridge, 1859)

Barth, Karl, *Das Wort Gottes und die Theologie* (Munich, 1925)

Kirchliche Dogmatik (13 vols.: Zurich, 1932–68)

Baxter, Richard, *Aphorisms on Justification* (London, 1649)

A Treatise of Justifying Righteousness (London, 1676)

[Benedetto da Mantova, Dom?], *Trattato utilissimo di Giesu Cristo crocifisso verso i Cristiani*, ed. Salvatore Caponetto (Florence, 1972)

Beveridge, William, *Theological Works* (12 vols.: Oxford, 1844–8)

Beza, Theodore, *Tractationes theologicae*, 2nd edn (Geneva, 1632)

Biel, Gabriel, *Collectorium circa quattuor Iibros sententiarum*, ed. W. Werbeck and U. Hofmann (4 vols.: Tübingen, 1973–84)

Canonis missae expositio, ed. H. A. Oberman and W. J. Courtenay (4 vols.: Wiesbaden, 1963–67)

Sermones dominicales de tempore (Hagenau, 1510)

Bonaventure *Opera Omnia* (10 vols.: Quaracchi, 1882–1902)

Bradwardine, Thomas *De causa Dei contra Pelagium* (London, 1618)

Bramhall, John, *Works* (5 vols.: Oxford, 1842–5)

Brochmand, Jesper Rasmussen, *Universae theologiae systema* (Ulm, 1638)

Bucanus, Guillaume, *Institutiones theologicae* (n.p., 1604)

Bucer, Martin, *Praelectiones in epistolam ad Ephesios* (Basel, 1561)

Metaphrasis et enarratio in epistolam ad Romanos (Basel, 1562)

Budde, Johann Franz, *Institutiones theologiae dogmaticae* (Jena, 1723)

Bull, George, *Harmonia Apostolica* (London, 1842)

Bullinger, Heinrich, *Sermonum decades quinque* (Zurich, 1552)

De gratia Dei iustificante (Zurich, 1554)

Burmann, Franz, *Synopsis theologiae* (Amsterdam, 1699)

Calov, Abraham, *Systema Locorum theologicorum* (Wittenberg, 1655)

Calvin, John, *Opera omnia quae supersunt* (59 vols.: Brunswick, 1863–1900)

Opera selecta, ed. P. Barth and W. Niesel (5 vols.: Munich, 1922–36)

Bibliography

Chemnitz, Martin, *Loci theologici* (3 vols.: Frankfurt, 1599)
   Examinis Concilii Tridentini (Frankfurt, 1646)
Clarke, Samuel, *The Saints Nosegay, or, 741 Spiritual Flowers* (London, 1642)
Cocceius, Johannes, *Summa theologiae* (Amsterdam, 1665)
   Opera (8 vols.: Amsterdam, 1673–5)
Contarini, Gasparo, *Regesten und Briefen*, ed. F. Dittrich (Braunsberg, 1881)
   Gegenreformatorische Schriften 1530–42 (Aschendorf, 1923)
Cosin, John, *Works* (5 vols.: Oxford, 1843–55)
Cotton, John, *Gods Mercie mixed with his Iustice* (London, 1641)
   Christ the Fountaine of Life (London, 1651)
   A Treatise of the Covenant of Grace (London, 1659)
Cranmer, Thomas, *Works* (2 vols.: Cambridge, 1844–6)
Dante Aligheri, *La divina commedia*, ed. D. Mattalia (3 vols.: Milan, 1975)
Davenant, John, *A Treatise on Justification, or the 'Disputatio de Iustitia Habituali et Actuali'* (London, 1844)
Downham, George, *A Treatise of Justification* (London, 1639)
Duns Scotus, *Commentaria Oxoniensia* (2 vols.: Quaracchi, 1912–14)
   Opera Omnia, ed. C. Balic (Rome, 1950–)
Durandus of St Pourçain, *In Petri Lombardi sententias theologicas commentariorum* (2 vols.: Venice, 1571)
Eck, Johannes, *Chrysospassus praedestinationis* (Augsburg, 1514)
   In primum librum sententiarum annotatiunculae, ed. W. L. Moore (Leiden, 1976)
Edwards, Jonathan, *Five Discourses on Justification by Faith* (Boston, 1738)
   Works, ed. E. Hickman (2 vols.: Edinburgh, 1974)
Erasmus, Desiderius, *Novum Instrumentum omne* (Basel, 1516)
   Opera Omnia, ed. J. Clericus (10 vols.: Leiden, 1703–6)
Fisher, John, *Opera* (Würzburg, 1597)
   English Works, ed. J. E. B. Mayor (EETS extra series 27: London, 1876)
Forbes, William, *Considerationes modestae et pacificae* (2 vols.: London, 1850–6)
Frith, John, *Whole Workes* (London, 1573)
Gerhard, Johann, *Loci communes*, ed. Cotta (10 vols.: Tübingen, 1768)
Godescalc of Orbais, *Œuvres théologiques et grammaticales*, ed. C. Lambot (Louvain, 1945)
Goodwin, John, *Imputatio fidei; or A Treatise of Justification* (London, 1615)
Gregory of Rimini, *Lectura super primum et secundum sententiarum*, ed. A. D. Trapp (6 vols.: Berlin/New York, 1979–84)
Gropper, Johann, *Enchiridion Christianae Institutiones* (Cologne, 1536)
Hafenreffer, Matthias, *Loci theologici* (Tübingen, 1603)
Hall, Joseph, *Works* (12 vols.: Oxford, 1837–9)
Hammond, Henry, *A Practical Catechism* (London, 1847)

Bibliography

Heidegger, Johann Heinrich, *Medulla theologiae Christianae* (Zurich, 1616)

Henke, Heinrich Philipp Konrad, *Lineamenta institutionum fidei Christianae* (Helmstedt, 1793)

Hincmar of Reims, 'Zwei Schriften des Erzbischofs Hinkmar von Reims', ed. W. Gundlach, *ZKG* 10 (1889), 92–145, 258–310

Holcot, Robert, *Opus super sapientiam Salomonis* (Hagenau, 1494)
Quaestiones super IV libros sententiarum (Leiden, 1497)

Hooker, Richard, *Works*, ed. J. Keble, 3rd edn (3 vols.: Oxford, 1845)

Hooker, Thomas, *The Soules Preparation for Christ* (London, 1632)
The Unbeleevers Preparing for Christ (London, 1638)
The Soules Humiliation (London, 1638)
Thomas Hooker: Writings in England and Holland 1626–33 (Harvard Theological Studies 28: Cambridge, Mass., 1975)

Huss, John, *Opera Omnia*, ed. V. Flajshans (3 vols.: Prague, 1903–8)

Hutter, Leonhard, *Compendium locorum theologicorum* (Wittenberg, 1652)

Jackson, Thomas, *Works* (12 vols.: Oxford, 1844)

Jansenius, Cornelius, *Augustinus* (Paris, 1641)

John of La Rochelle, *Die neuen Quästionen der Gnadentheologie des Johannes von Rupella*, ed. L. Hodl (Munich, 1964)

Kant, Immanuel, *Gesammelte Schriften* (22 vols.: Berlin, 1902–42)

Knewstub, John, *Lectures upon the Twentieth Chapter of Exodus* (London, 1577)

Knox, Alexander, *Remains*, ed. J. H. Newman, 2nd edn (4 vols.: London, 1836–7)

Koenig, Johann Friedrich, *Theologia positiva acroamatica*, 11th edn (Rostok/Leipzig, 1703)

Locke, John, *Reasonableness of Christianity*, in *Works* VII (London, 1823), 1–159
Essay concerning Human Understanding, ed. P. H. Nidditch (Oxford, 1975)

Luther, Martin, *Kritische Gesamtausgabe* (Weimar, 1883–)

Maresius, Samuel, *Collegium theologicum* (Geneva, 1662)

Mastricht, Peter van, *Theoretico-practica theologia* (Rhenum/Amsterdam, 1725)

Matthew of Aquasparta *Quaestiones disputatae de gratia*, ed. V. Doucet (Quaracchi, 1935)

Melanchthon, Philip, *Opera omnia quae supersunt* (28 vols.: Brunswick, 1834–60)
Werke in Auswahl, ed. R. Stupperich (8 vols.: Gutersloh, 1951–)

Molina, Luis de, *Concordia liberii arbitrii cum gratiae donis* (Lisbon, 1588)

Morgan, Thomas, *The Moral Philosopher* (3 vols.: London, 1738–40)

Mosheim, Lorenz vom, *Elementa theologiae dogmaticae* (Nuremburg, 1758)

Mosse, Miles, *Iustifying and Saving Faith distinguished from the Faith of the Devils* (Cambridge, 1614)

Musculus, Wolfgang, *Loci communes sacrae theologiae* (Basel, 1561)

Newman, John Henry, *Remarks on Certain Passages in the Thirty-Nine Articles* (Tract 90: Oxford, 1841)

 Lectures on the Doctrine of Justification, 3rd edn (London/Cambridge, 1874)

Odo Rigaldi, *In II Sent. dist. xxvi–xxix*, ed. J. Bouvy, in 'Les questions sur la grâce dans le Commentaire des Sentences d'Odon Rigaud', *RThAM* 27 (1960), 305–43; 'La nécessité de la grâce dans le Commentaire des Sentences d'Odon Rigaud', *RThAM* 28 (1961), 69–96

Owen, John, *Works*, ed. T. Russell (21 vols.: London, 1826)

Perkins, William, *Workes* (3 vols.: Cambridge, 1608–9)

Petavius, Dionysius, *Opus de theologicus dogmatibus* (3 vols.: Antwerp, 1700)

Peter Aureoli, *Commentarorium in primum librum sententiarum* (Rome, 1596)

Peter of Bergamo, *Summa Aurea* (Venice, 1593)

Peter Cantor, *Summa de sacramentis et animae consiliis*, ed. J.-A. Dugauquier (5 vols.: Louvain/Lille, 1954–67)

Peter Lombard, *Libri IV Sententiarum*, 2nd edn (2 vols.: Quaracchi, 1916)

Peter of Tarantaise, *In IV libros sententiarum commentaria* (4 vols.: Toulouse, 1649–52)

Pfaff, Christoph Matthaeus, *Institutiones theologiae dogmaticae et moralis* (Tubingen, 1720)

Polanus a Polansdorf, Amandus, *Syntagma theologiae Christianae* (Geneva, 1612)

Quenstedt, Johannes Andreas, *Theologia didactico-polemica* (Wittenberg, 1685)

Richard of Middleton, *Supra quattuor libros sententiarum* (4 vols.: Brescia, 1591)

Rijssen, Leonhard van, *Compendium theologiae didactico elencticae* (Amsterdam, 1695)

Ritschl, A. B., *Die christliche Lehre von der Rechtfertigung und Versöhnung*. III. *Die positive Entwickelung der Lehre*, 3rd edn (Bonn, 1888)

Robert of Melun, *Questiones theologice de epistolis Pauli*, ed. R. M. Martin (Louvain, 1938)

Roger of Marston, *Quaestiones disputatae de statu naturae lapsae* (Quaracchi, 1932)

Roland of Cremona, *Summae magistri Rolandi Cremonensis*, ed. A. Cortesi (Bergamo, 1962)

Sanderson, Robert, *Sermons*, ed. P. Montgomery (2 vols.: London, 1841)

Scherzer, J. A., *Breviculus theologicus*, 3rd edn (Leipzig, 1680)

Schleiermacher, F. D. E., *Der christliche Glaube*, 4th edn (2 vols.: Berlin, 1842–3)

Simon of Tournai, *Les disputations de Simon de Tournai*, ed. J. Warichez (Louvain, 1932)

Bibliography

Soto, Domingo de, *De natura et gratia* (Paris, 1549)

    In epistolam ad Romanos commentarii (Antwerp, 1550)

Stapleton, Thomas, *Opera* (4 vols.: Paris, 1620)

Steinbach, Wendelin, *Opera Exegetica quae supersunt omnia*, ed. H. Feld (Wiesbaden, 1976)

Steinbart, Gotthelf Samuel, *System der reinen Philosophie oder Gluckselig-keitslehre des Christenthums* (Zullichau, 1778)

Suarez, Francisco de, *Opera omnia* (28 vols.: Paris, 1856–78)

Taylor, Jeremy, *Works*, ed. C. P. Eden (10 vols.: London, 1847–54)

Teller, Wilhelm Abraham, *Die Religion der Vollkommnern* (Berlin, 1792)

Thomas Aquinas, *Opera Omnia* (31 vols.: Rome, 1882–1947)

    Scriptum super libros sententiarum Magistri Petri Lombardi, ed. P. Mandonnet and F. Moos (4 vols.: Paris, 1929–47)

    Quaestiones disputatae, 2nd edn, ed. R. Spiazzi (2 vols.: Rome, 1949)

    Quaestiones quodlibetales, 9th edn, ed. R. Spiazzi (Rome, 1956)

Thomas of Strasbourg, *Commentaria in IIII libros sententiarum* (Venice, 1564)

Tindal, Matthew, *Christianity as Old as the Creation*, ed. G. Gawlick (Stuttgart, 1968)

Töllner, Johann Gottlieb, *Der thatige Gehorsam Christi untersucht* (Breslau, 1768)

    Theologische Untersuchungen (2 vols.: Riga, 1772–4)

Toland, John, *Christianity not Mysterious*, ed. G. Gawlick (Stuttgart, 1964)

Turrettini, Franciscus, *Institutio theologiae elencticae* (Geneva, 1688)

Tyndale, William, *Works* (3 vols.: Cambridge, 1848)

Ussher, James, *Whole Works*, ed. C. R. Elrington and J. H. Todd (17 vols.: Dublin/London, 1847–64)

Valdés, Juan de, *Diálogo de doctrina Cristiana*, ed. B. F. Stockwell (Mexico, 1946)

    Los ciento diez divinas consideraciones, ed. J. I. T. Idigoras (Salamanca, 1975)

Vega, Andrés de, *Opusculum de iustificatione* (Venice, 1546)

    De iustificatione doctrina universa (Cologne, 1572)

Walker, George, *A Defence of the True Sense and Meaning of the Words of the Holy Apostle: Rom. 4 ver. 3.5.9* (London, 1641)

Wendelin, Friedrich, *Christianae theologiae libri II* (Amsterdam, 1646)

Wesley, John, *Works* (14 vols.: London, 1829–31)

    Standard Sermons (2 vols.: London, 1921)

William of Auvergne, *Opera Omnia* (2 vols.: Paris, 1674)

William of Auxerre, *Summa Aurea in quattuor libros sententiarum* (Paris, 1500)

William of Ockham, *Commentaria in quattuor libros sententiarum* (Leiden, 1495)

    Tractatus de praedestinatione et de praescientia Dei et de futuris contingentibus, ed. P. Boehmer (New York, 1945)

Bibliography

Opera philosophica et theologica (9 vols.: New York, 1966–)

Wollebius, Johannes, *Christianae theologiae compendium* (Amsterdam, 1637)

Zwingli, Huldrych, *Sämtliche Werke* (4 vols.: Zurich, 1905–)

2. Secondary studies

Abercrombie, N., *The Origins of Jansenism* (Oxford, 1936)

Alfaro, J., 'Sobrenatural y pecado original en Bayo', *RET* 12 (1952), 3–76

Althaus, P., 'Gottes Gottheit als Sinn der Rechtfertigungslehre Luthers', *Luther Jahrbuch* 13 (1931), 1–28

Alzeghy, S., *Nova creatura: la nozione della grazia nei commentari medievali di S. Paolo* (Rome, 1956)

Amand, D., *Fatalisme et liberté dans l'antiquité grecque* (Louvain, 1945)

Anciaux, P., *La théologie du sacrament du pénance au XIIe siècle* (Louvain, 1949)

Armstrong, B. G., *Calvinism and the Amyraut Heresy: Protestant Scholasticism and Humanism in Seventeenth-Century France* (Madison, 1969)

Auer, J., *Die menschliche Willensfreiheit im Lehrsystem des Thomas von Aquin und Johannes Duns Skotus* (Munich, 1938)

Die Entwicklung der Gnadenlehre in der Hochscholastik (2 vols.: Freiburg, 1942–51)

Bakhuizen van den Brink, J. N., 'Mereo(r) and meritum in some Latin Fathers', *Studia Patristica* 3 (Berlin, 1961), 333–40

Ball, D., 'Libre arbitre et liberté dans Saint Augustin', *AThA* 6 (1945), 368–82

'Les développements de la doctrine de la liberté chez Saint Augustin', *AThA* 7 (1946) 400–30

Bannach, K., *Die Lehre von der doppelten Macht Gottes bei Wilhelm von Ockham* (Wiesbaden, 1975)

Baur, J., *Salus Christiana: Die Rechtfertigungslehre in der Geschichte des christlichen Heilsverständnisses* (Gutersloh, 1968)

Bavaud, G., 'La doctrine de la justification d'après Saint Augustin et la Réforme', *REAug* 5 (1959), 21–32

'La doctrine de la justification d'après Calvin et le Concile de Trent', *Verbum Caro* 22 (1968), 83–92

Beck, H., *Vorsehung und Vorherbestimmung in der theologischen Literatur der Byzantiner* (Rome, 1937)

Becker, K. J., *Die Rechtfertigungslehre nach Domingo de Soto: Das Denken eines Konzilsteilnehmers vor, in und nach Trient* (Rome, 1967)

Beltran de Heredia, V., 'Controversia de certitudine gratiae entre Domingo de Soto y Ambrosio Catarino', *Ciencia Tomista* 62 (1941), 33–62

Beumer, J., 'Gratia supponit naturam. Zur Geschichte eines theologischen Prinzips', *Gregorianum* 20 (1939), 381–406, 535–52

Bizer, E., *Theologie der Verheissung: Studien zur theologische Entwicklung des jungen Melanchthon 1519–1524* (Neukirchen, 1964)

Fides ex auditu: Eine Untersuchung über die Entdeckung der Gerechtigkeit Gottes durch Martin Luther, 3rd edn (Neukirchen, 1966)

Blomme, R., *La doctrine de la péché dans les écoles théologiques de la première moitié du XIIe siècle* (Louvain, 1958)

Boisset, J., 'Justification et sanctification chez Calvin', in *Calvinus Theologus: Die Referate des Congrés Européen de recherches Calviniennes*, ed. W. H. Neuser (Neukirchen, 1976), 131–48

Bornkamm, H., 'Zur Frage der Iustitia Dei beim jungen Luther', *ARG* 52 (1961), 16–29; 53 (1962), 1–60

Bouillard, H., *Conversion et grâce chez S. Thomas d'Aquin* (Paris, 1944)

Braunisch, R., *Die Theologie der Rechtfertigung im 'Enchiridion' (1538) des Johannes Gropper: Sein kritischer Dialog mit Philipp Melanchthon* (Münster, 1974)

Bruch, R., 'Die Urgerechtigkeit als Rechtheit des Willens nach der Lehre des hl. Bonaventuras', *FS* 33 (1951), 180–206

Brunner, P., 'Die Rechtfertigungslehre des Konzils von Trient', in *Pro veritate: Eine theologischer Dialog* (Münster/Kassel, 1963), 59–96

Burger, C. P., 'Das auxilium speciale Dei in der Gnadenlehre Gregors von Rimini', in *Gregor von Rimini: Werk und Wirkung bis zur Reformation*, ed. H. A. Oberman (Berlin, 1981), 195–240

Burnaby, J., *Amor Dei: A Study of the Religion of St. Augustine* (London, 1947)

Buuck, F., 'Zum Rechtfertigungsdekret', in *Das Weltkonzil von Trient*, ed. G. Schreiber, 117–43

Capánaga, V., 'La deificacíon en la soteriología agustiniana', *Augustinus Magister* (Paris, 1954), 2.745–54

Chéné, J., 'Que significiaient "initium fidei" et "affectus credulitatis" pour les sémipelagiens?', *RSR* 35 (1948), 566–88

'Le sémipelagianisme du Midi et de la Gaule d'après les lettres de Prosper d'Aquitaine et d'Hilaire à Saint Augustin', *RSR* 43 (1955), 321–41

Cosgrove, C. H., 'Justification in Paul: A Linguistic and Theological Reflection', *Journal of Biblical Literature* 106 (1987), 653–70

Courtenay, W. J., 'Covenant and Causality in Pierre d'Ailly', *Speculum* 46 (1971) 94–119

'The King and the Leaden Coin. The Economic Background of Sine Qua Non Causality', *Traditio* 28 (1972), 185–209

Adam Wodeham: An Introduction to his Life and Writings (Leiden, 1978)

Courtney, F., *Cardinal Robert Pullen: An English Theologian of the Twelfth Century* (Rome, 1954)

Dalmau, J. M., 'La teología de la disposición a la justificación en vísperas de la revolución protestante', *RET* 6 (1946), 249–75

Bibliography

Davids, E. A., *Das Bild vom neuen Menschen: Ein Beitrag zum Verständnis des Corpus Macarianum* (Salzburg/Munich, 1968)

Dettloff, W., *Die Lehre von der acceptatio divina bei Johannes Duns Scotus mit besonderer Berücksichtigung der Rechtfertigungslehre* (Werl, 1954)

Die Entwicklung der Akzeptations- und Verdienstlehre von Duns Scotus bis Luther mit besonderer Berücksichtigung der Franziskanertheologen (Münster, 1963)

'Die antipelagianische Grundstruktur des scotischen Rechtfertigungslehre', *FS* 48 (1966), 267–70

Dhont, R.-C., *Le problème de la préparation à la grâce: débuts de l'école franciscain* (Paris, 1946)

Doms, H., *Die Gnadenlehre des sel. Albertus Magnus* (Breslau, 1929)

Donfried, K. 'Justification and Last Judgement in Paul', *Zeitschrift für Neutestamentlichen Wissenschaft* 67 (1976), 90–110

Douglass, E. J. D., *Justification in Late Medieval Preaching: A Study of John Geiler of Strassburg* (Leiden, 1966)

Dunn, J. D. G., 'The New Perspective on Paul', *Bulletin of the John Rylands Library* 65 (1983), 95–122

Ehrle, F., *Der Sentenzenkommentar Peters von Candia des pisanerpapstes Alexander V* (Münster, 1925)

Ernst, W., *Gott und Mensch am Vorabend der Reformation: Eine Untersuchung zur Moralphilosophie und -theologie bei Gabriel Biel* (Leipzig, 1972)

Feckes, C., *Die Rechtfertigungslehre des Gabriel Biel und ihre Stellung innerhalb der nominalistischen Schule* (Münster, 1925)

Flick, M., *L'attimo della giustificazione secondo S. Tomasso* (Rome, 1947)

Fock, O., *Der Socianismus nach seiner Stellung* (Kiel, 1847)

Gibbs, Lee W., 'Richard Hooker's Via Media Doctrine of Justification', *HThR* 74 (1991), 211–20

Gillon, B., 'La grâce incréée chez quelques théologiens du XIVe siècle', *Divinitas* 11 (1967), 671–80

Gohler, A., *Calvins Lehre von der Heiligung* (Munich, 1934)

Gonzáles Rivas, S., 'Los teólogos salmantinos y el decreto de la justificación', *EE* 21 (1947), 147–70

Grabmann, M., *Mittelalterliches Geistesleben: Abhandlungen zur Geschichte der Scholastik und Mystik* (3 vols.: Munich, 1926–56)

Die Geschichte der scholastischen Methode (2 vols.: Darmstadt, 1956)

Grane, L., *Contra Gabrielem: Luthers Auseinandersetzung mit Gabriel Biel in der Disputatio contra scholasticam theologiam 1517* (Gyldendal, 1962)

'Gregor von Rimini und Luthers Leipziger Disputation', *StTh* 22 (1968), 29–49

'Augustins "Expositio quarumdam propositionum ex Epistola ad Romanos" in Luthers Römerbriefvorlesung', *ZThK* 69 (1972), 304–30

Grass, H., 'Die durch Jesum von Nazareth vollbrachte Erlösung: Ein

Bibliography

Beitrag zur Erlösungslehre Schleiermachers', in *Denkender Glaube: Festschrift für Carl Heinz Ratschow* (Berlin/New York, 1976), 152–69

Greschat, M., *Melanchthon neben Luther: Studien zur Gestalt der Rechtfertigungslehre zwischen 1528 und 1537* (Witten, 1965)

Gross, J., *La divinisation du chrétien d'après les pères grecs* (Paris, 1938)

Guerard des Lauriers, M. L., 'Saint Augustin et la question de la certitude de la grâce au Concile de Trente', *Augustinus Magister* (Paris, 1954), 2.1057–69

Gundry, R. H., 'Grace, Works and Staying Saved in Paul', *Biblia* 60 (1985), 1–38

Gyllenkrok, A., *Rechtfertigung und Heiligung in der fruhen evangelischen Theologie Luthers* (Uppsala, 1952)

Häring, N., *Die Theologie der Erfurter Augustiner-Eremiten Bartholomäus Arnoldi von Usingen* (Limburg, 1939)

Hamm, B., *Promissio, pactum, ordinatio: Freiheit und Selbstbindung Gottes in der scholastischen Gnadenlehre* (Tübingen, 1977)

von Harnack, A., *History of Dogma* (7 vols.: Edinburgh, 1894–9)

Hefner, J., *Die Entstehungsgeschichte des Trienter Rechtfertigungsdekretes: Ein Beitrag zur Geschichte des Reformationszeitalters* (Paderborn, 1939)

Hermann, R., *Luthers These 'Gerecht und Sünder zugleich': Eine systematische Untersuchung* (Darmstadt, 1960)

Heynck, V., 'Die aktuelle Gnade bei Richard von Mediavilla', *FS* 22 (1935) 297–325

'Untersuchungen uber die Reuelehre der tridentinischen Zeit', *FS* 29 (1942), 25–44, 120–50; 30 (1943), 53–73

'A Controversy at the Council of Trent concerning the Doctrine of Duns Scotus', *FcS* 9 (1949), 181–258

'Der Anteil des Konzilstheologen Andreas de Vega O.F.M. an dem ersten amtlichen Entwurf des Trienter Rechtfertigungsdekretes', *FS* 33 (1951), 49–81

'Zum Problem der unvollkommenen Reue auf dem Konzil von Trient', in *Das Weltkonzil von Trient*, ed. G. Schreiber, 231–80

'Zur Kontroverse uber die Gnadengewissheit auf dem Konzil von Trient', *FS* 37 (1955) 1–17, 161–88

'Die Bedeutung von "mereri" und "promereri" bei dem Konzilstheologen Andreas de Vega', *FS* 50 (1968), 224–38

Hirsch, E., *Die Theologie des Andreas Osiander und ihre geschichtlichen Voraussetzungen* (Göttingen, 1919)

Hocedez, E., *Richard de Middleton: sa vie, ses œuvres, sa doctrine* (Louvain, 1925)

Hochstetter, E., 'Nominalismus?', *FrS* 9 (1949), 370–403

Holfelder, H. H., *Tentatio et consolatio: Studien zu Bugenhagens Interpretatio in librum psalmorum* (Berlin/New York, 1974)

Solus Christus: Die Ausbildung von Bugenhagens Rechtfertigungslehre in der Paulusauslegung (1524/25) und ihre Bedeutung für die theologische Argu-

Bibliography

mentation im Sendbrief 'Von dem christlichen Glauben' (Tübingen, 1981)

Holl, K., *Gesammelte Aufsatze zur Kirchengeschichte* (3 vols.: Tübingen, 1928)

Horn, S., *Glaube und Rechtfertigung nach dem Konzilstheologer Andres de Vega* (Paderborn, 1972)

Hultgren, A. J., *Paul's Gospel and Mission* (Philadelphia, 1985)

Hunermann, F., *Wesen und Notwendigkeit der aktuellen Gnade nach dem Konzil von Trient* (Paderborn, 1926)

Huthmacher, H., 'La certitude de la grâce au Concile de Trente', *Nouvelle Revue Théologique* 60 (1933), 213–26

Iserloh, E., *Gnade und Eucharistie in der philosophischen Theologie des Wilhelm von Ockham. Ihre Bedeutung fur die Ursachen der Reformation* (Wiesbaden, 1956)

Jansen, F.-X., *Baius et la Baïanisme* (Louvain, 1927)

Jedin, H., *Kardinal Contarini als Kontroverstheologe* (Münster, 1949)
Geschichte des Konzils von Trient (4 vols.: Freiburg, 1951–75)

Joest, W., 'Die tridentinische Rechtfertigungslehre', *KuD* 9 (1963), 41–59

Kähler, E., *Karlstadt und Augustin: Der Kommentar des Andreas Bodenstein von Karlstadt zu Augustins Schrift De spiritu et litera* (Halle, 1952)

Kaiser, A., *Natur und Gnade im Urstand: Eine Untersuchung der Kontroverse zwischen Michael Baius und Johannes Martinez de Ripaldi* (Munich, 1965)

Käsemann, E., *New Testament Questions of Today* (London, 1969)
Commentary on Romans (Grand Rapids, 1980)

Kaup, J., 'Zum Begriff der iustitia originalis in der alteren Franziskanerschule', *FS* 29 (1942), 44–55

Knox, D. B., *The Doctrine of Faith in the Reign of Henry VIII* (London, 1961)

Kolb, R., *Nikolaus von Amsdorf: Popular Polemics in the Preservation of Luther's Legacy* (Nieuwkoop, 1978)

Kriechbaum, F., *Grundzüge der Theologie Karlstadts: Eine systematische Studie zur Erhellung der Theologie Andreas von Karlstadts* (Hamburg, 1967)

Kruger, F., *Bucer und Erasmus: Eine Untersuchung zum Einfluss des Erasmus auf die Theologie Martin Bucers* (Wiesbaden, 1970)

Küng, H., *Rechtfertigung: Die Lehre Karl Barths und eine katholische Besinnung* (Einsiedeln, 1957)

Landgraf, A. M., 'Untersuchungen zu den Eigenlehren Gilberts de la Porrée', *ZKTh* 54 (1930), 180–213
'Mitteilungen zur Schule Gilberts de la Porrée', *CFr* 3 (1933), 185–208
'Neue Funde zur Porretanerschule', *CFr* 6 (1936), 354–63
'Der Porretanismus der Homilien des Radulphus Ardens', *ZKTh* 64 (1940), 132–48
Einführung in die Geschichte der theologischen Literatur der Frühscholastik (Regensburg, 1948)

Dogmengeschichte der Frühscholastik (8 vols.: Regensburg, 1952–6)

Laplanche, F., *Orthodoxie et prédication: l'œuvre d'Amyraut et la querelle de la grâce universelle* (Paris, 1965)

Laun, J. F., 'Die Prädestination bei Wiclif und Bradwardin', in *Imago Dei: Festschrift fur G. Kruger*, ed. H. Bornkamm (Giessen, 1932), 63–84

Leff, G., *William of Ockham: The Metamorphosis of Scholastic Discourse* (Manchester, 1975)

Lennerz, H., 'De historia applicationis principii "omnis ordinate volens prius vult finem quam ea quae sunt ad finem" ad probandam gratuitatem praedestinationis ad gloriam', *Gregorianum* 10 (1929), 238–66

Lennerz, J., 'Voten auf dem Trienter Konzil uber die Rechtfertigung', *Gregorianum* 15 (1934), 577–88

Lindbeck, G., 'Nominalism and the Problem of Meaning as illustrated by Pierre d'Ailly on Predestination and Justification', *HThR* 52 (1959), 43–60

Loewenich, W. von, *Von Augustin zu Luther* (Witten, 1959)

Duplex Iustitia: Luthers Stellung zu einer Unionsformel des 16. Jahrhunderts (Wiesbaden, 1972)

Logan, E. M. T., 'Grace and Justification: Some Italian Views on the 16th and Early 17th centuries', *JEH* 20 (1969), 67–78

Lonergan, B. J. F., *Grace and Reason: Operative Grace in the Thought of St. Thomas Aquinas* (London, 1971)

Loofs, F., *Leitfaden zum Studien der Dogmengeschichte* (Halle, 1906)

'Der articulus stantis et cadentis ecclesiae', *Theologische Studien und Kritiken* 90 (1917), 323–400

Lottin, O., 'Le concept de justice chez les théologiens du moyen âge avant l'introduction d'Aristôte', *Revue Thomiste* 44 (1938), 511–21

Psychologie et morale aux XIIe et XIIIe siècles (8 vols.: Louvain/Gembloux, 1942–60)

McGrath, A. E., 'The Anti-Pelagian Structure of "Nominalist" Doctrines of Justification', *EThL* 57 (1981), 107–19

'Justification: Barth, Trent and Küng', *SJTh* 34 (1981), 517–29

'Rectitude: The Moral Foundations of Anselm of Canterbury's Soteriology', *Downside Review* 99 (1981), 201–13

'"Augustinianism"? A Critical Assessment of the So-Called "Medieval Augustinian Tradition" on Justification', *Augustiniana* 31 (1981), 247–67

'Forerunners of the Reformation? A Critical Examination of the Evidence for Precursors of the Reformation Doctrines of Justification', *HThR* 75 (1982) 219–42

'Humanist Elements in the Early Reformed Doctrine of Justification', *ARG* 73 (1982) 5–30

'"The Righteousness of God" from Augustine to Luther', *StTh* 36 (1982), 63–78

Bibliography

'Justice and Justification. Semantic and Juristic Aspects of the Christian Doctrine of Justification', *SJTh* 35 (1982), 403–18

'Divine Justice and Divine Equity in the Controversy between Augustine and Julian of Eclanum', *Downside Review* 101 (1983), 312–19

'Mira et nova diffinitio iustitiae: Luther and Scholastic Doctrines of Justification', *ARG* 74 (1983), 37–60

'John Henry Newman's "Lectures on Justification": The High Church Misrepresentation of Luther', *Churchman* 97 (1983), 112–22

'Karl Barth and the Articulus Iustificationis: The Significance of His Critique of Ernst Wolf within the Context of His Theological Method', *Theologische Zeitschrift* 39 (1983), 349–61

'The Influence of Aristotelian Physics upon St. Thomas Aquinas' Discussion of the "Processus Iustificationis"', *RThAM* 51 (1984), 223–9

'ARCIC II and Justification: Some Difficulties and Obscurities relating to Anglican and Roman Catholic Teaching on Justification', *Anvil* 1 (1984), 27–42

'Der articulus iustificationis als axiomatischer Grundsatz des christlichen Glaubens', *ZThK* 81 (1984), 273–83

'The Emergence of the Anglican Tradition on Justification', *Churchman* 98 (1984), 28–43

'Karl Barth als Aufklärer? Der Zusammenhang seiner Lehre vom Werke Christi mit der Erwählungslehre', *KuD* 30 (1984), 273–83

'Justification and Christology: The Axiomatic Correlation between the Proclaimed Christ and the Historical Jesus', *Modern Theology* 1 (1984–5), 45–54

'The Moral Theory of the Atonement: An Historical and Theological Critique', *SJTh* 38 (1985), 205–20

Luther's Theology of the Cross: Martin Luther's Theological Breakthrough (Oxford, 1985)

'John Calvin and Late Medieval Thought: A Study in Late Medieval Influences upon Calvin's Theological Thought', *ARG* 77 (1986), 58–78

The Intellectual Origins of the European Reformation (Oxford, 1987)

'Justification and the Reformation. The Significance of the Doctrine of Justification by Faith to Sixteenth Century Urban Communities', *ARG* 81 (1990), 5–19

MacQueen, D. J., 'John Cassian on Grace and Free Will, with Particular Reference to Institutio XII and Collatio XII', *RThAM* 44 (1977), 5–28

McSorley, H. J., *Luther – Right or Wrong? An Ecumenical-Theological Study of Luther's Major Work, The Bondage of the Will* (New York/Minneapolis, 1969)

Martin, R. M., *La controverse sur le péché originel au début du XIVe siècle* (Louvain, 1930)

Bibliography

Mitzka, F., 'Die Lehre des hl. Bonaventura von der Vorbereitung auf die heiligmachende Gnade', *ZKTh* 50 (1926) 27–72, 220–52

'Die Anfange der Konkurslehre im 13. Jahrhundert', *ZKTh* 54 (1930), 161–79

Modalsi, O., *Das Gericht nach den Werken: Ein Beitrag zu Luthers Lehre vom Gesetz* (Göttingen, 1963)

Molteni, P., *Roberto Holcot O.P. Dottrina della grazia e della giustificazione* (Pinerolo, 1968)

Moltmann, G., 'Prädestination und Heilsgeschichte bei Moyse Amyraut', *ZKG* 65 (1954), 270–303

Müller, O., *Die Rechtfertigungslehre nominalistischer Reformationsgegner, Bartholomäus Arnoldi von Usingen und Kaspar Schatzgeyer über Erbsunde, erste Rechtfertigung und Taufe* (Breslau, 1940)

Niesel, W., 'Calvin wider Osianders Rechtfertigungslehre', *ZKG* 46 (1982), 410–30

Nygren, A., 'Simul iustus et peccator bei Augustin und Luther', *ZSTh* 16 (1940), 364–79

Nygren, G., *Das Prädestinationsproblem an der Theologie Augustins* (Göttingen, 1956)

Oakley, F., 'Pierre d'Ailly and the Absolute Power of God. Another Note on the Theology of Nominalism', *HThR* 56 (1963), 59–73

Oberman, H. A., *Archbishop Thomas Bradwardine: A Fourteenth Century Augustinian* (Utrecht, 1957)

'Facientibus quod in se est Deus non denegat gratiam. Robert Holcot O.P. and the Beginnings of Luther's Theology', *HThR* 55 (1962), 317–42

The Harvest of Medieval Theology: Gabriel Biel and Late Medieval Nominalism (Cambridge, Mass., 1963)

'Das tridentinische Rechtfertigungsdekret im Lichte spätmittelalterlicher Theologie', *ZThK* 61 (1964), 251–82

'"Iustitia Christi" and "Iustitia Dei": Luther and the Scholastic Doctrines of Justification', *HThR* 59 (1966), 1–26

Forerunners of the Reformation: The Shape of Late Medieval Thought (New York, 1966)

'Wir sind pettler. Hoc est verum. Bund und Gnade in der Theologie des Mittelalters und der Reformation', *ZKG* 78 (1967), 232–52

'Headwaters of the Reformation: Initia Lutheri – Initia Reformationis', in *Luther and the Dawn of the Modern Era*, ed. H. A. Oberman (Leiden, 1974) 40–88

Werden und Wertung der Reformation: Vom Wegestreit zum Glaubenskampf (Tübingen, 1977)

Olazarán, J., *Documentos inéditos tridentinos sobre la justificación* (Madrid, 1957)

Oltra, M., *Die Gewissheit des Gnadenstandes bei Andres de Vega: Ein Beitrag zum Verständnis des Trienter Rechtfertigungsdekretes* (Dusseldorf, 1941)

Bibliography

Pannenberg, W., *Die Prädestinationslehre des Duns Skotus in Zusammenhang der scholastischen Lehrentwicklung* (Göttingen, 1954)

Pas, P., 'La doctrine de la double justice au Concile de Trente', *EThL* 30 (1954), 5–53

Peñamaria de Llano, A., *La salvación por la fe. La noción 'fides' in Hilario de Poitiers. Estudio filológico-teológico* (Burgos, 1981)

Pesch, O. H., *Die Theologie der Rechtfertigung bei Martin Luther und Thomas von Aquin* (Mainz, 1967)

Peters, A., *Glaube und Werk: Luthers Rechtfertigungslehre im Lichte der heiligen Schrift*, 2nd edn (Berlin/Hamburg, 1967)

Pfnur, V., *Einig in der Rechtfertigungslehre? Die Rechtfertigungslehre der Confessio Augustana (1530) und die Stellungsnahme der katholischen Kontroverstheologie zwischen 1530 und 1535* (Wiesbaden, 1970)

Philips, G., 'La justification luthérienne et la Concile de Trente', *EThL* 47 (1971), 340–58

'La théologie de la grâce chez les préscholastiques', *EThL* 48 (1972), 479–508

'La théologie de la grâce dans la "Summa Fratris Alexandris"', *EThL* 49 (1973), 100–23

L'union personnelle avec le Dieu vivant: essai sur l'origine et le sens de la grâce créée (Gembloux, 1974)

Rich, A., *Die Anfänge der Theologie Huldrych Zwinglis* (Zurich, 1949)

Ritschl, A. B., *The Christian Doctrine of Justification and Reconciliation* (Edinburgh, 1871)

Ritter, G. *Studien zur Spätscholastik I. Marsilius von Inghen und die okkamistischen Schule in Deutschland* (Heidelberg, 19)

Studien zur Spätscholastik II Via Antiqua und Via Moderna auf den deutschen Universtitäten des XV. Jahrhunderts (Heidelberg, 1922)

Rivière, J., *Le dogme de la rédemption au début du moyen âge* (Paris, 1934)

'Le dogme de la rédemption au XIIe siècle d'après les dernières publications', *Revue du Moyen Age Latin* 2 (1946), 101–12

Ruckert, H., *Die Rechtfertigungslehre auf dem Tridentinischen Konzil* (Bonn, 1925)

'Promereri: Eine Studie zum tridentinischen Rechtfertigungsdekret als Antwort an H. A. Oberman', *ZThK* 68 (1971), 162–94

Rupp, E. G., *The Righteousness of God: Luther Studies* (London, 1953)

Studies in the Making of the English Protestant Tradition (Cambridge, 1966)

Sagues, J., 'Un libro pretridentino de Andrés de Vega sobre la justificación', *EE* 20 (1946), 175–209

Salguiero, T., *La doctrine de Saint Augustin sur la grâce d'après le traité à Simplicien* (Porto, 1925)

Sanders, E. P., *Paul and Palestinian Judaism* (London, 1977)

Paul, The Law, and the Jewish People (London, 1983)

Santoro, S., 'La giustificazione in Giovanni Antonio Delfini, teologo del Concilio di Trento', *Miscellanea Franciscana* 40 (1940), 1–27

Bibliography

Schafer, R., 'Die Rechtfertigungslehre bei Ritschl und Kähler', *ZThK* 62 (1965), 66–85

Schelkle, K. H., *Paulus Lehrer der Väter. Die altkirchliche Auslegung von Römer 9–11* (Düsseldorf, 1959)

Schierse, F. J., 'Das Trienterkonzil und die Frage nach der christliche Gewissheit', in *Das Weltkonzil von Trient*, ed. G. Schreiber, 145–67

Schreiber, G. (ed.), *Das Weltkonzil von Trient: Sein Werden und Wirken* (2 vols.: Freiburg, 1951)

Schrenk, G., *Gottesreich und Bund im alteren Protestantismus* (Darmstadt, 1967)

Schupp, J., *Die Gnadenlehre des Petrus Lombardus* (Freiburg, 1932)

Schwarz, R., *Fides, spes und caritas beim jungen Luther, unter besonderer Berücksichtigung der mittelälterlichen Tradition* (Berlin, 1962)

Seifrid, M. A., *Justification by faith: The Origin and Development of a Central Pauline Theme* (Leiden, 1992)

Serry, J. H., *Historia congregationis de auxiliis* (Louvain, 1700)

Seybold, M., *Glaube und Rechtfertigung bei Thomas Stapleton* (Paderborn 1967)

Sider, R. J., *Andreas Bodenstein von Karlstadt: The Development of his Thought 1517–1525* (Leiden, 1974)

Siewerth, G., *Thomas von Aquin. Die menschliche Willensfreiheit* (Dusseldorf, 1954)

Stadtland, T., *Rechtfertigung und Heiligung bei Calvin* (Neukirchen, 1972)

Staedtke, J., *Die Theologie des jungen Bullinger* (Zurich, 1962)

Stakemeier, A., *Das Konzil von Trient über die Heilsgewissheit* (Heidelberg, 1949)

Stakemeier, E., 'Die theologischen Schulen auf dem Trienter Konzil während der Rechtfertigungsverhandlung', *Theologisches Quartalschrift* 117 (1936), 188–207, 322–50, 446–504

　　Der Kampf um Augustin: Augustinus und die Augustiner auf dem Tridentinum (Paderborn, 1937)

Stegmüller, F., *Francisco de Vitoria y la doctrina de gracia en la escuela salmantina* (Barcelona, 1934)

Steinmetz, D. C., *Misericordia Dei. The Theology of Johannes von Staupitz in its Late Medieval Setting* (Leiden, 1968)

Stoeckle, B., *'Gratia supponit naturam.' Geschichte und Analyse eines theologischen Axioms* (Rom, 1962)

Studer, B., 'Jesucristo, nuestra justicia, según san Augustín', *Augustinus. Revista Trimestral* 26 (1981) 253–82

Stufler, J., 'Die entfernte Vorbereitung auf die Rechtfertigung nach dem hl. Thomas', *ZKTh* 47 (1923), 1–23, 161–83

　　'Der hl. Thomas und das Axiom omne quod movetur ab alio movetur', *ZKTh* 47 (1923), 369–90

Stuhlmacher, P. *Gerechtigkeit Gottes bei Paulus* (Göttingen, 1966)

Bibliography

Stupperich, R., 'Der Ursprung des Regensburger Buches von 1541 und seine Rechtfertigungslehre', *ARG* 36 (1939), 88–116

Subilia, V., *La giustificazione per fede* (Brescia, 1976)

Tellechea, I., 'El articulus de iustificatione de Fray Bartolomeo de Carranza', *RET* 15 (1955), 563–635

Toner, N., 'The Doctrine of Justification according to Augustine of Rome (Favaroni)', *Augustiniana* 8 (1958), 164–89, 229–327, 497–515

Trape, A., *Il concorso divino nel pensiero di Egidio Romano* (Tolentino, 1942)

Trapp, D., 'Augustinian Theology of the Fourteenth Century', *Augustiniana* 6 (1956), 146–274

Vanneste, A., 'Nature et grâce dans la théologie du XIIe siècle', *EThL* 50 (1974), 181–214

'Nature et grâce dans la théologie de Saint Augustin', Recherches Augustiniennes 10 (1975), 143–69

Van't Spijker, W., 'Prädestination bei Bucer und Calvin', in *Calvinus Theologus*, ed. W. Neuser (Neukirchen, 1976), 85–111

Vignaux, P., *Justification et prédestination au XIVe siècle* (Paris, 1934)

'Sur Luther et Ockham', *FS* 32 (1950), 21–30

Villalmonte, A. de, 'Andrés de Vega y el proceso de la justificación según el Concilio Tridentina', *RET* 5 (1945), 311–74

Vogelsang, E., *Die Anfänge von Luthers Christologie nach der ersten Psalmenvorlesung* (Berlin/Leipzig, 1929)

Vulfila oder die gotische Bible ed. W. Streitberg (Heidelberg, 1965)

Walz, A., 'La giustificazione tridentina', *Angelicum* 28 (1951), 97–138

Weingart, R. E., *The Logic of Divine Love. A Critical Analysis of the Soteriology of Peter Abailard* (Oxford, 1990)

Weisweiler, H., 'L'école de Laon et de Guillaume de Champeaux', *RThAM* 4 (1932), 237–69, 371–91

Werbeck, W., *Jacobus Perez von Valencia. Untersuchungen zu seiner Psalmenkommentar* (Tübingen, 1959)

Westerholm, W., *Israel's Law and the Church's Faith: Paul and his Recent Interpreters* (Grand Rapids, 1988)

Wolf, E., 'Die Rechtfertigungslehre als Mitte und Grenze reformatorischer Theologie', in *Peregrinatio II: Studien zur reformatorischen Theologie, zum Kirchenrecht und zur Sozialethik* (Munich, 1965), 11–21

Worter, F., *Die christliche Lehre über das Verhältnis von Gnade und Freiheit von den apostolischen Zeiten bis zu Augustinus* (2 vols.: Freiburg, 1855–60)

Wright, N. T., *The Climax of the Covenant: Christ and the Law in Pauline Theology* (Edinburgh, 1991)

Xiberta, B., 'La causa meritoria de la justificación en las controversias pretridentinas', *RET* 5 (1945), 87–106

Zimmermann, A., 'Calvins Auseinandersetzung mit Osianders Rechtfertigungslehre', *KuD* 35 (1989), 236–56

Bibliography

Zumkeller, A., *Dionysius de Montina. Ein neuentdeckter Augustinertheologe des Spätmittelalters* (Würzburg, 1948)

'Hugolin von Orvieto über Urstand und Erbsünde', *Augustiniana* 3 (1953), 35–62; 165–93; 4 (1954) 25–46

'Hugolin von Orvieto über Prädestination, Rechtfertigung und Verdienst', *Augustiniana* 4 (1954) 109–56; 5 (1955) 5–51

'Der Wiener Theologieprofessor Johannes von Retz und seine Lehre von Urstand, Erbsünde, Gnade und Verdienst', *Augustiniana* 22 (1972) 118–84; 540–82

'Johannes Klenkok O.S.A. im Kampf gegen den "Pelagianismus" seiner Zeit. Seine Lehre über Gnade, Rechtfertigung und Verdienst', *Recherches Augustiniennes* 13 (1978), 231–333

'Die Lehre des Erfurter Augustinertheologen Johannes von Dorsten über Gnade, Rechtfertigung und Verdienst', *Theologie und Philosophie* 53 (1978), 7–64; 127–219

'Der Augustinertheologe Johannes Hiltalingen von Basel über Erbsünde, Gnade und Verdienst', *Analecta Augustiniana* 43 (1980), 57–162

'Erbsunde, Gnade und Rechtfertigung im Verständnis der Erfurter Augustinertheologen des Spätmittelalters', *ZKG* 92 (1981), 39–59

'Der Augustiner Angelus Dobelinus, erster Theologieprofessor der Erfurter Universität, über Gnade, Rechtfertigung und Verdienst', *Analecta Augustiniana* 44 (1981), 69–147

Index of names

Index of names

Flaminio, Marcantonio, 248
Florus of Lyons, 132–4
Forbes, William 295–6
Francke, August Herrmann, 239–40
Frexius, Antonius, 265
Frith, John, 286

Gataker, Thomas, 290
Geiler, Johann, 89–90
Gerhard, Johann, 233, 235
Gerson, Jean, 207
Gilbert de la Porrée, 93
Giles of Rome, 152, 177–8, 179
Giustiniani, Paolo, 234–4
Godescalc of Orbais, 139–1, 140
Godfrey of Fontaines, 68
Godfrey of Poitiers, 62
Gomarus, Franciscus, 228
Goodwin, John, 290, 303–4
Graile, John, 290
Gratian of Bologna, 155
Gregory the Great, 58, 91
Gregory of Nyssa, 32
Gregory of Padua, 257
Gregory of Rimini, 87, 116, 117, 123,
    142–3, 152–3, 157, 167, 168,
    176–7, 178, 179, 206, 251
Gropper, Johann, 222, 242, 244–7,
    254, 262
Grotius, Hugo, 352–3

Haimo of Auxerre, 92
Hall, Joseph, 294
Hammond, Henry, 293, 295
Hegel, G. W. F., 345–6, 365
Heidegger, Martin, 372–4
Henry of Friemar, 178
Henry of Ghent, 68, 121, 162
Herbert, Edward, 324
Hervaeus of Bourg-Dieu, 43, 93
Hilary of Poitiers, 15
Hiltalingen, Johann, 87, 143, 154,
    177, 178
Hincmar of Reims, 131–4
Hobbes, Thomas, 327, 350–1, 354

Holcot, Robert, 88, 165, 166, 167, 169
Holl, Karl, 198–200, 357, 363–4
Hollaz, David, 236
Honorius of Autun, 93
Hooker, Richard, 291–3, 296–7, 298,
    313, 319
Hooker, Thomas, 304–5, 306
Hopkins, Samuel, 307
Hugh of Rouen, 67
Hugh of St Cher, 67
Hugh of St Victor, 61, 62, 93, 102,
    156
Hugolino of Orvieto, 87, 143, 153,
    157, 168, 174, 179, 254
Huss, Johann, 117, 142, 176, 185

Irenaeus of Lyons, 20, 83
Isidore of Seville, 23, 131
Ivo of Chartres, 155

Jackson, Thomas, 294
Jacobus Perez of Valencia, 174, 178,
    254, 263
Jansen, Cornelius, 283–4
Jerome, 11, 74, 75
Jewel, John, 298, 319
John of La Rochelle, 48, 62, 78–9,
    84–5
John of St Giles, 156, 157
Joye, George, 286
Julian of Eclanum, 25, 26, 34, 35,
    53–4, 129, 293
Julian of Toledo, 37
Justin Martyr, 20

Kähler, Martin, 356, 362, 370
Kant, Immanuel, 336–41, 356
Karlstadt, Andreas Bodenstein von,
    294, 307–9, 310, 318
Käsemann, E., 382–3
Kierkegaard, Søren, 373
Klenkok, Johann, 143, 154, 177
Knewstub, John, 300
Knox, Alexander, 309
Küng, Hans, 388–9

529

Index of names

Index of names